GALÁPAGOS
ISLANDS

GALÁPAGOS ISLANDS

A SHOWCASE OF EVOLUTION

TOM JACKSON

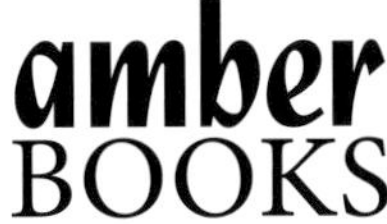

First published in 2025

Copyright © 2025 Amber Books Ltd

Published by
Amber Books Ltd
United House
North Road
London N7 9DP
United Kingdom

www.amberbooks.co.uk
Facebook: amberbooks
YouTube: amberbooksltd
Instagram: amberbooksltd
X(Twitter): @amberbooks

ISBN: 978-1-83886-617-4

Project Editor: Anna Brownbridge
Designer: Keren Harragan
Picture Research: Adam Gnych

Printed in China

Contents

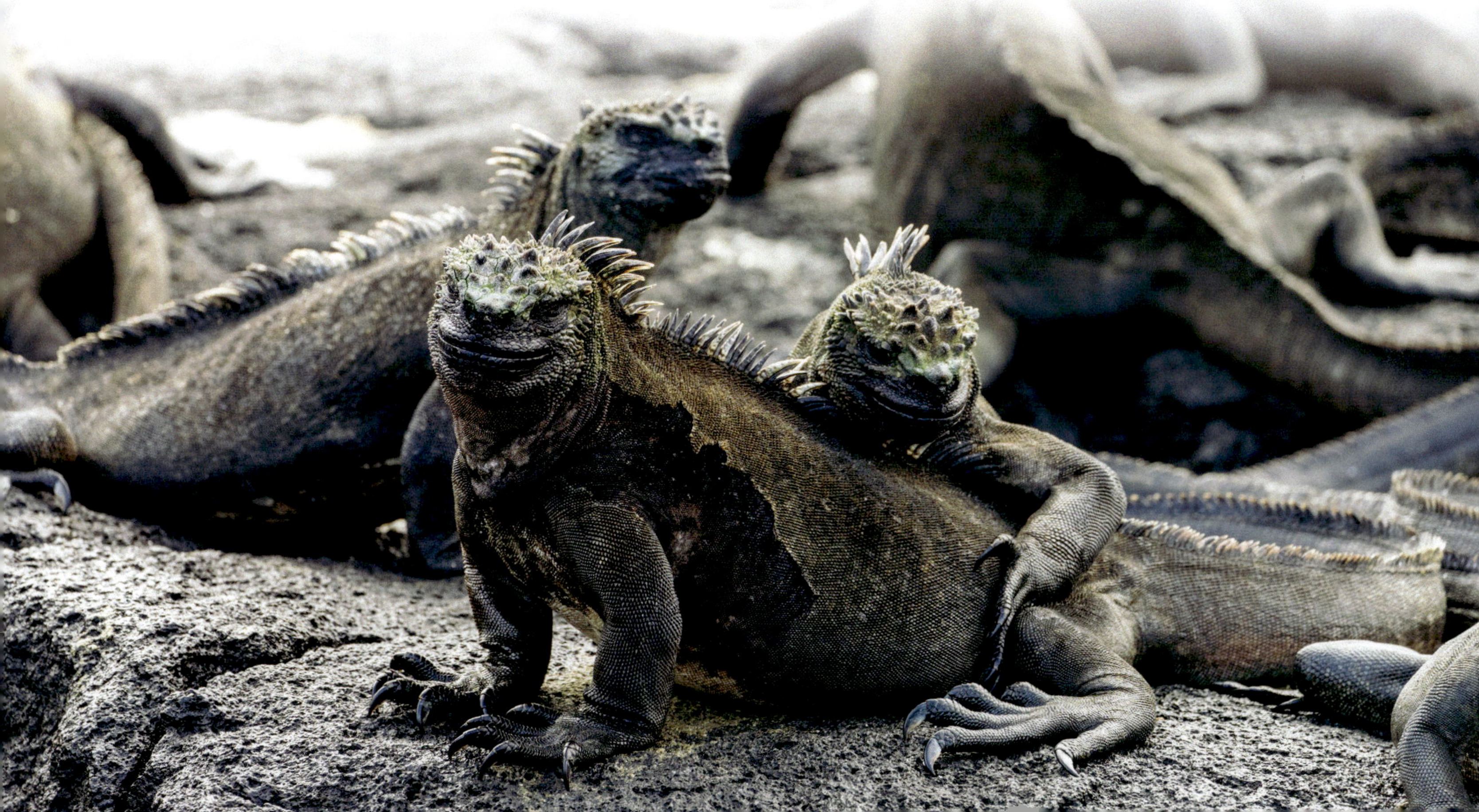

Introduction

Rising from the Pacific Ocean not far from Ecuador in South America, the Galápagos Islands are a world within a world. Cut off from the rest of us by nearly 1000km (600 miles) of ocean, the volcanic archipelago has been a blank canvas decorated by natural selection to create a near-magical world of wildlife. It was here that Charles Darwin solidified his theory of evolution after visiting in 1835 aboard the British research vessel HMS *Beagle*. Darwin found a flora and fauna unlike any other. Many

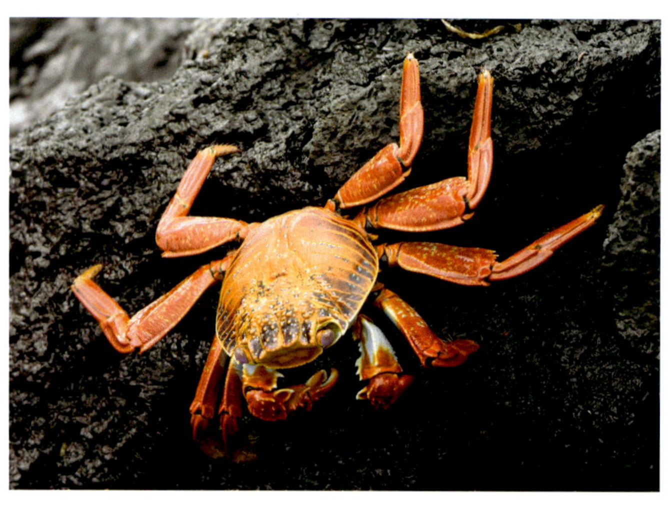

animal types were missing – for example, the large mammals and frogs – but in their place were giant tortoises, diving lizards and birds galore. Darwin used much of what he saw there to explain the process of evolution to a sceptical public. Most notable were Darwin's finches, several species that evolved from a single ancestral songbird and adapted to survive in myriad ways on their island homes. Those same islands that inspired Darwin feature in the following pages. Read on to visit the awesome Galápagos.

Sally Lightfoot crab
This agile red crab stands out among the dark rocks along the Galápagos's lava shores. The crab, which grows brighter as it ages, is seen clambering on the rocks and paddling through the shallows. It is said to be named after a 19th-century dancer.

OPPOSITE:
Nazca booby
A pair of Nazca boobies (*Sula granti*) get acquainted in the evening light atop a coastal cliff on Wolf Island. This is one of the more rugged and remote islands in the Galápagos and is home to vast colonies of breeding seabirds.

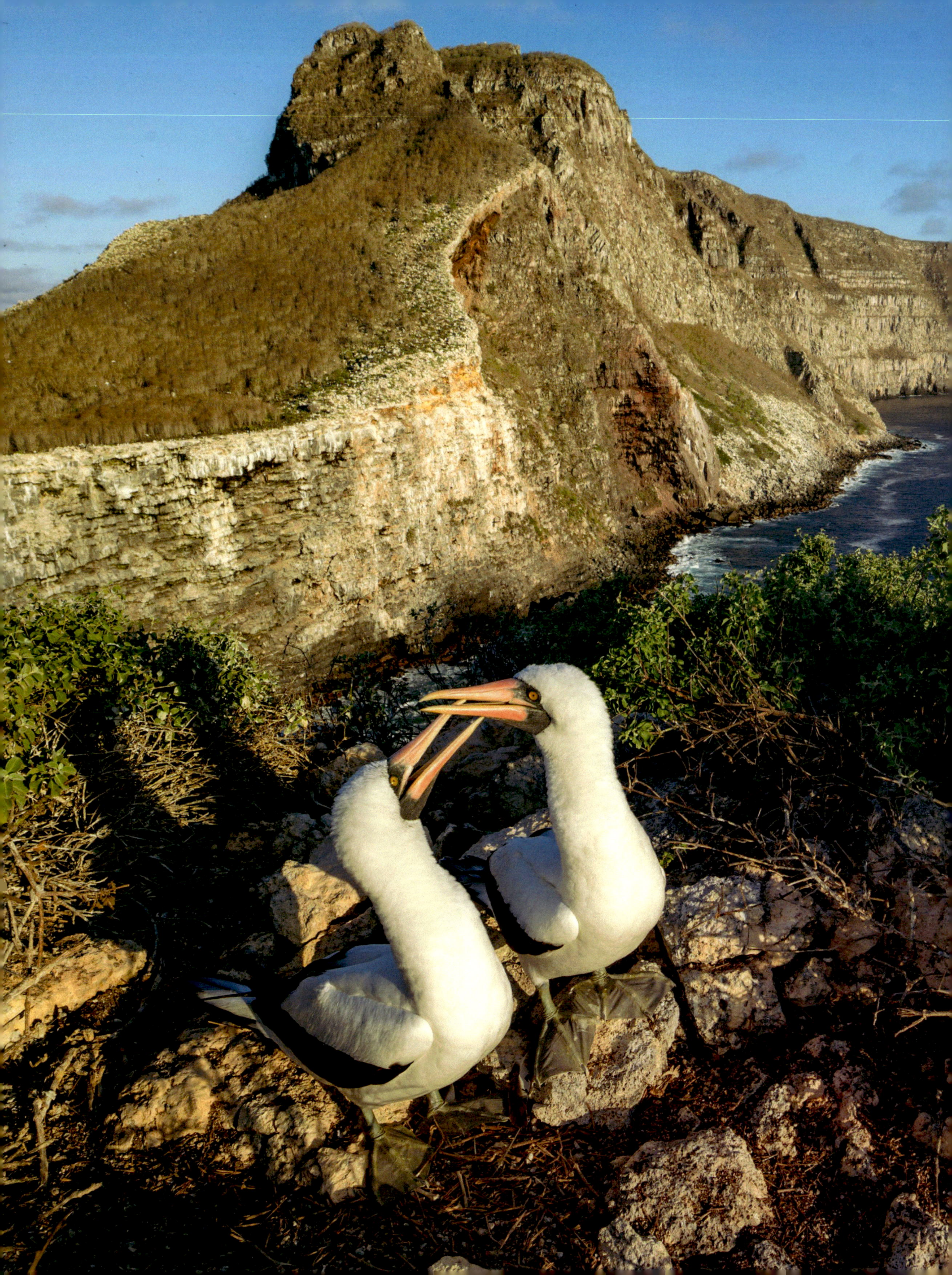

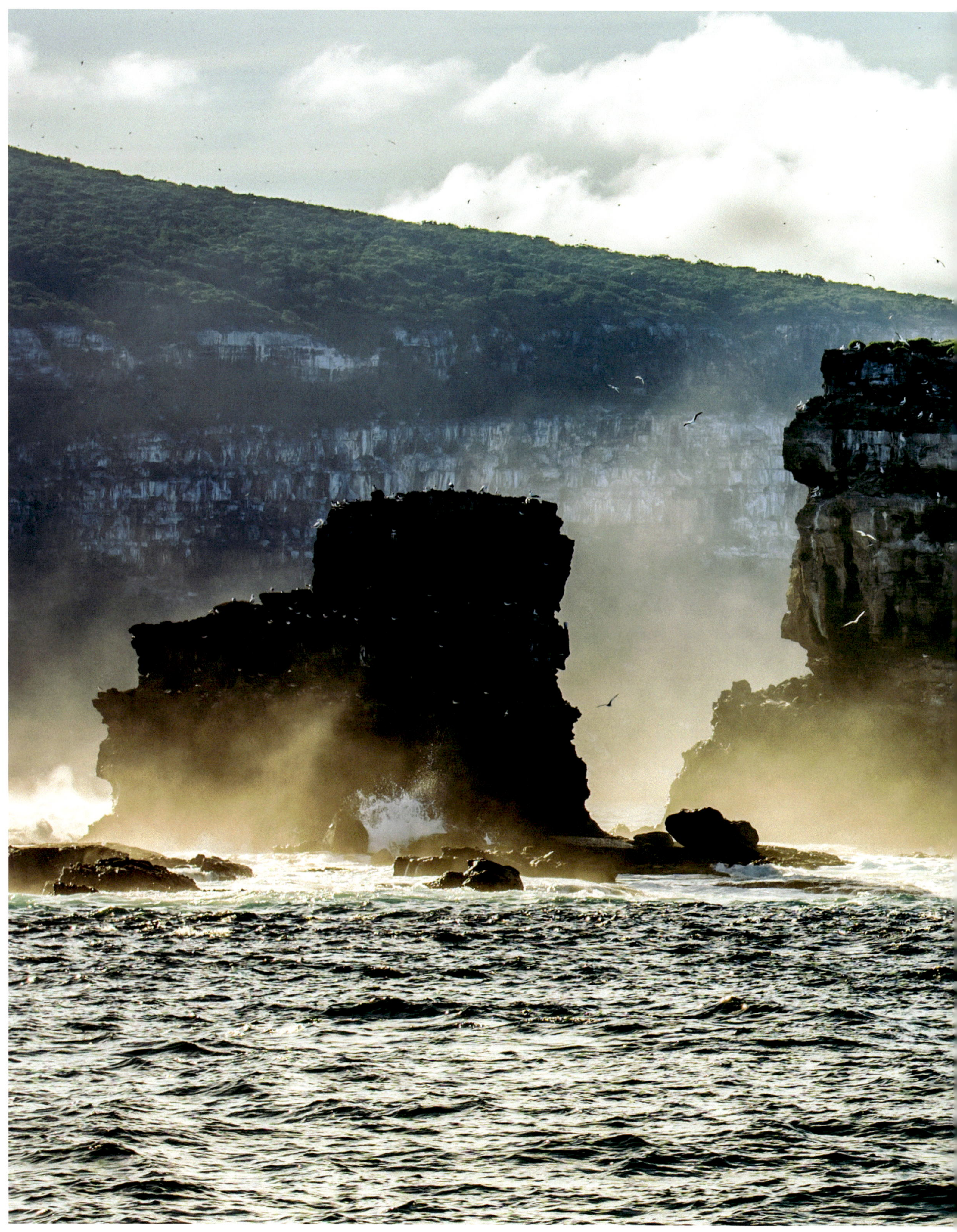

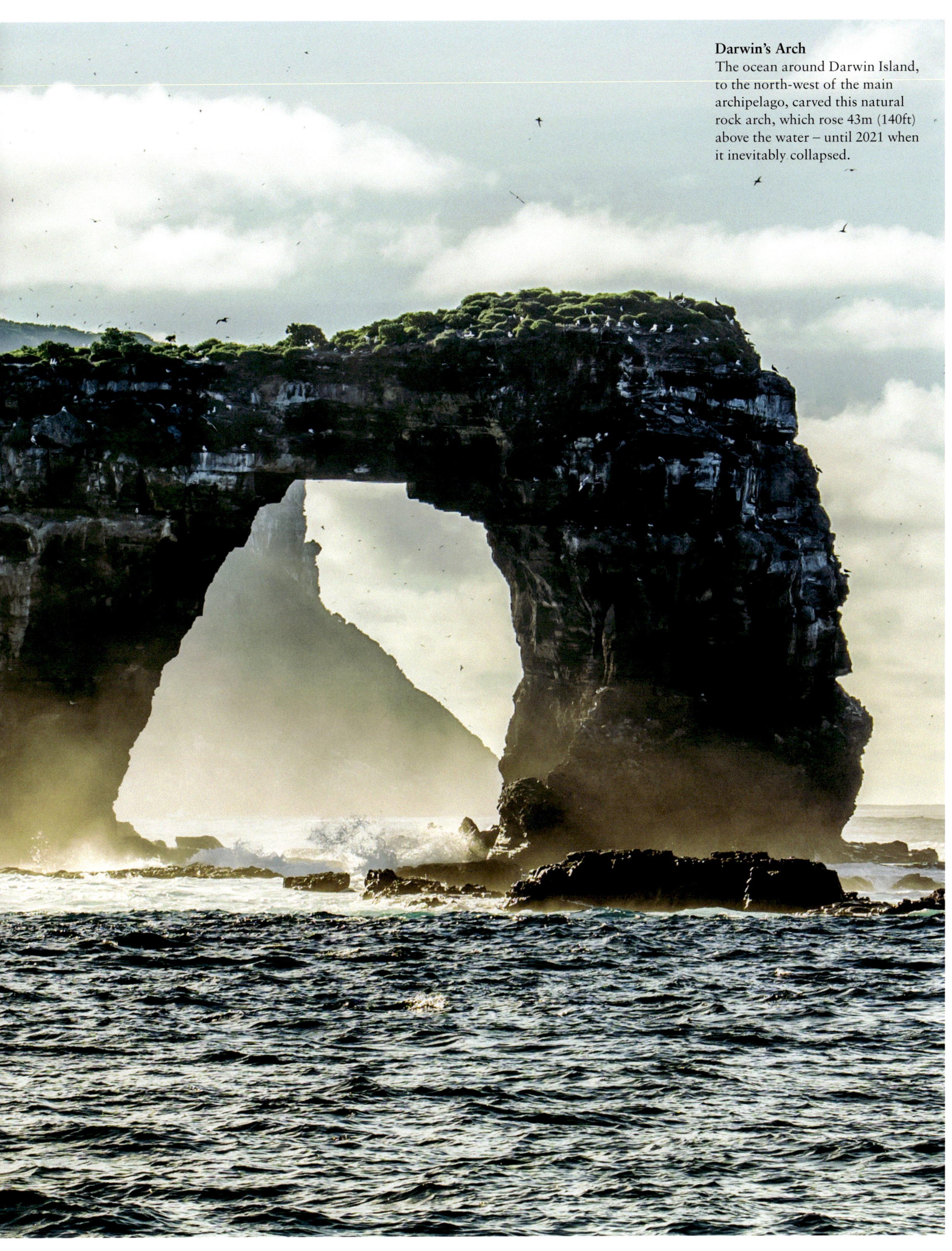

Darwin's Arch
The ocean around Darwin Island,
to the north-west of the main
archipelago, carved this natural
rock arch, which rose 43m (140ft)
above the water – until 2021 when
it inevitably collapsed.

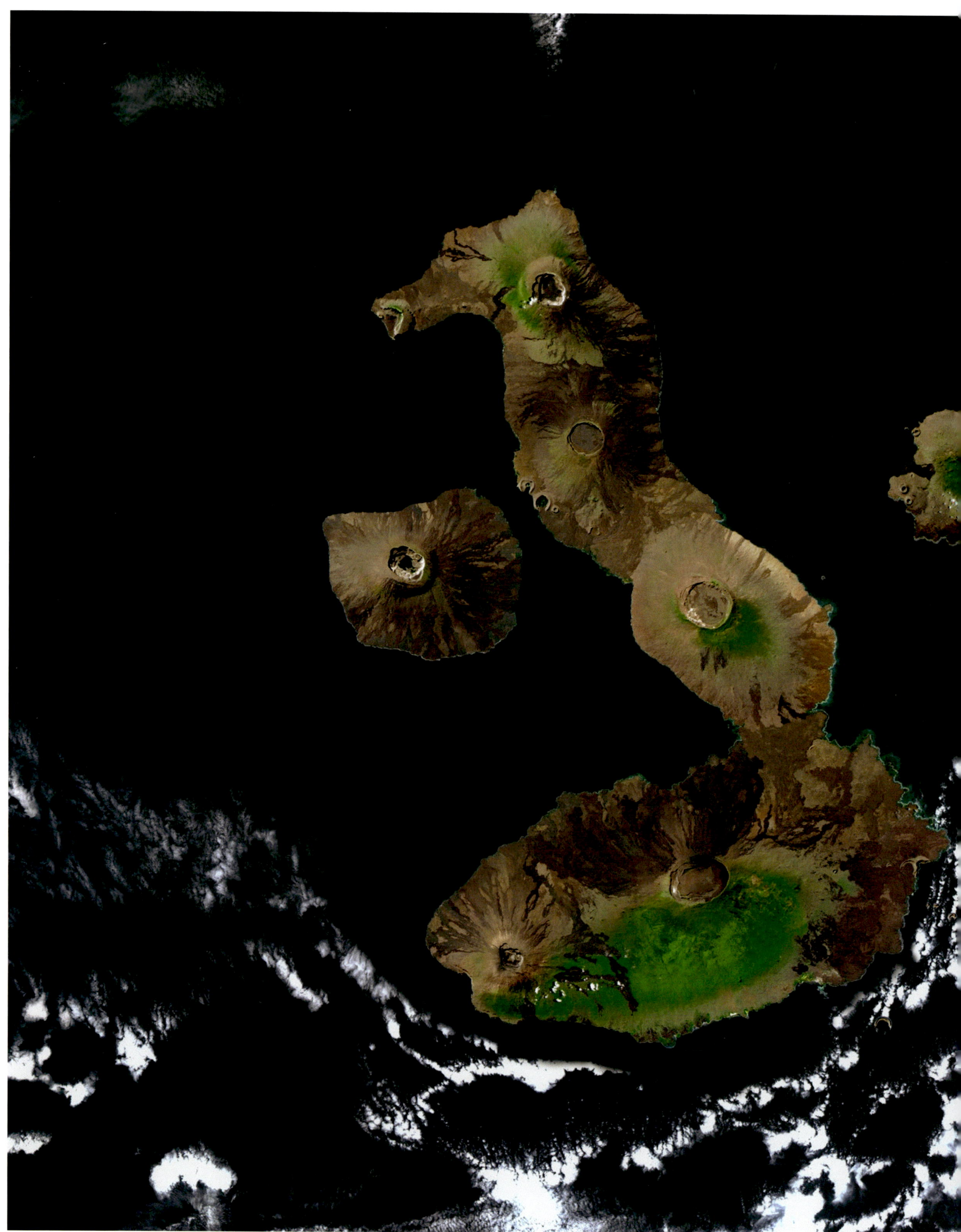

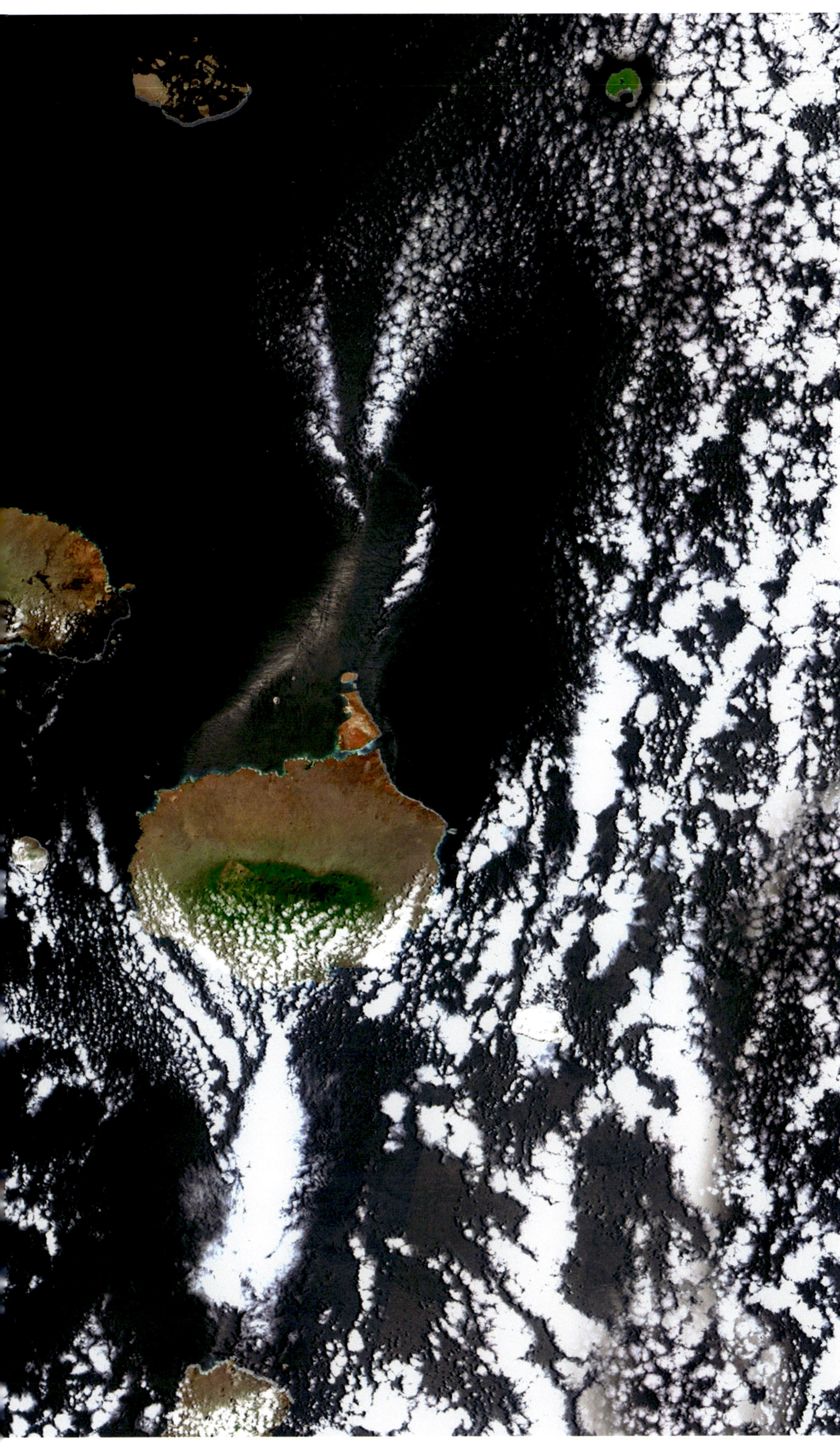

View from space
A satellite image shows the main islands of the Galápagos with San Cristóbal in the east and Fernandina (with clouds hugging the volcano) in the west, beside Isabela, the largest land mass. The most populous island is Santa Cruz (roughly centre).

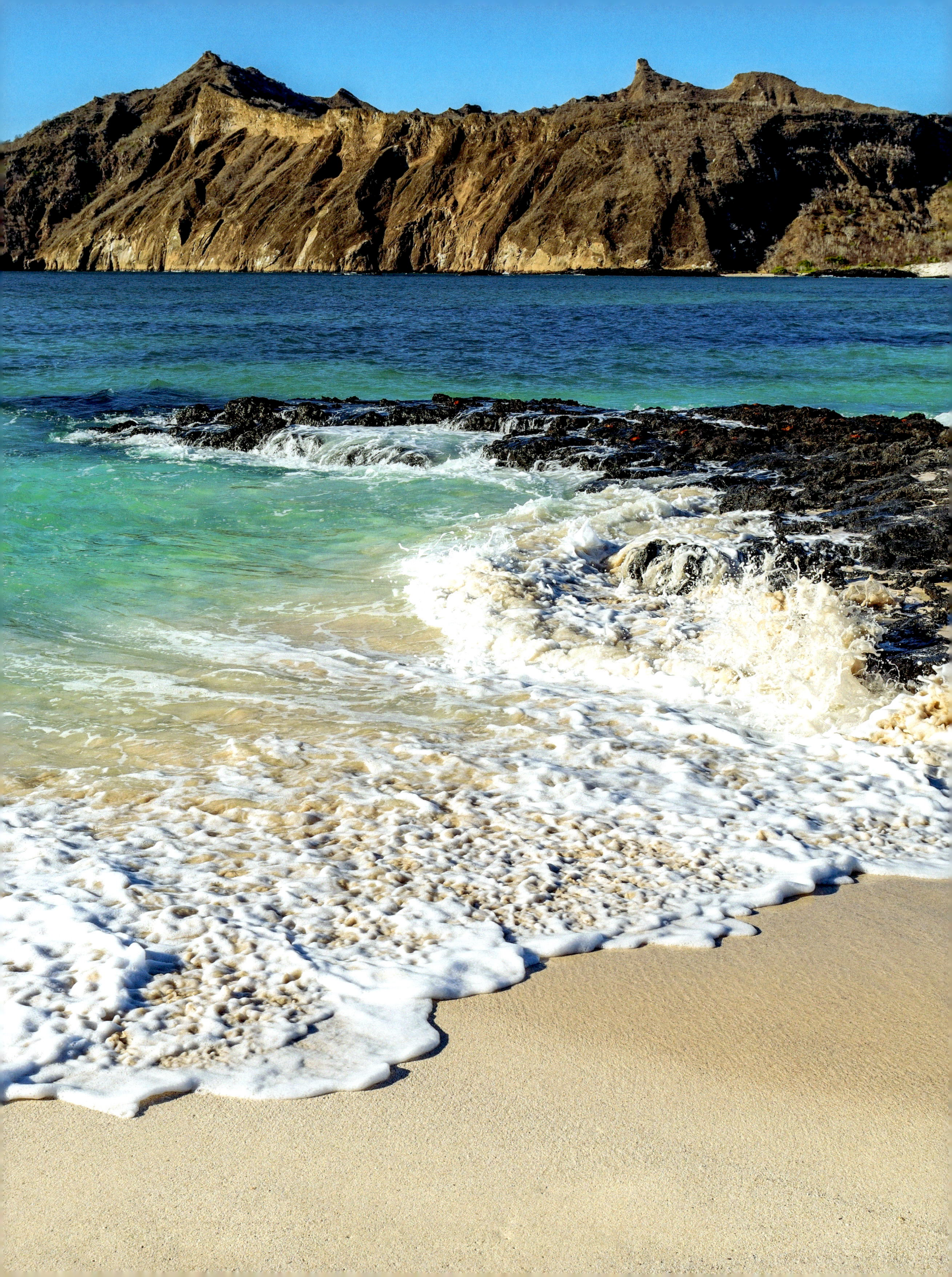

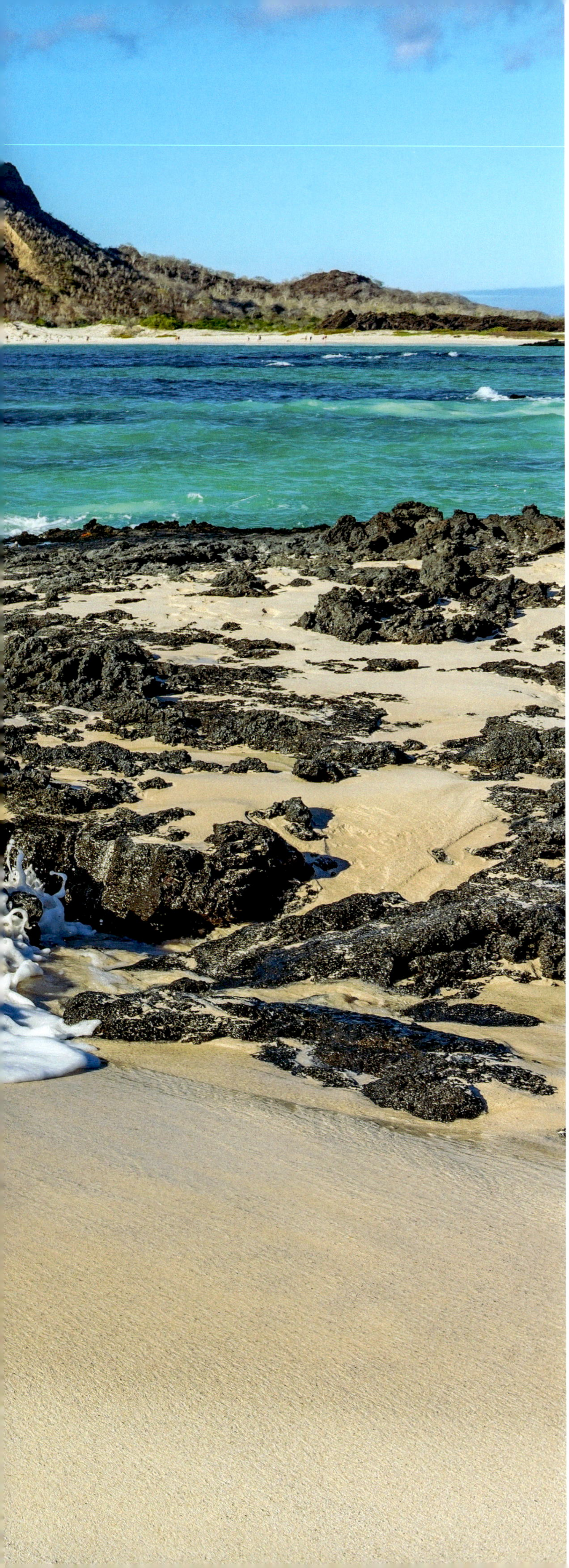

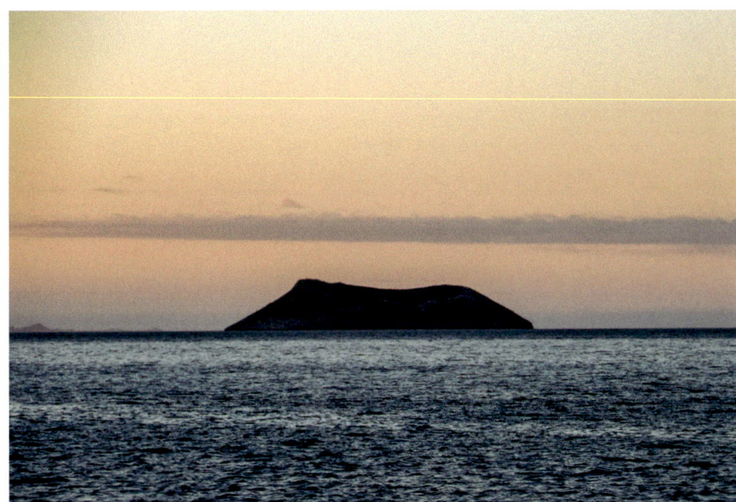

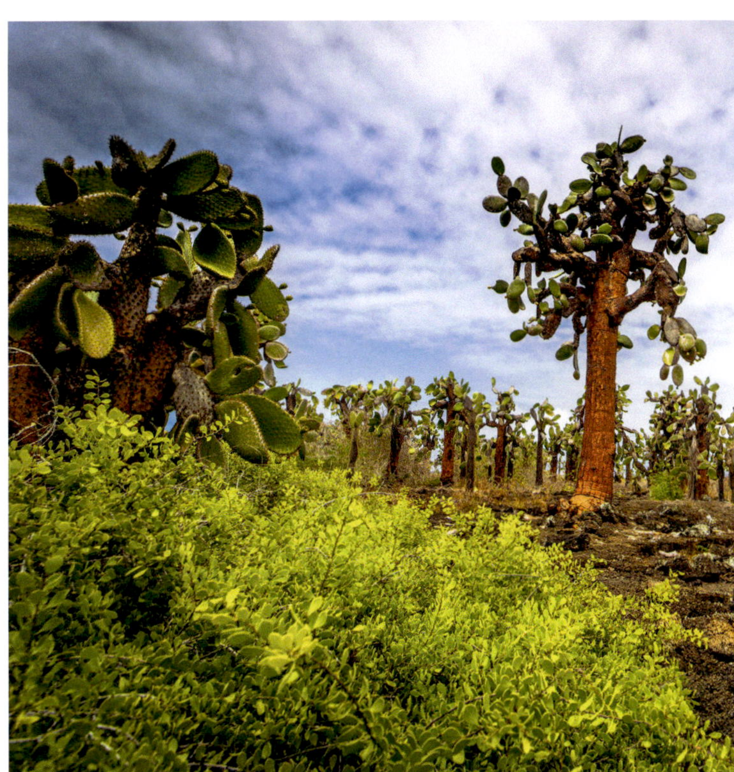

LEFT:
San Cristóbal
This island was the first port of call for HMS *Beagle* and its naturalist passenger, Charles Darwin, on 15 September 1835. Darwin would have known it by the British name Chatham.

ABOVE TOP:
Daphne Major
This tuff cone, rising more than 100m (320ft) above the water, is roughly halfway between the Galápagos islands of Santa Cruz and Santiago.

ABOVE BOTTOM:
Cactus forest
Tall cacti of endemic *Opuntia galapageia* plants form a backdrop to Tortuga Bay, a popular sightseeing spot on Santa Cruz. This is one of the few places on the Galápagos where tourists can swim off the beach (in part of the bay).

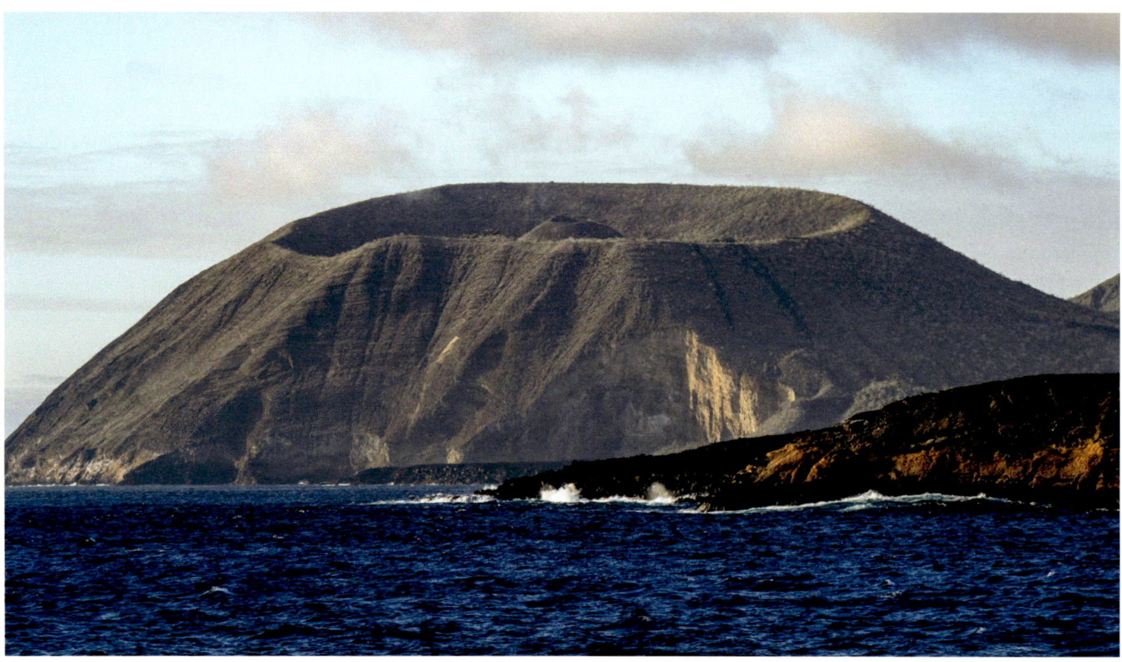

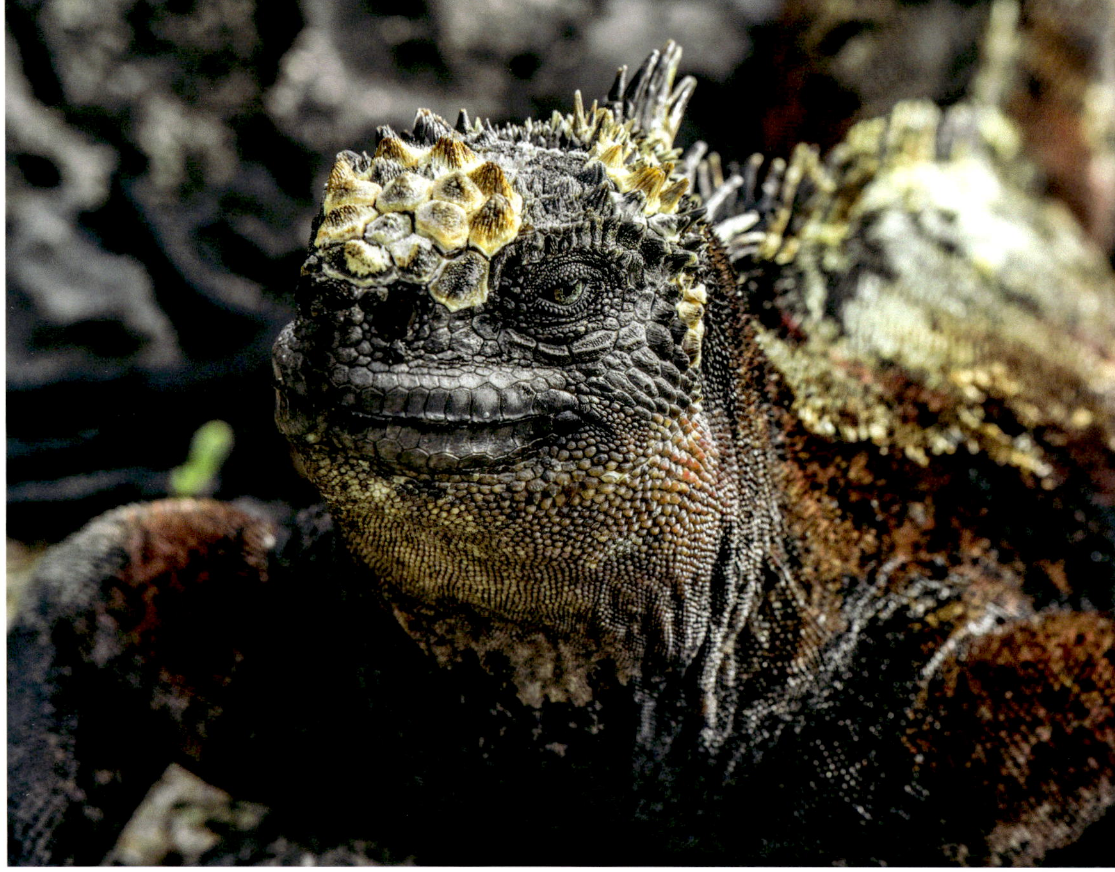

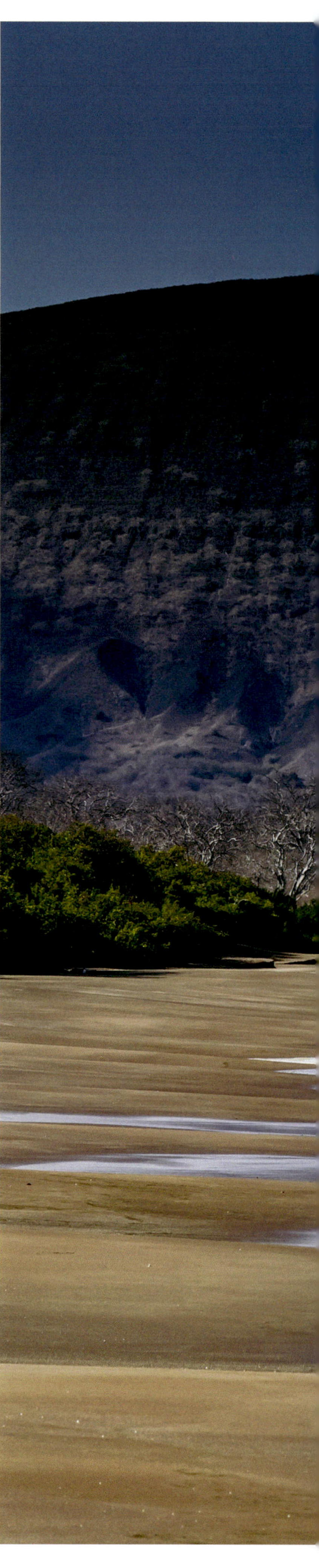

Volcanic feature

The tall tuff cone of the Ecuador Volcano, looking rather like a well-worn hat and made from deposits of ash from volcanic eruptions, stands above the northern coast of Isabela. This volcano has not erupted for 900 years.

Marine iguana

A male marine iguana has taken on bright colours, turning its normally dark, drab scales into an eye-catching calling card intended to attract mates during the breeding season.

Brown pelican

One of the largest bird species on the islands, this brown pelican watches the ocean as it prepares to take to the air and snatch some fish food from the ocean in its large, sack-shaped bill.

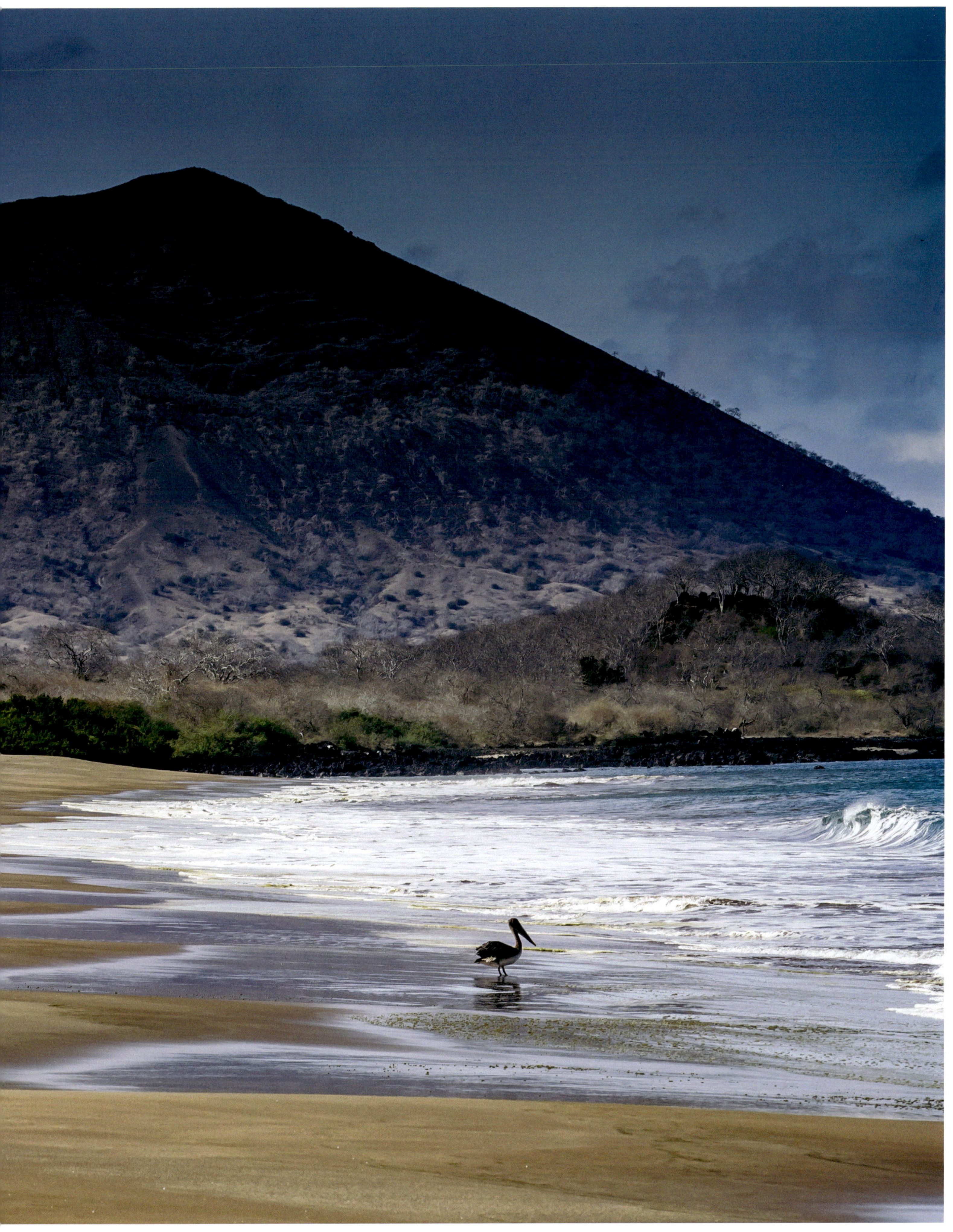

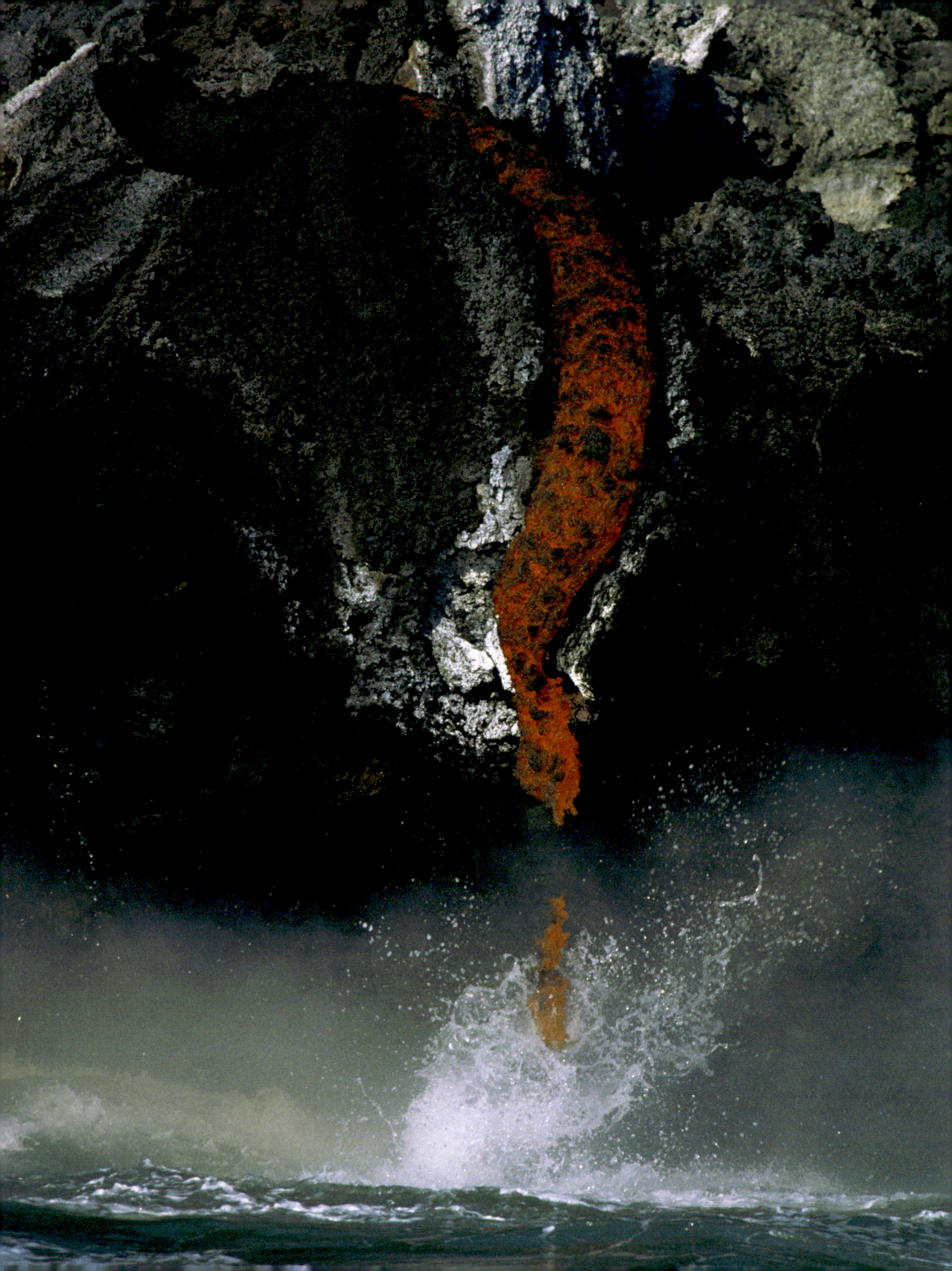

Geology

There are 128 islands in the Galápagos archipelago, most of them small rocky islets that poke above the waves. There are 18 main islands, all of which are volcanic in origin. The islands have been formed over the last 4.5 million years by a hotspot. A hotspot is a chamber of magma that sits below the crust and erupts through volcanoes frequently, first on the seabed and then, as repeated layers of rock are laid down, an island that breaks the surface is formed. The Galápagos Islands are on the Nazca Plate that is shifting slowly eastward, plunging below the South American continent and helping push up the tallest parts of the Andes Mountains. The motion of the plate drags the islands with it but the hotspot stays where it is. As a result a chain of islands has formed. The oldest one is Española in the south east and the islands become younger to the north and west.

There are 21 volcanoes above the surface in the Galápagos, of which six are still active. There is an eruption somewhere in the islands almost every year. The youngest island is Fernandina, which has La Cumbre, one of the most active volcanoes in the archipelago. The largest island, Isabela, is just to the east and has four active craters. Six other volcanoes are regarded as dormant, but most have erupted in the last thousand years. As a result there is evidence of volcanic activity all over the archipelago – from craters spitting fire and smouldering fumaroles to ancient craters and long-cooled lava tubes that now create unique habitats for the island's special wildlife.

OPPOSITE:
Lava flow
A torrent of fast-flowing lava or pahoehoe (pronounced pa-hoy-hoy) slides down from the La Cumbre volcano on Fernandina island.

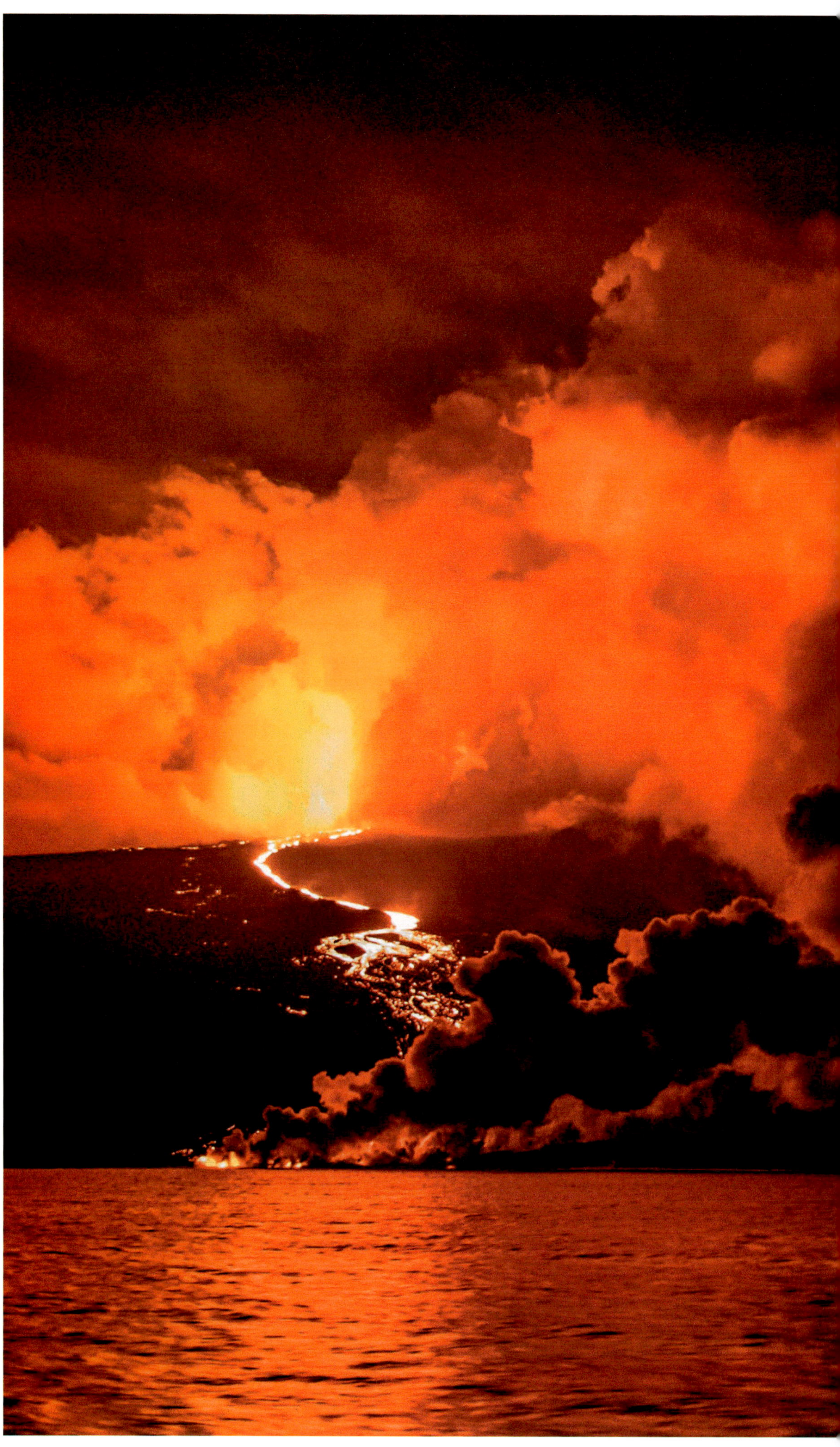

Smoke on the water
The glow of an eruption in 2022 illuminates a plume of smoke and steam rising from where the red-hot lava from Wolf Volcano hits the sea.

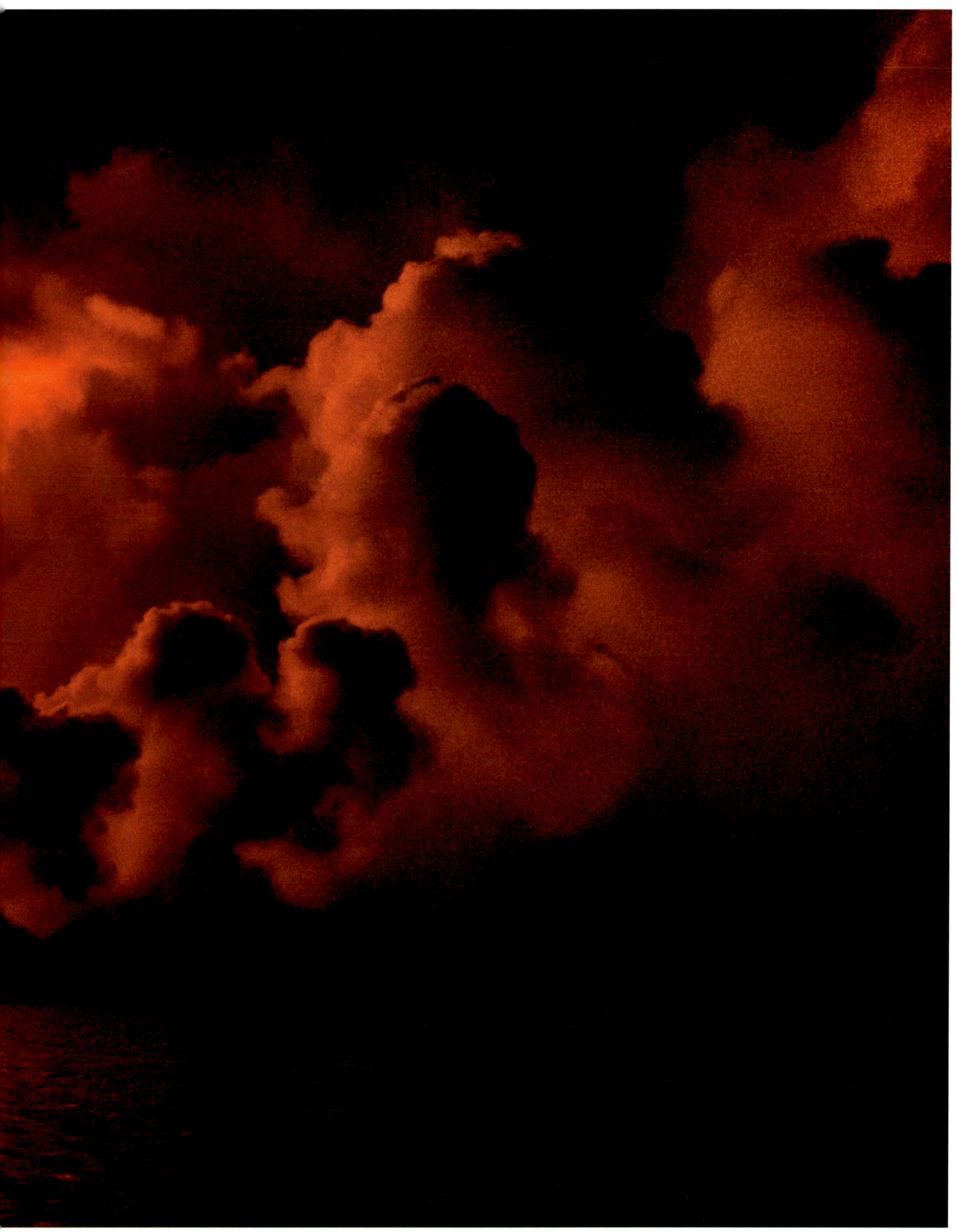

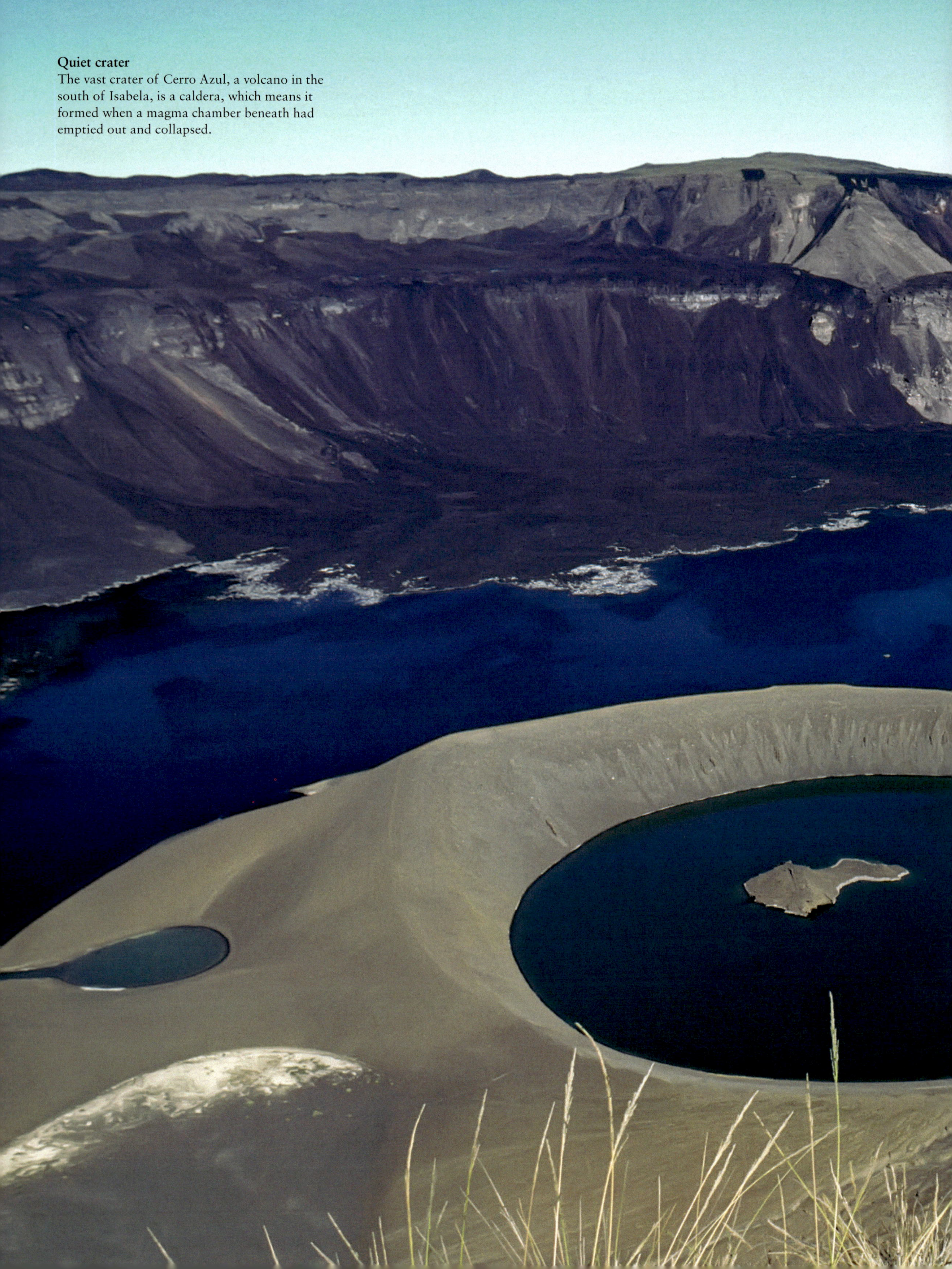

Quiet crater
The vast crater of Cerro Azul, a volcano in the
south of Isabela, is a caldera, which means it
formed when a magma chamber beneath had
emptied out and collapsed.

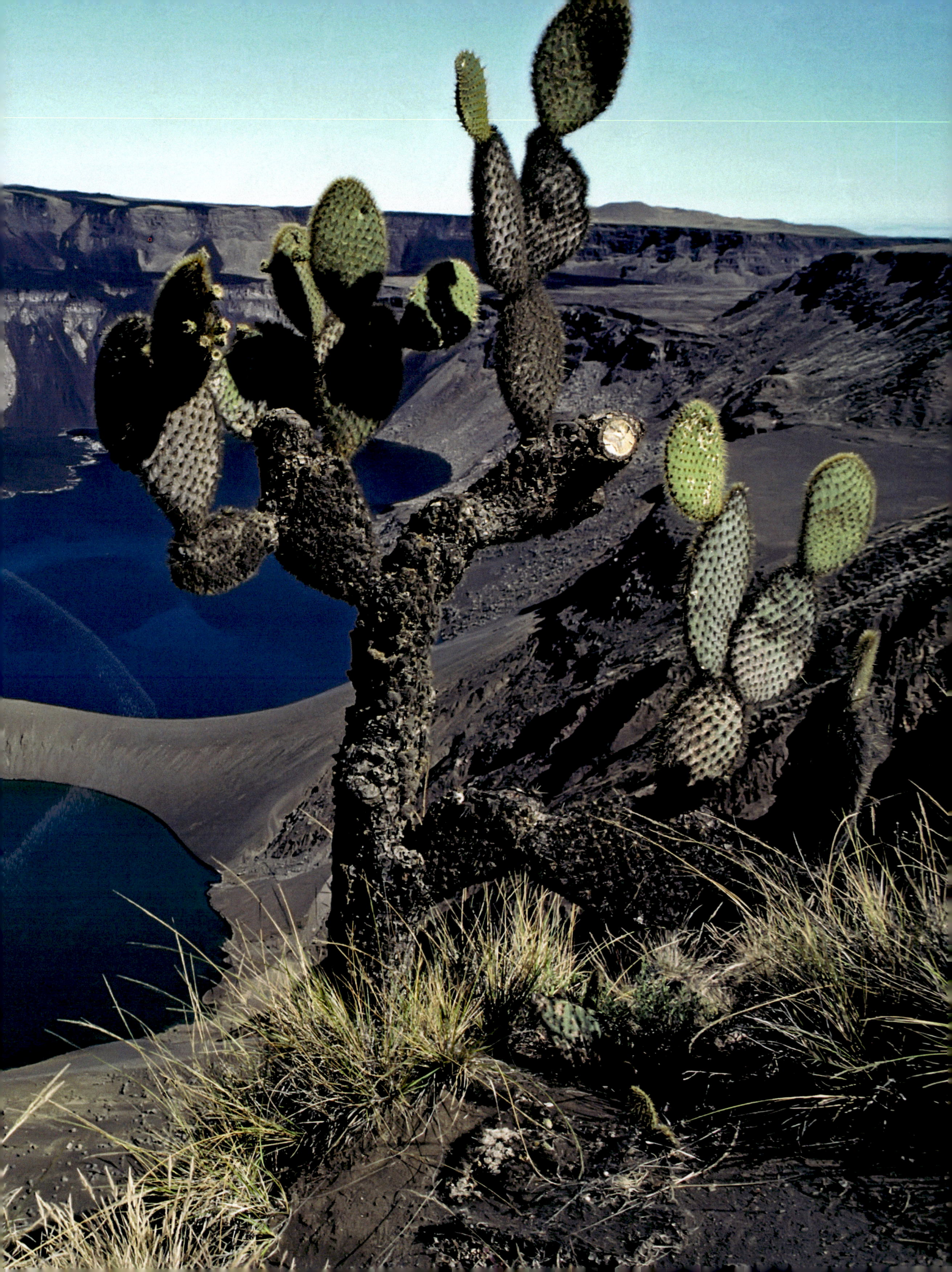

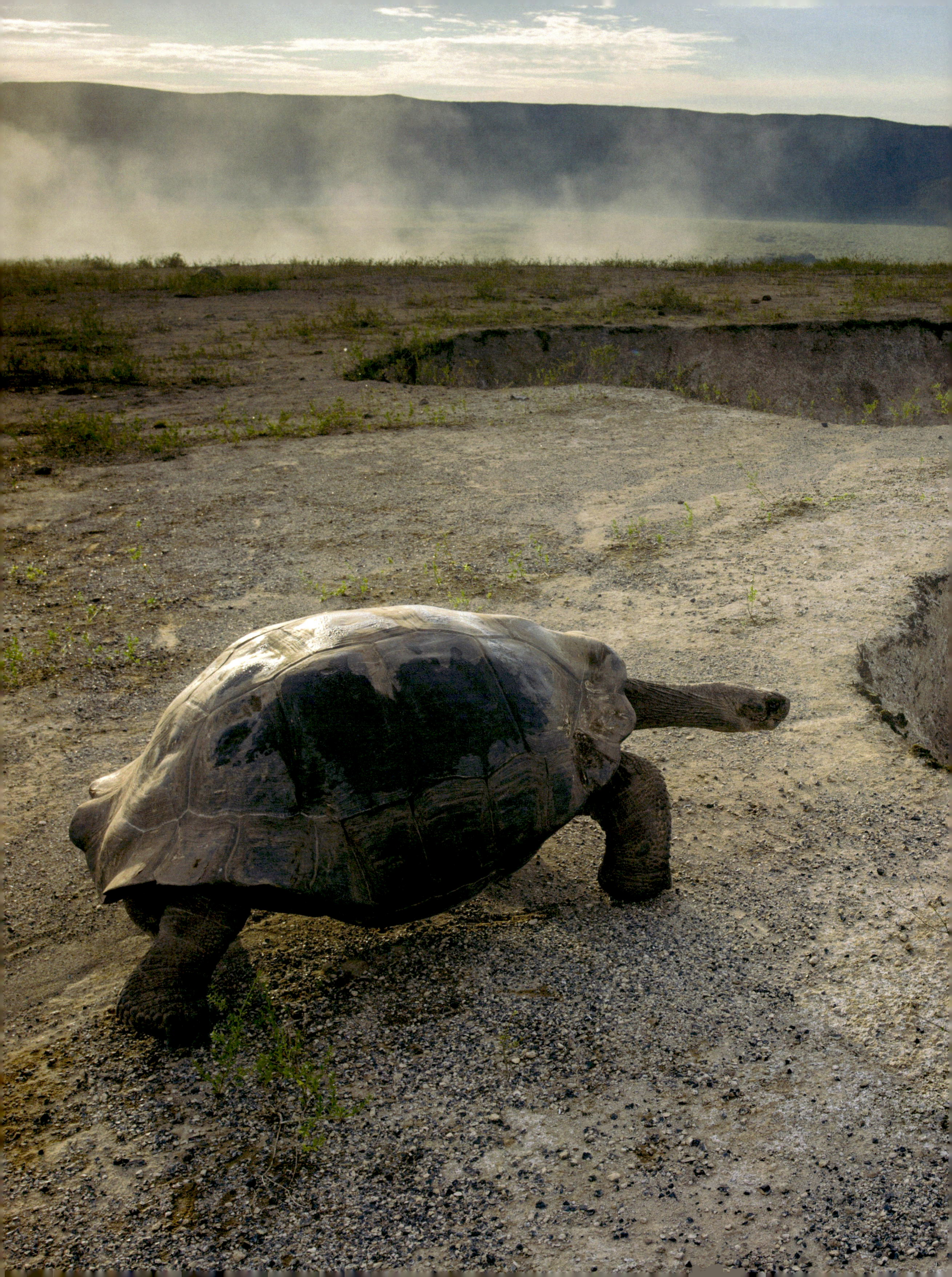

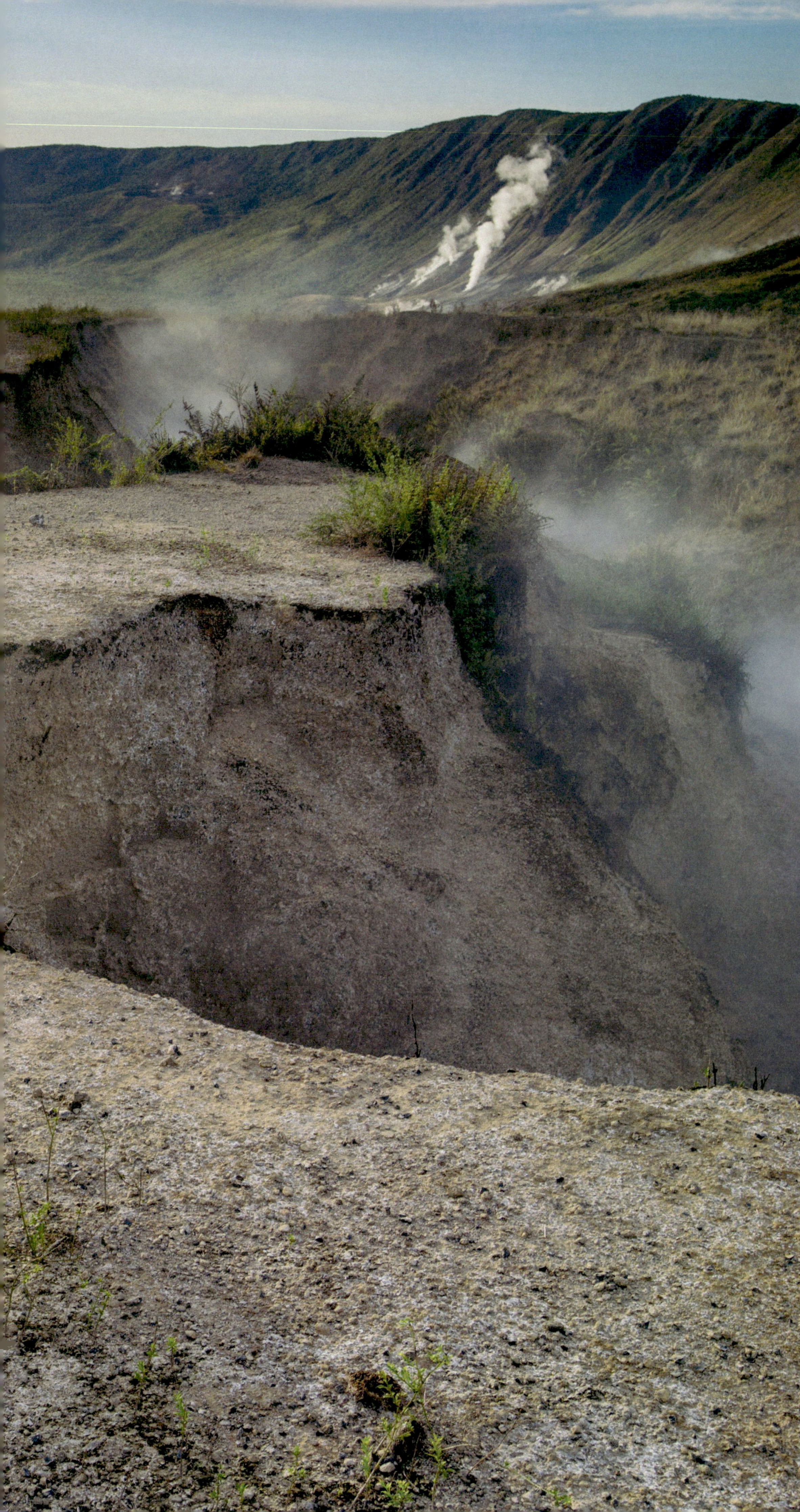

Alcedo giant tortoise
The volcanoes of the Galápagos generally have their own species of giant tortoise, which graze on their slopes. This Alcedo giant tortoise is found around the vents and fumaroles of the Alcedo Volcano in central Isabela.

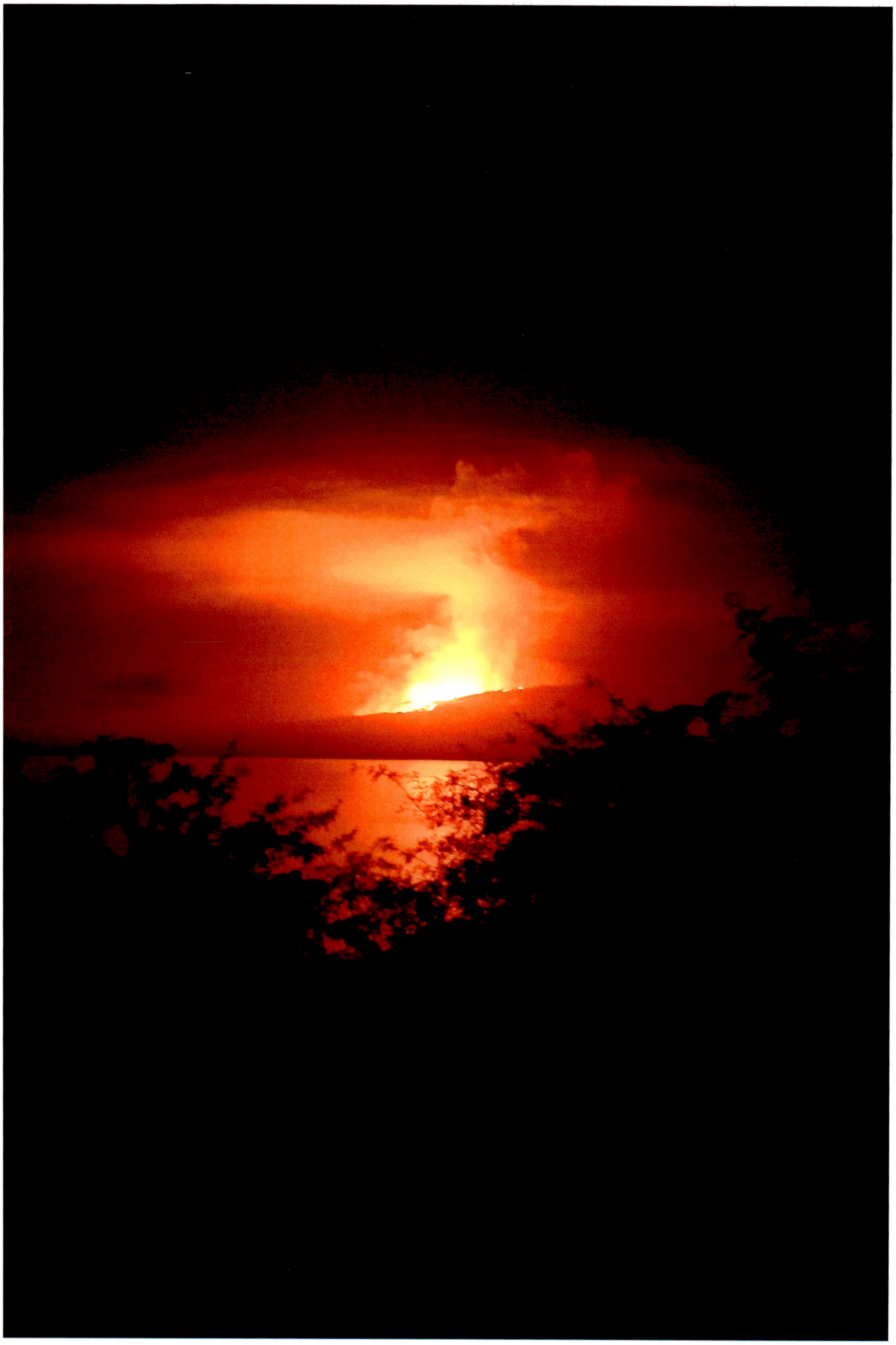

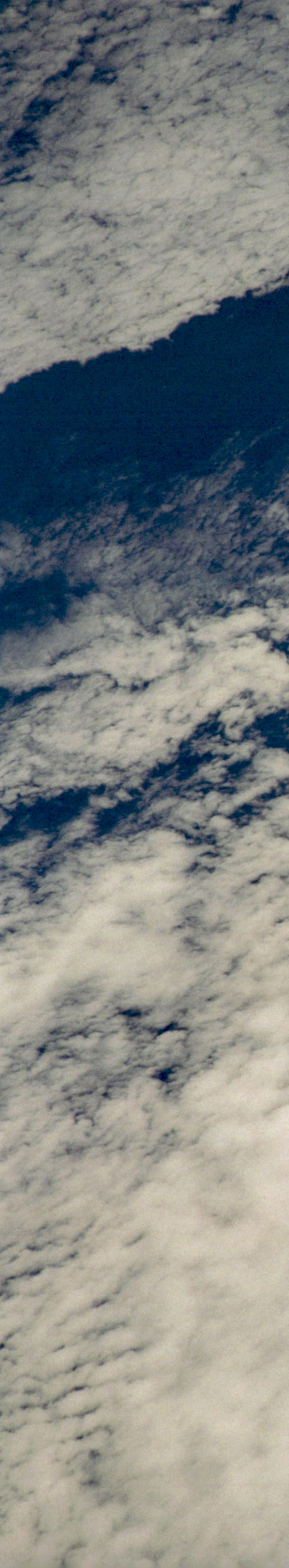

Latest eruption
A fountain of lava can be seen during the eruption of La Cumbre volcano on Fernandina, which began in March 2024 and went on for two months.

Quieter time
The La Cumbre volcano crater is pictured from the air before the latest eruption. La Cumbre erupts on average every few years. As a result Fernandina is uninhabited.

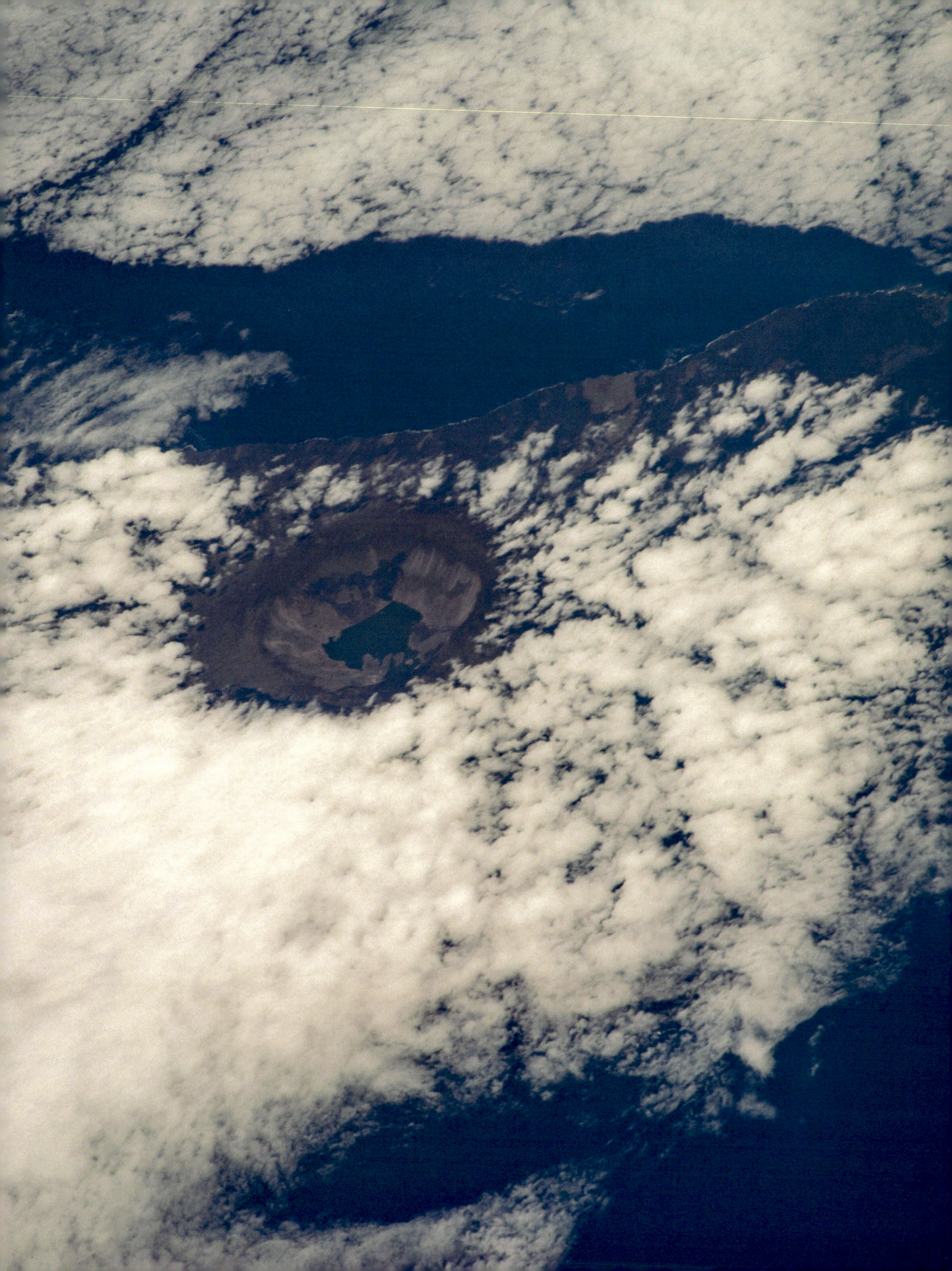

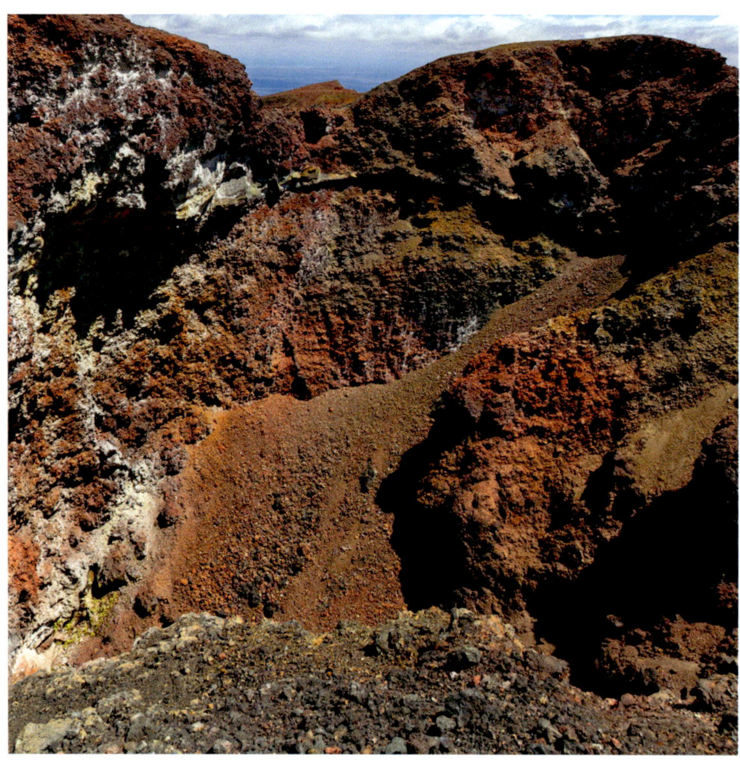

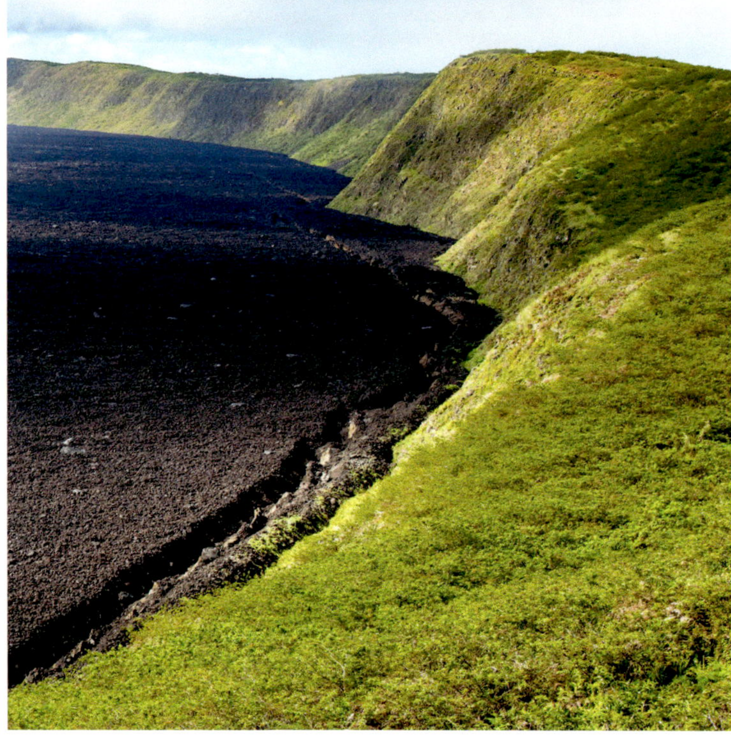

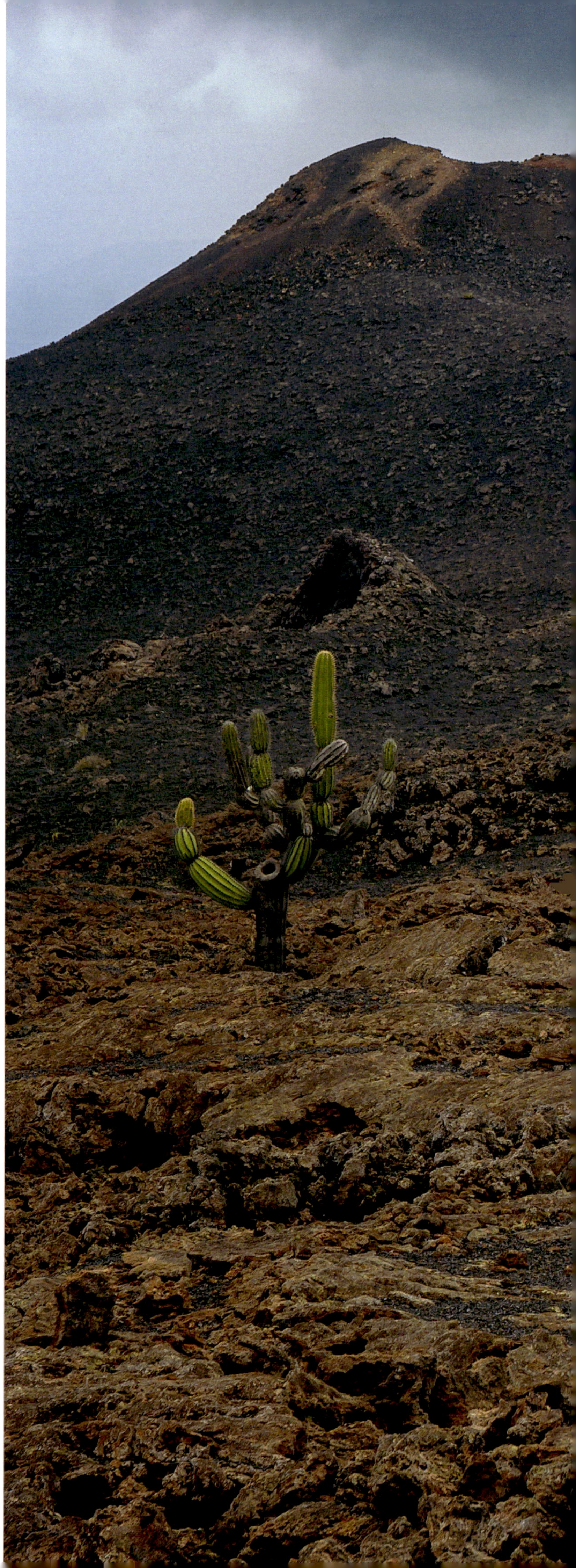

Sierra Negra volcano
The Sierra Negra is the largest crater on the islands at 9km (5 miles) wide. That also makes it the second-largest crater in the world. Sierra Negra last erupted in 2018. Desert plants, like cacti, are quick to colonize the empty rocks.

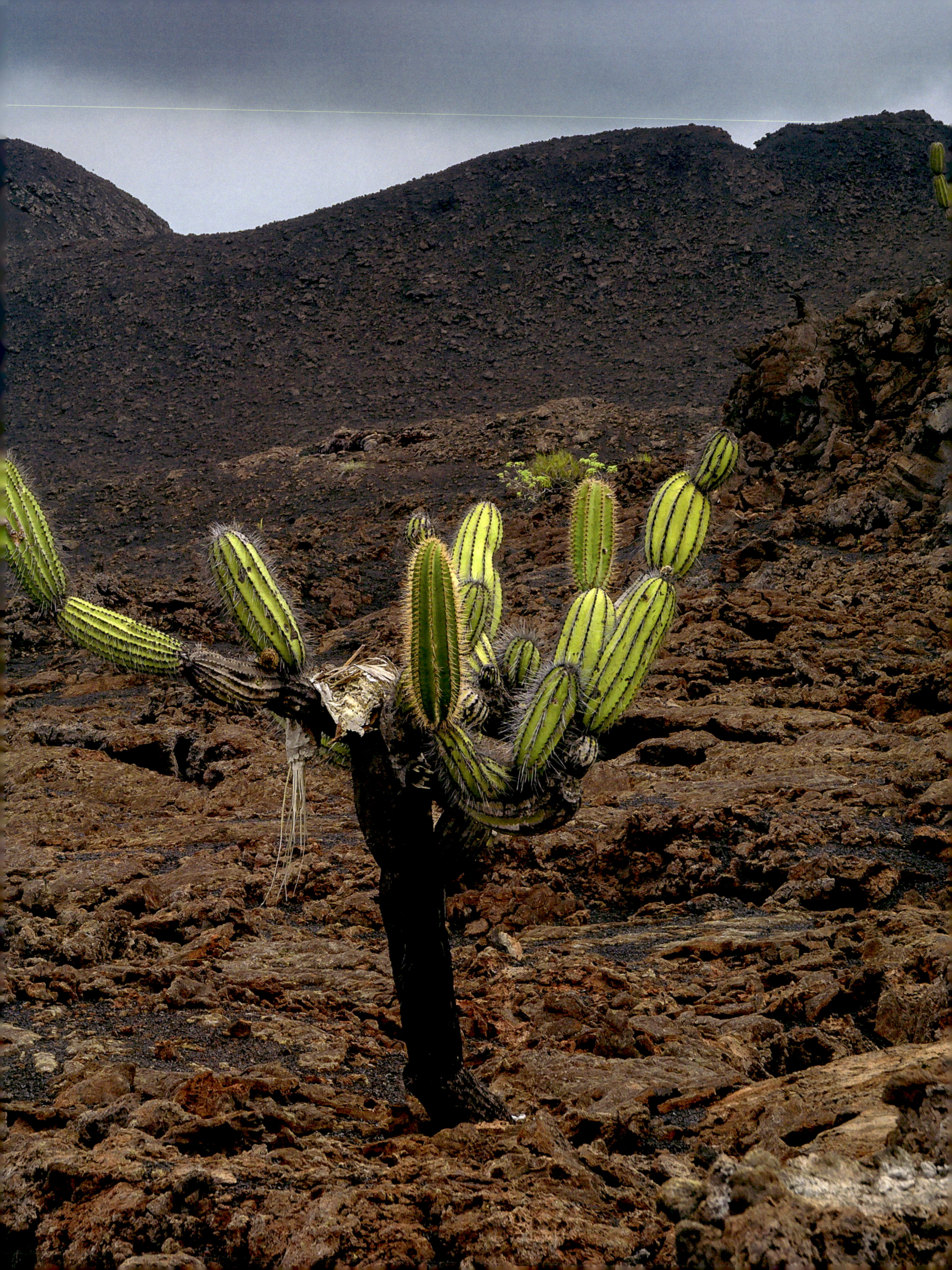

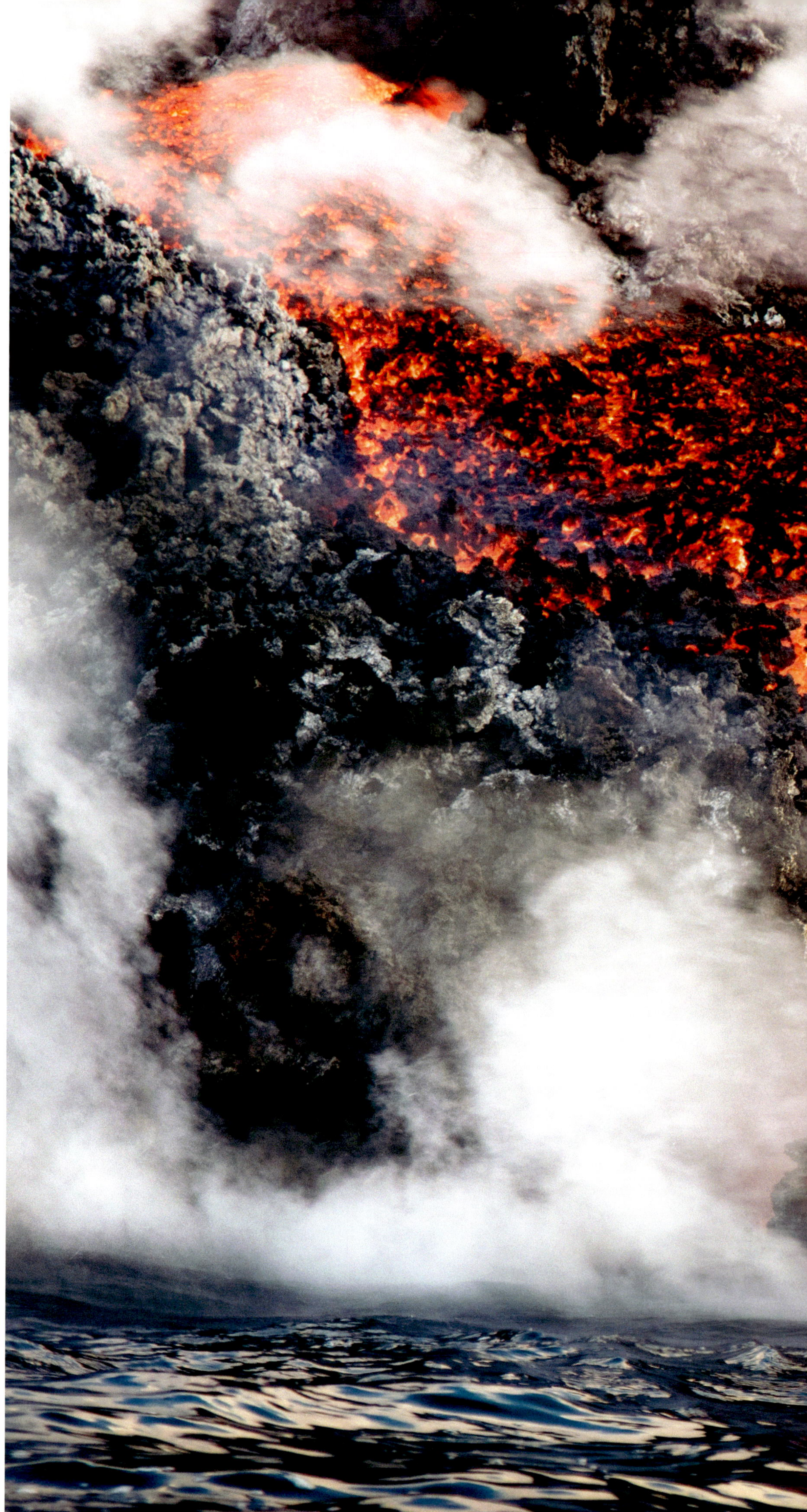

Thick lava
A thick, chunky lava, known
as aa (from the Hawaiian word
a'a), flows slowly into the ocean
near Punta Moreno from the July
2018 eruption of Sierra Negra on
Isabela Island.

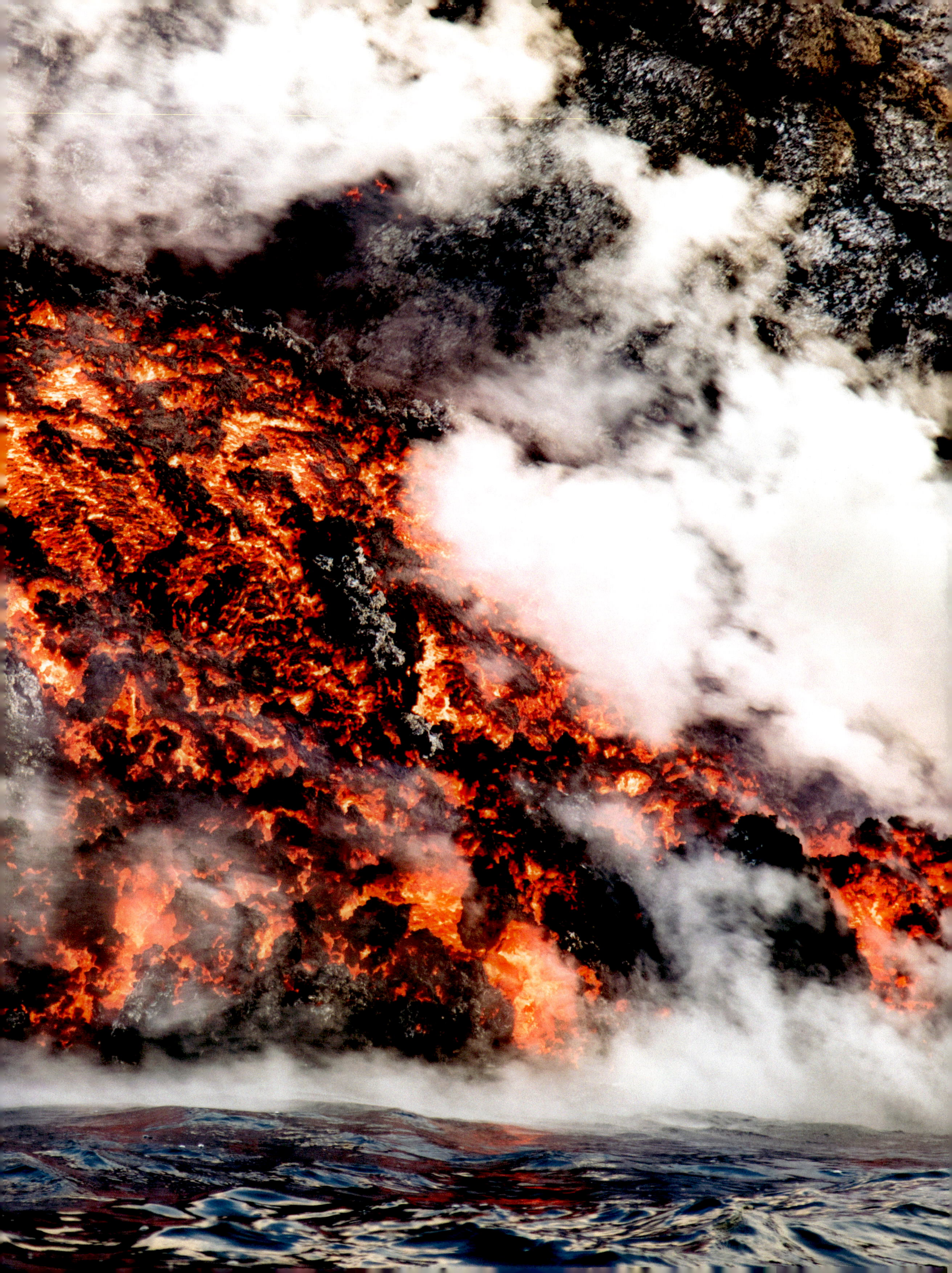

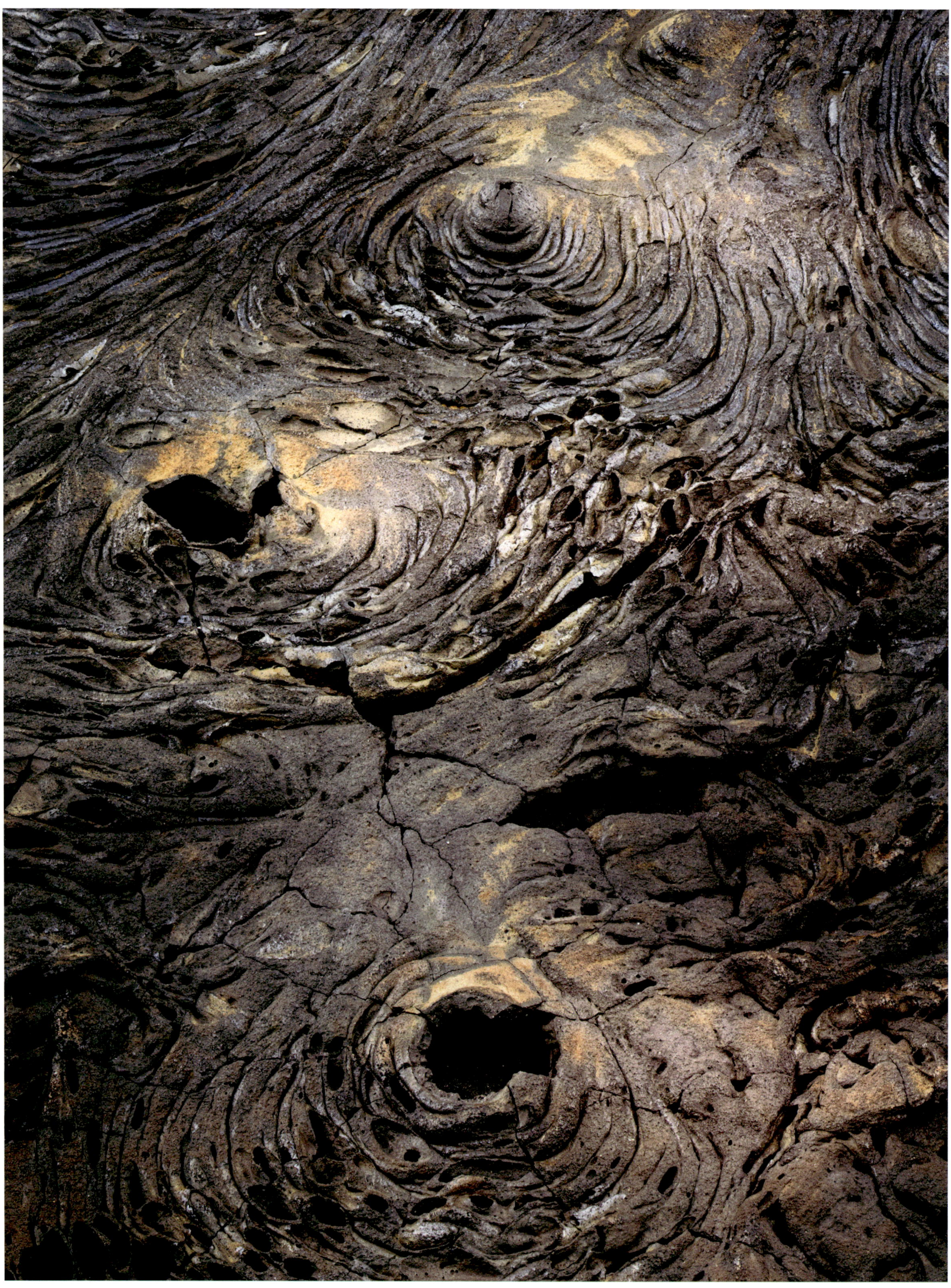

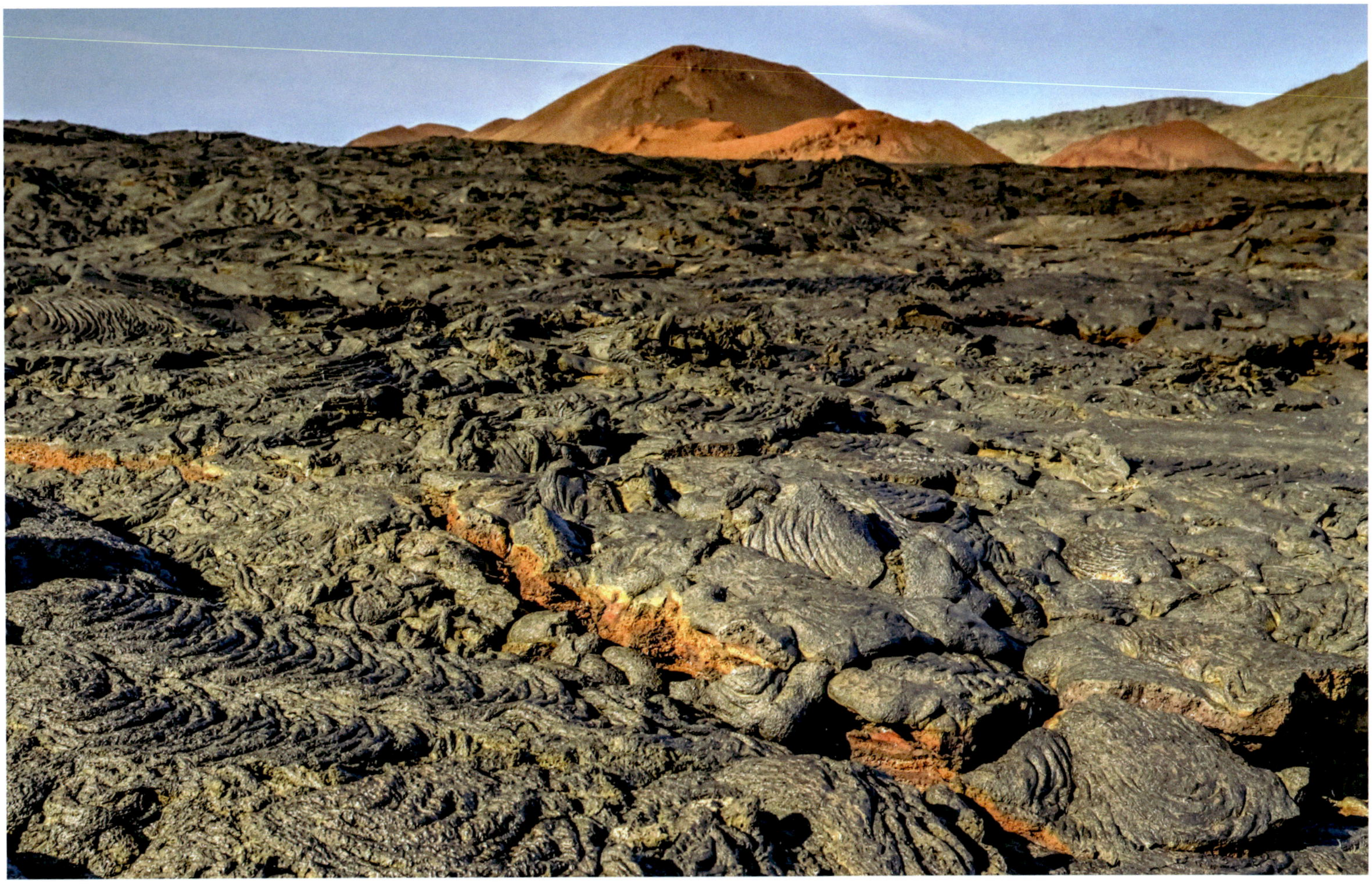

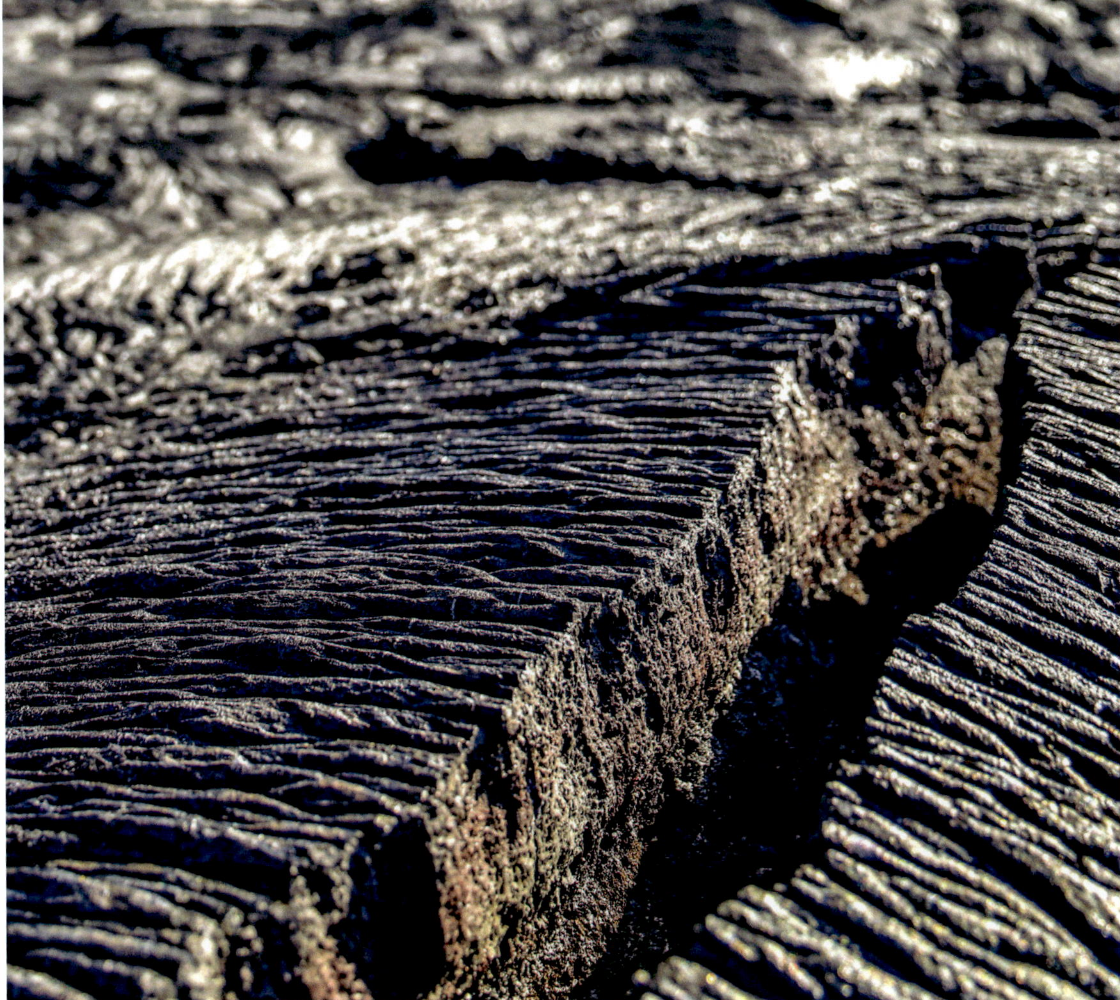

Pahoehoe lava

These cooled lava flows all show evidence of pahoehoe lava (originally from a Hawaiian word meaning rope-like). The slick lava cools first at the top, creating a crust that is dragged on underneath by the continued flow of hot, liquid rock. That dragging creates the rippled or corded effects in the crusts shown here.

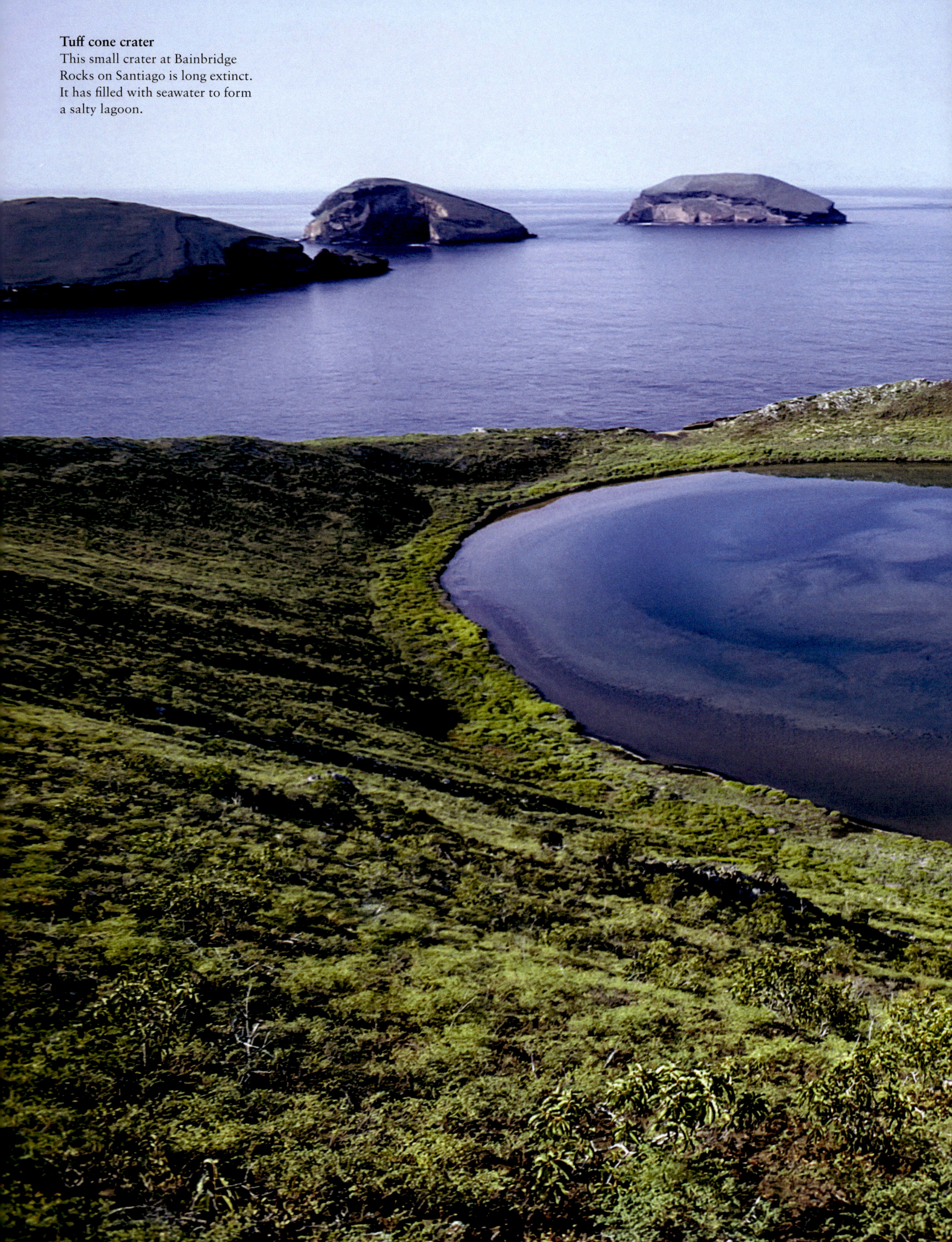

Tuff cone crater
This small crater at Bainbridge
Rocks on Santiago is long extinct.
It has filled with seawater to form
a salty lagoon.

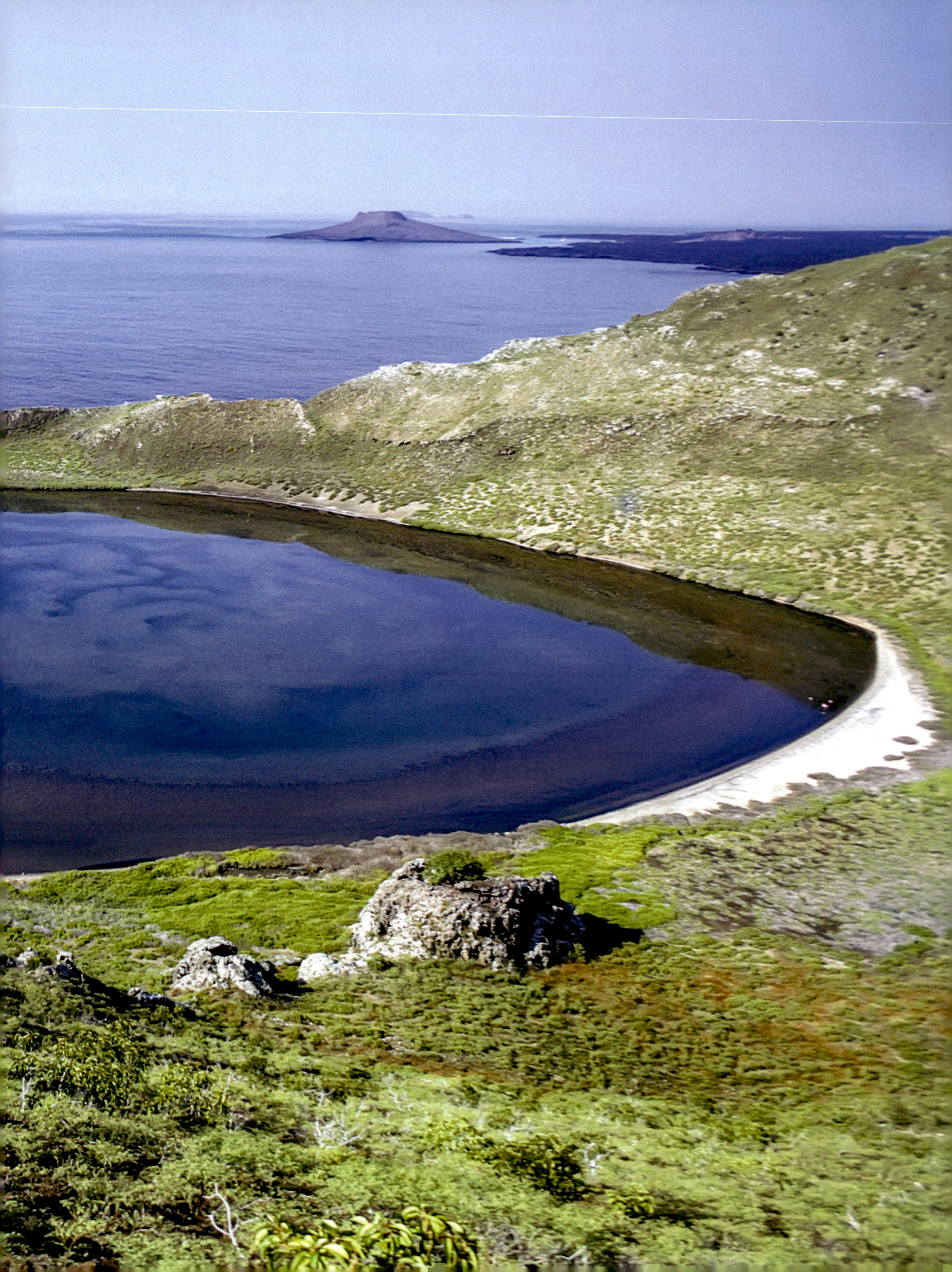

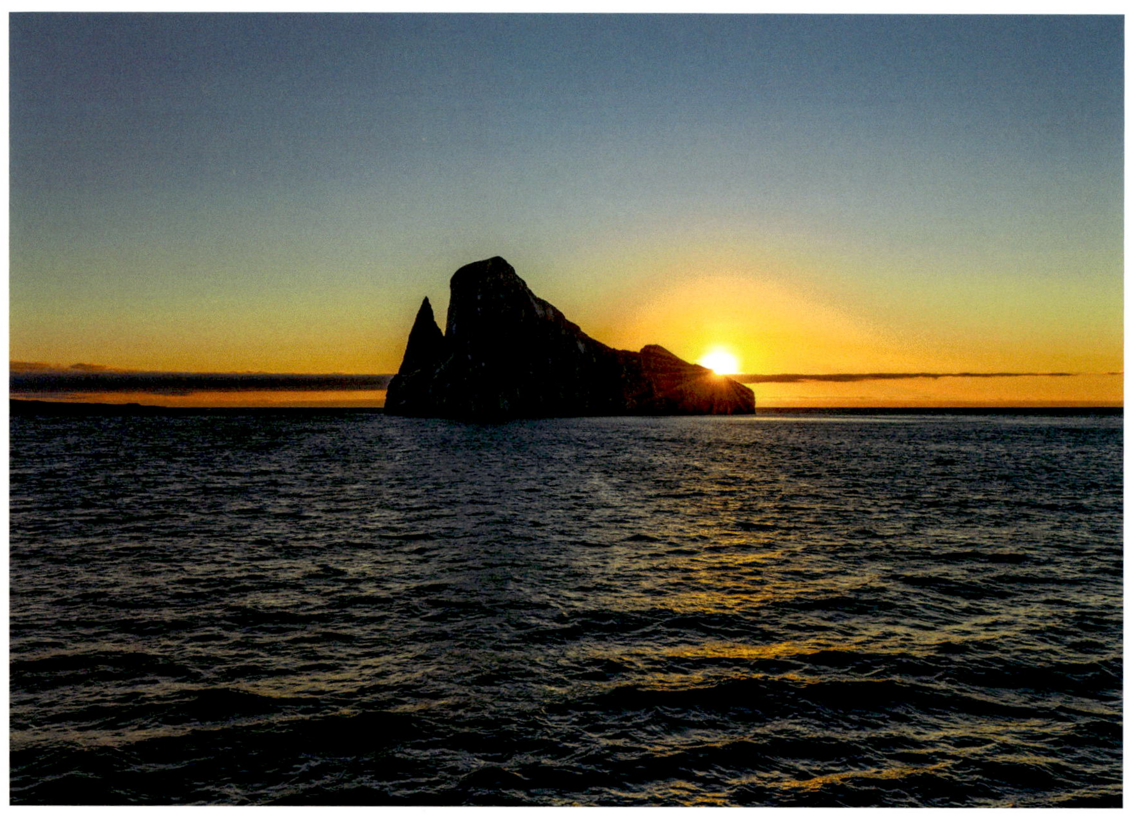

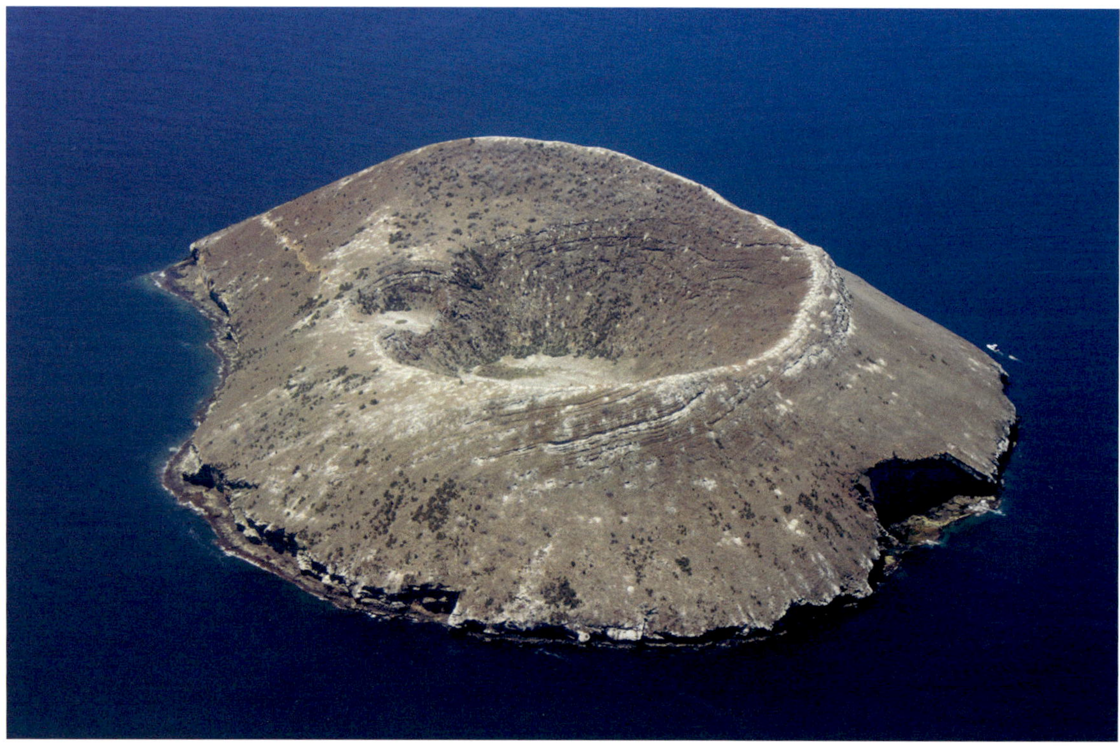

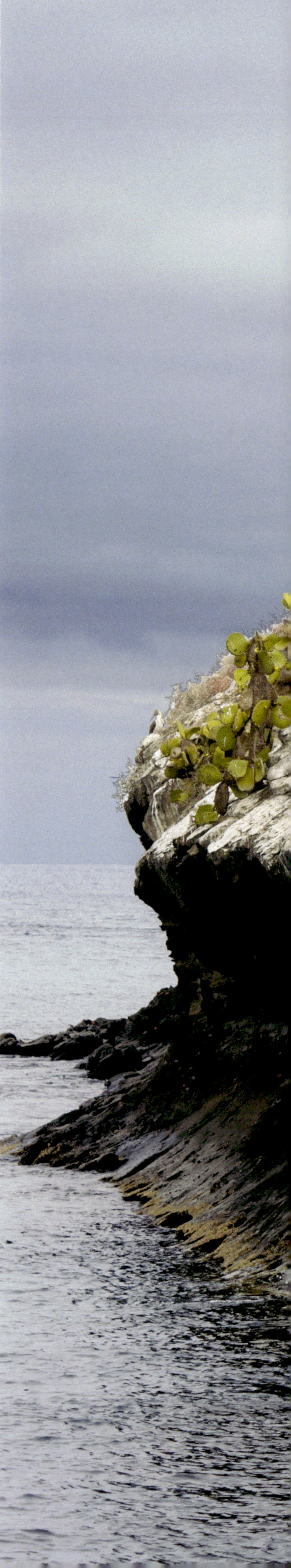

ABOVE TOP:

Kicker Rock
Also known as Leon Dormido
('sleeping lion'), this rock is
the last remnant of an ancient
volcano. Picked out by the sunset
to the west of San Cristóbal, the
edifice is gradually eroding away.

ABOVE BOTTOM AND RIGHT:

Daphne Major
This isolated, long-extinct crater is
largely off-limits to visitors apart
from a few scientists. They are
especially interested in the finches
that live there and how they are
evolving into a new species.

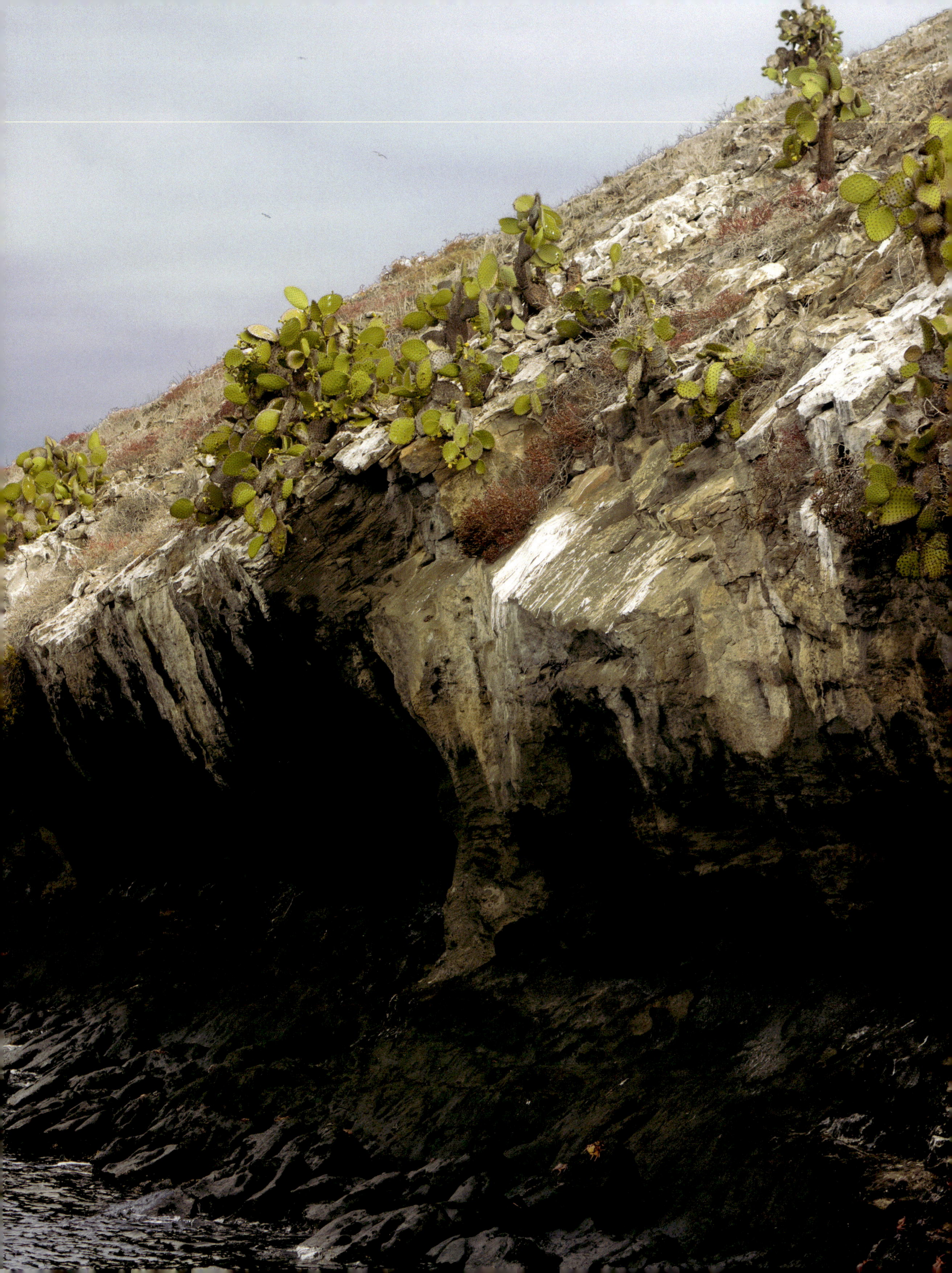

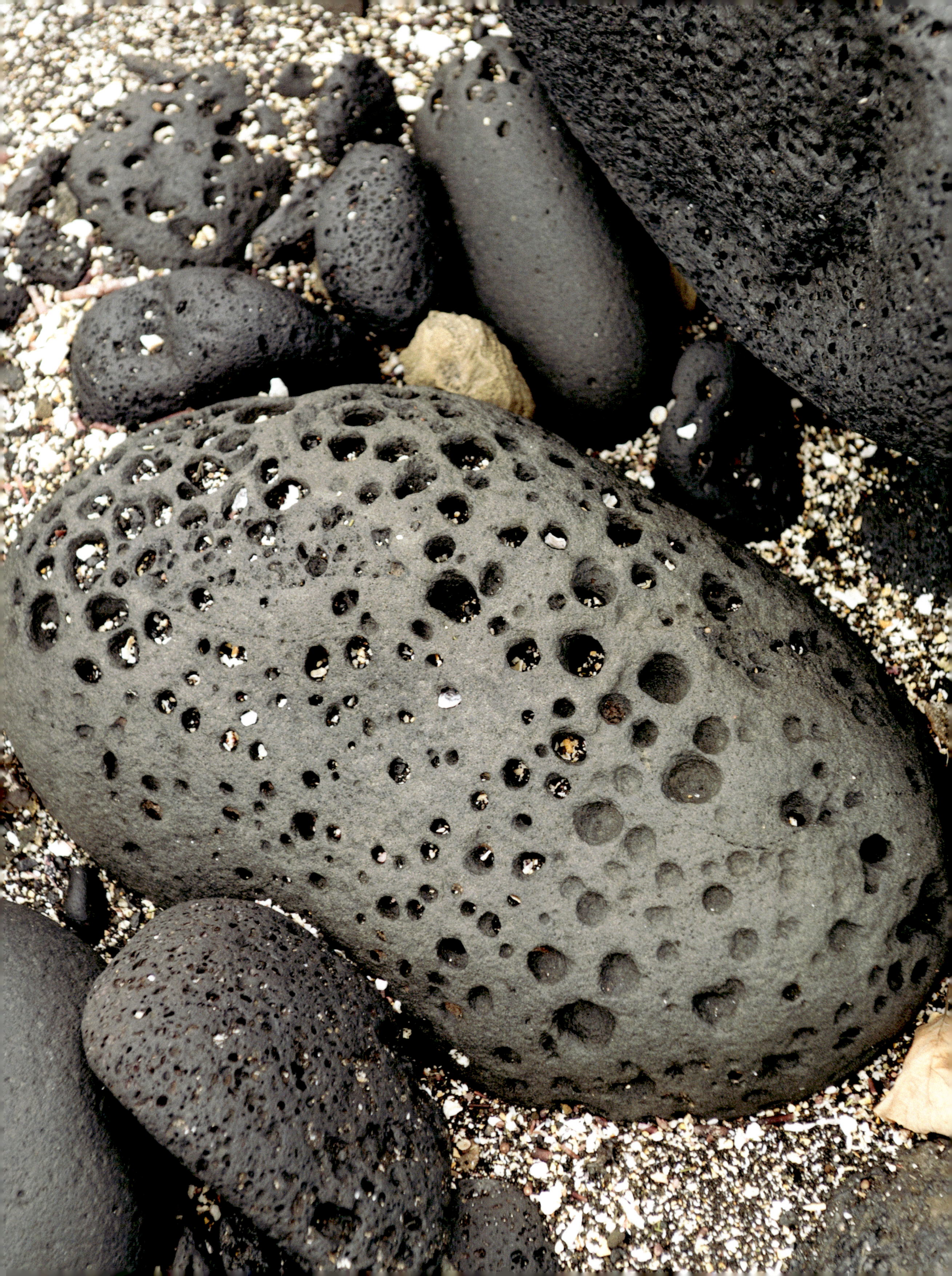

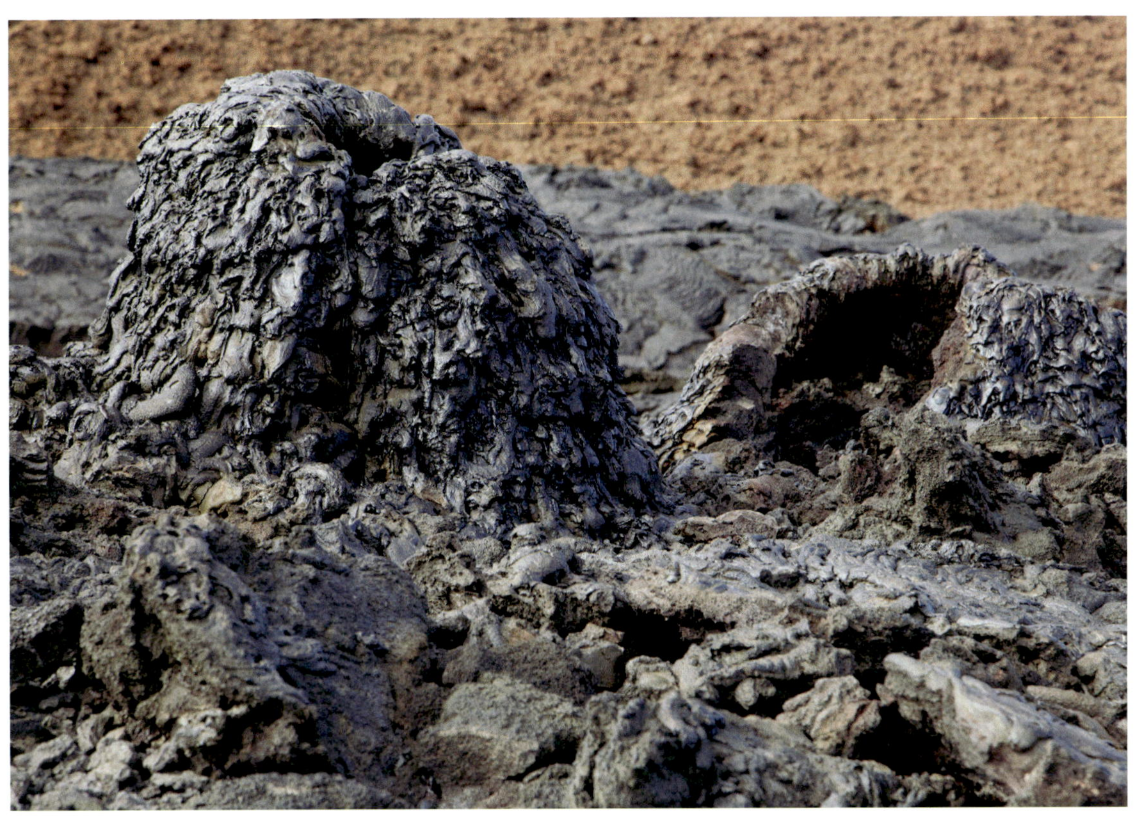

Lava stones
Beaches of the Galápagos are littered with perforated stones. They are the remnants of lava rocks rounded by the waves. The holes are caused by gas vesicles that were trapped in the lava as it solidified.

LEFT:
Volcanic hornitos
A hornito is a small cone of glassy lava formed by a gas or water pocket bursting out of the surface of a pahoehoe lava flow.

BELOW:
Lava terrain
Evidence of its volcanic past is seen widely across the Galápagos, especially in the western islands. Across the dark lava rocks of Santiago a volcanic plug can be seen. The plug is the hard rock that closed up an ancient volcano making it extinct. The surrounding volcano has long since eroded away.

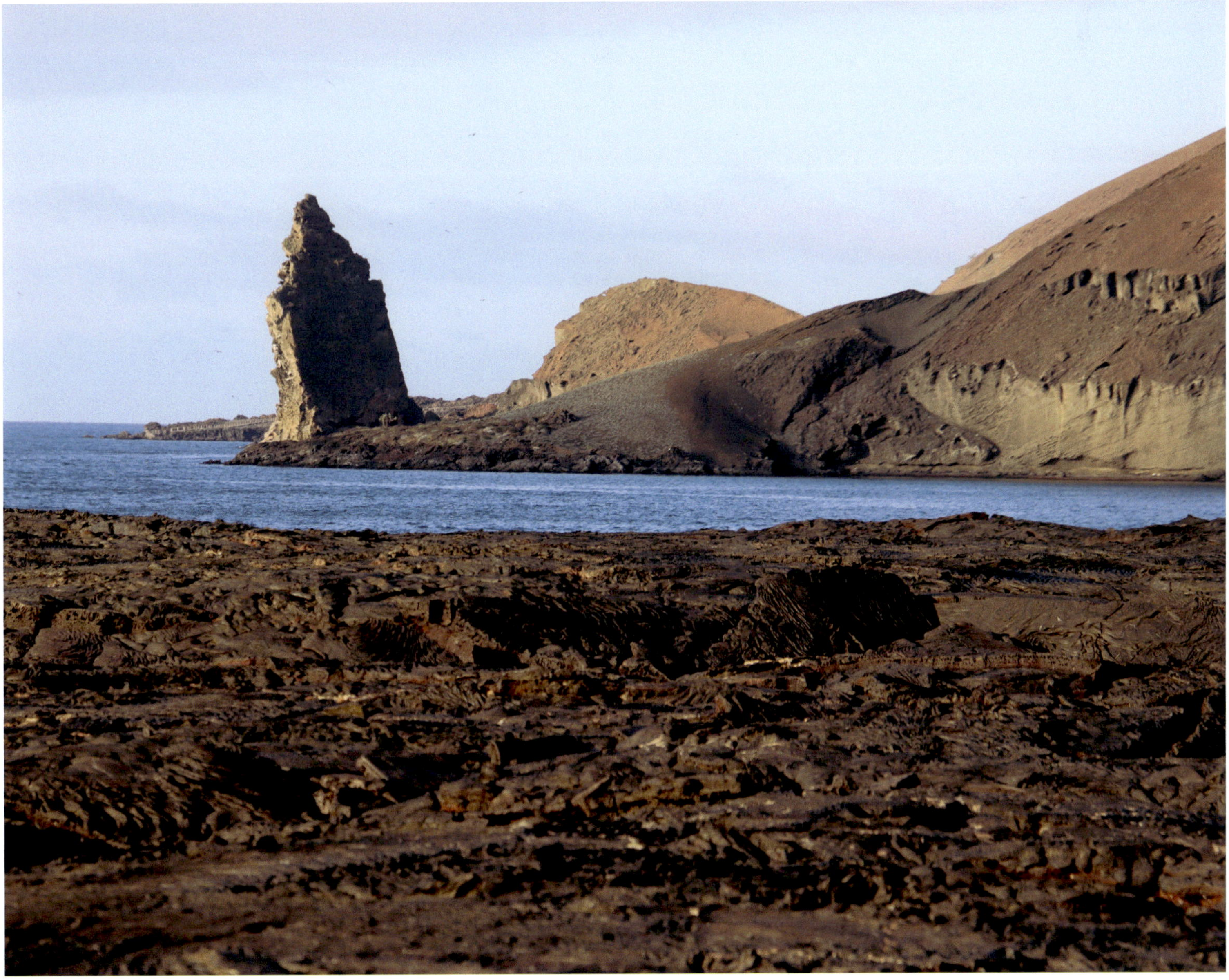

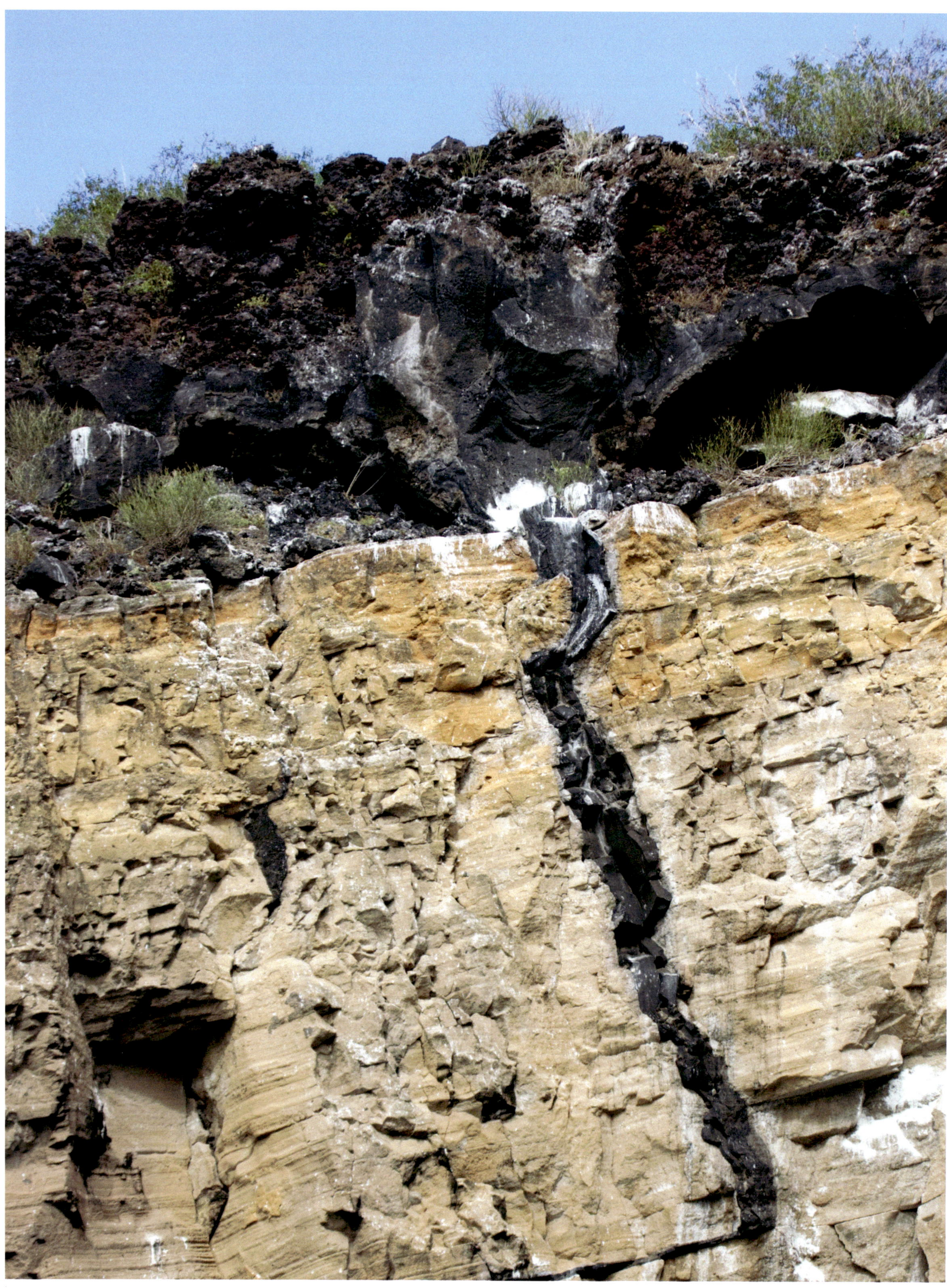

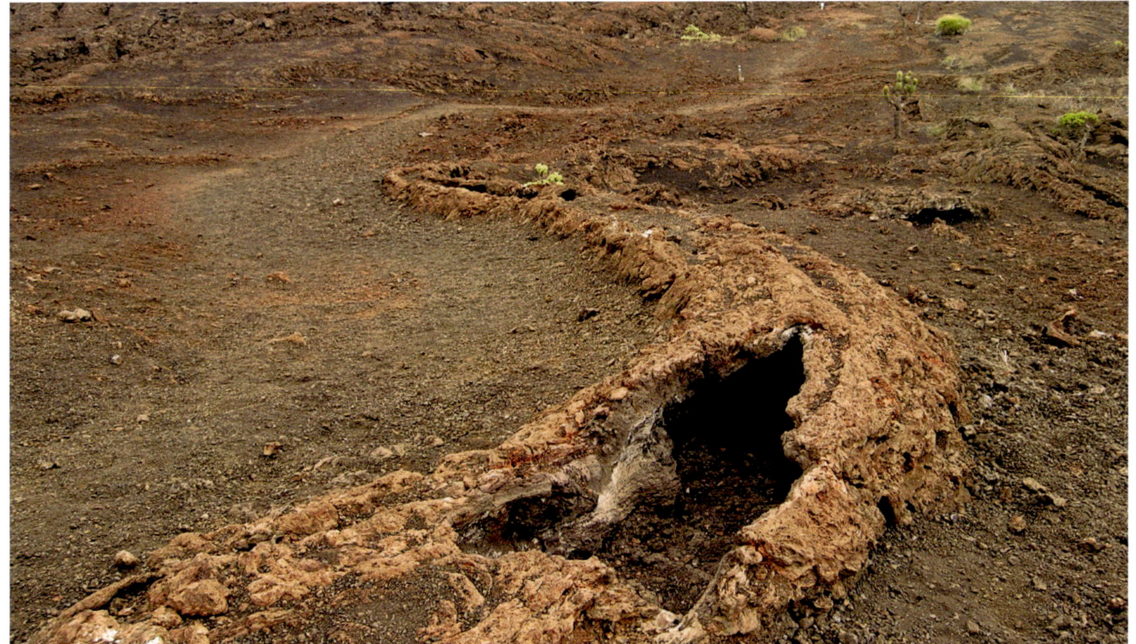

OPPOSITE:
Volcanic dike
This dark seam of rock is a dike, created when magma pushed its way into a crack between older rocks and cooled.

LEFT ALL PHOTOGRAPHS:
Lava tubes
The Galápagos has many examples of lava tubes, which are subterranean conduits that form as the top of a deep lava flow cools into a solid ceiling. Insulated beneath, a stream of hot liquid lava flows along for some time. In these cases, the lava flowed out the lower end leaving a natural tunnel. Like other kinds of caves, the lava tube develops stalactites and other speleothems (mineral deposits).

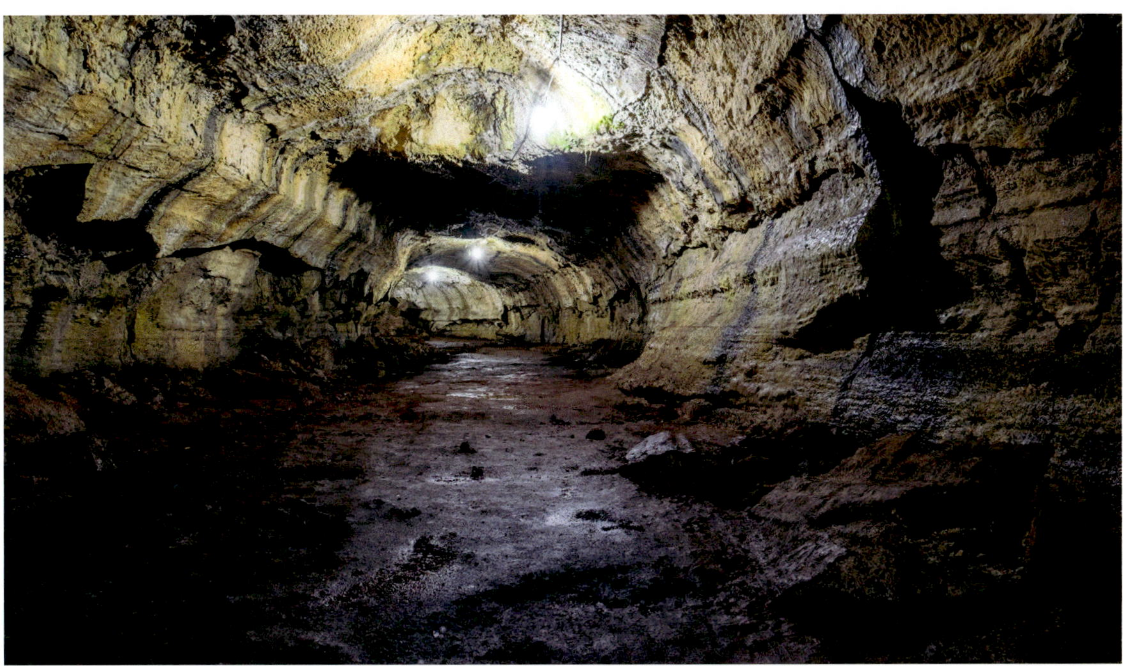

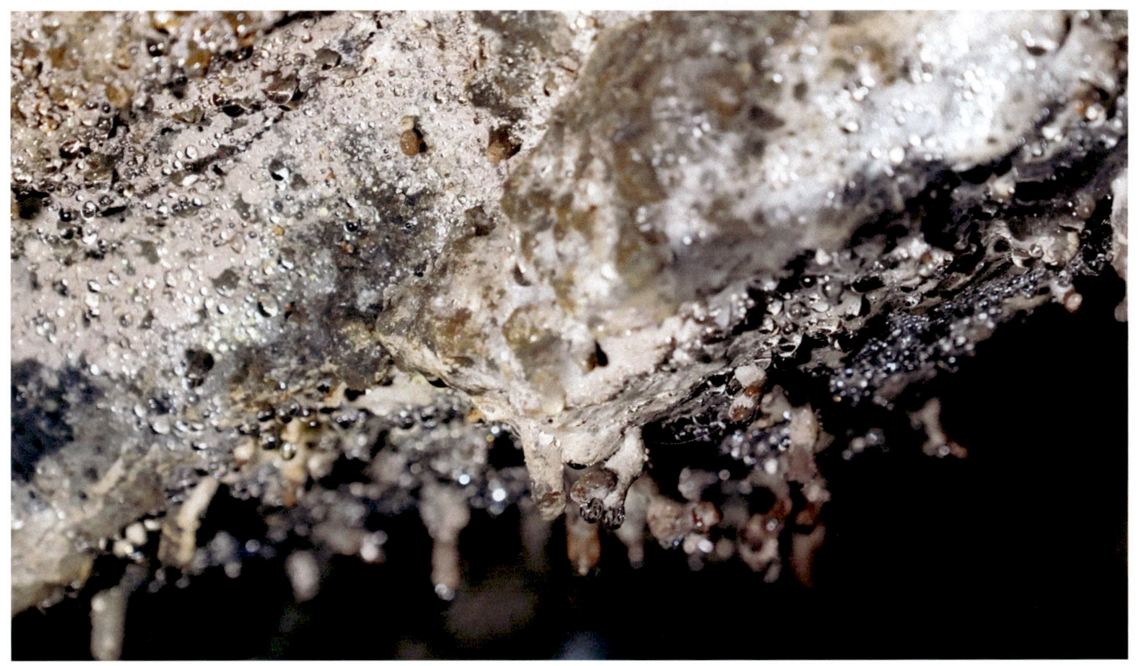

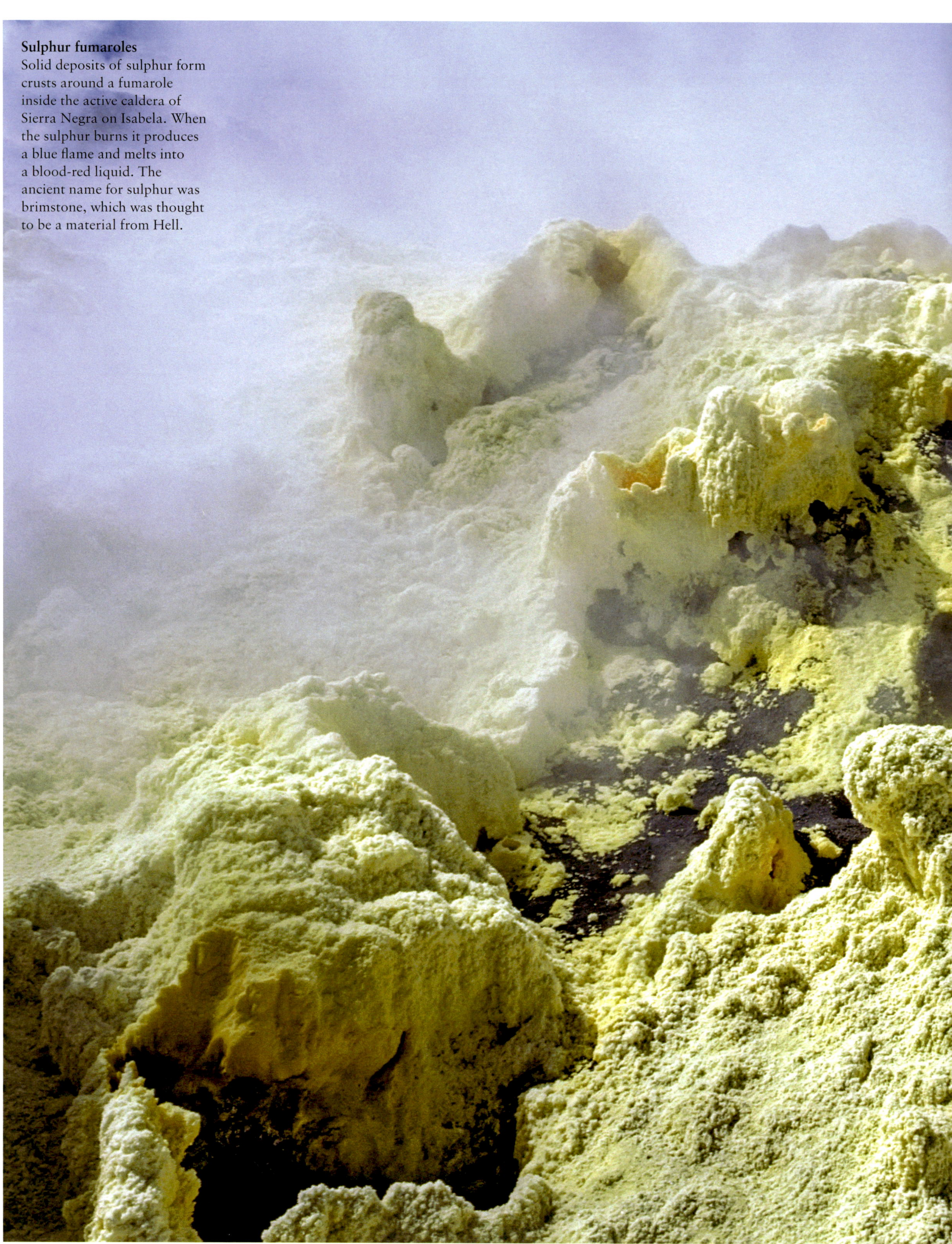

Sulphur fumaroles
Solid deposits of sulphur form
crusts around a fumarole
inside the active caldera of
Sierra Negra on Isabela. When
the sulphur burns it produces
a blue flame and melts into
a blood-red liquid. The
ancient name for sulphur was
brimstone, which was thought
to be a material from Hell.

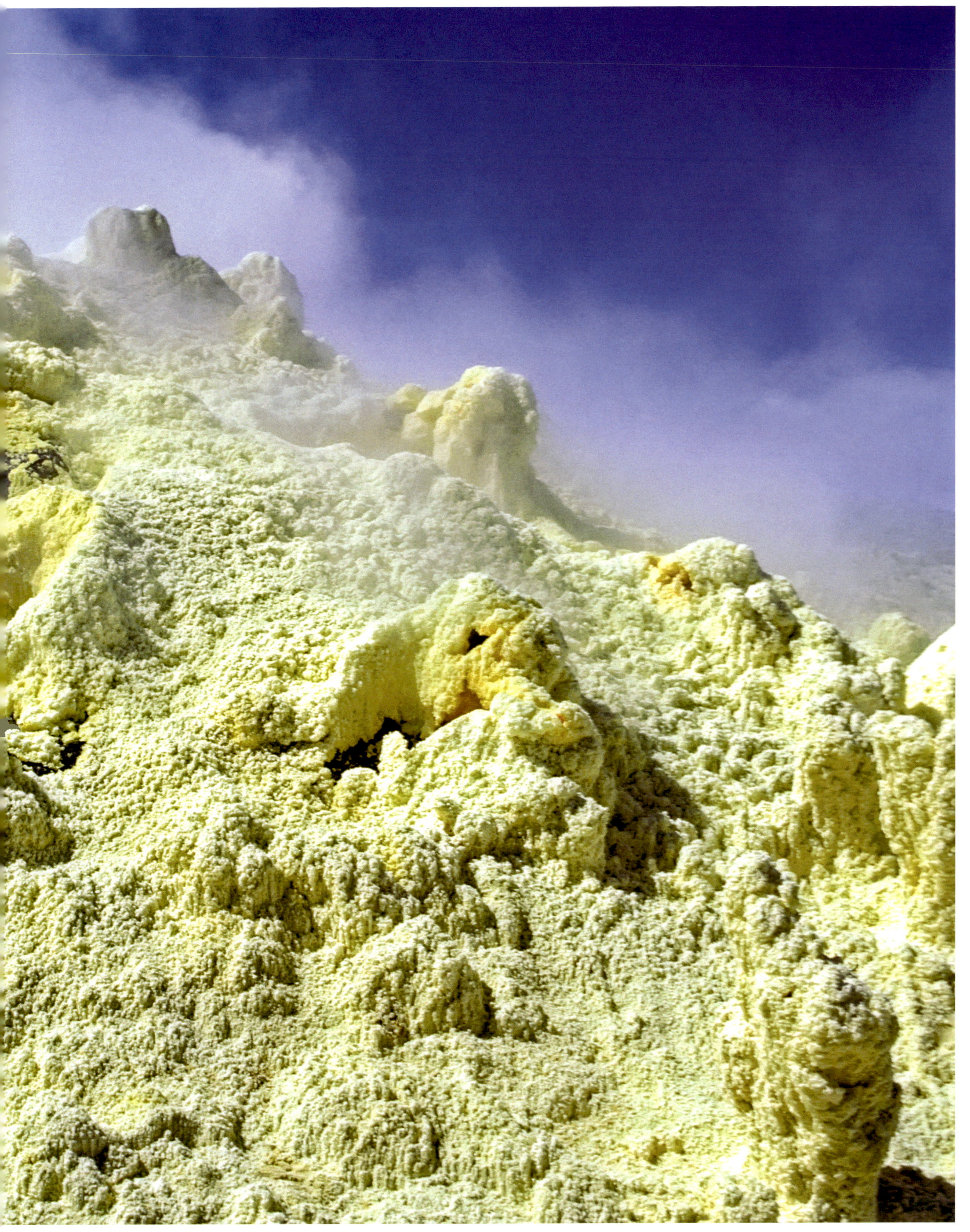

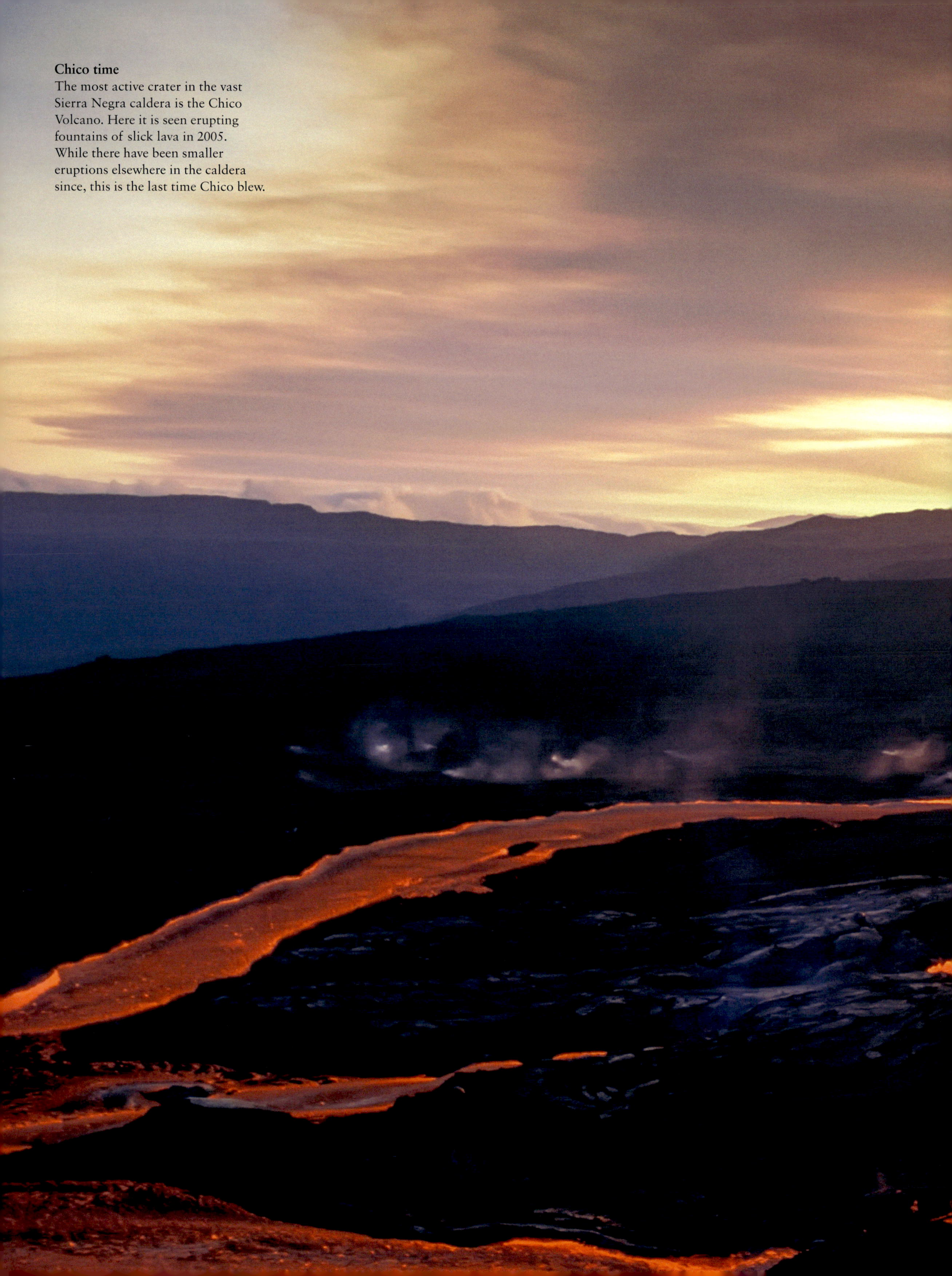

Chico time
The most active crater in the vast Sierra Negra caldera is the Chico Volcano. Here it is seen erupting fountains of slick lava in 2005. While there have been smaller eruptions elsewhere in the caldera since, this is the last time Chico blew.

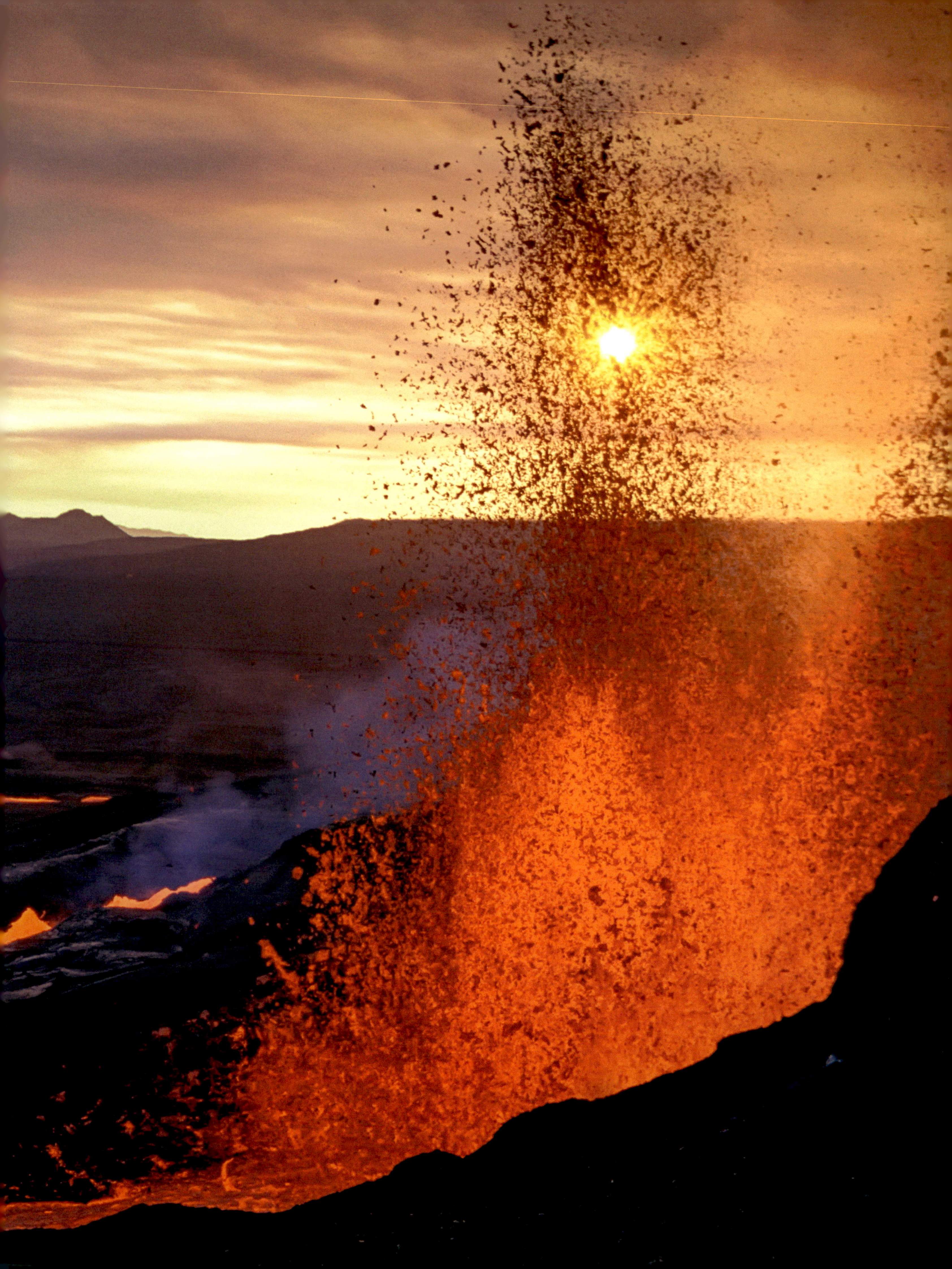

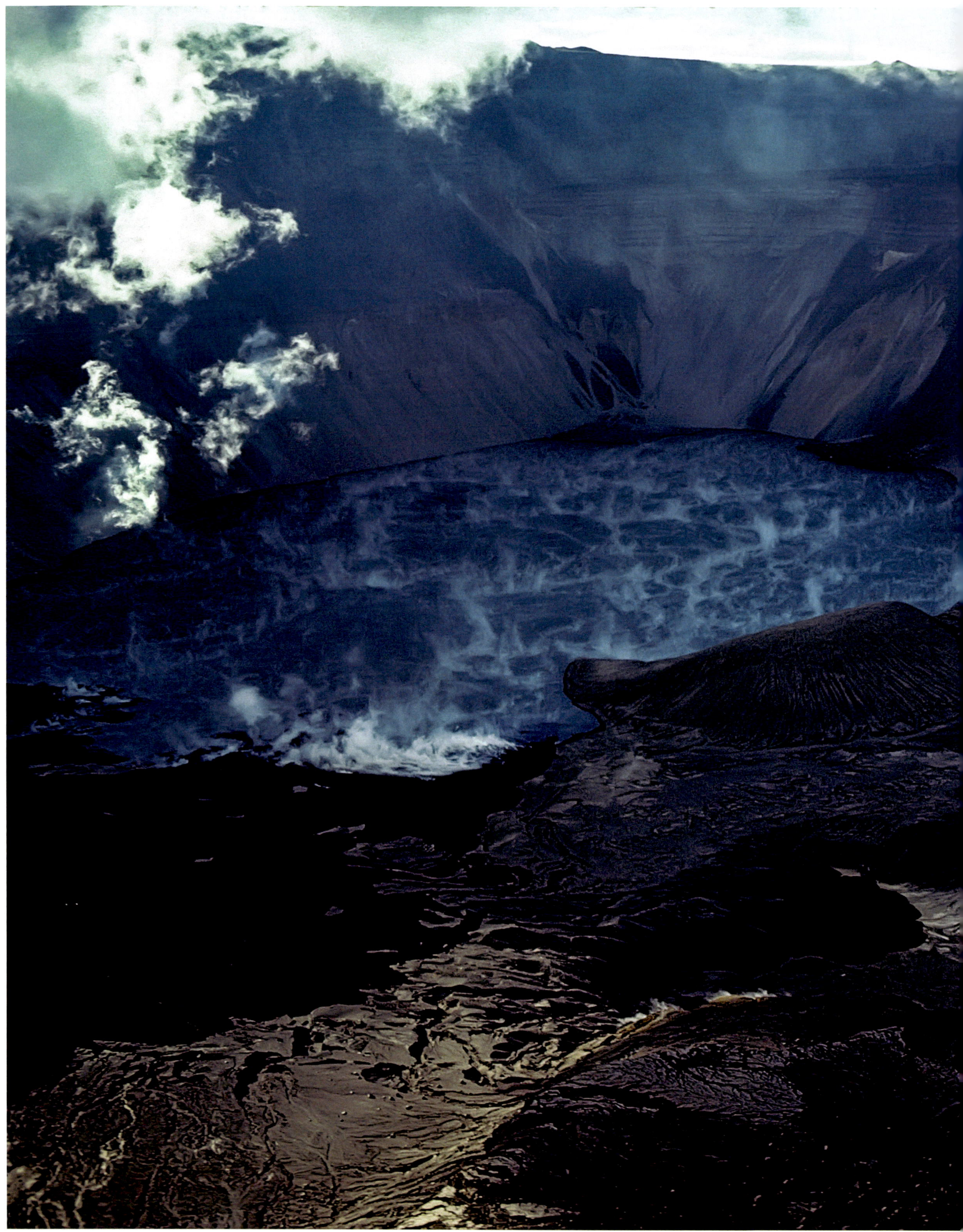

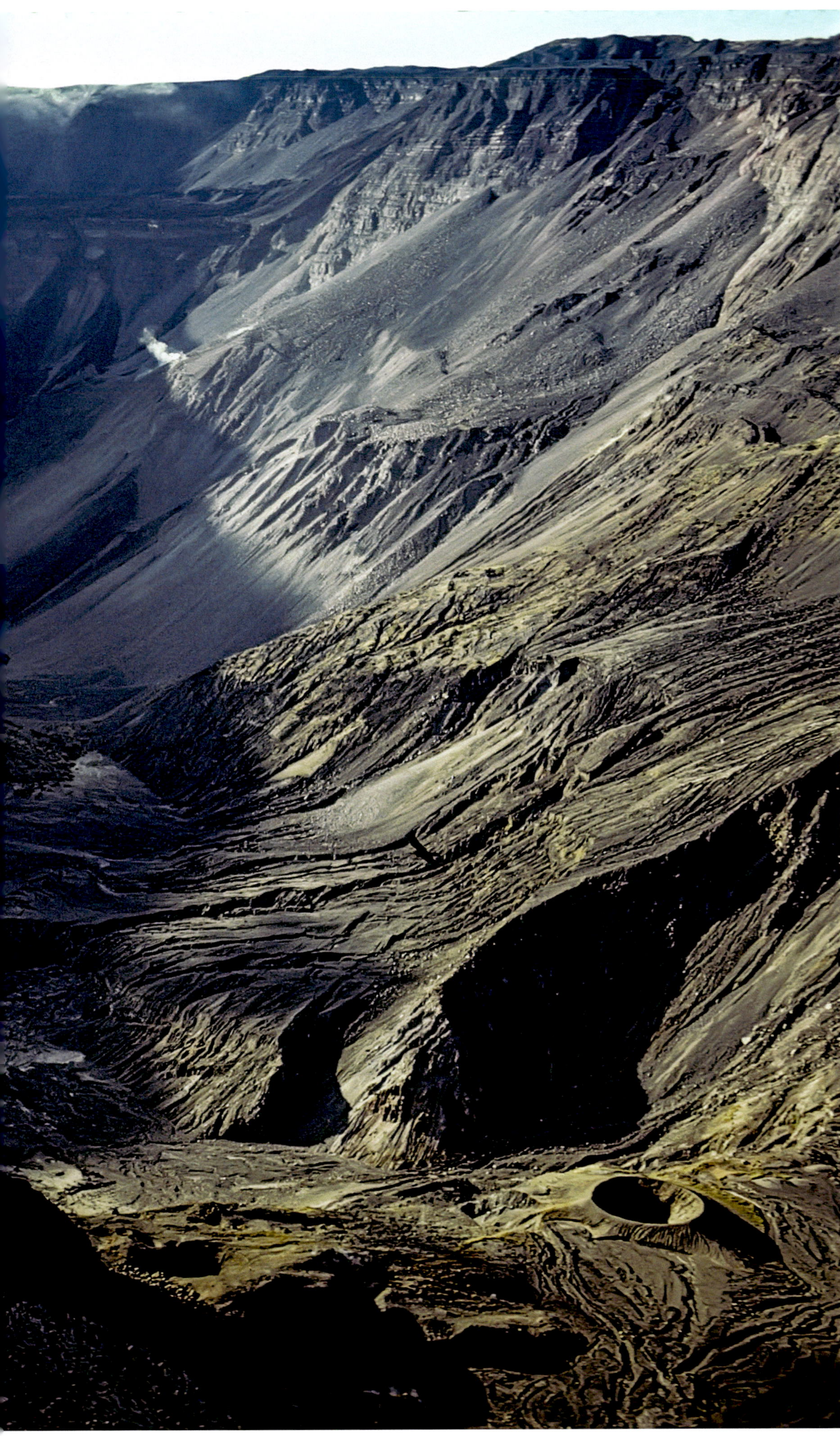

Unstable landscape
The stark crater of La Cumbre on Fernandina in the west of the Galápagos, appears quiet. However, this volcano is closely monitored and produces medium-sized eruptions every few years.

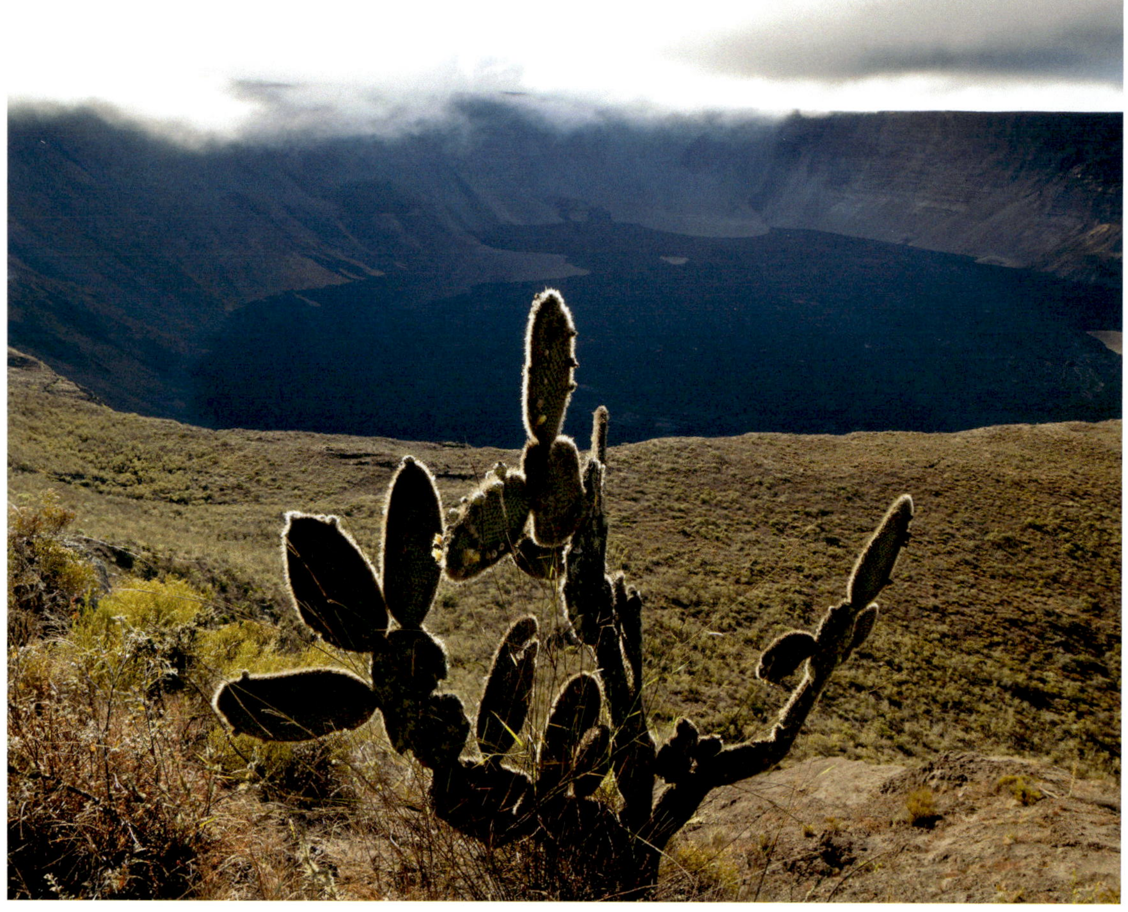

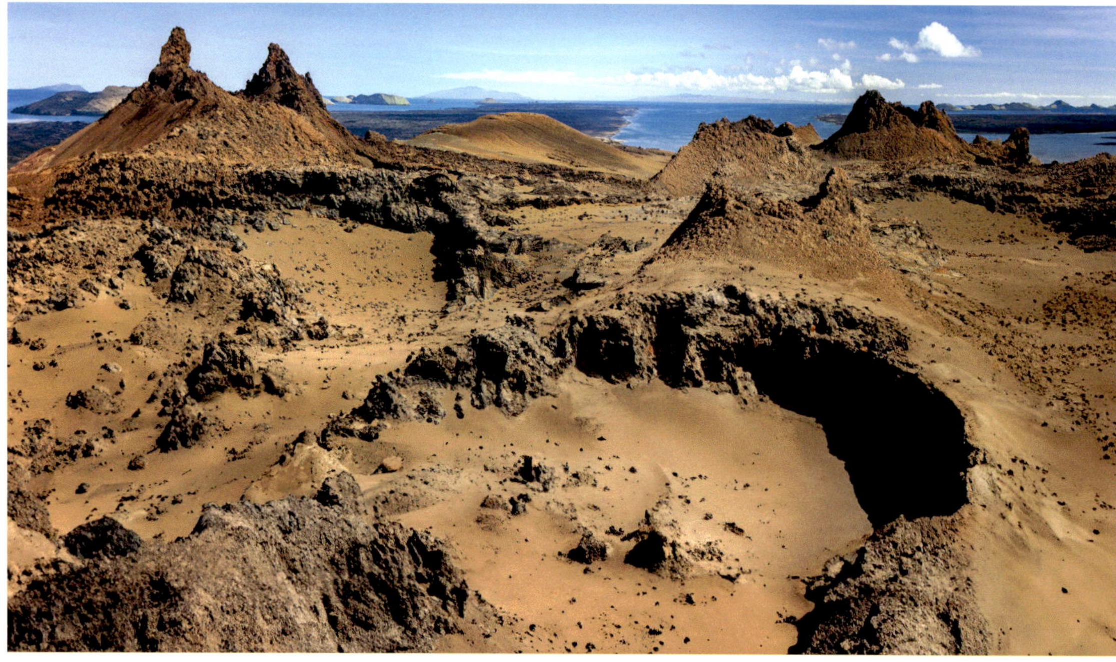

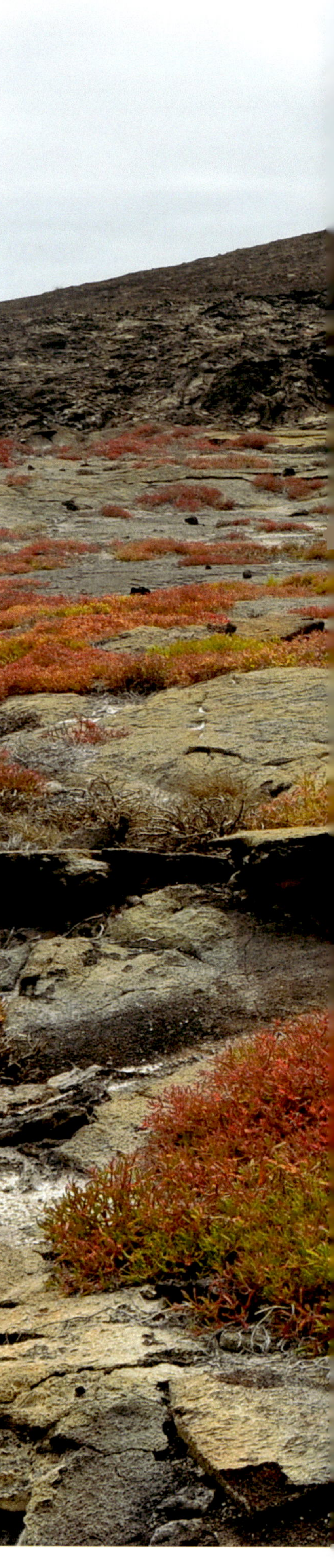

ABOVE TOP:

Life finds a way

An endemic cactus grows defiantly on the lip of the crater of Volcano Wolf, the tallest and one of the most active of the islands' volcanoes. The volcano has erupted twice since this picture was taken. If this cactus has not survived, another will be sure to grow here again.

ABOVE BOTTOM:

Cinder cones

This almost alien landscape on Bartolomé, a barren uninhabited islet east of Santiago, was created by heaps of ash ejected from volcanic craters.

RIGHT:

Hat-shaped volcano

This island south of Santiago is called Sombrero Chino, or Chinese Hat Island, due to the distinctive gently sloping shape of the ancient volcano – an example of a feature known as a spatter cone.

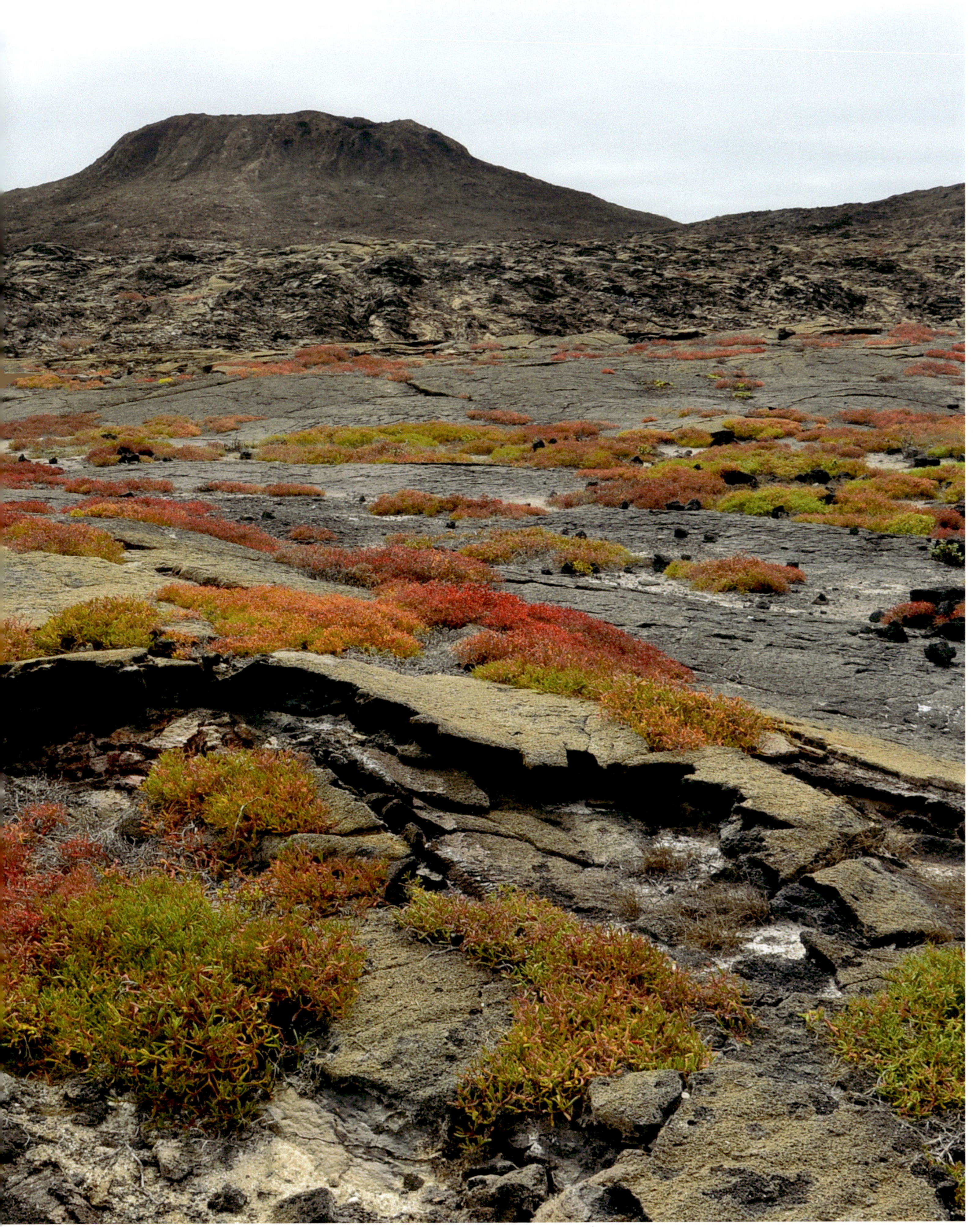

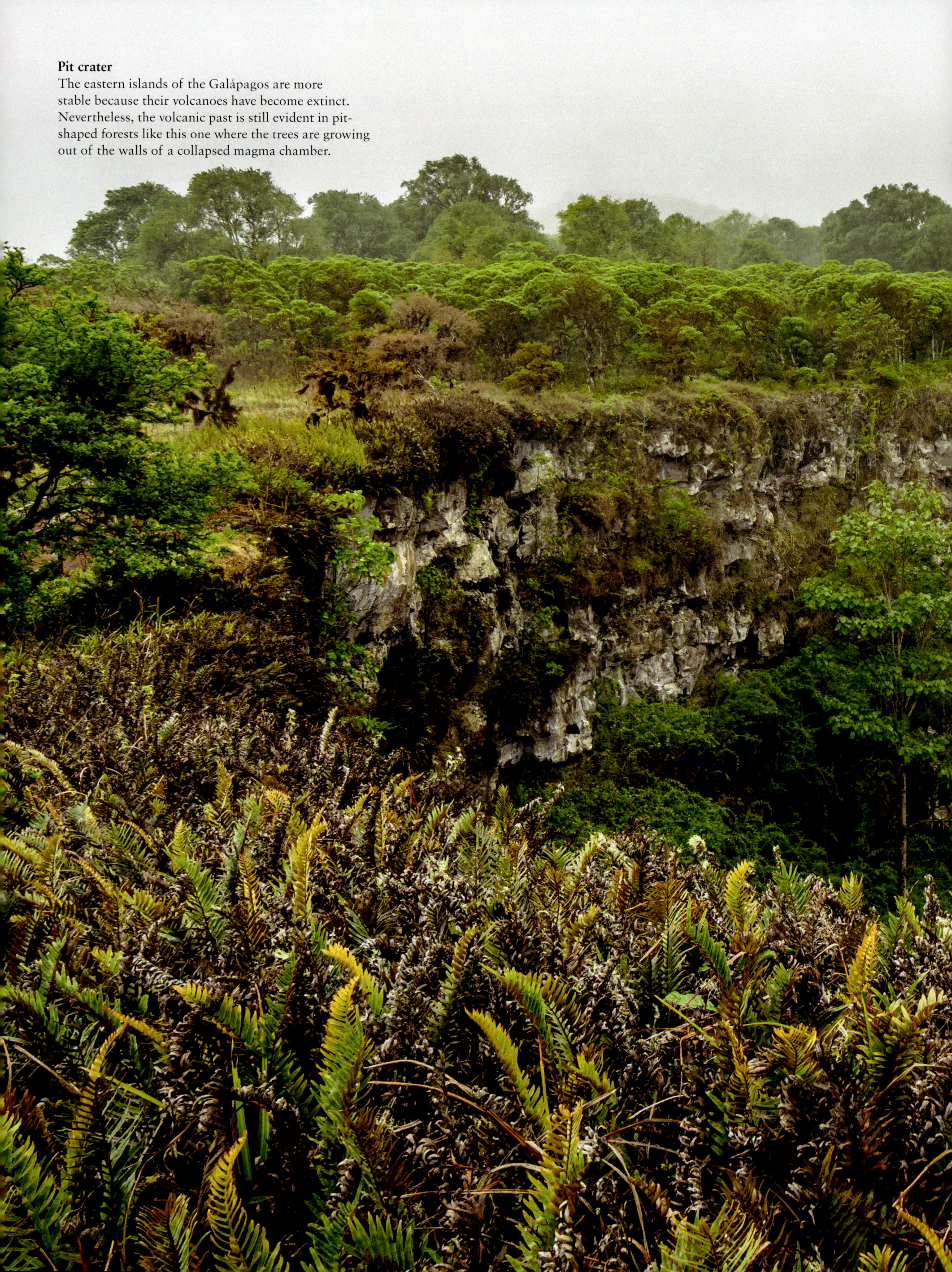

Pit crater
The eastern islands of the Galápagos are more stable because their volcanoes have become extinct. Nevertheless, the volcanic past is still evident in pit-shaped forests like this one where the trees are growing out of the walls of a collapsed magma chamber.

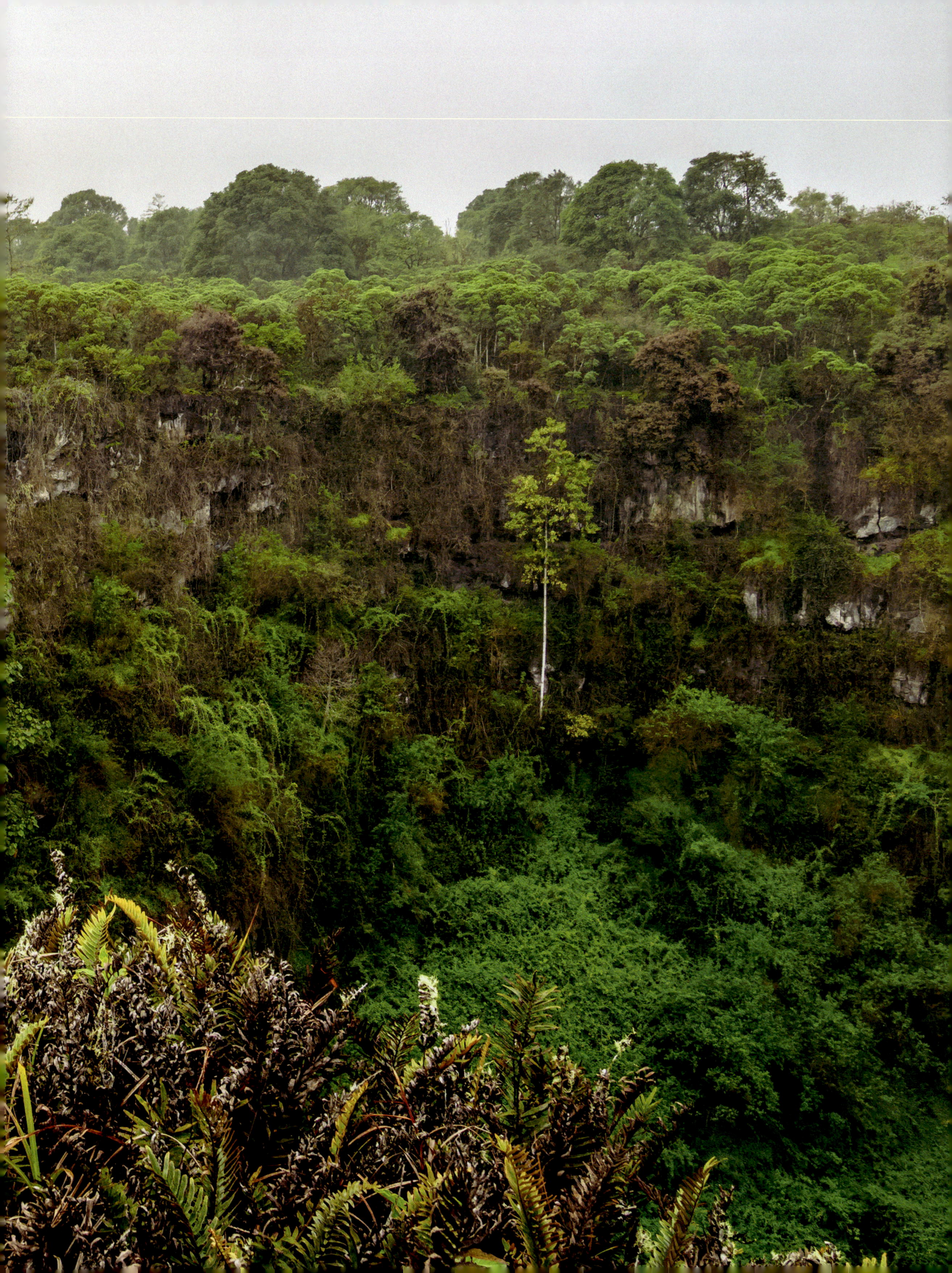

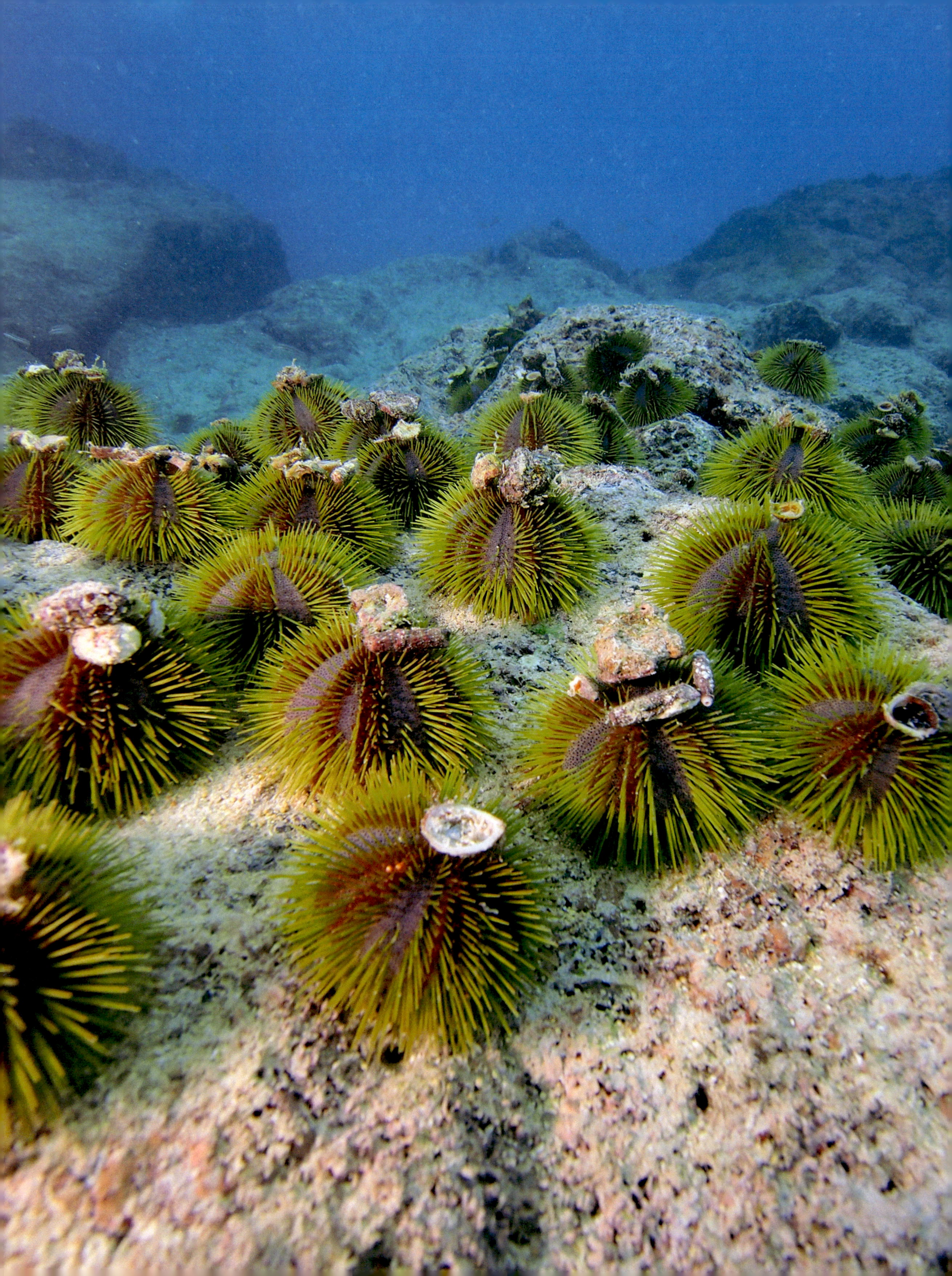

The Surrounding Seas

The Galápagos Islands are at a crossroads in the oceans. There three ocean currents meet creating a fertile sea around the islands that teems with life. Recent observations suggest that the waters around Wolf and Darwin islands host the largest congregations of oceanic sharks recorded anywhere on the planet. As well as sharks there are almost 3000 fish and other marine animal species that live around the islands or are frequent visitors. They include sea lions, dolphins and many different kinds of whale. The inspiration for the story of the classic American novel *Moby Dick* (1851) came from an 1820 battle between a giant sperm whale and the crew of the New England whaling ship *Essex* that played out in these waters. The *Essex* was sunk.

It was the ocean currents and associated winds that brought life to the Galápagos. Insects and birds were blown over by storms, while large land animals arrived on rafts of floating logs. The currents that collide at the islands each bring an important feature that helps to create the fertile surrounding seas. The Humboldt Current brings cold water from the Antarctic filled with oxygen and nutrients. The Panama Current from the north is driven by warm winds that buffet the islands and act to pull water up from the deep, adding to the mineral content of the seas. Finally, the Cromwell Countercurrent brings cold water from the west. This has the effect of chilling the ocean around the Galápagos, all in spite of the islands straddling the Equator. This cooling makes the seas more fertile.

OPPOSITE:
Green sea urchin
These small urchins, barely
5cm (2in) wide, are a common
feature of the waters around the
Galápagos and are found mostly
in the clear, bright waters just
below the low-tide mark.

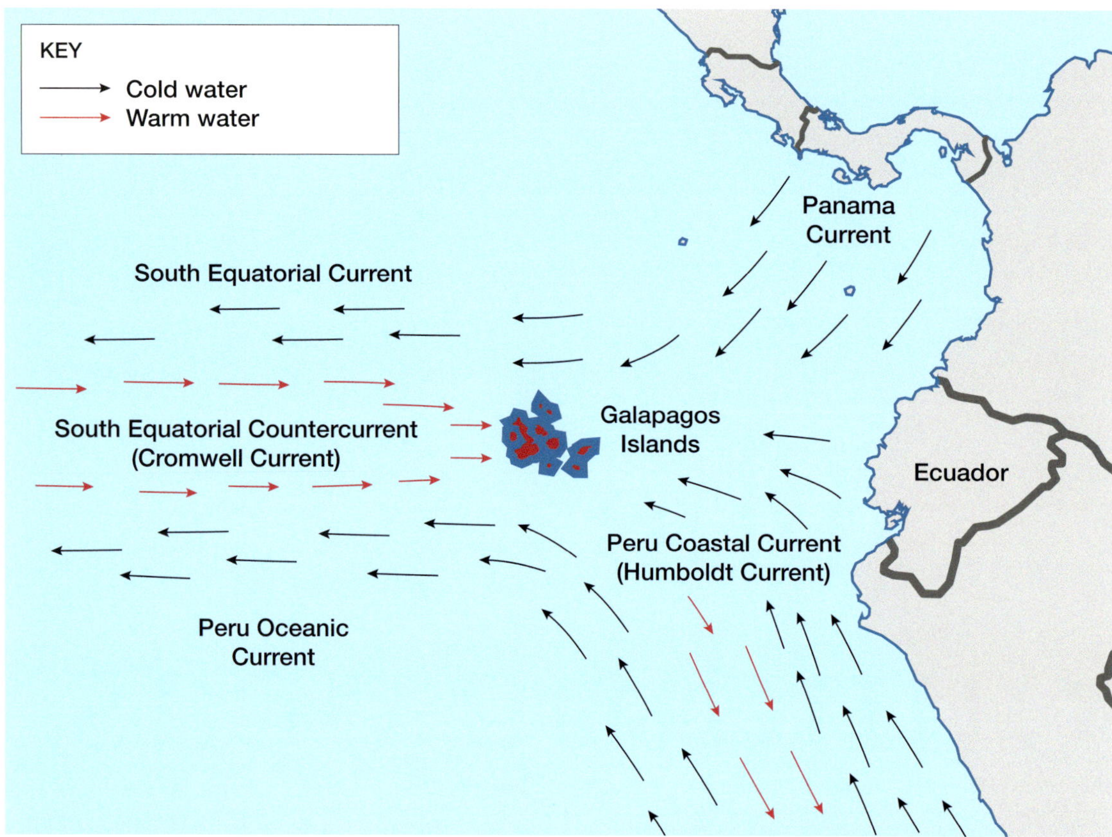

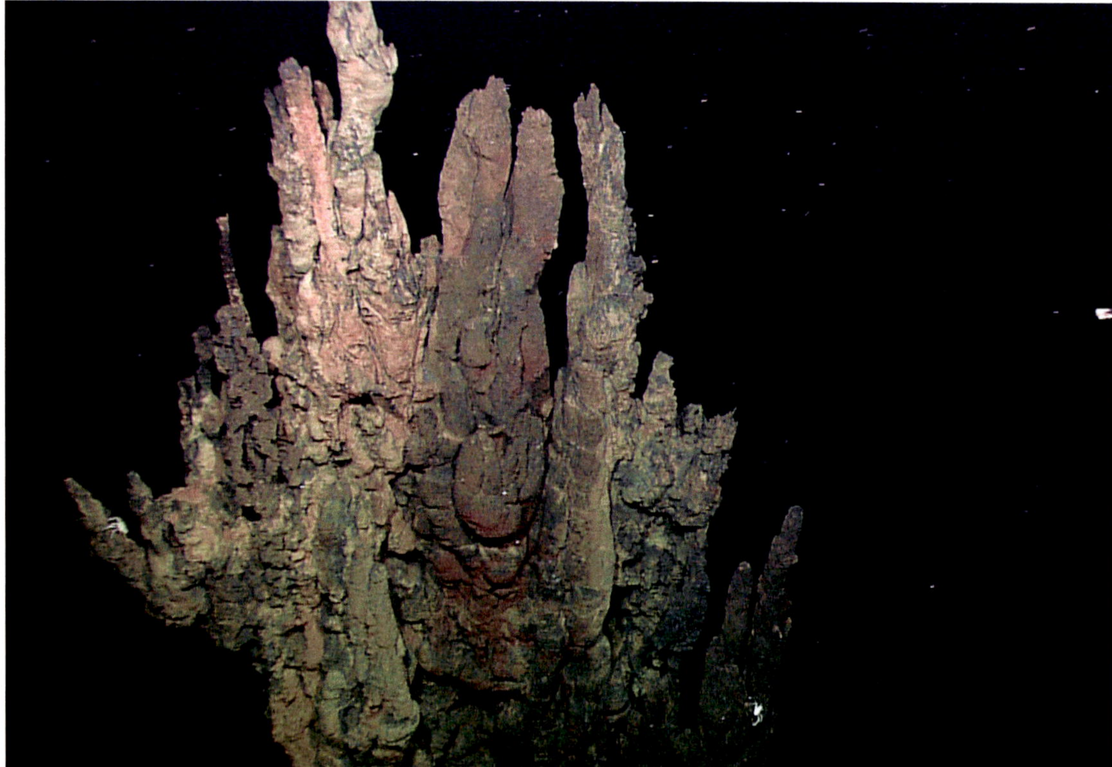

ABOVE TOP:

Ocean currents

The islands are buffeted by three currents. The Humboldt Current is especially significant because it sometimes changes in direction, taking warmer water south. The years when this happens are called El Niño events. Each event is caused by heat being released from the deep Pacific Ocean and that creates hotter weather around the world.

ABOVE BOTTOM:

Hydrothermal vent

The volcanic activity of the archipelago is not restricted to land. In the deeper parts of the seafloor, there are hydrothermal vents where hot water, heated deep in the rocks of the seabed, gushes into the ocean, creating mineral chimneys and bringing nutrients for deep-sea life.

RIGHT:

Tectonic plates

This map shows the major tectonic plates in the south-eastern Pacific Ocean. The Galápagos lie along the northern edge borders on a satellite map of areas adjacent to the Nazca Plate area. To the north and west, upwelling magma is pushing the plates apart, and in the east the plates are pushing together.

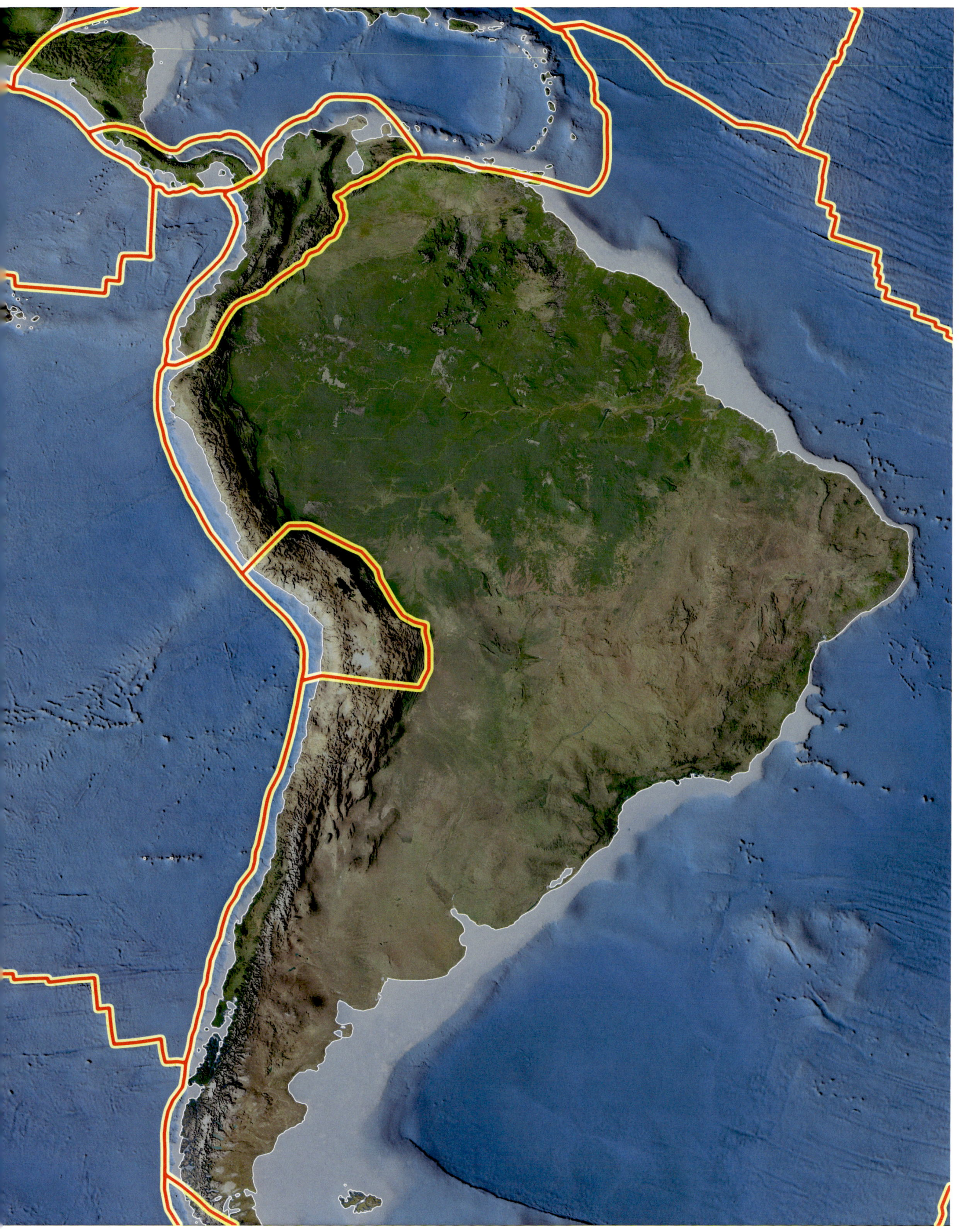

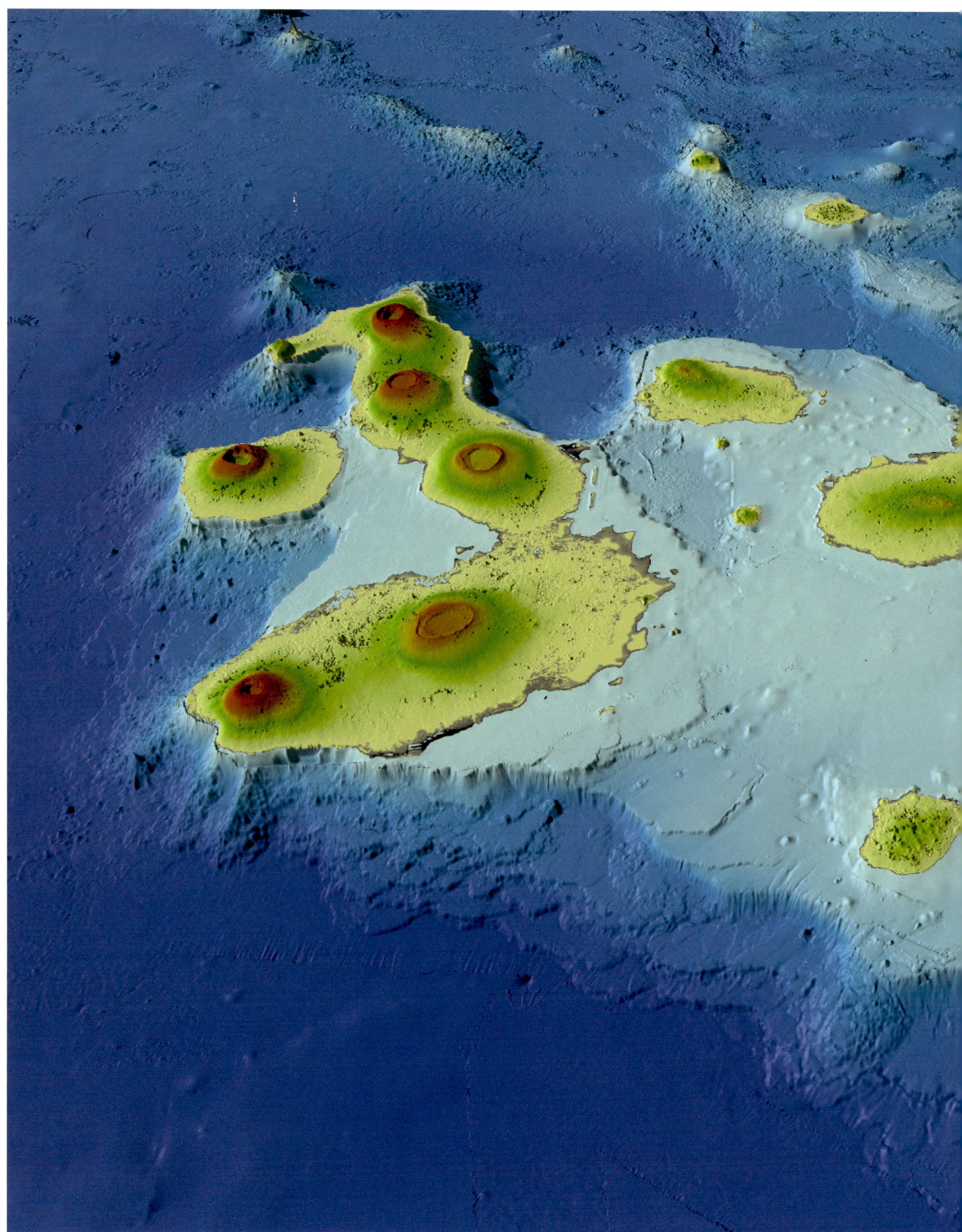

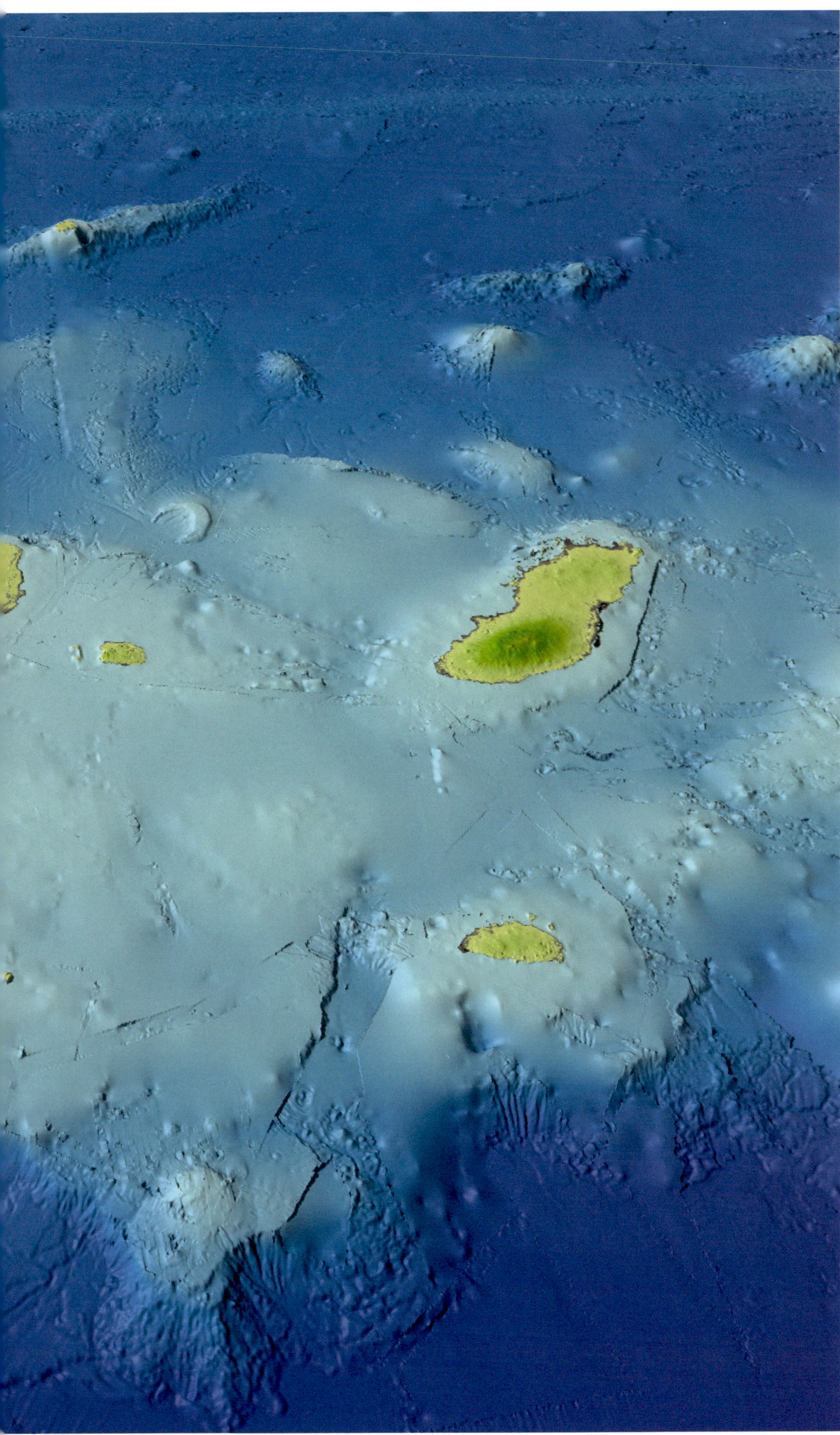

Topographic seafloor map
This map of the seafloor shows that the Galápagos Islands sit on a wider undersea shelf laid down by millions of years of volcanic eruptions. Today the most volcanically active region (red areas) is along the western edge where that shelf plunges to the deep ocean. This deep western sea is considerably colder than the waters around other parts of the archipelago.

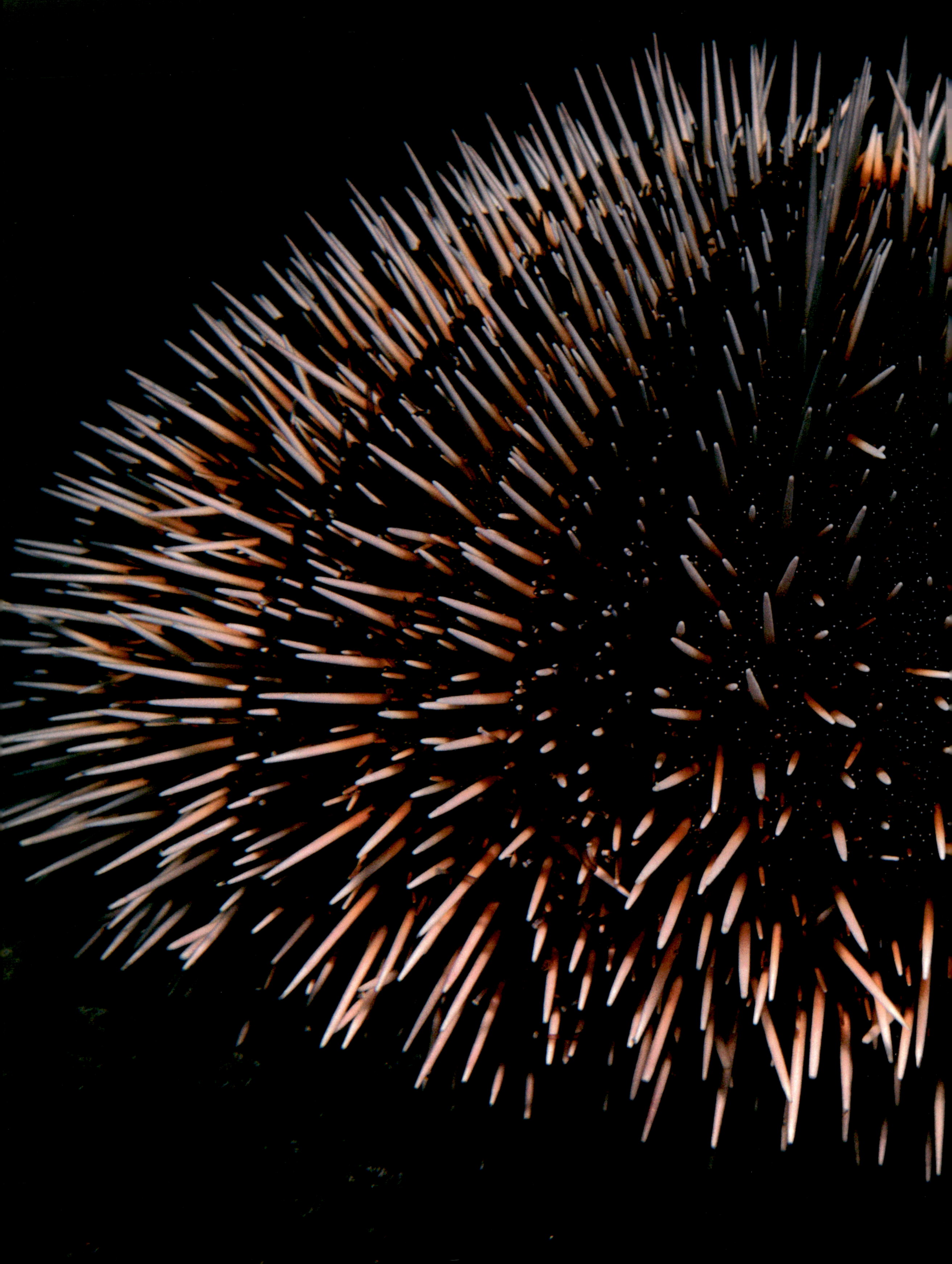

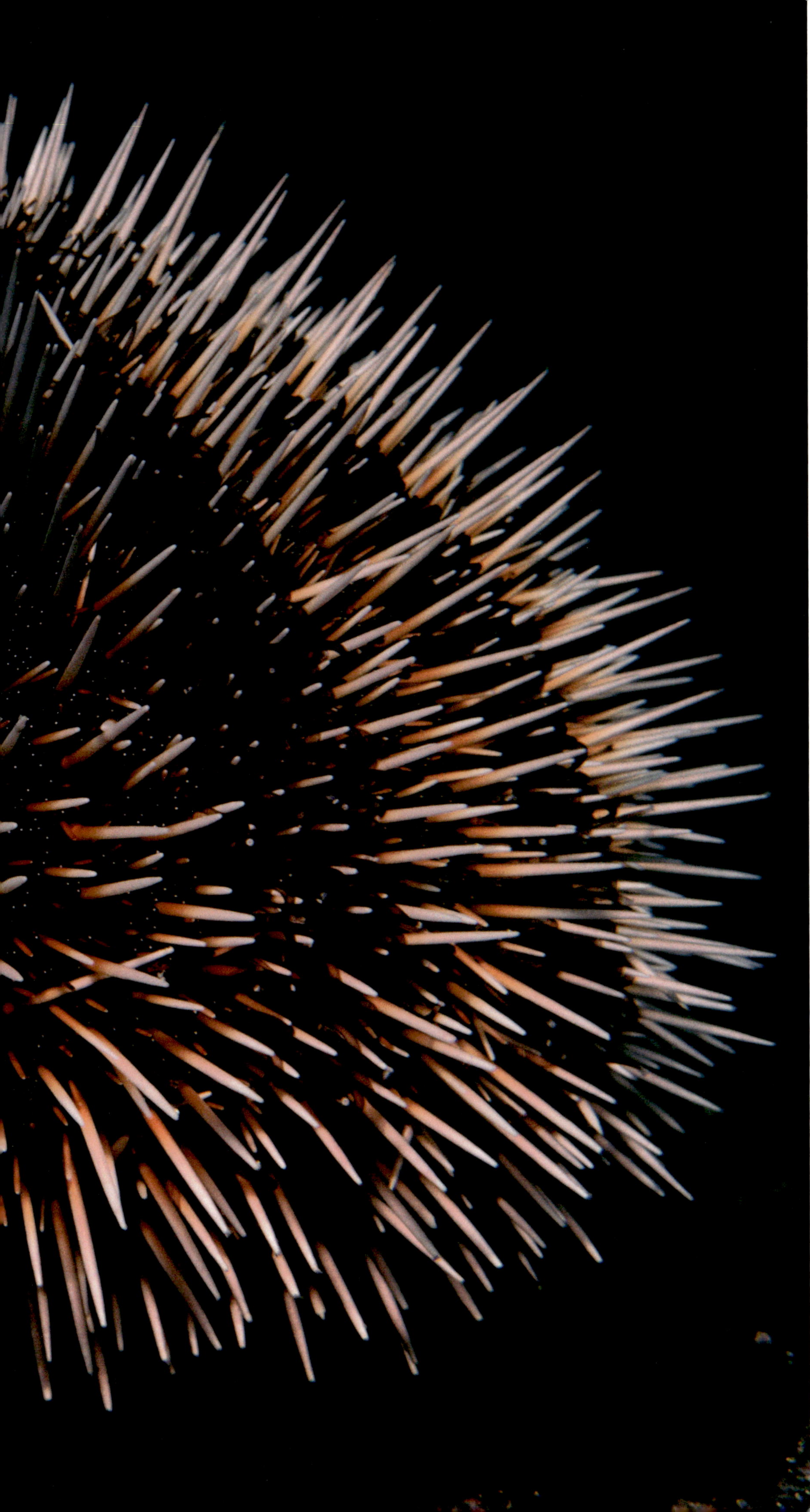

White sea urchin
Mostly this 10cm (4in) filter feeder
is found underwater growing
on rocky areas of seabed. In the
lowest tides around the spring/
autumn equinox, the spiked
animal may be seen for a short
while above the surface.

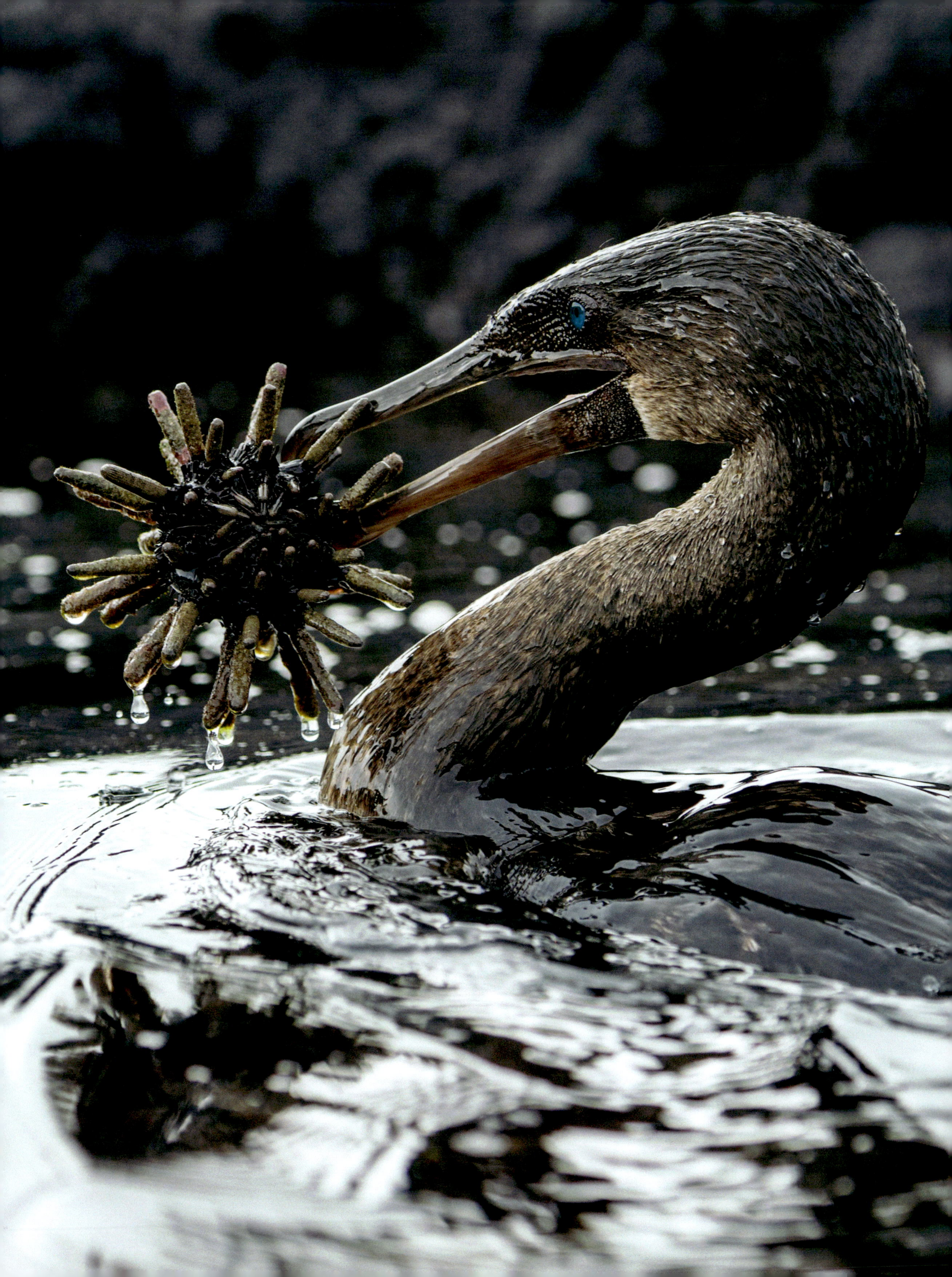

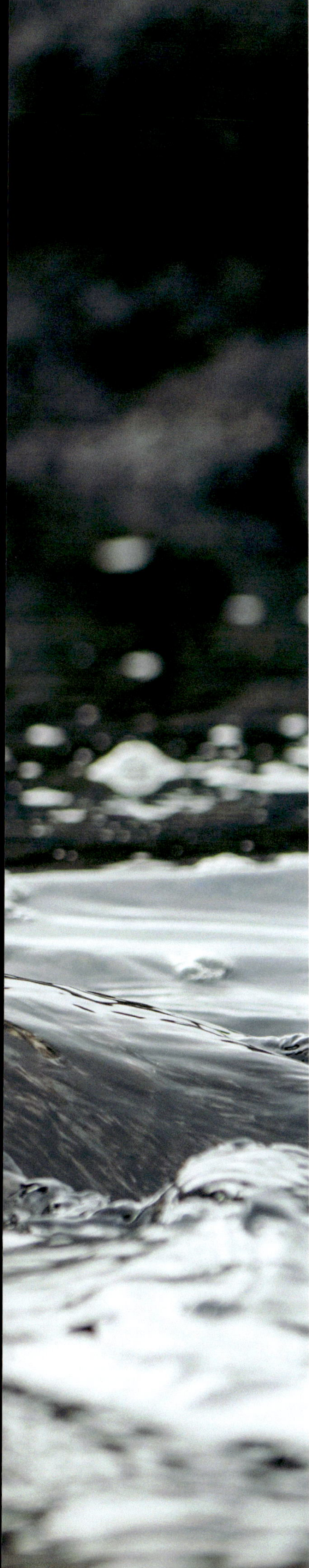

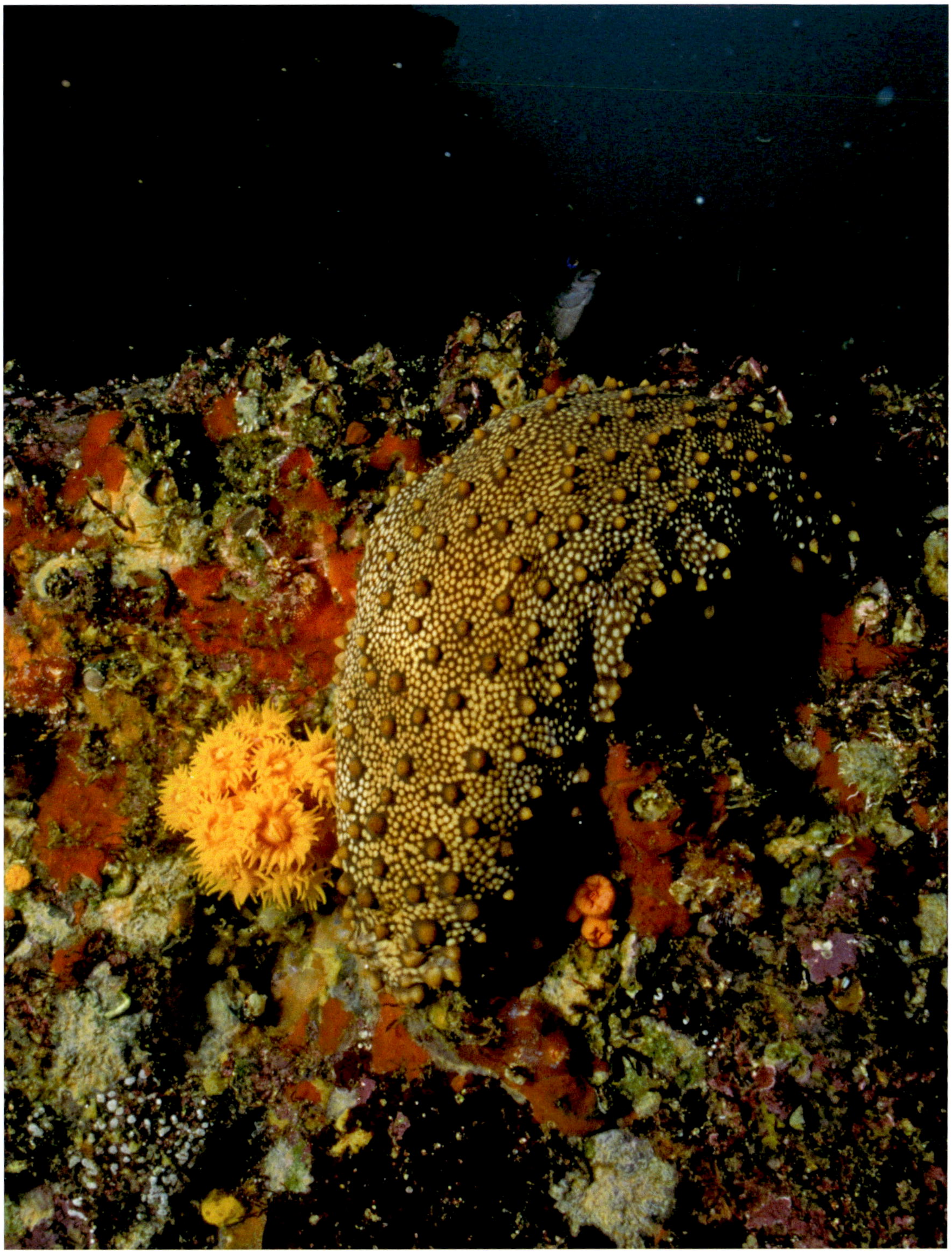

Flightless cormorant
The flightless cormorant is one of
the more active shoreline hunters.
Its bottom-heavy body is suited for
diving, not flying. Here, the bird
has surfaced with a slate pencil
sea urchin.

Giant sea cucumber
Despite its name this is an
animal rather than a plant. More
surprisingly, it is an echinoderm,
which makes it a relative of starfish
and urchins. This soft-bodied
seafloor creature grows to a length
of 20cm (8in). Numbers around
the islands are low today as local
fishermen sell them to Asian
consumers as a delicacy.

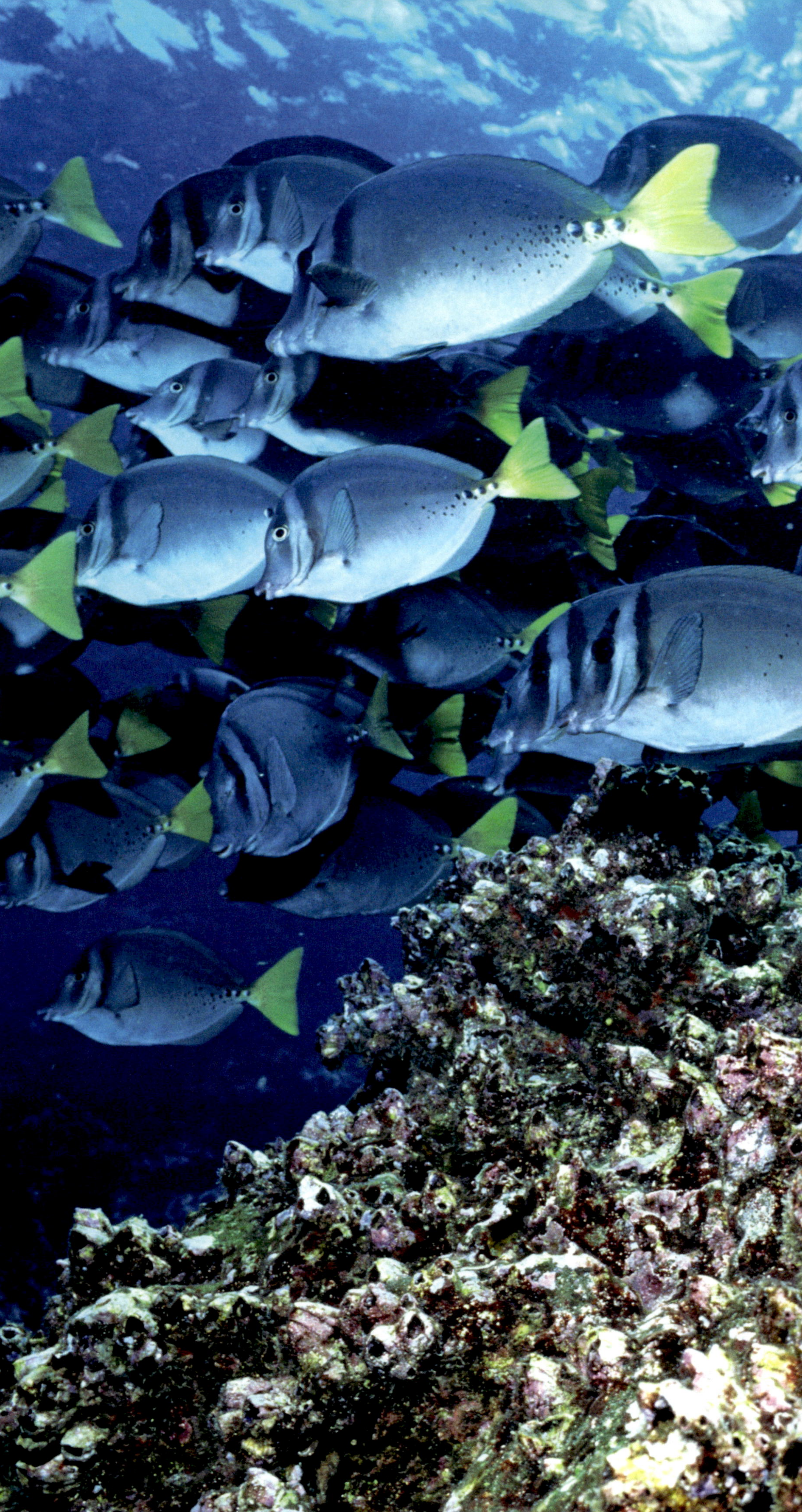

Yellowtail surgeonfish
A school of these round-bodied fish – a kind of tang – glides past a rocky reef in the shallow coastal waters off the Galápagos Islands. These fish consume algae using tiny teeth to scrape it from rocks.

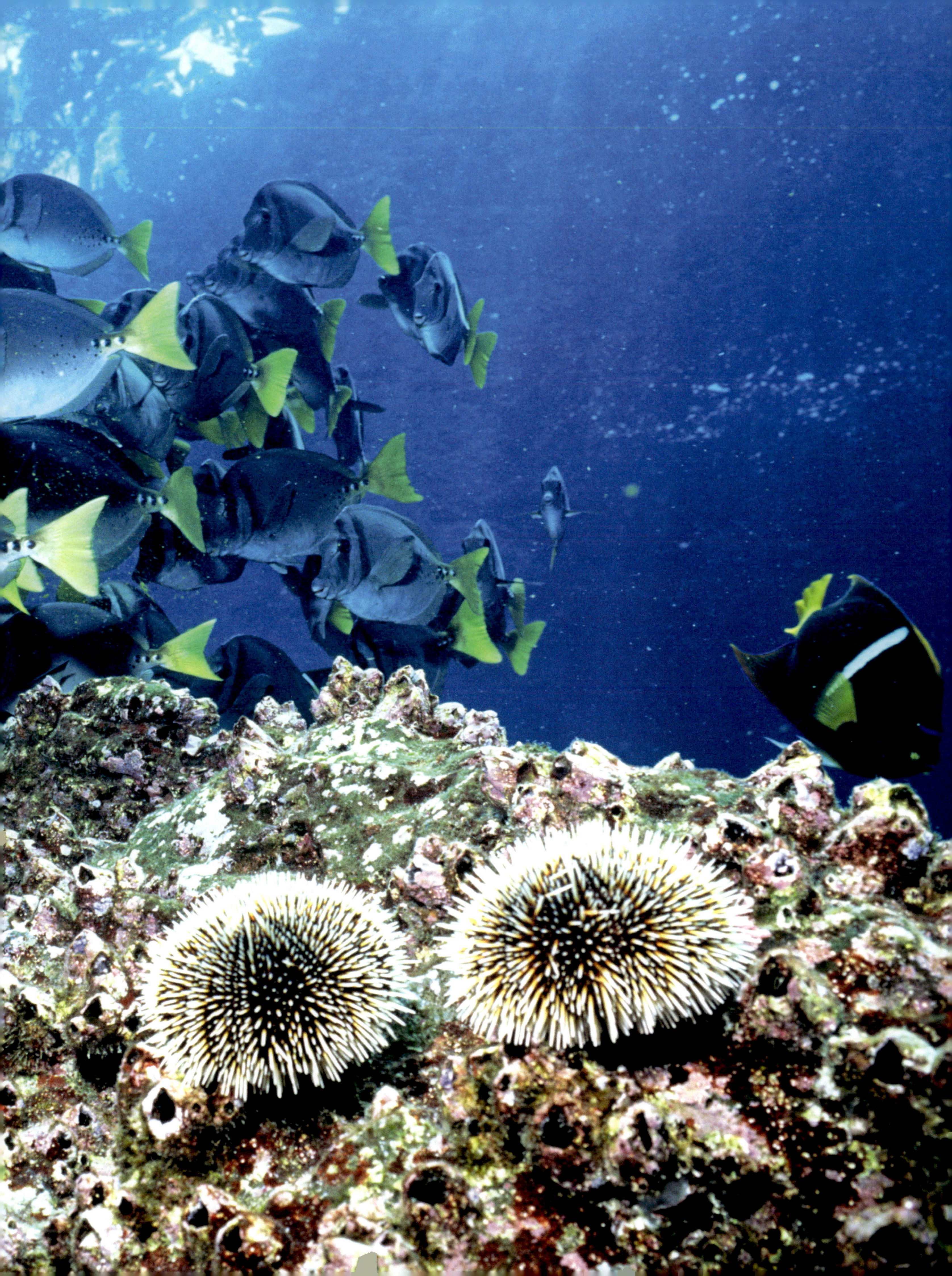

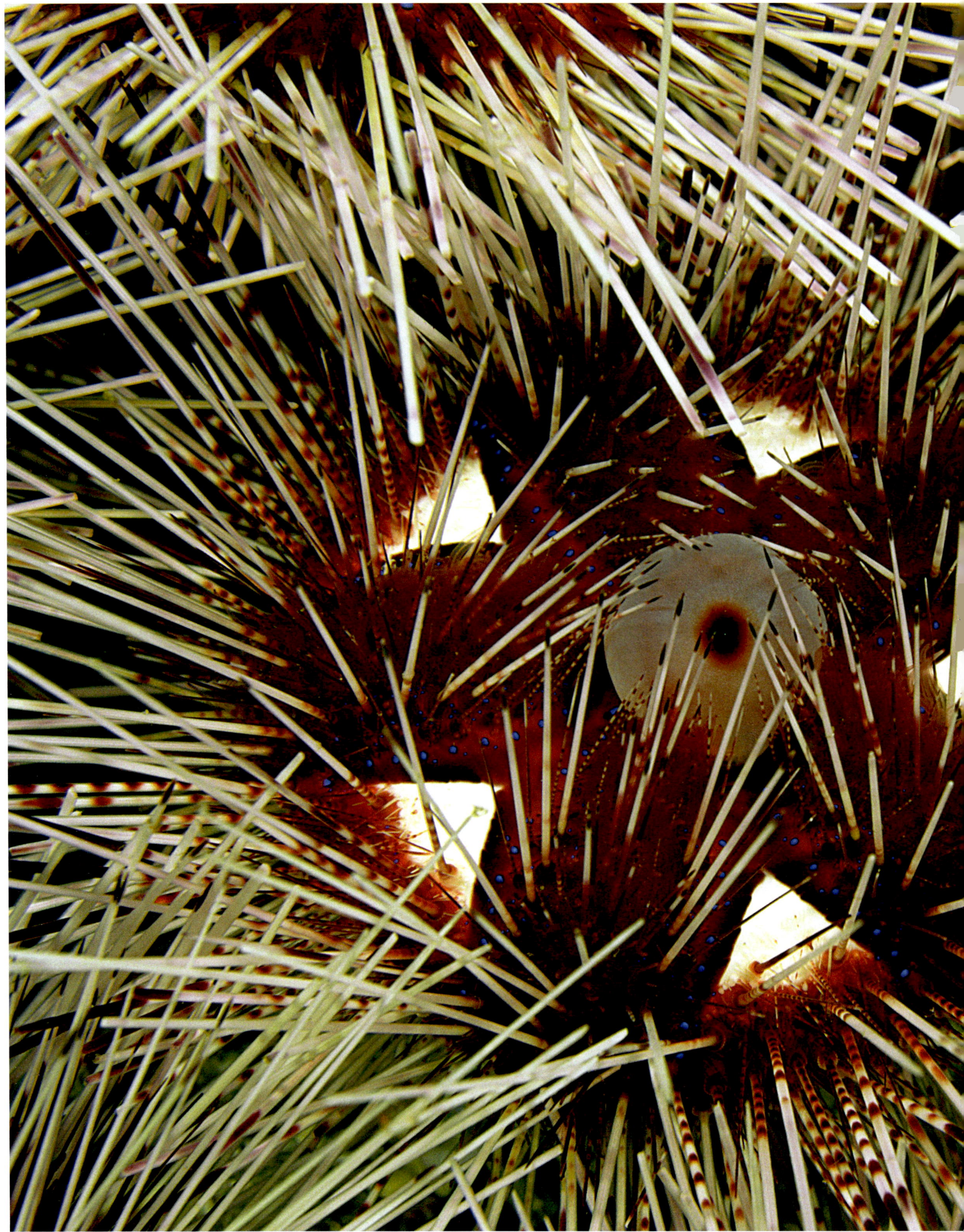

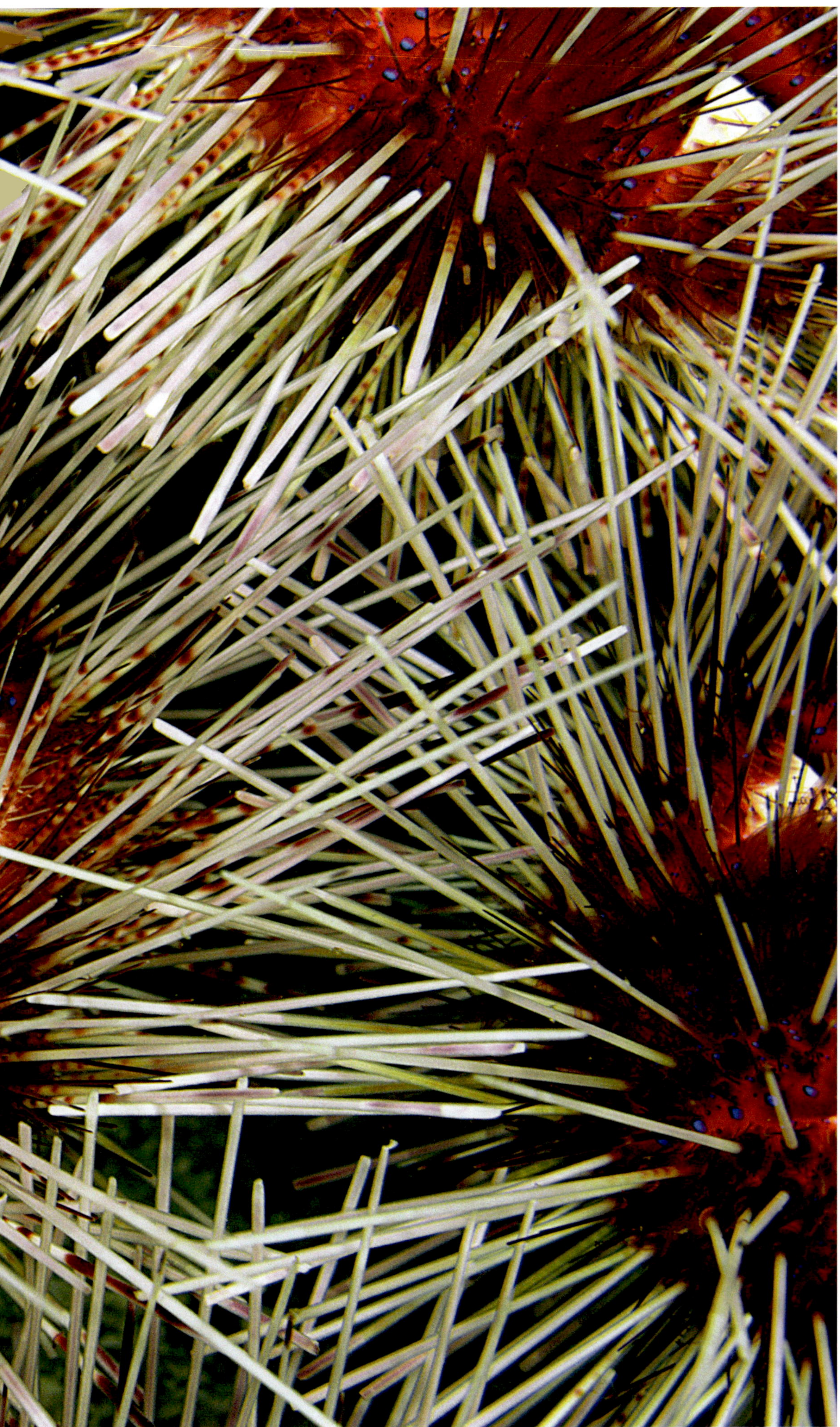

Red sea urchin
Also called the false fire urchin, this species is widespread across the Indian and Pacific oceans, from the coast of Africa to Australia and the Galápagos Islands. It is mostly found in the darker waters around 30m (98ft) down.

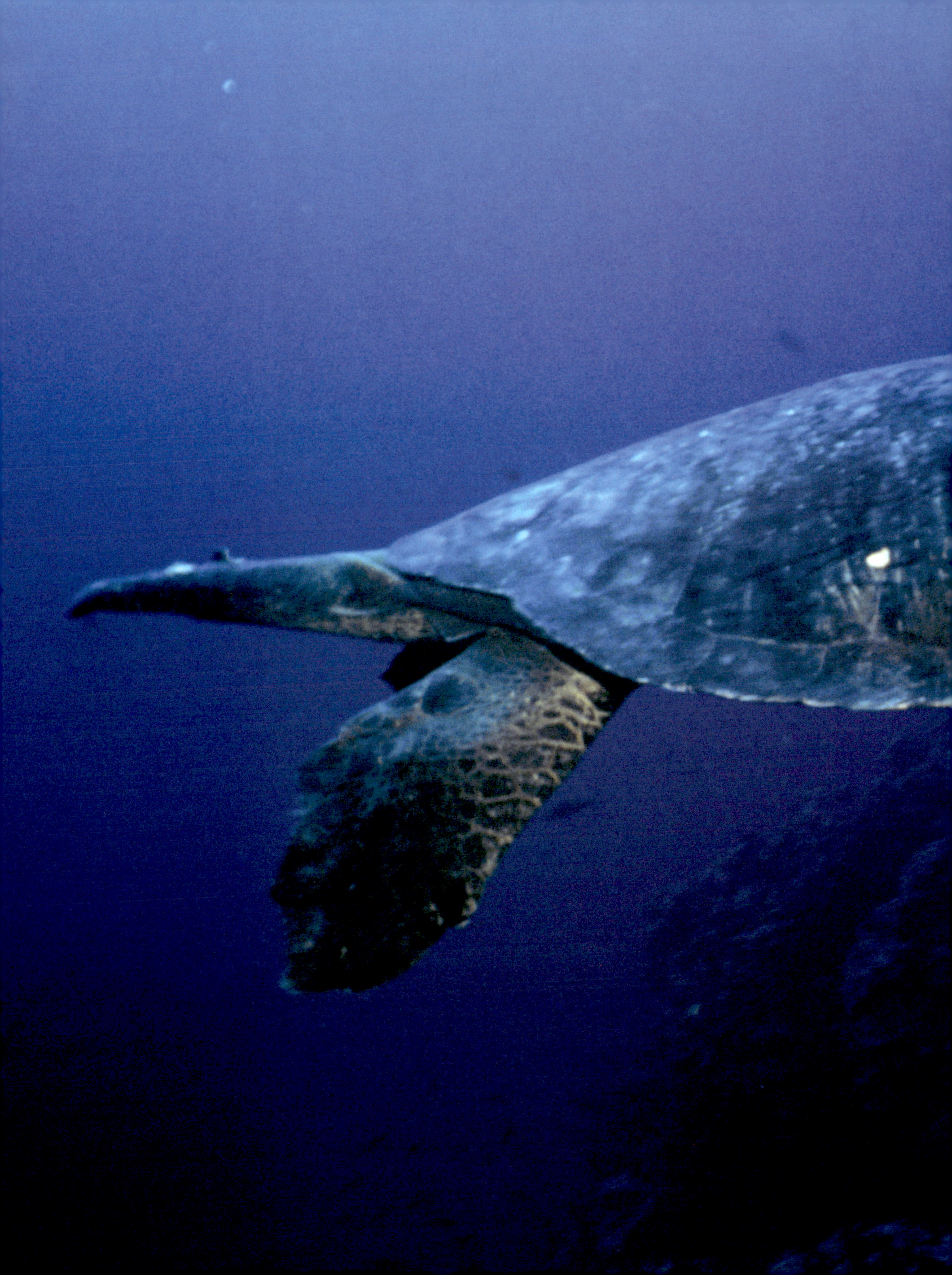

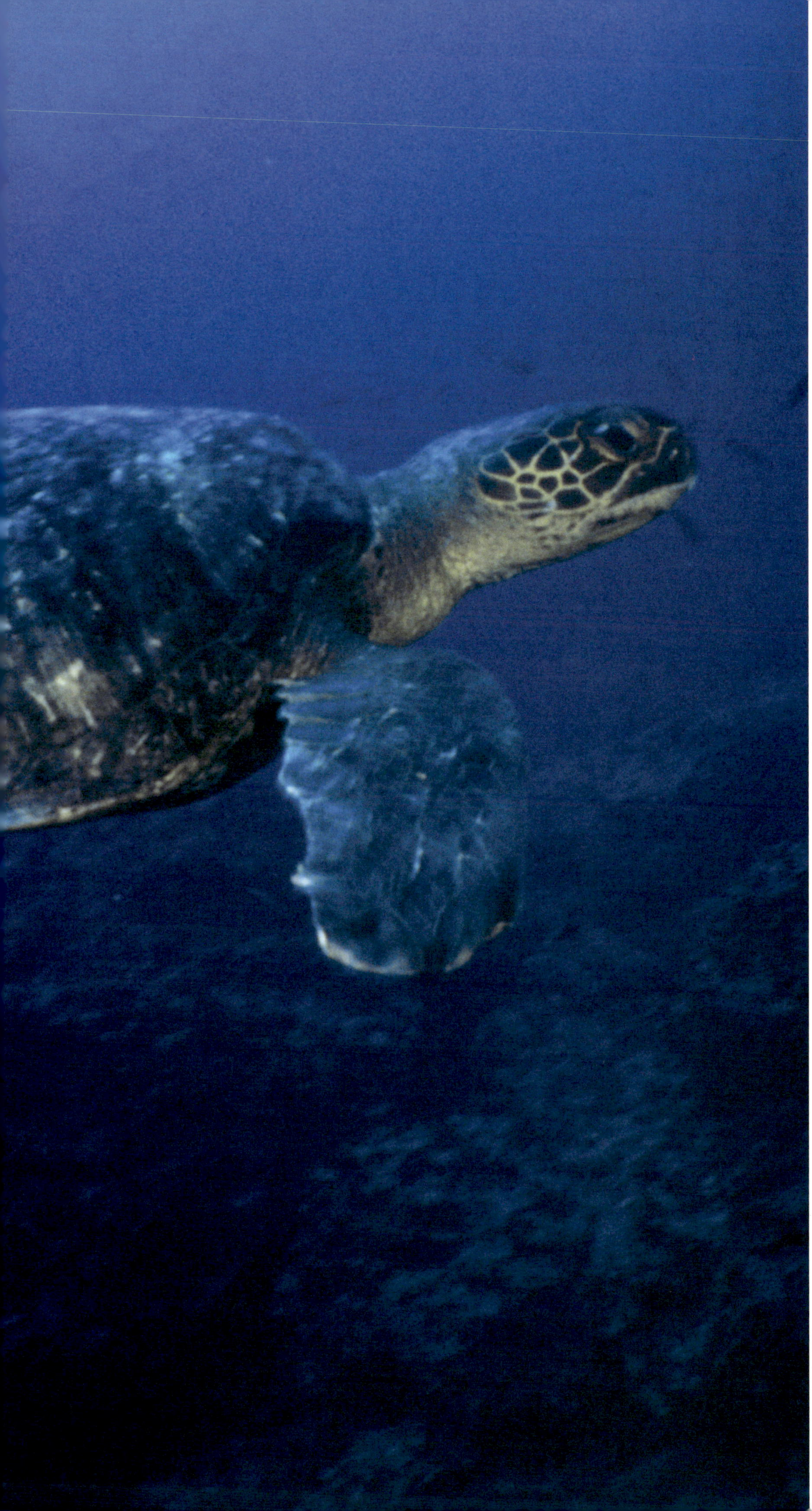

Hawksbill sea turtle
This is one of the smaller sea
turtles seen in the seas around the
Galápagos. It is rare the world
over due to being hunted for its
shell, but small numbers are seen
frequently in this area. The turtle
is an omnivore and eats seaweed,
jellyfish and crab.

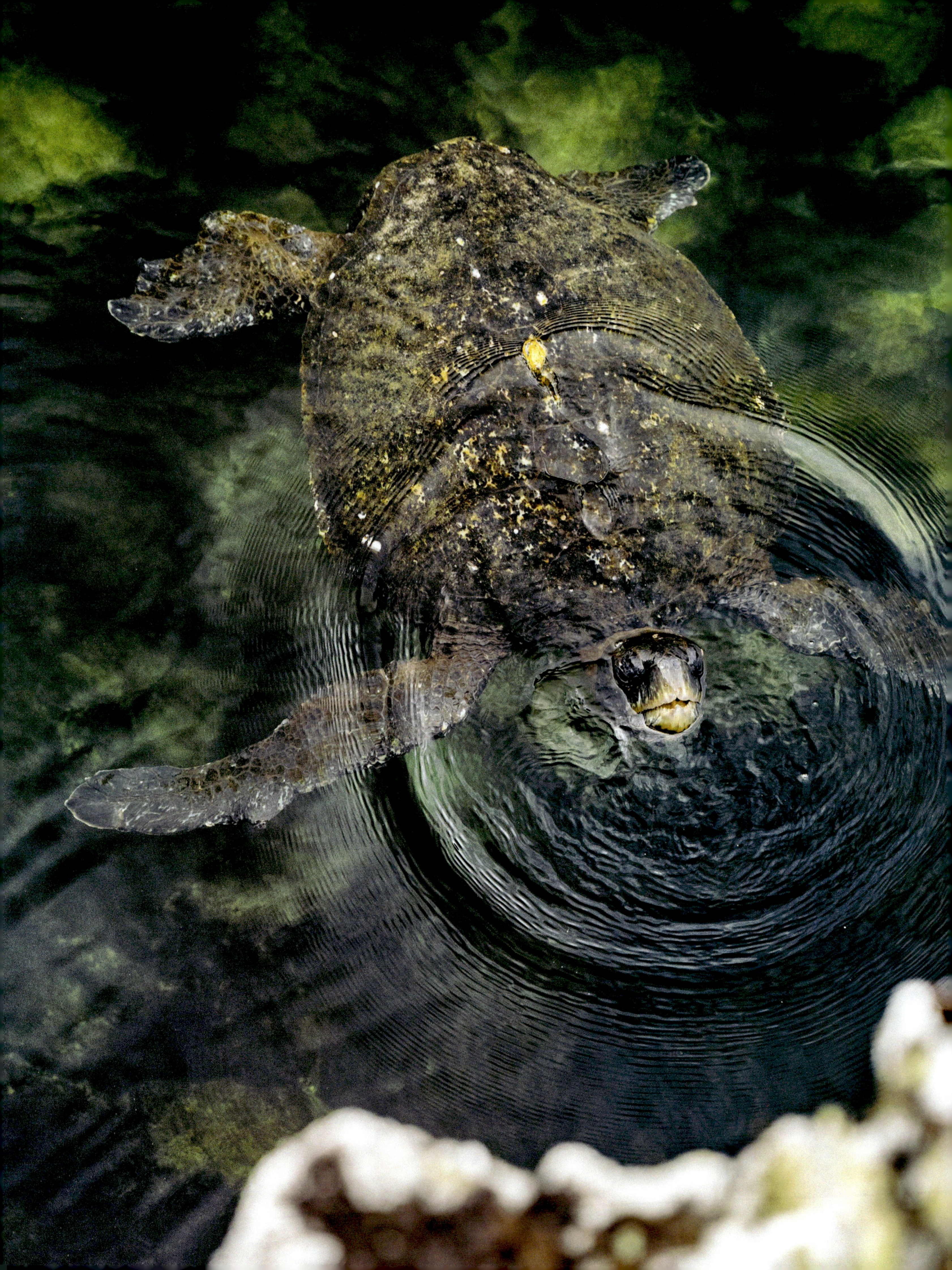

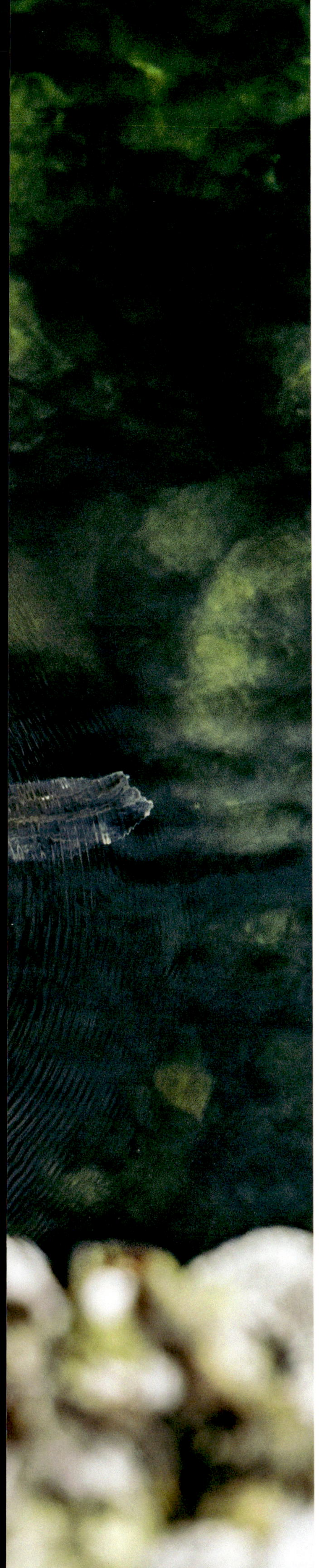

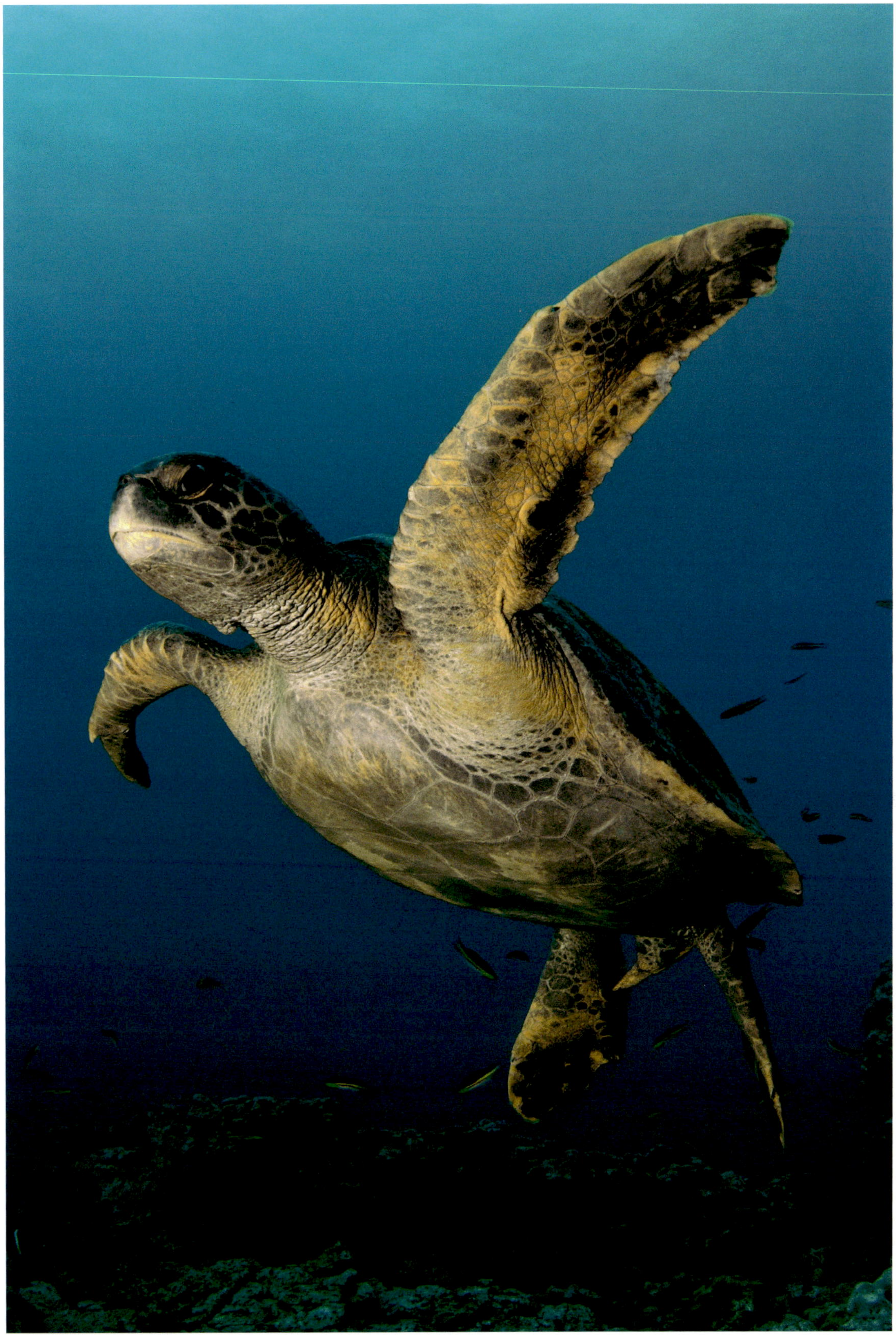

BOTH PHOTOGRAPHS:
Galápagos green turtle
The islands have their own resident
subspecies of green turtle. They
lay eggs in pits dug into the
island's many sandy beaches. The
name does not relate to the shell,
which grows darker with age,
but comes from the colour of the
seaweed-eating animal's internal
fat deposits.

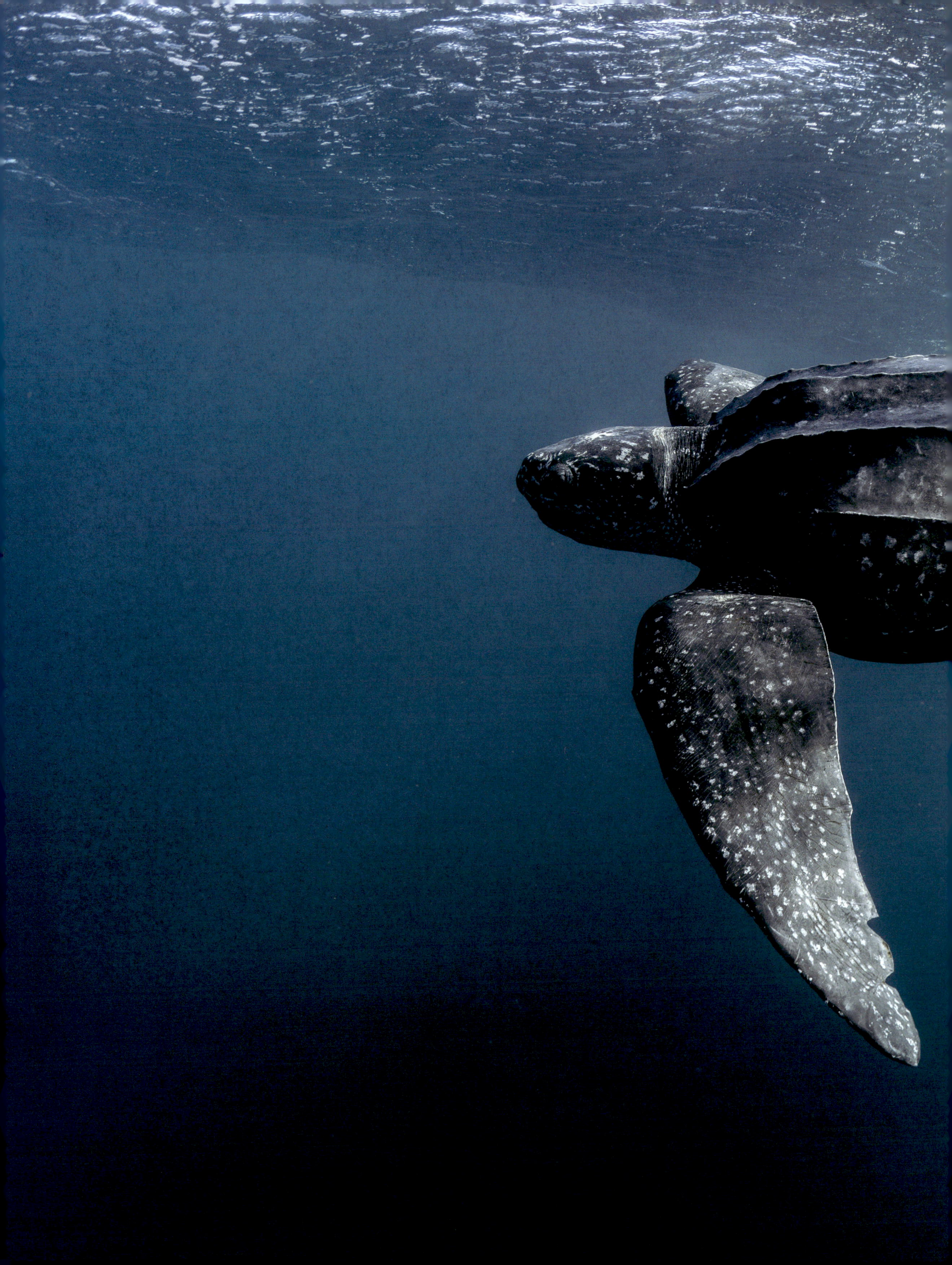

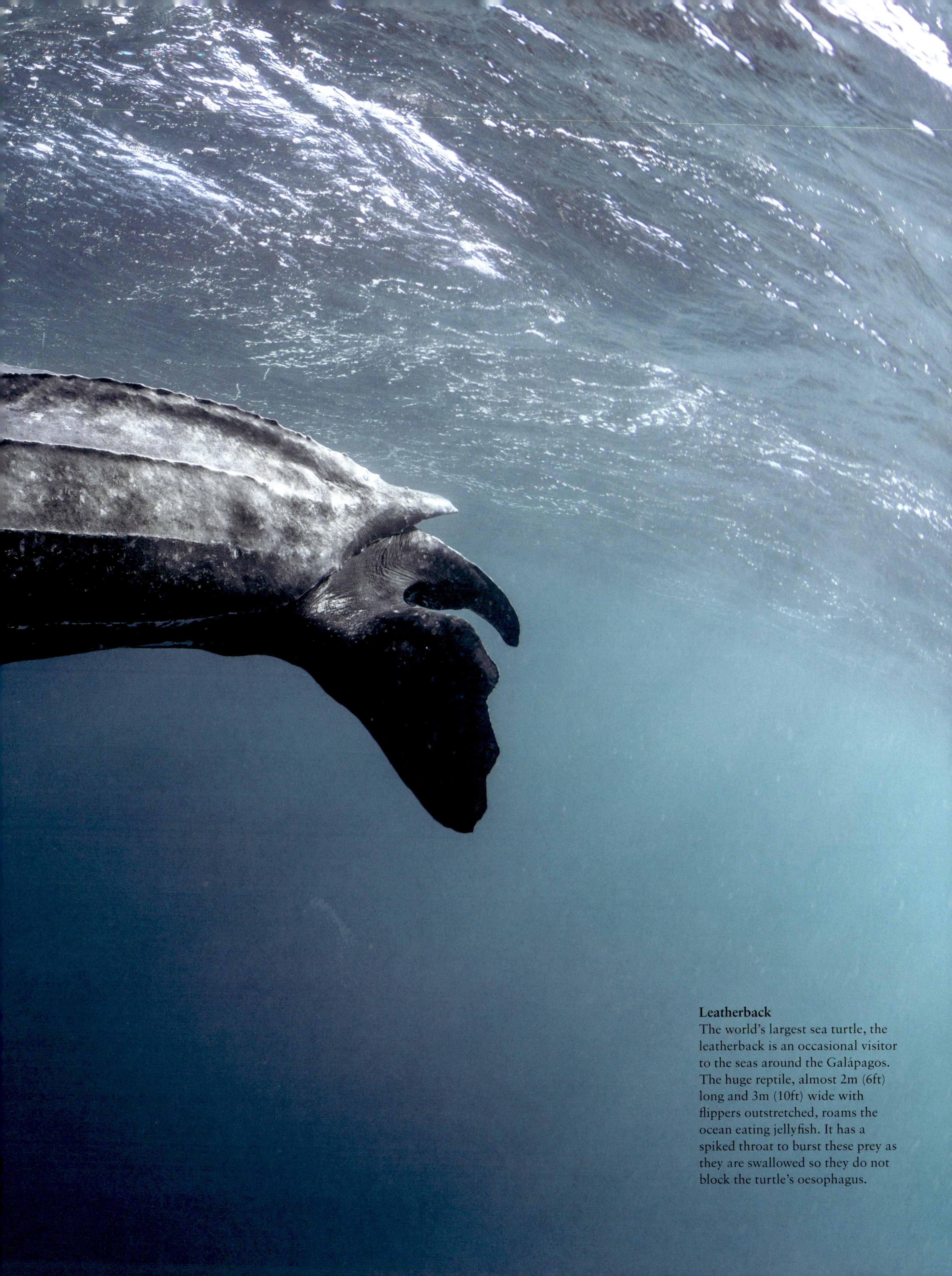

Leatherback
The world's largest sea turtle, the leatherback is an occasional visitor to the seas around the Galápagos. The huge reptile, almost 2m (6ft) long and 3m (10ft) wide with flippers outstretched, roams the ocean eating jellyfish. It has a spiked throat to burst these prey as they are swallowed so they do not block the turtle's oesophagus.

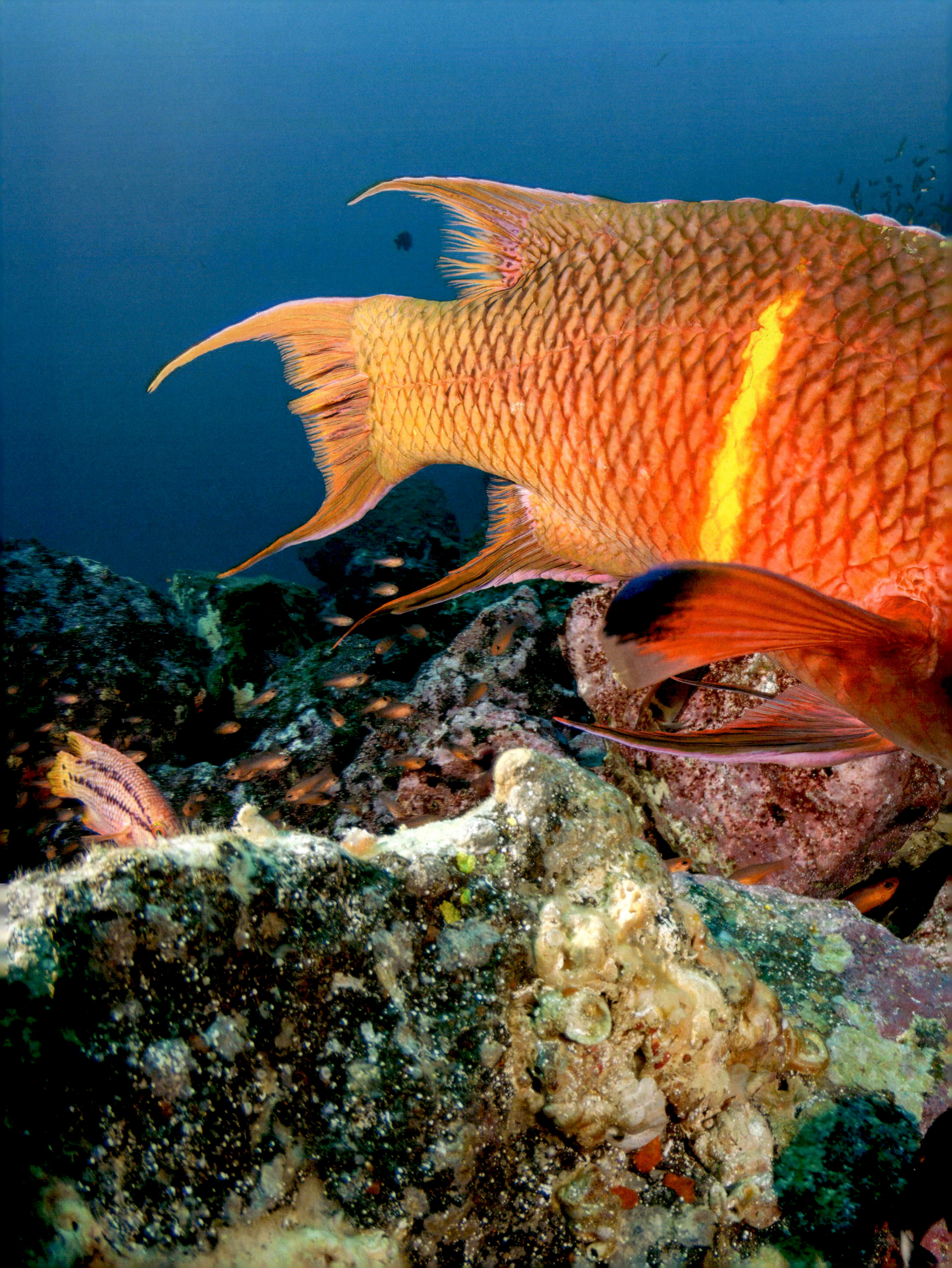

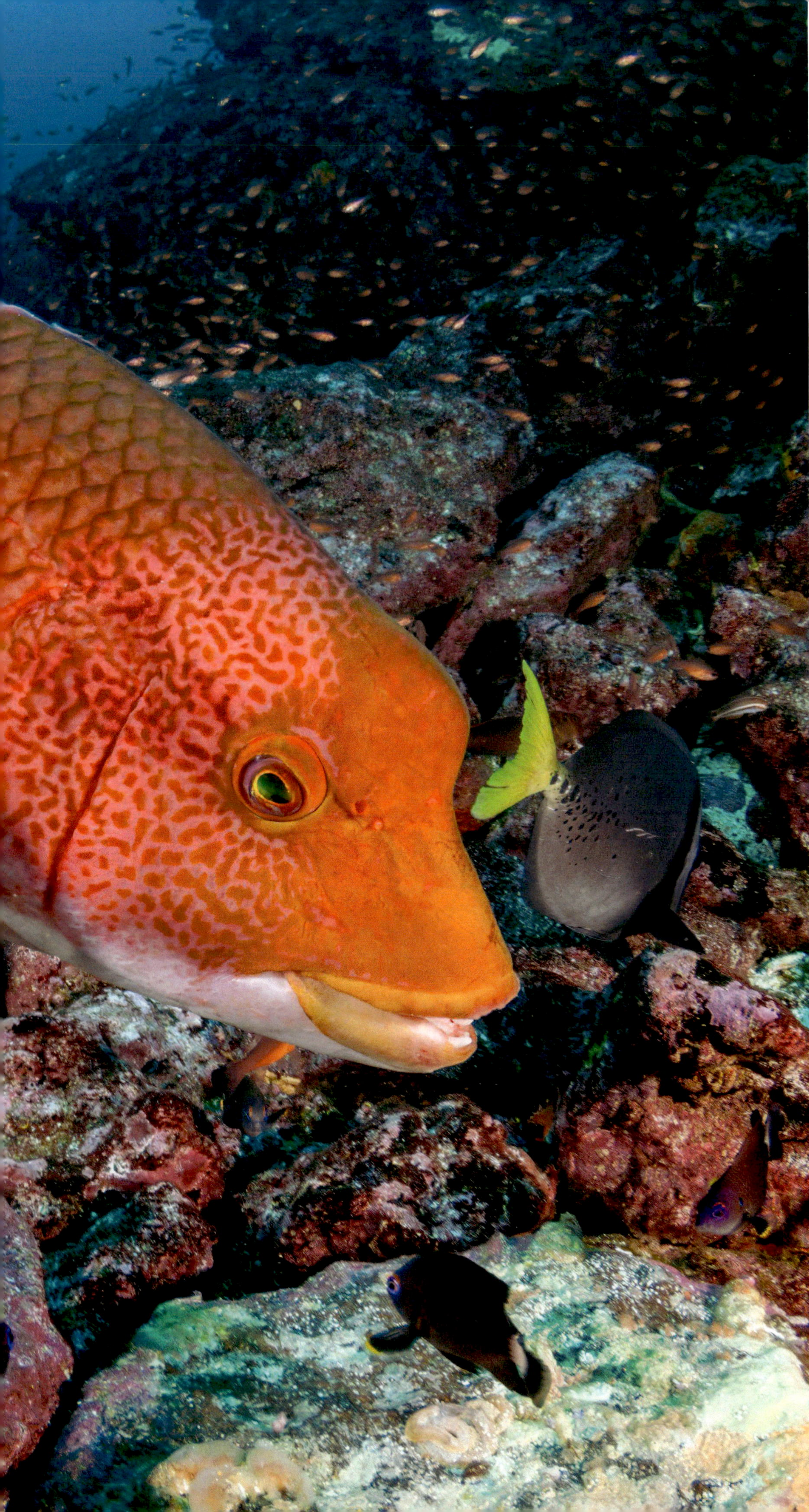

Mexican hogfish
Growing to 70cm (2ft) in length, this sturdy reef fish has a distinctive bump on its head, which swells with age, and streamers trailing from its anal and pelvic fins and tail. It forages for shellfish and sea urchins among the rocks and crushes prey with its large jaw.

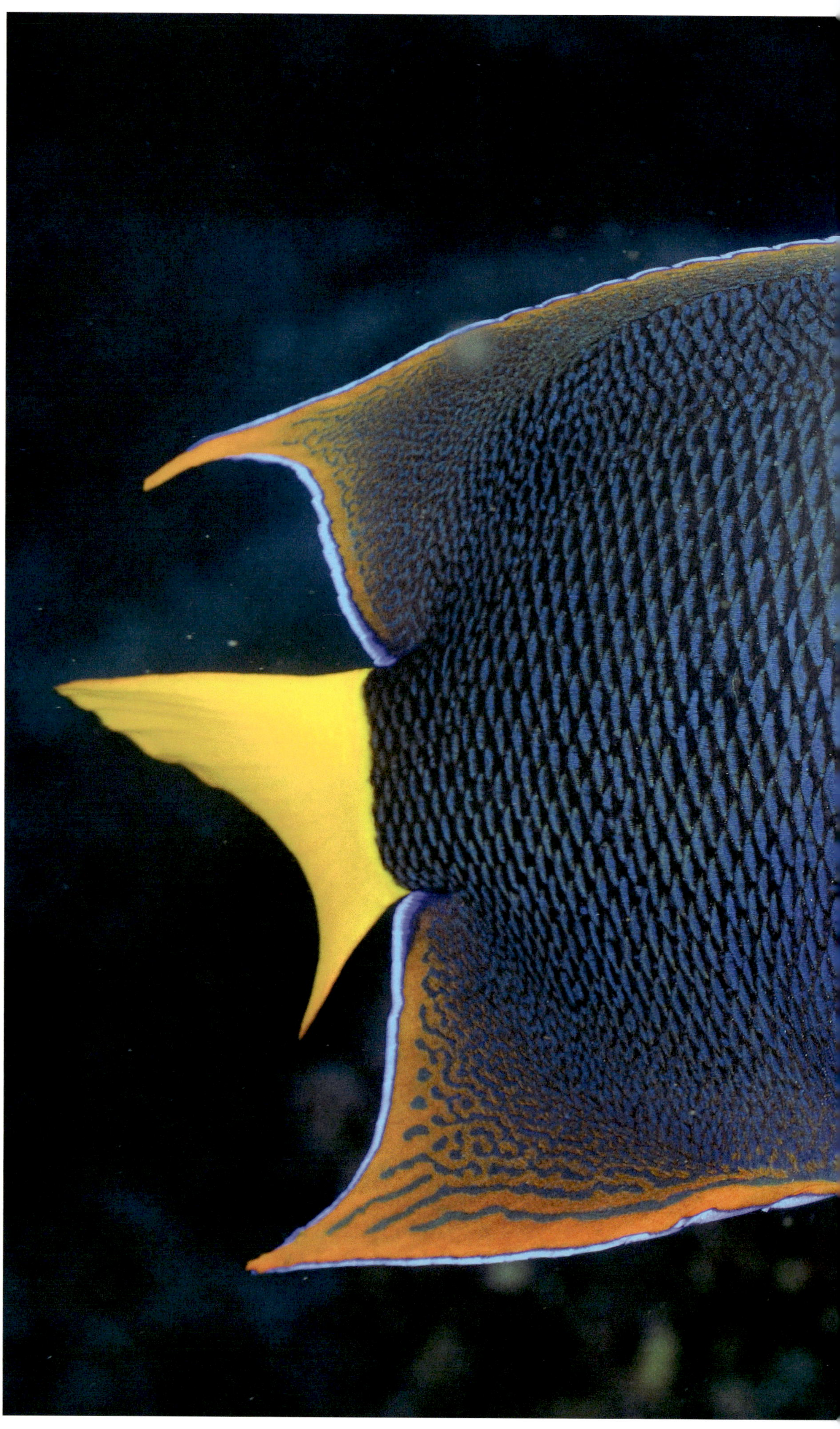

King angelfish
This striking fish gathers in small shoals around the rocks and reefs in shallow water. They target sponges on the seafloor and will also nibble morsels from the skin of other fish.

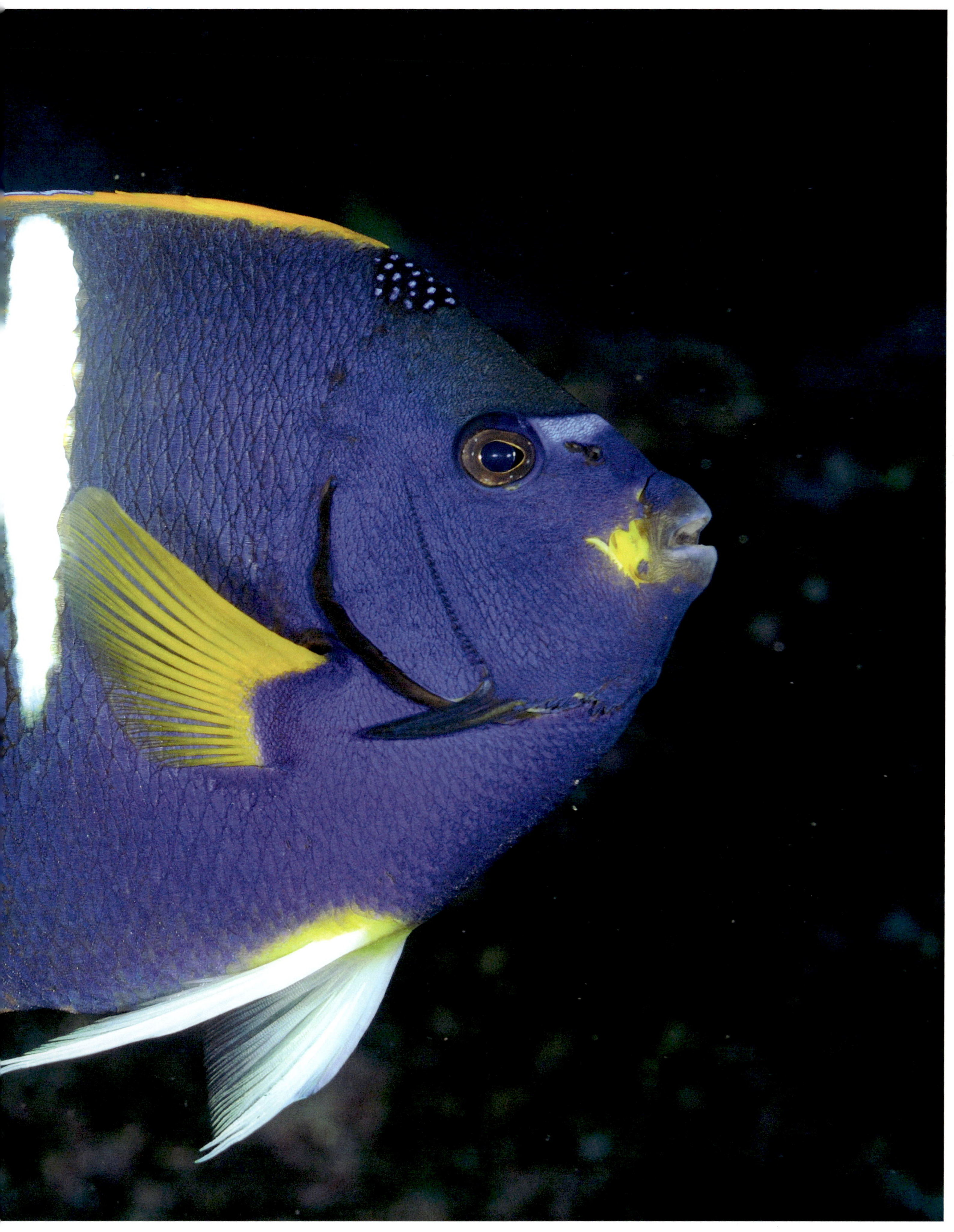

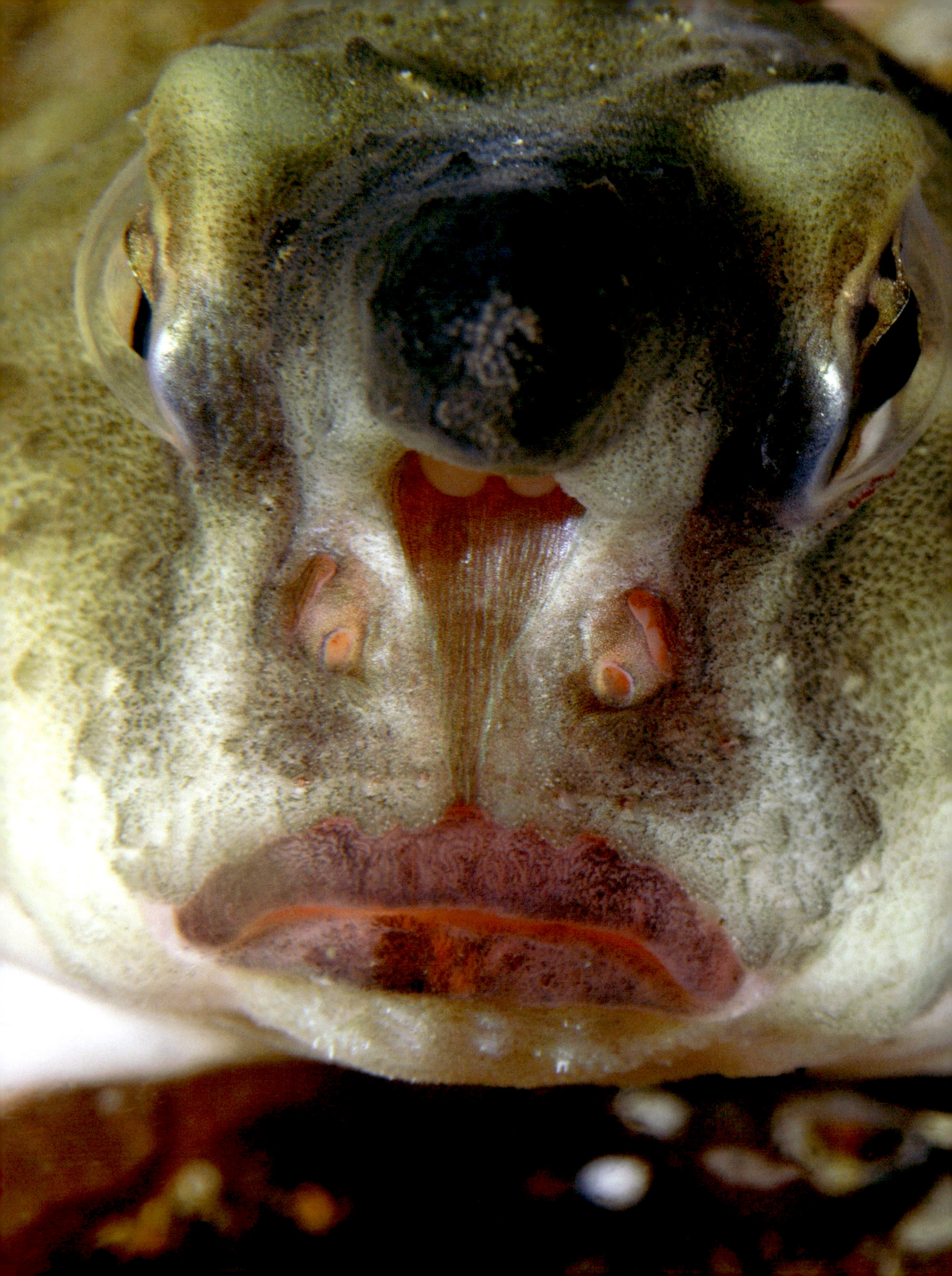

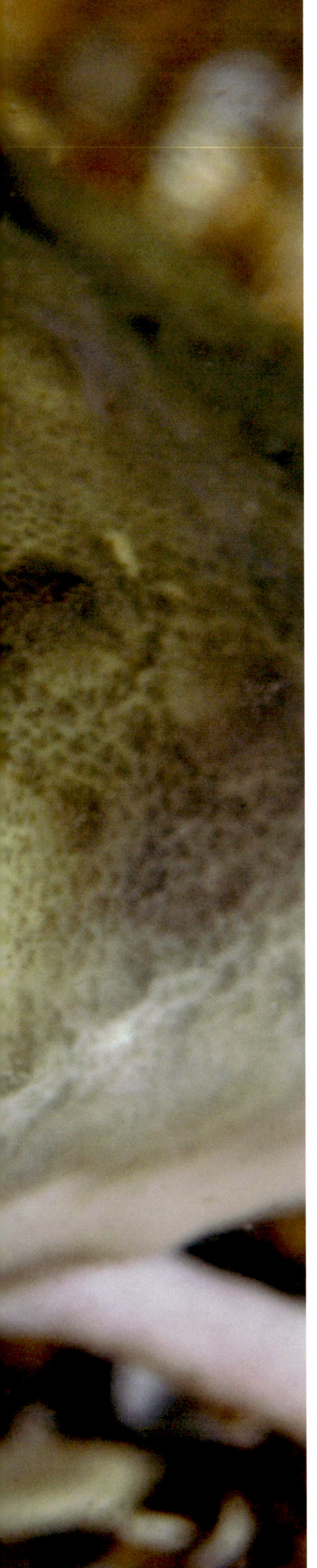

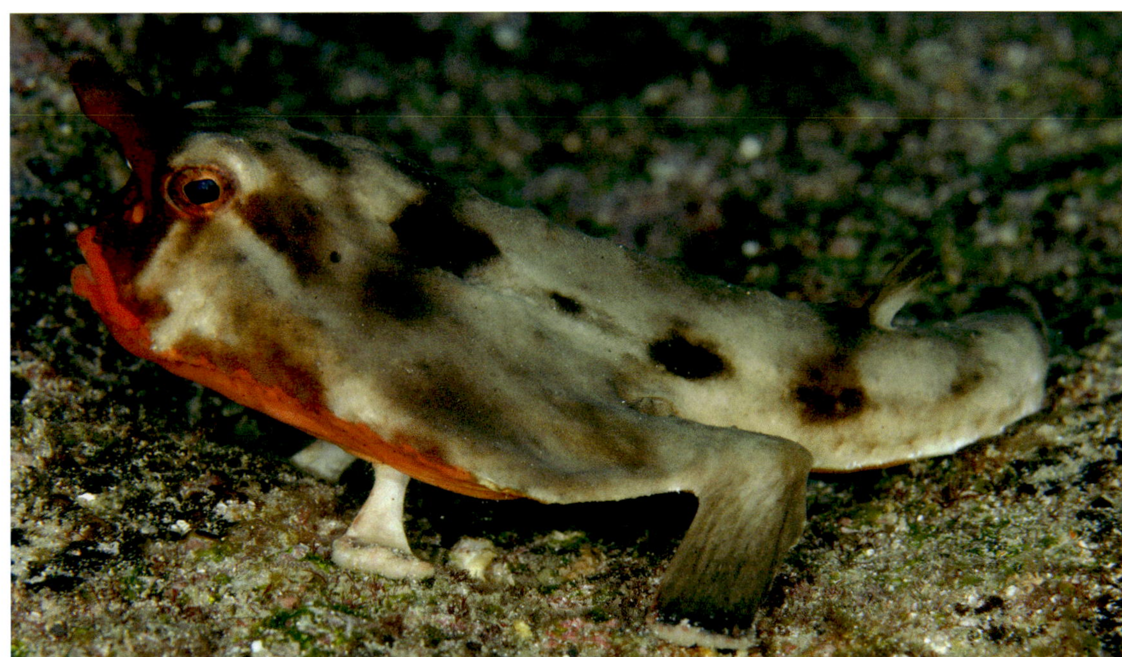

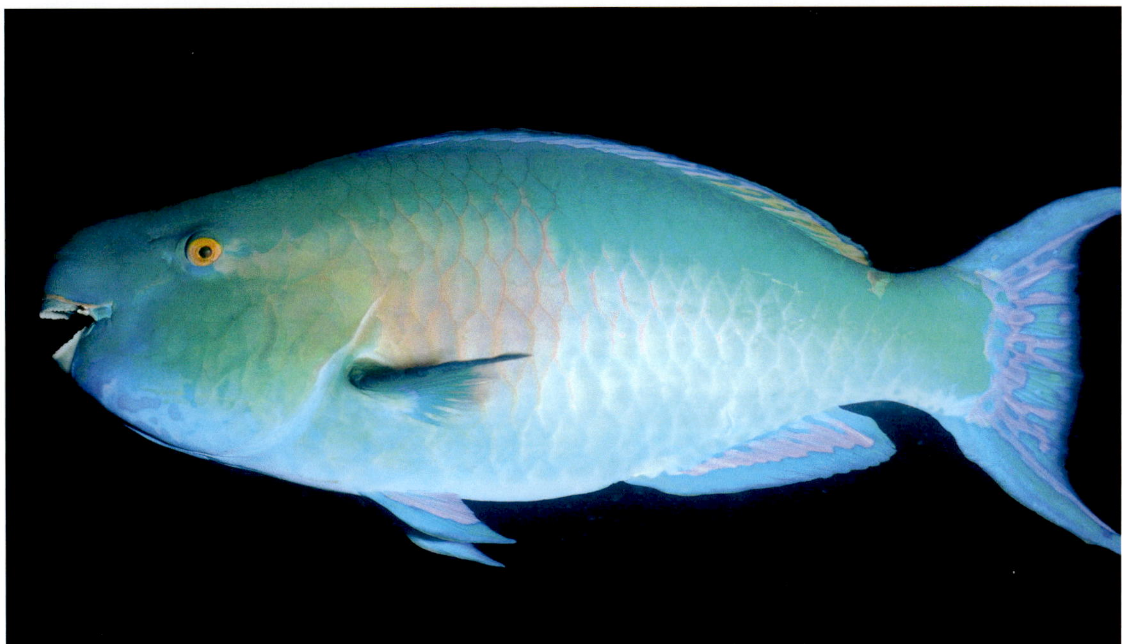

Red-lipped batfish

In one way it is obvious where this striking creature got part of its name. The thick red lips and hooded eyes give the fish a stern look. Then there is a unicorn-like horn on the forehead and leg-like fins that are used to walk, not swim, across the seabed. This gangly way of moving is similar to the way bats walk on land.

Bicolour parrotfish

This brilliantly blue fish is so named because in lower light conditions the front of the body appears darker than the rear, presumably to break up its shape and make it harder for predators to pick out against the background. Parrotfish scrape algae from rocks using their hard, beak-like mouths.

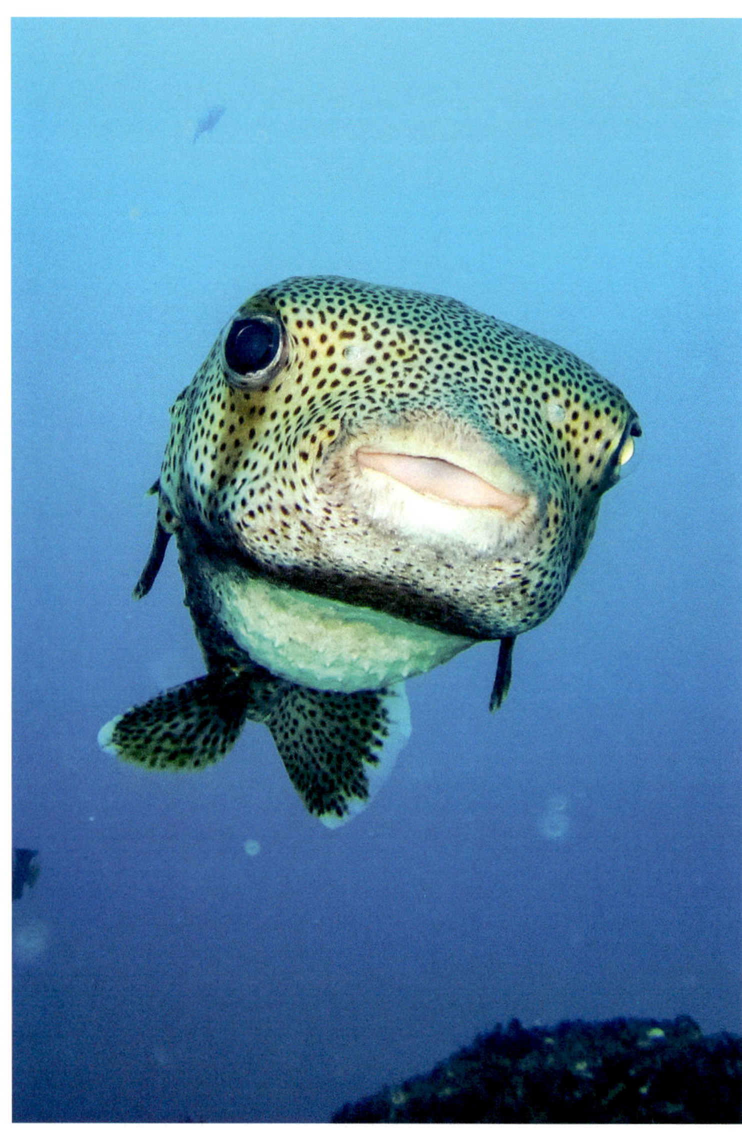

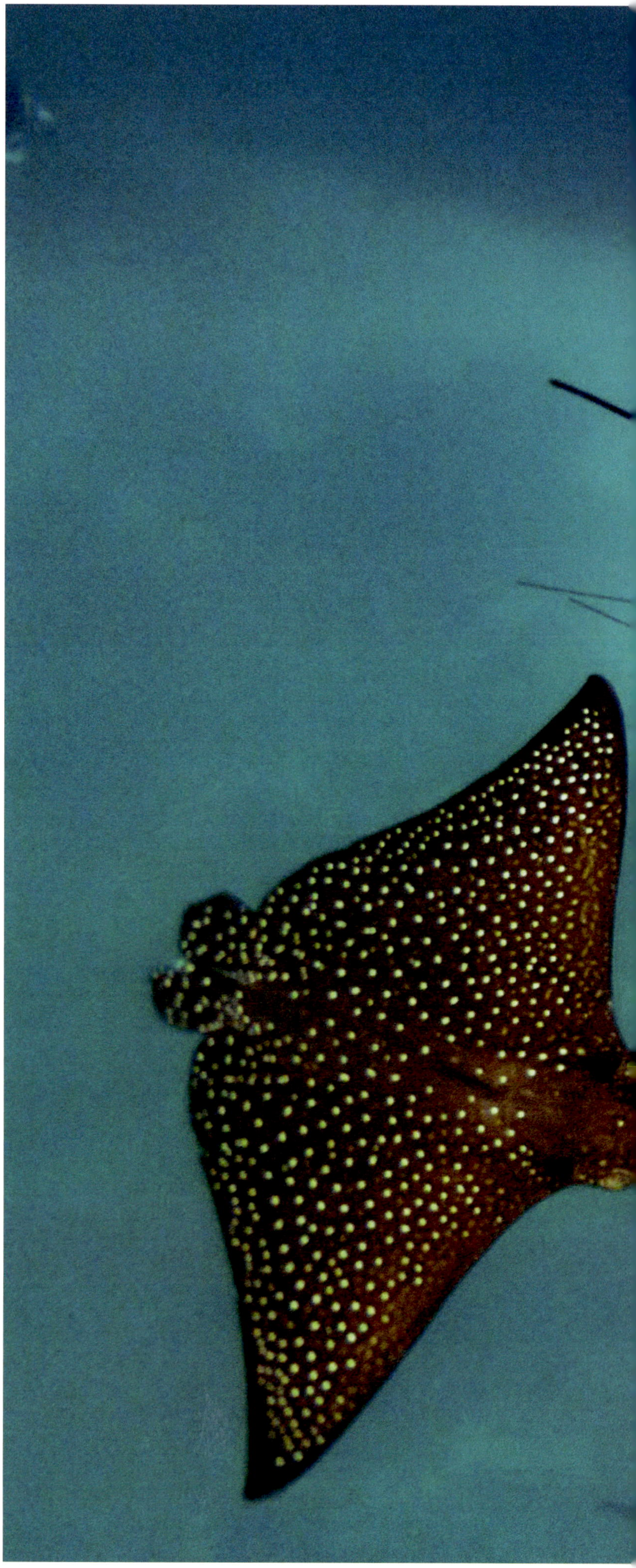

White-spotted puffer
This medium-sized fish is a
cosmopolitan marine species
that is a resident of the islands.
It inflates, or puffs up, its boxy
body to expose venomous spines
when threatened.

Spotted eagle ray
A flotilla of rays patrols the
seafloor. These 2m (6ft) wide fish
– relatives of sharks – are bottom
feeders. They use their downward-
facing mouths to excavate the sand
for buried shellfish.

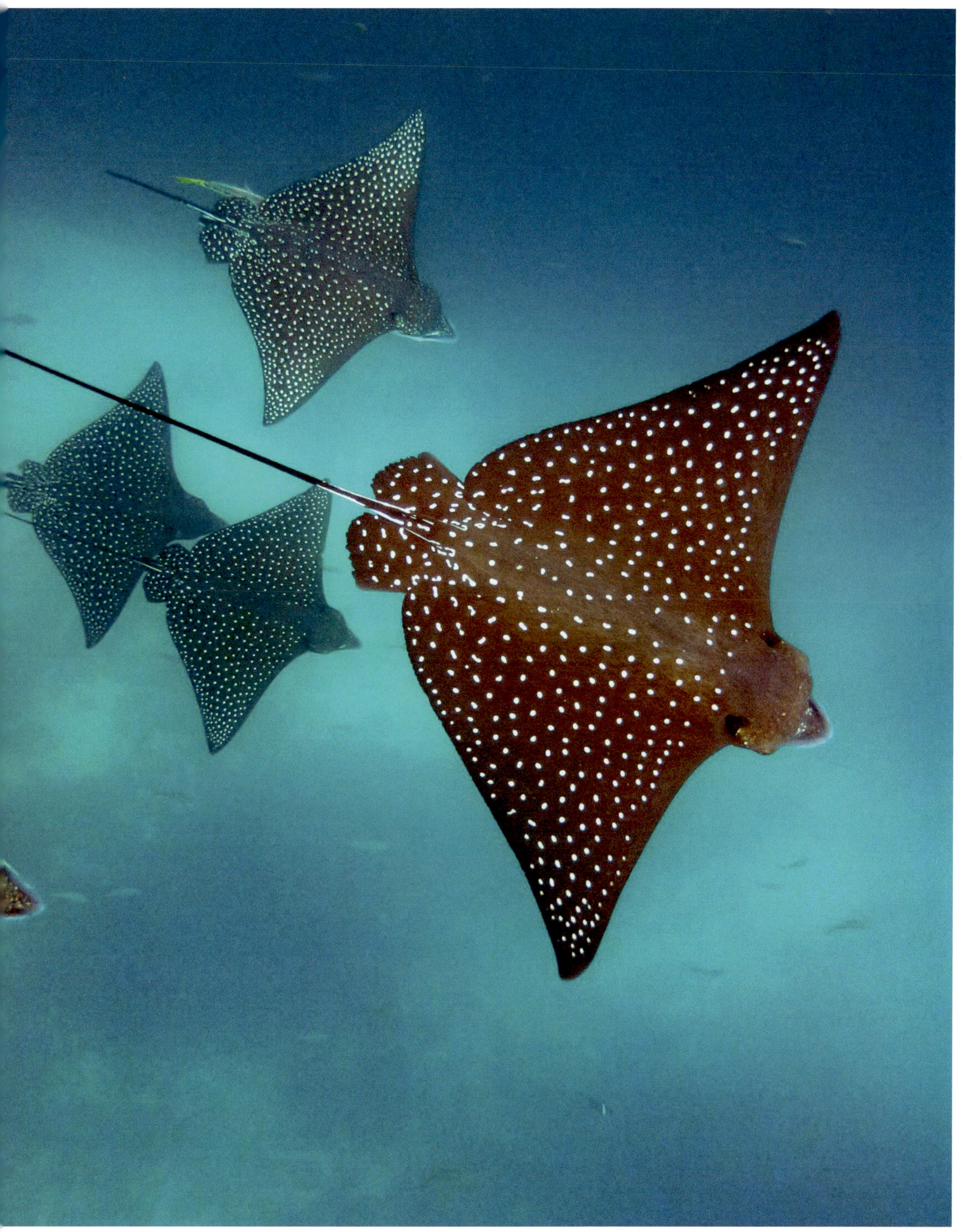

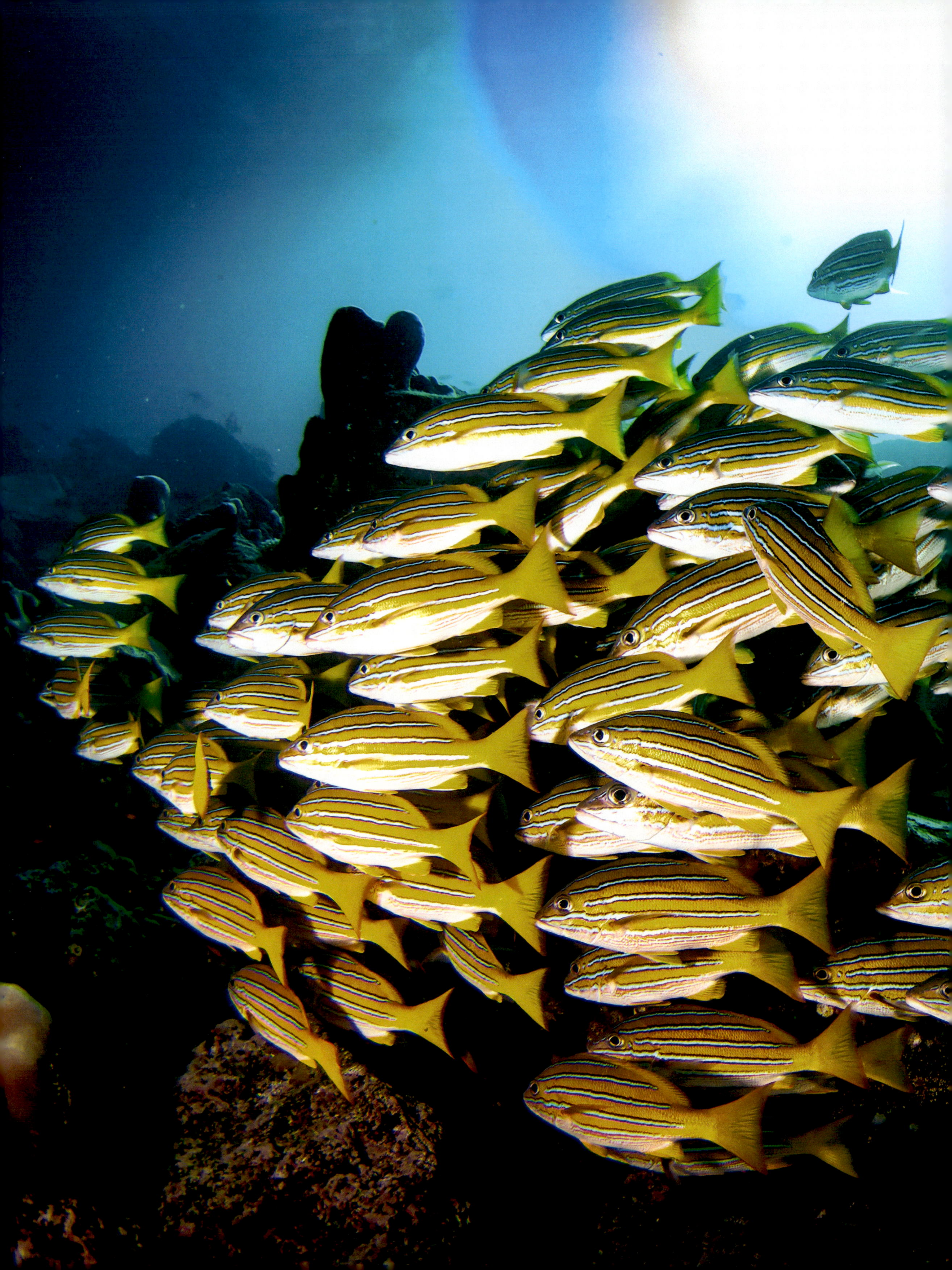

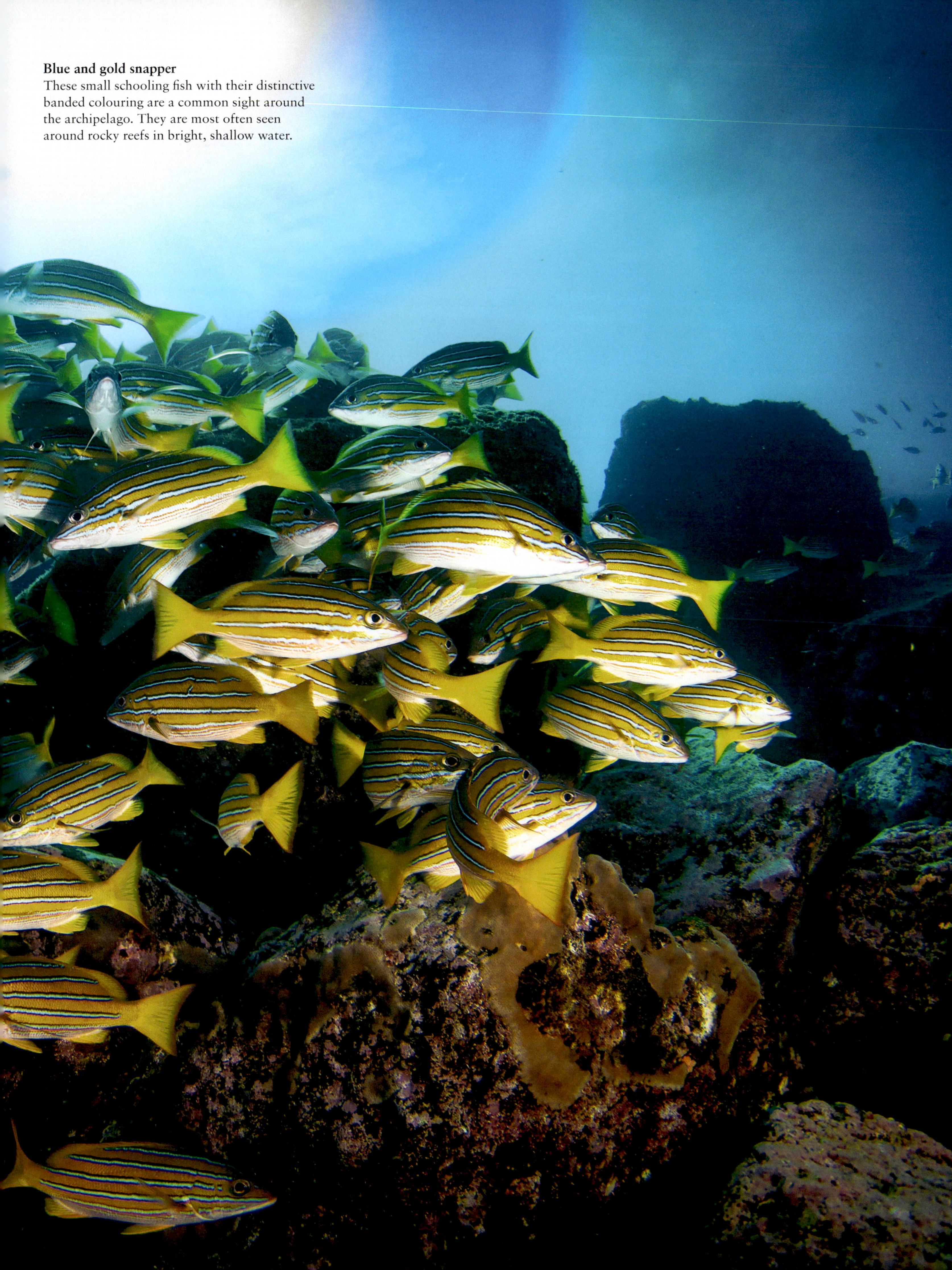

Blue and gold snapper
These small schooling fish with their distinctive banded colouring are a common sight around the archipelago. They are most often seen around rocky reefs in bright, shallow water.

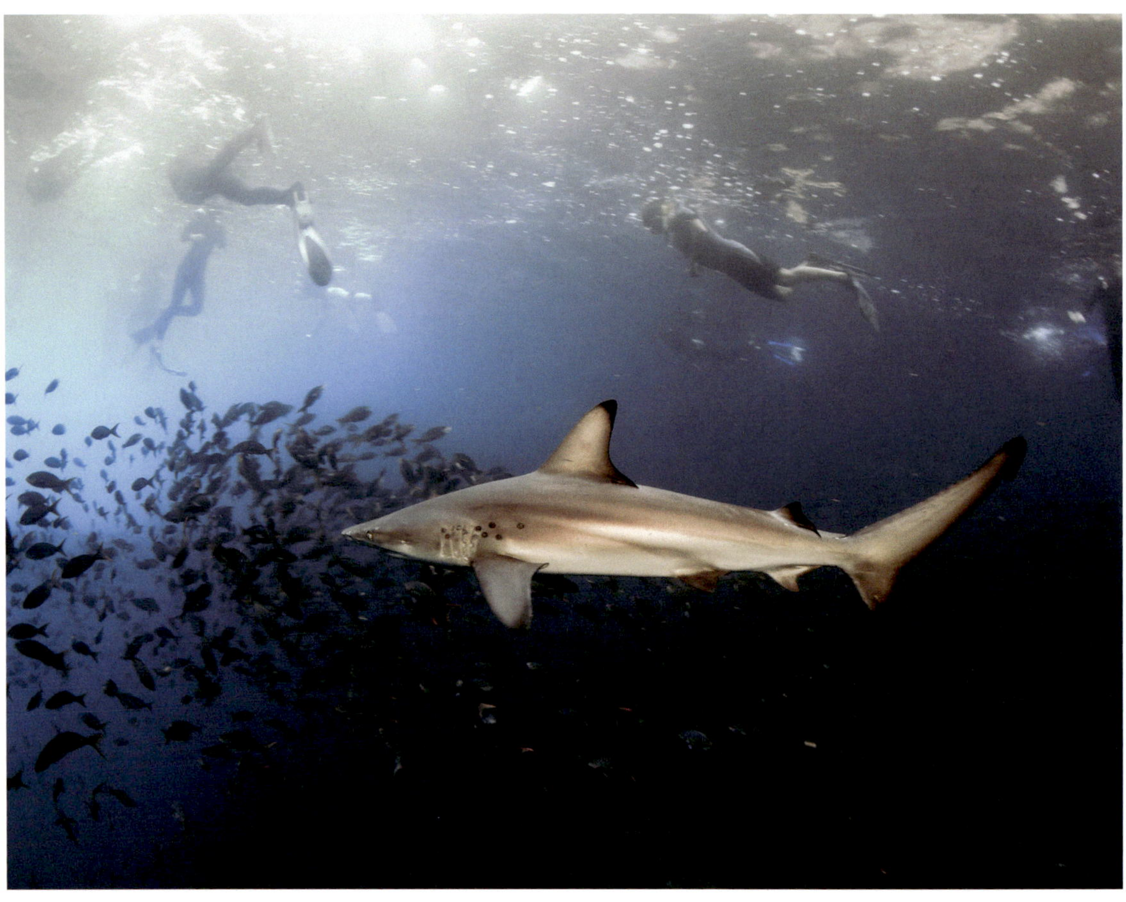

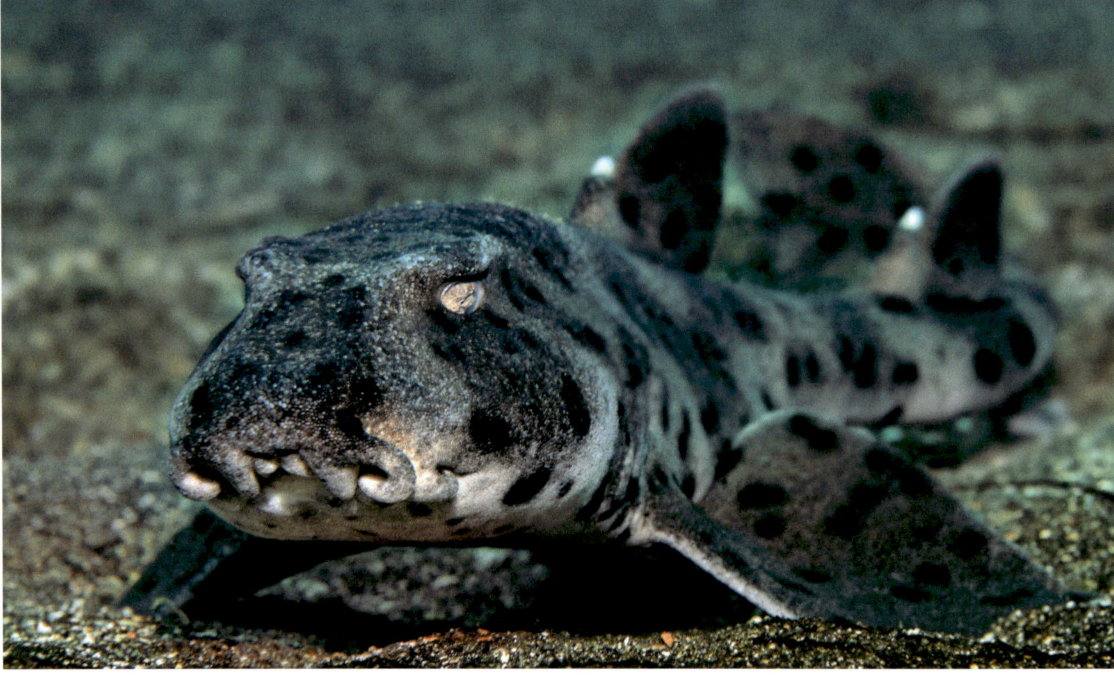

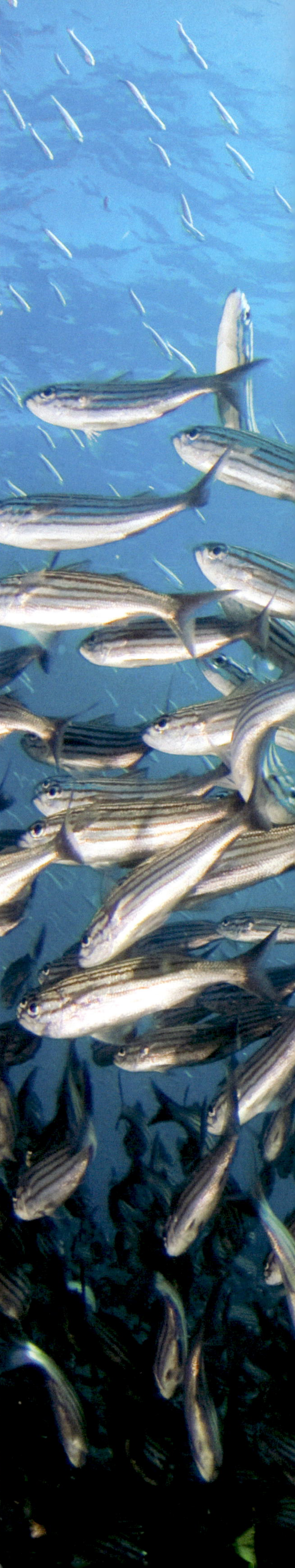

Blacktip shark

Not to be confused with its smaller relative the blacktip reef shark, this predatory fish is about 2.5m (8ft) long, which is medium-sized for a shark. This one is preparing to attack a shoal of fish, while divers look on. It is seldom found in shallow waters, preferring to live and hunt further out in the deep.

Galápagos bullhead shark

This is a small, bottom-dwelling species, barely 1m (3ft) in length. It is most common in the western part of the islands. It is active at night and forages for shellfish among the rocks.

Galápagos shark

This 2m (6ft) long species is endemic to the archipelago, according to some authorities as least. Others contend that the Galápagos is a hotspot for dusky sharks, which are widespread in coastal seas worldwide, and more or less indistinguishable from the Galápagos shark. Around the archipelago, the shark preys on sea lions, fish and rays.

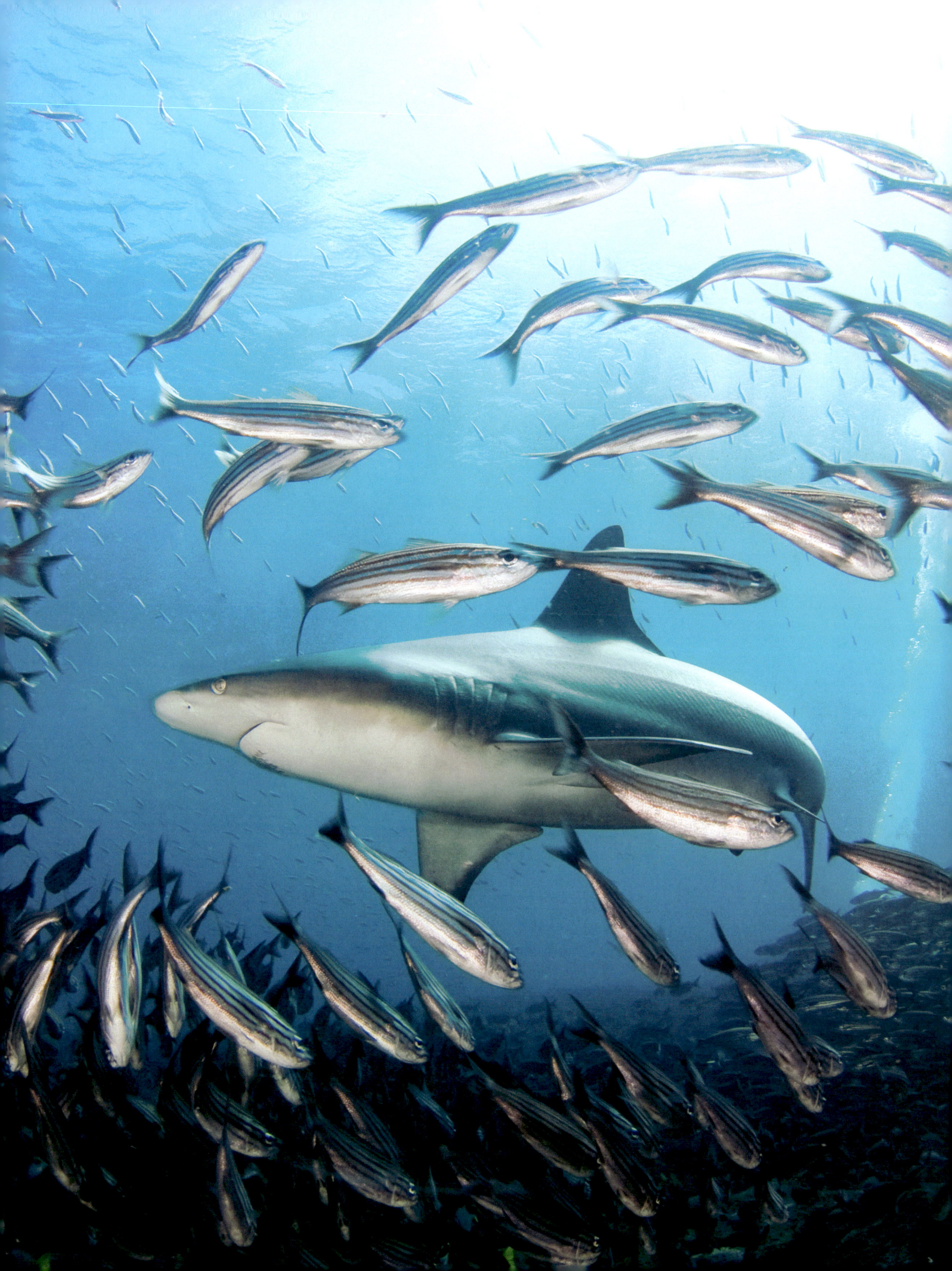

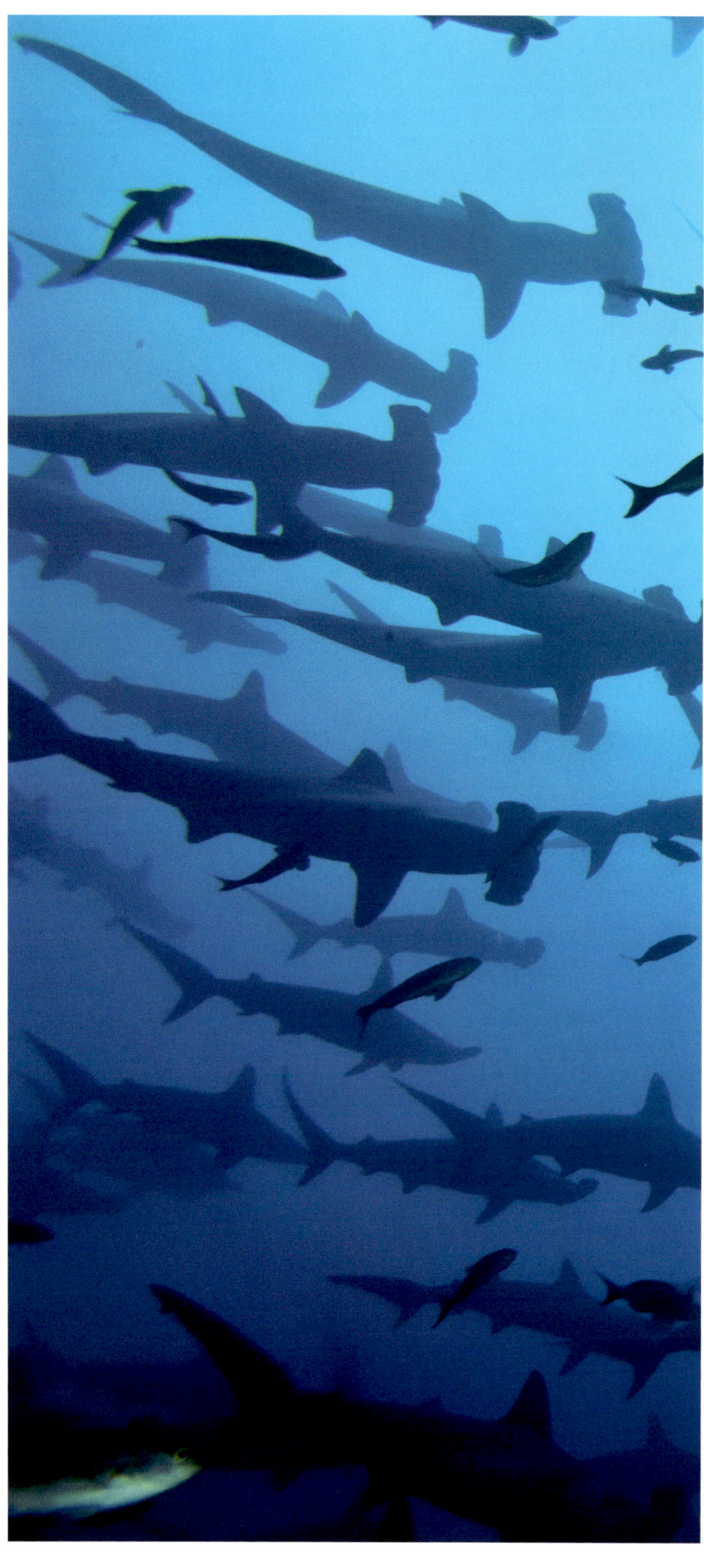

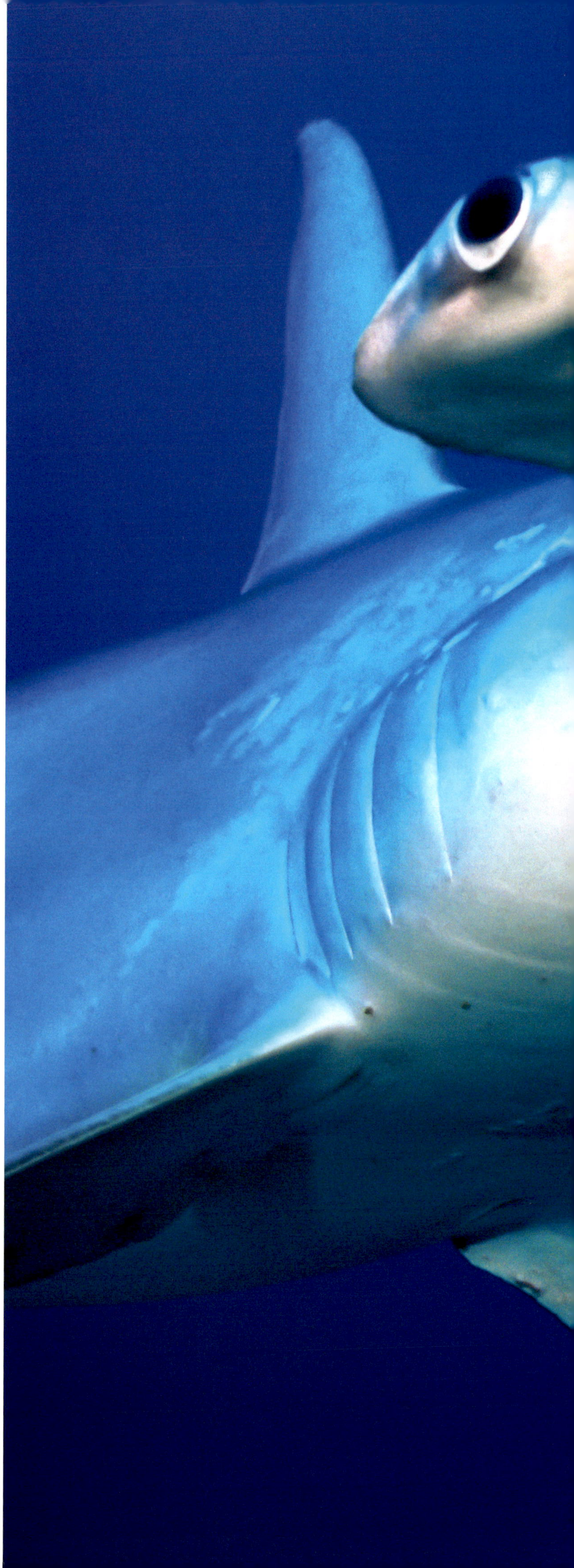

Scalloped hammerhead shark
Well-known for the unusual shape of its head, this species in common with other hammerheads, gathers in large numbers to breed. One of these breeding sites is around the isolated islands of Darwin and Wolf.

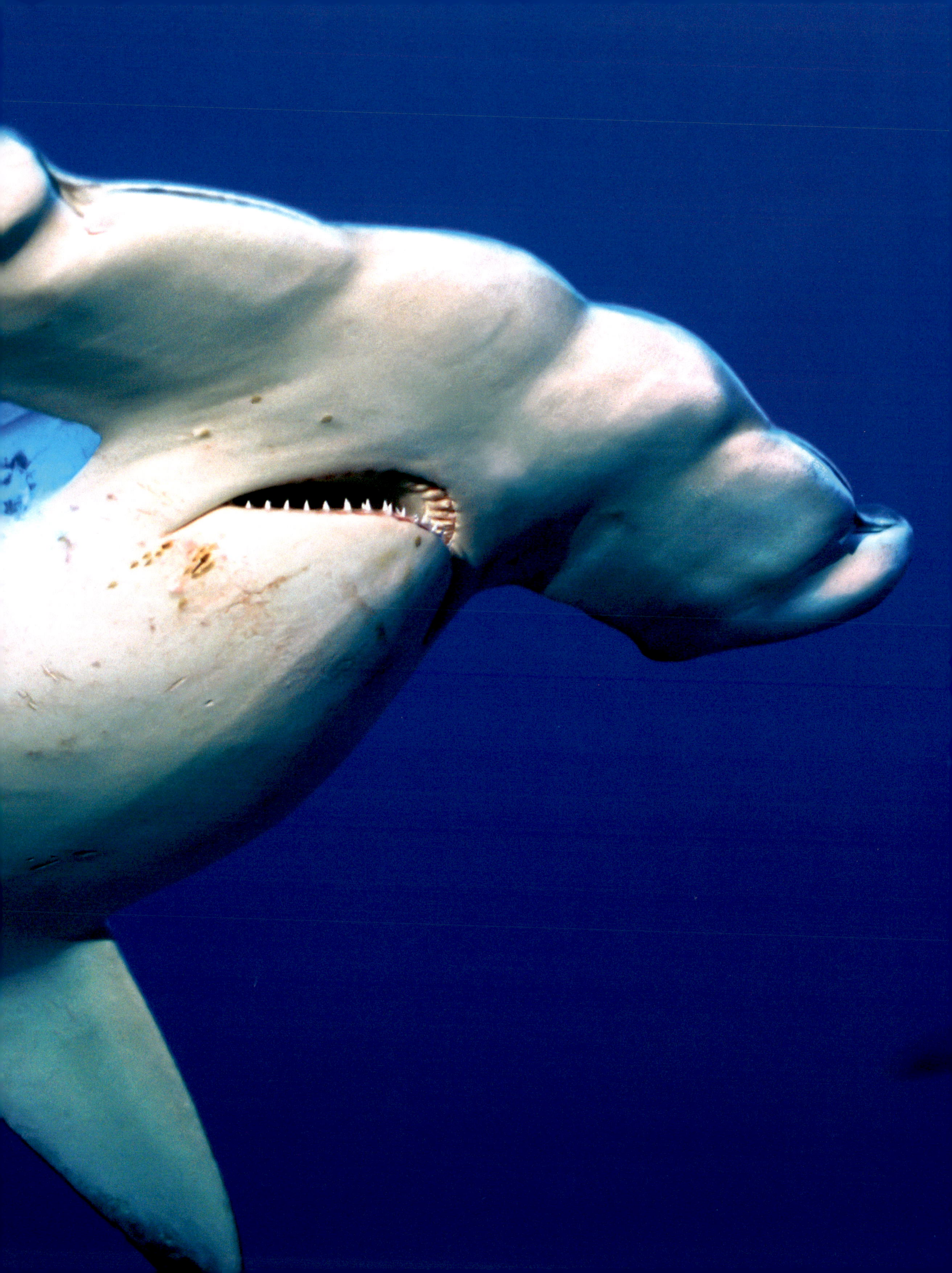

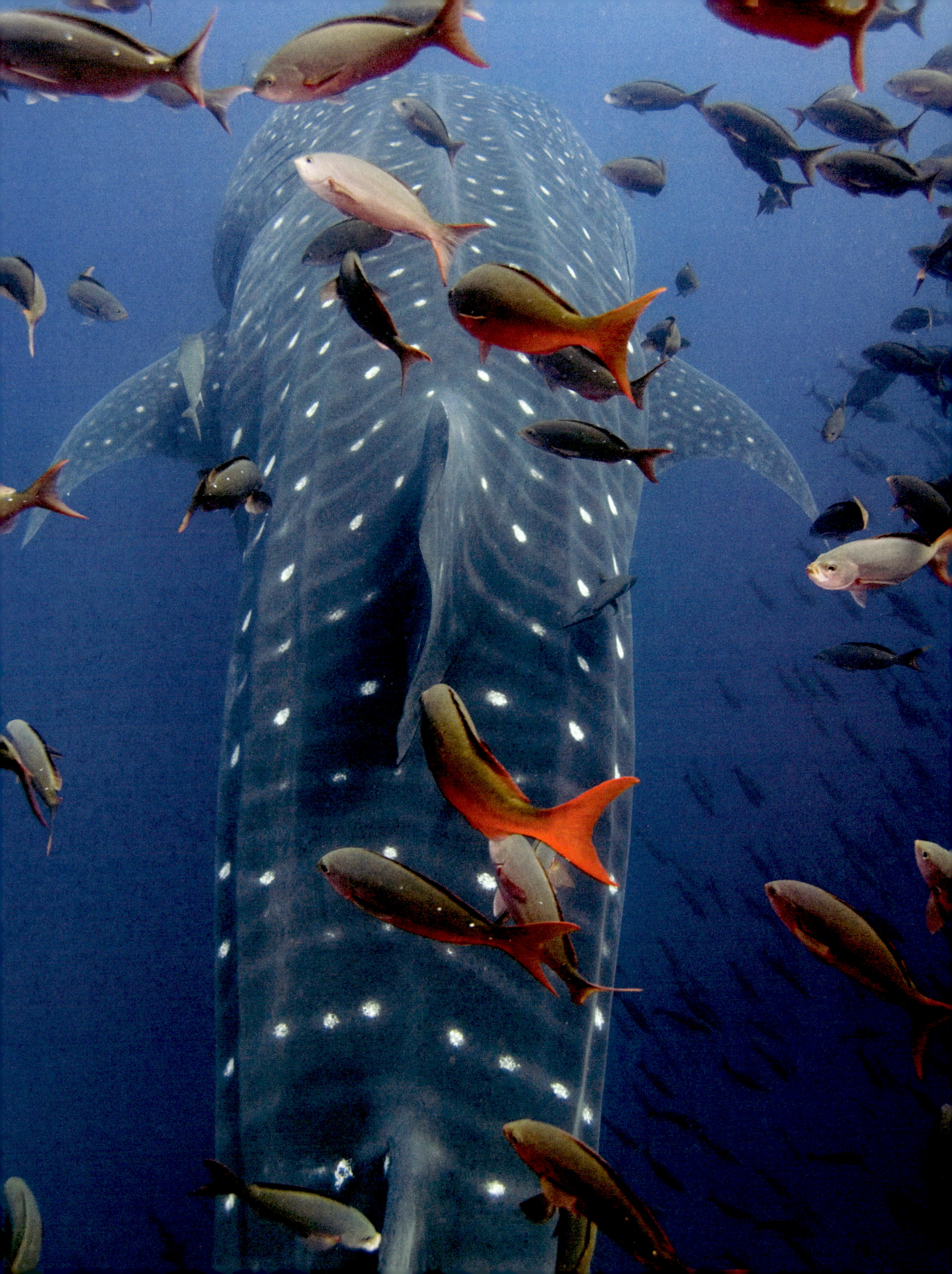

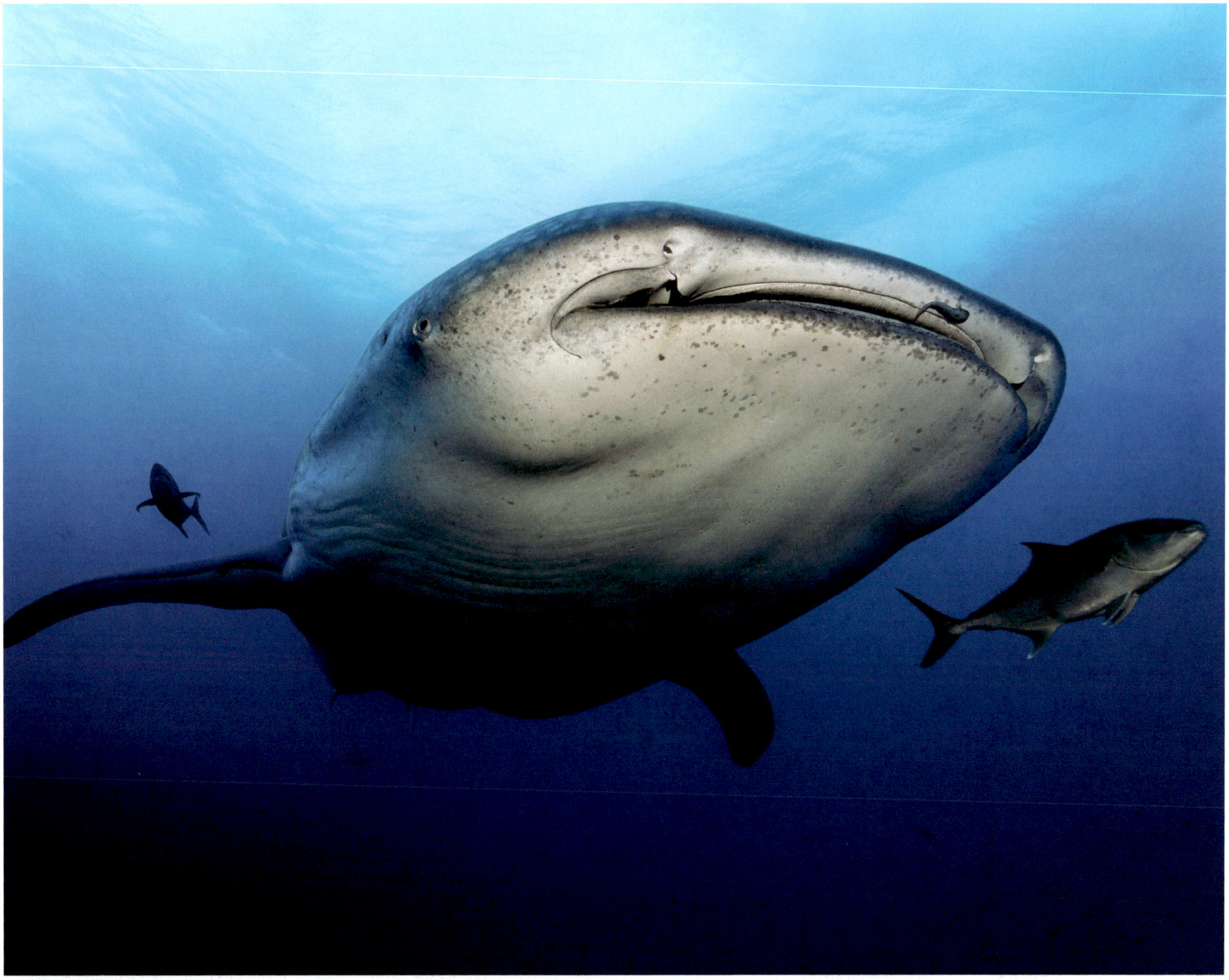

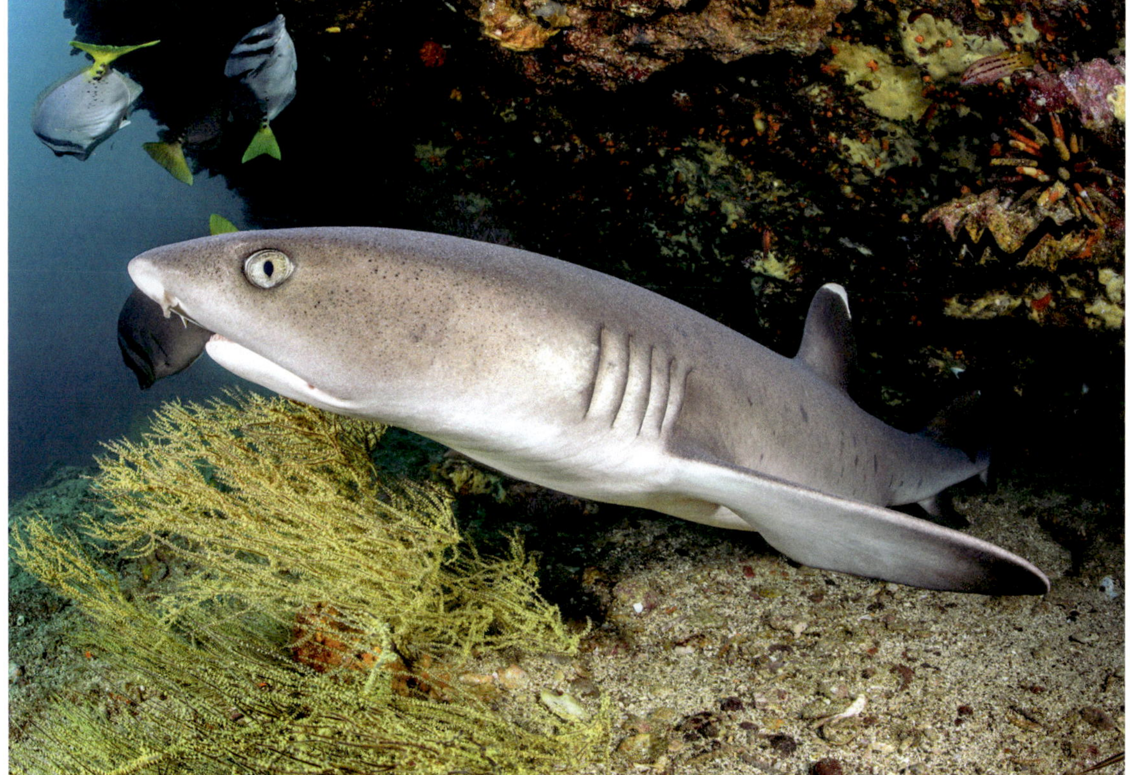

Whale shark

The world's largest shark and largest fish species, the whale shark can grow to 14m (46ft) long. However, it is a filter feeder and poses no threat to humans or fish that it meets. It is found throughout the archipelago all year round but is also more likely to congregate around Darwin and Wolf islands.

Whitetip reef shark

This small shark orbits areas of rocky seabed before making incursions to grab prey. This one is having a sleep, resting by day in a secluded spot.

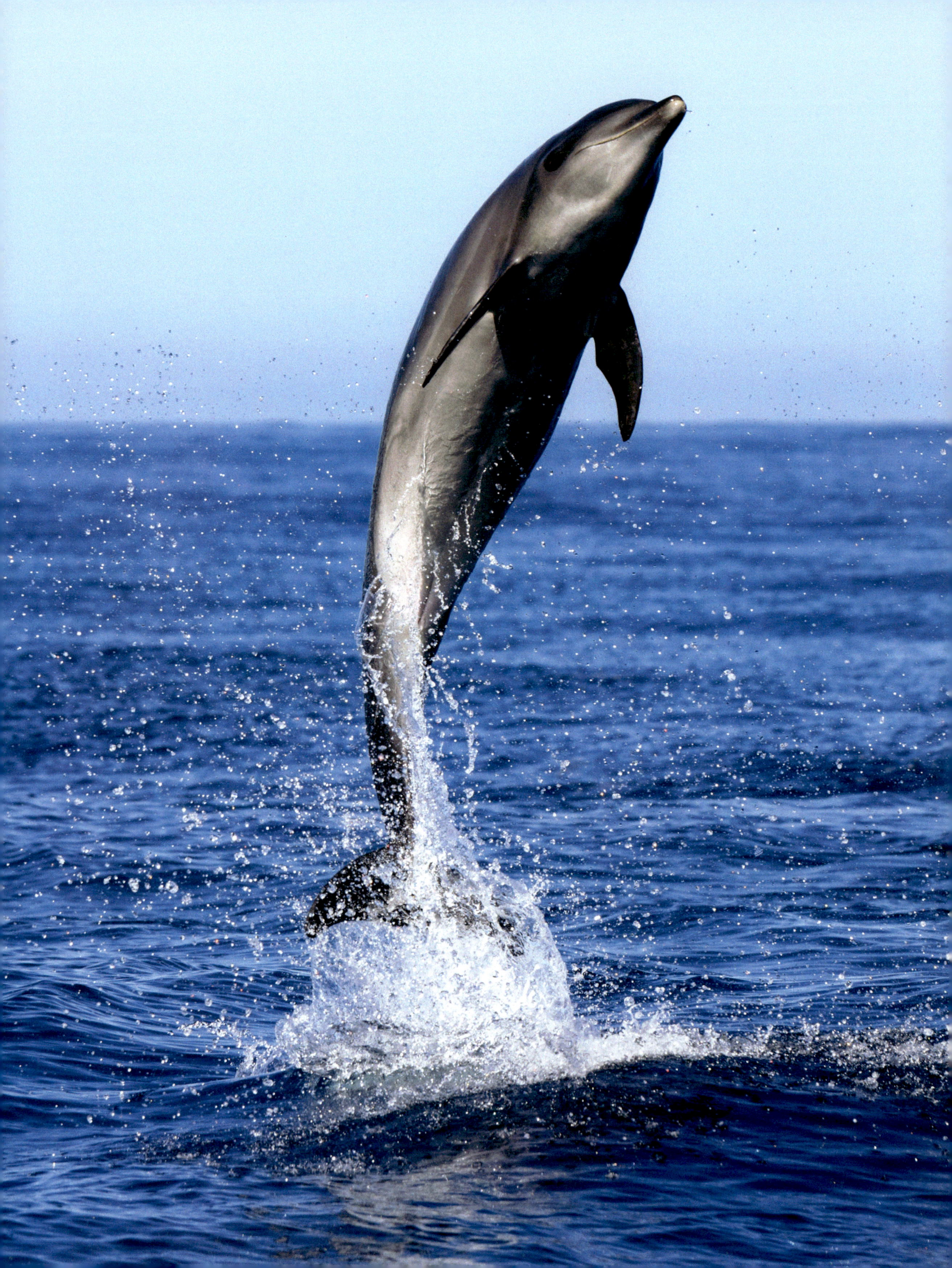

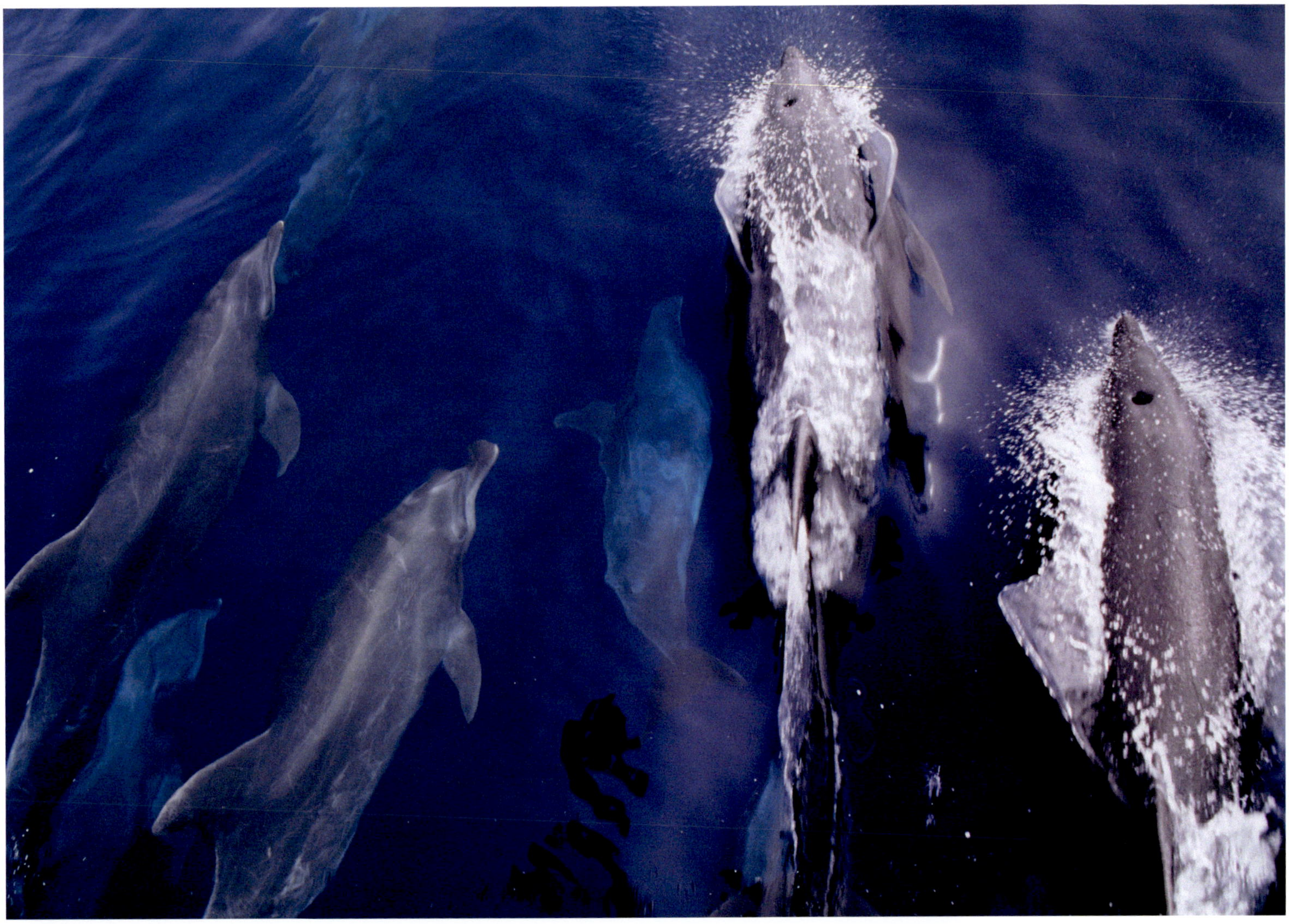

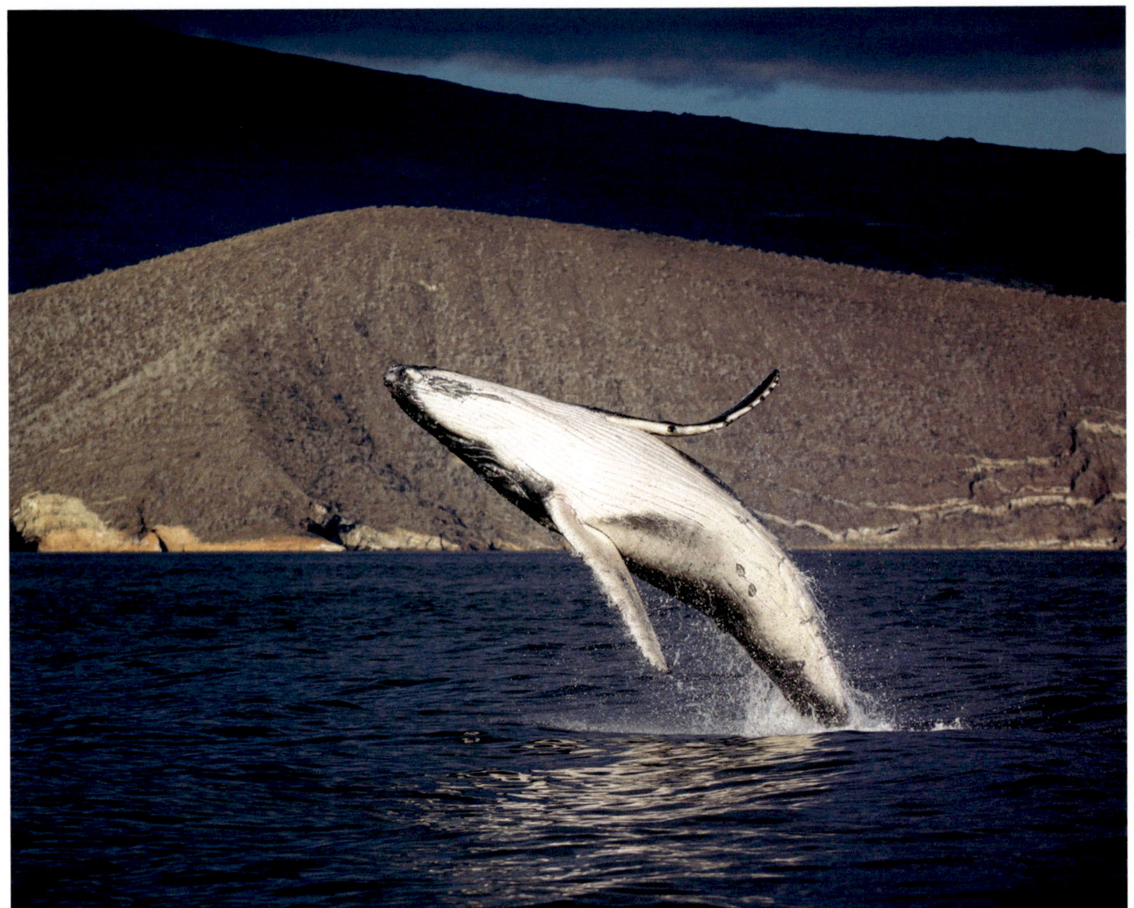

Bottlenose dolphin
One of the most familiar and
common of dolphins species are a
regular sight around the islands. It
is probable that there are resident
pods living here, but there are also
regular visits from oceanic pods,
and members will often move from
one group to the next.

LEFT:
Humpback whale
A mighty humpback breaches off
the coast of Isabela Island. Pods of
these big whales pass by the island
in the winter months.

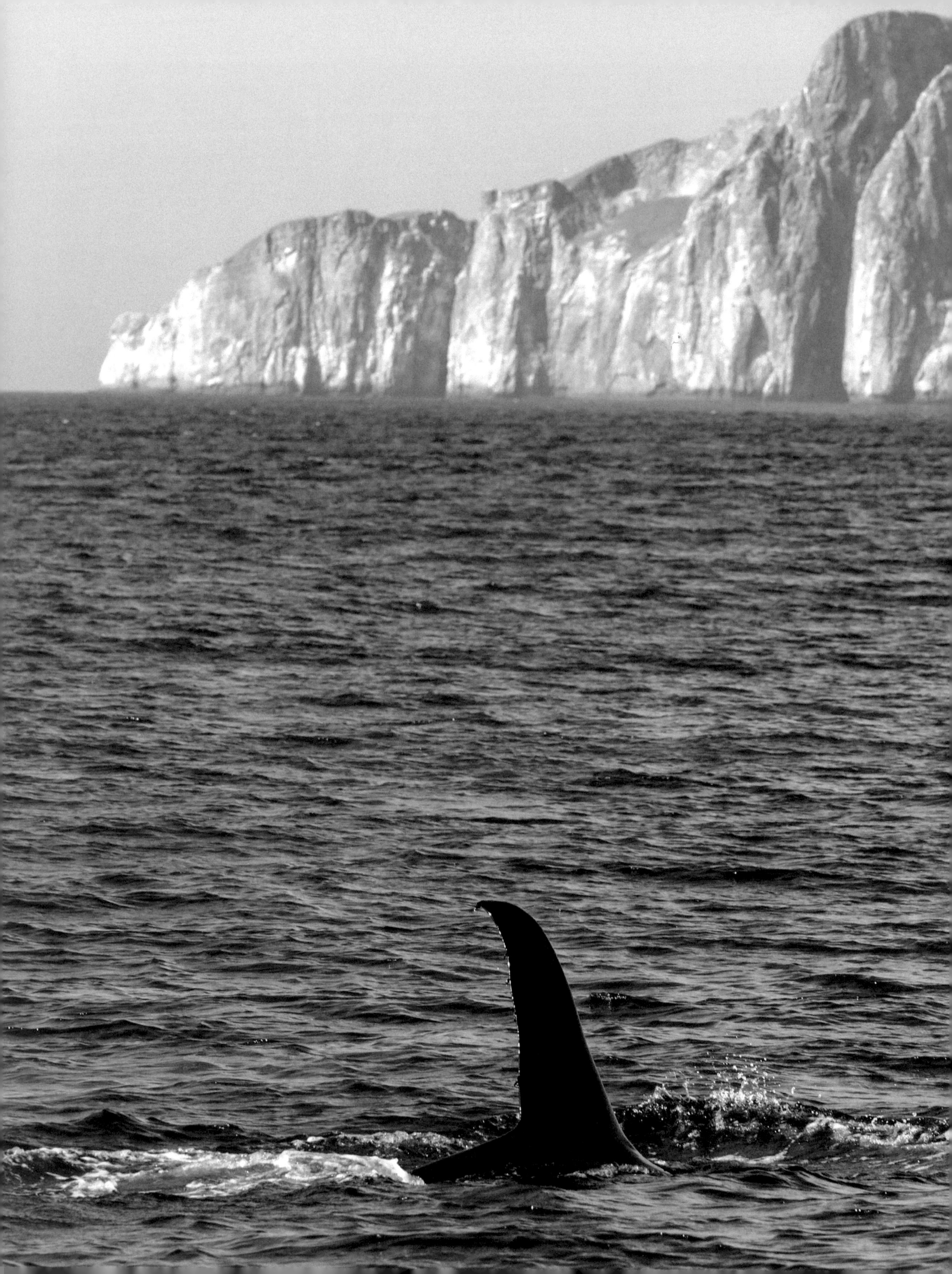

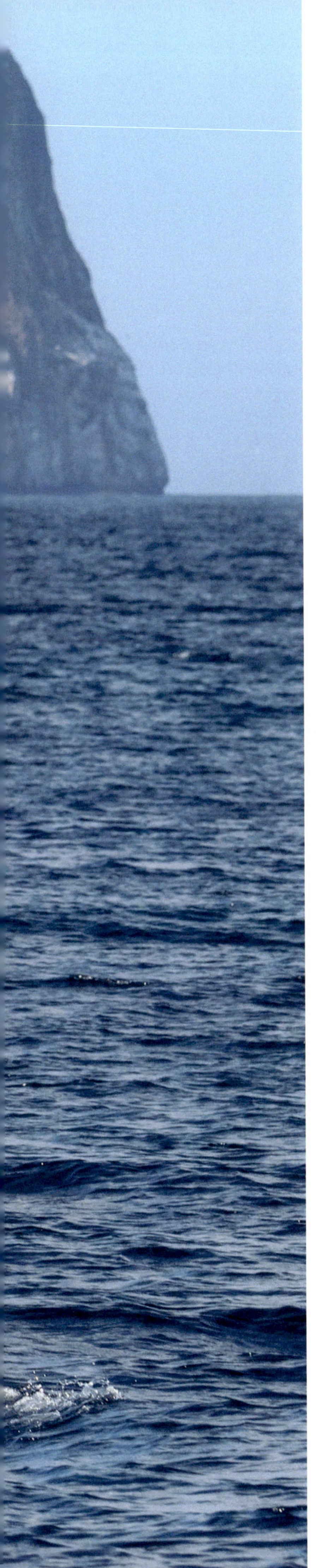

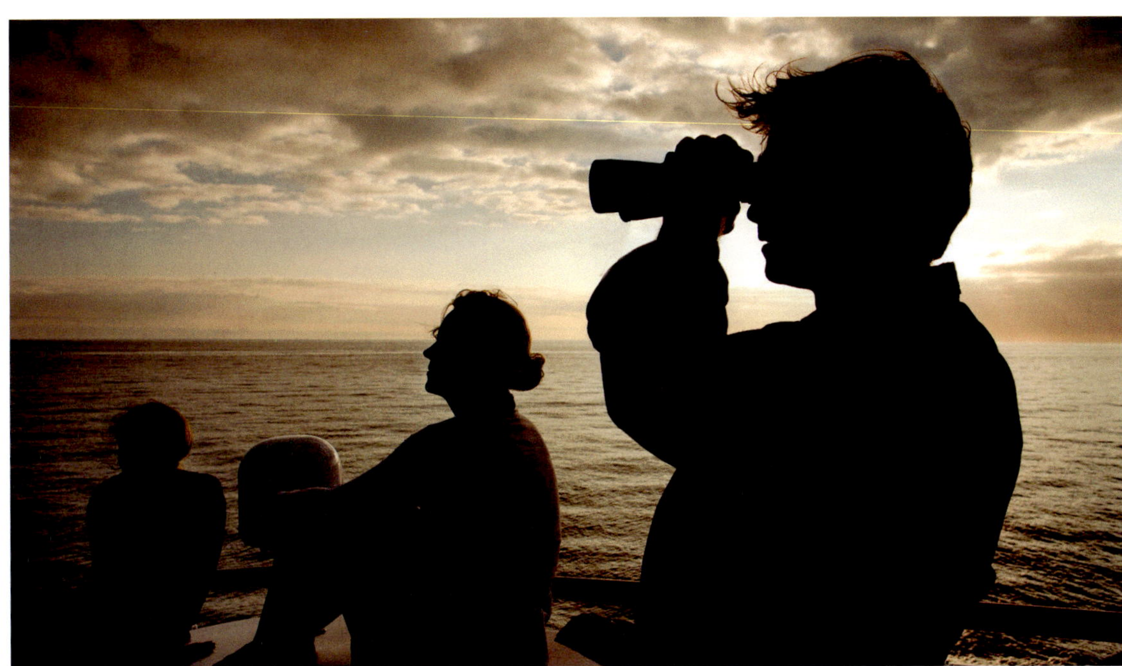

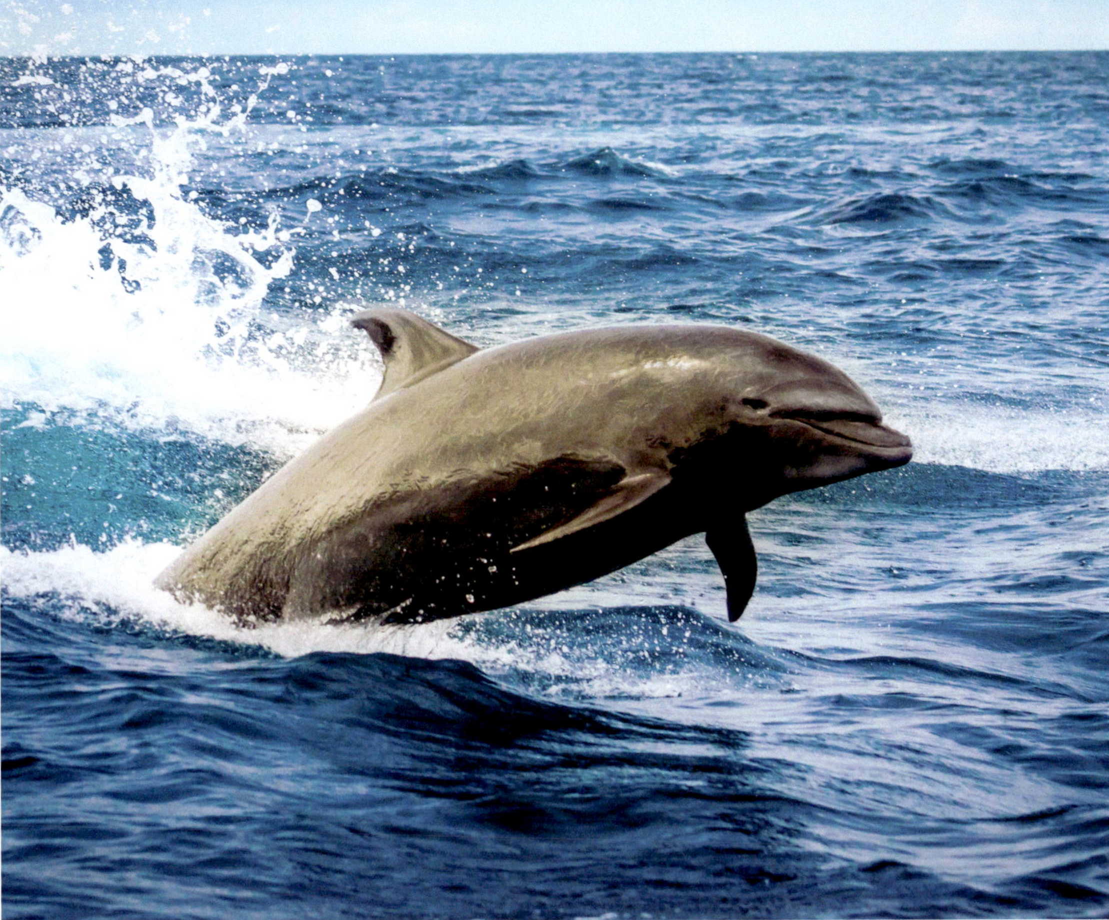

LEFT:

Killer whale

This is the distinctive tall fin of a killer whale, also known by the less brutal name of orca. This hunter travels in pods and preys on dolphins, seals and fish, with one pod often being a specialist in one type of prey.

ABOVE TOP:

Whale watching

The opportunity to see so many whales is one of the attractions that brings tourists to the Galápagos Islands.

ABOVE BOTTOM:

Bottlenose dolphin

Along with killer whales, bottlenose dolphins can be seen all year round in the Galápagos Islands. Most visitors will see at least one of these species during their stay.

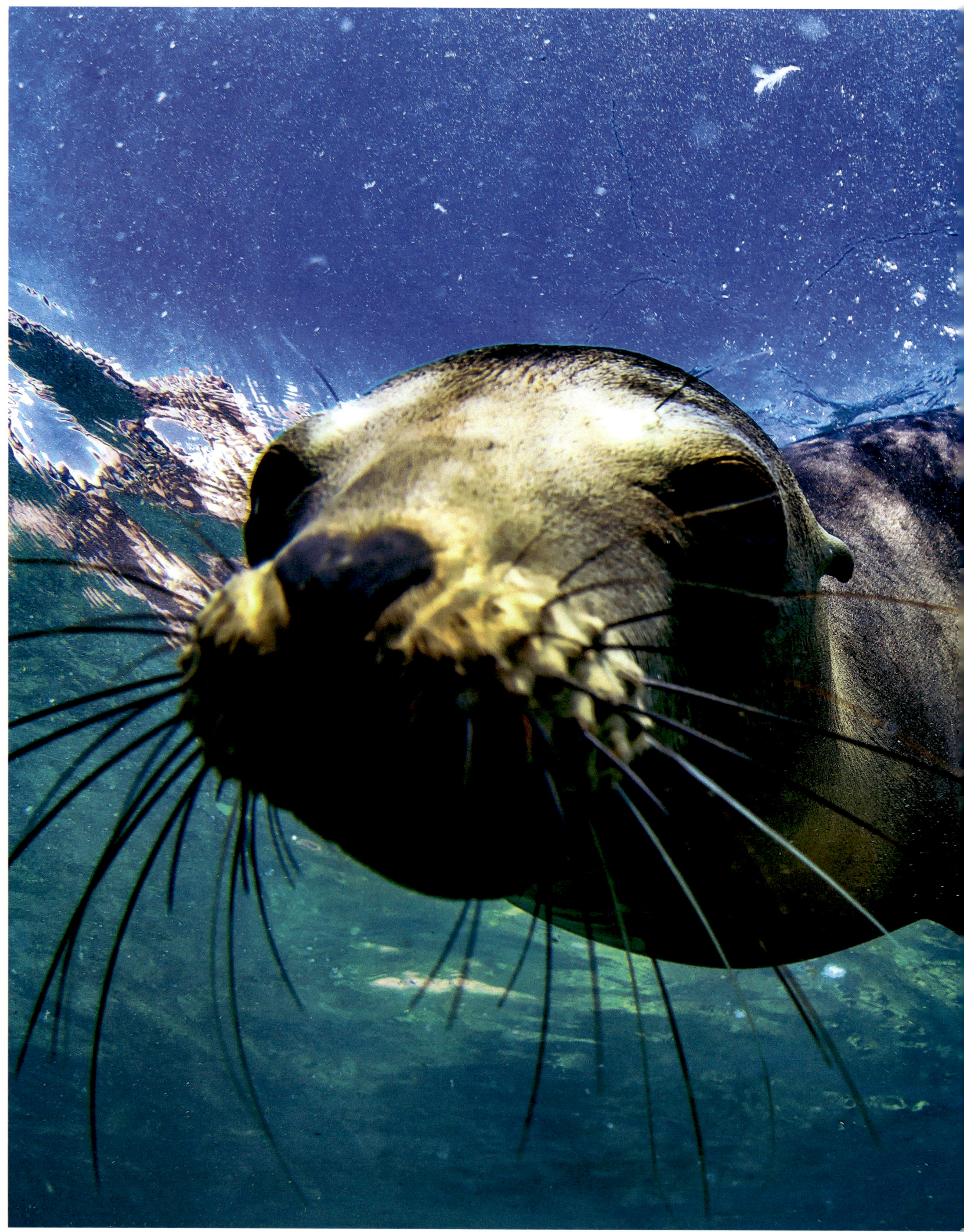

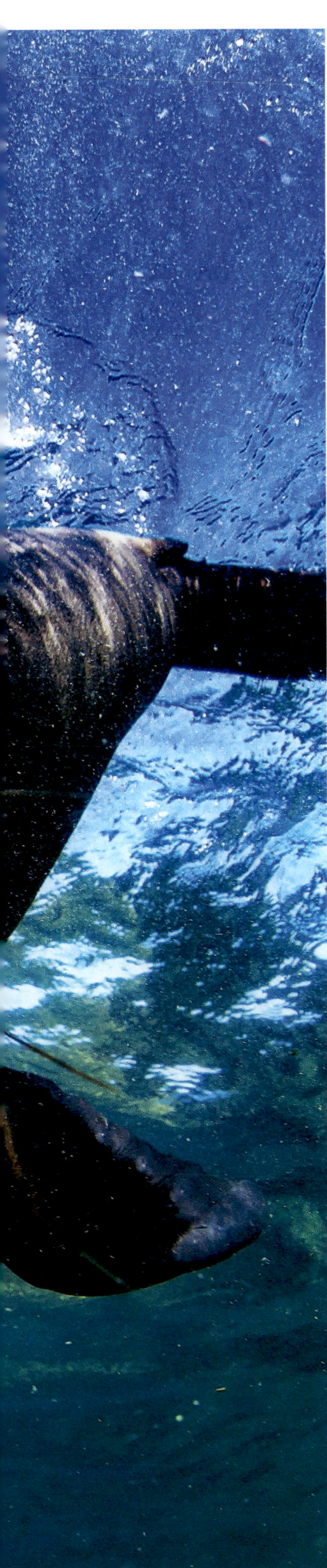

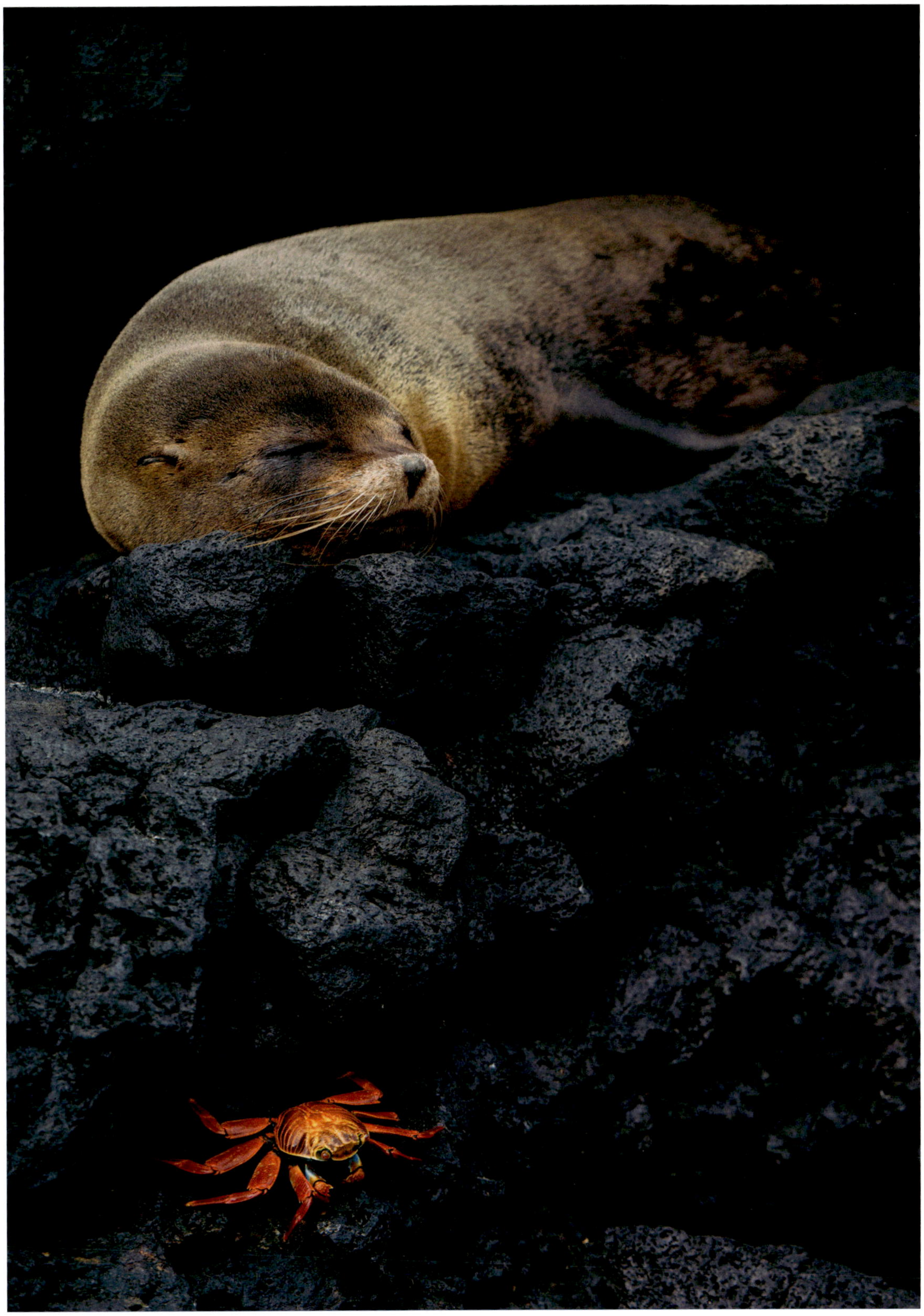

BOTH PHOTOGRAPHS:
Galápagos sea lion
This is the smaller of the two
species of sea lion that live on the
islands. The visible ears show that
this is not a seal, but a sea lion.
The fur seal has thicker fur than
the Galápagos sea lion, but both
species live a similar life, spending
sleepy hours in rocky coves and
then heading out to sea to hunt fish.

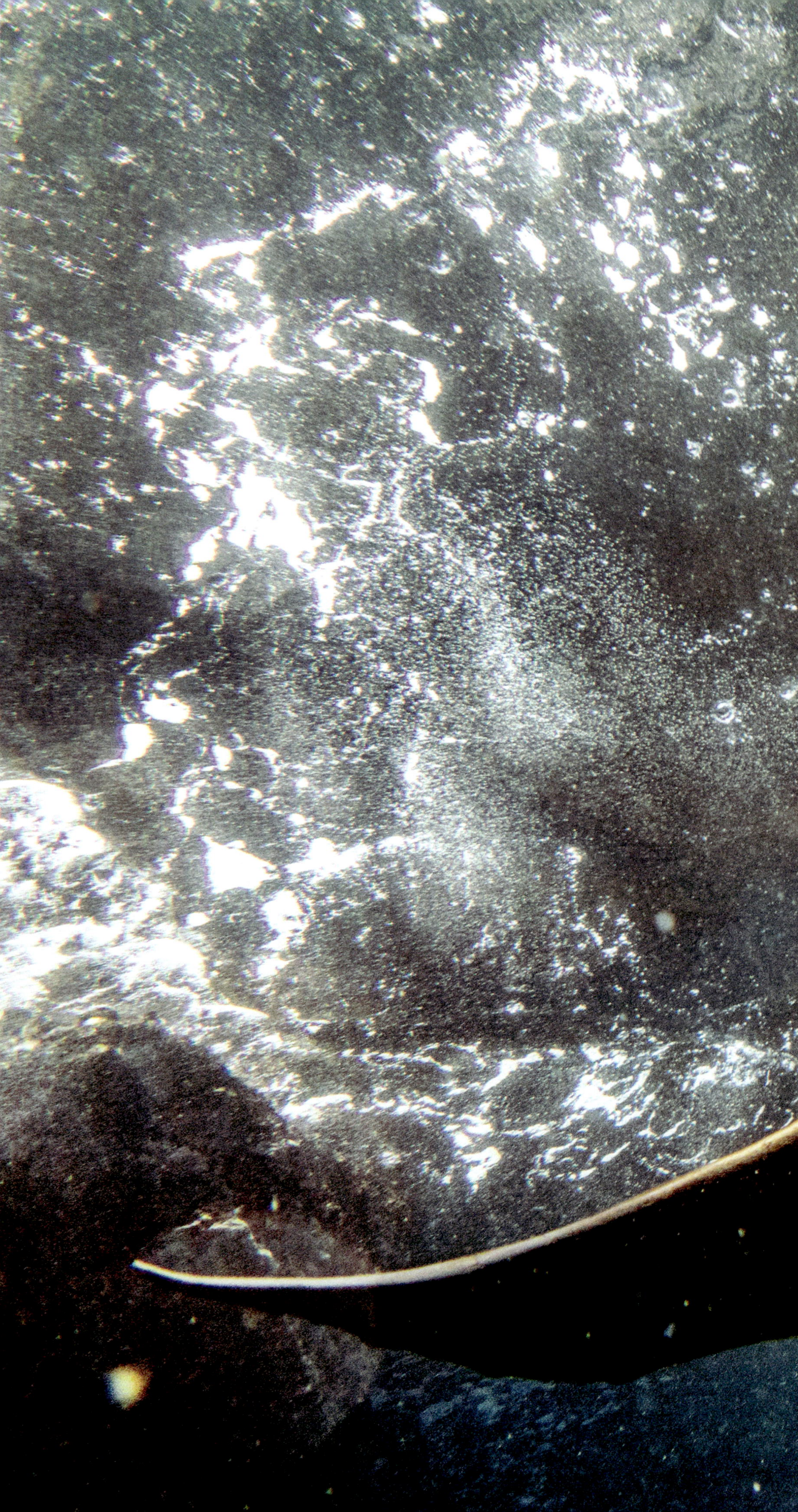

Largest land animal
At 2m (6ft) long and usually weighing 250kg (550lb), this is the largest animal found on dry land in the Galápagos, but it is primarily a water animal. The ultra-sensitive whiskers can pick up currents in the water made by fish, so the sea lion can find prey even in the dark.

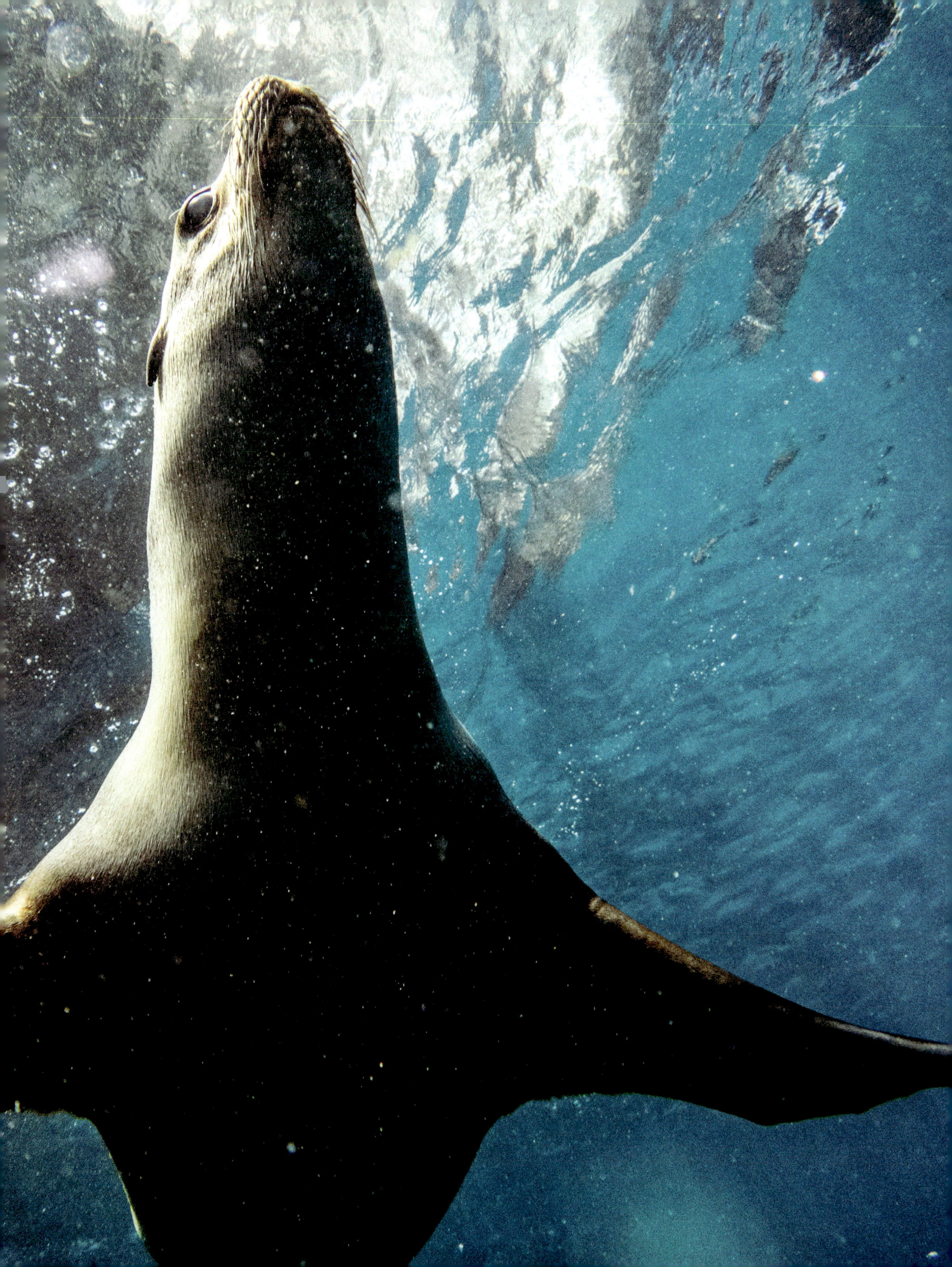

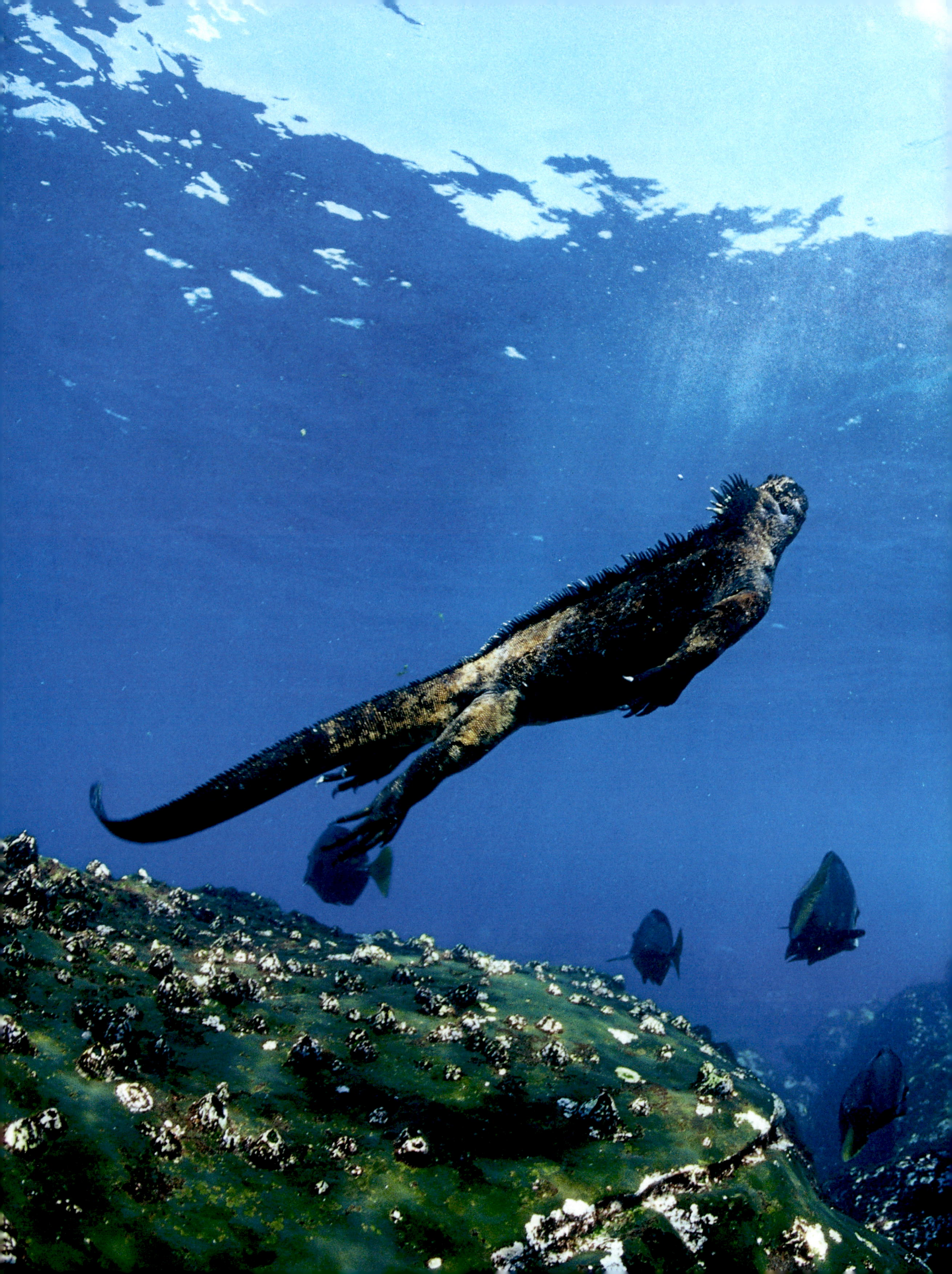

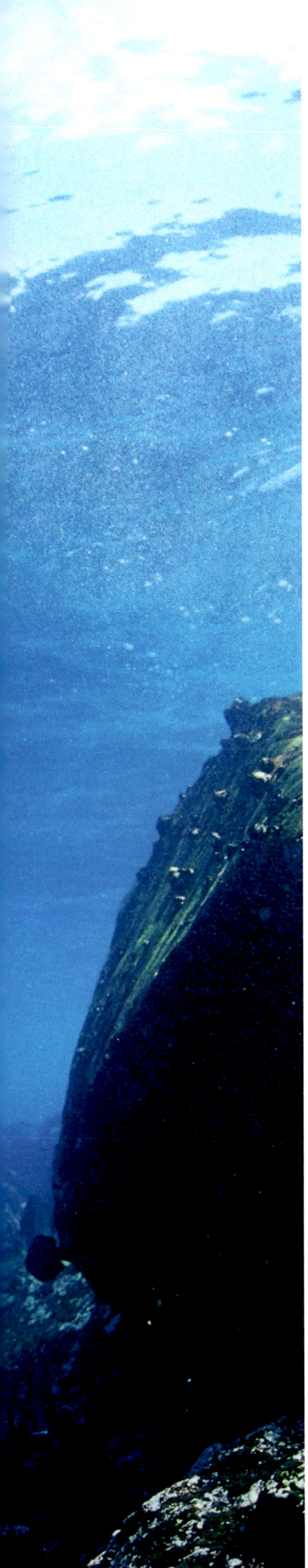

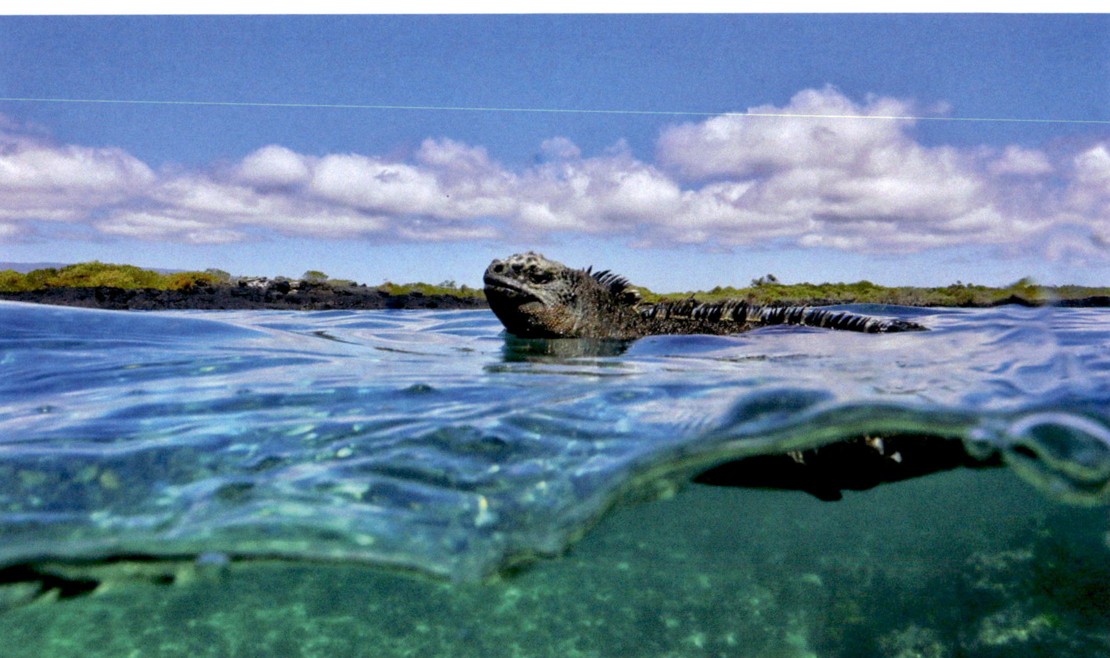

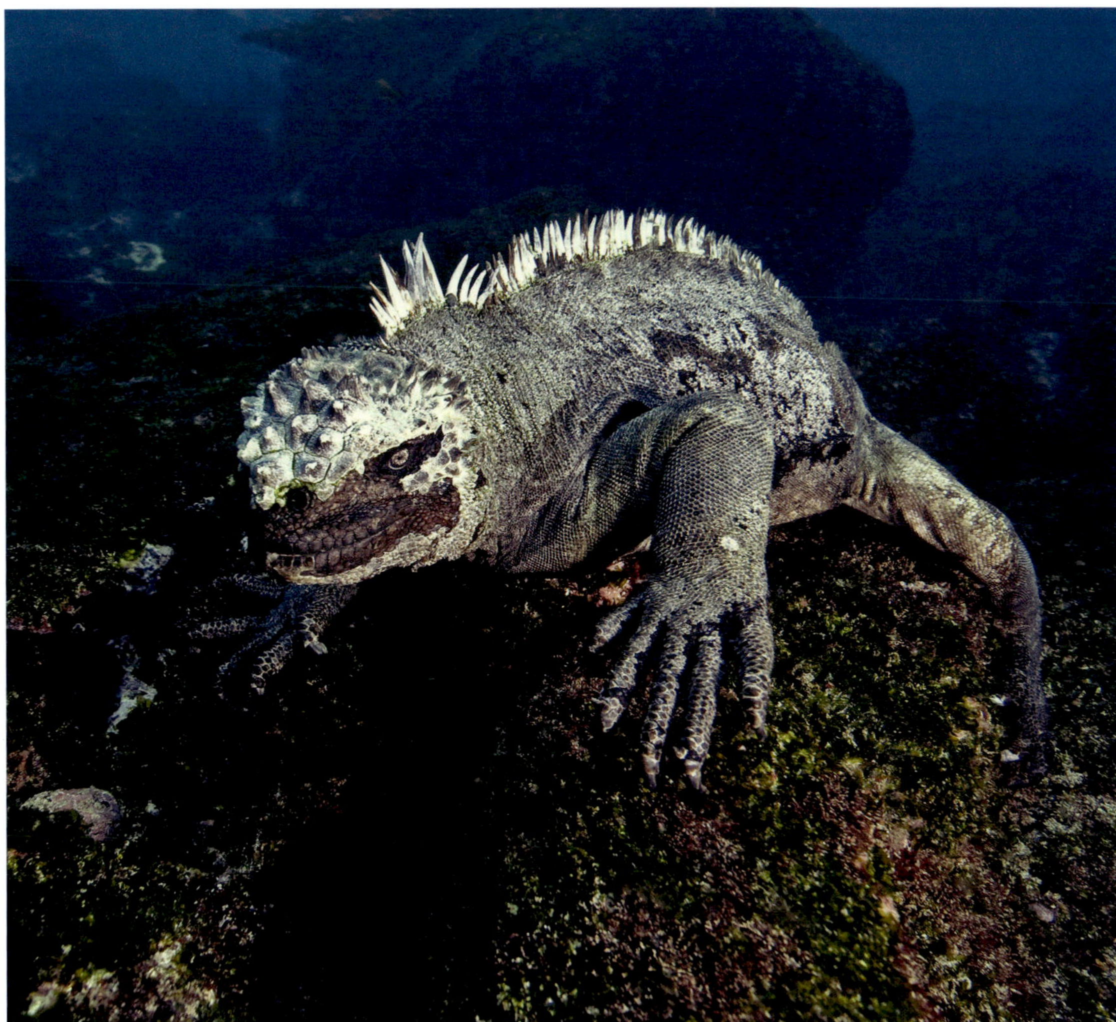

ALL PHOTOGRAPHS:

Sea lizard

The marine iguana, unique to the Galápagos, is the only lizard that finds its food in seawater. Although it breathes air, it can stay under water for 20 minutes. It swims with its short legs folded against the body and paddles with the long flattened tail. On the seabed, the blunt snout allows the lizard to crop short seaweeds.

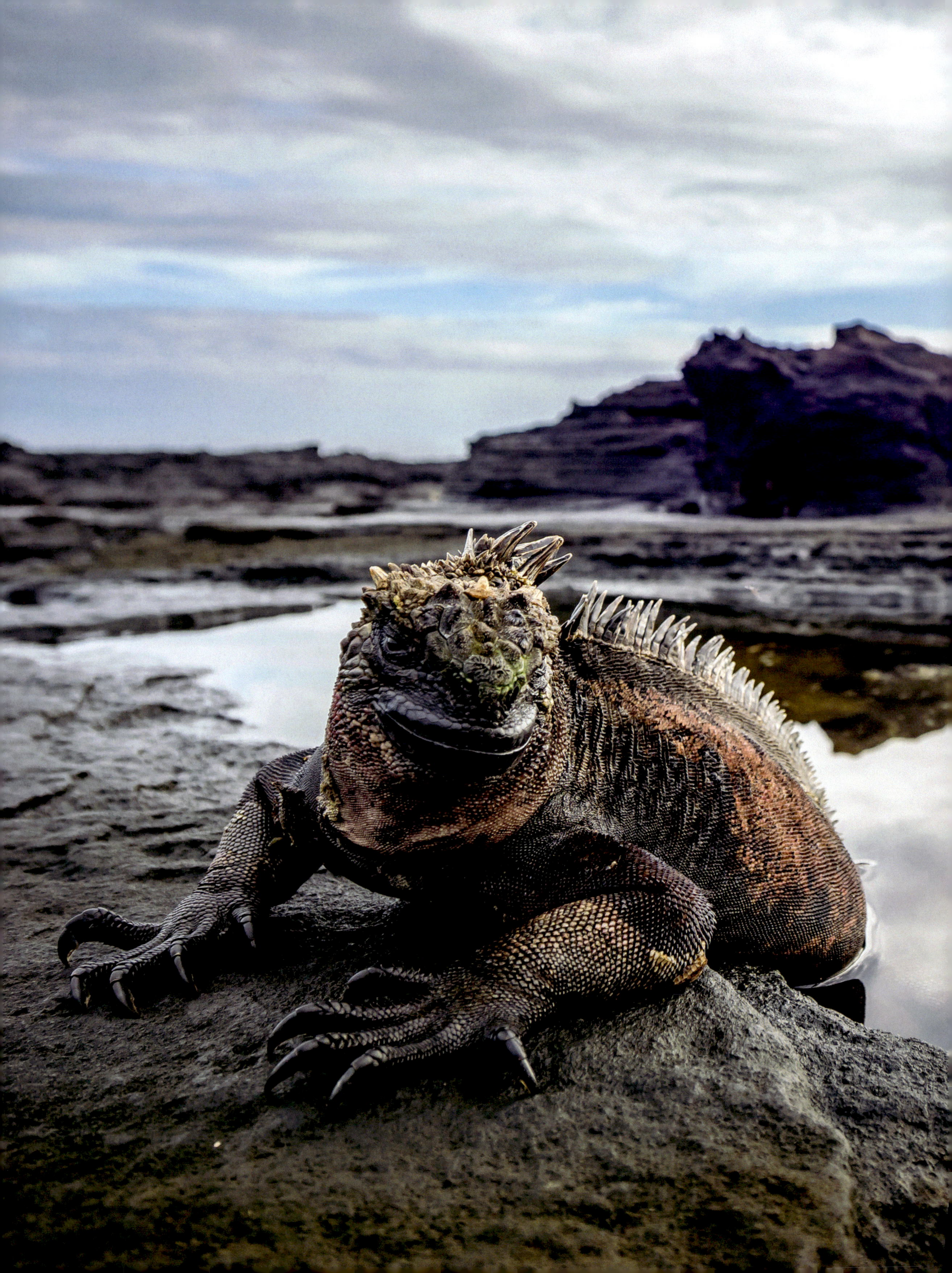

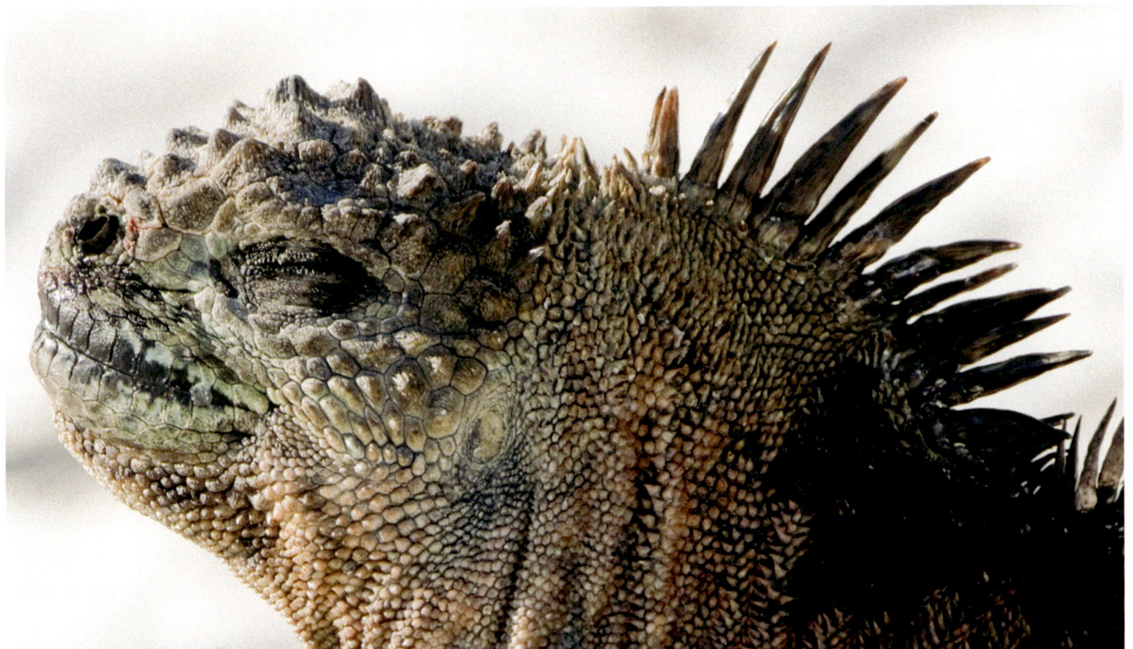

Land lizard

The marine iguana cannot stay in the water between dives – it is too cold. So the iguana climbs up the rocky shore using its long claws. The body is dark when wet and that helps the lizard to absorb heat and warm up. The crest helps to capture heat and maintains stability in the water.

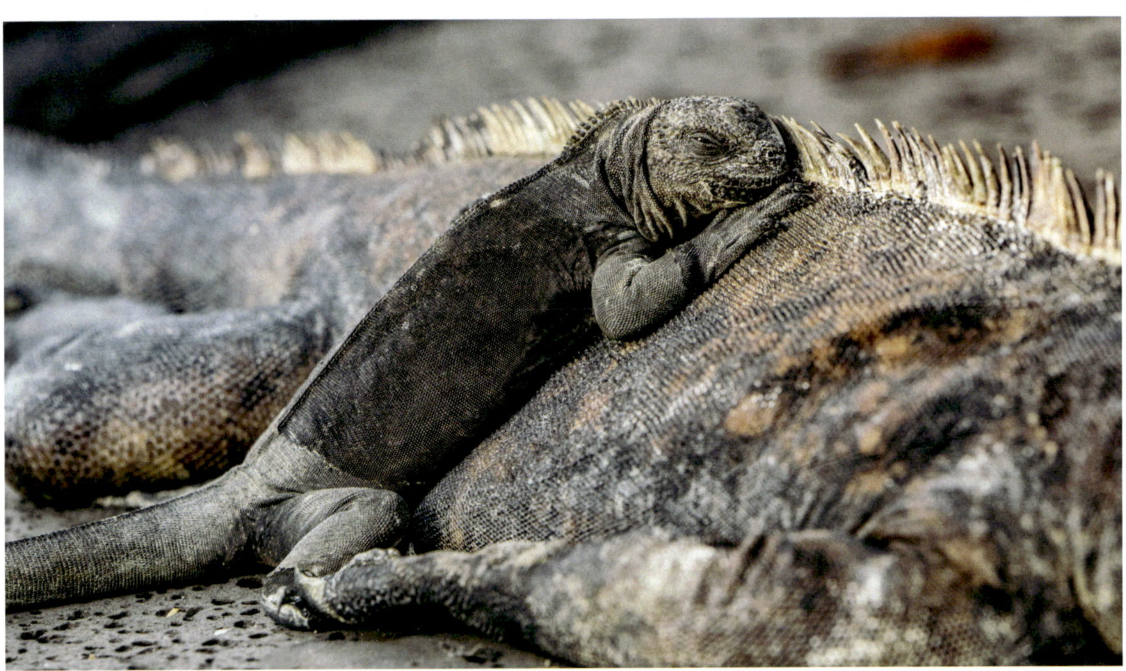

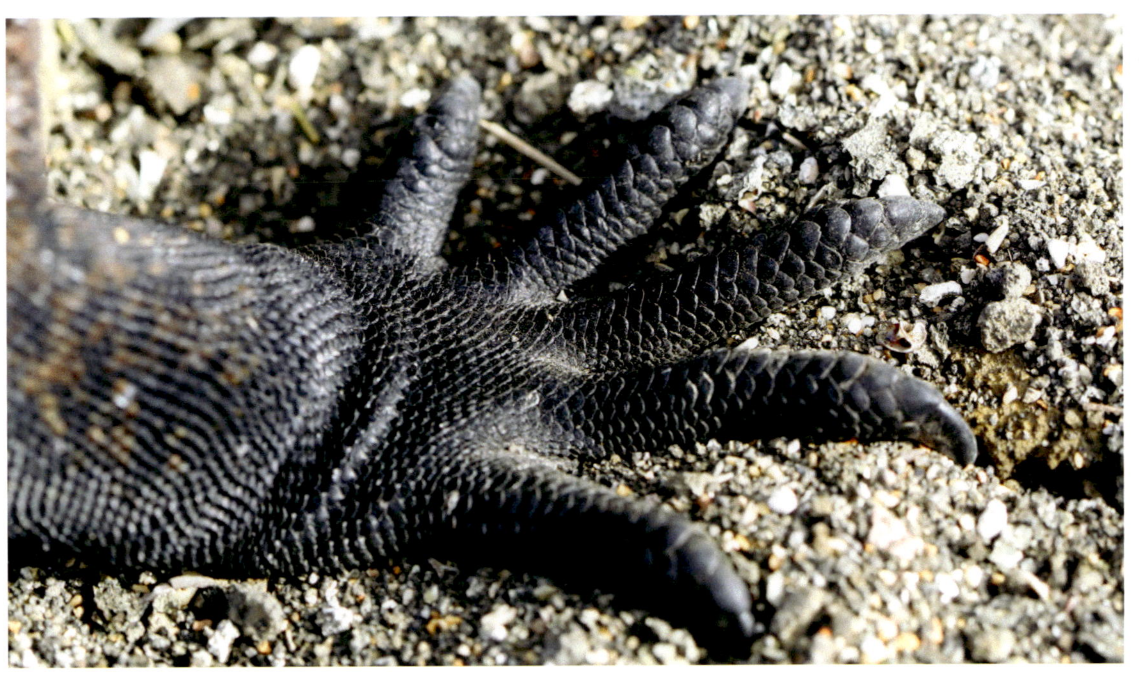

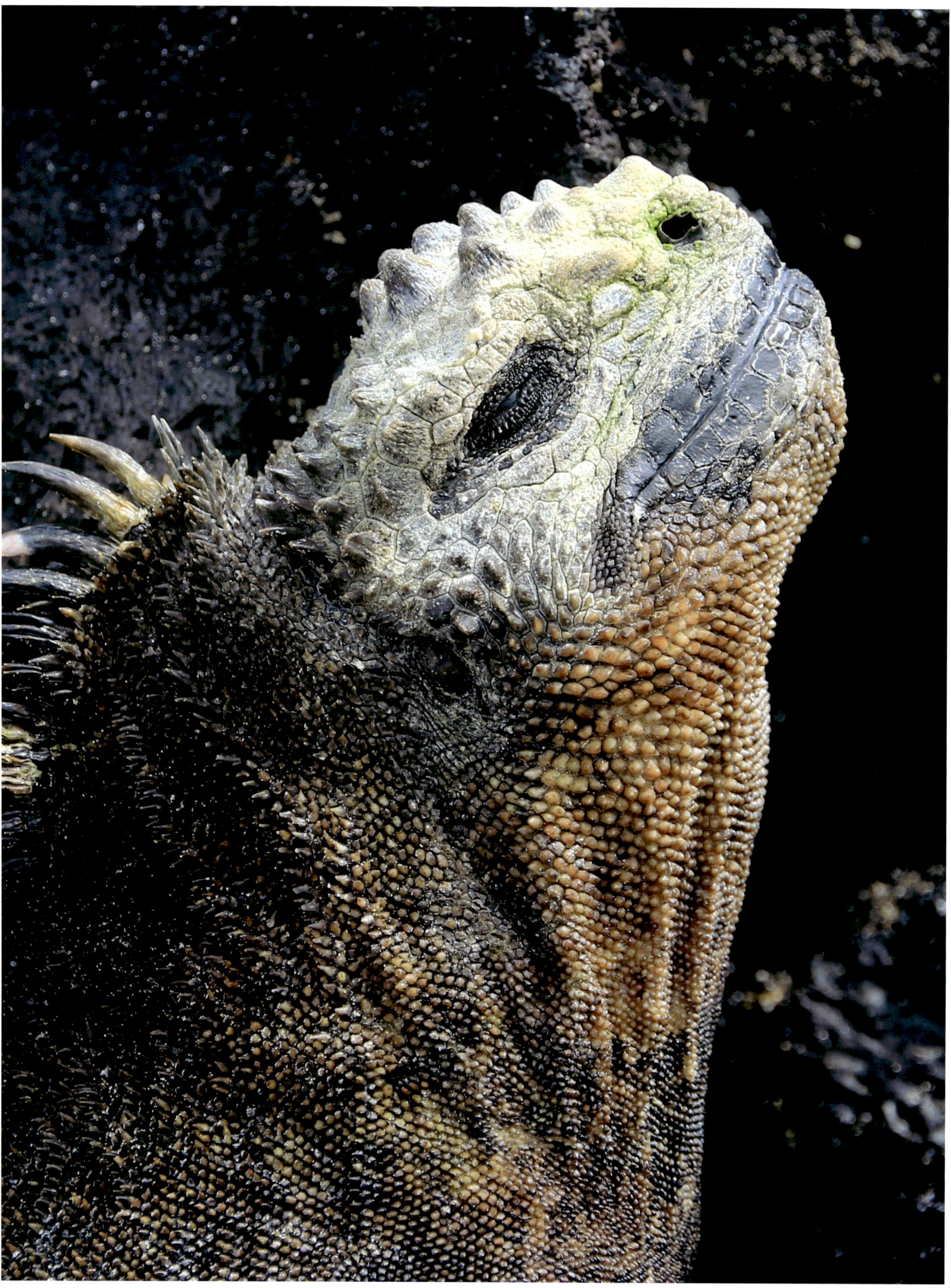

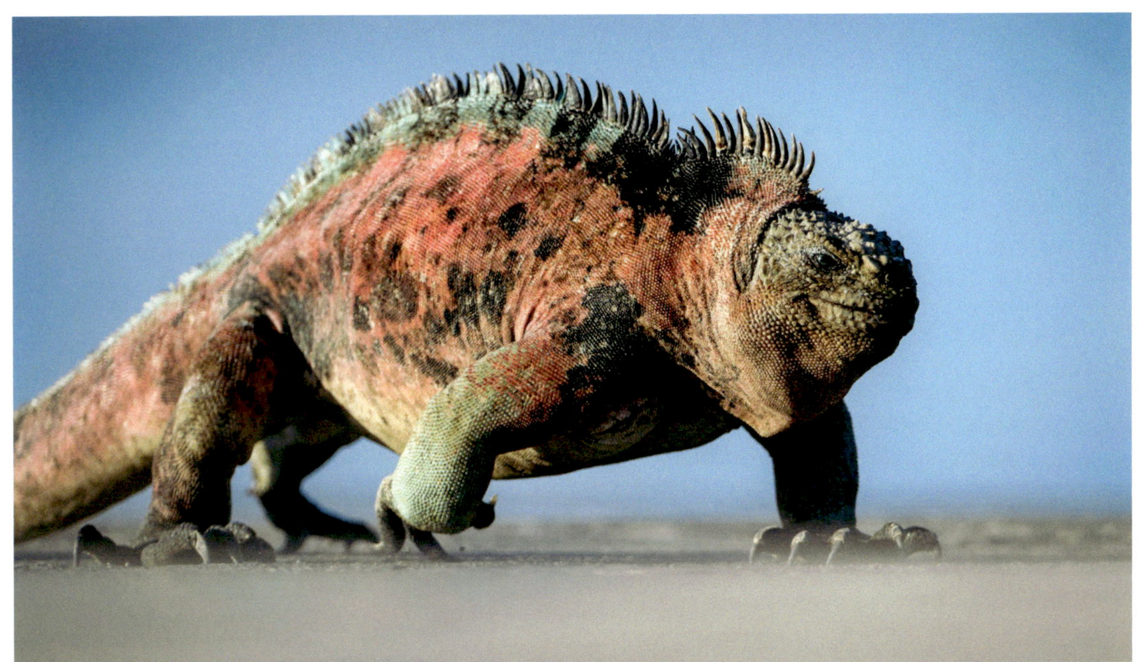

OPPOSITE:
Skypointing
When the marine iguana gets too hot it will lift its head so it faces straight up. Known as skypointing, this behaviour minimizes the body area exposed to sunlight.

LEFT TOP, MIDDLE AND BOTTOM:
Breeding colours
During the breeding season, the male marine iguanas develop bright colouring to attract females. The pigments are derived from chemicals in the lizards' seaweed foods. The biggest and brightest males fight for territorial control.

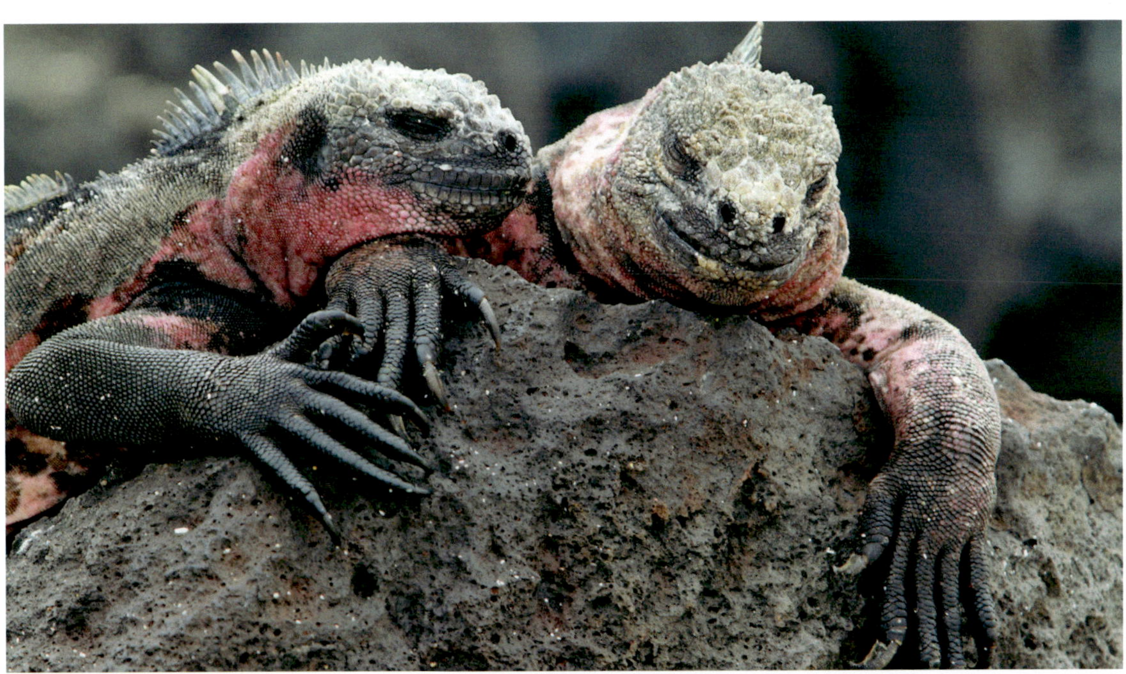

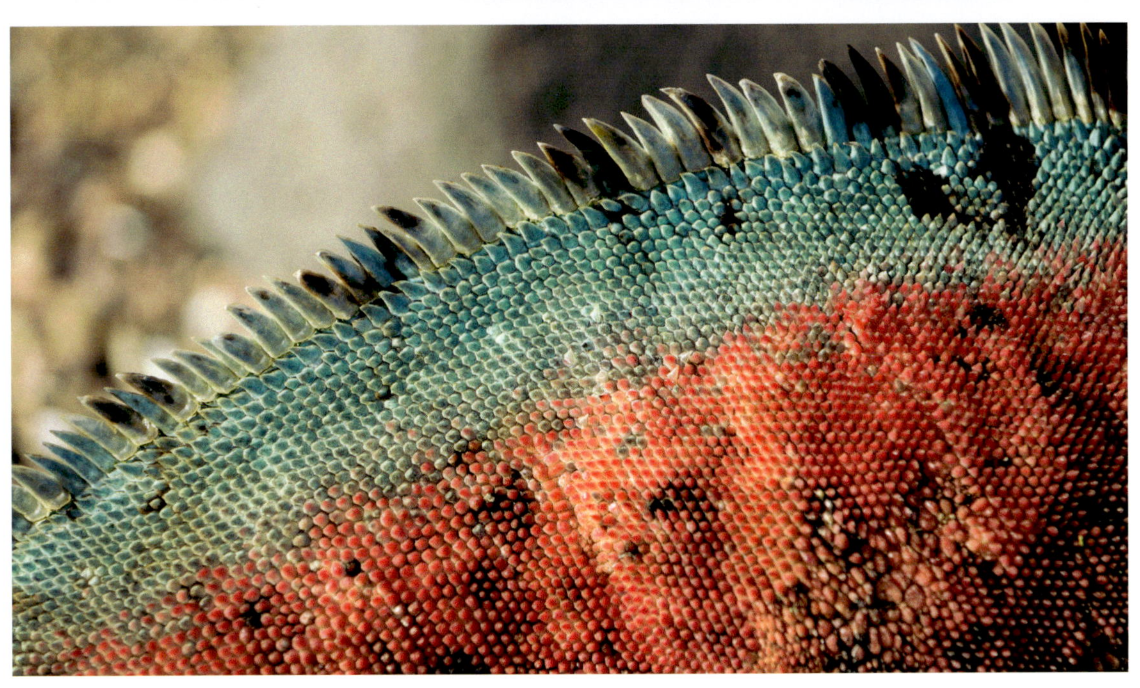

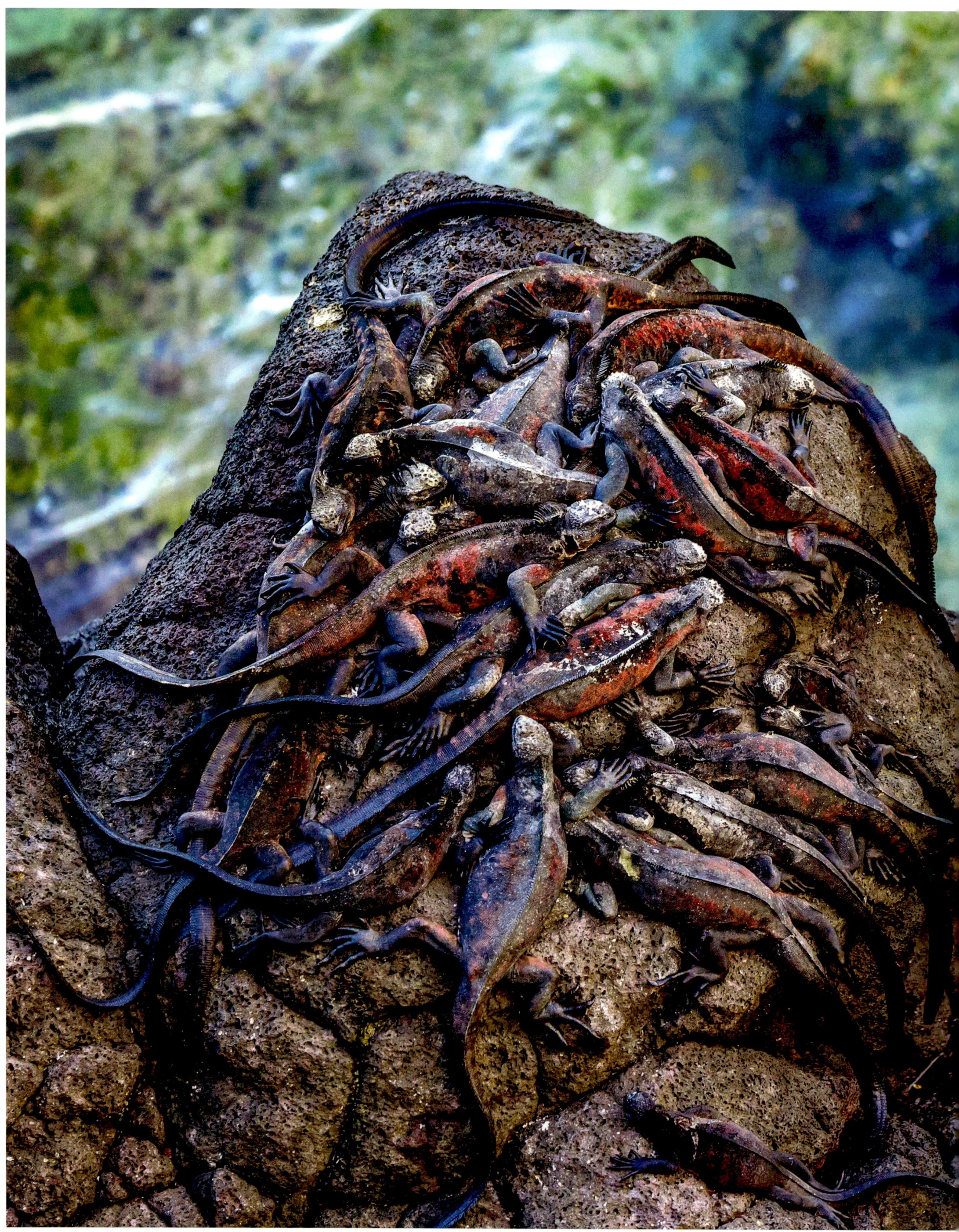

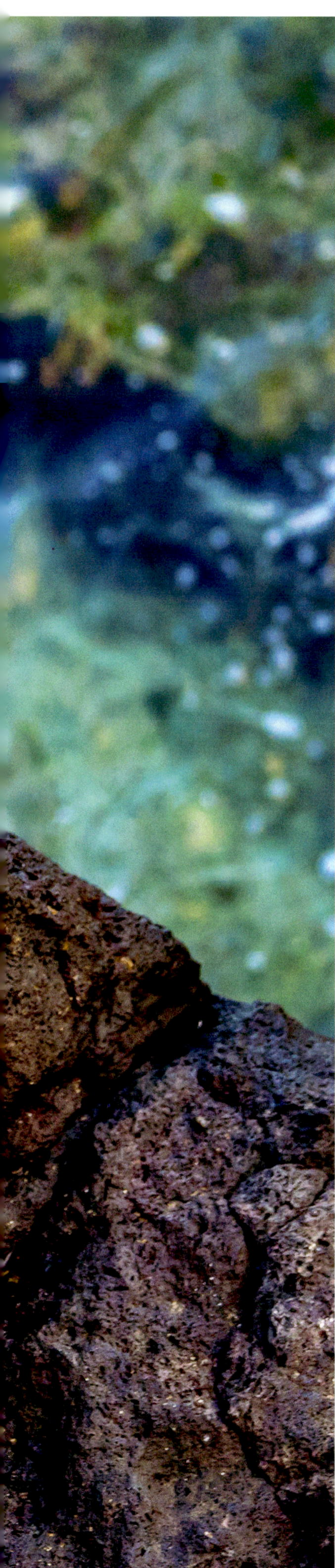

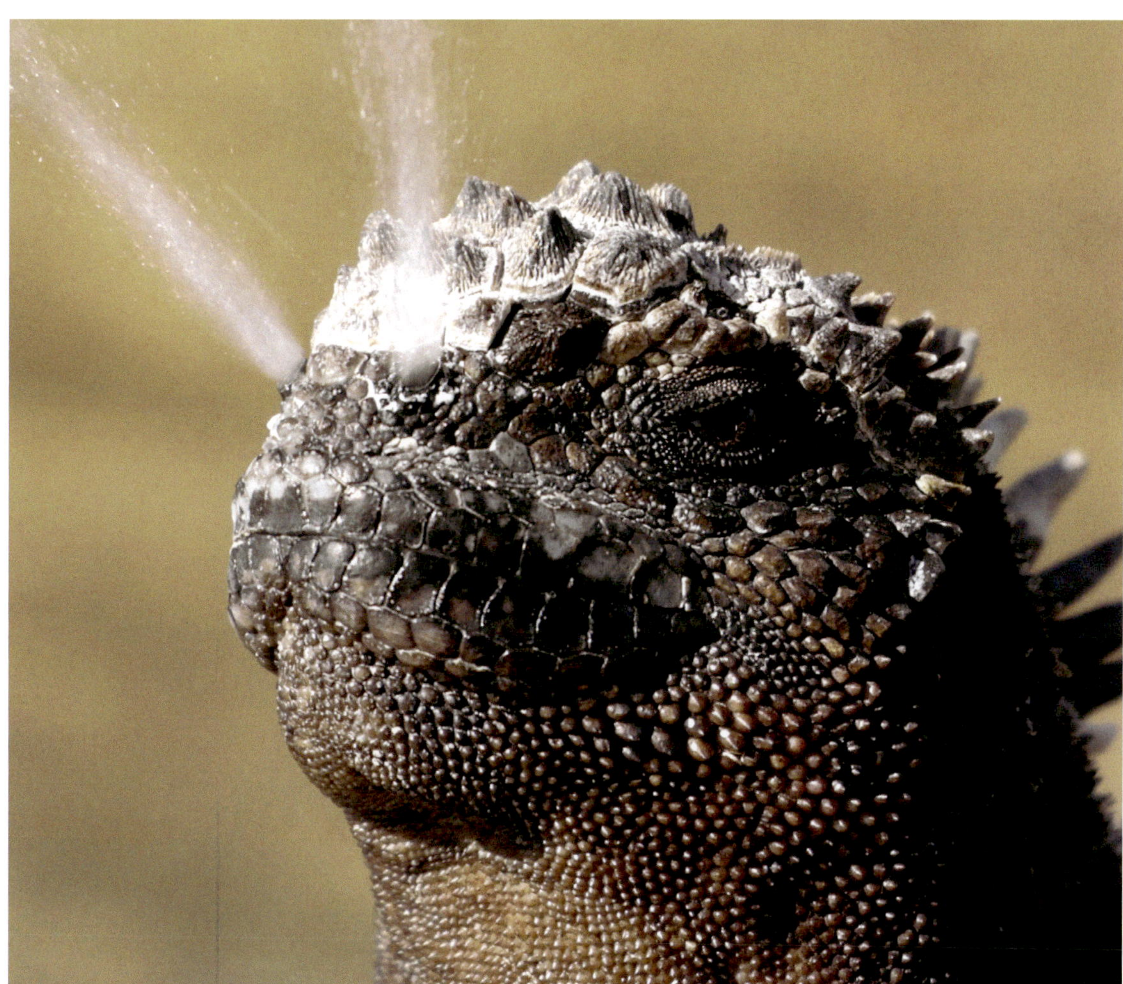

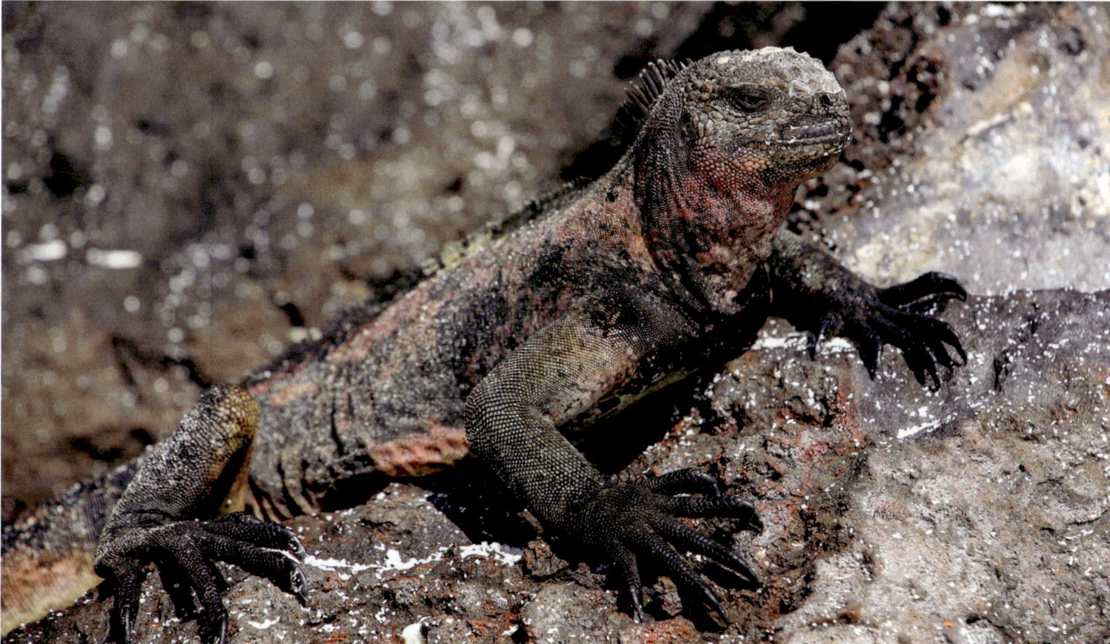

LEFT:

Body heat

As night falls, marine iguanas crowd together to share body heat as they sleep.

ABOVE TOP AND BOTTOM:

Salt glands

Feeding in seawater means the lizard has to get rid of extra salt. They squirt it out of their nostrils in a salty snot. The salts form a pale crust on the lizard's face.

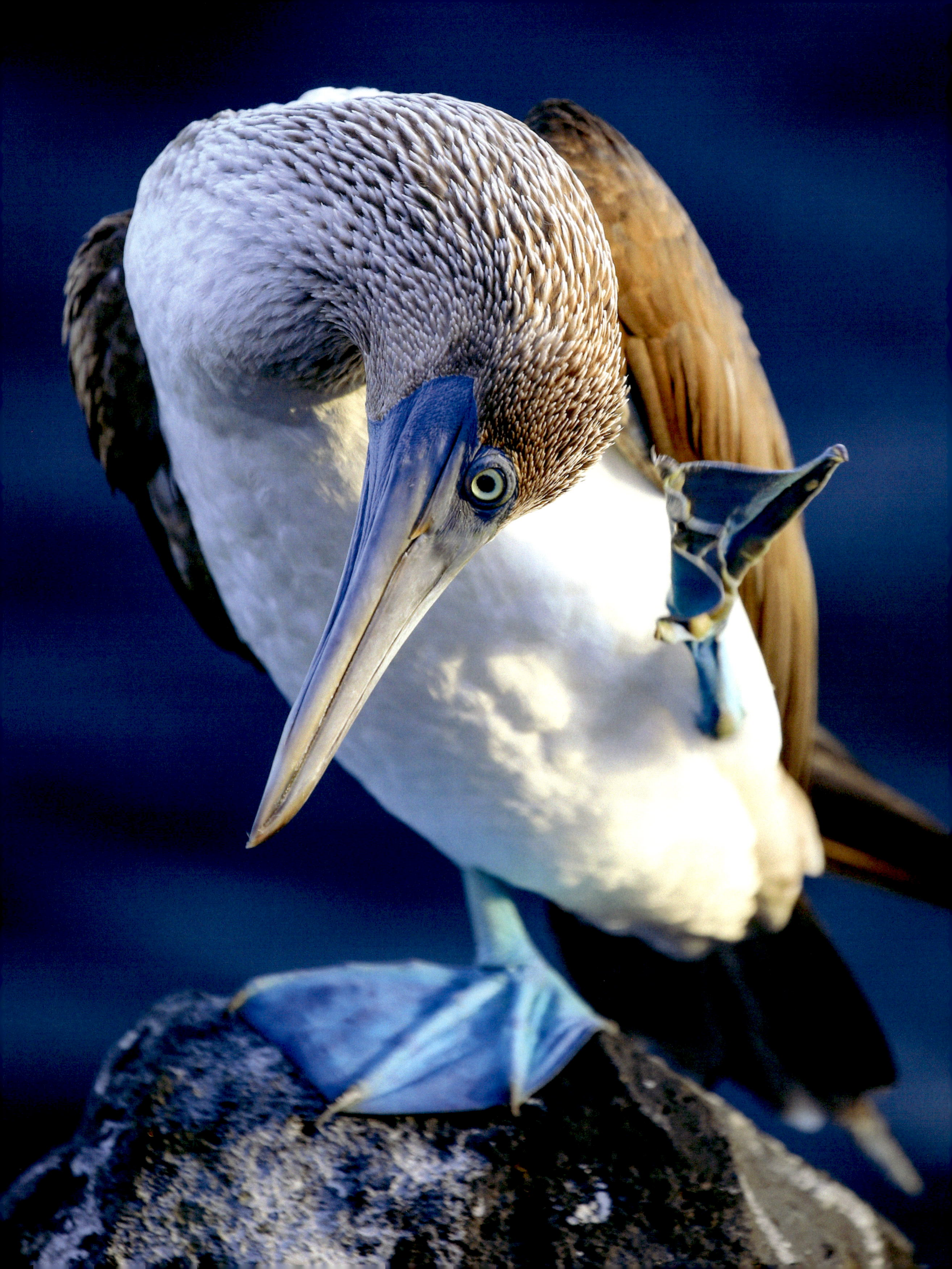

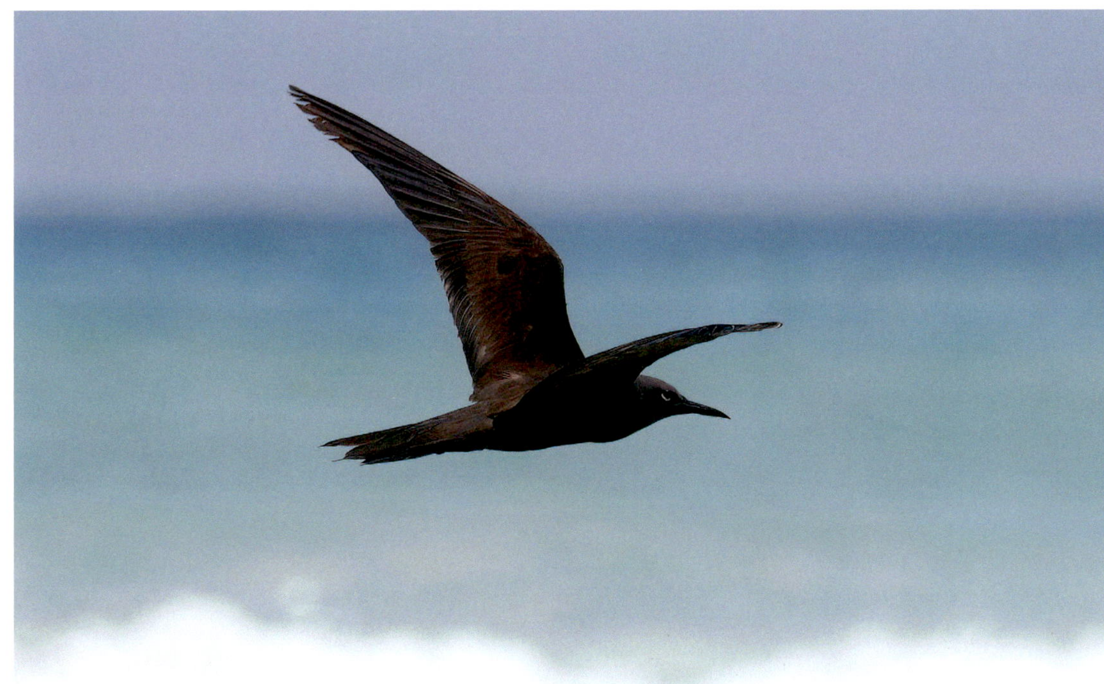

Blue-footed booby
This bird's name comes from the Spanish word *bobo,* meaning clown. The bird is ungainly on the ground, especially when landing. It hunts fish by plunge diving and air sacs in the cheeks cushion the impact of hitting the water.

Brown noddy
This tern is a common seabird on the Galápagos. It lives in two large colonies, one on Fernandina, the other on Baltra, an island north of Santa Cruz.

Brown pelican
This big fish eater does not stray far from shore. After a foray in the water, the wet bird is too heavy to fly. It swims ashore and stands with its wings out to dry.

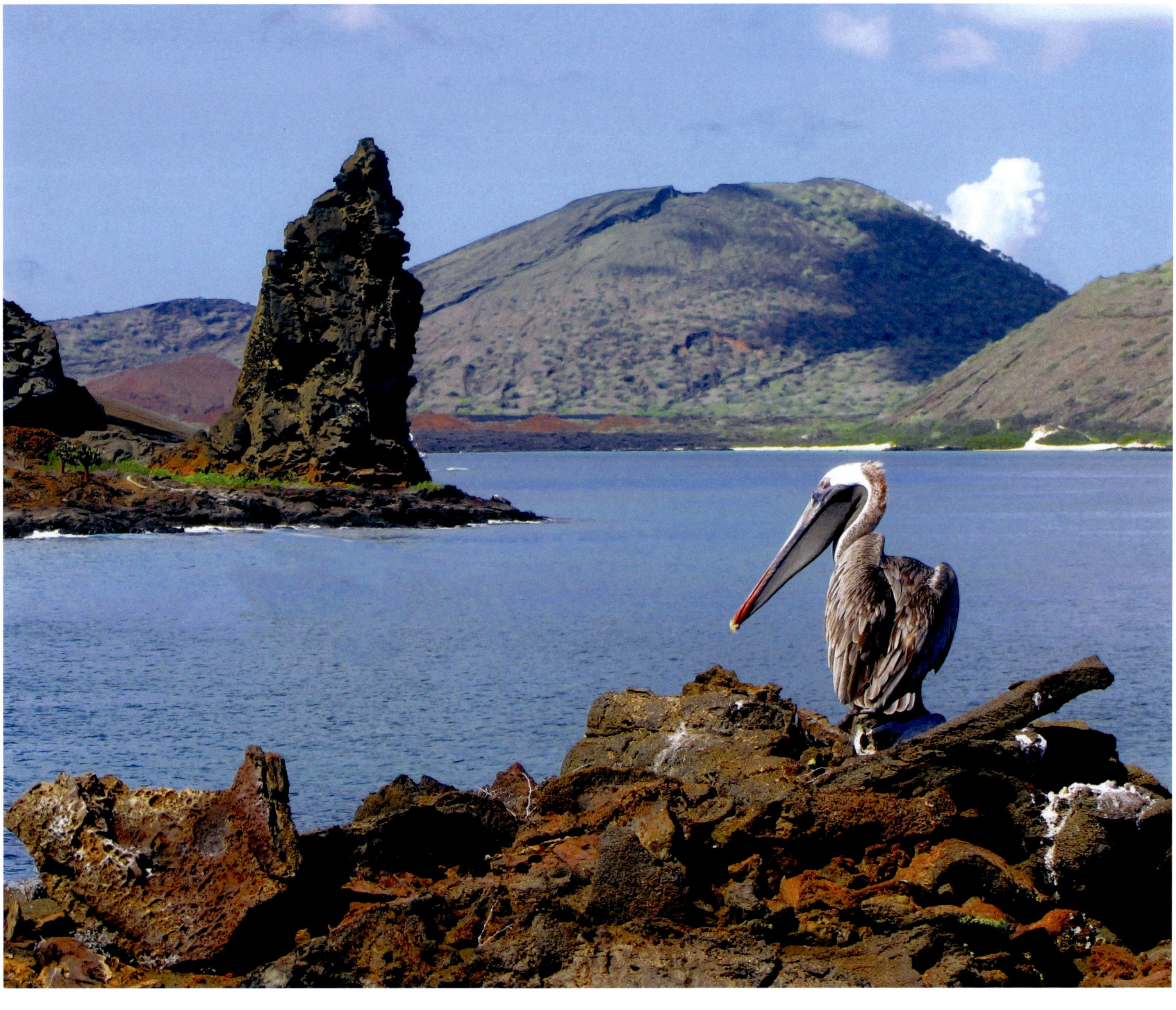

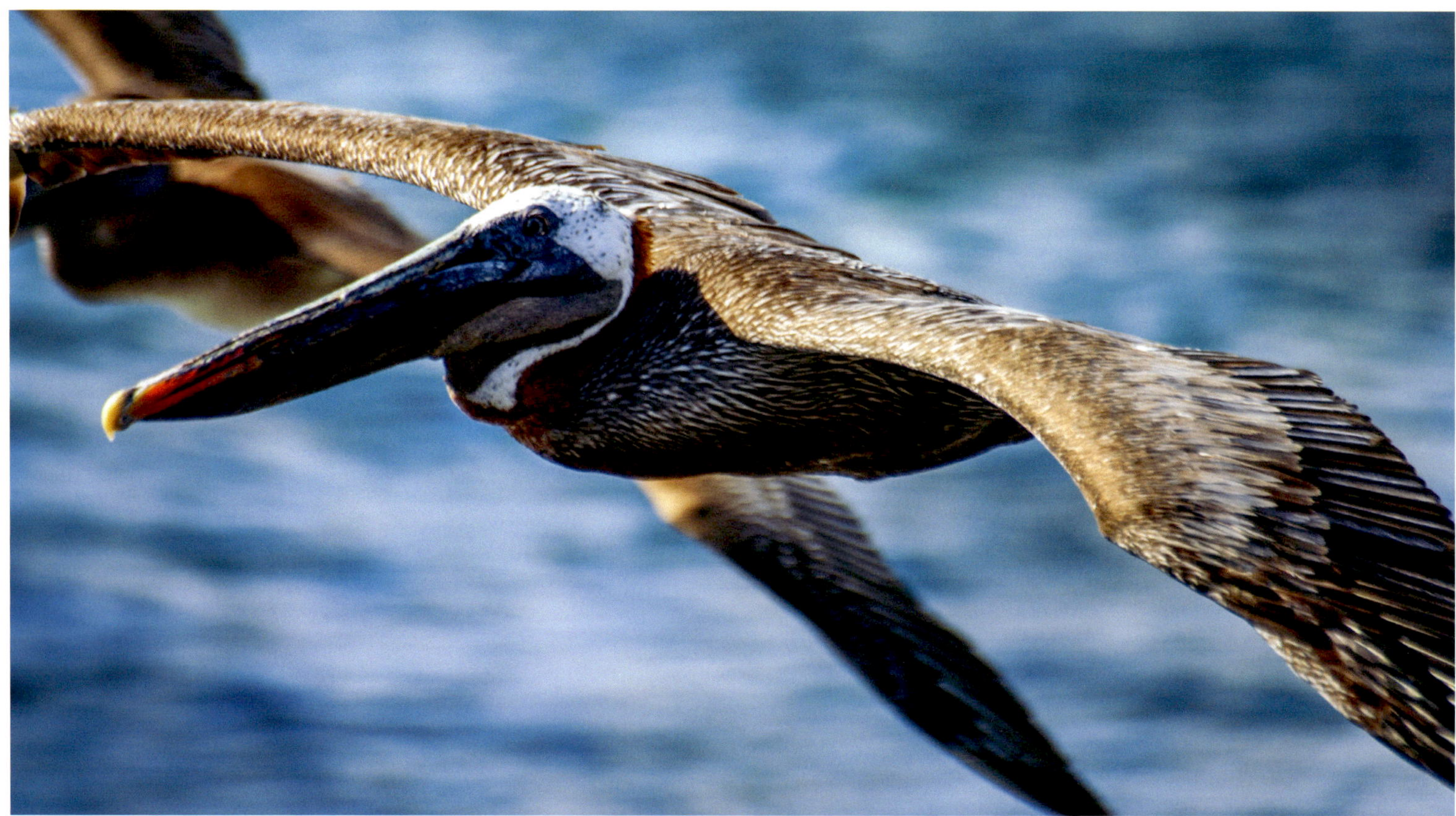

Folded up

The brown pelican folds its neck so the long bill points forward during flight. The flexible throat sac is contracted to reduce wind resistance.

Red-billed tropicbird

This plunge-diving, fish eater has long streamers on the tail that almost double its length. At ease in the air, the bird is less agile on land. Its short legs and small feet are too weak for walking so it shuffles around rocky refuges high up on the cliffs. To get into the air it just takes a leap off the edge.

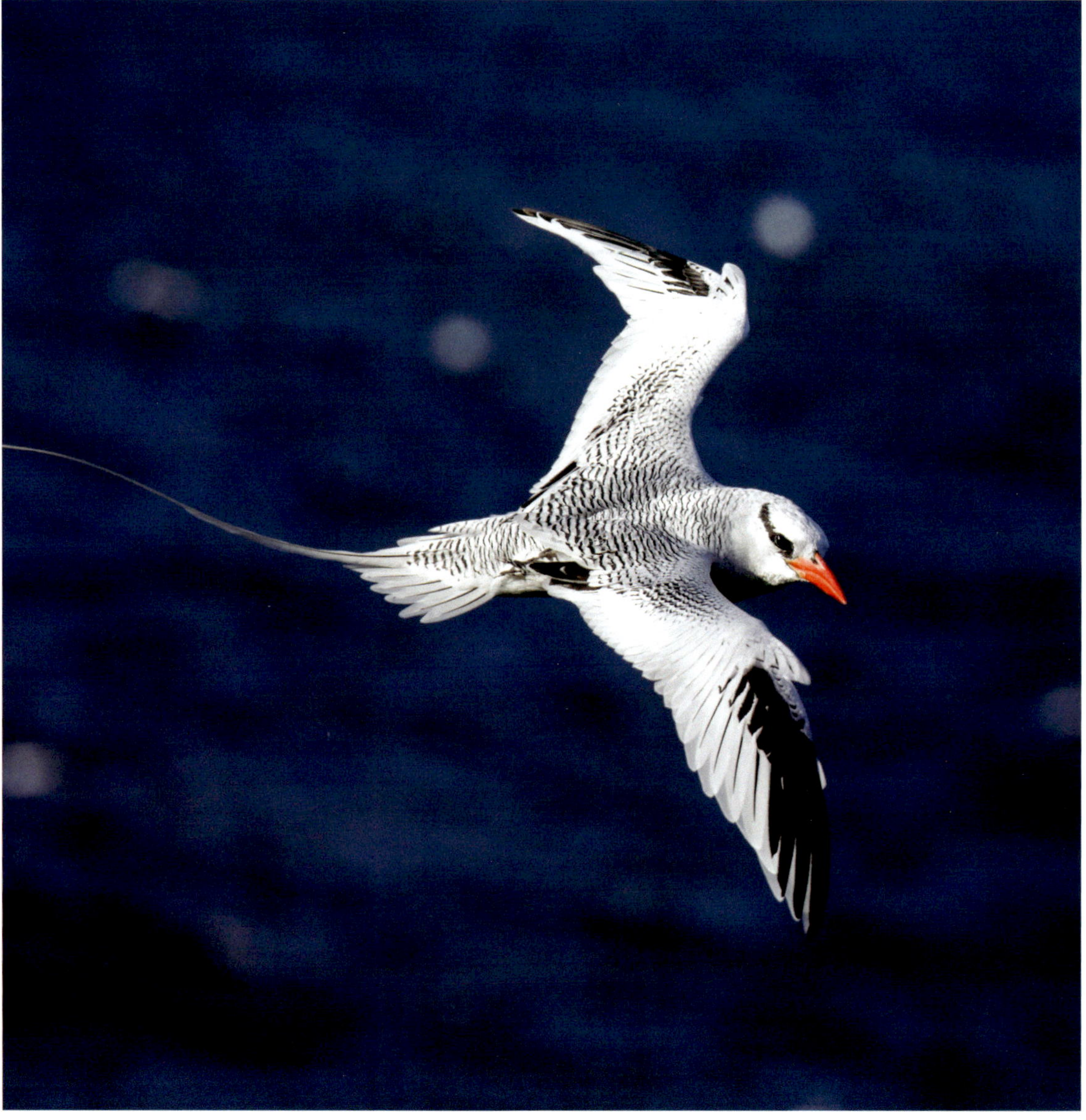

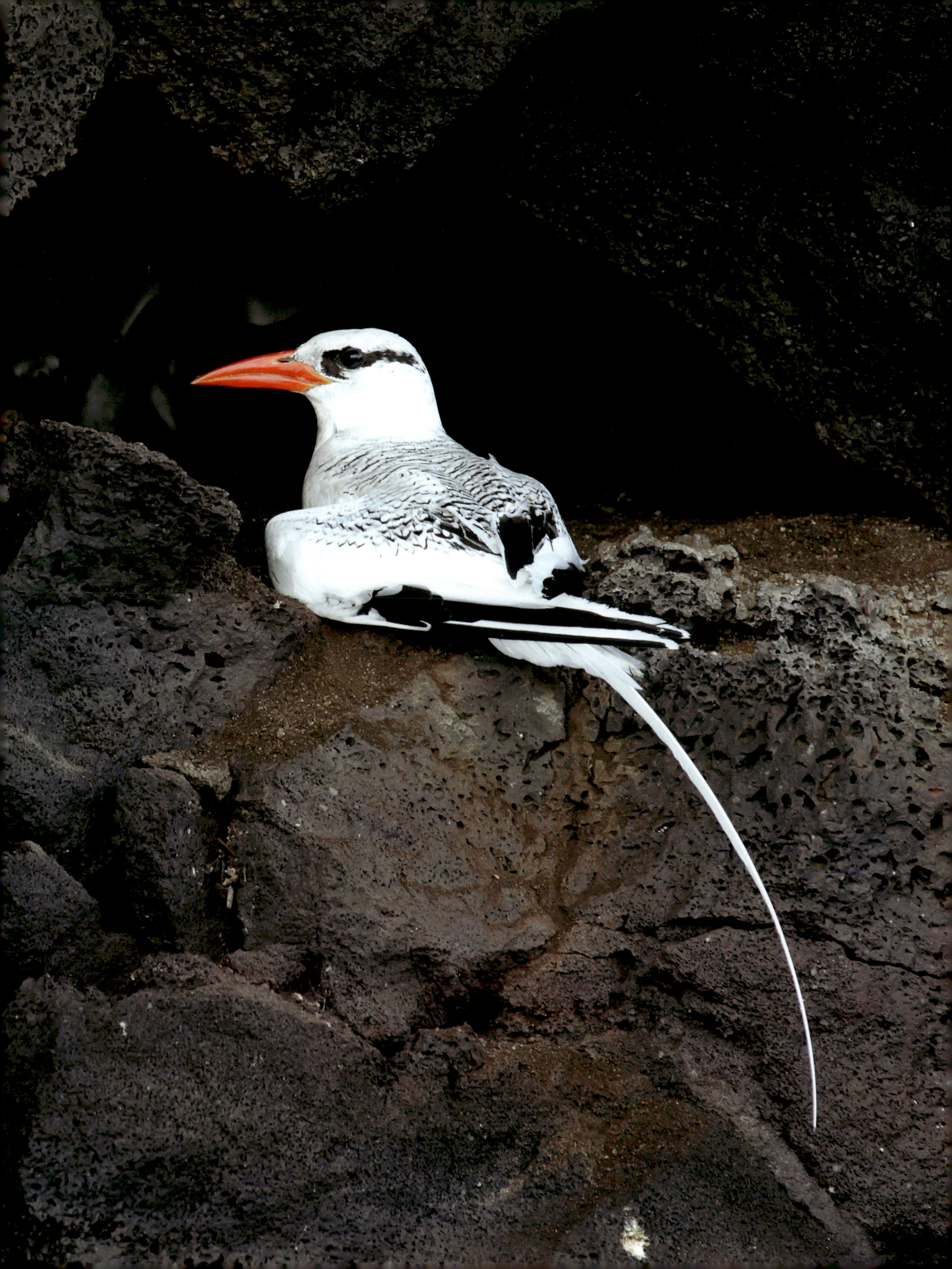

Designed to swim
Without the need to fly, this bird has small breast muscles and much larger ones to power the legs for swimming. This makes the body bottom heavy so it floats low in the water, thus making it easier for the bird to poke its long neck under the surface in search of fish.

Galápagos shearwater
This seabird is endemic to the islands and is seen hunting in large flocks. It nests in colonies on steep cliffs.

Galápagos penguins
One of the smaller penguin species, this seabird is the only penguin species to live wild in the northern hemisphere. Penguin colonies are most often found on the western coasts where the water is colder and the fishing opportunities are greater.

Nazca booby
The largest of the booby species living on the Galápagos, this seabird can be seen diving for fish out at sea and forms major breeding colonies on Genovesa and Española.

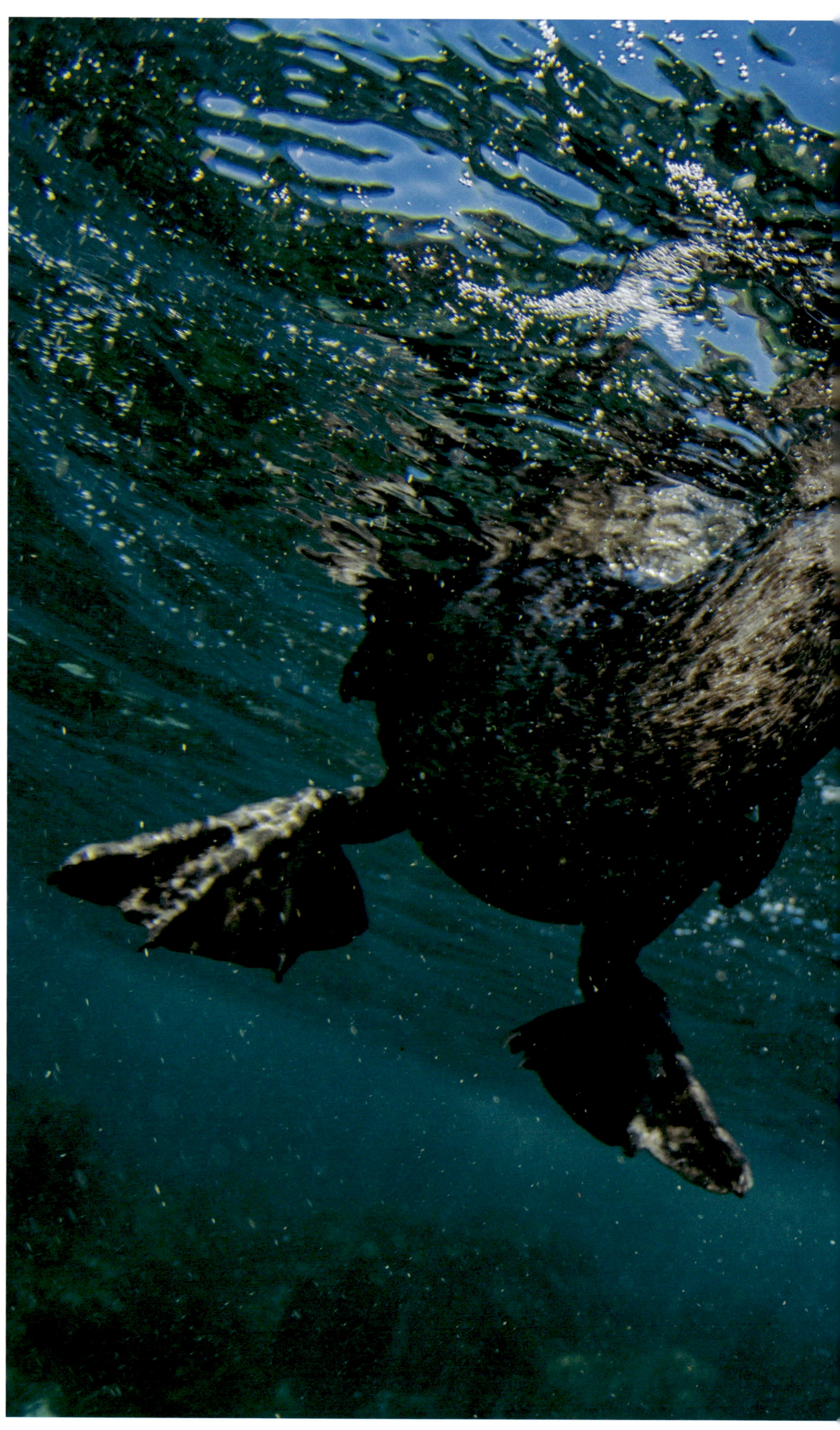

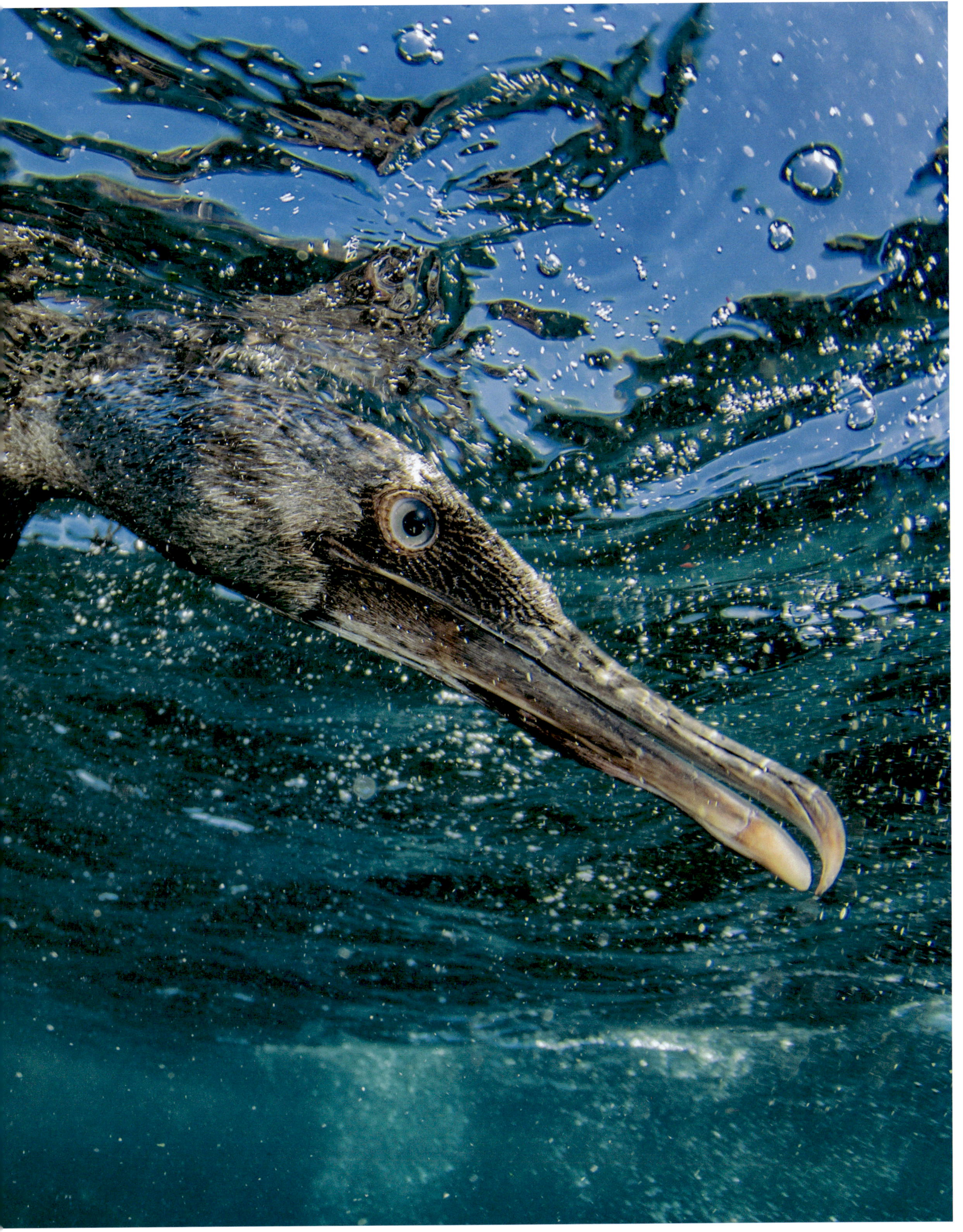

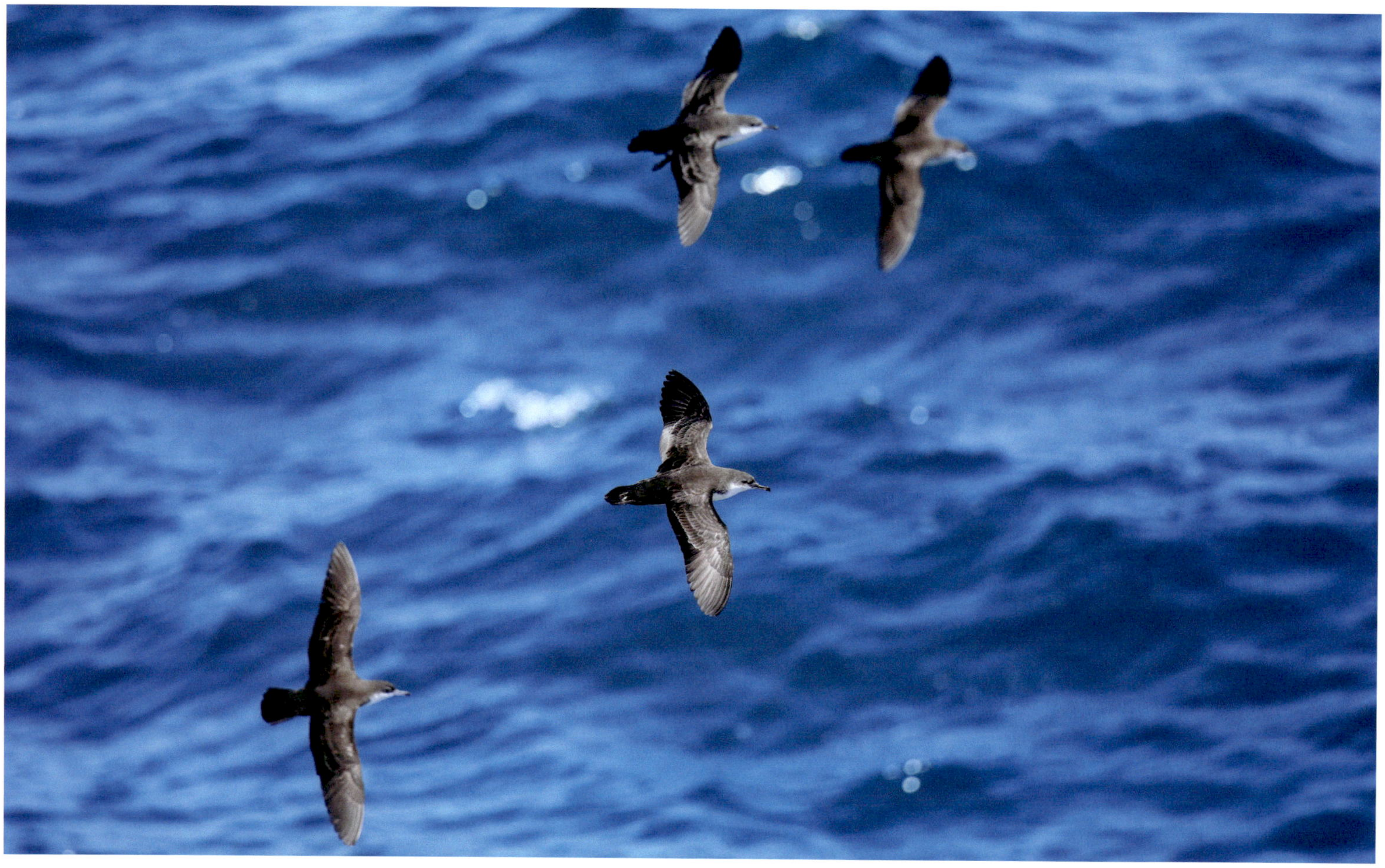

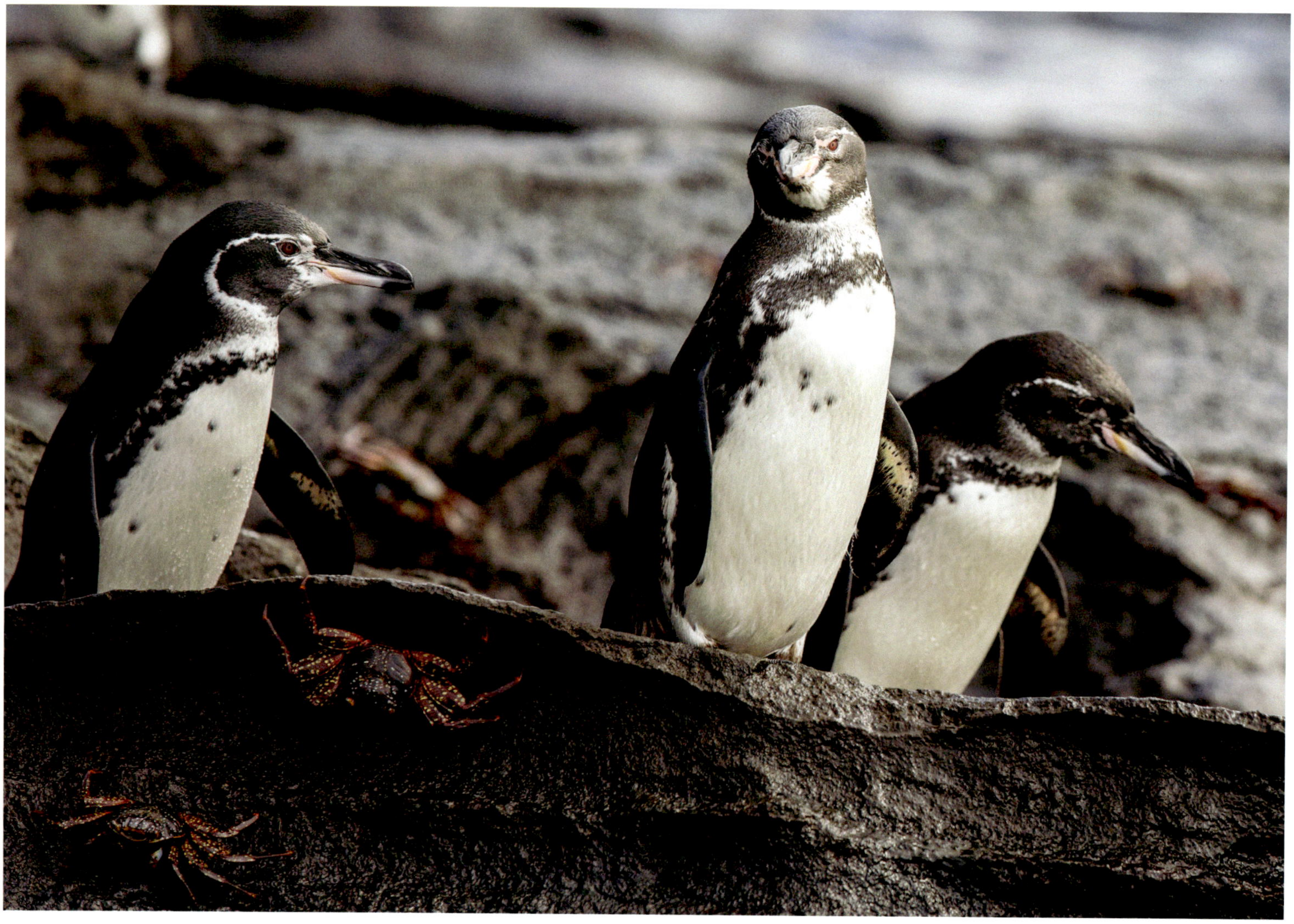

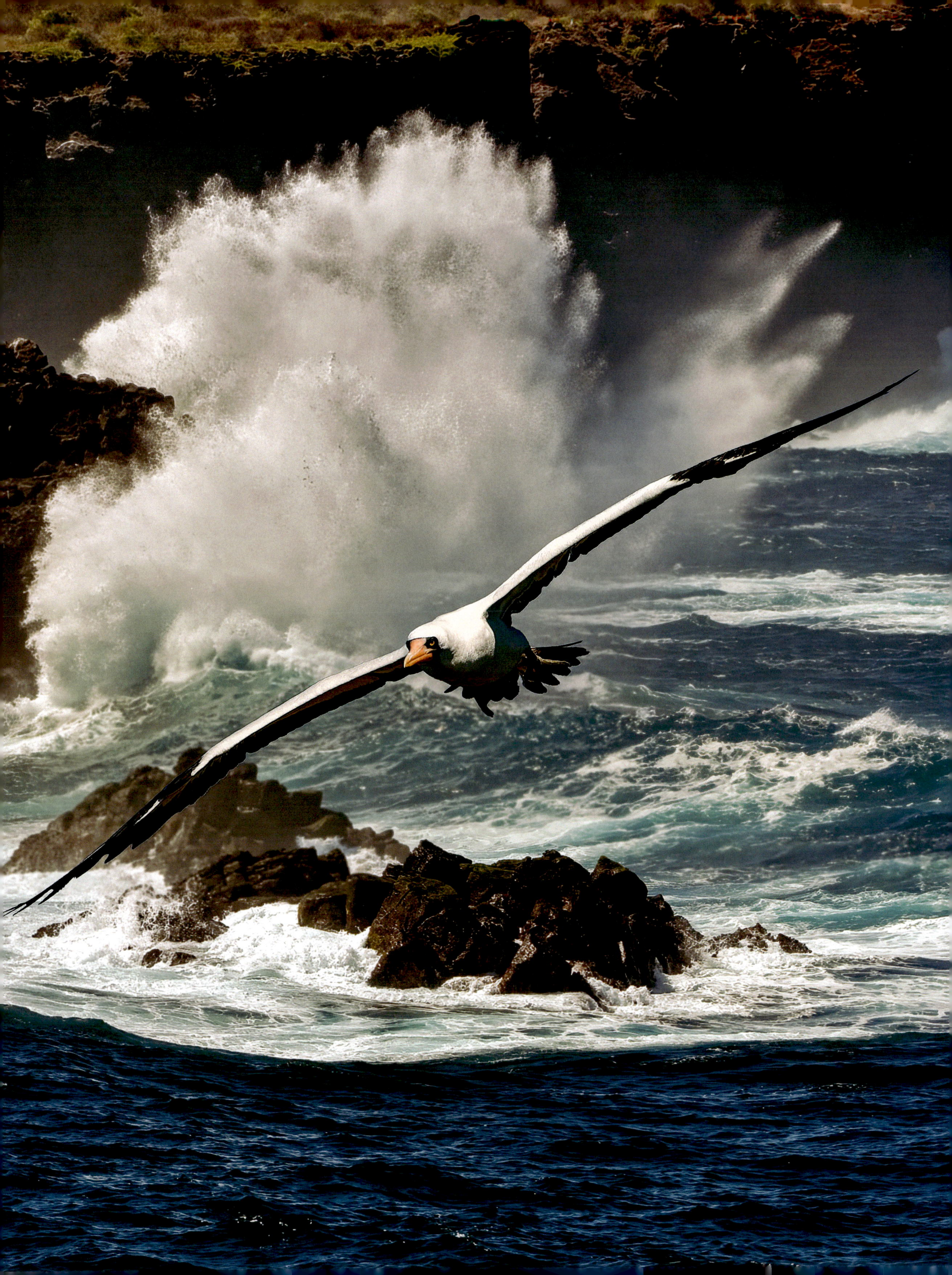

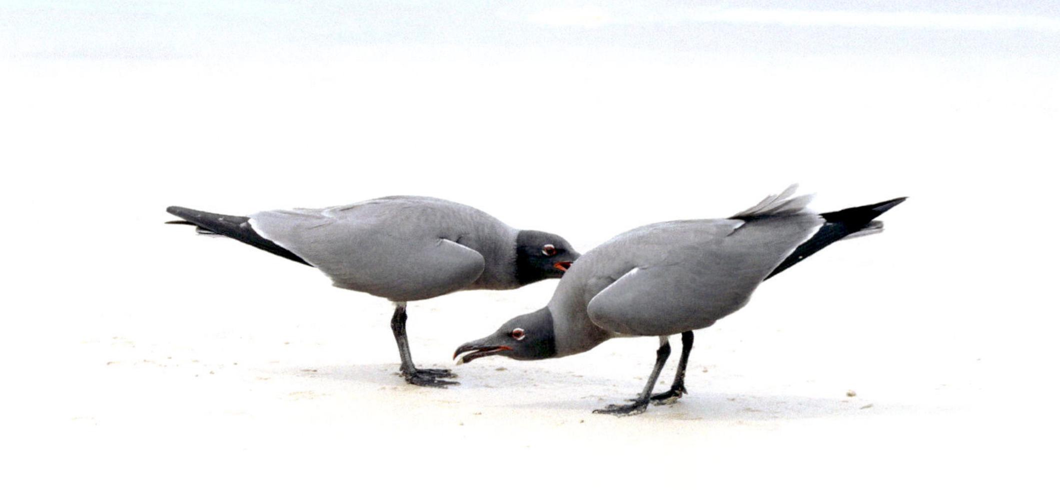

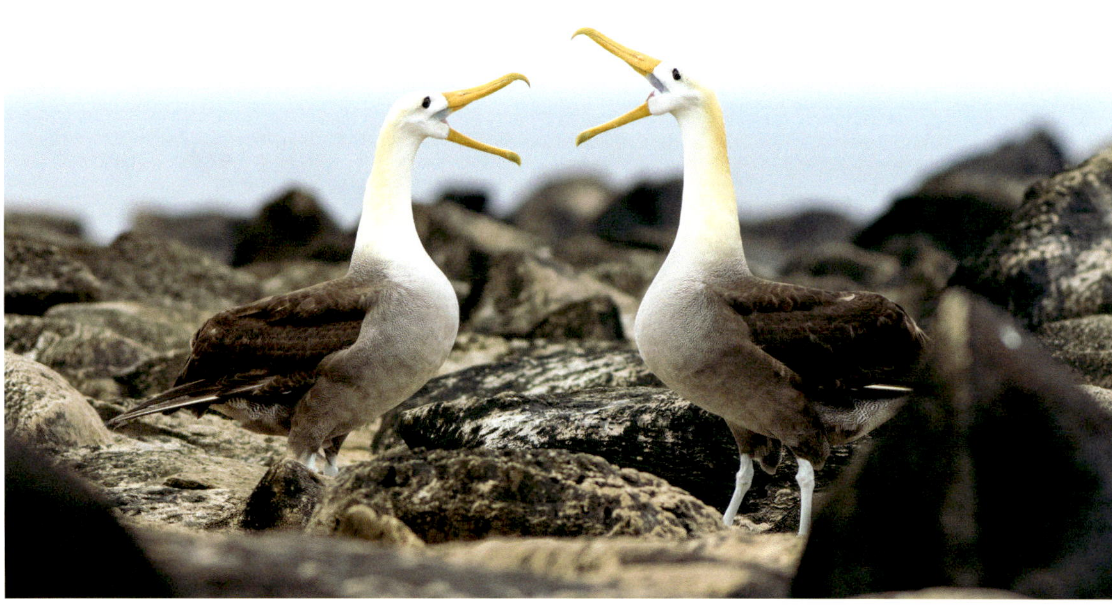

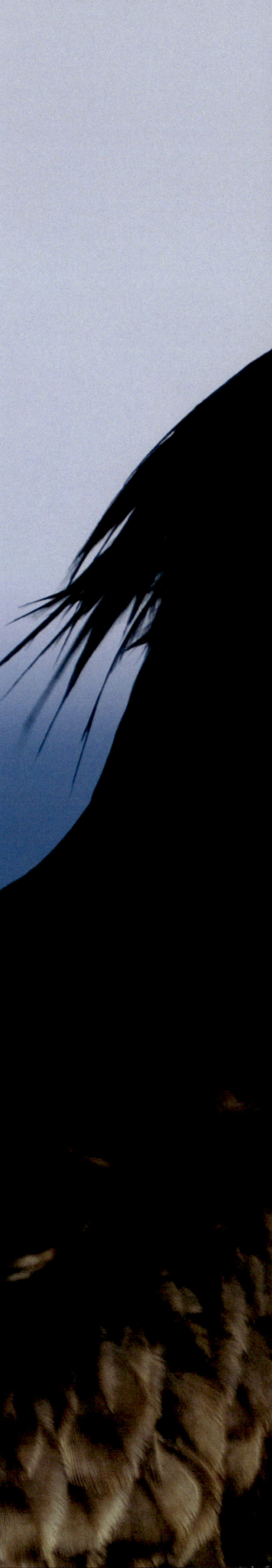

Lava gull
Coloured grey to blend in with lava fields along the coast, this species of gull lives only on the Galápagos. It feeds on all kinds of food, including lizards that scurry over the rocks.

Waved albatross
This is the largest bird that visits the Galápagos with a wingspan of 2.5m (8ft). The birds spend most of the year out at sea, soaring on the winds by day and diving to the surface to snatch fish. They also rest on the water, crowded into groups called rafts. In March thousands of albatrosses start to congregate on Española to breed, greeting mates with an elaborate display. Nearly all of the world's population of waved albatrosses will have hatched on this single island.

Magnificent frigatebird
Why is this seabird quite so magnificent? It is perhaps the eye-catching red throat pouch used by males to attract mates, or the elaborately hooked bill for snaring fish. Others might refer to the incredible aerodynamics. This species has the highest wingspan to body weight ratio of any bird, which means it requires minimum effort to stay aloft.

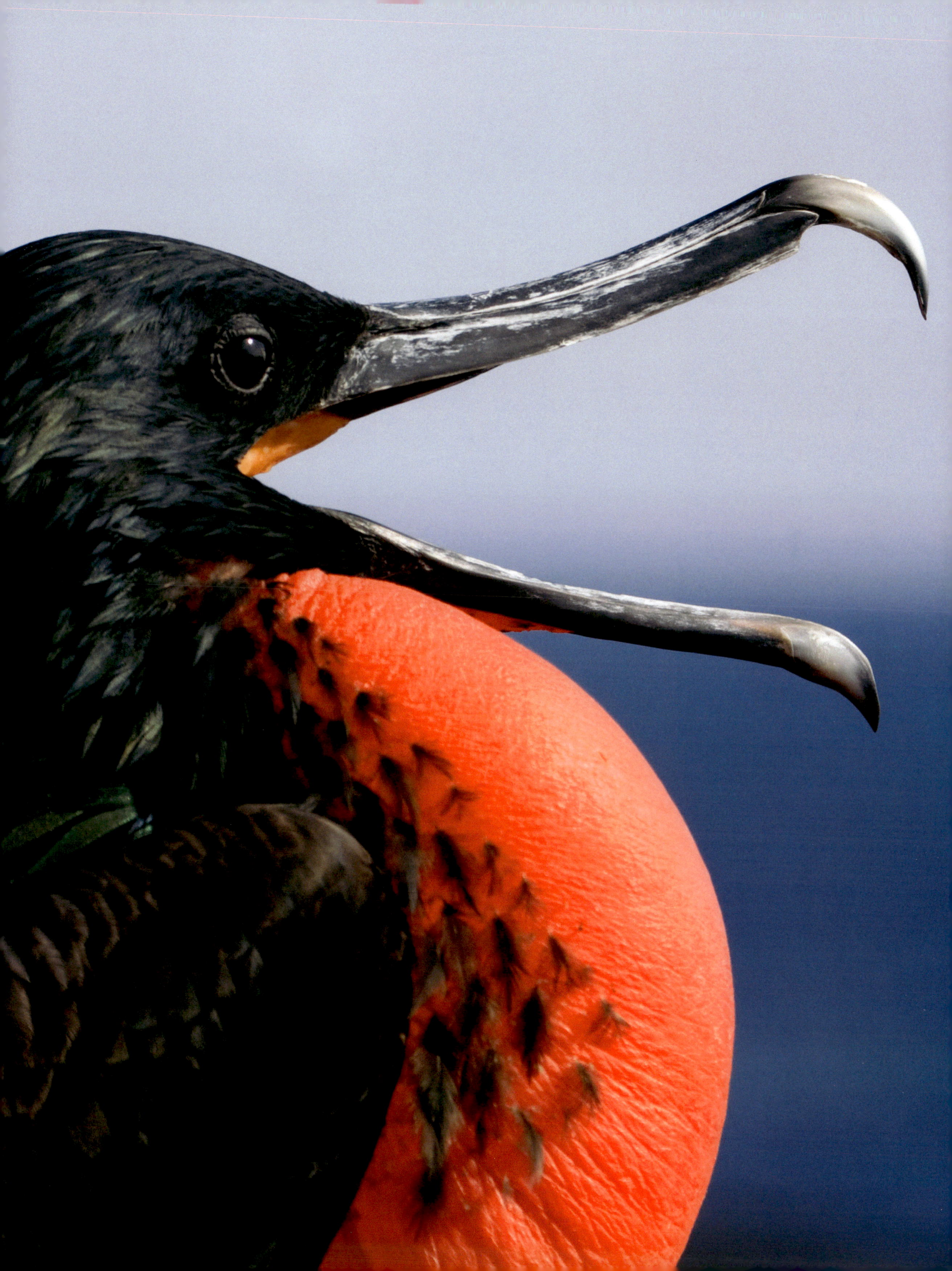

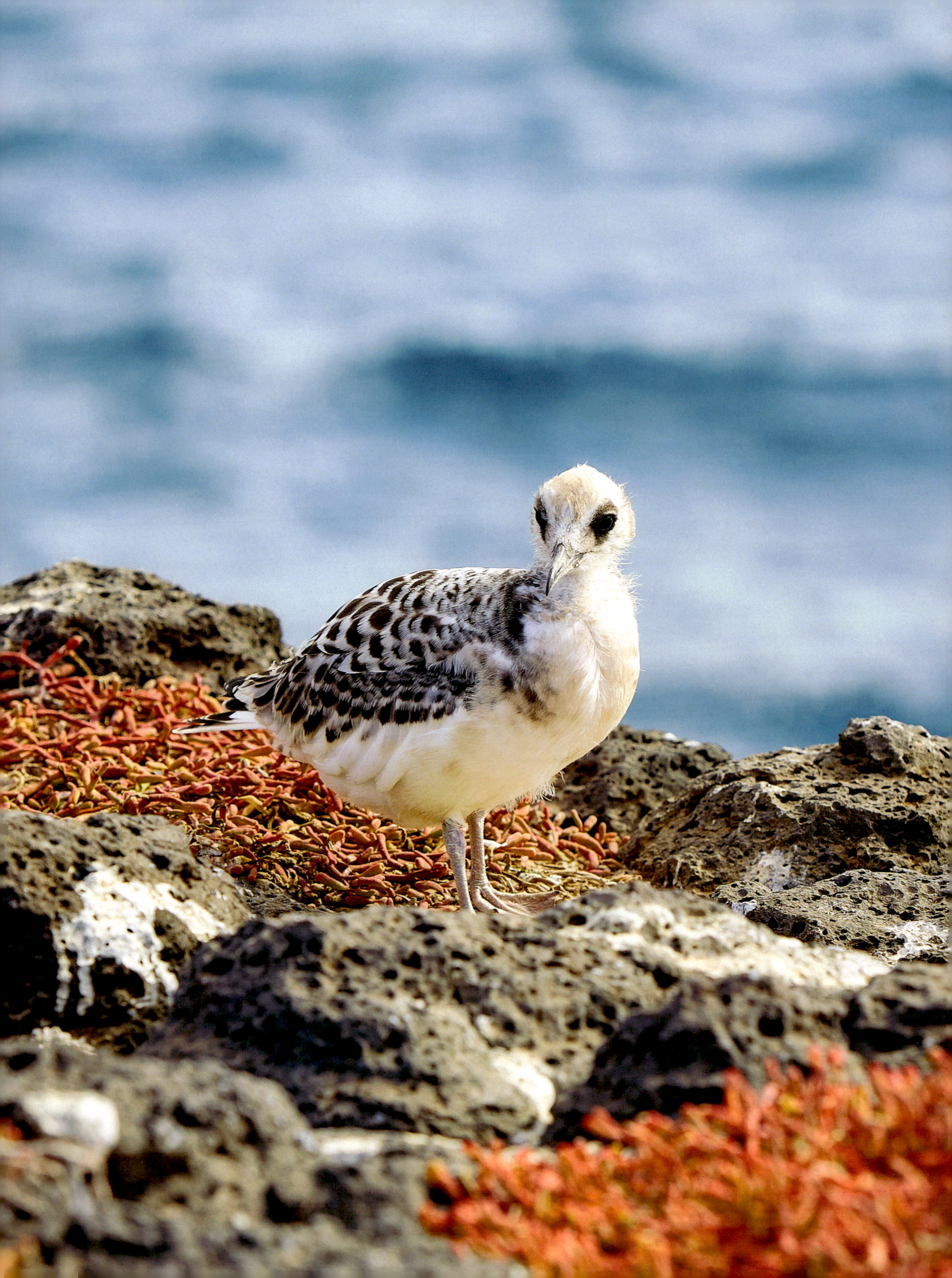

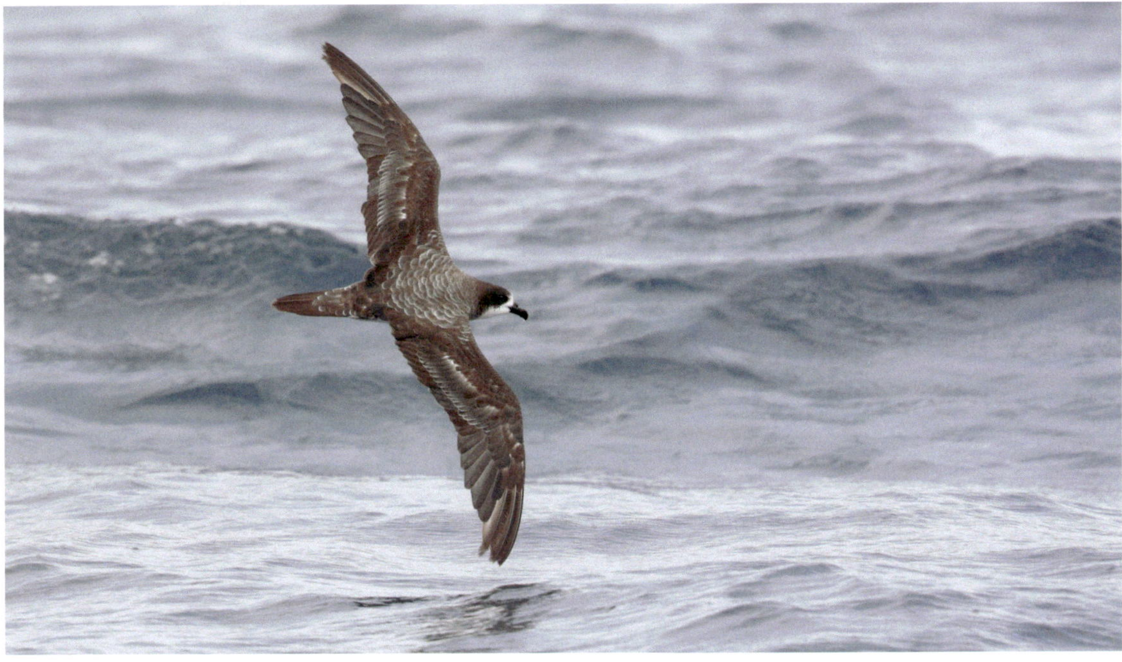

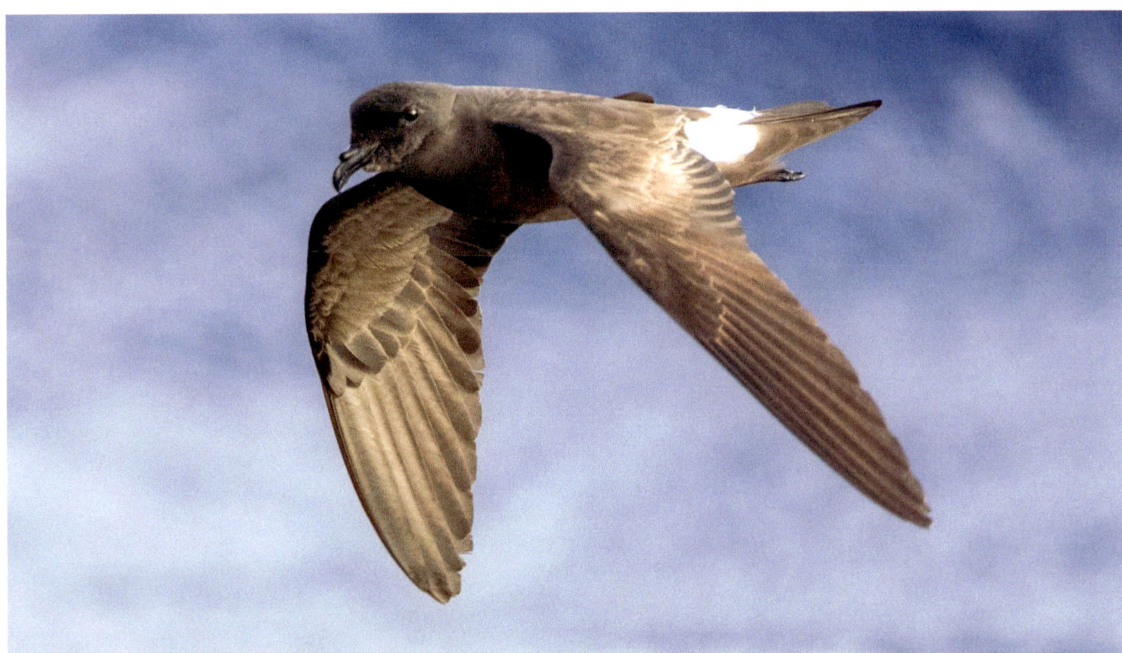

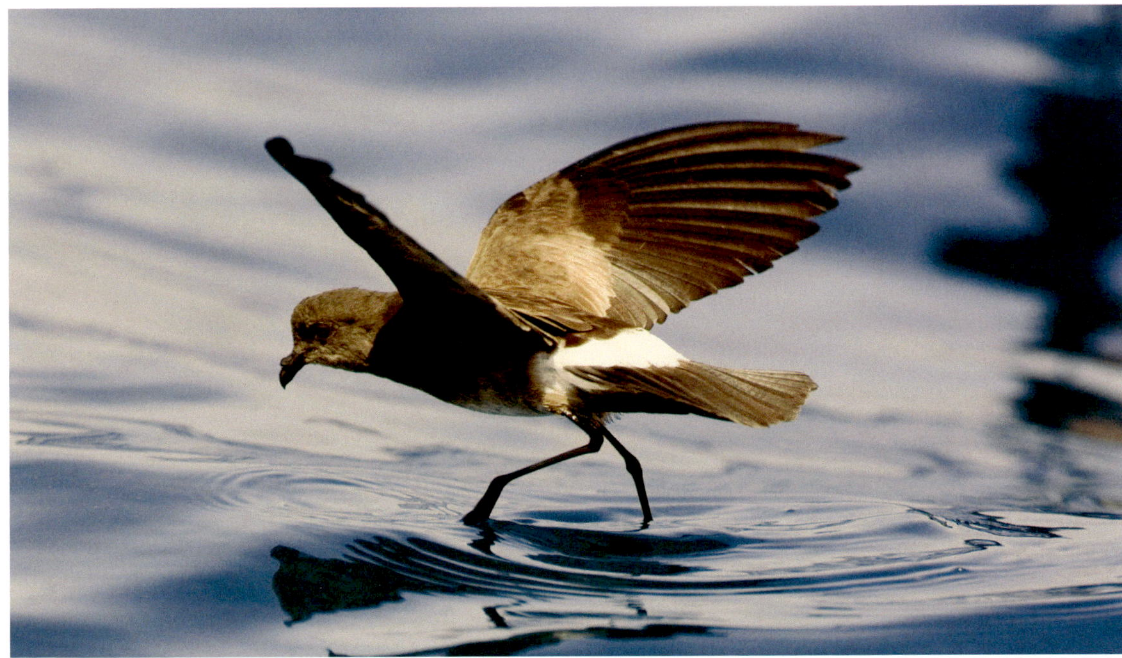

Galápagos petrel
Another endemic species, this seabird flies in land to breed in the lush hill forests. It is sadly endangered by rats and other introduced vermin attacking its nests.

Madeiran storm petrel
Named after a stormy isle in the Atlantic, this species of seabird is found all over the world. It is the largest petrel in these islands with several breeding colonies in isolated rocky coastal areas.

White-vented storm petrel
Although these seabirds are often seen flying around the coasts of the islands, their breeding grounds have not yet been located.

Swallow-tailed gull
This fledgling will one day join its parents preying on shoals of fish and squid. The endemic gull species, named after its unusual tail-shape – for a gull, that is – is the only bird on the Galápagos that hunts at night.

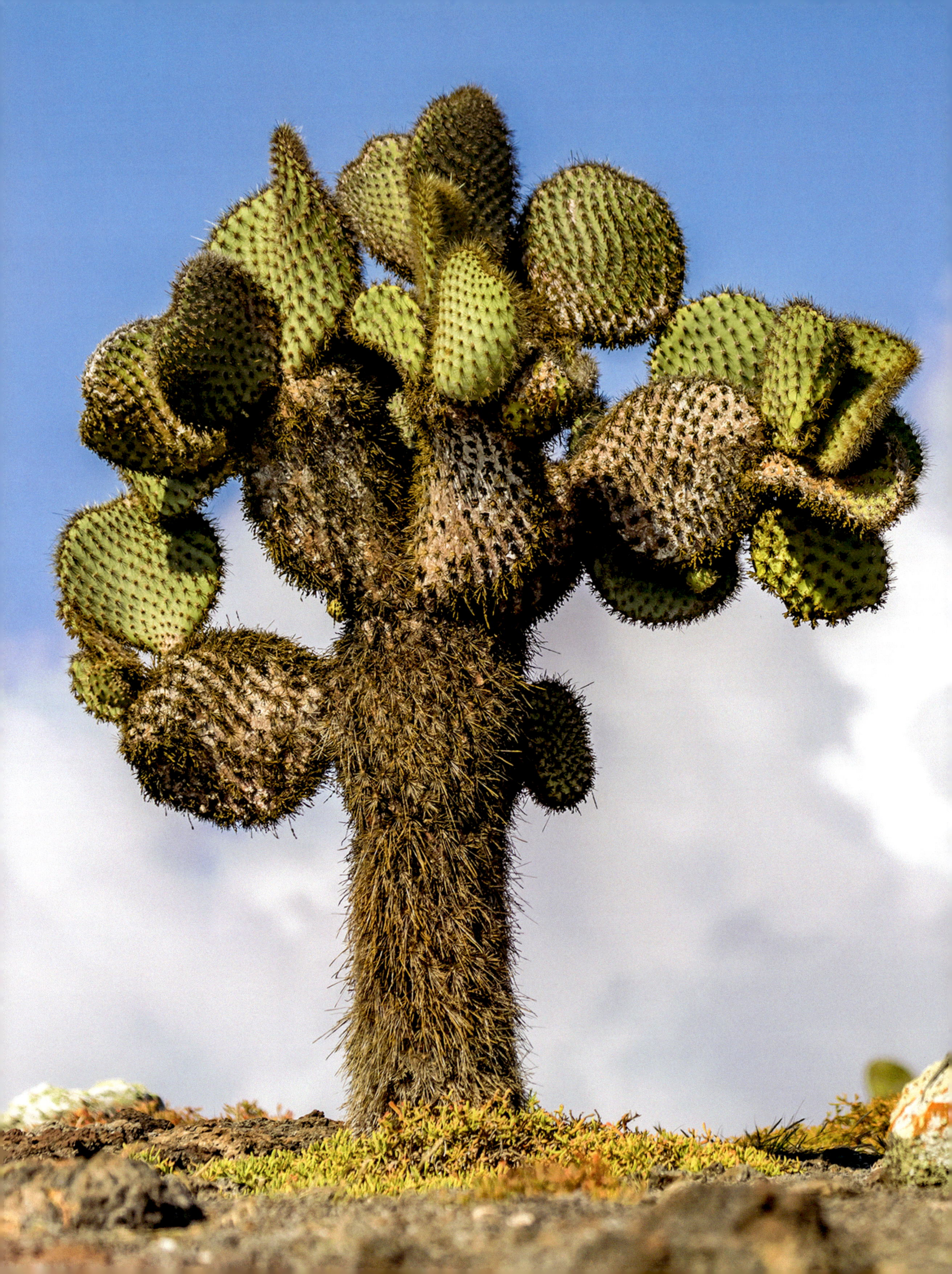

Flora

There are only 500 plant species living on the Galápagos, and a third of them are found nowhere else on Earth. This plant life offers a chance like few other places on the planet to admire the power of convergent evolution. This is where unrelated species from far distant places evolve to adapt to a common ecological niche or way of life, and end up looking the same thanks to natural selection. The Galápagos has areas of forest composed of Scalesia trees. At first glance these trees look unremarkable until one learns that their nearest relatives living elsewhere in the world are plants like daisies and marigolds.

The Scalesia forests are one of four main plant zones based on varying climate conditions on the islands.

The zones are driven largely by the varying landscapes of the different islands. The older islands in the east have been worn away by the ages and so present a low profile. As a result warm and wet ocean winds pass overhead dropping little rain. These islands are generally arid and the plants are adapted to dry salty conditions. In the western islands, the younger landscape is steeper and taller. The wet wind forced up and over these mountains forms clouds that shroud the slopes in mist and frequently drop rain. Above the arid lowlands, the Scalesia forests grow, and higher still the humid hills are filled with fern forests. The tallest islands top out with a pampas zone, filled with moss and thickets of sedge.

Prickly pear cactus
This is the most common kind of cactus on the islands, found in the arid zones, especially in the east of the archipelago. It can grow to almost 12m (39ft) high in some places. The fruits – the prickly pears – are a valuable source of food for the giant tortoises.

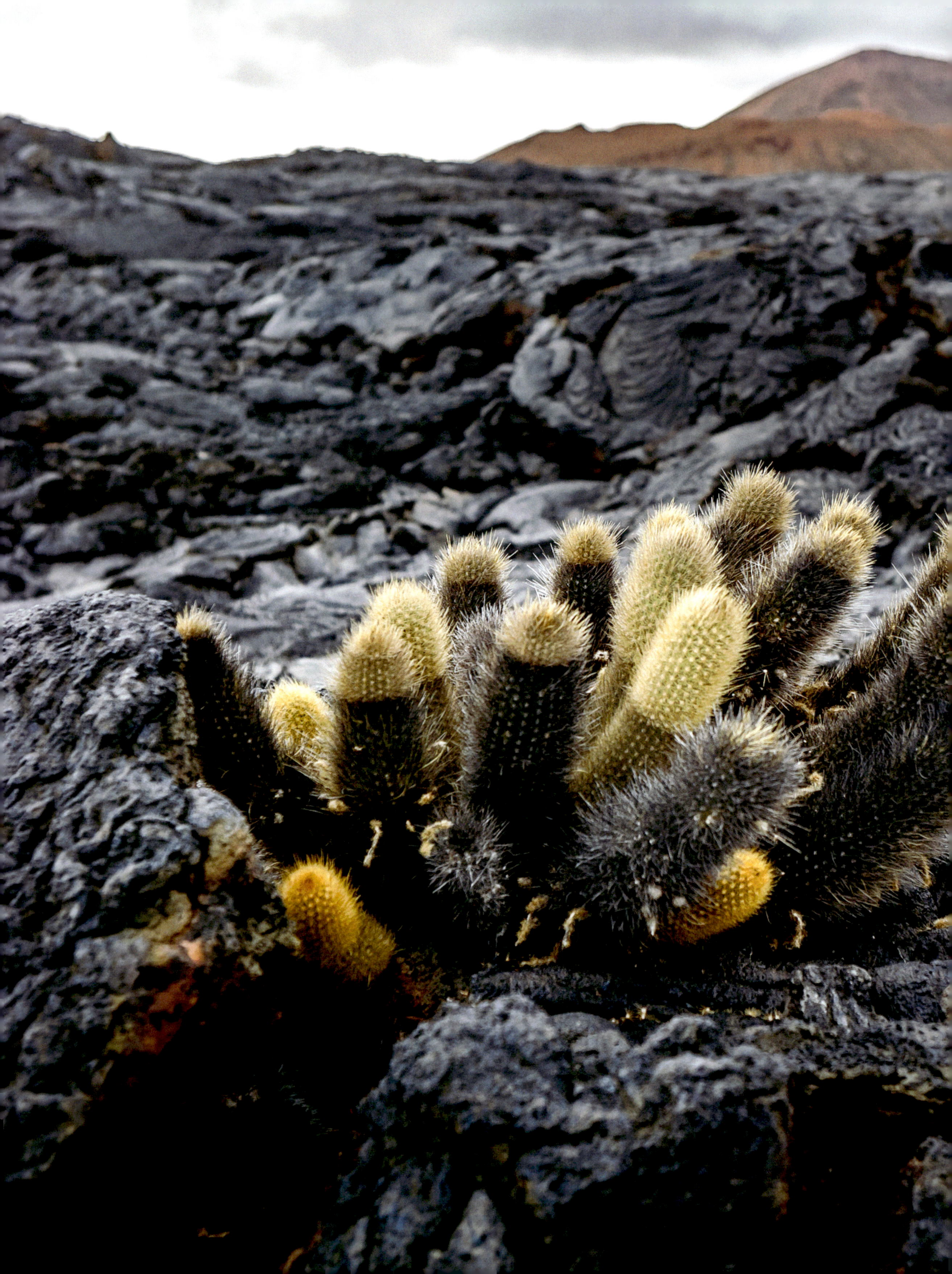

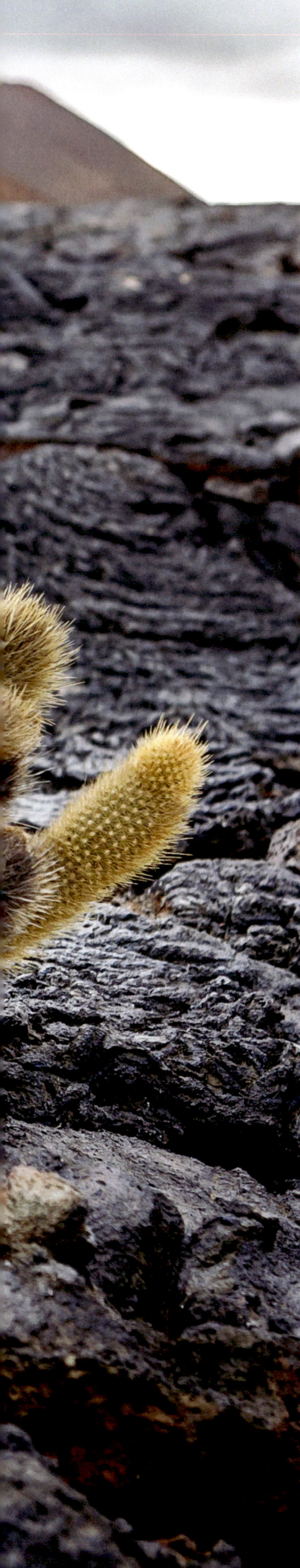

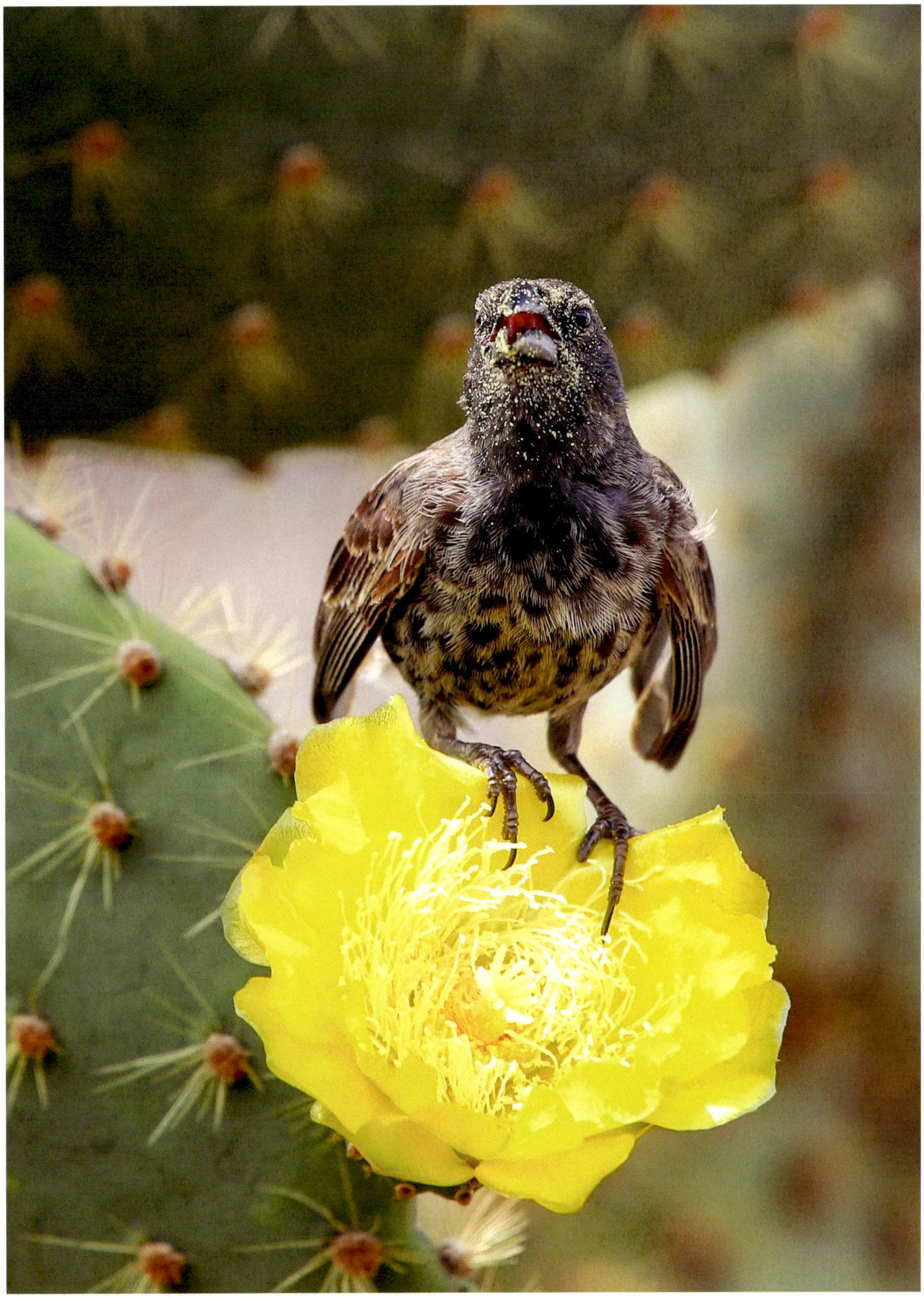

Lava cacti
Small compared to other cacti, at a maximum height of about 60cm (23in), this endemic species is one of the first plants to colonzse fresh lava fields.

Common cactus finch
With its long, pointed beak, this bird – one of the fabled Darwin's finches – is a specialized predator of prickly pear cactus seeds and flowers. While eating these foods, however, the bird helps to pollinate the plants.

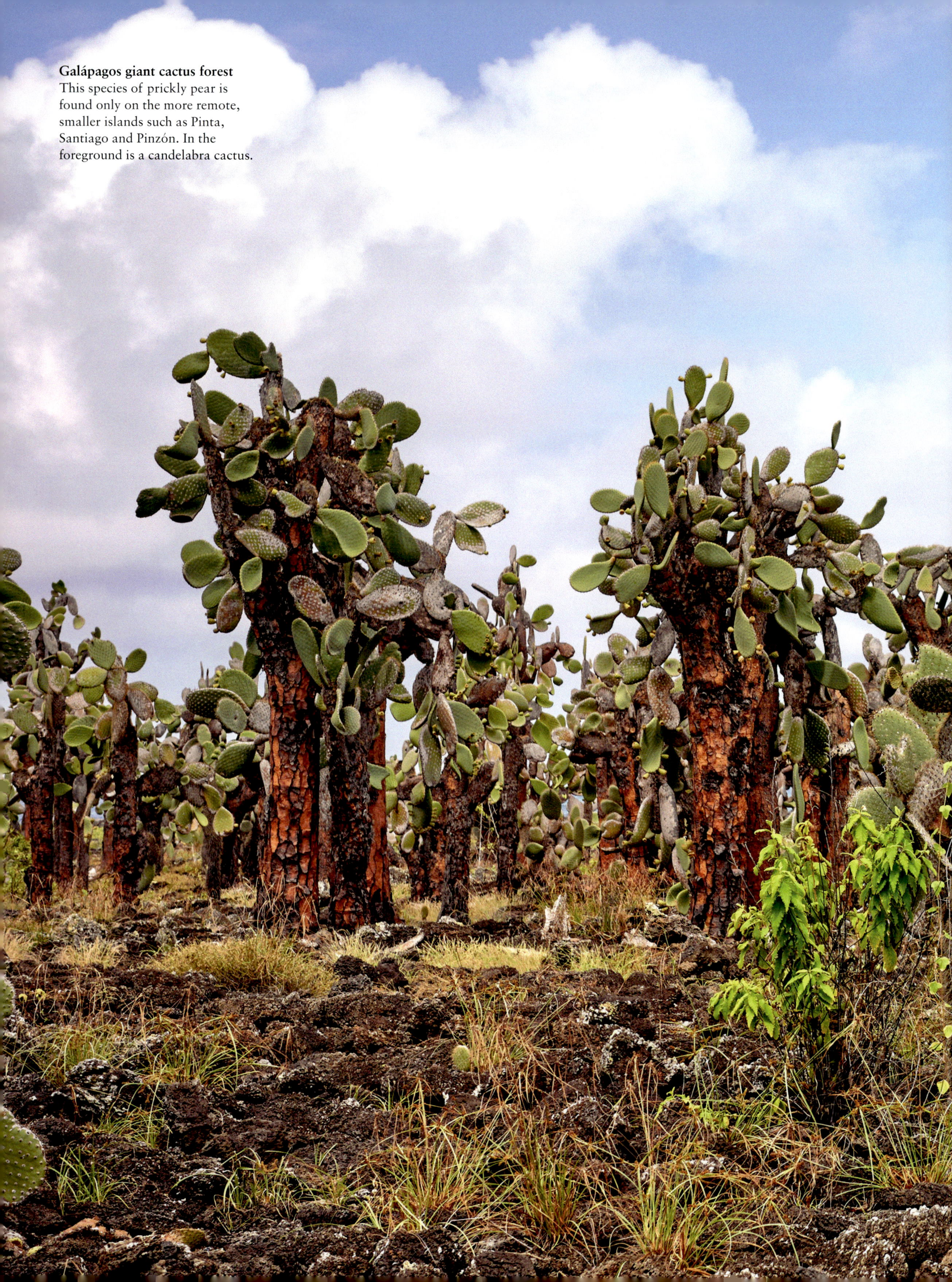

Galápagos giant cactus forest
This species of prickly pear is
found only on the more remote,
smaller islands such as Pinta,
Santiago and Pinzón. In the
foreground is a candelabra cactus.

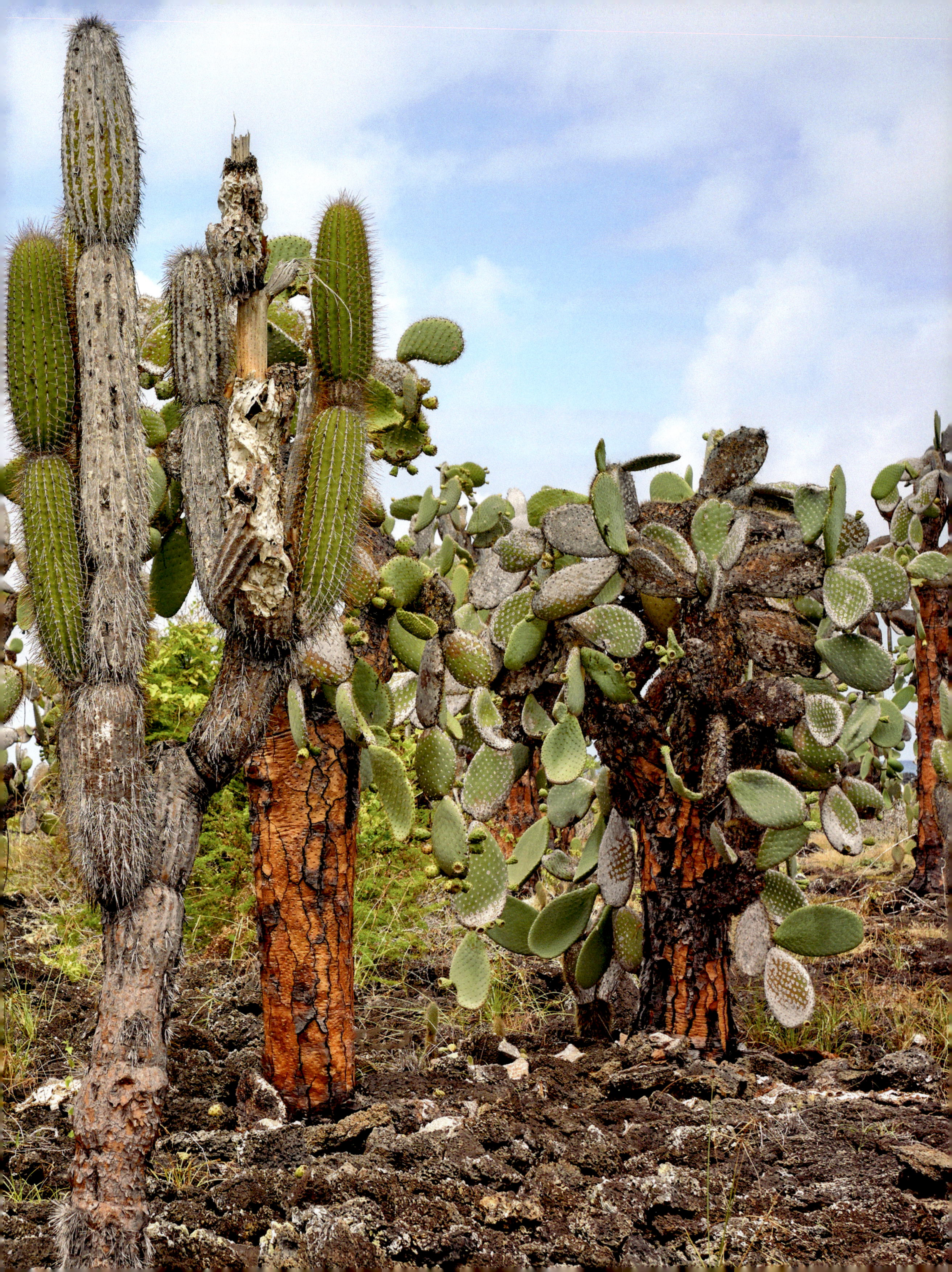

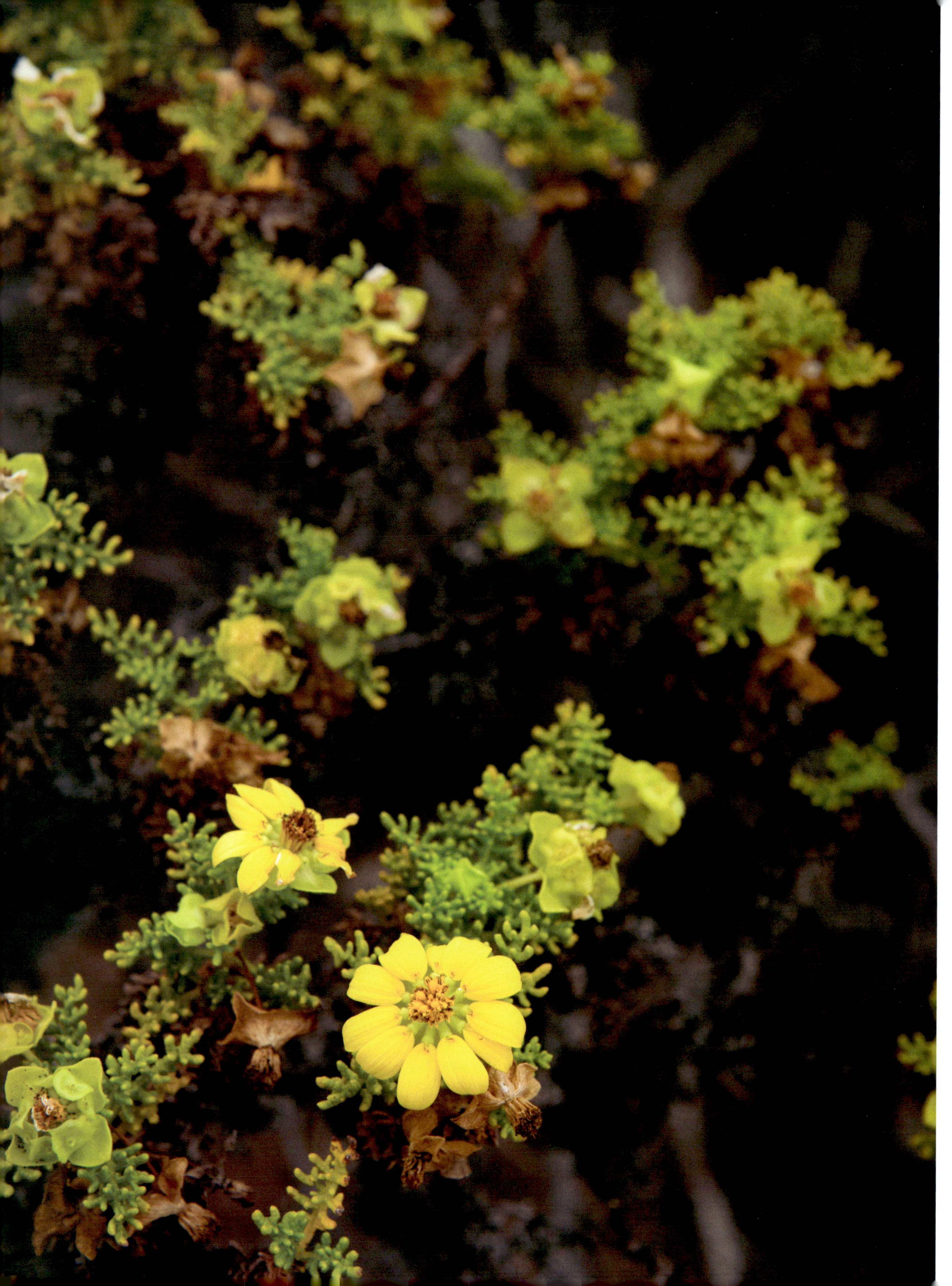

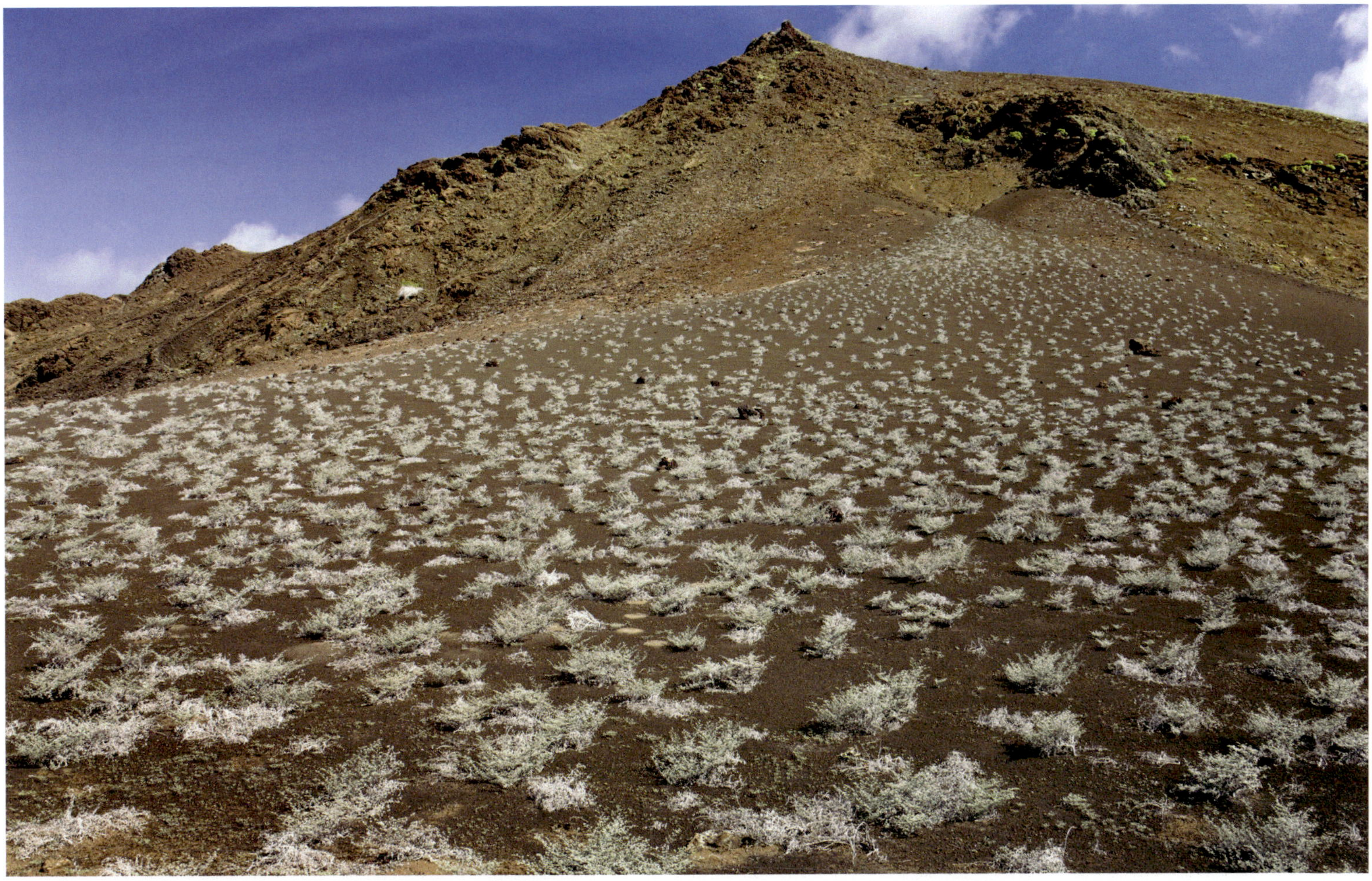

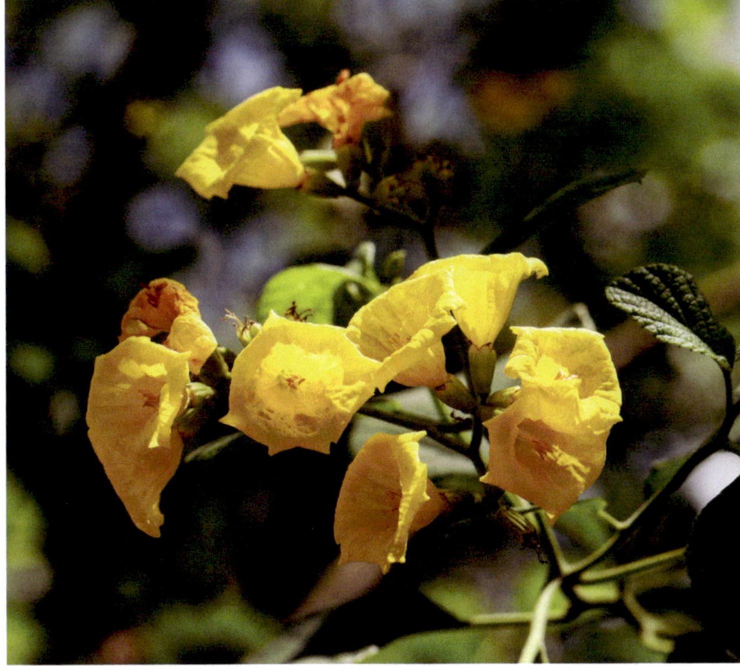

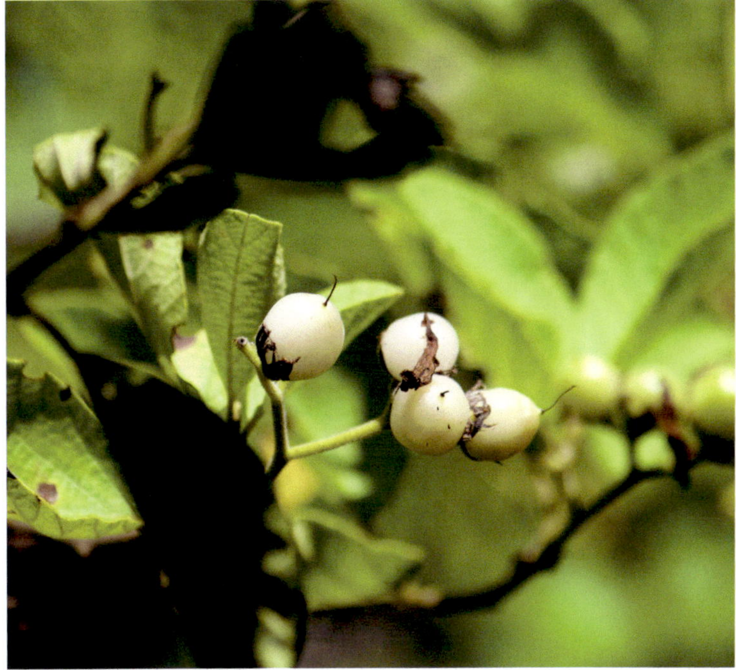

Floreana daisy
A small bushy evergreen shrub that grows on bare lava or in cinder soils, this endemic flowering plant can reach 2m (6ft) high.

Grey matplant
This small grey-green plant grows in low thickets in arid soils. When flowering, areas of matplant are alive with lava lizards that come to feast on the flies drawn to the blooms.

Muyuyo
This yellow-flowered species is also called the glue bush because the pearly berries contain a single seed that is coated in a sticky secretion, which is useful as a paper adhesive.

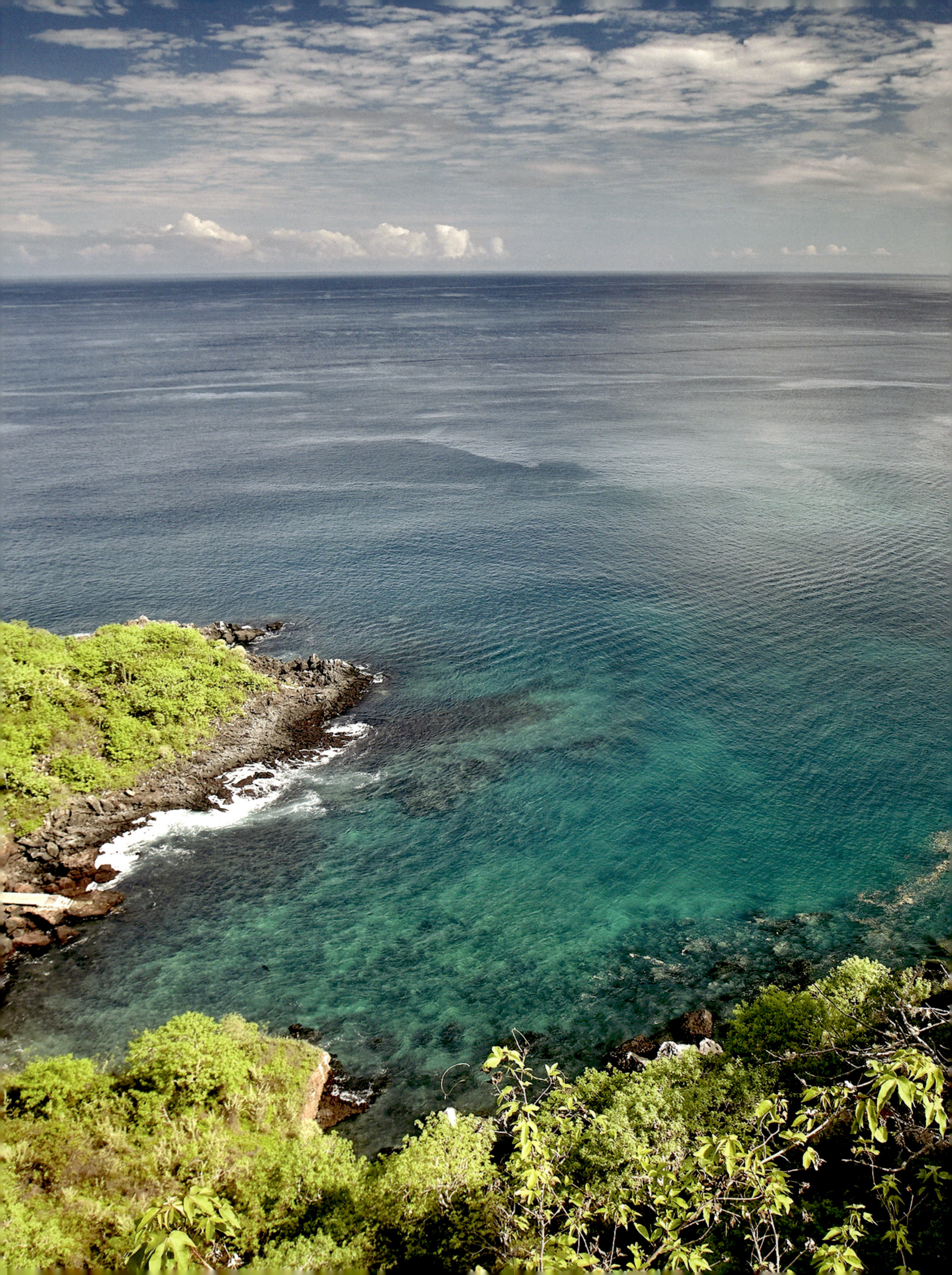

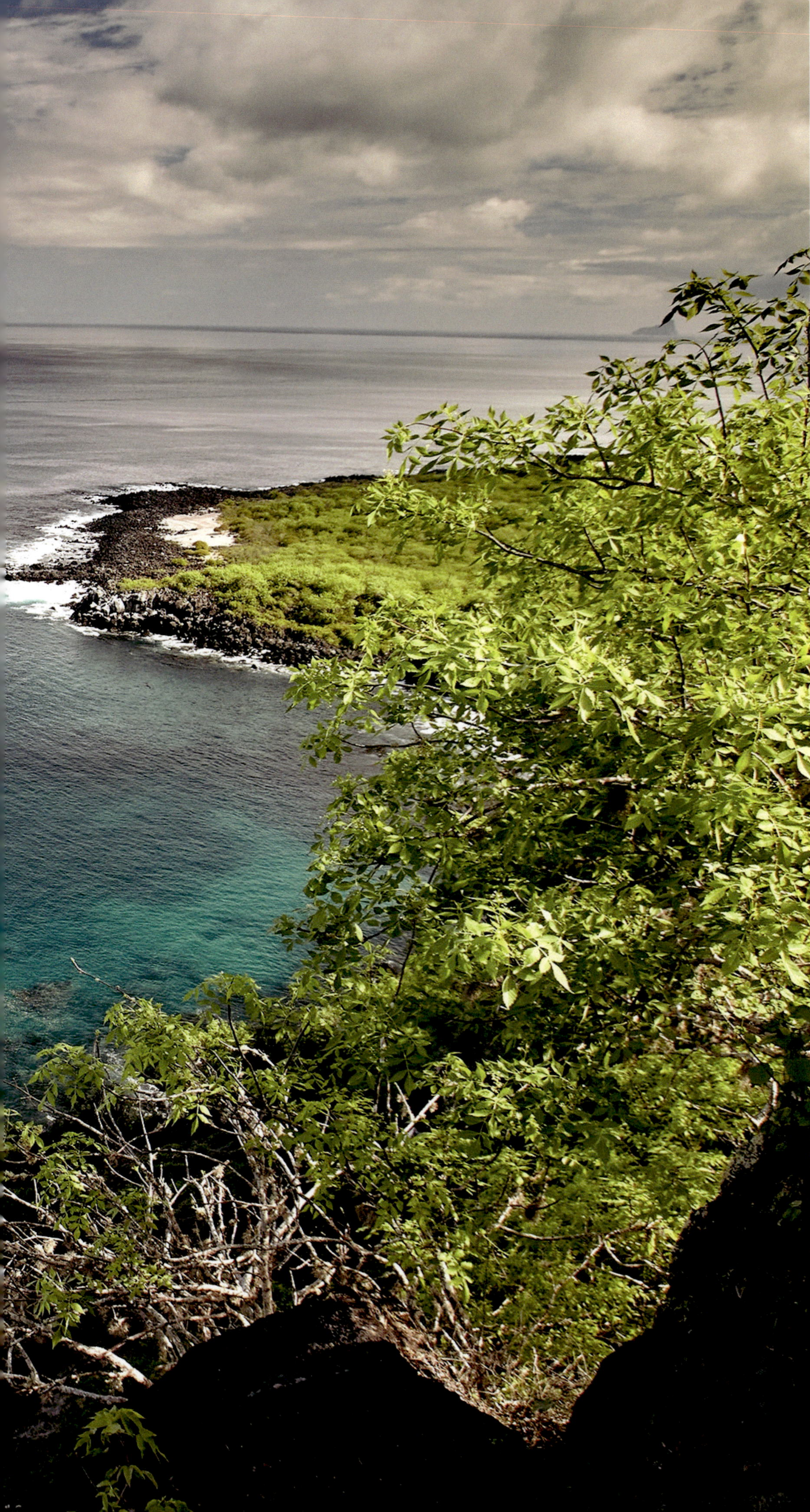

Mangroves
The coastline of the islands has many mangrove swamps where trees grow out of the sediment of the shallow tidal seabed. The mangrove roots form a sheltered habitat that is a haven for marine wildlife.

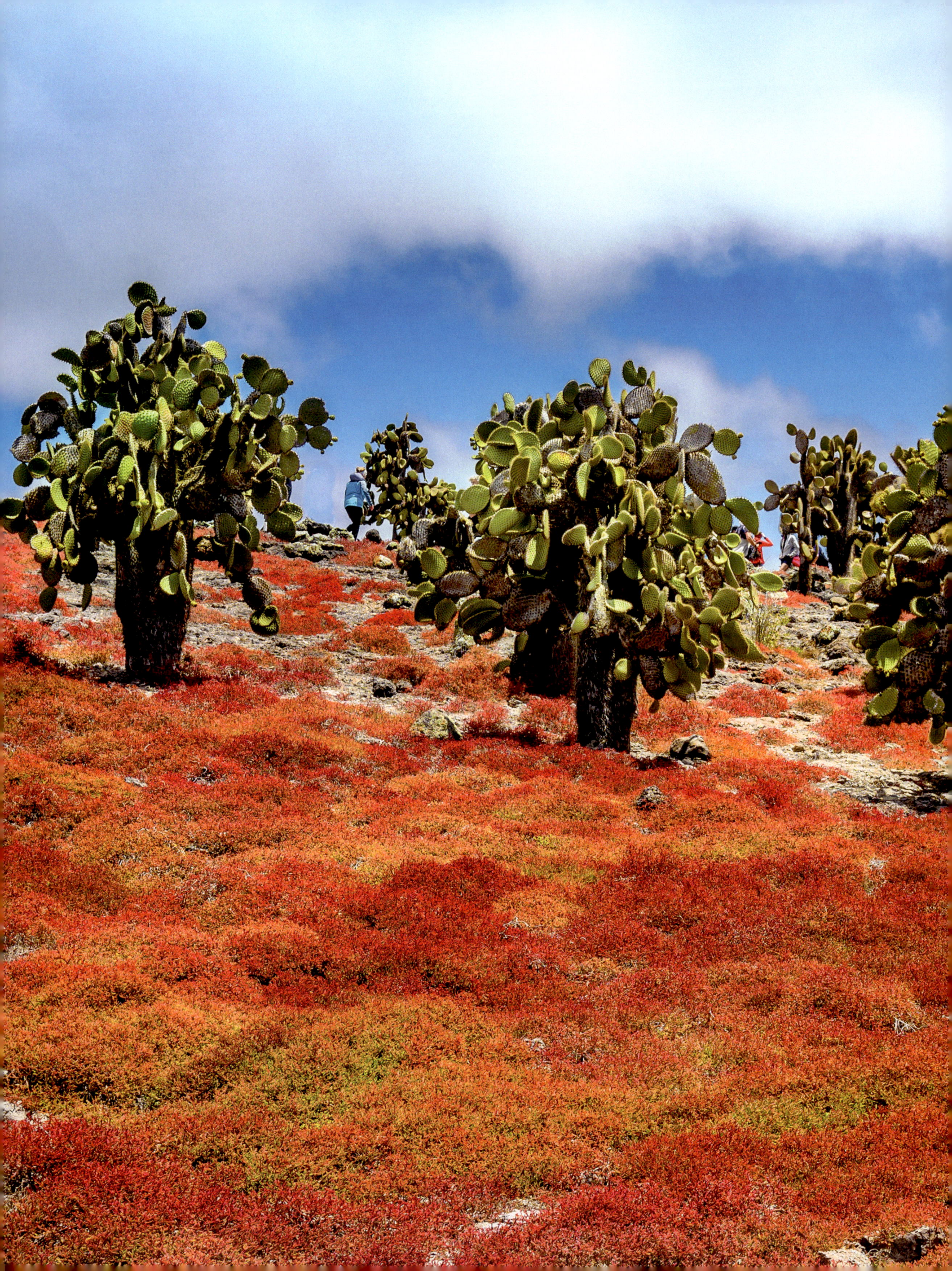

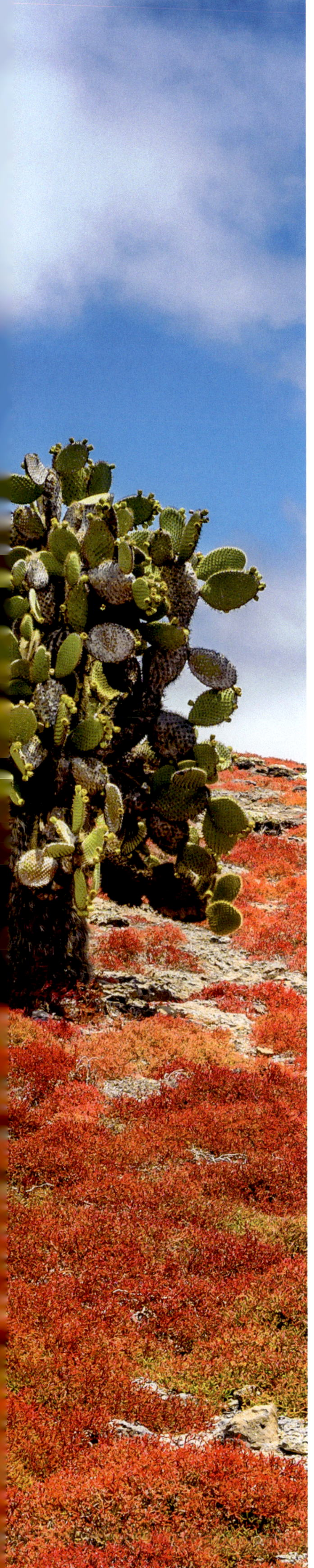

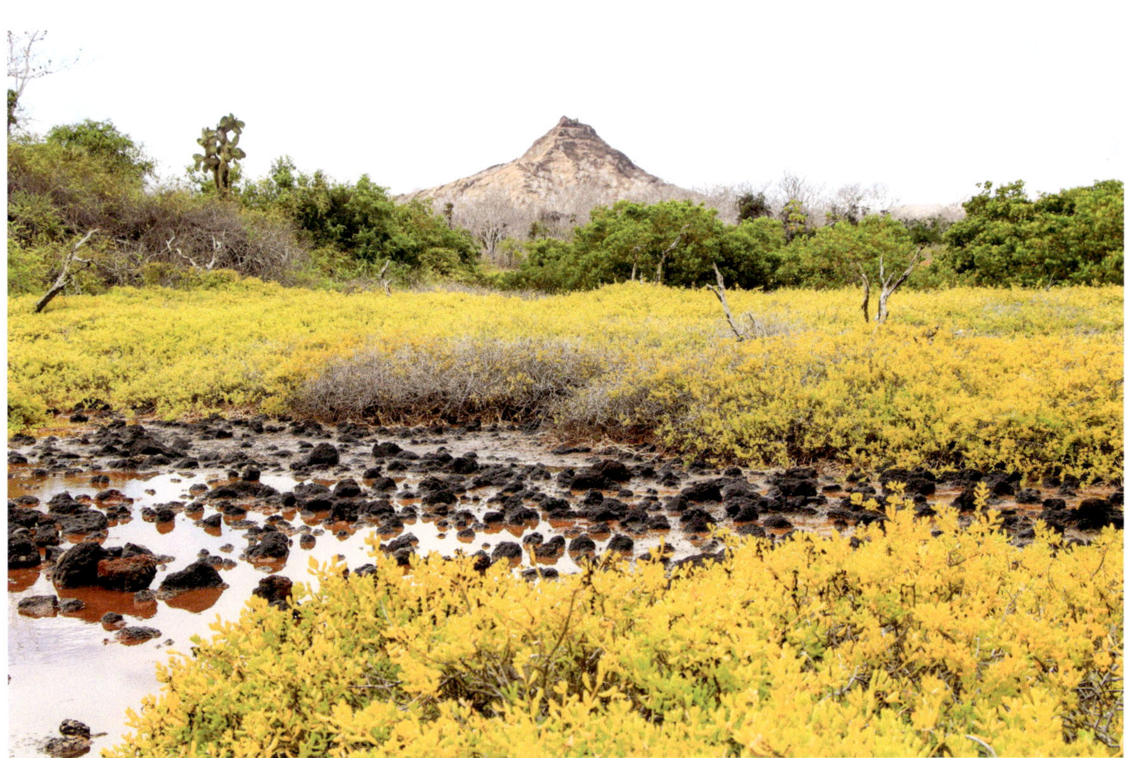

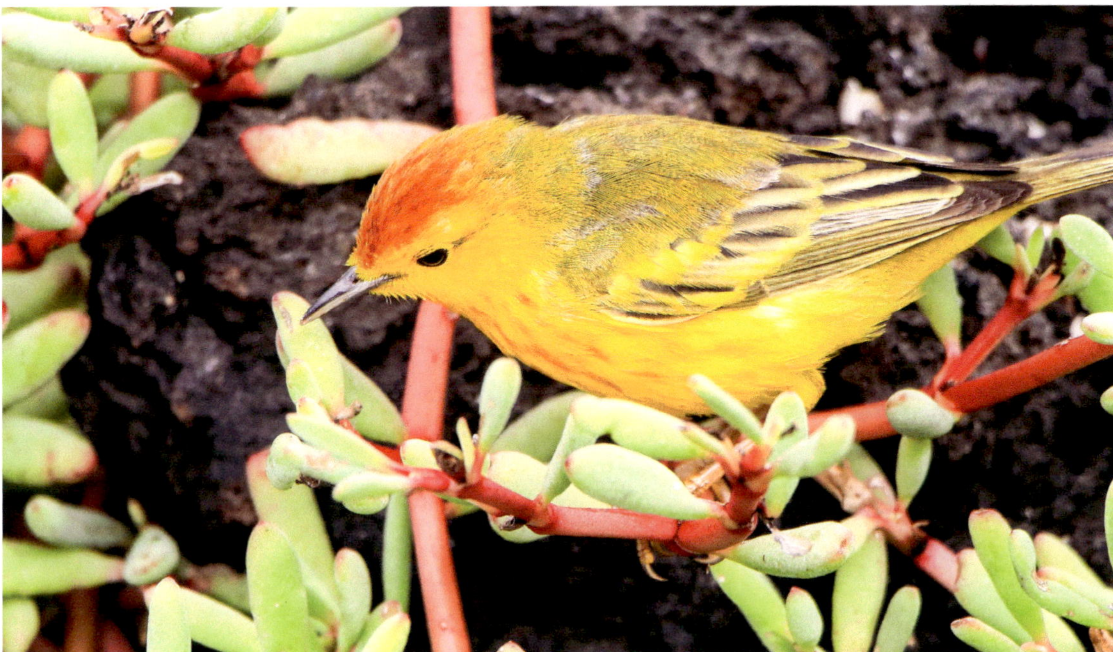

Galápagos carpetweed
Much of the arid zone is covered by this low-lying herb. The fleshy leaves have turned a rust colour indicating that this is the dry season and the plant is protecting itself from intense sunlight. When the rains return, the carpetweed will sprout fresh green leaves.

Galápagos purslane
Dragon Hill on Santa Cruz island can be seen here across a field of purslane flowers. This fleshy perennial grows out of lava close to the shore.

Yellow warbler
A small songbird is perching on purslane as it scours the lava in search of insect prey.

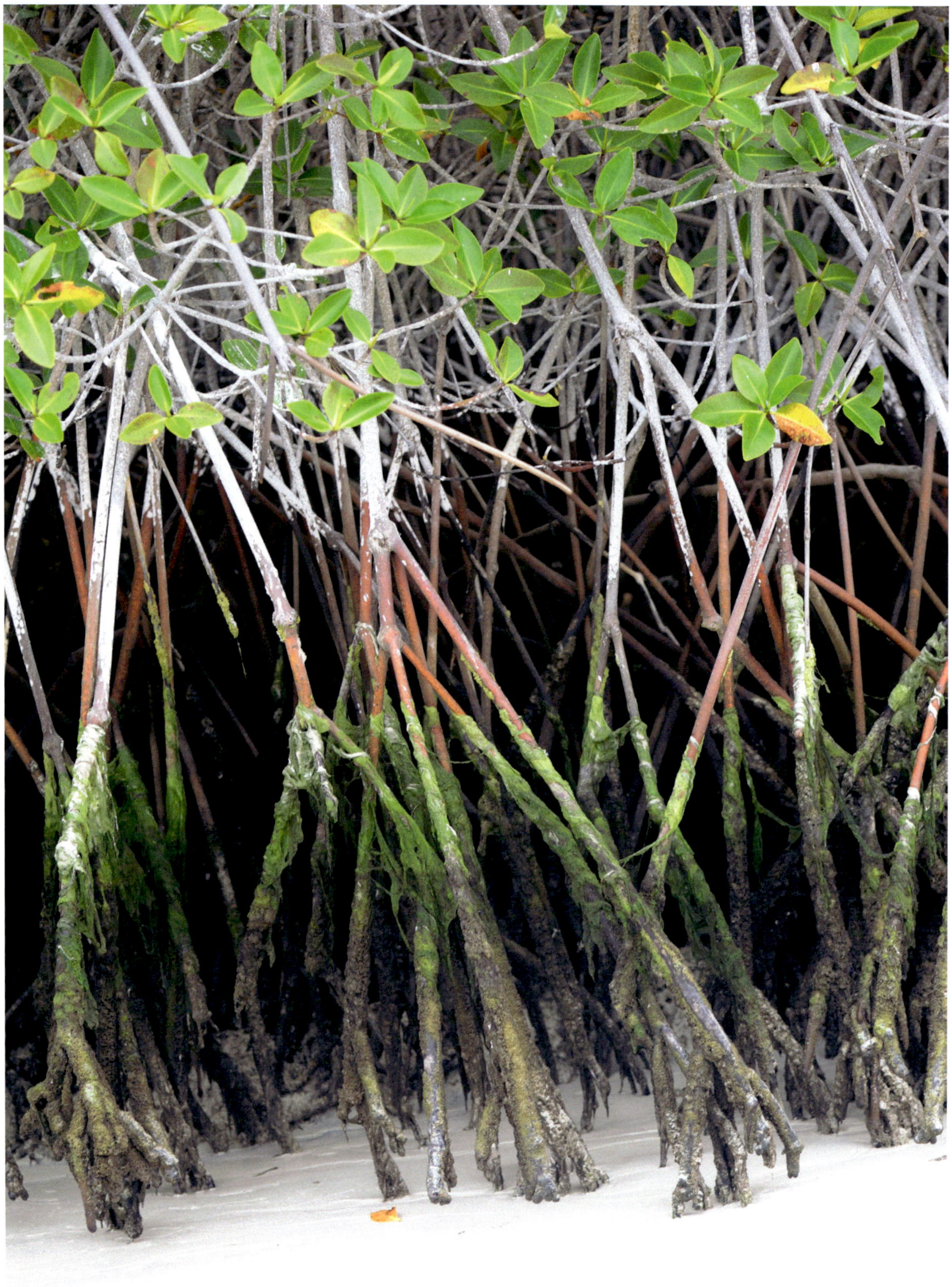

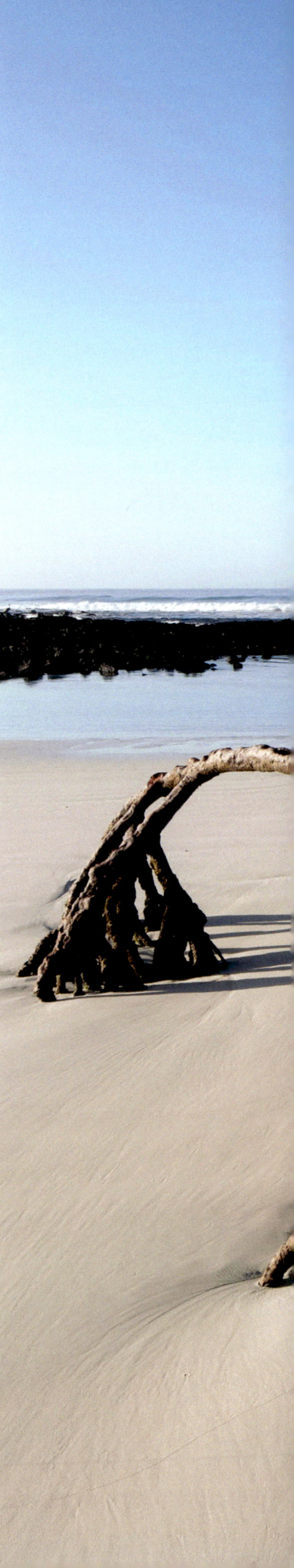

ABOVE AND RIGHT:
Red mangrove
This is the most common
mangrove plant on the islands,
the roots of which are exposed to
the air by low tide. In common
with all mangroves, the aerial
roots of the red mangrove are
able to take in air directly.

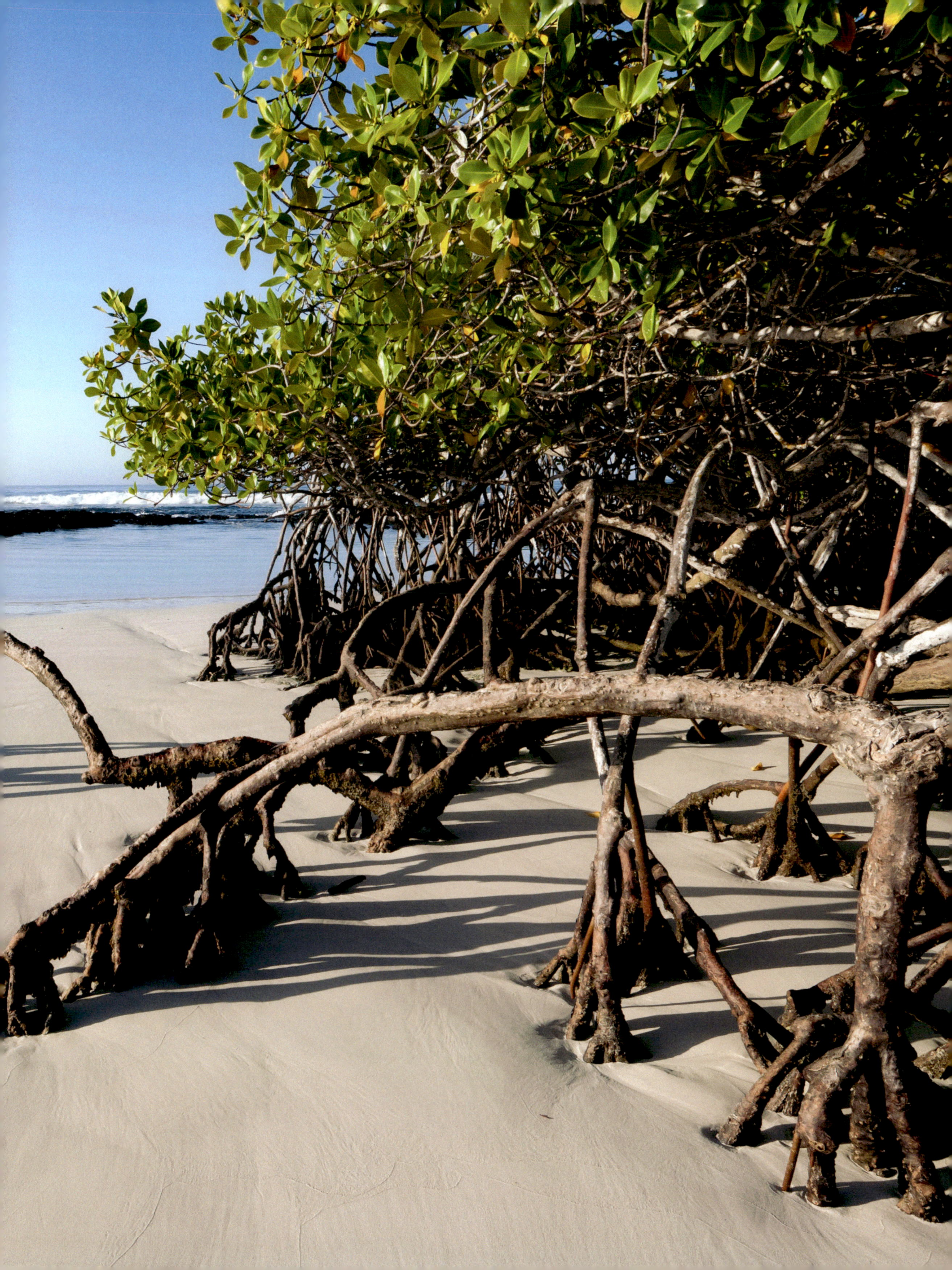

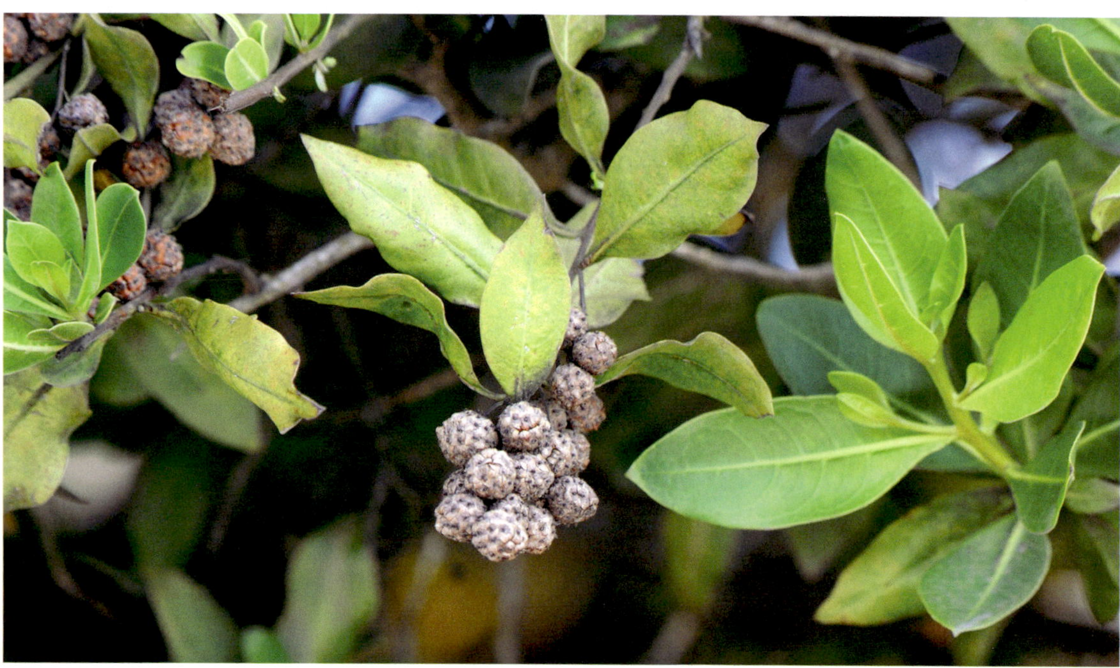

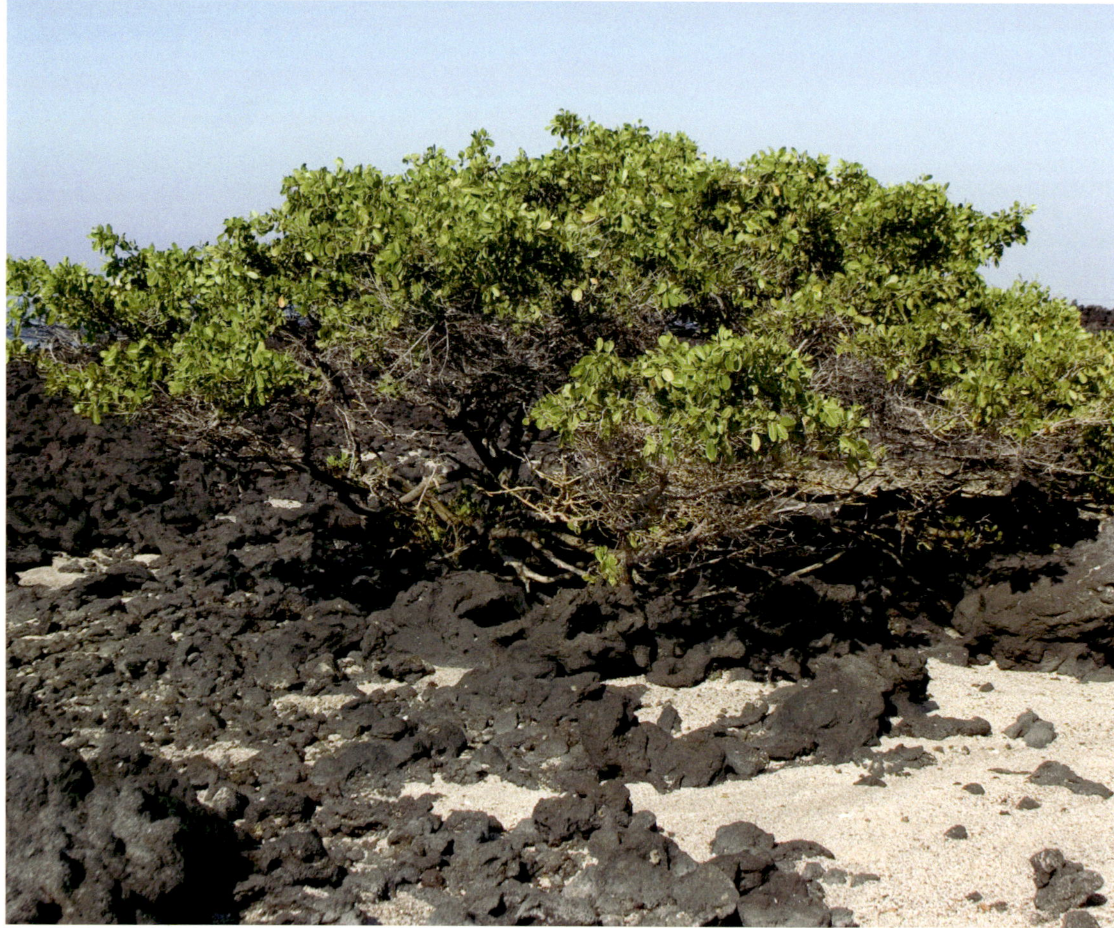

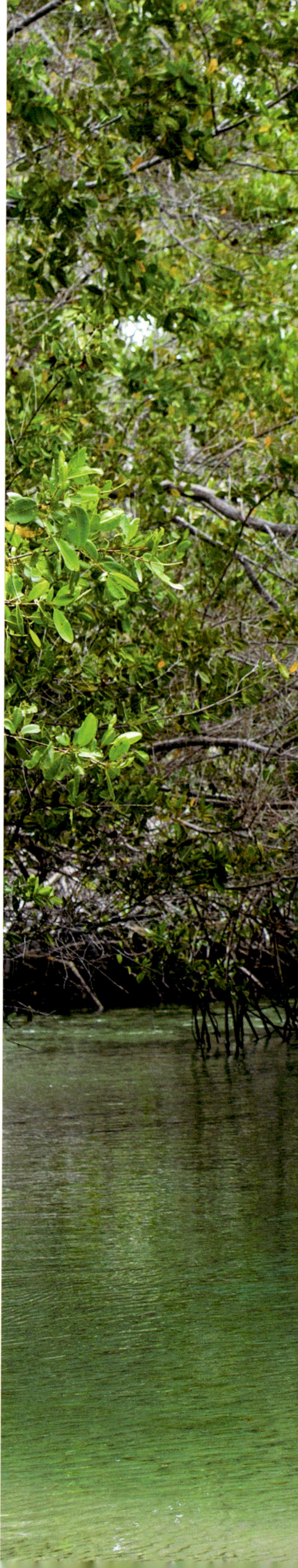

ABOVE TOP:

Button mangrove
This is the least common type of mangrove tree in the Galápagos. It is named after the small rounded flowers.

ABOVE BOTTOM:

White mangrove
Although not quite white, the leaves of this species are paler than the others. This is due in part to the plants expelling unwanted salts through the leaves at night, forming a coating of white crystals.

RIGHT:

Black mangrove
This species forms the largest mangrove forests on the islands. It is named for the darkness – black, almost – of the bark. As well as taking in air from roots above the water, the plants grow pneumatophores, which are snorkel-like pipes that stick up out of the sand.

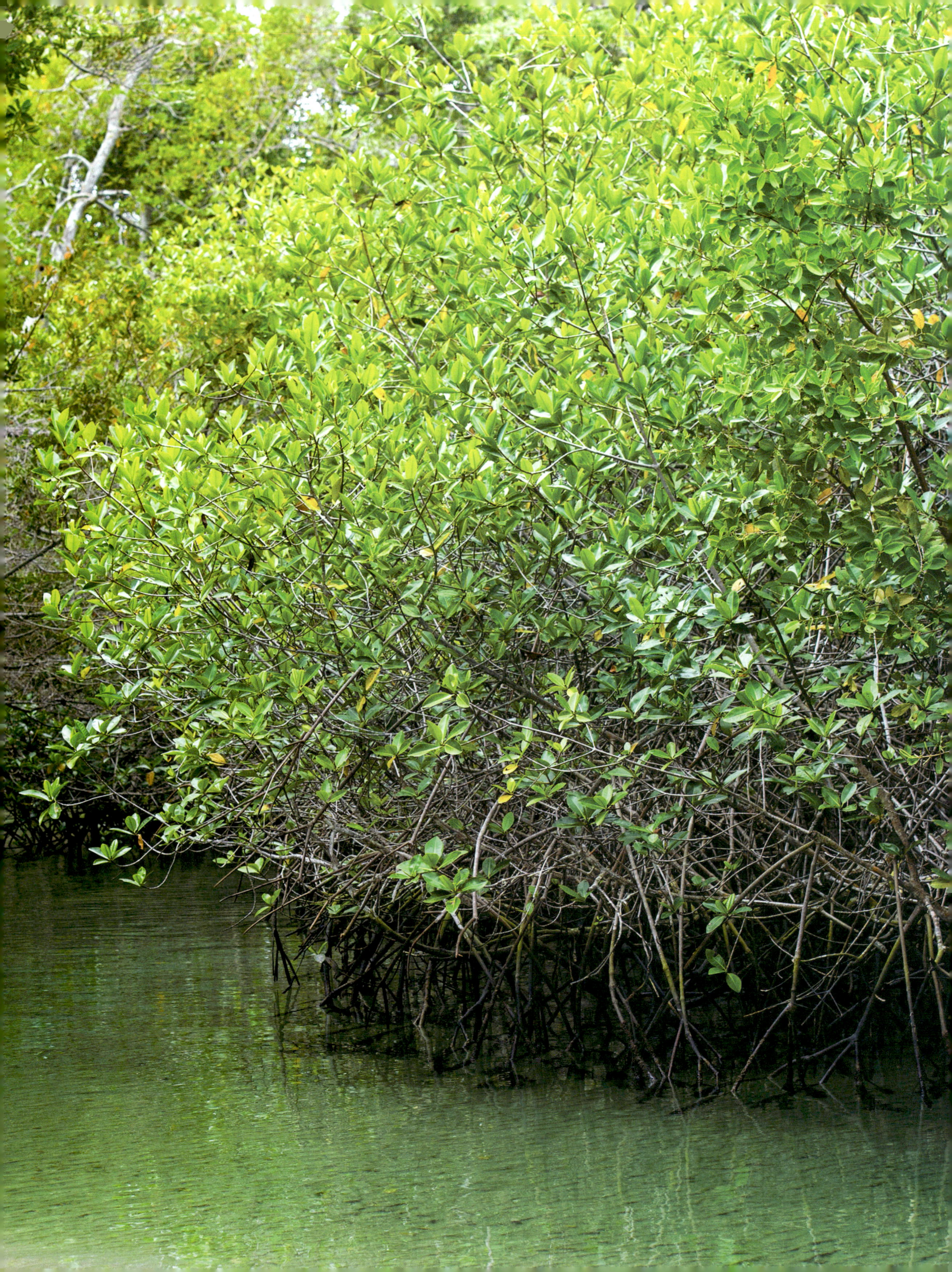

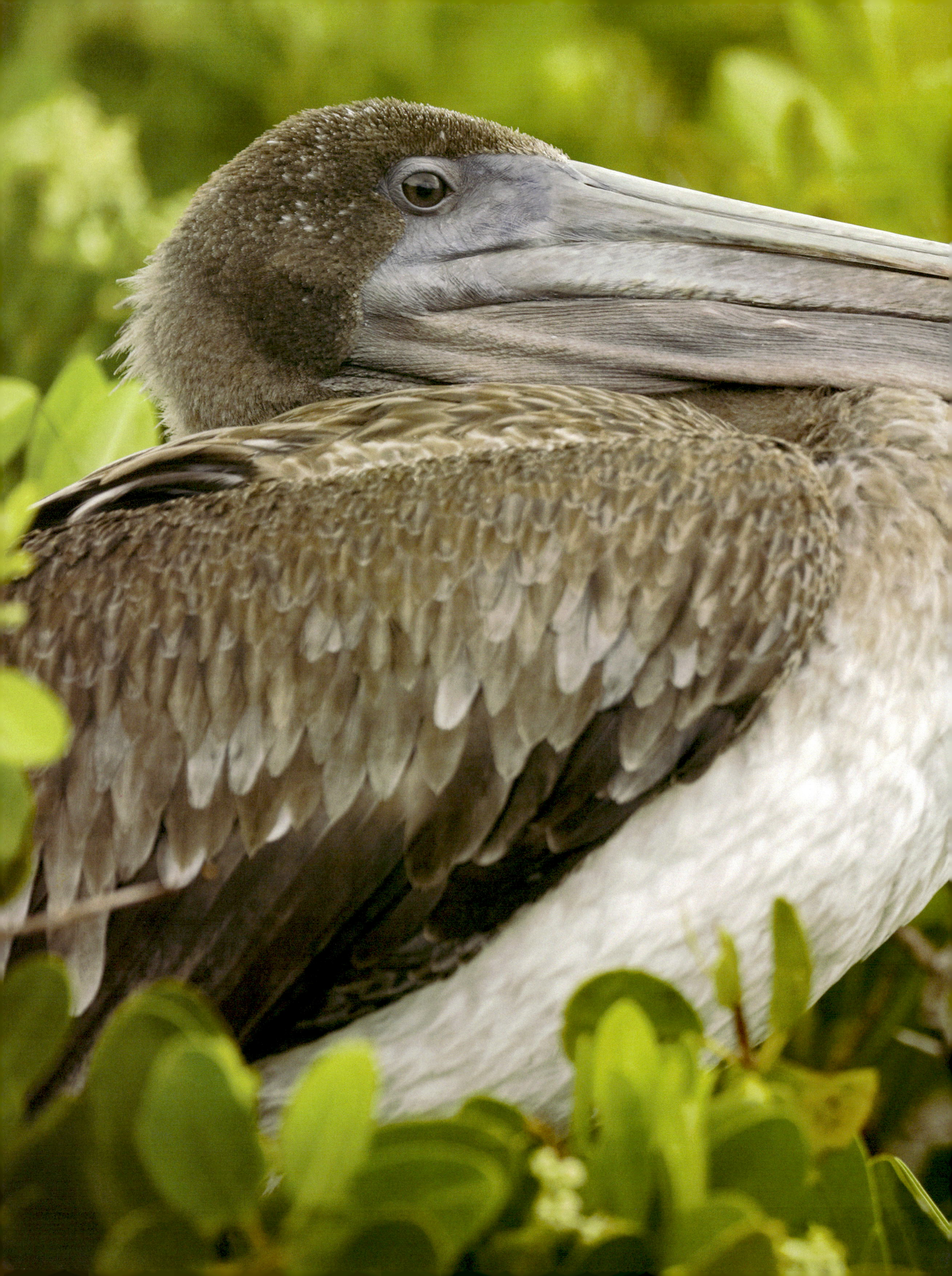

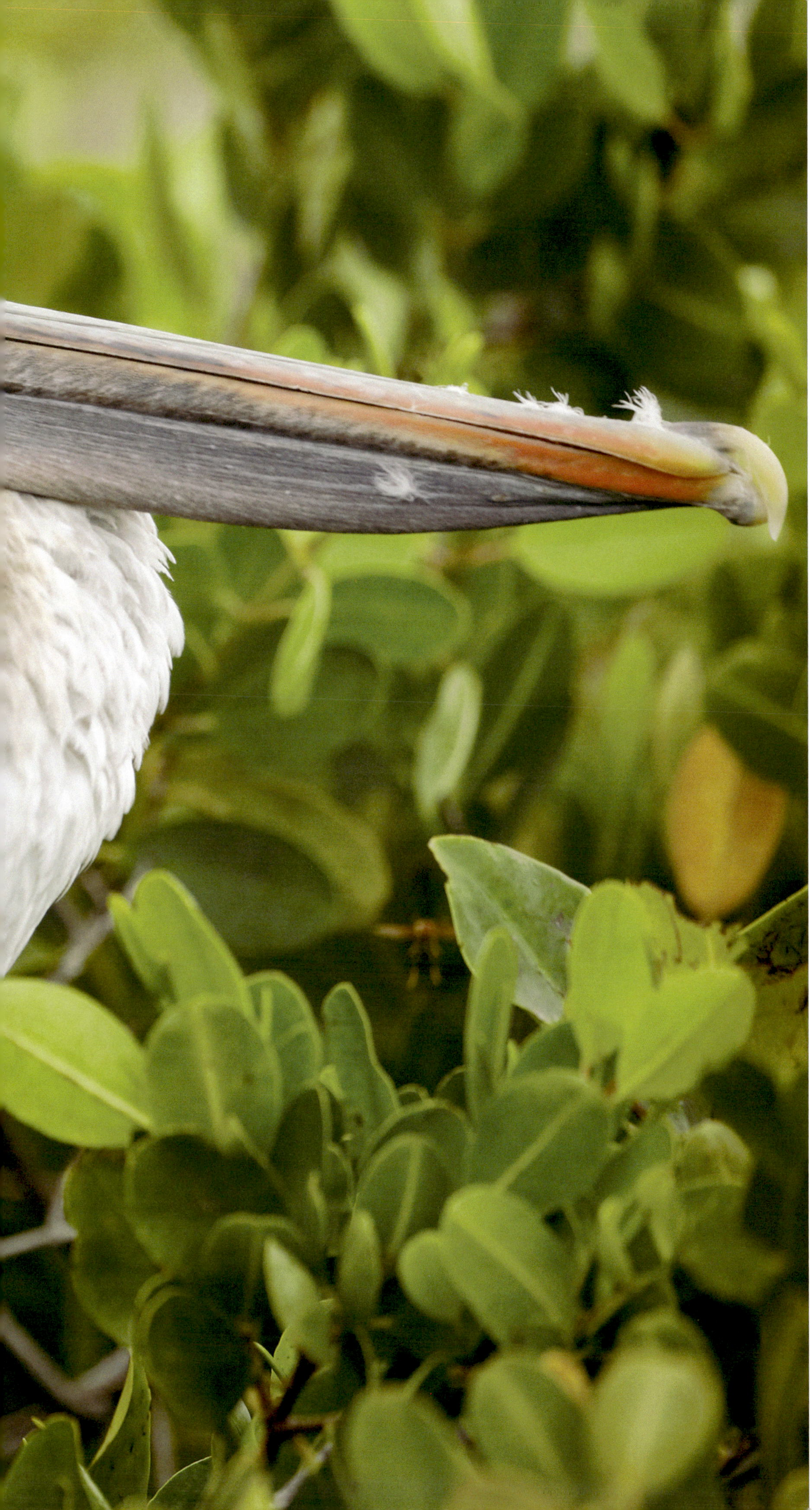

Haven for wildlife
A young brown pelican takes a rest
on a perch in a mangrove tree. The
fringe of forest along the coast
provides safe nursery habitats
for young fish. This ensures that
further out there will be plenty
of older and larger prey for this
ravenous bird.

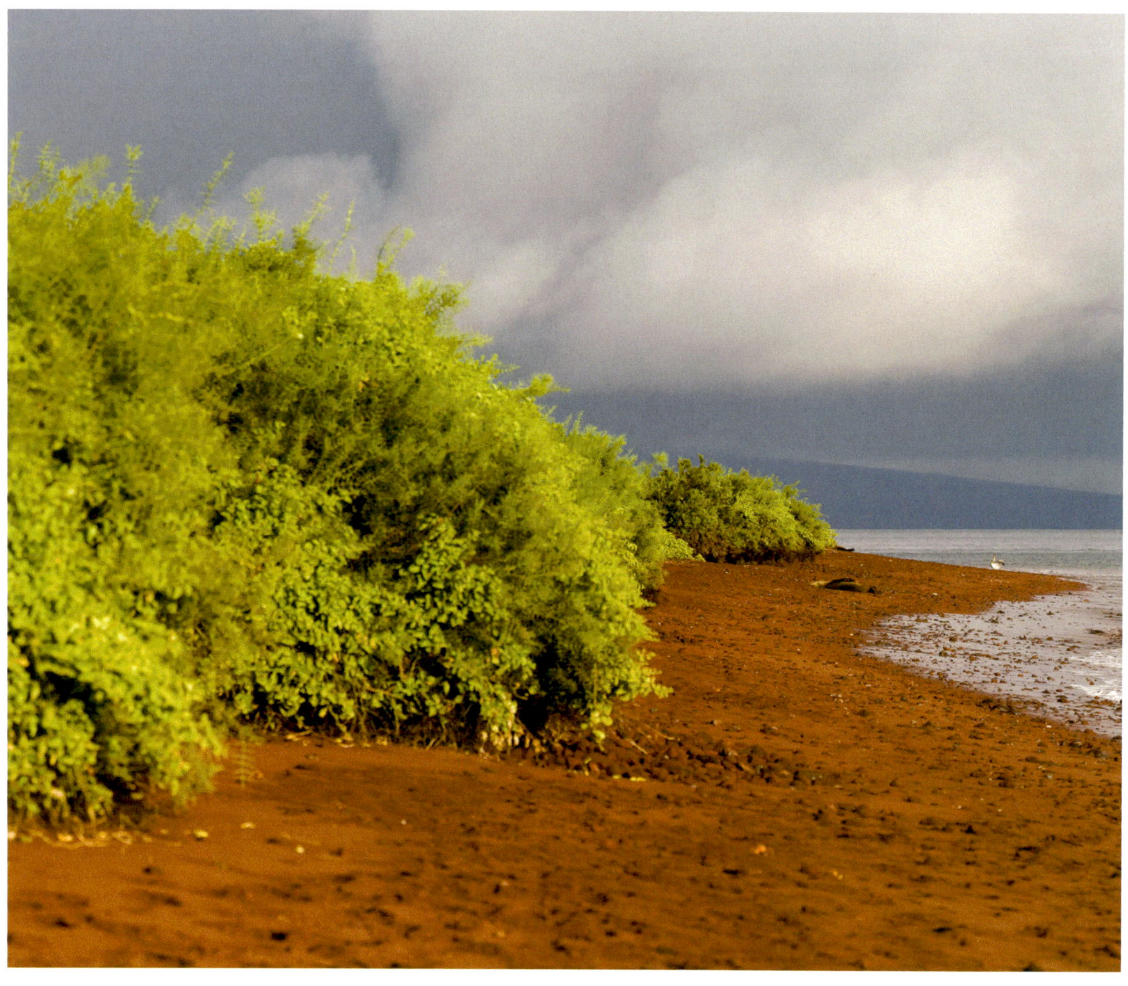

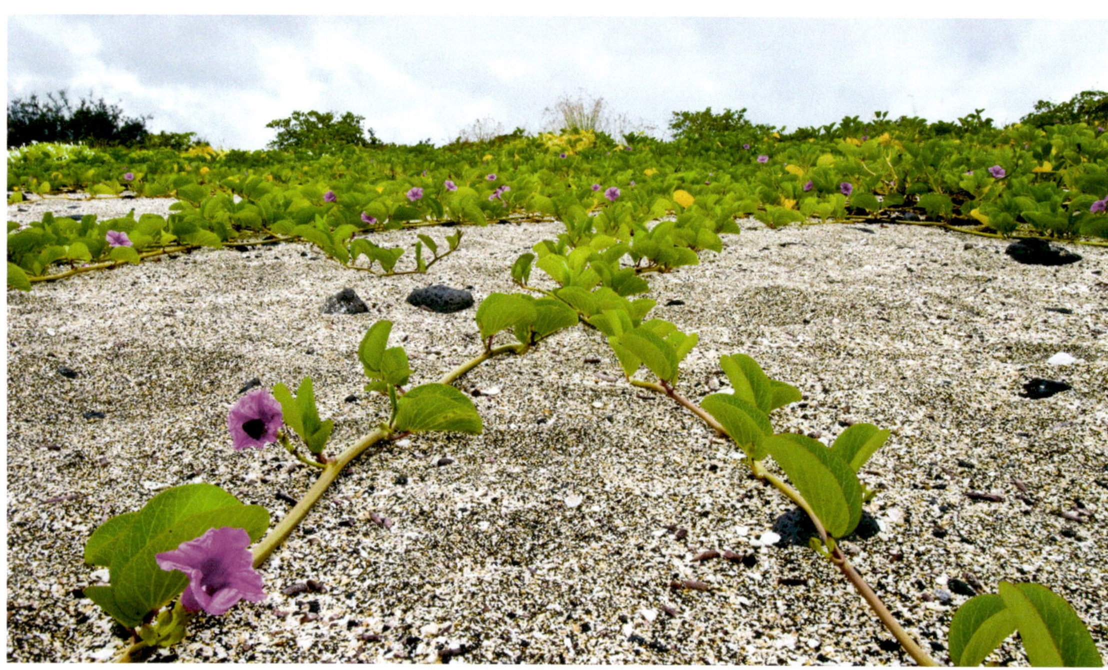

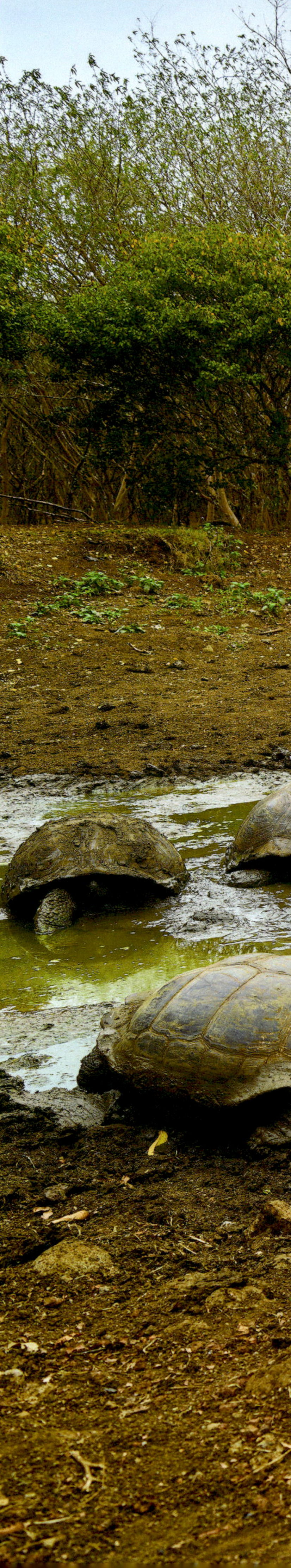

ABOVE TOP:

Saltbush

Much of the land behind beaches on the Galápagos Islands is covered in thickets of this small shrub. It is able to survive in salty conditions that would kill most green plants.

ABOVE BOTTOM:

Beach morning glory

A common sight in coastal areas, this beach plant is unmistakable for its long creepers – often several metres long – that spread over sandy areas.

RIGHT:

Down at the swamp

On the flatter, drier islands, swampy ponds and mud holes form during the dry season. Giant tortoises wallow in the mud to help regulate their body temperature.

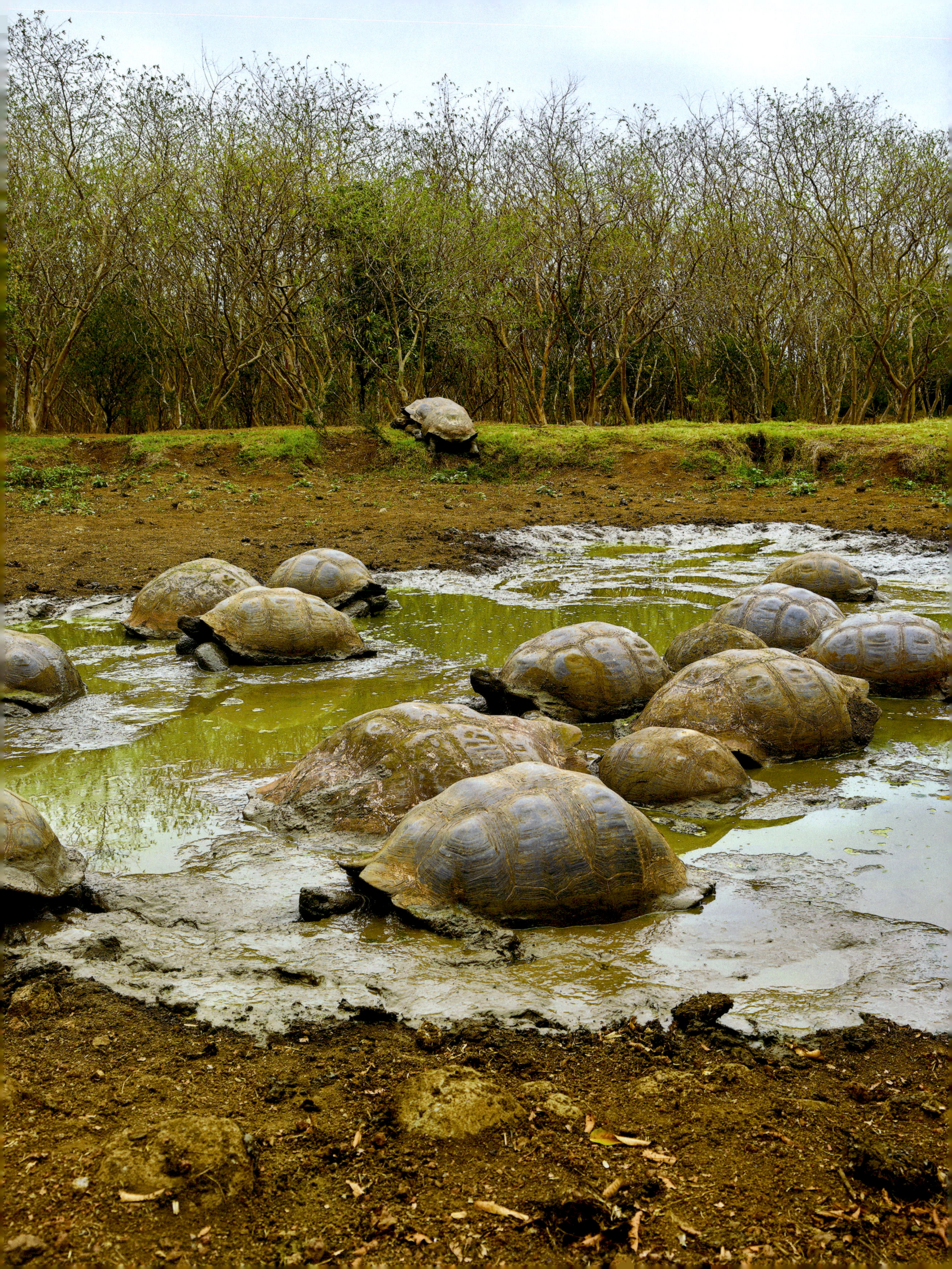

Stay cool
This female giant tortoise is
relaxing in a muddy pool to
stay cool but also as a means of
protection from swarms of biting
insects and ticks.

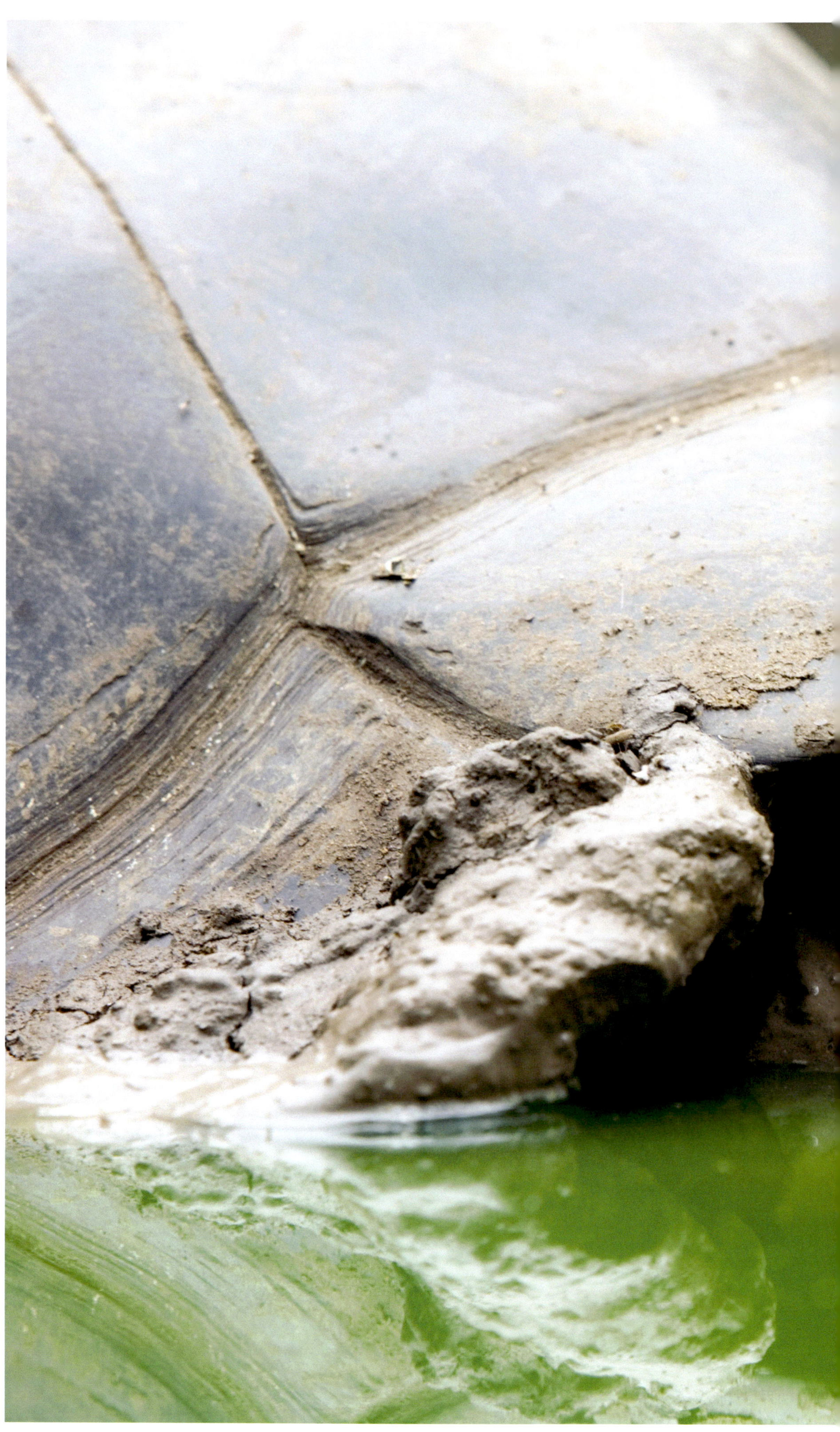

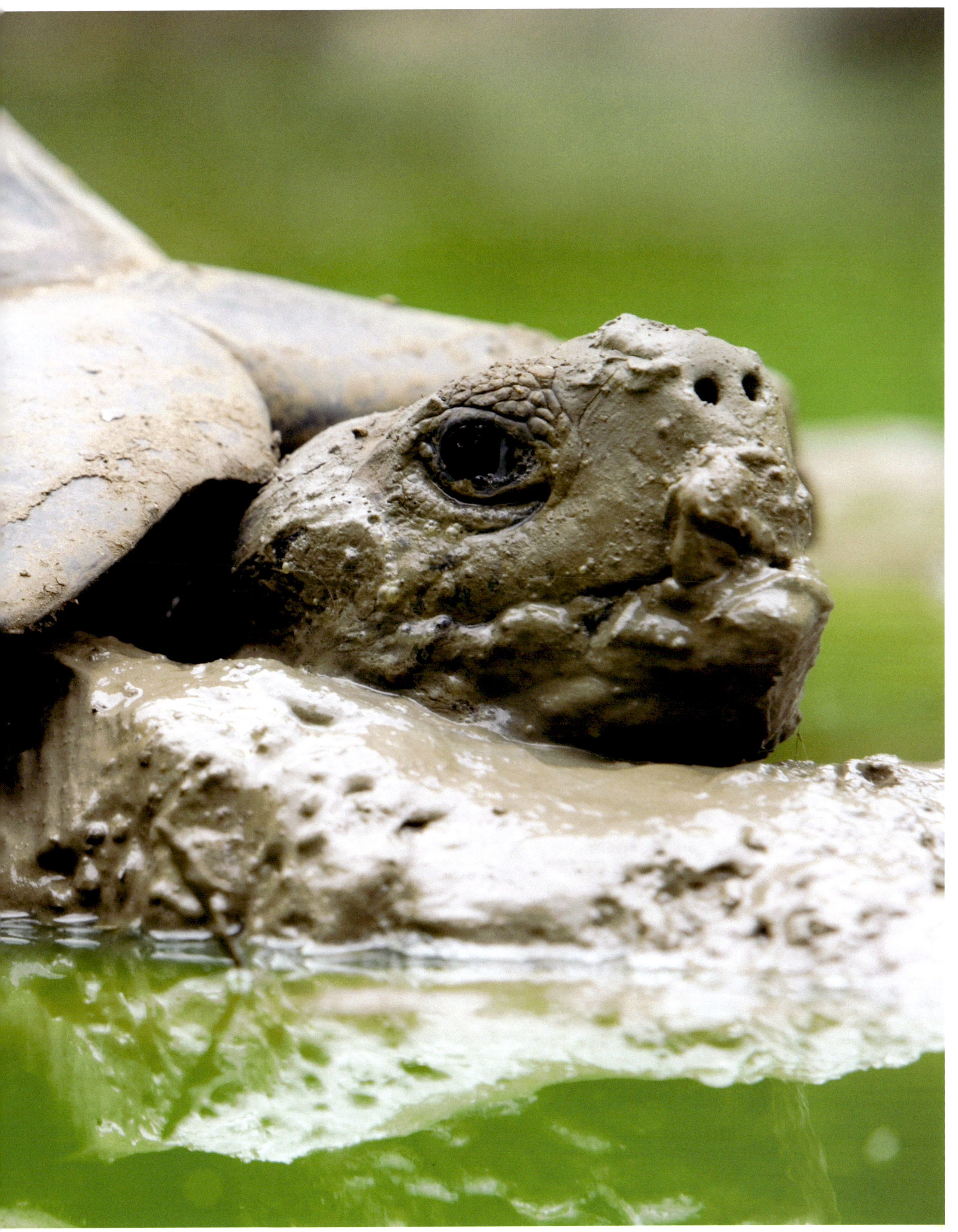

Galápagos cotton
This big shrub – it grows to 3m
(10ft) high – produces a flower
with a dark purple band in the
centre. The seeds are protected
inside a capsule of fluffy fibres.
Finches and other Galápagos
songbirds use the fibres as
nesting materials.

Miconia
This flowering shrub grows in the
humid zone on steeper islands.
It has clusters of small pink
flowers among long, waxy leaves,
which have a pink hue for much
of the year.

Brown zone
The humid highland regions in the
interior of the islands is covered in
a forest of ferns and miconia. The
region is also known as the brown
zone because of the colour of the
mosses and lichens growing on the
taller plants.

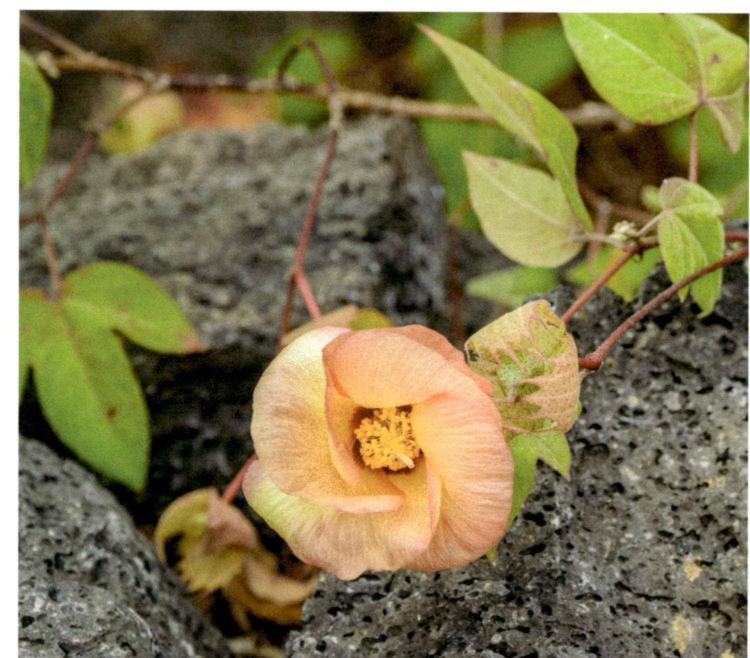

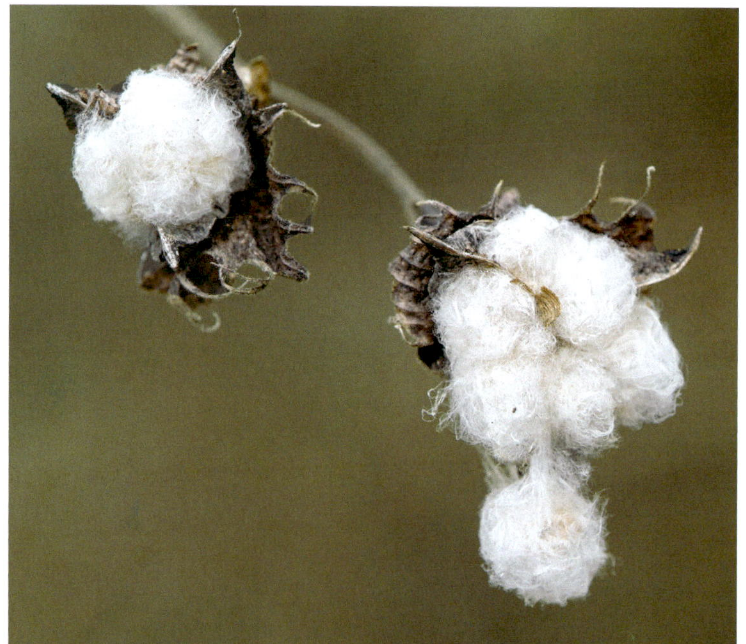

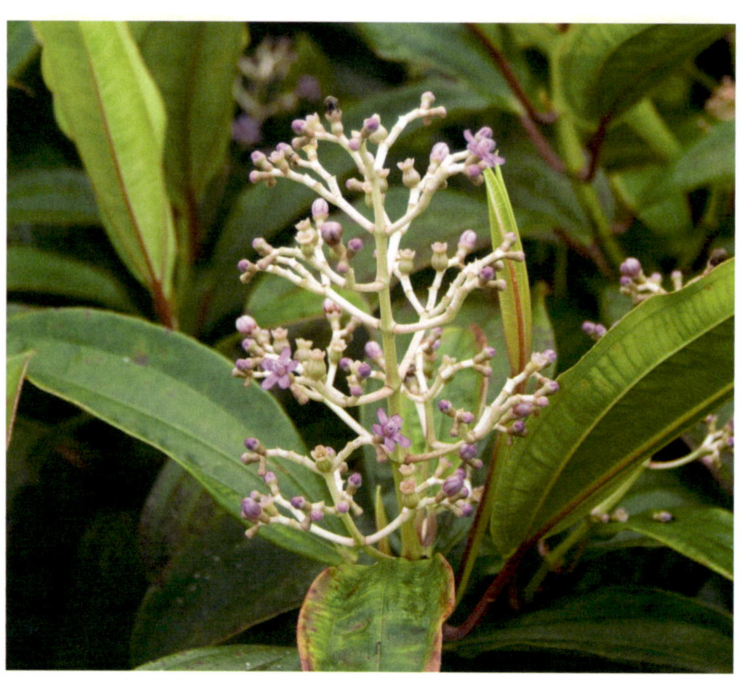

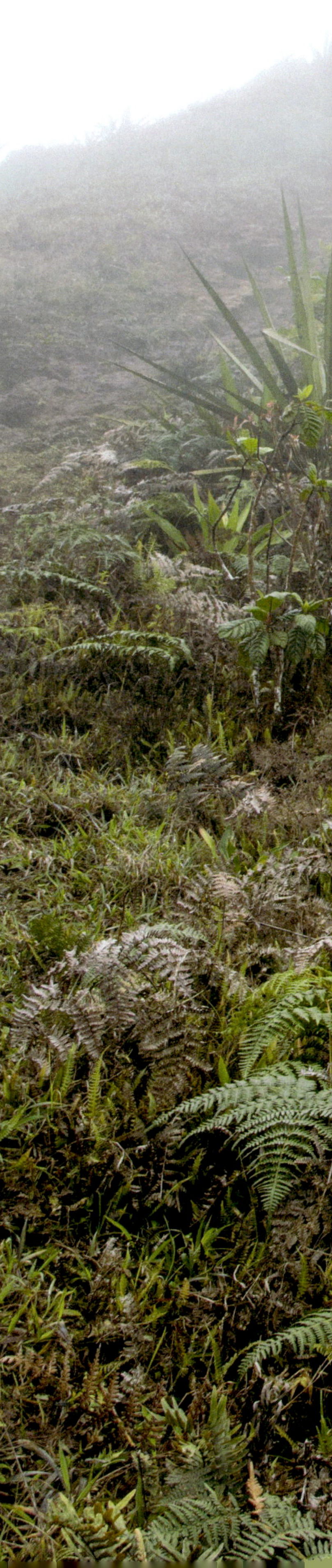

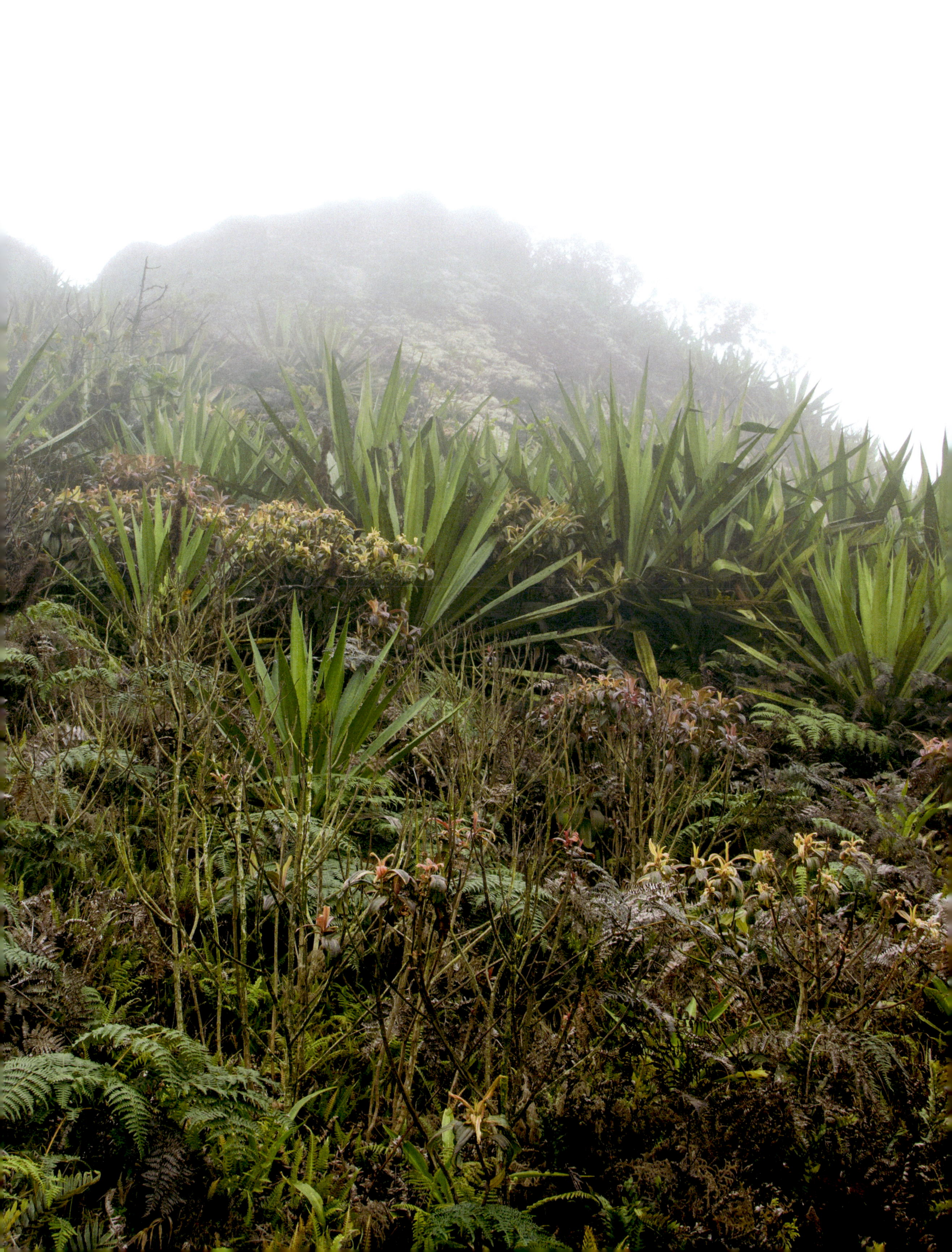

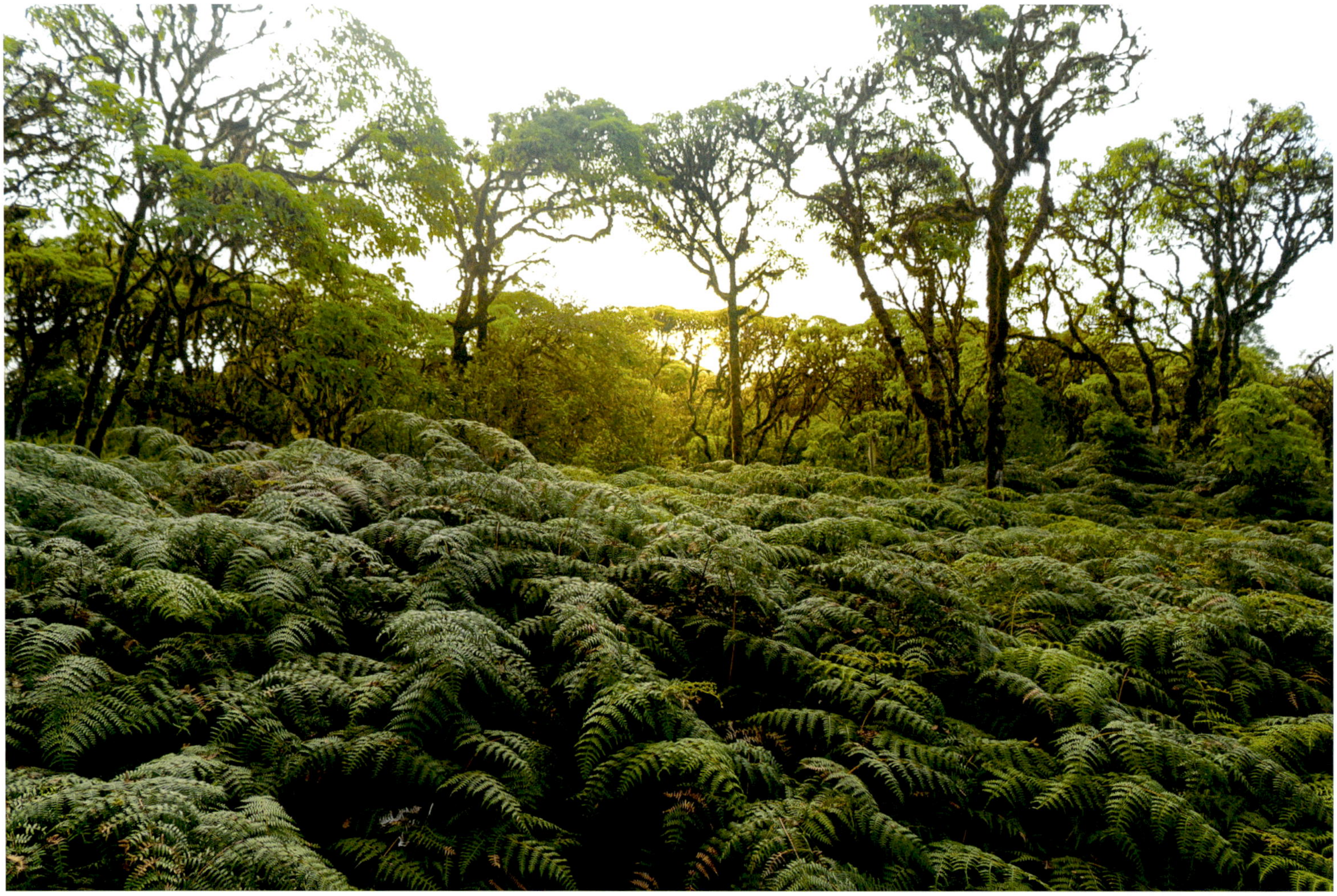

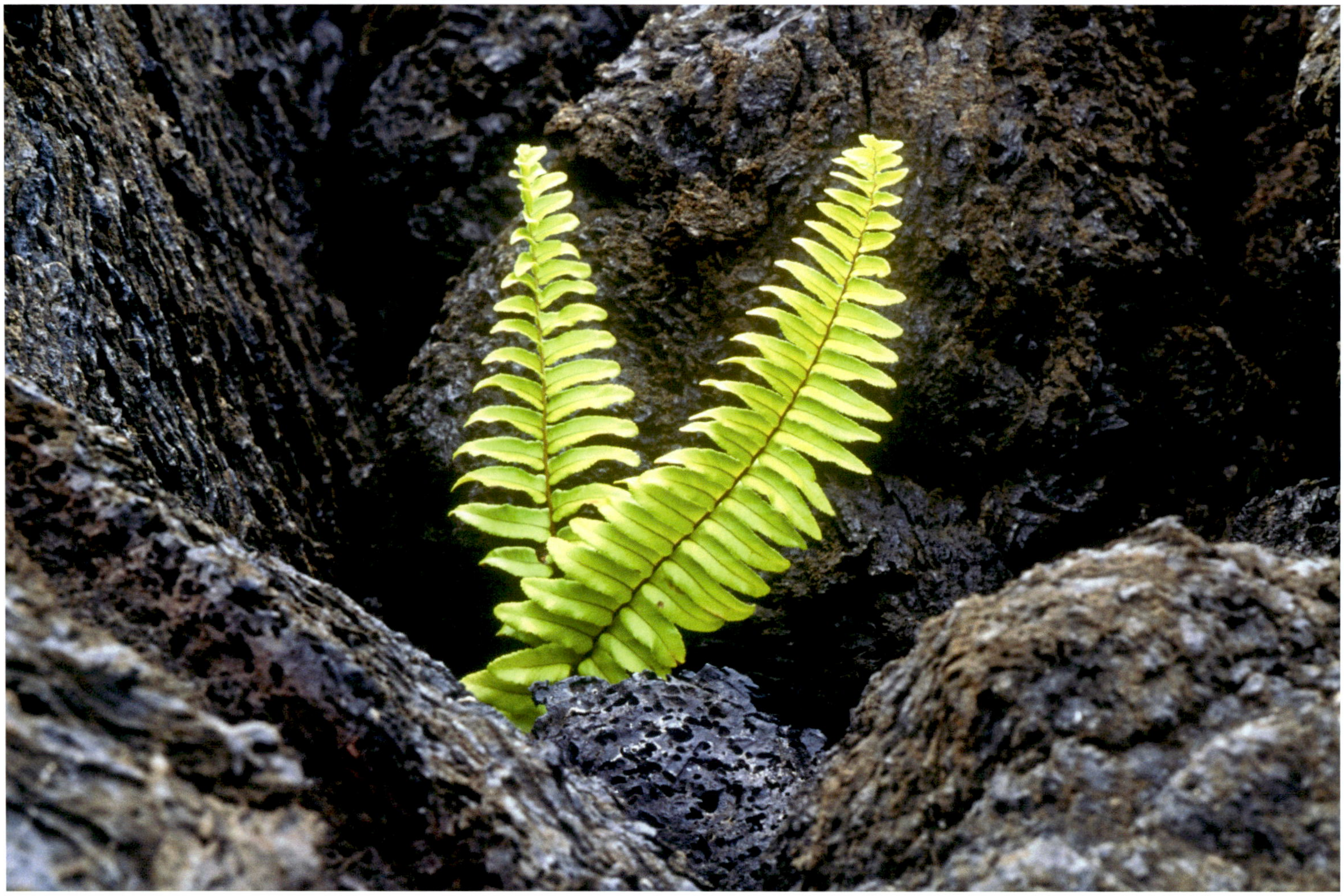

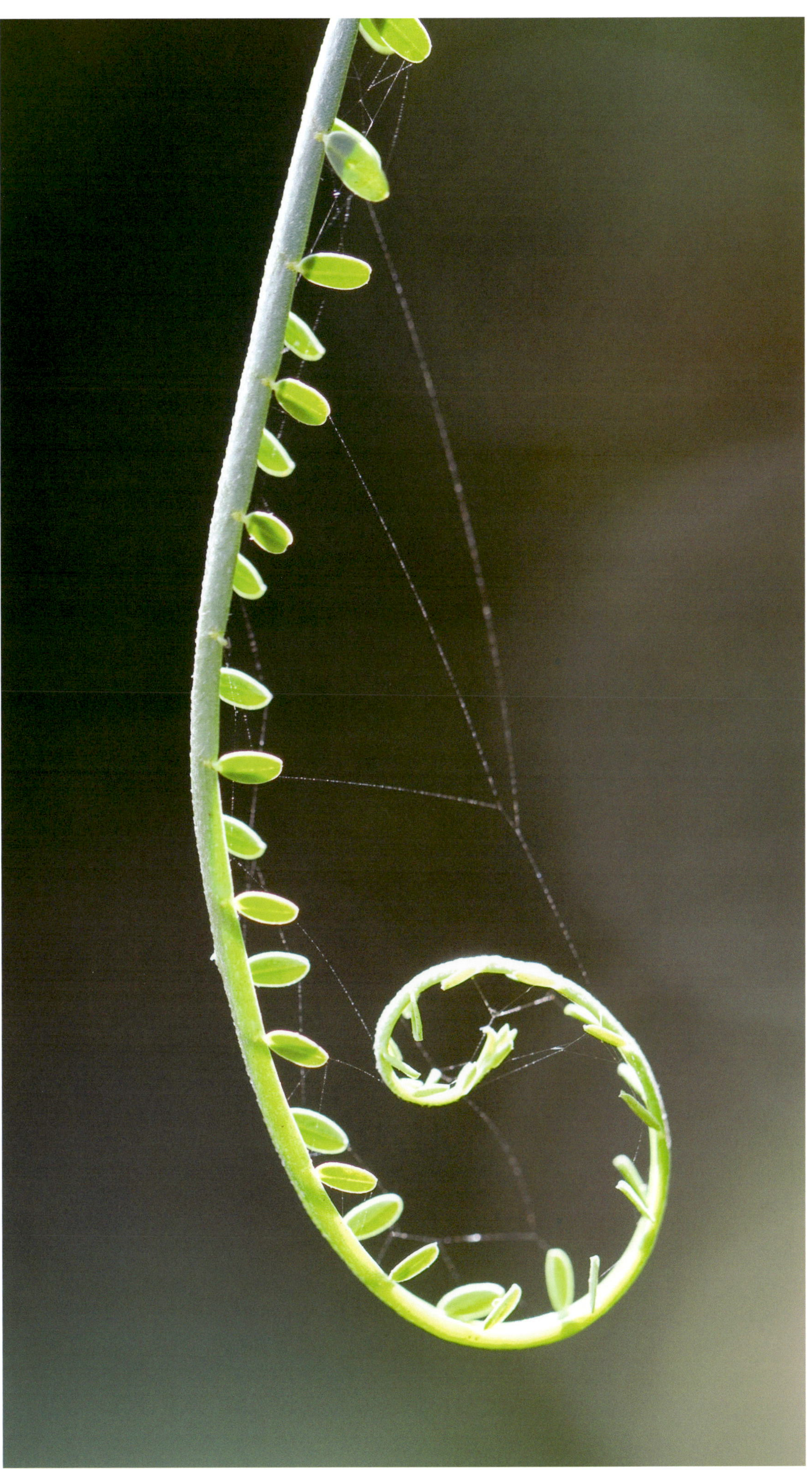

OPPOSITE TOP:
Sunset over Scalesia
Trees are built to capture sunlight,
shrouding smaller rival plants
in shade. The tallest trees in the
Galápagos are Scalesia species, a
giant, woody relative of the daisy.

OPPOSITE BOTTOM:
Ladder fern
Plants on the Galápagos are
prepared to grow in lifeless land
made empty by volcanic eruptions.
This ladder fern is one of the
pioneer species that is first to
arrive on the islands.

LEFT:
Fern coil
A new frond uncoils as the fern
grows. Ferns are a common feature
of the Galápagos Islands. They
dominate in lush highland regions,
often taking over above the
miconia line. They are also able
to find living space on the walls
of collapsed craters.

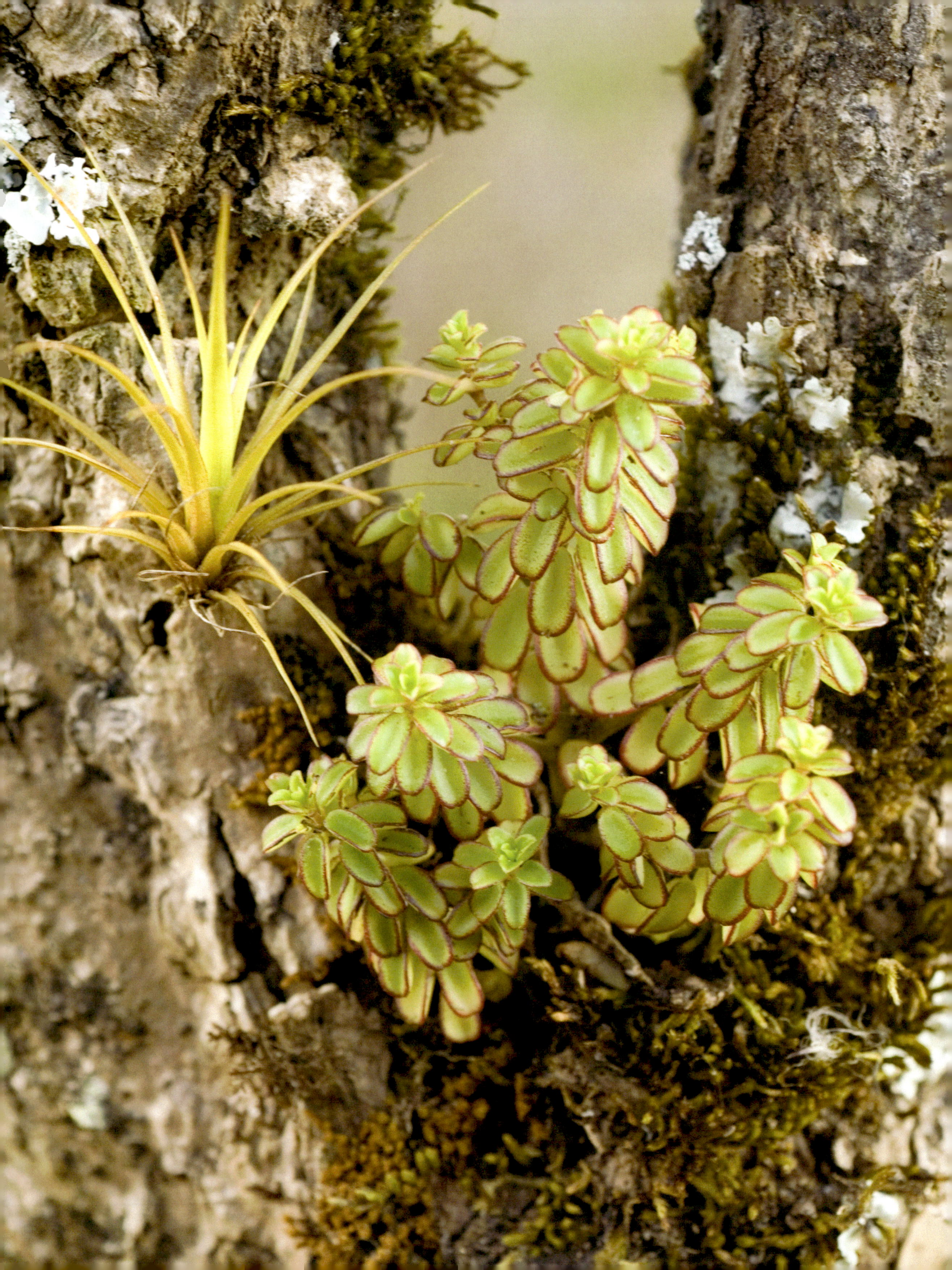

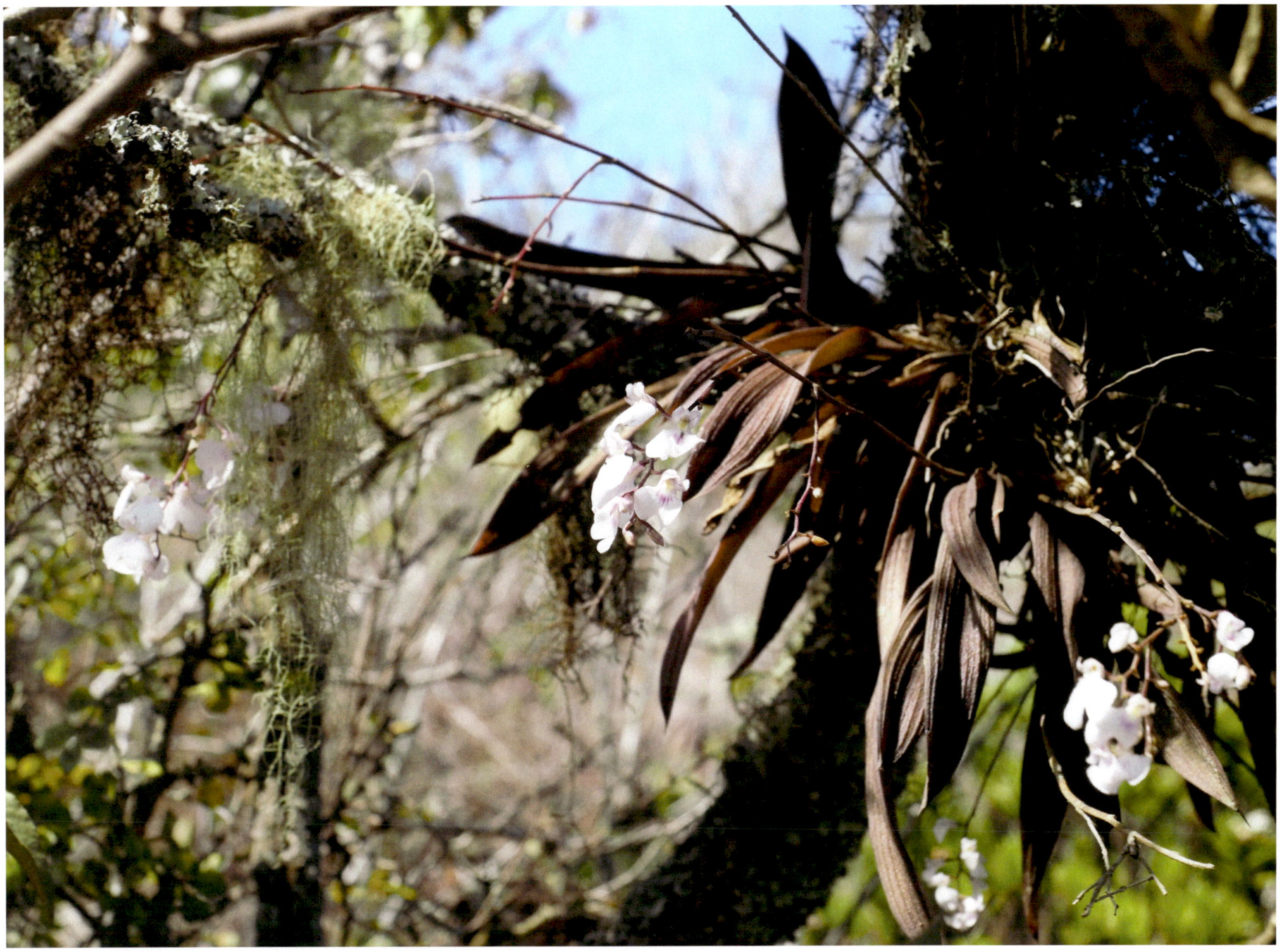

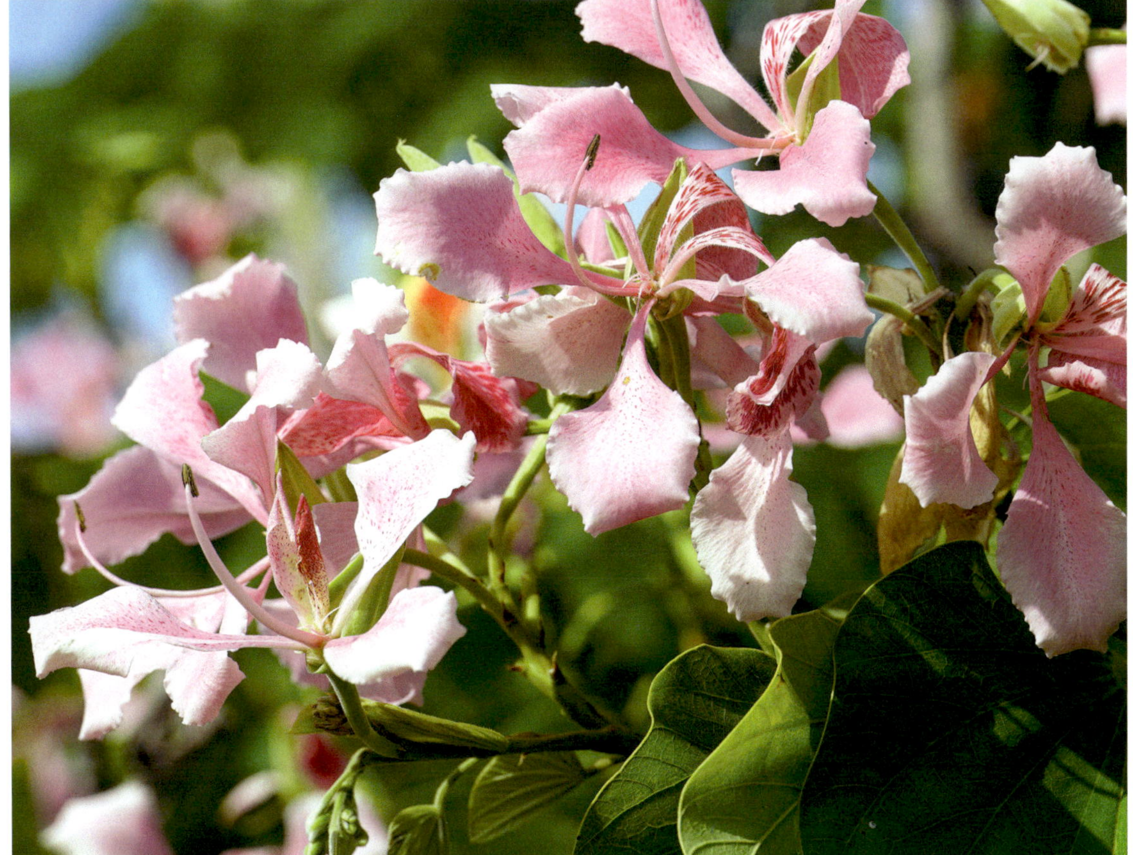

Galápagos peperomia
With succulent spoon-shaped leaves fringed in dark red, this endemic pepper species is another Galápagos epiphyte.

ABOVE:

Galápagos orchid
A naturally trailing epiphyte (a plant that grows on larger plants), this is the endemic orchid of the Galápagos. The white flowers droop from the end of a spray of stems. The seeds are almost microscopically small.

LEFT:

Pink bauhinia
This orchid tree is considered a weed in the Galápagos. It was originally from Madagascar but has spread widely to other tropical islands with dry forests.

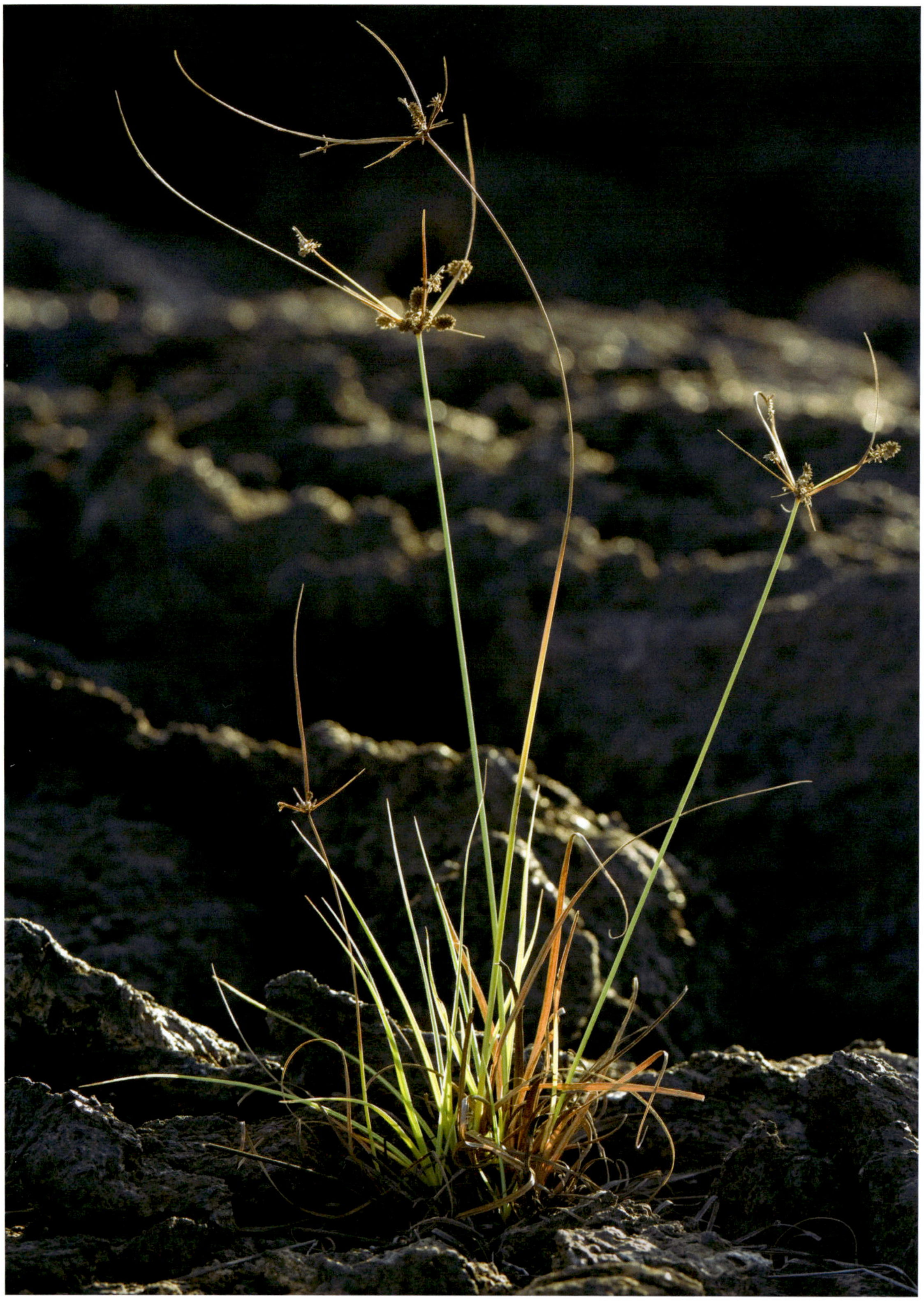

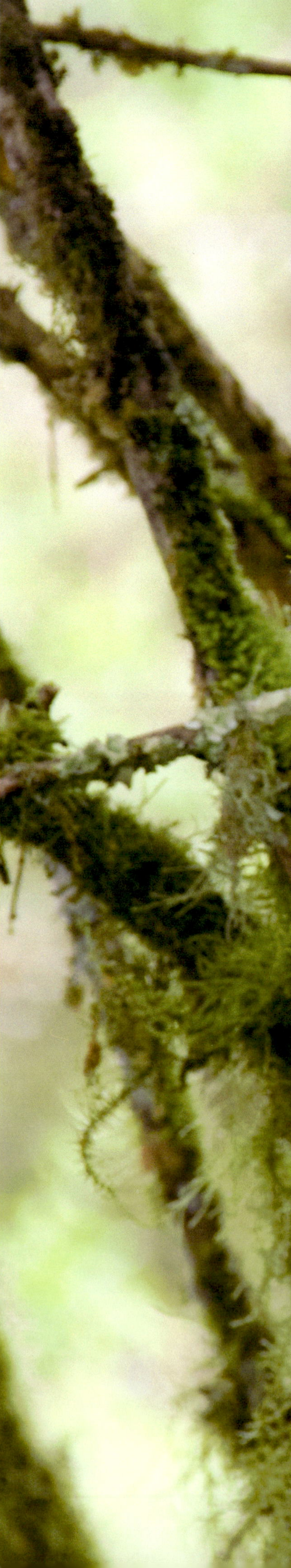

Galápagos sedge

Looking rather like grass, this sedge has a distinctive triangular stem. The endemic sedge can be found in most parts of the islands but is most obvious in the wet pampas zone at the very highest elevations.

Highland lichen

A lichen is an intriguing symbiosis of algae and fungus. The fungus provides the body while the algae live inside, photosynthesizing to create the food that both symbionts need. Lichen are slow growing and can survive cold and dry conditions. The Galápagos lichens get their moisture from the mist, known locally as *garúa*, that often clothes higher slopes.

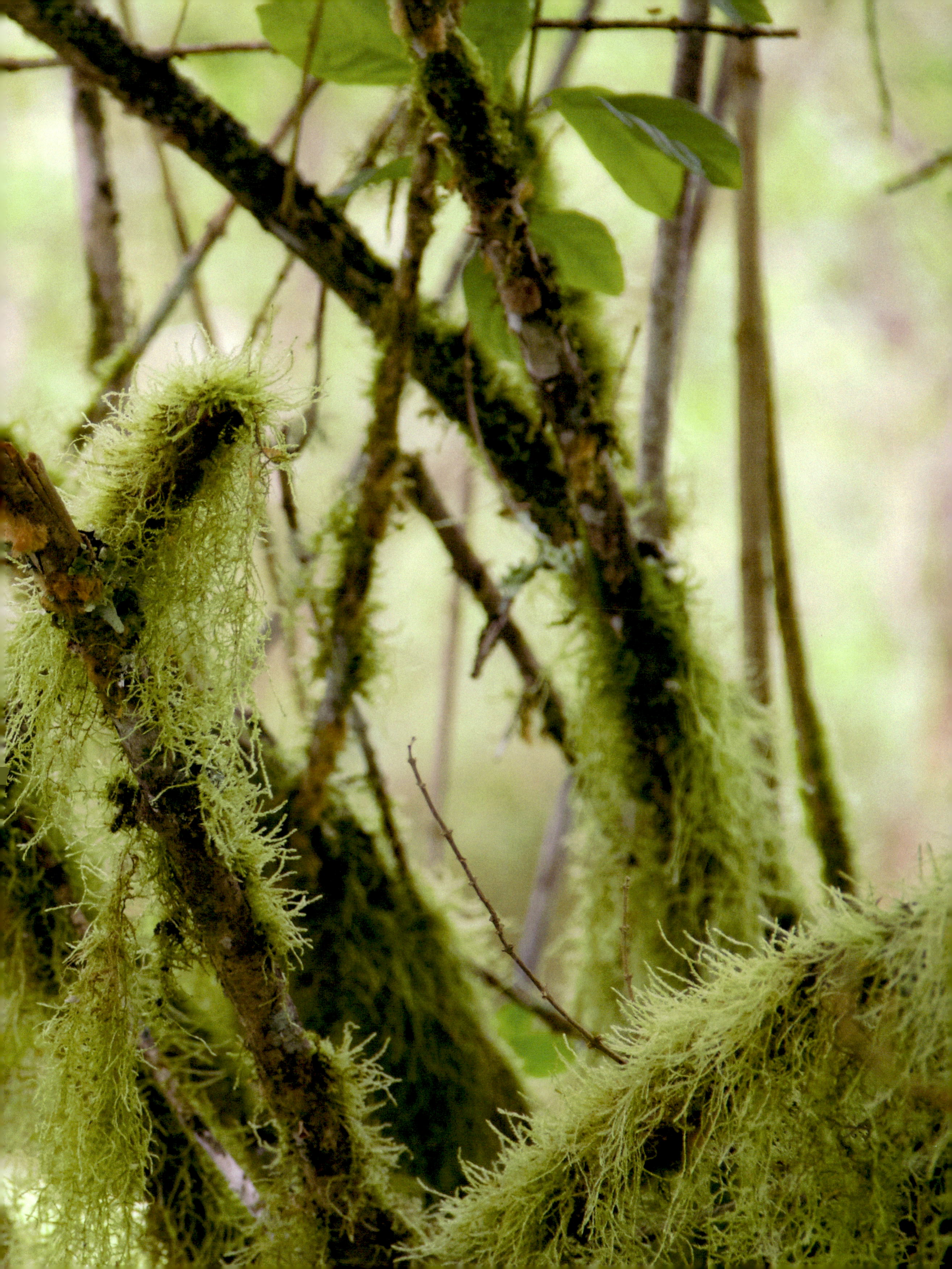

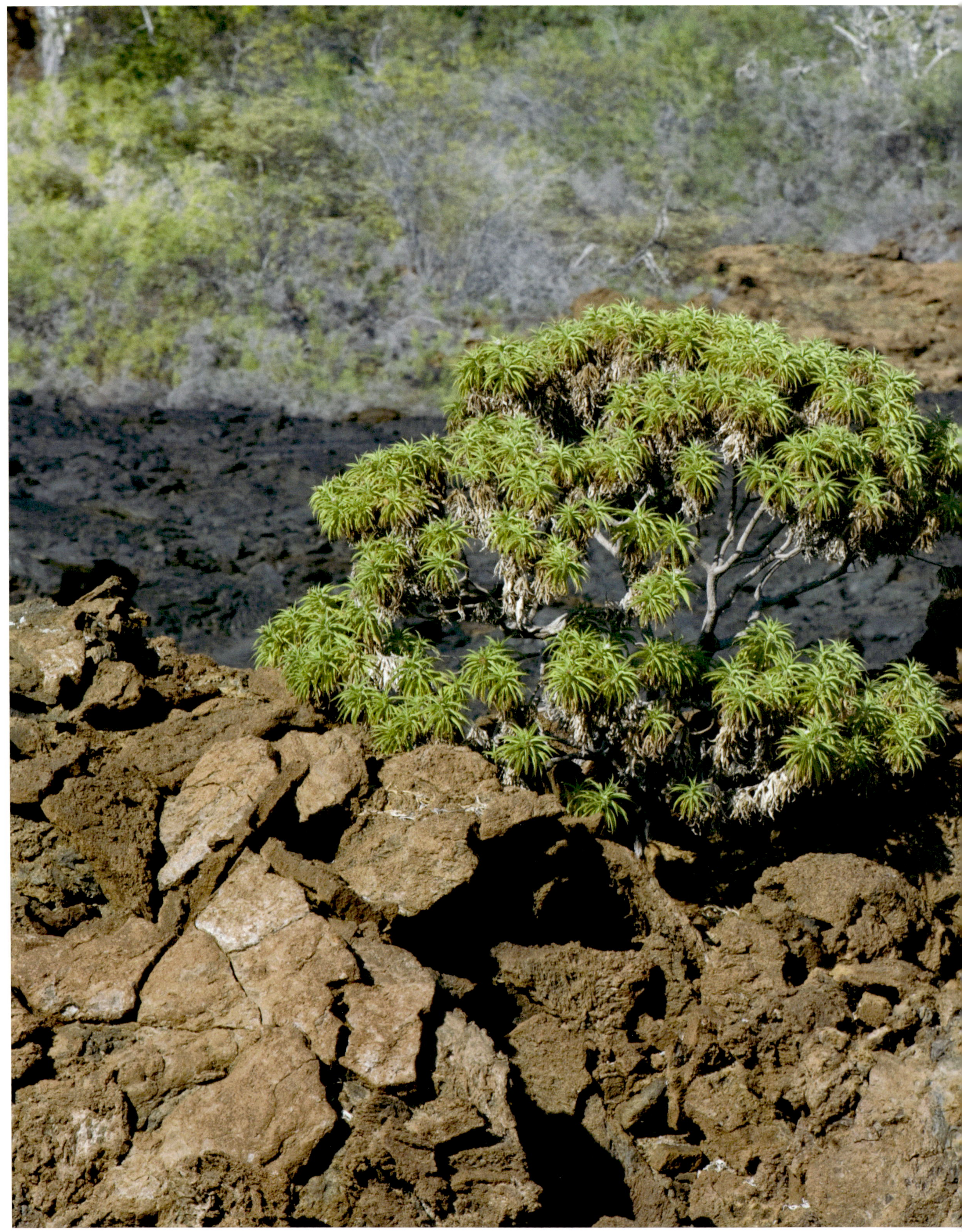

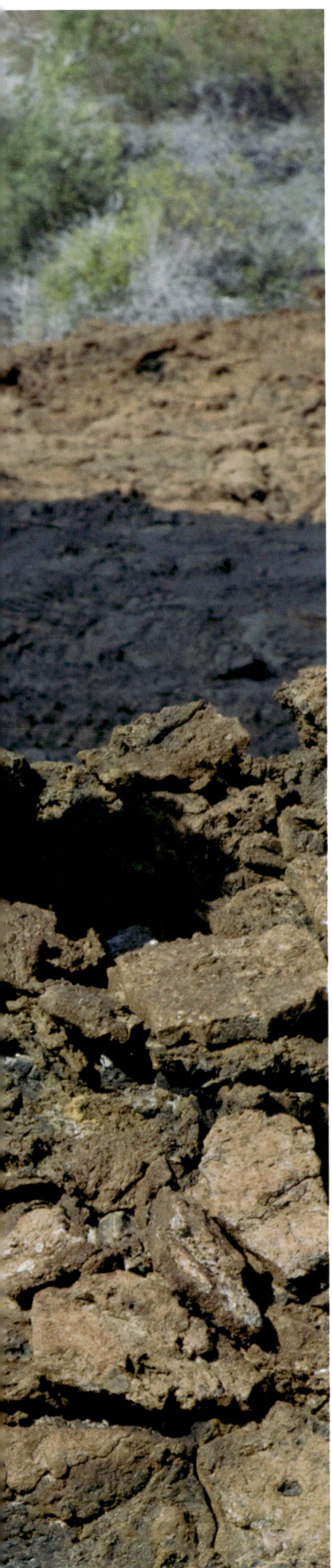

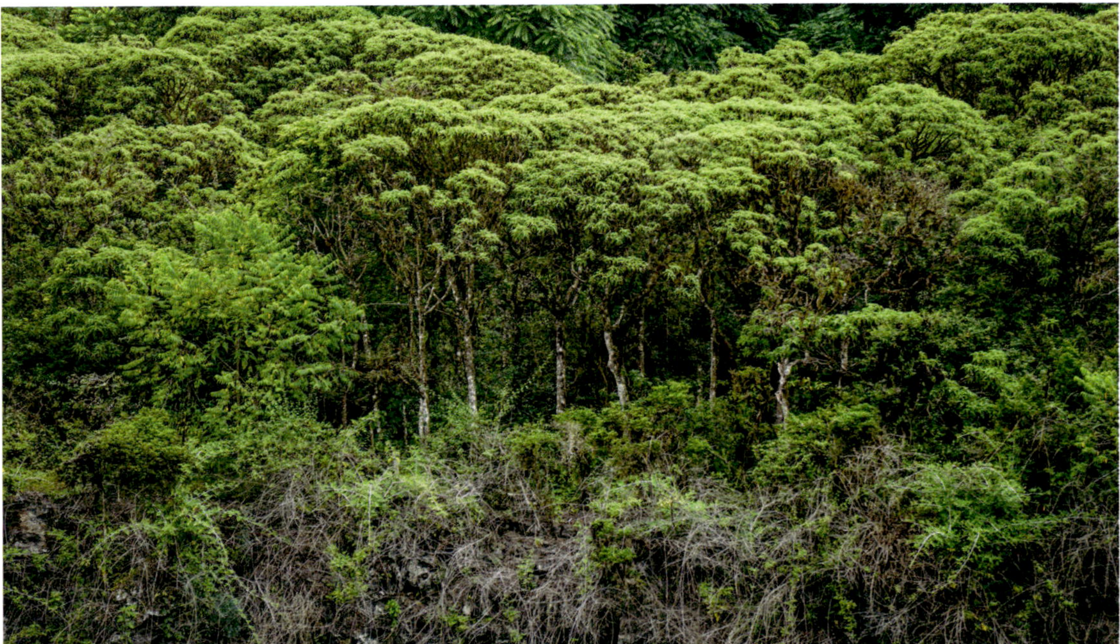

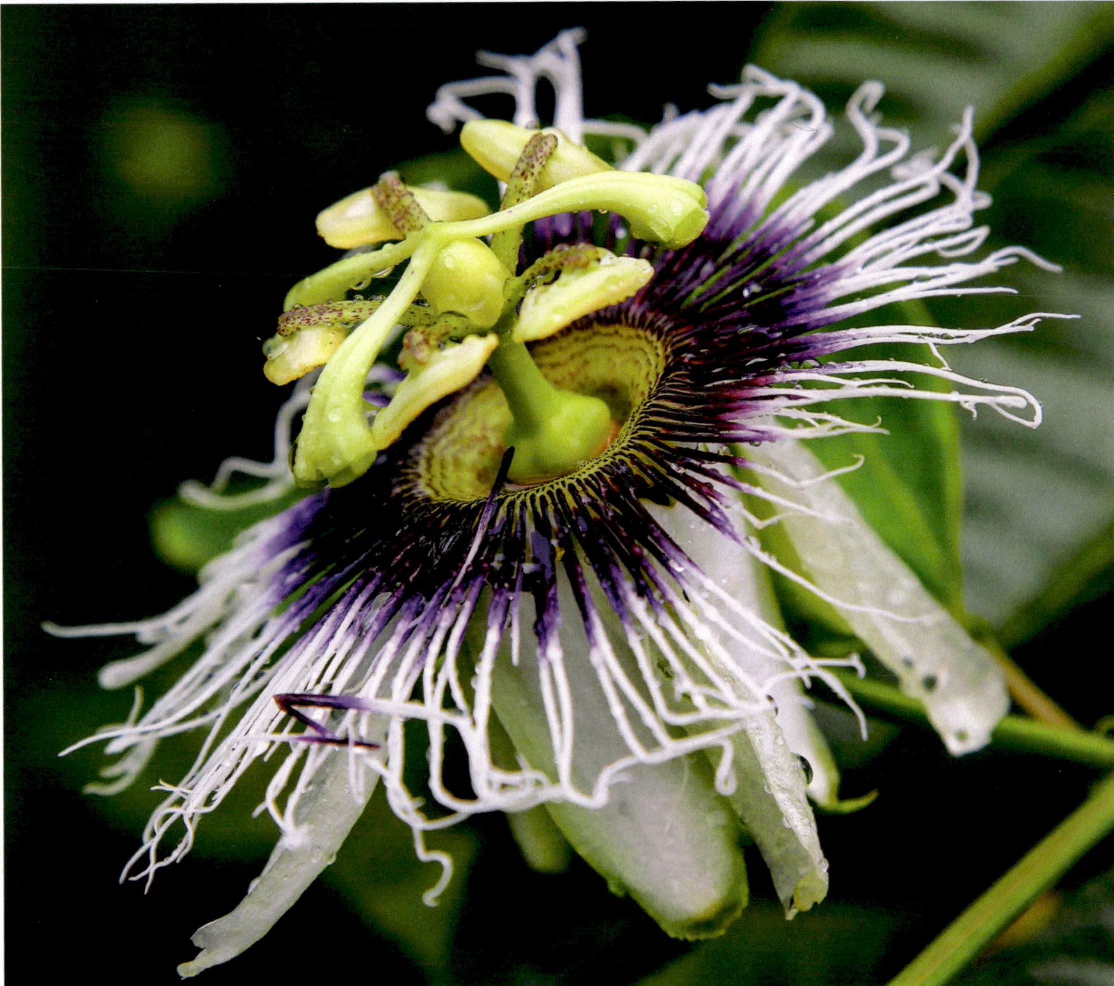

Scalesia

A young Scalesia tree grows on a lava field at Sullivan Bay on Santiago Island.

Scalesia forest

The forests on the Galápagos Islands grow fastest during cool years with more rain. During the hotter, drier weather of El Niño periods the taller trees die back, and younger saplings lurking on the forest floor race up to the light to take their place.

Invasive species

Passionflower is a damaging and invasive species on the Galápagos. Scientists heading for remote islands are not allowed to eat passion fruits or other, non-native fruits for a few days before travelling in case they leave seeds there in their faeces.

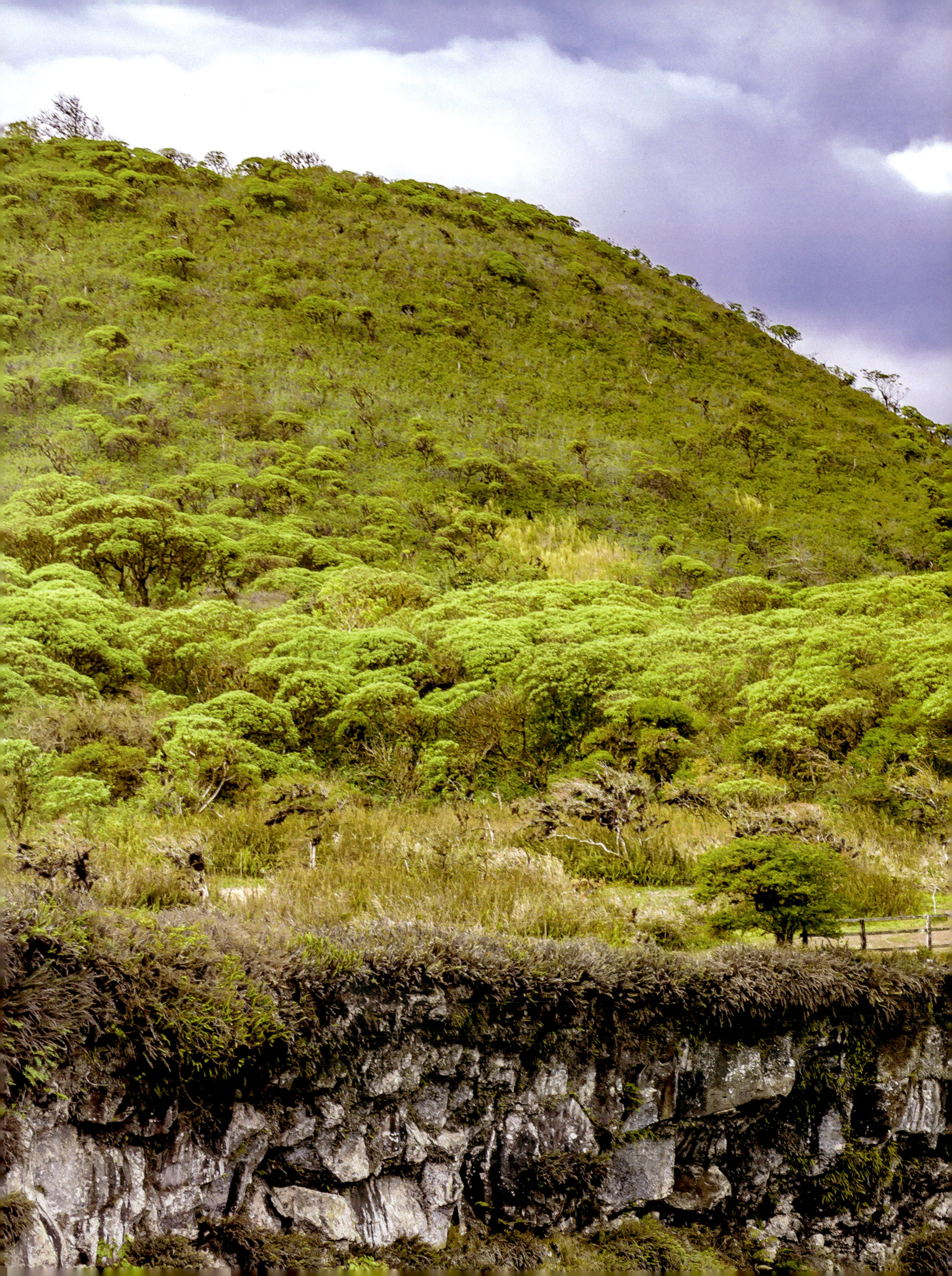

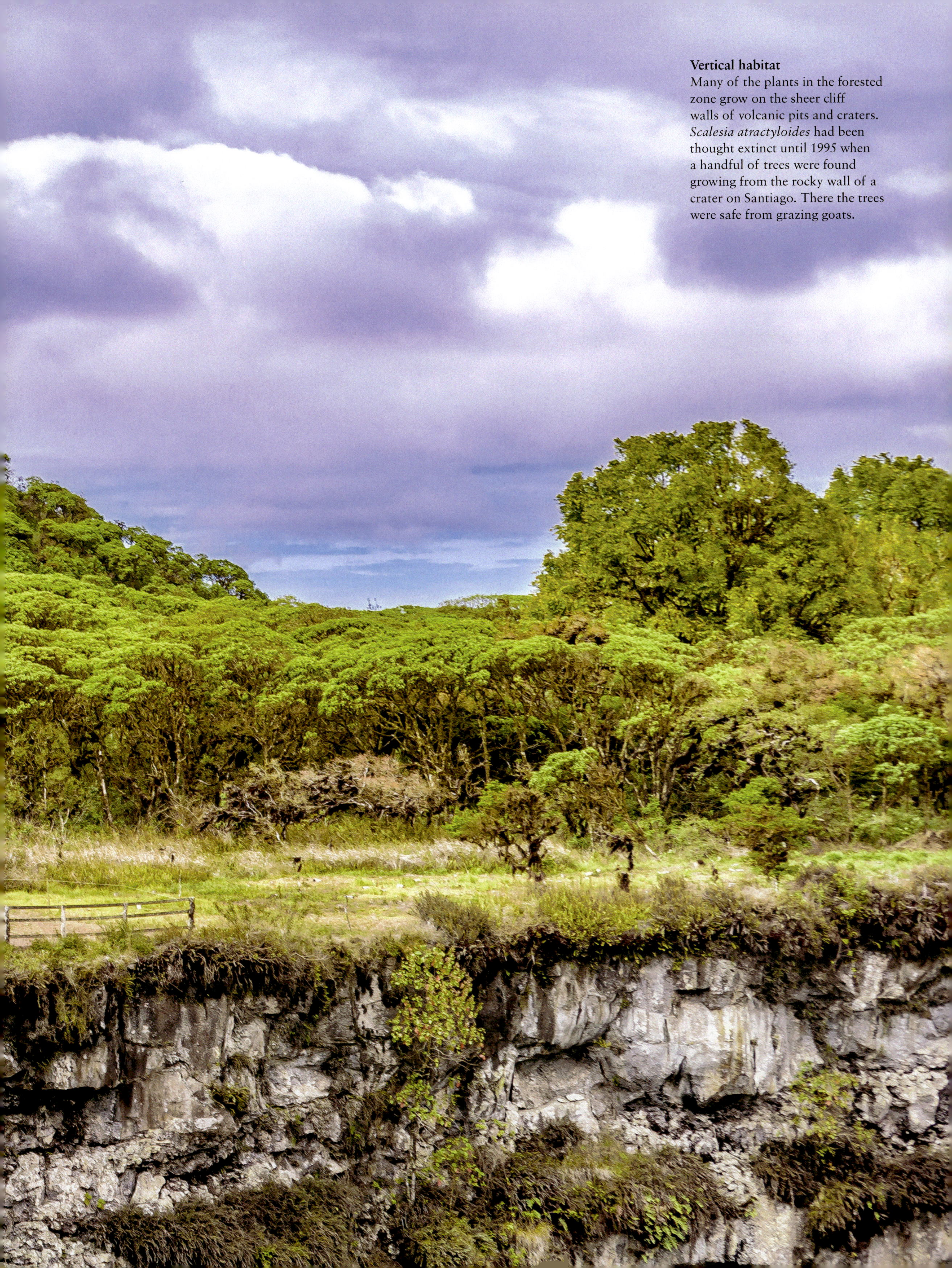

Vertical habitat
Many of the plants in the forested zone grow on the sheer cliff walls of volcanic pits and craters. *Scalesia atractyloides* had been thought extinct until 1995 when a handful of trees were found growing from the rocky wall of a crater on Santiago. There the trees were safe from grazing goats.

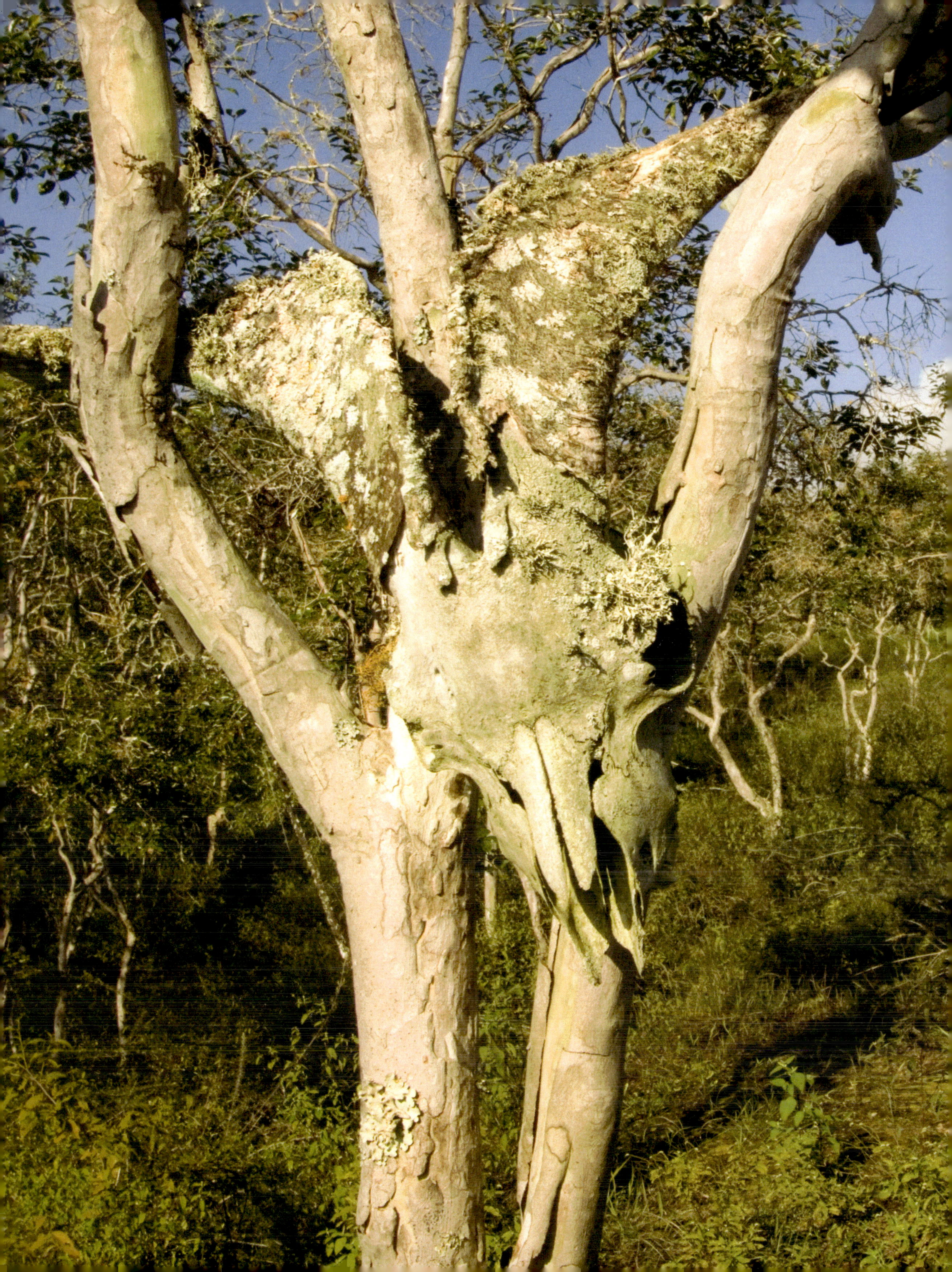

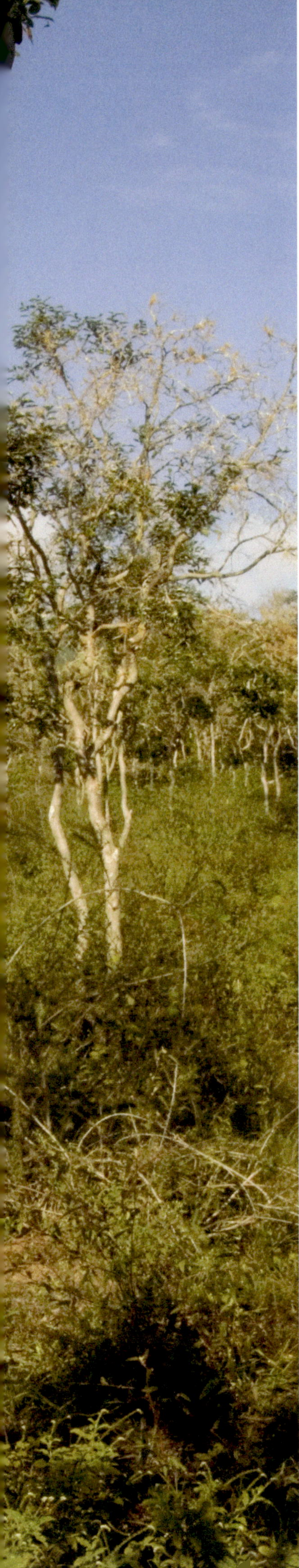

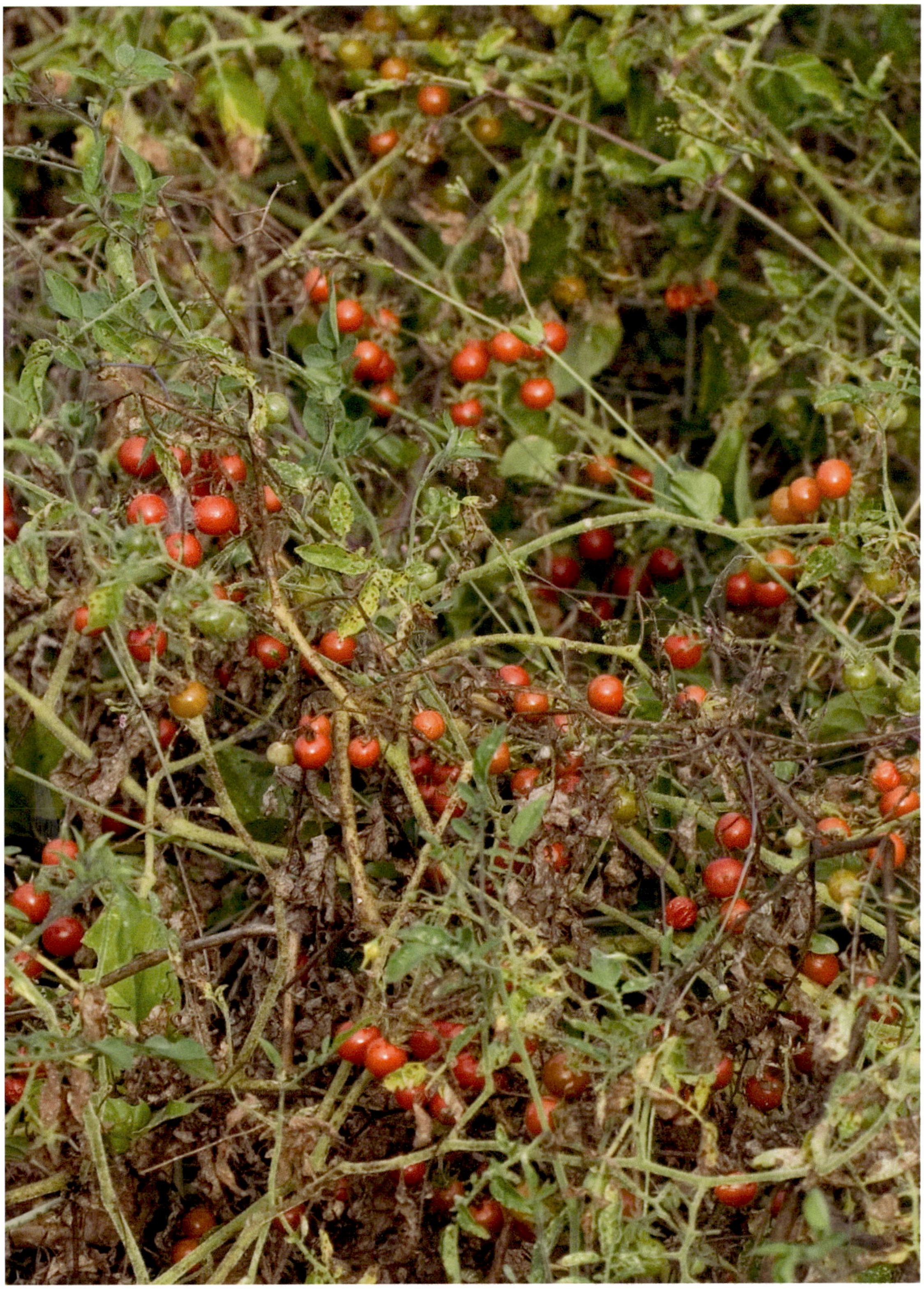

Goat problem

Many of the native plants of the Galápagos are at risk from goats, voracious grazers that were brought in by early settlers nearly 200 years ago. Since then goats have spread to all the larger islands and now live in feral herds. A major conservation project underway in the islands aims to completely eradicate goats from the islands.

Cherry tomato

There are two species of wild tomato native to the Galápagos. One has red fruits that are also rather hairy, while the other grows small yellow fruits. However, cherry tomatoes cultivated originally in kitchen gardens have escaped to the wild and are driving out the endemic fruits.

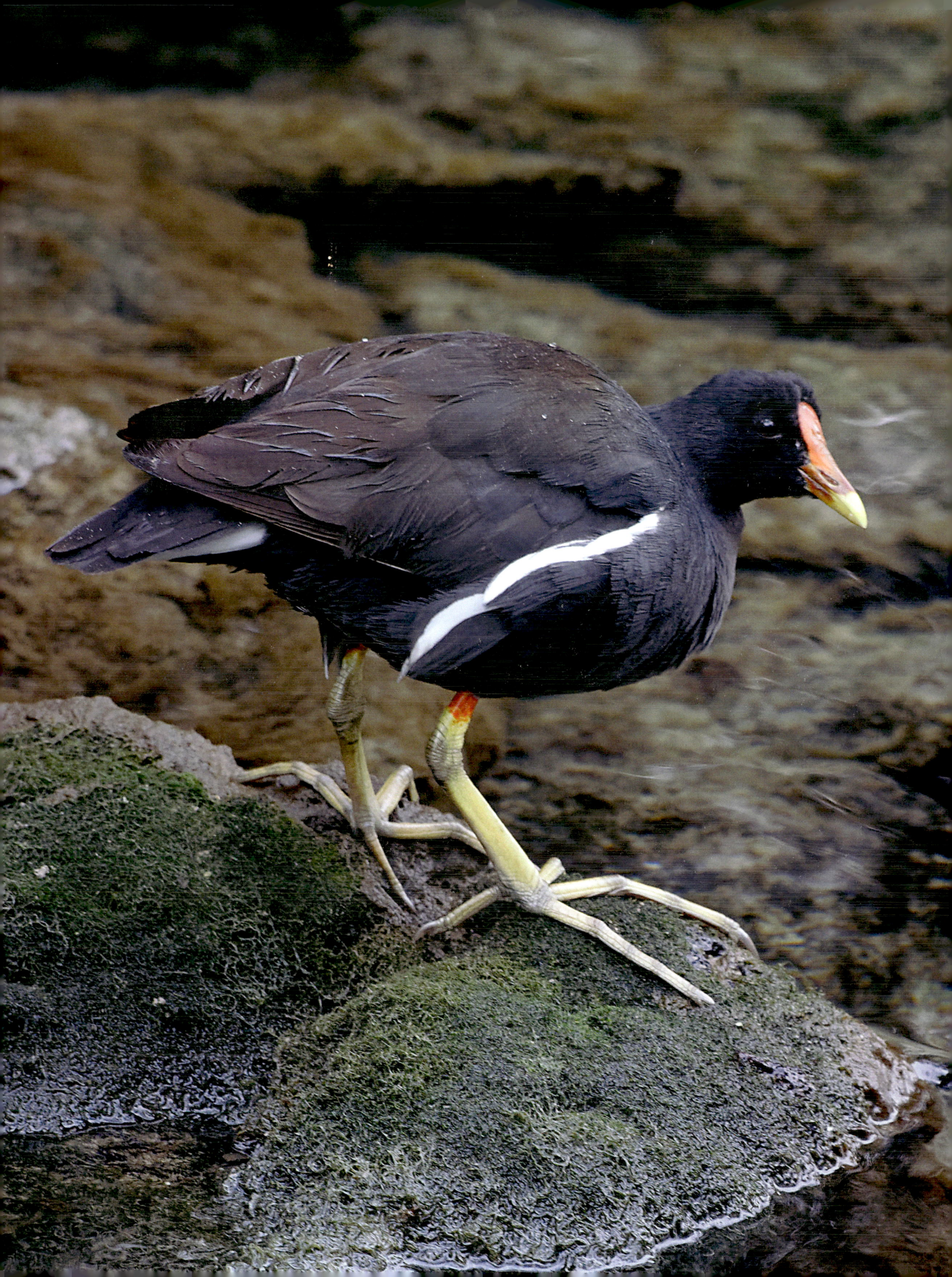

Fauna

The name Galápagos comes from an old Spanish word for tortoise. In fact, the region could be called the Islands of the Tortoises for very good reason. The most famous animal residents are the 12 or so (the exact number is an open question) living species of the giant tortoises. In the absence of large mammals, these immense reptiles are major herbivores here. Large mammals were unable to survive the weeks (or months) at sea that were required to reach the young islands. These long voyages were also impossible for frogs and other amphibians, which need fresh water to stay moist. In their place, the reptiles and birds have become the dominant animals on the islands. As well as giant tortoises, the Galápagos is famed for its iguanas, some of which live inland, as well as another more totemic marine species that lives on the shore, diving into the cold waters to graze on seaweeds. Nowhere else do lizards live like this.

The bird life on the islands also has its superstars. The Galápagos penguins are the only species to live in the northern hemisphere, whereas the flightless cormorant is another bird that has devoted itself to life in water at the expense of flight. Meanwhile the blue-footed booby, aptly named for its sensational webbed toes, provides entertainment with flamboyant courtship displays and an incredible tolerance of human visitors.

All Galápagos wildlife is under threat from encroaching human settlements and introduced species, but the animals are the most obvious victims. Already tortoise and birds species have become extinct and great efforts are being made to remove goats, rodents, cats, dogs, ants and several other animals that have damaged the fragile natural balance of the islands since humans arrived in the 19th century.

Common gallinule
Sometimes called the moorhen (although now seen as a separate species from the Eurasian moorhen), this long-legged bird spends most of its time on the ground, poking around leaf litter for insects. It flies only rarely.

Dark-billed cuckoo
Despite the name, this bird is not
the callous nest invader (or social
parasite) like many other cuckoos.
Instead it builds its own nest,
mostly in the arid zone where there
are plenty of insects to catch.

Galápagos flycatcher
This large flycatcher – though
still only about 16cm (6in) long
– is found only on the islands. It
nests in the warm season between
December and March taking over
holes in tree cacti or settling in
cracks in the lava.

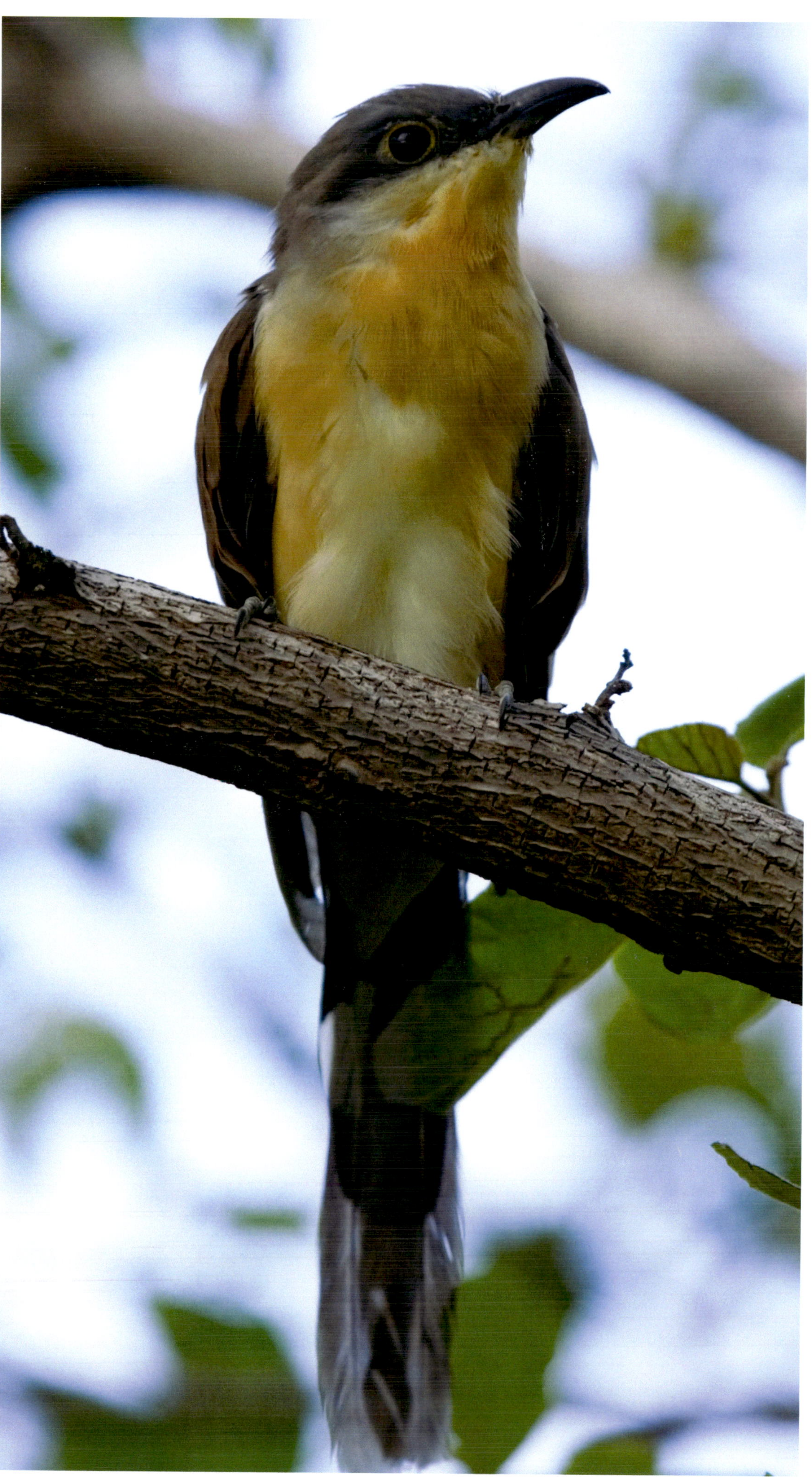

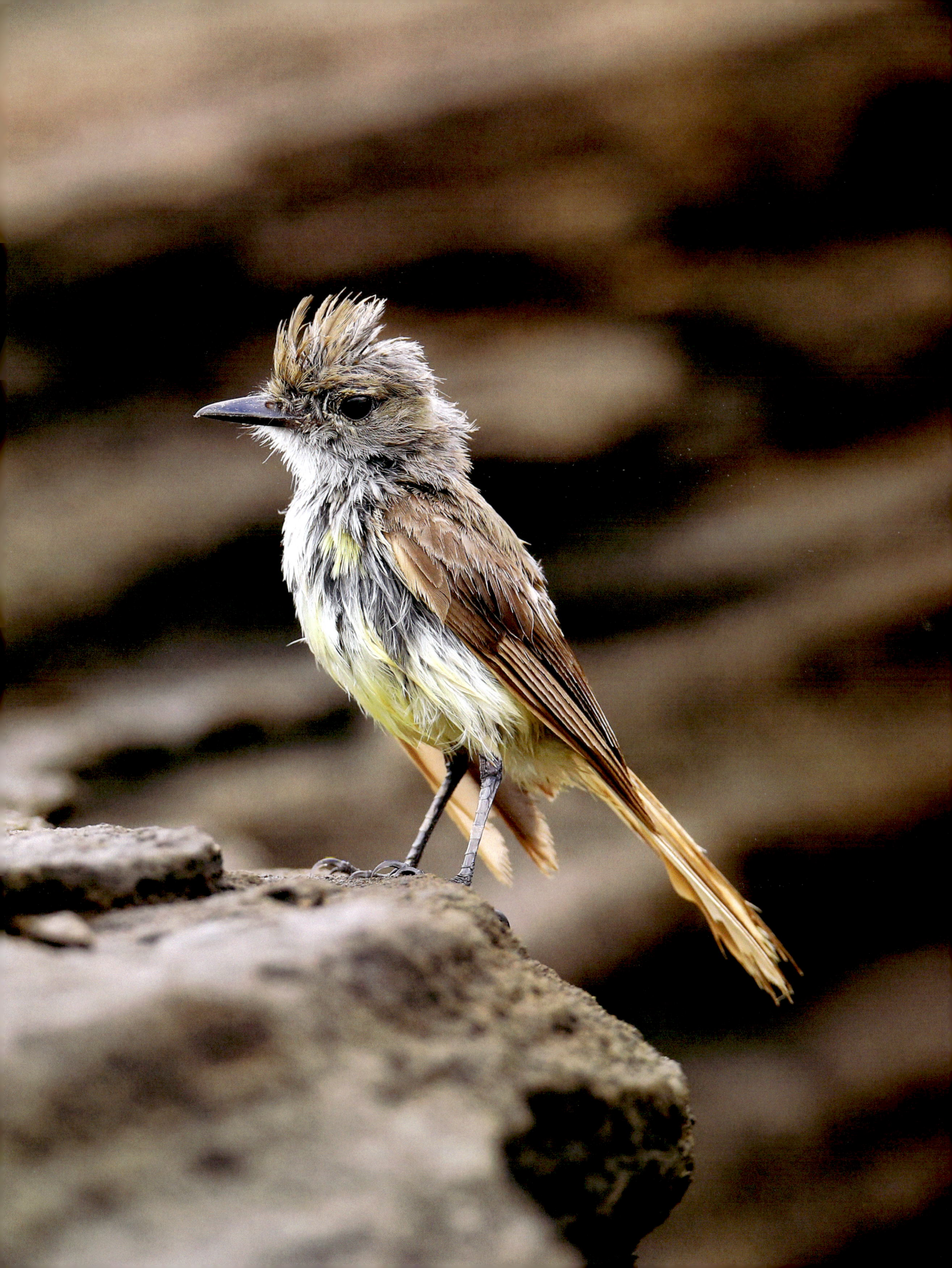

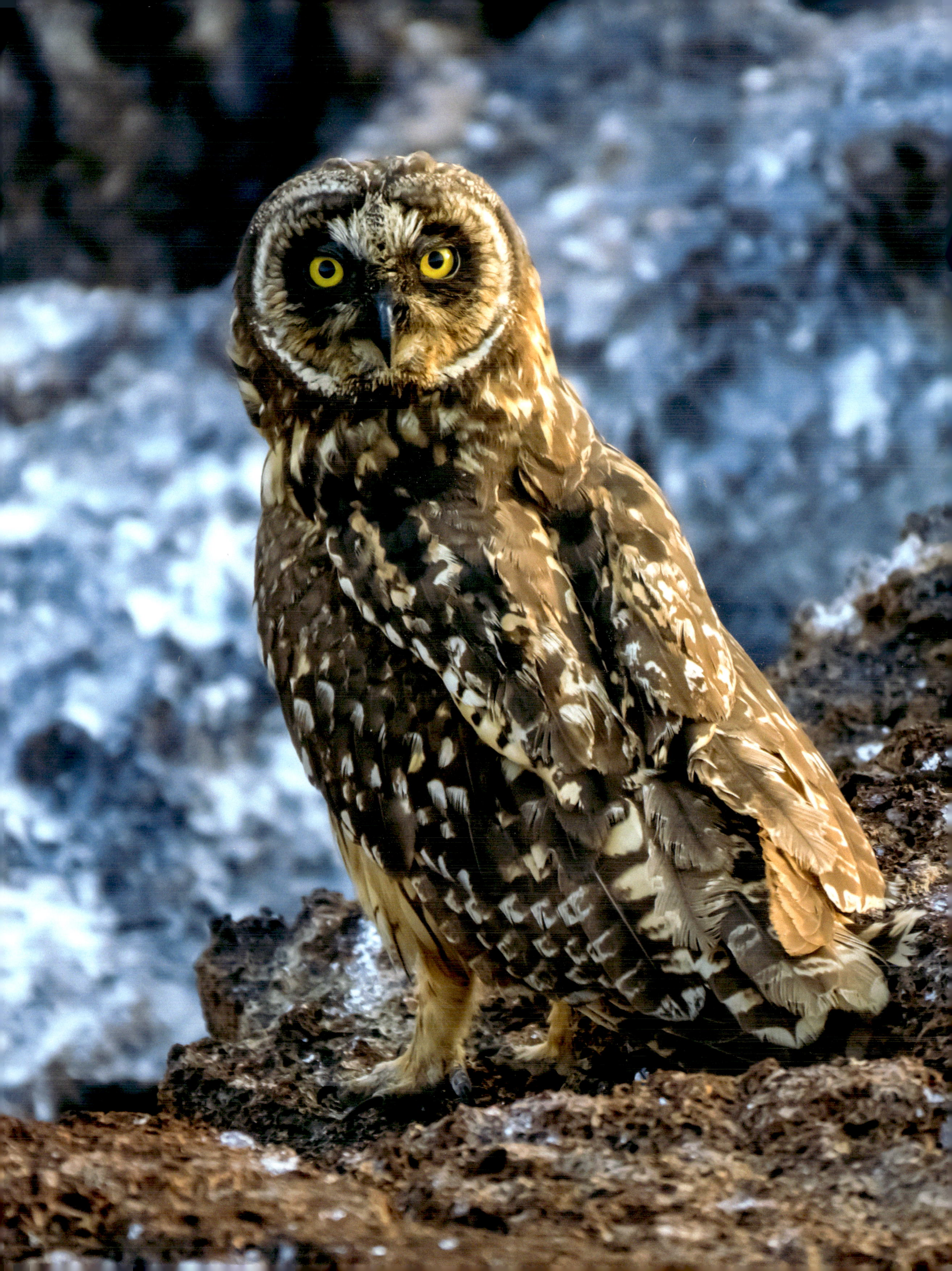

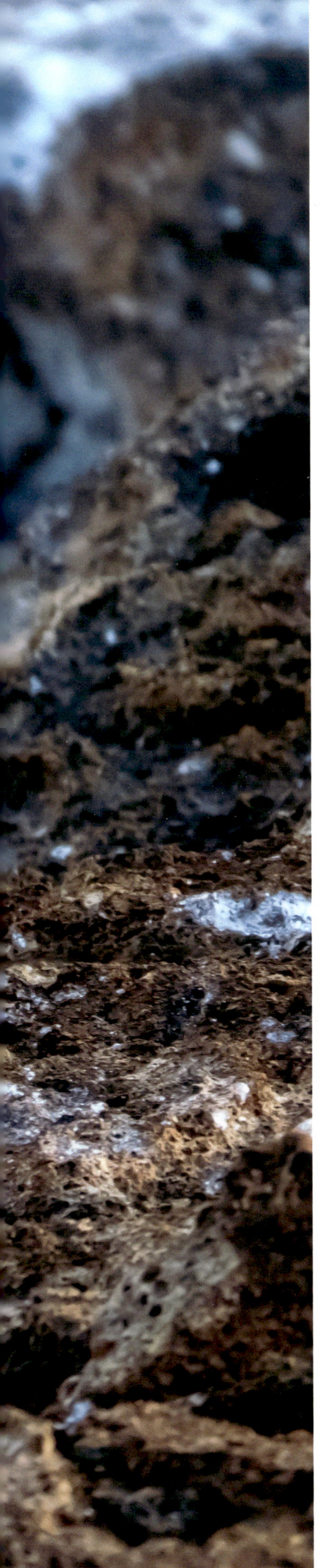

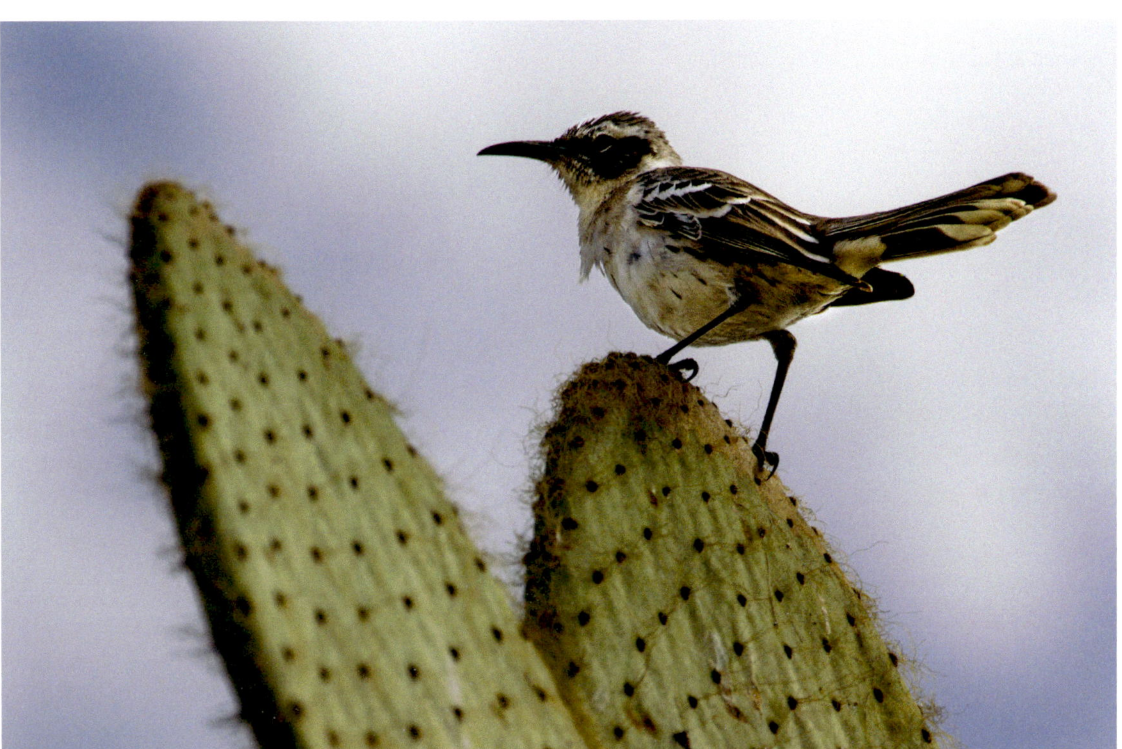

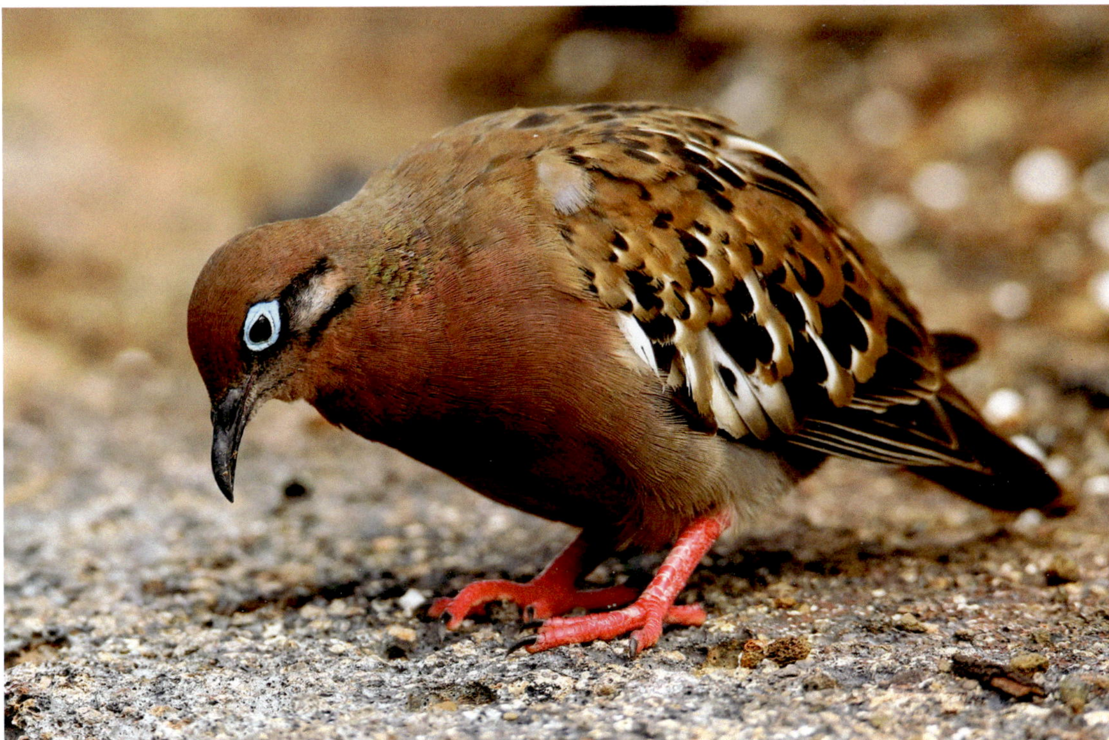

LEFT:
Short-eared owl
The Galápagos has its own endemic subspecies of this owl. It is more active during the day than other owl species on the islands. The owl specializes in hunting smaller birds, but has since switched to targeting introduced mice and rats.

ABOVE TOP:
Galápagos mockingbird
There are four species of mockingbird on the Galápagos, all endemic and found nowhere else in the world. Like their relatives across the ocean, they are excellent mimics. This species is the most widespread and has a diet typical of all four species that includes everything from sea lion placenta to seeds.

ABOVE BOTTOM:
Galápagos dove
The islands' pigeon is naturally unafraid of humans, simply because it is not adapted to protecting itself from any large animals. During his stay in 1835 Charles Darwin commented that he could kill a dove for that evening's stew by throwing his hat at it.

Galápagos hermit crab
This is the only endemic species
of crab on the Galápagos. It is an
otherwise unremarkable soft-
shell species that seeks out the
protection of abandoned seashells.
It is a common resident of the
rocky shores and beaches around
the islands.

Fiddler crab
This species is famed for the
male's oversized, pincer-like claw,
seen here, which is used to attract
mates. It is too big to be of much
other use since the crabs are
herbivores that scrape algae from
rocks and roots. These little crabs
live in colonial burrows in and
around the stems of mangrove trees.

Ghost crab
A squad of little crabs, with their
distinctive tall eye stalks, patrols
the sand. They dig through the
sand looking for food morsels,
discarding balls of sand as they go.

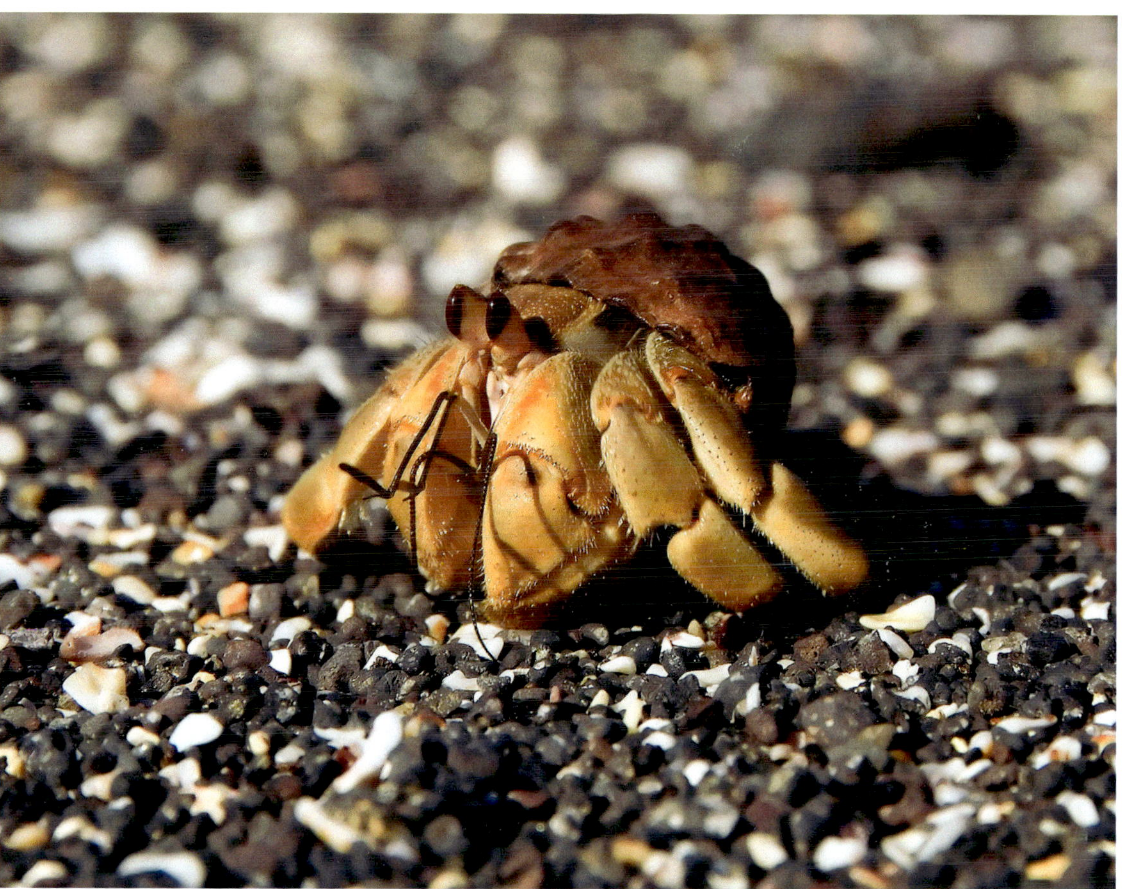

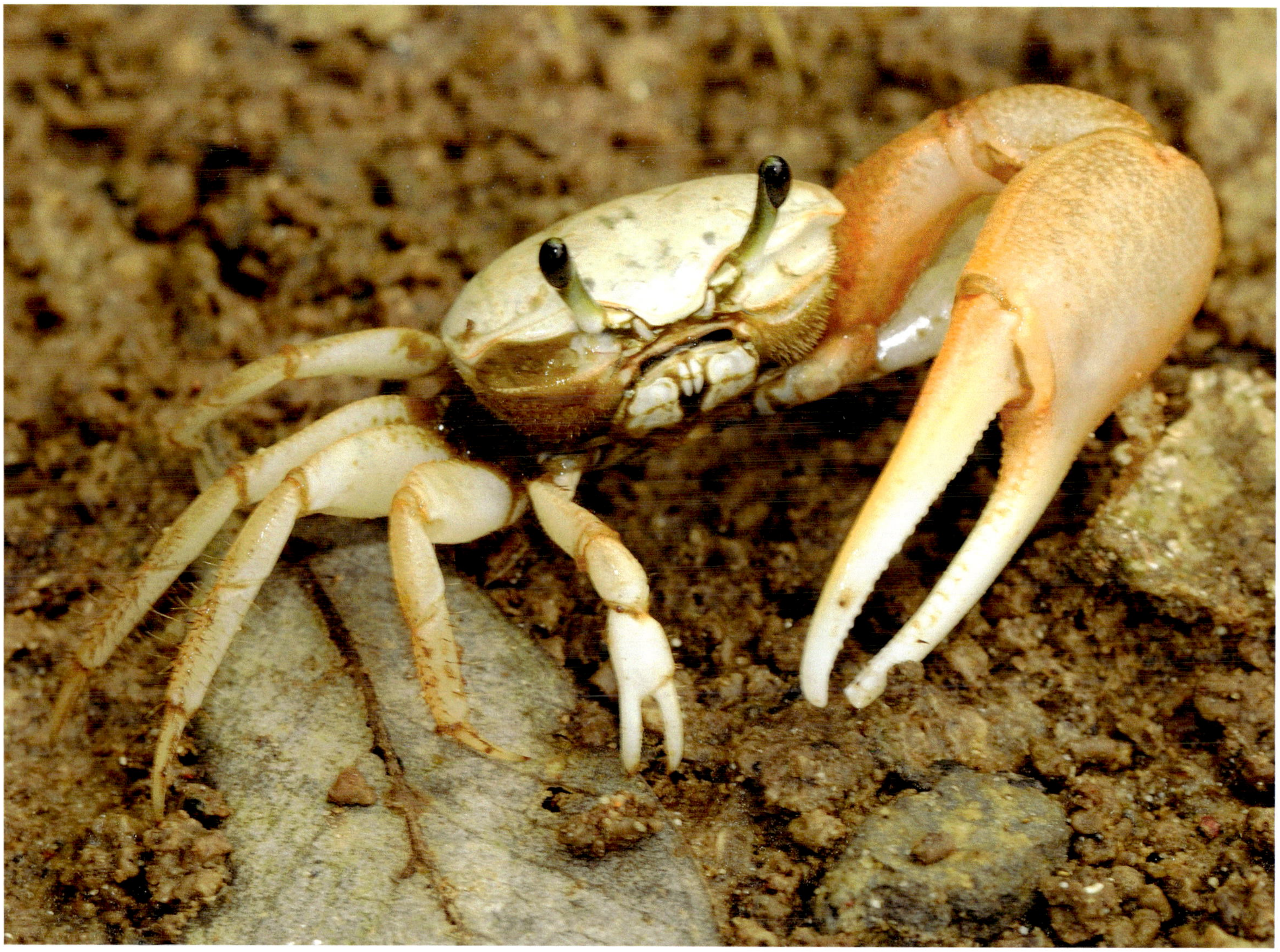

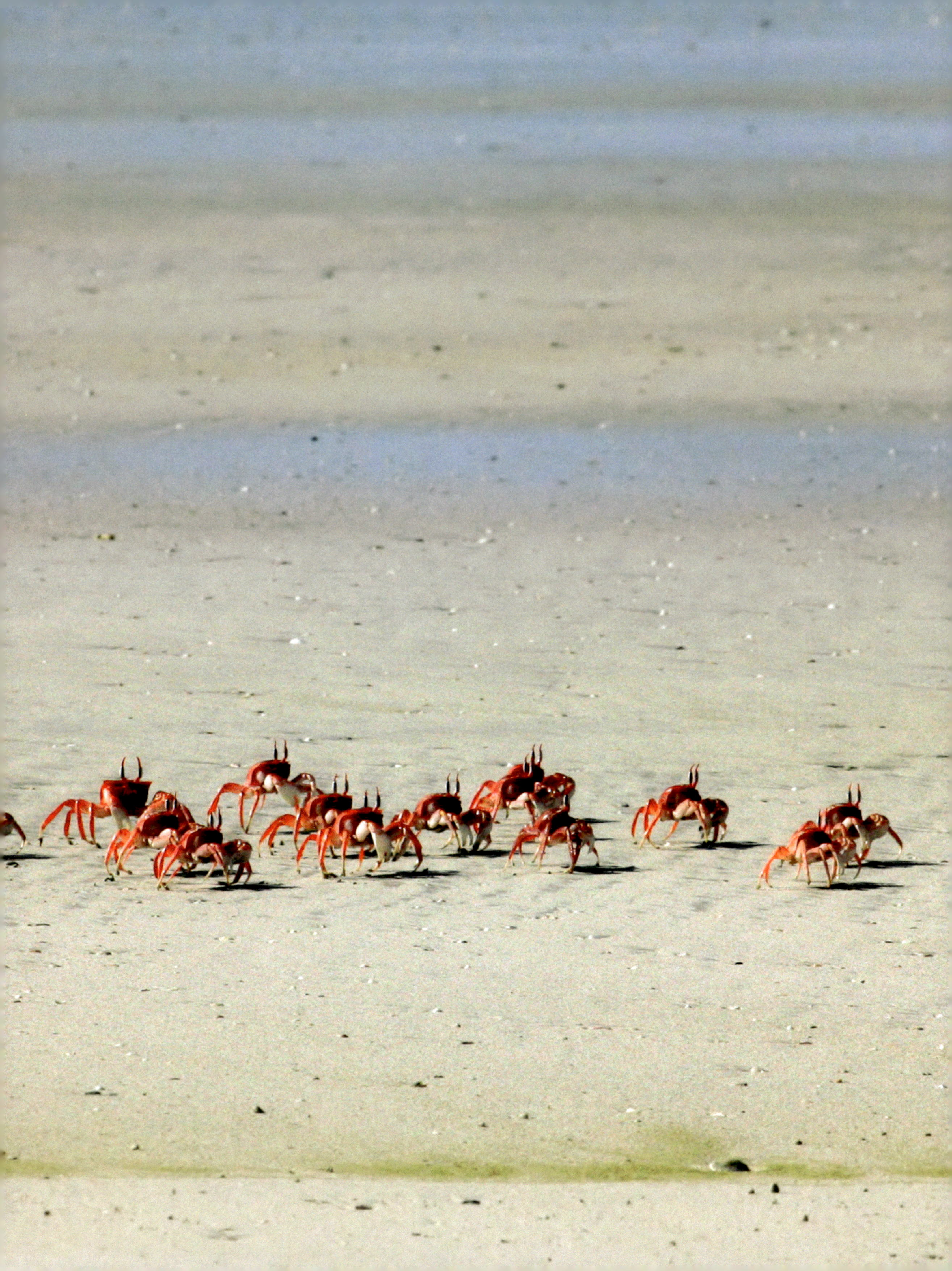

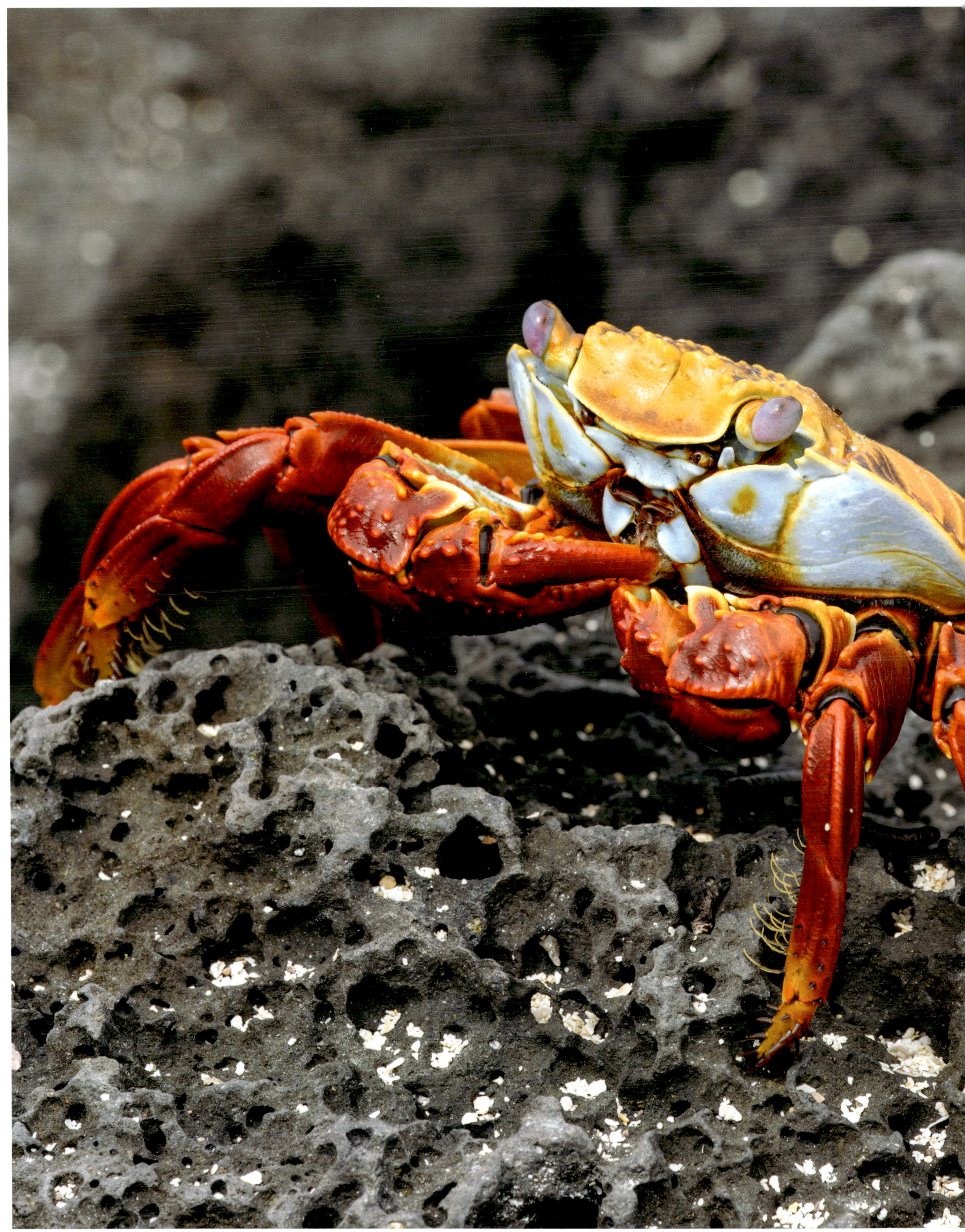

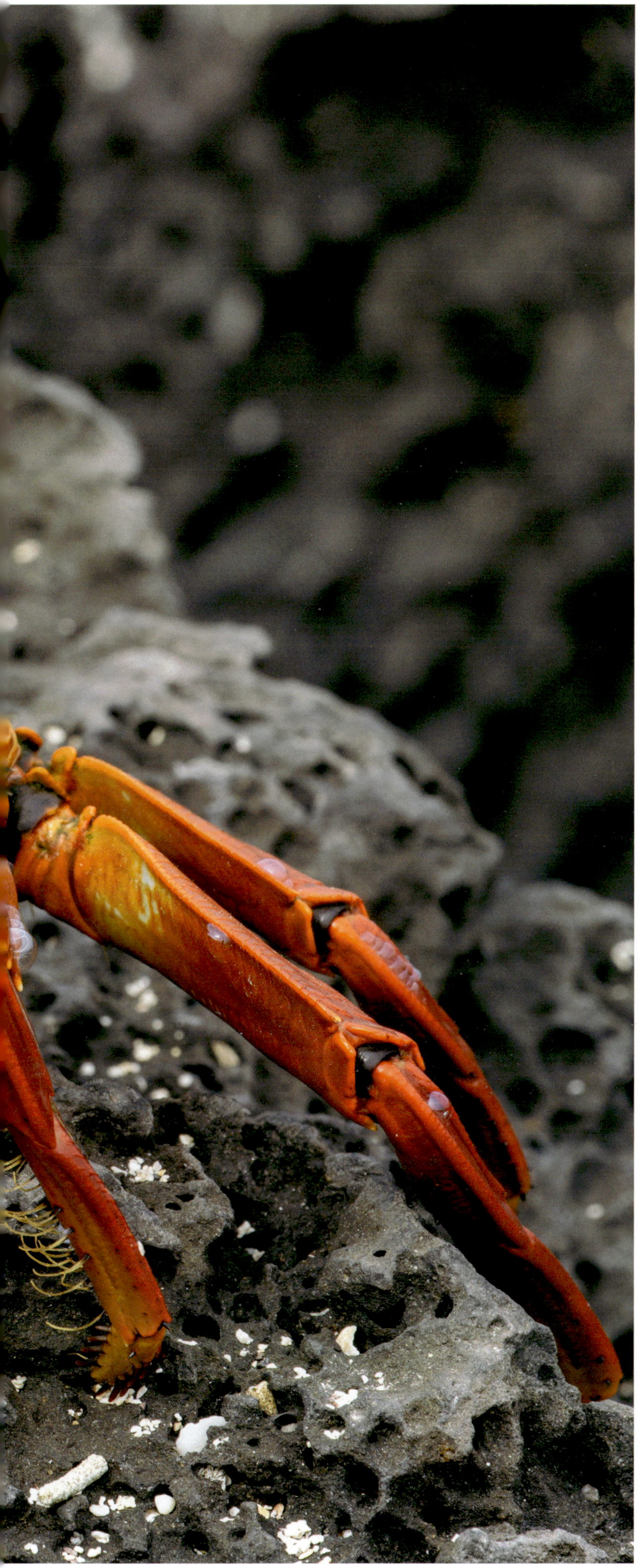

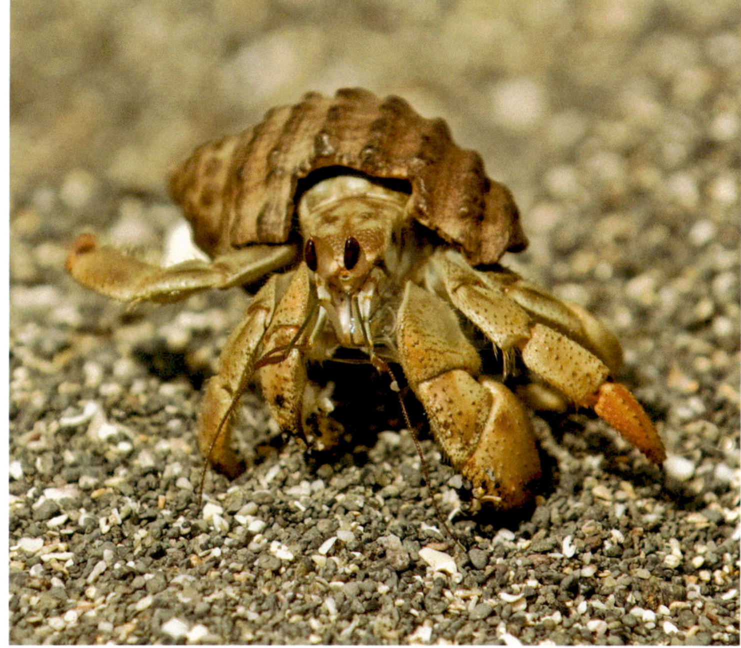

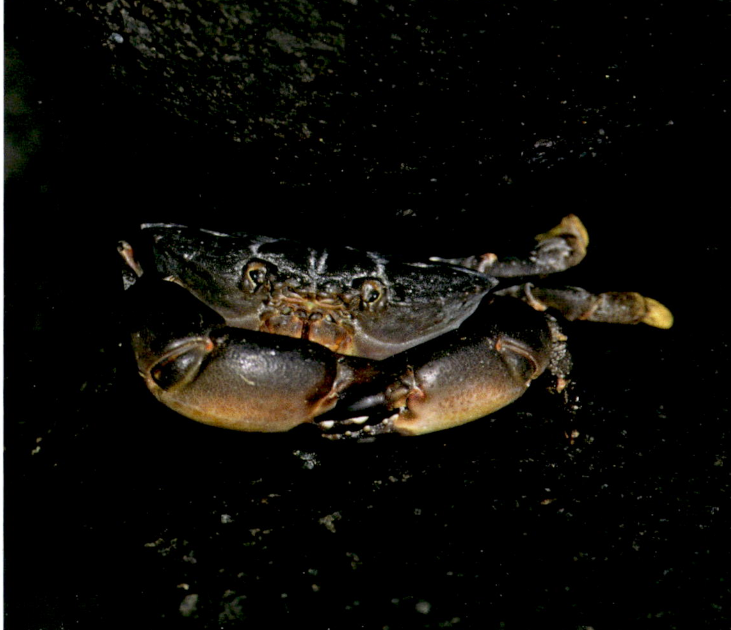

Sally Lightfoot crab

This is the largest crab on the islands, and it is often seen in large numbers, its yellow and red colouring making it easy to pick out against the dark rocks. The crab is known for its agility, able to run, climb and even jump between rocks as it searches for food. These crabs are also cannibals with the larger, brighter individuals eating their younger neighbours. This is one reason why younger crabs have a darker, more camouflaged carapace, which brightens with age.

Semi-terrestrial hermit crab

This is a native species of hermit crab that is also found living in other parts of the south-eastern Pacific. Despite its name, the crab is as shackled to the seashore and the ocean as any other hermit crab. It needs to take regular baths in seawater to moisten its gills.

Velvet-fingered ozius

This small crab is not commonly seen since it is often hiding out in damp nooks when the tide is low. It has a blue-green shell and chunky pincers for cracking into the shells of sea snails, its principal prey.

Iconic Galápagos animal
The giant tortoise is the iconic
animal of the Galápagos Islands
with around a dozen species
living here. The tortoises that
live on the humid islands or in
lusher habitats have a domed
shell. That is because their food
is mostly low-growing herbs that
thrive in the damper conditions.
In drier locations, the tortoises
have saddleback shells, where the
shell behind the neck has curved
up so that the tortoise can lift
its head higher. This allows the
tortoises in arid zones to reach
up and graze on the leaves of
taller, hardier shrubs that are
getting their water by tapping
into deeper groundwater.

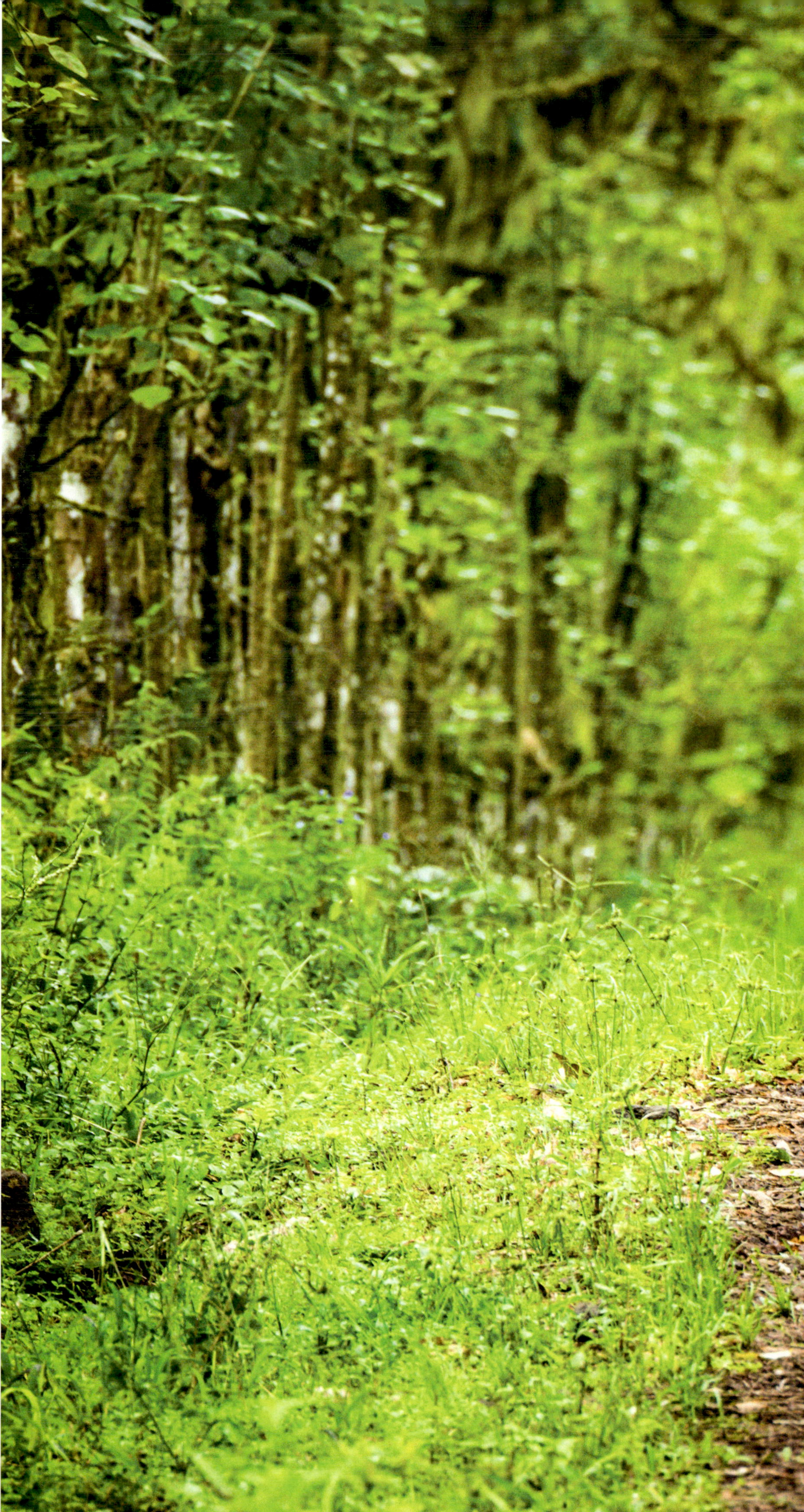

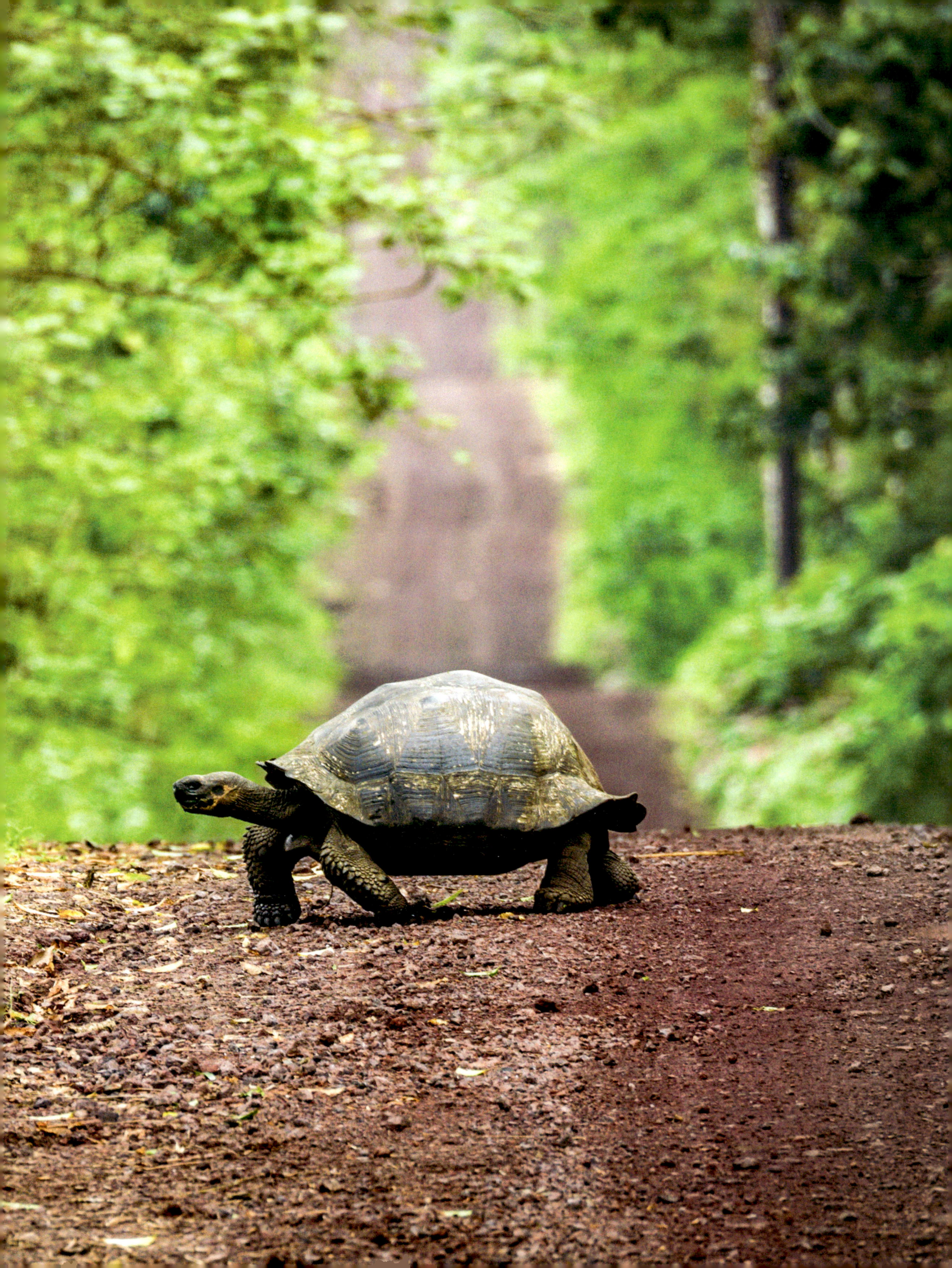

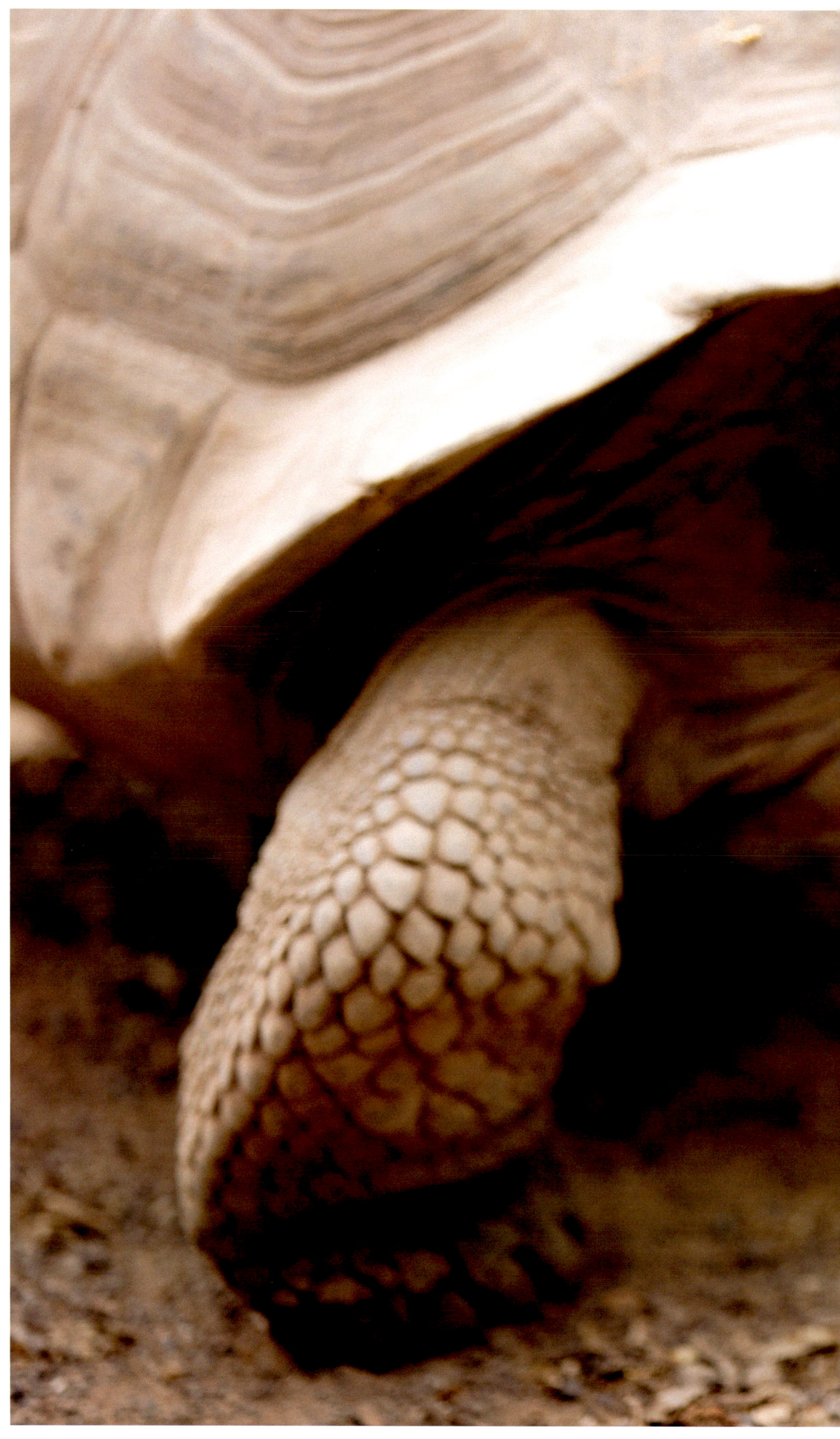

Largest land animal

The giant tortoises of the Galápagos are a remnant of a once much wider community. Tortoises of this size lived across the mainland but were outcompeted by mammal rivals. However, the few that made it across to remote islands like the Galápagos – probably aboard rafts of floating vegetation – found a home free of these rivals and have remained the biggest animals ever since. (The largest giant tortoises of all are actually found on the Seychelles in the Indian Ocean.)

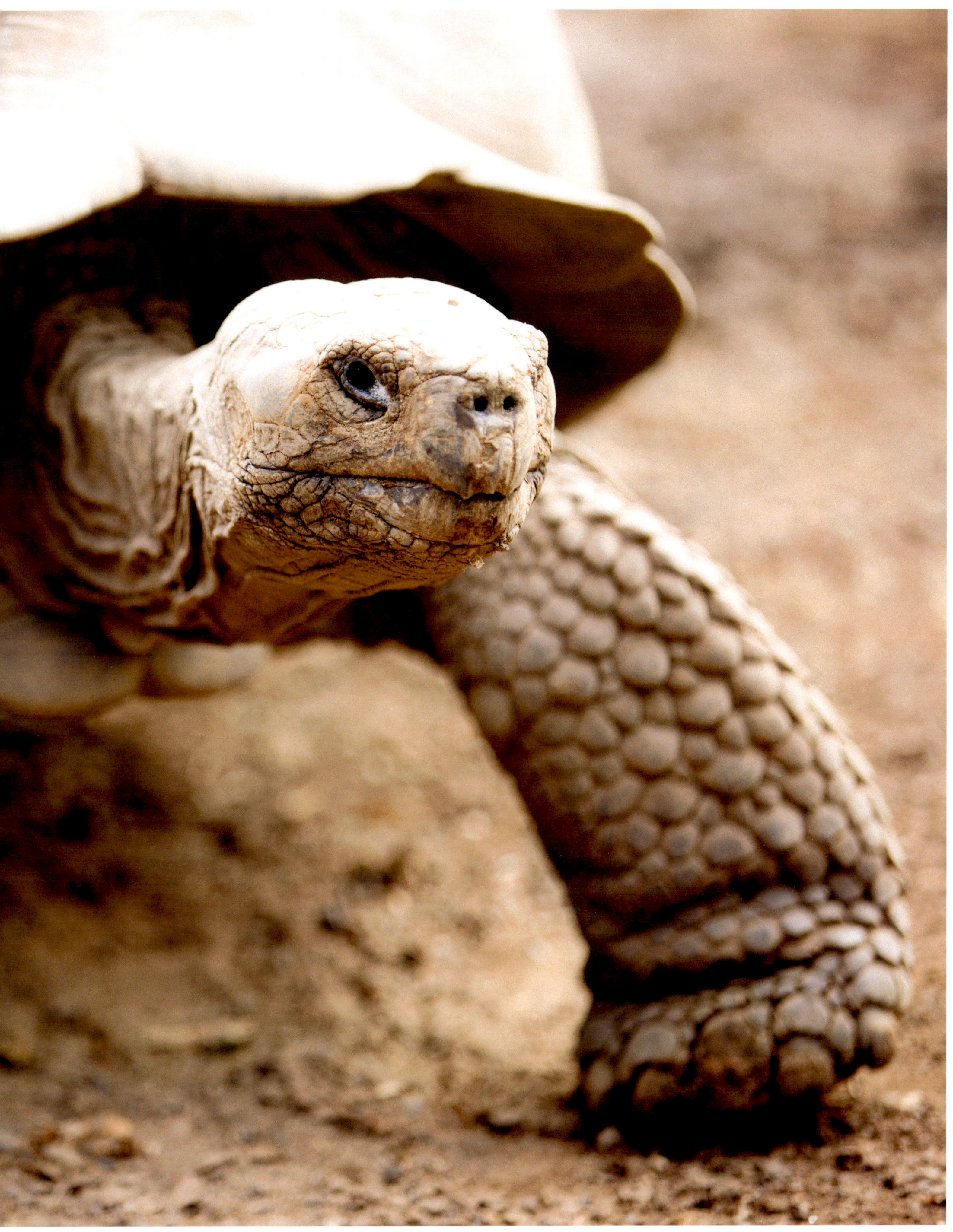

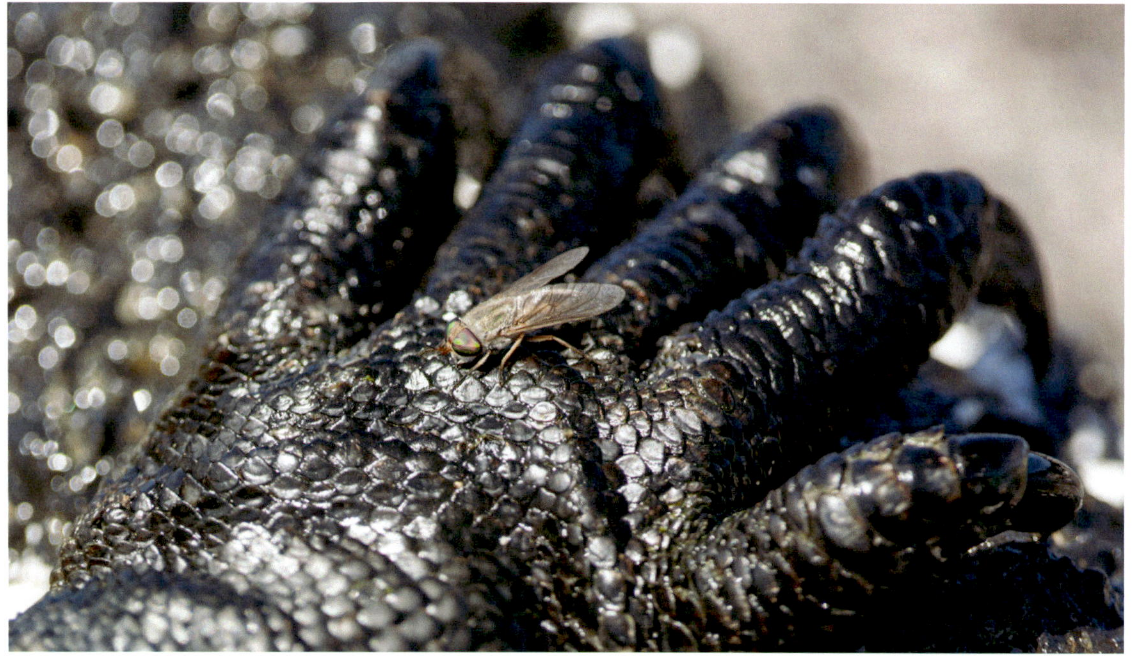

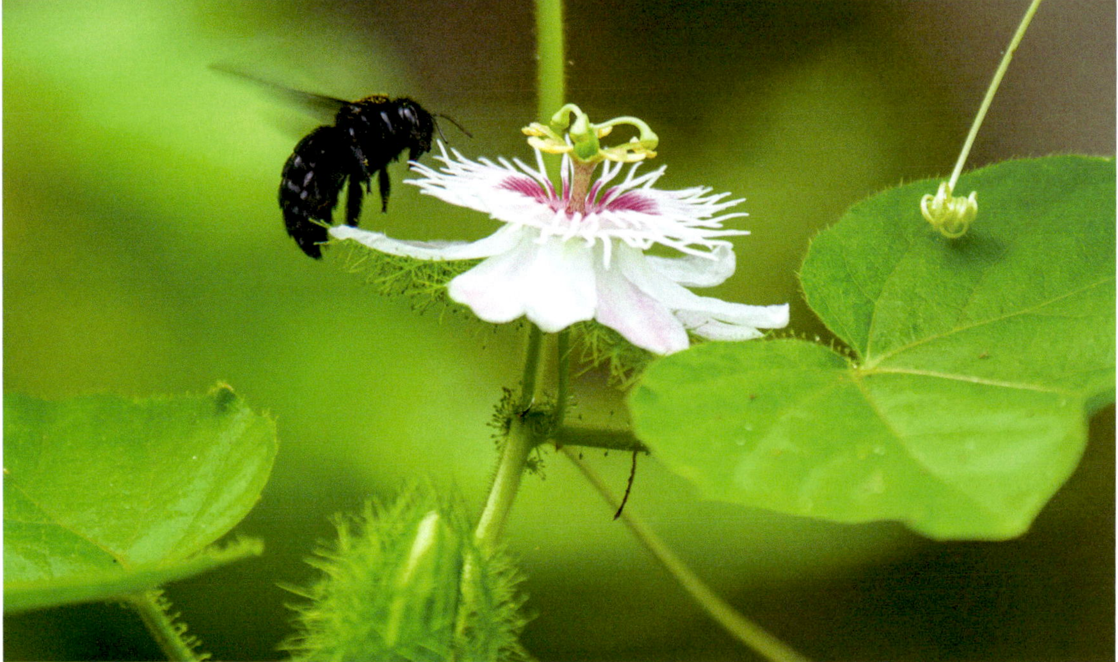

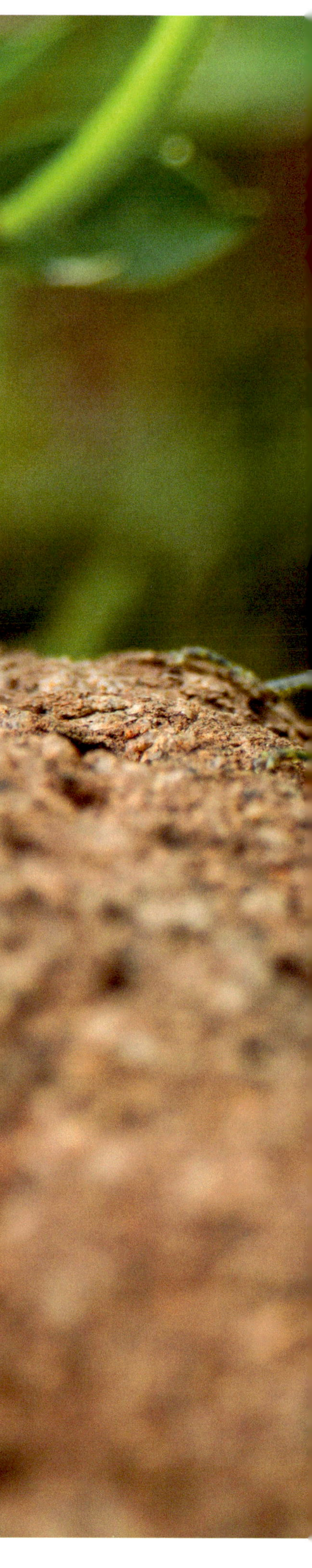

Galápagos green-eyed horse fly
The largest fly on the Galápagos, this female horse fly is taking a blood meal from a marine iguana's foot. The horse fly slashes a wound in the skin and laps up the blood that emerges. The males feed on nectar or pollen.

Galápagos carpenter bee
With the scientific name *Xylocopa darwini* (the name *darwini* is common here), this is the only bee species on the islands. It makes nests in dead wood, with the females chewing a tunnel inside and laying a single egg within. When the egg hatches the female will feed her baby with nectar until it is ready to pupate.

Large painted locust
One of four endemic orthopterans (grasshoppers and crickets) on the Galápagos, this is the largest, with the adults growing to 8cm (3in) long. Despite the name, this is not a swarming insect. It will swell in numbers after the rains when there is plenty of fresh plant food around. The younger wingless nymphs are green and they take on the painted browns and yellows when sexually mature.

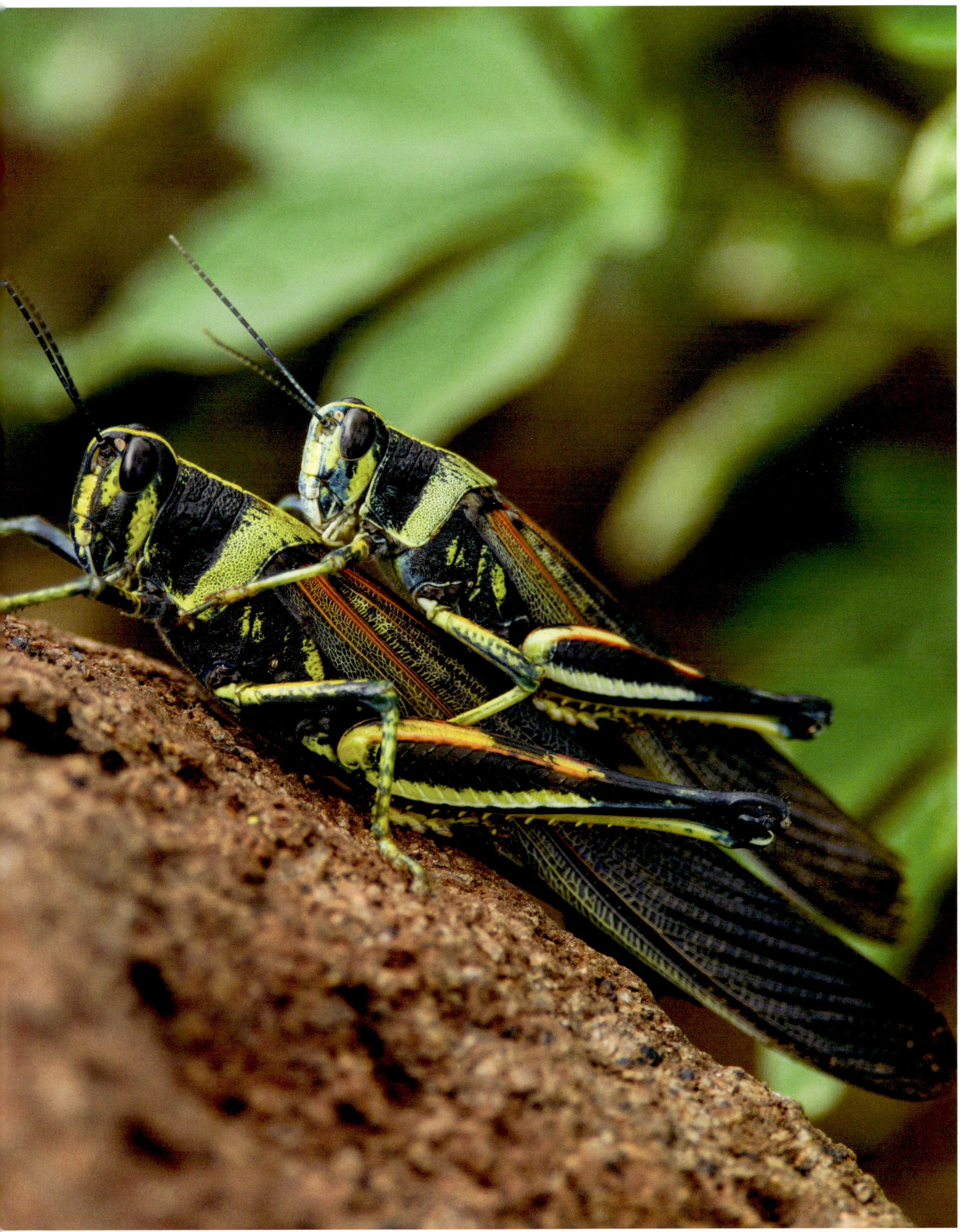

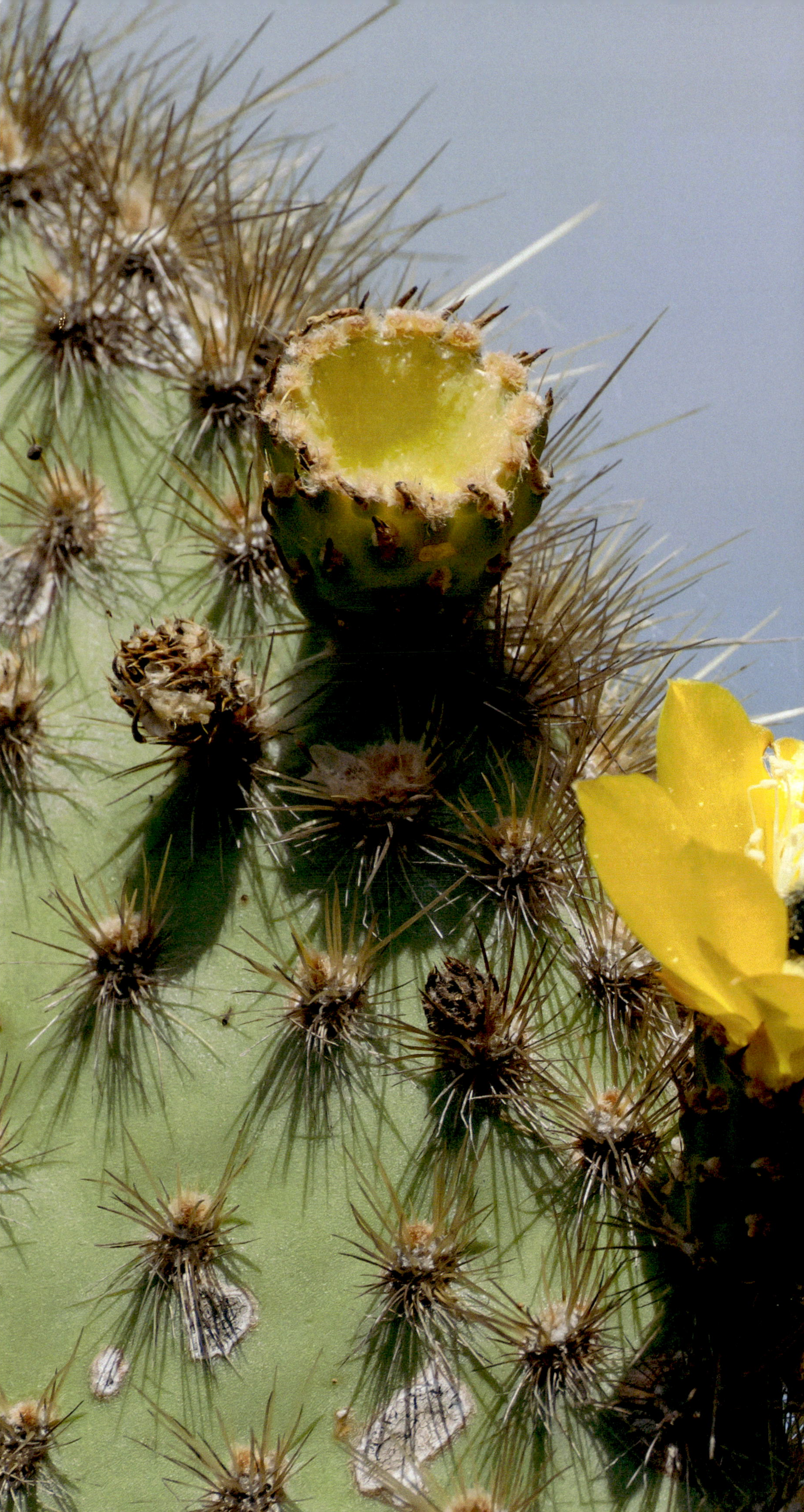

Galápagos sulphur butterfly
The simple yellow-green colouring
of this native species makes it one
of the easier butterflies to identify.
It is widely seen in lowland areas
fluttering between blooms on
sunny days.

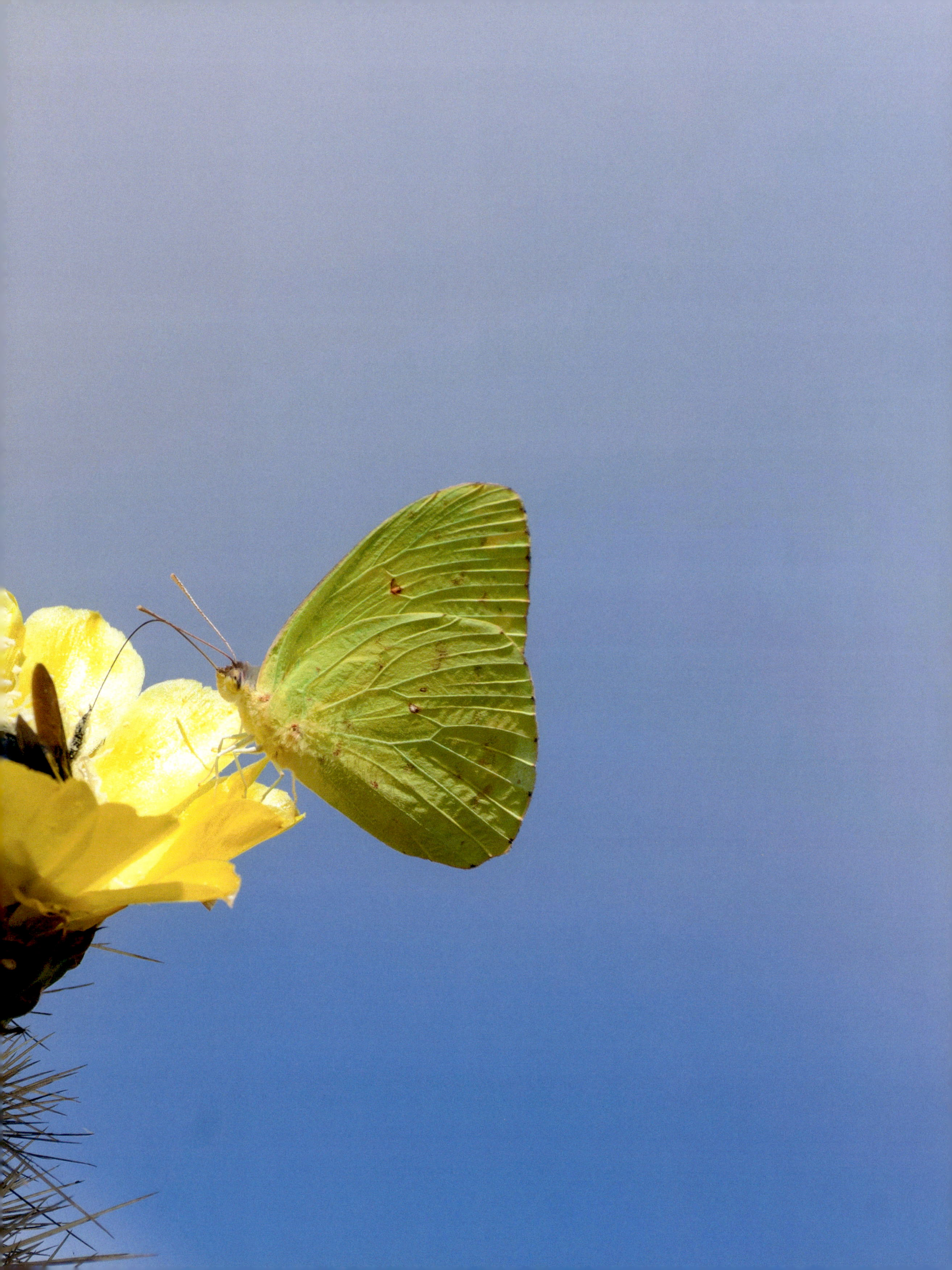

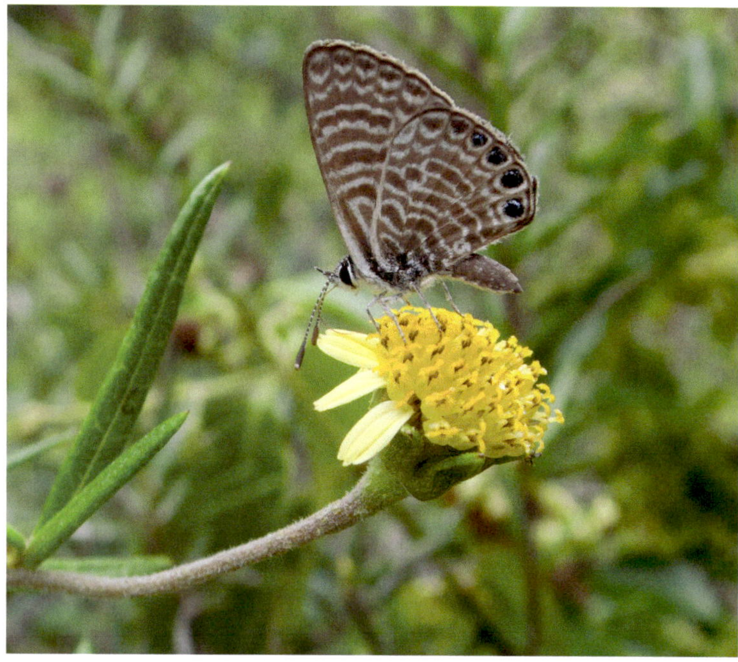

Galápagos blue butterfly

This is a small but striking endemic butterfly species. When at rest the underside of the wings are a nondescript brown typical of many butterflies. However, in flight the upper surfaces of the wings flash blue.

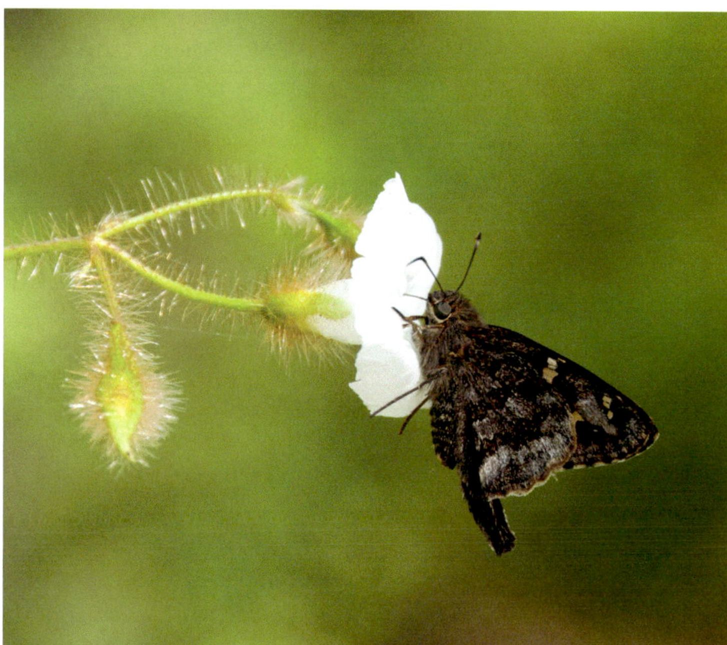

Long-tailed skipper

A skipper is halfway between a butterfly and a moth. For most of us the difference is that moths fly at night (and are frightening, ugly or a nuisance) while butterflies are more of a welcome sight, a flash of colourful activity on a summer's day. A more precise difference is to do with the way the four wings connect, and skippers show similarities between both. This endemic species is distinctive for its tail-like protrusion on the hind wings.

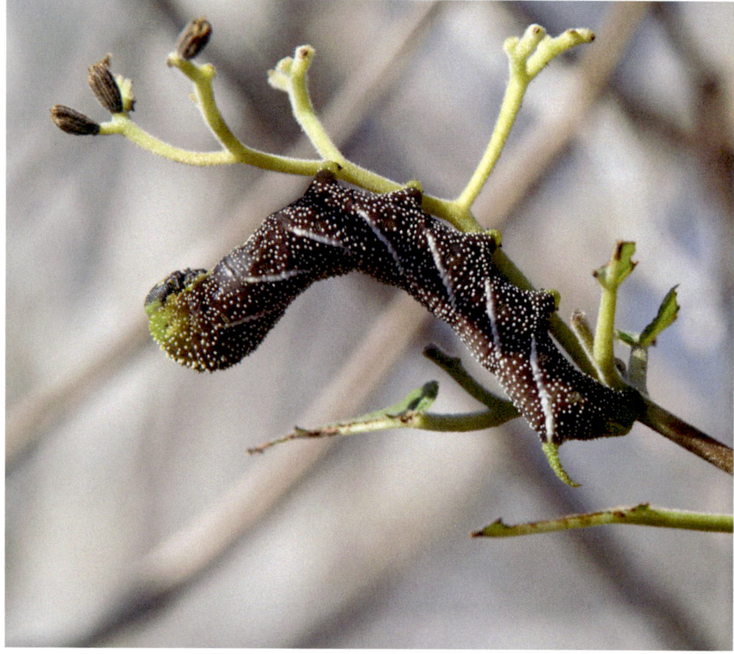

Galápagos silver fritillary

This is an endemic subspecies of the gulf fritillary, which is found widely in warmer parts of the Americas. Its caterpillars feed on the leaves of passionflowers, both the endemic Galápagos species and invasive ones.

Green hawk-moth

One of several kinds of hawk-moth that lives on the Galápagos, these sturdy lepidopterans fly at night and are drawn to lights, even travelling out from the coast to buzz around lamps on boats and ships at sea. They are nectar feeders and use their powerful wings to hover before blooms as they suck up food.

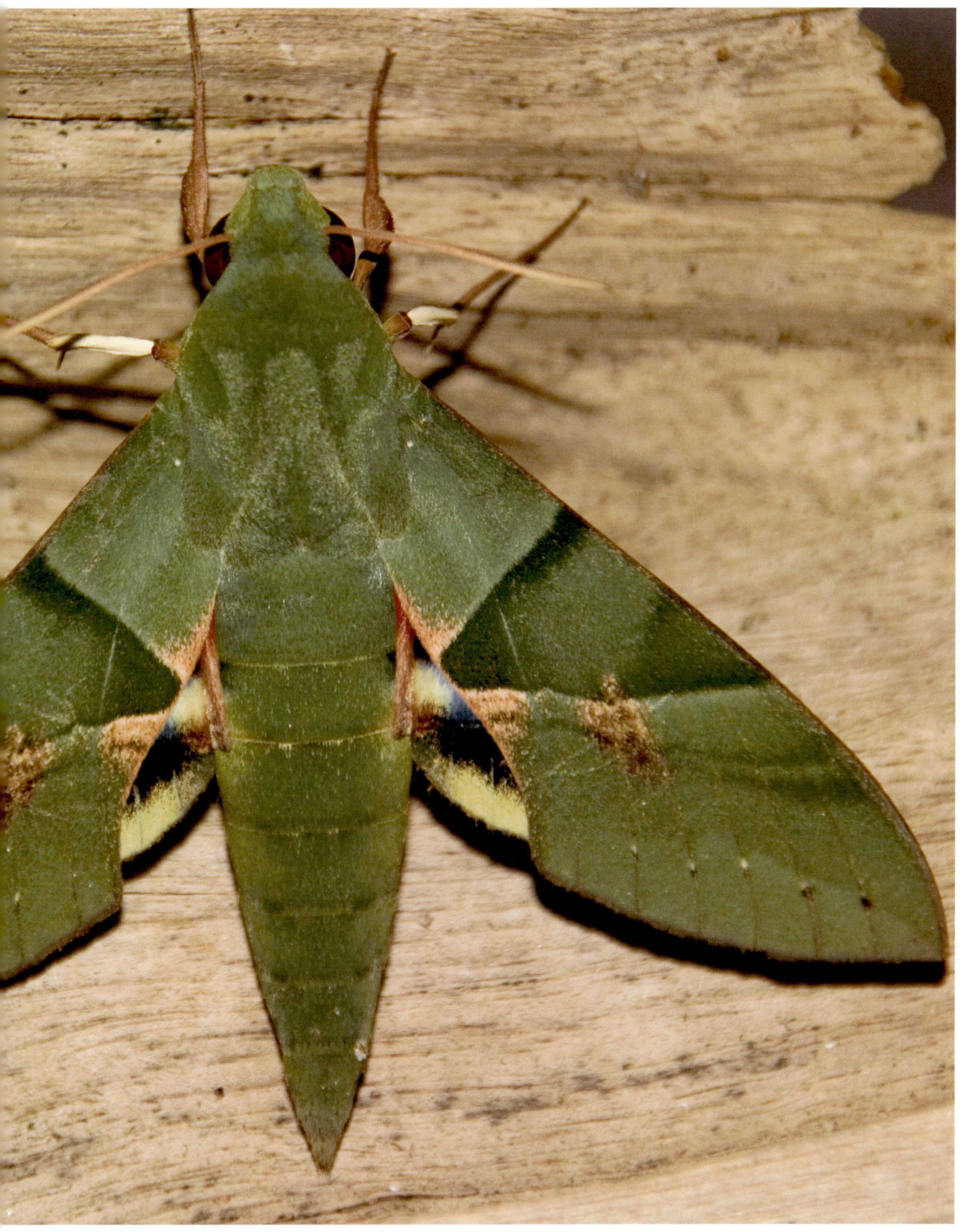

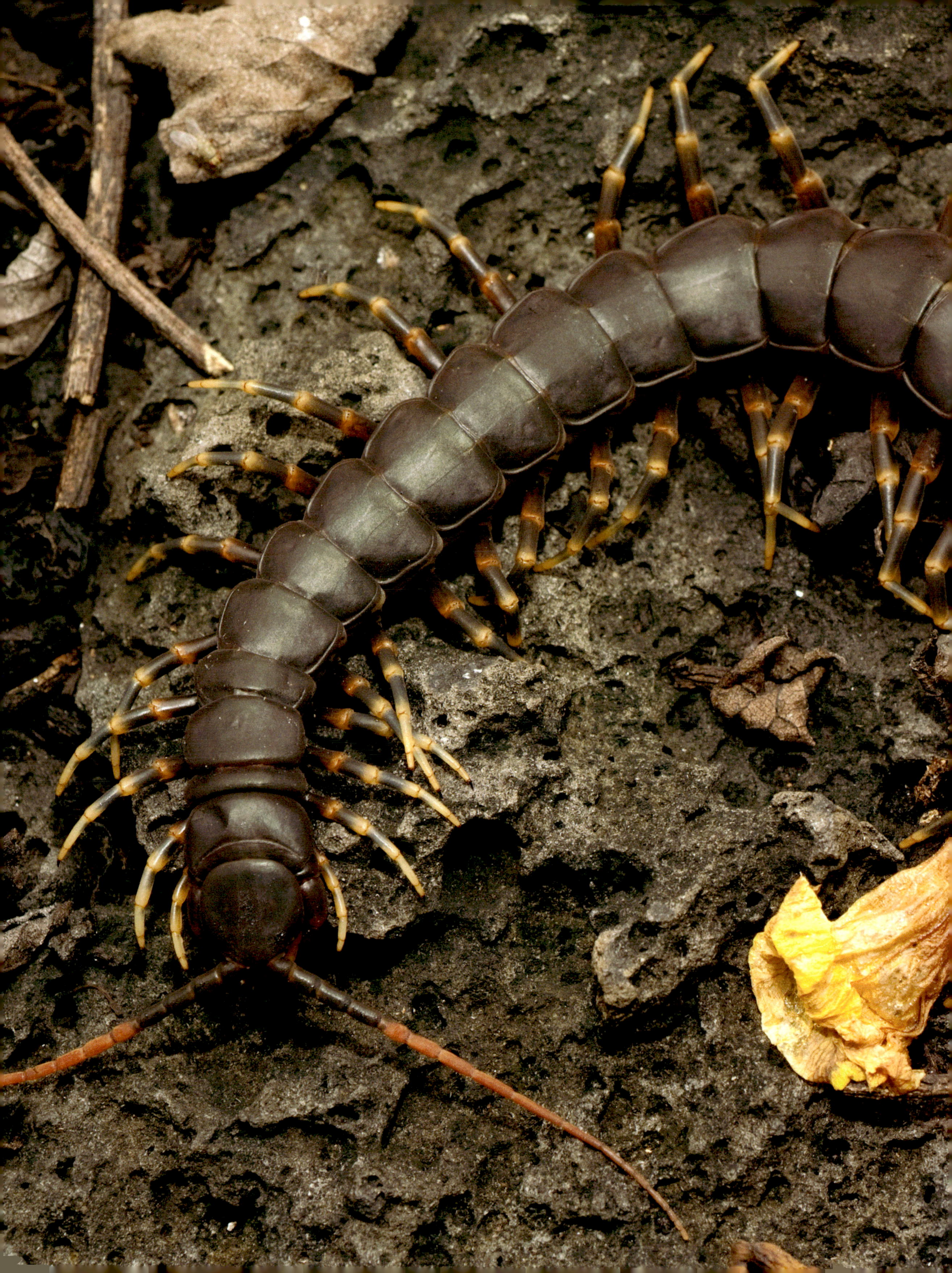

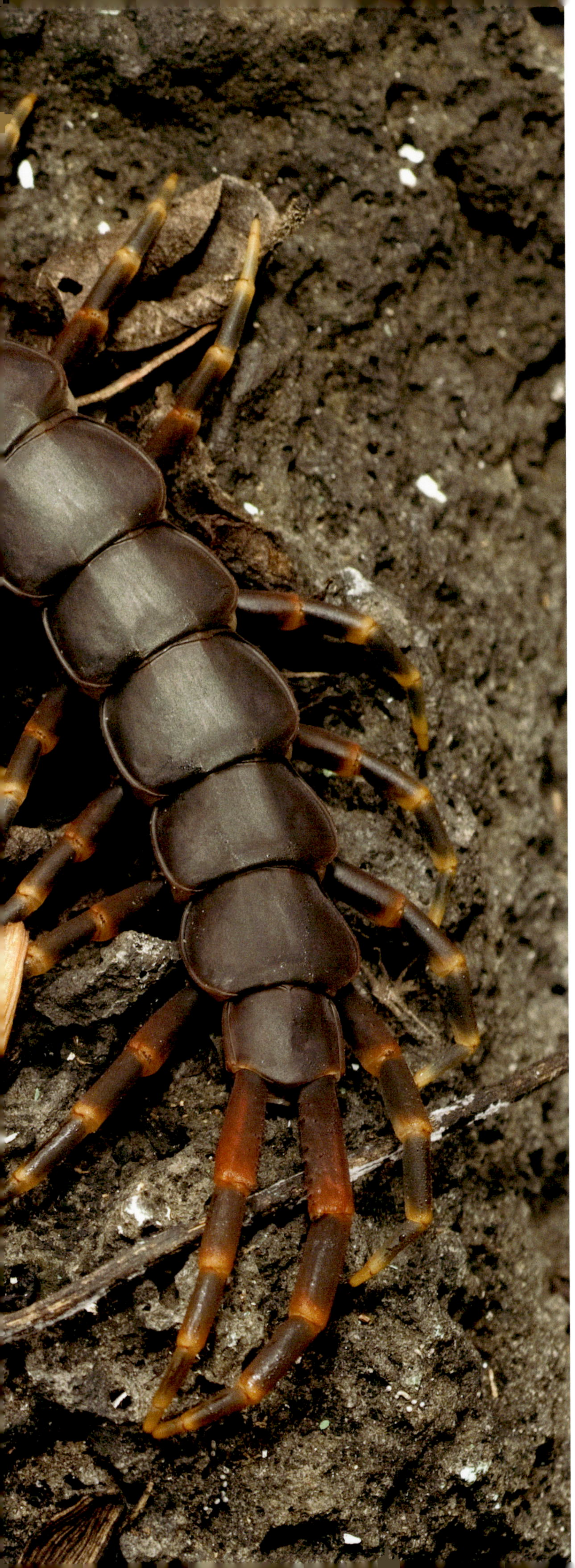

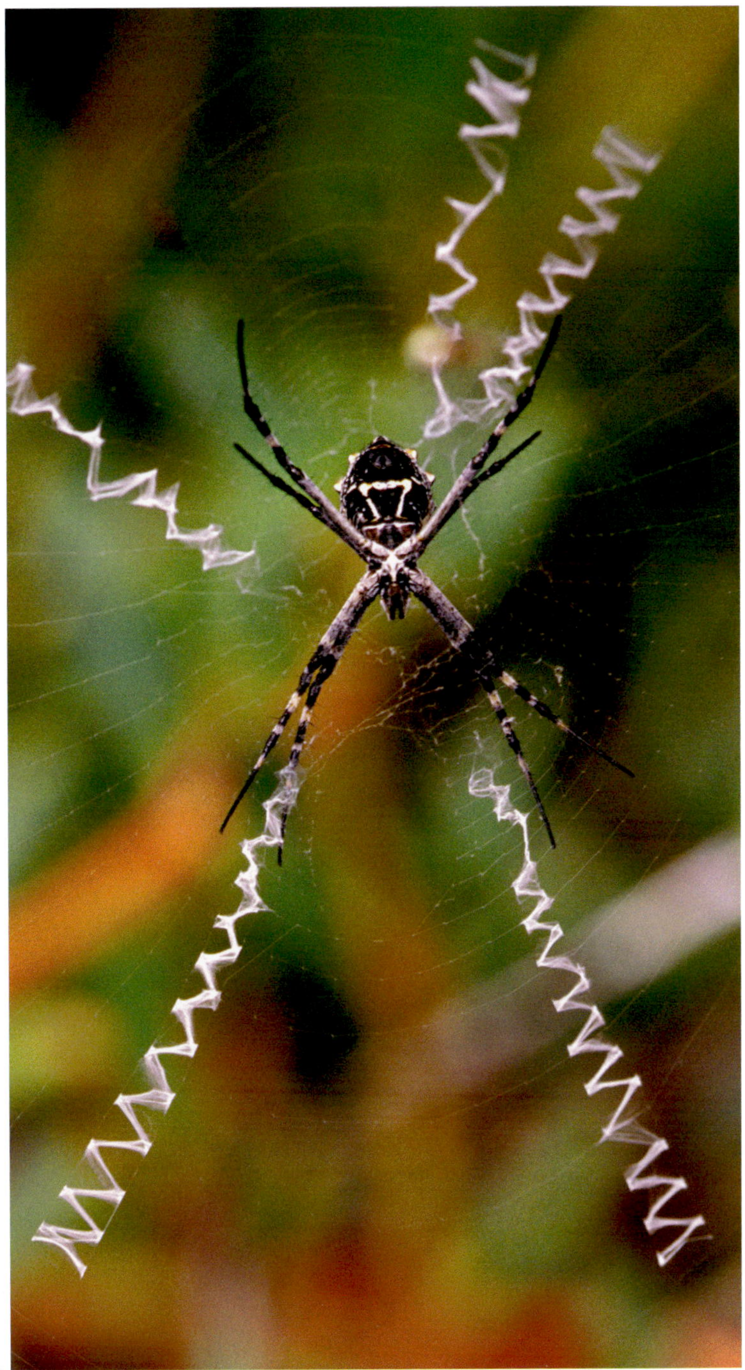

LEFT:

Galápagos giant centipede

Also known as Darwin's goliath centipede, this insect grows to 30cm (12in) long and is the largest invertebrate on the island. It is a hunter that lives mostly in the arid zone. It has a venom that can subdue lizards and small birds. Bites from this critter are painful but not dangerous.

ABOVE:

Silver argiope

This garden spider is a naturally occurring resident of the arid zone. The 12-mm (0.4-in) harmless spider spins an X-shaped pattern in the centre of its web – it is not known why. Perhaps it highlights the web to larger animals so they do not blunder into it or it alters the way light reflects making it harder for flying insects to detect the trap.

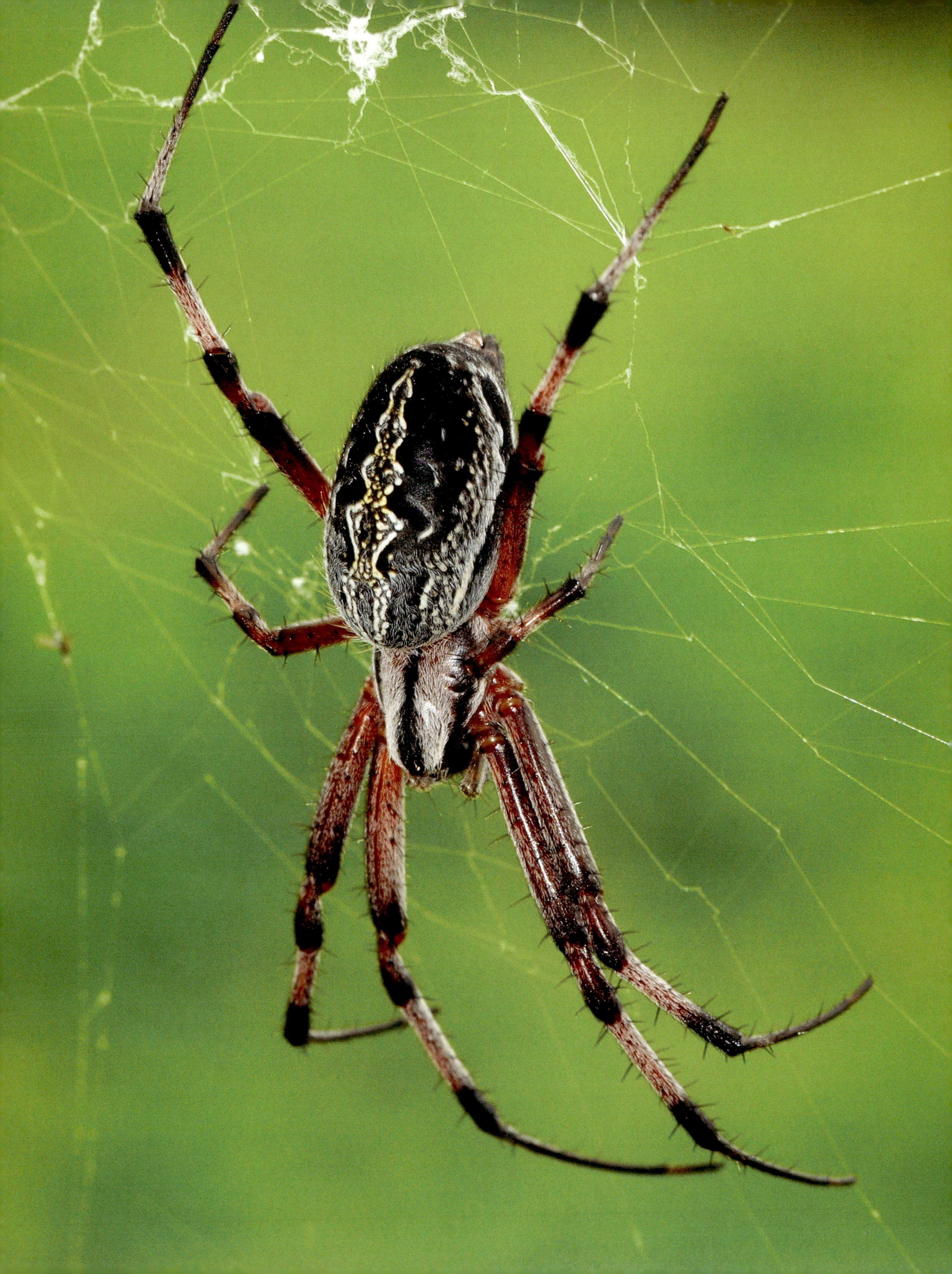

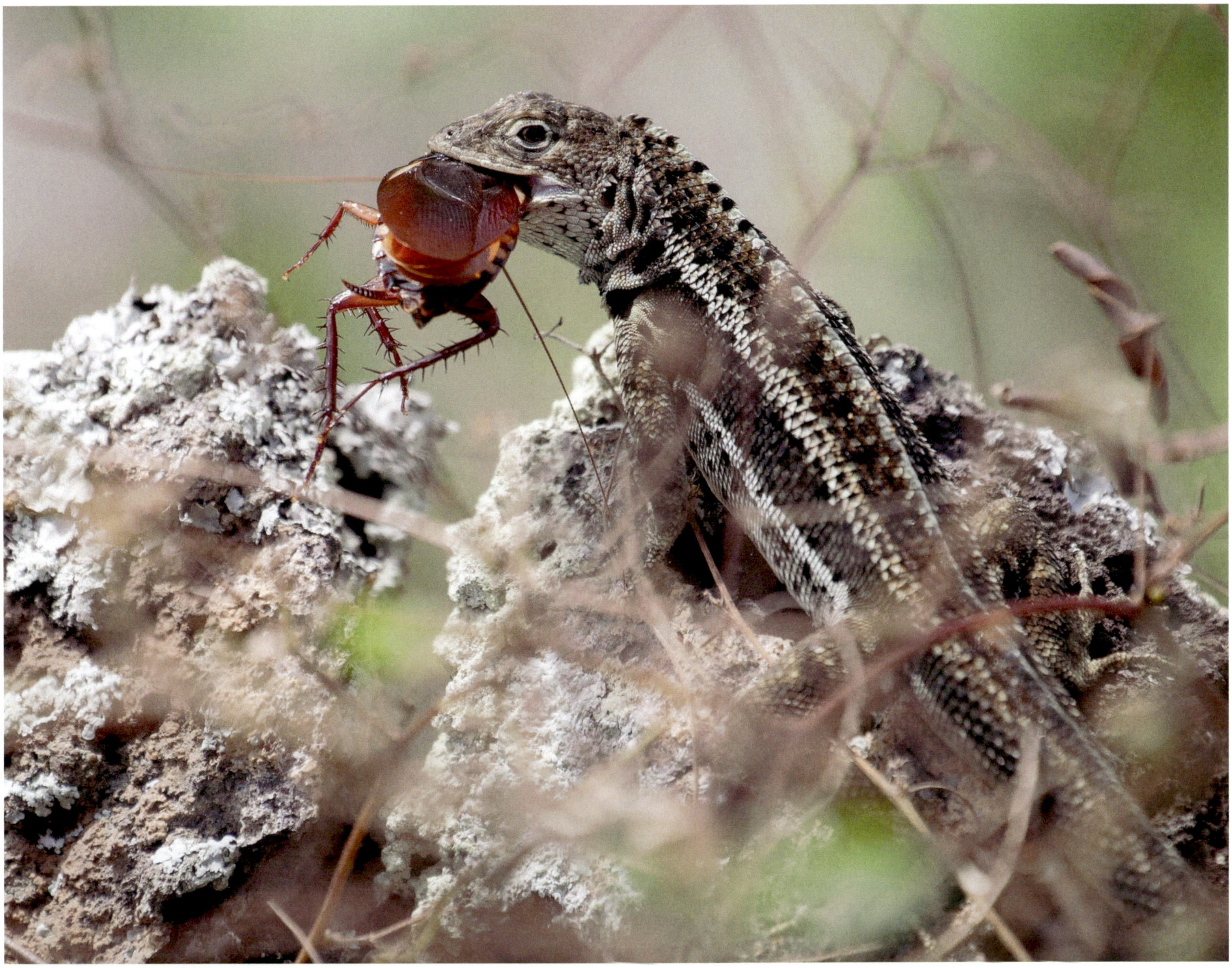

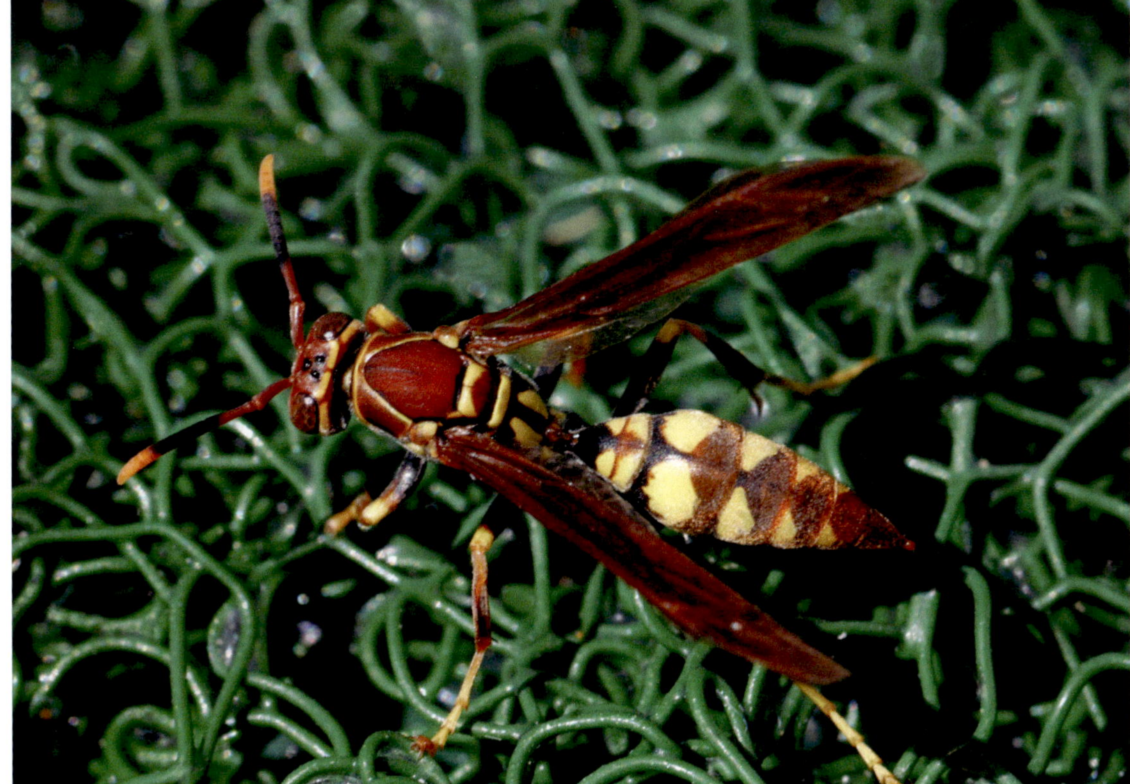

Zigzag spider
This orb-weaver is endemic
to the islands. It builds its nest in
insect flyways and often across
trails used by tourists.

Galápagos lava lizard
This is the most widespread of the
ten lava lizard species found on
the islands, often seen scurrying
around dark rocks. This one is
eating a cockroach; they will eat
whatever they can find from seeds
and leaves to maggots and rotting
carcasses. Lava lizards are related
to iguanas but are considerably
smaller at 15cm (6in) in length.

Yellow paper wasp
This large wasp – with a potent
sting – is a recent incomer to the
Galápagos. It was first recorded
in 1988 and has since spread to all
islands, building its large colonial
nests near the coasts.

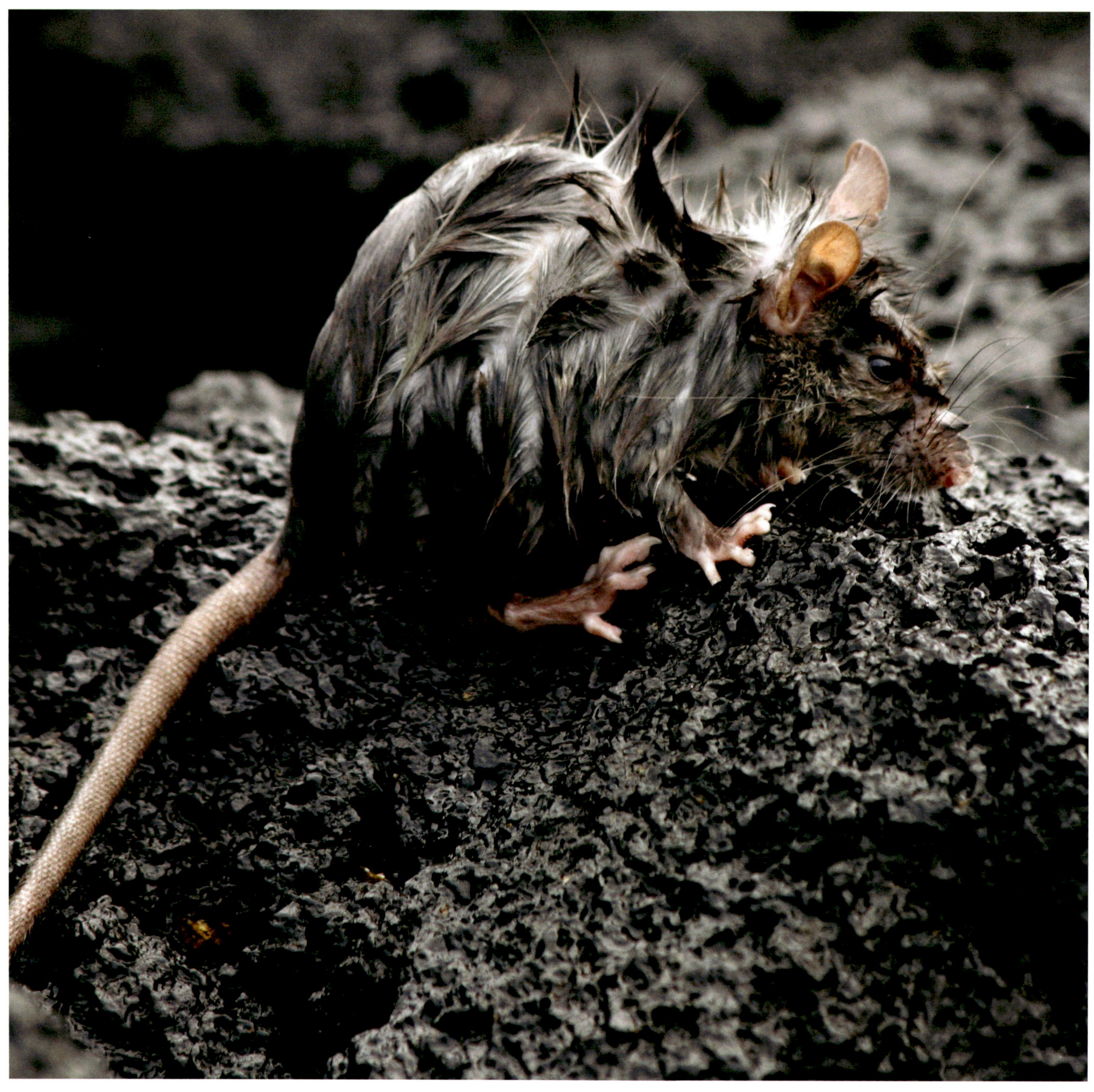

Black rat
The black rat (*Rattus rattus*) was accidentally introduced to many of the Galápagos islands by pirates and whalers in the 17th or 18th centuries. Successful rodent eradications have taken placeon some of the small and medium sized islands as they pose a threat to the endemic species of the archipelago.

Flamingos
The resident population of this distinctive wading bird are members of the American flamingo species. They feed in saltwater lagoons across the archipelago. The population rises and falls dramatically following the El Niño climate oscillation. The periodic heating of the oceans around the islands, reduces the availability of nutrients and impacts the animals that rely on the water for food.

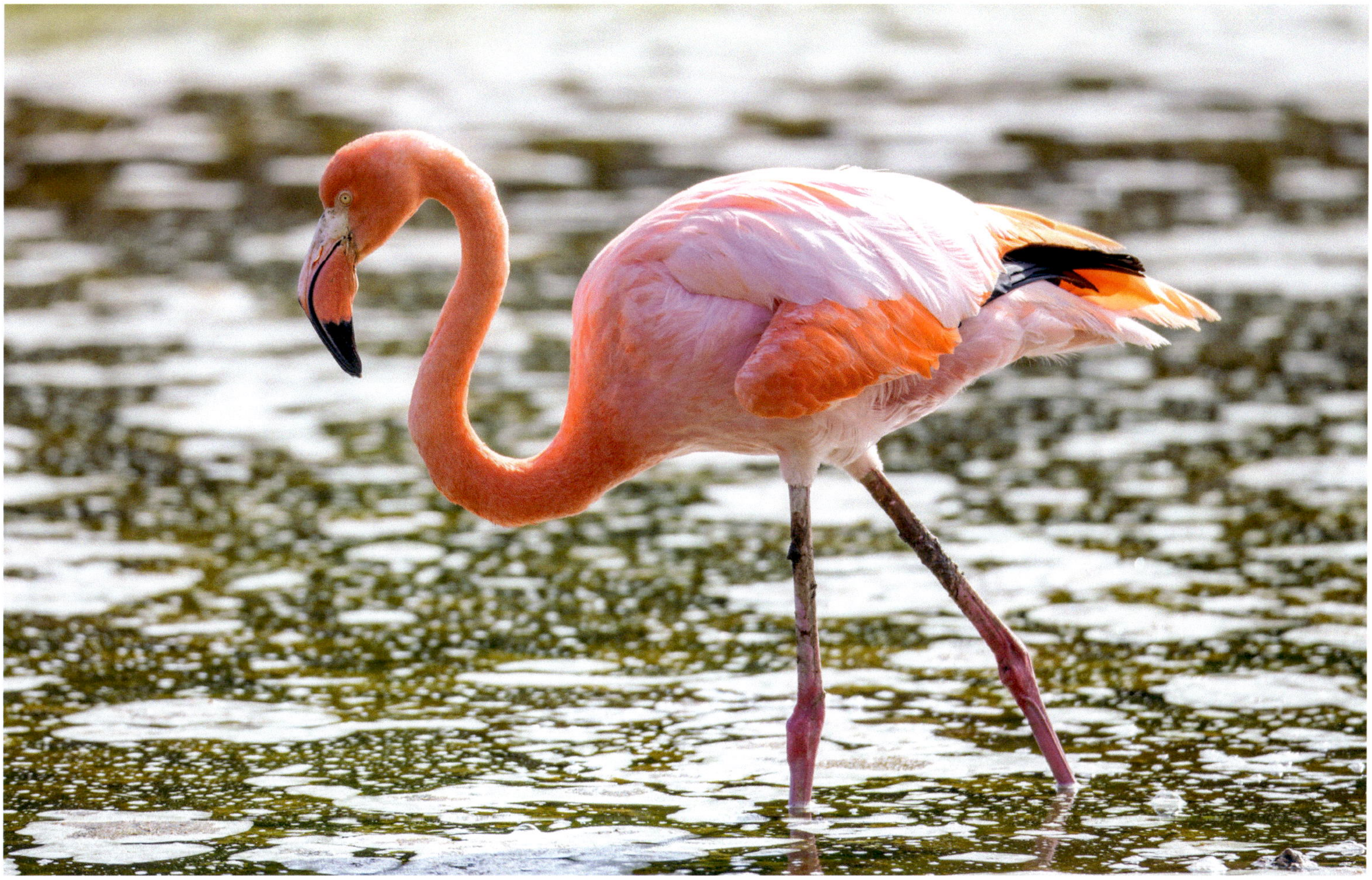

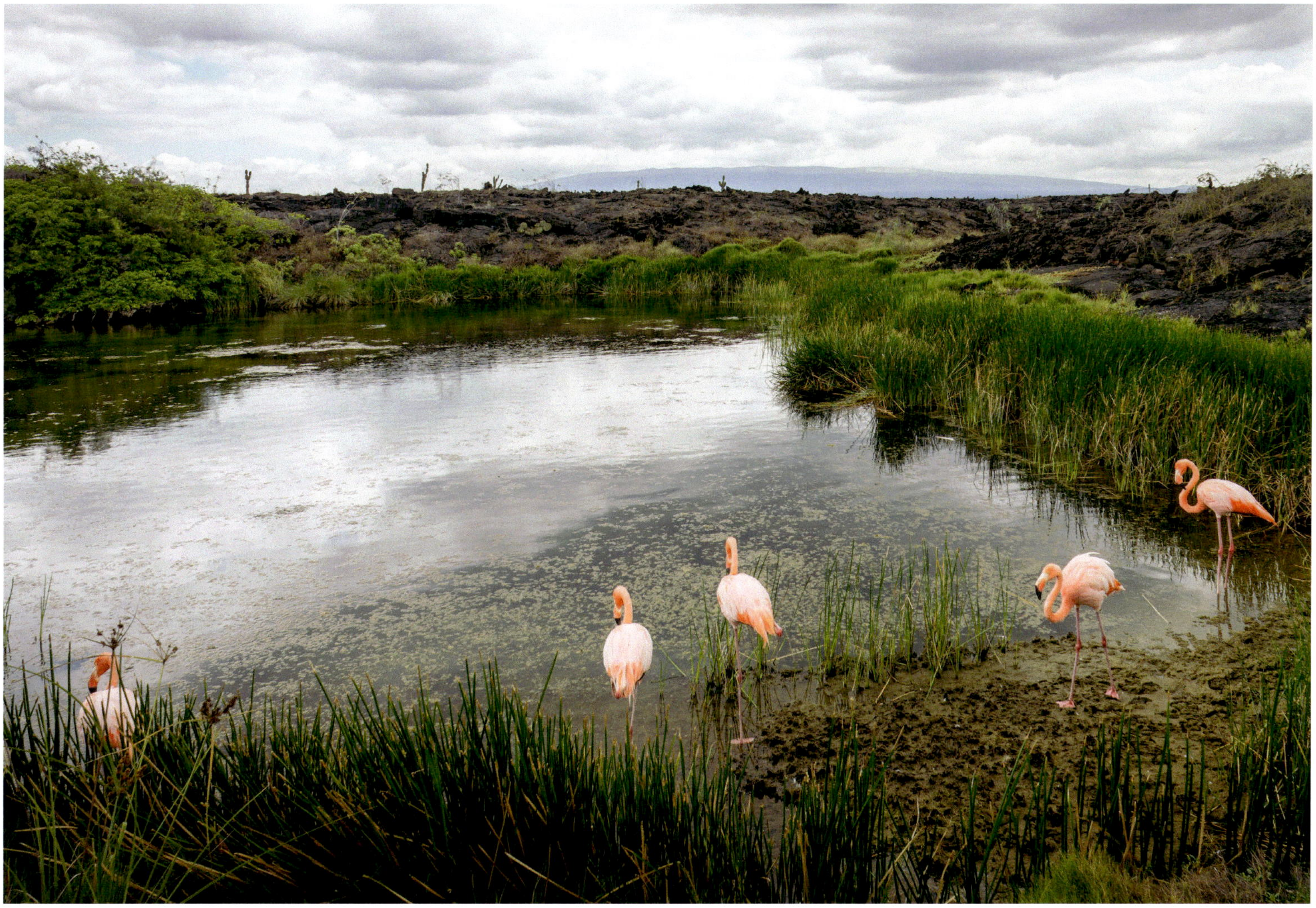

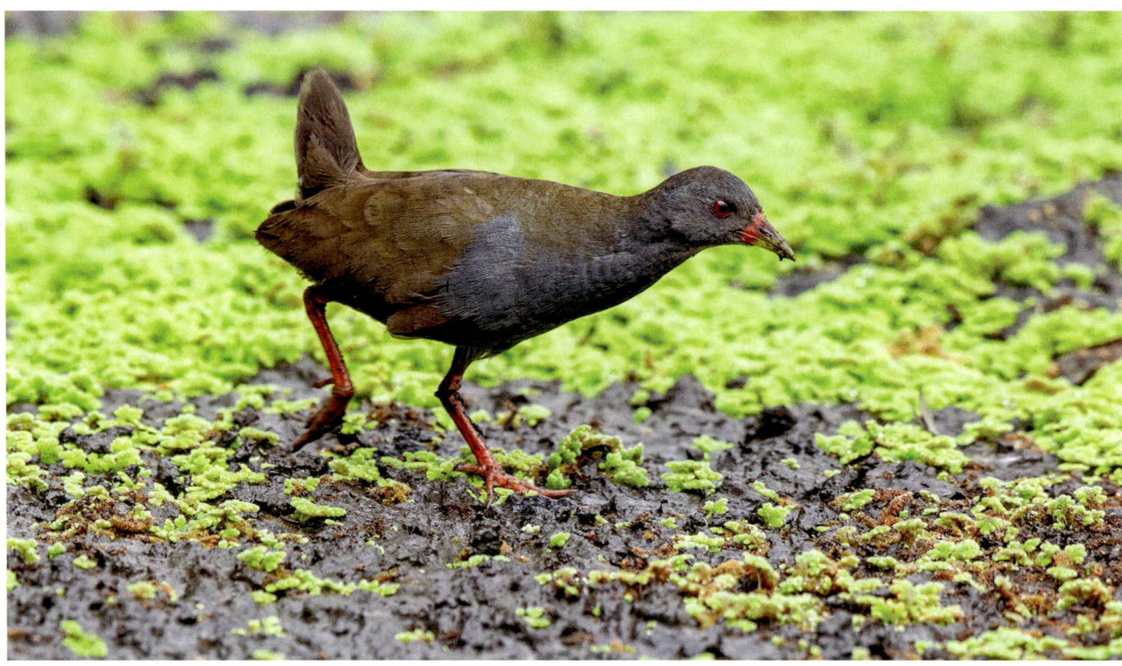

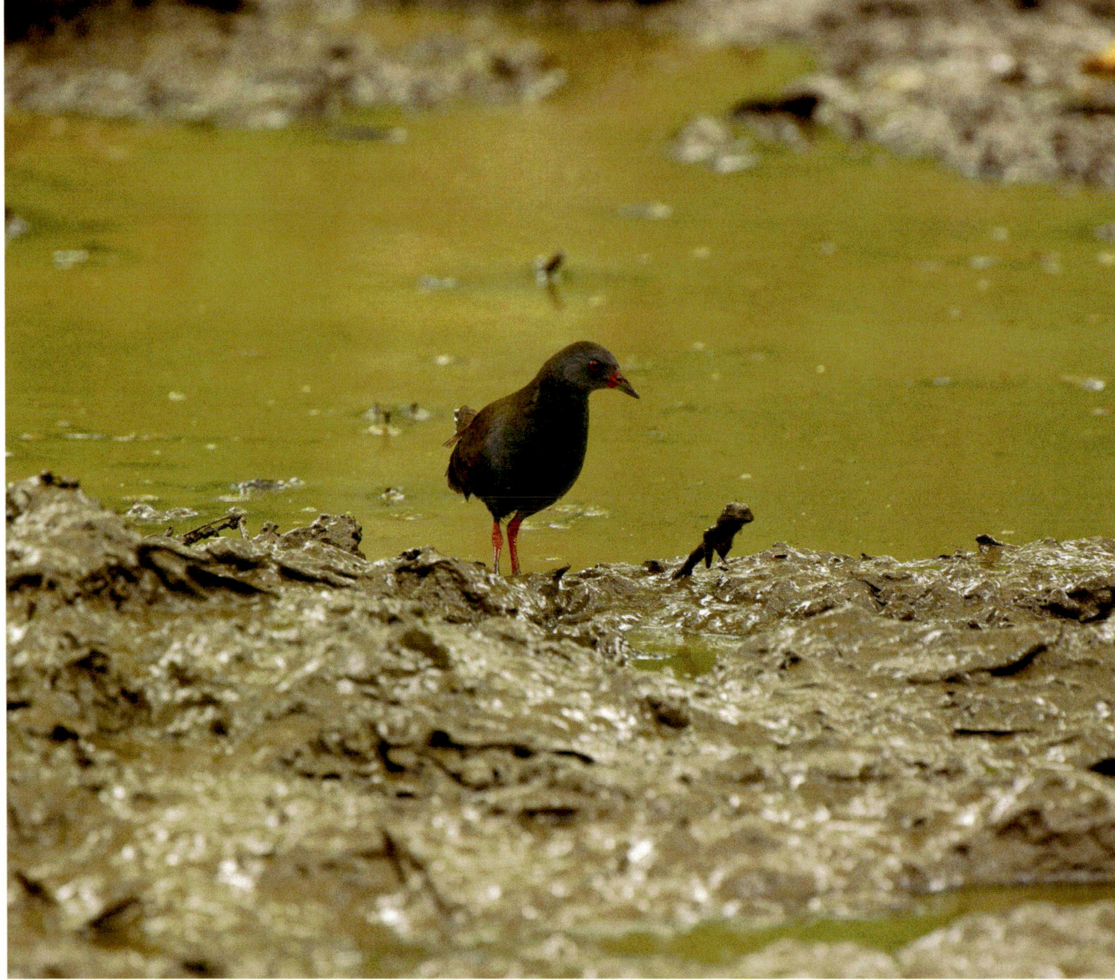

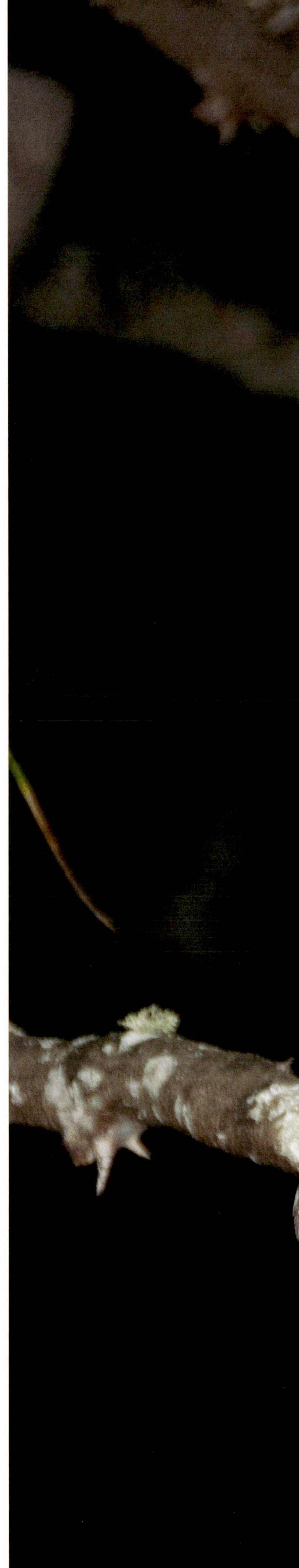

Paint-billed crake
This bird is a relative of the coot but lives away from wetlands in terrestrial habitats. Admittedly it prefers humid conditions but it can be found stalking the dry forests looking for insects and other invertebrates to eat among the leaves.

Galápagos crake
This is an endemic Galápagos species, also known as the Galápagos rail. It lives in the humid miconia forests in the island's upland interior. It is not completely flightless but seldom flies.

Galápagos barn owl
The islands host a distinct subspecies of this otherwise cosmopolitan owl. It is found mostly in the forests or the transitional zone between dry coast and humid interior.

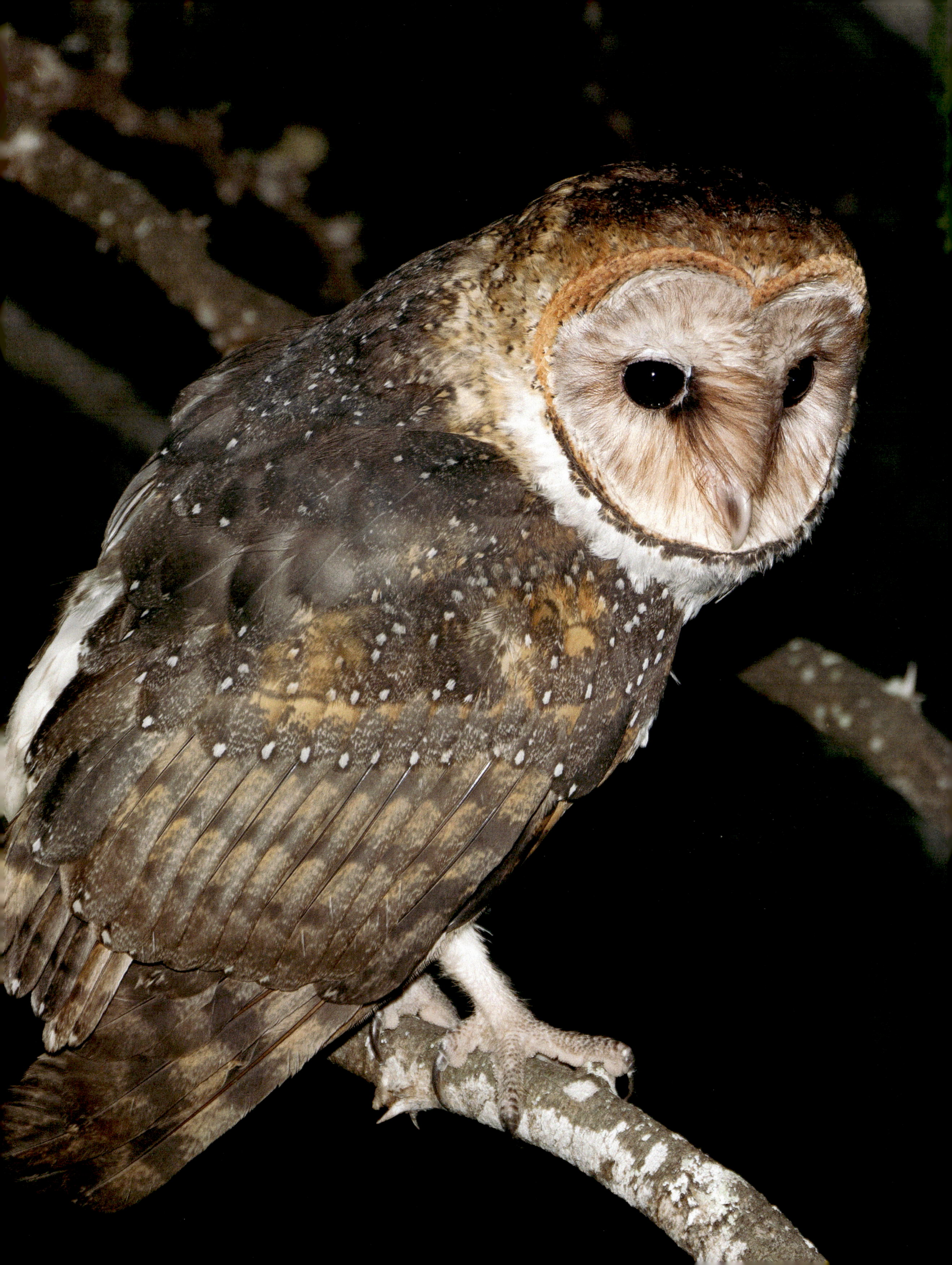

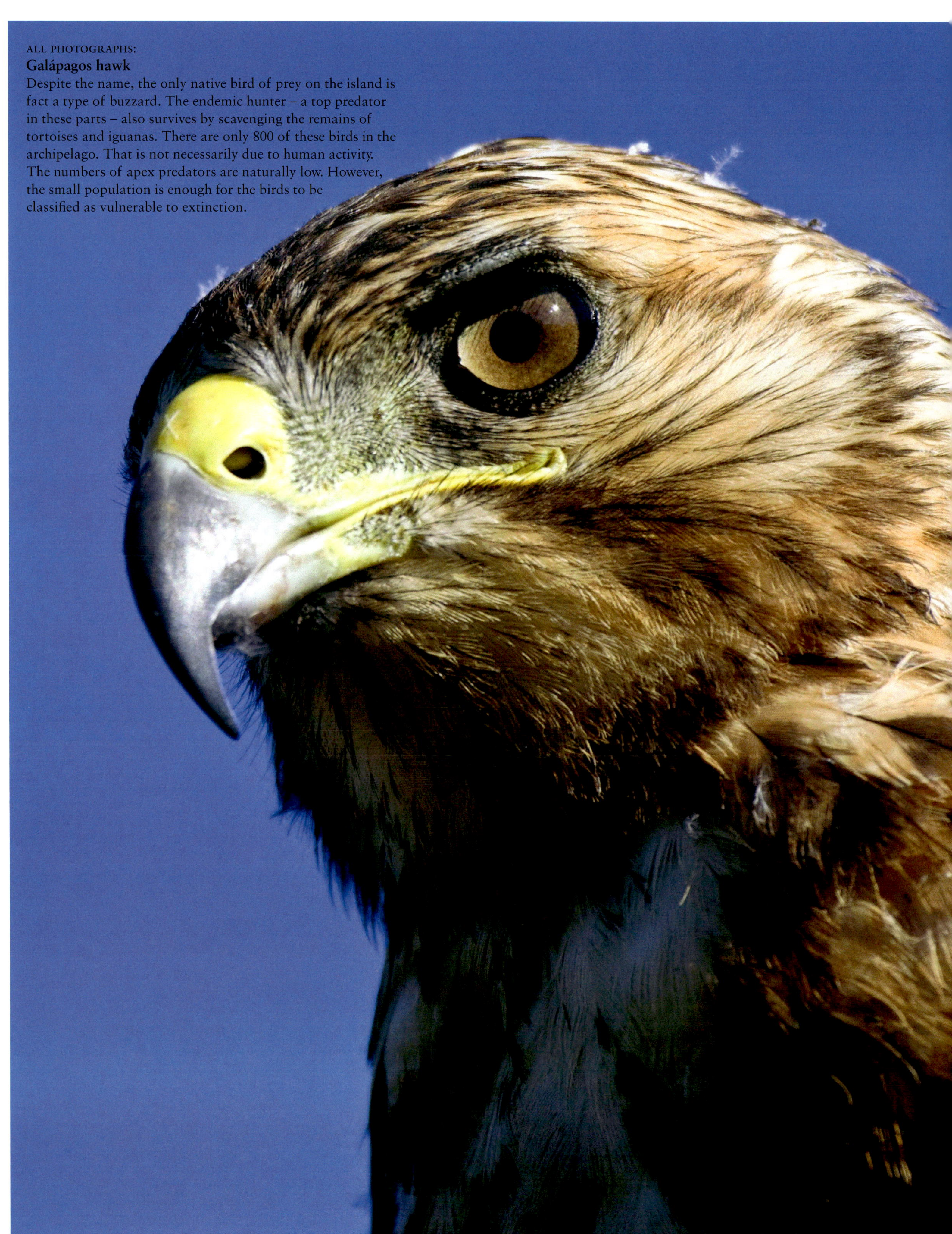

Galápagos hawk
Despite the name, the only native bird of prey on the island is
fact a type of buzzard. The endemic hunter – a top predator
in these parts – also survives by scavenging the remains of
tortoises and iguanas. There are only 800 of these birds in the
archipelago. That is not necessarily due to human activity.
The numbers of apex predators are naturally low. However,
the small population is enough for the birds to be
classified as vulnerable to extinction.

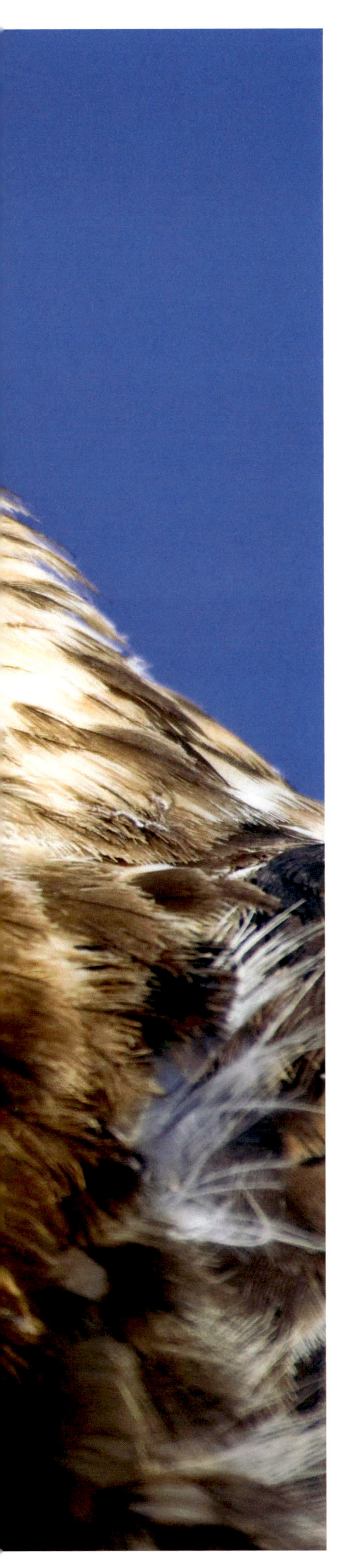
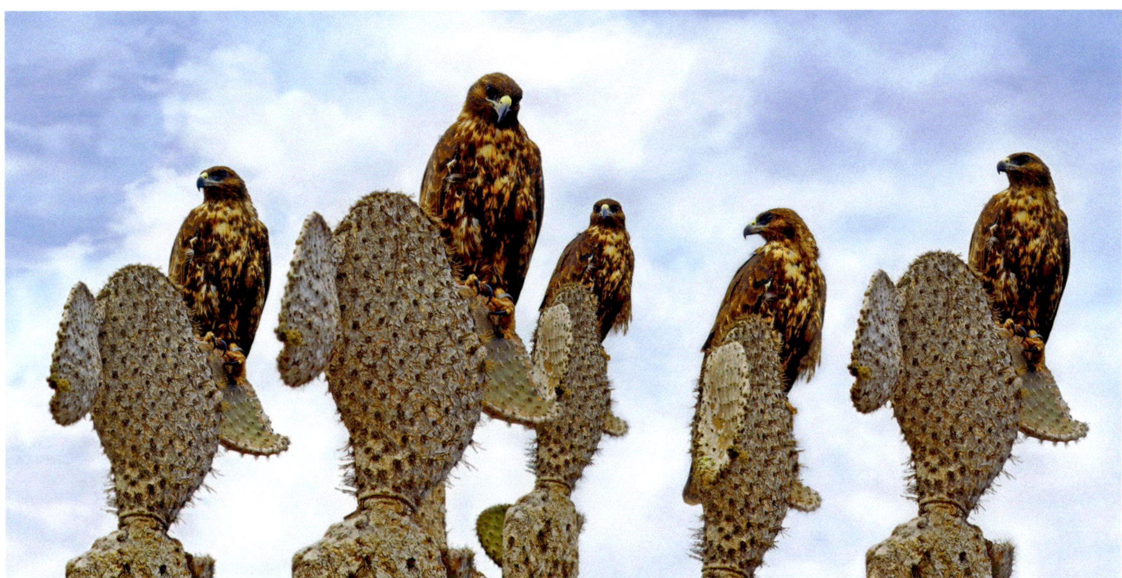
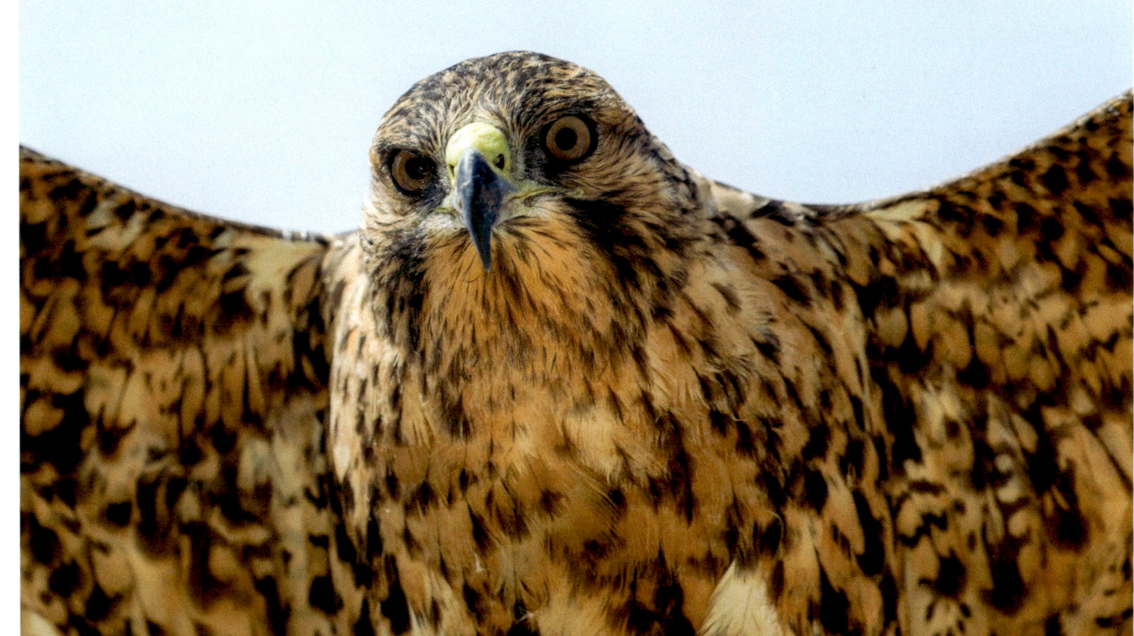
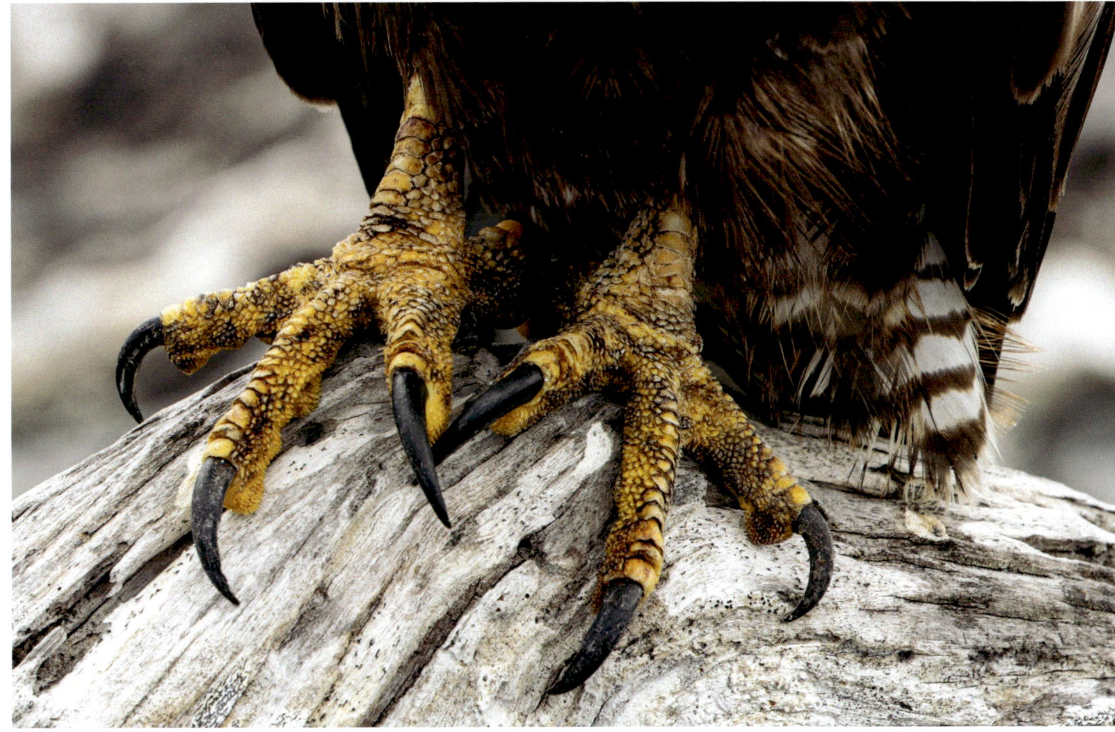

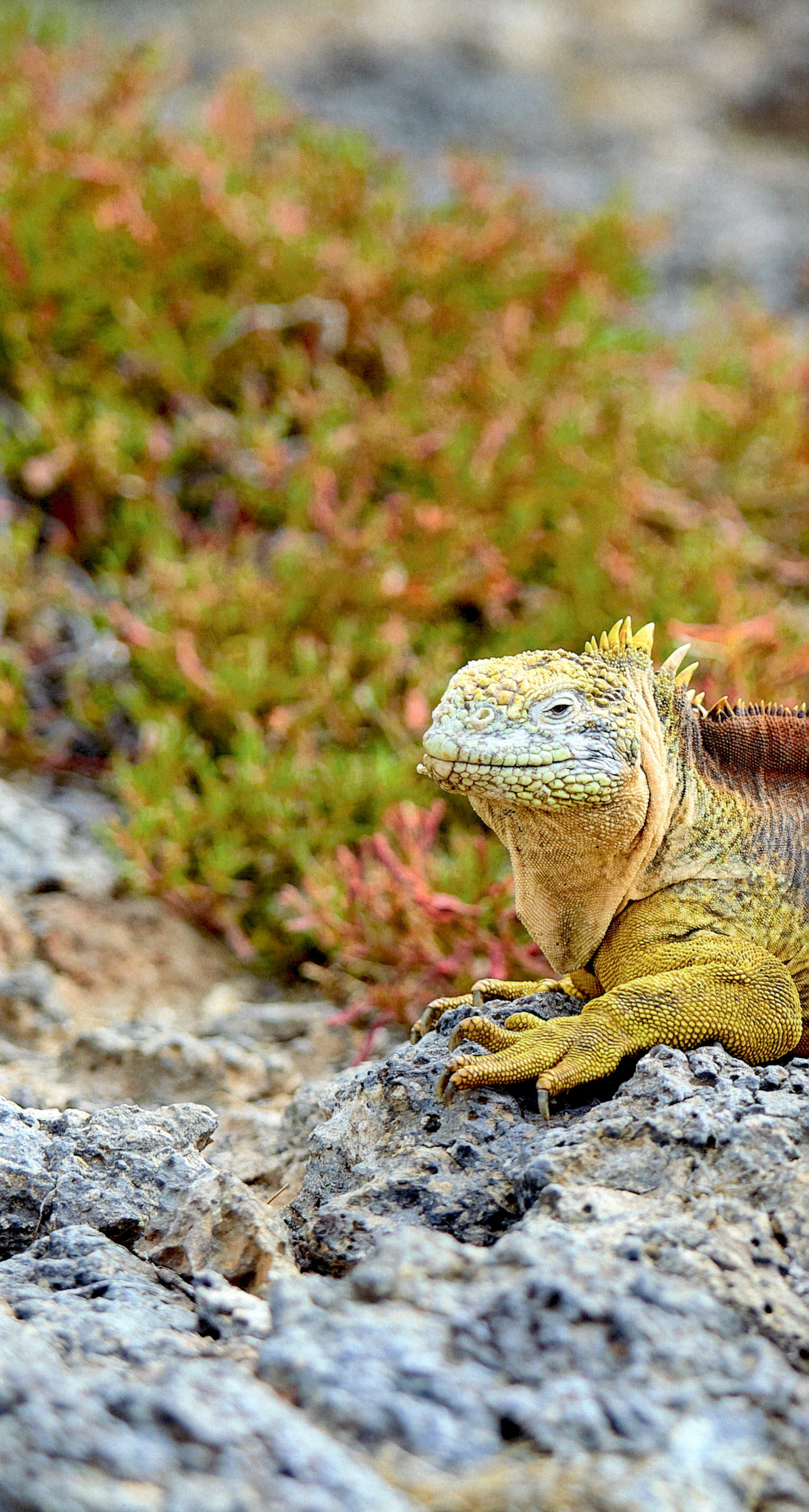

Land iguana
This beast is one of the longest terrestrial animals on the Galápagos. Older adults can be 1.5m (5ft) long, about twice the length (and more than twice the weight) of their coastal cousins, the marine iguanas. There are three species of land iguana. The main one seen here is found on all major islands. A smaller, paler species is limited to Santa Fé. The rarest is a pink species that lives only on the slopes of Wolf Volcano on Isabella. The iguanas on Fernandina incubate their eggs in the warm sands of the volcanic crater, but the hatchlings then need to climb to safety.

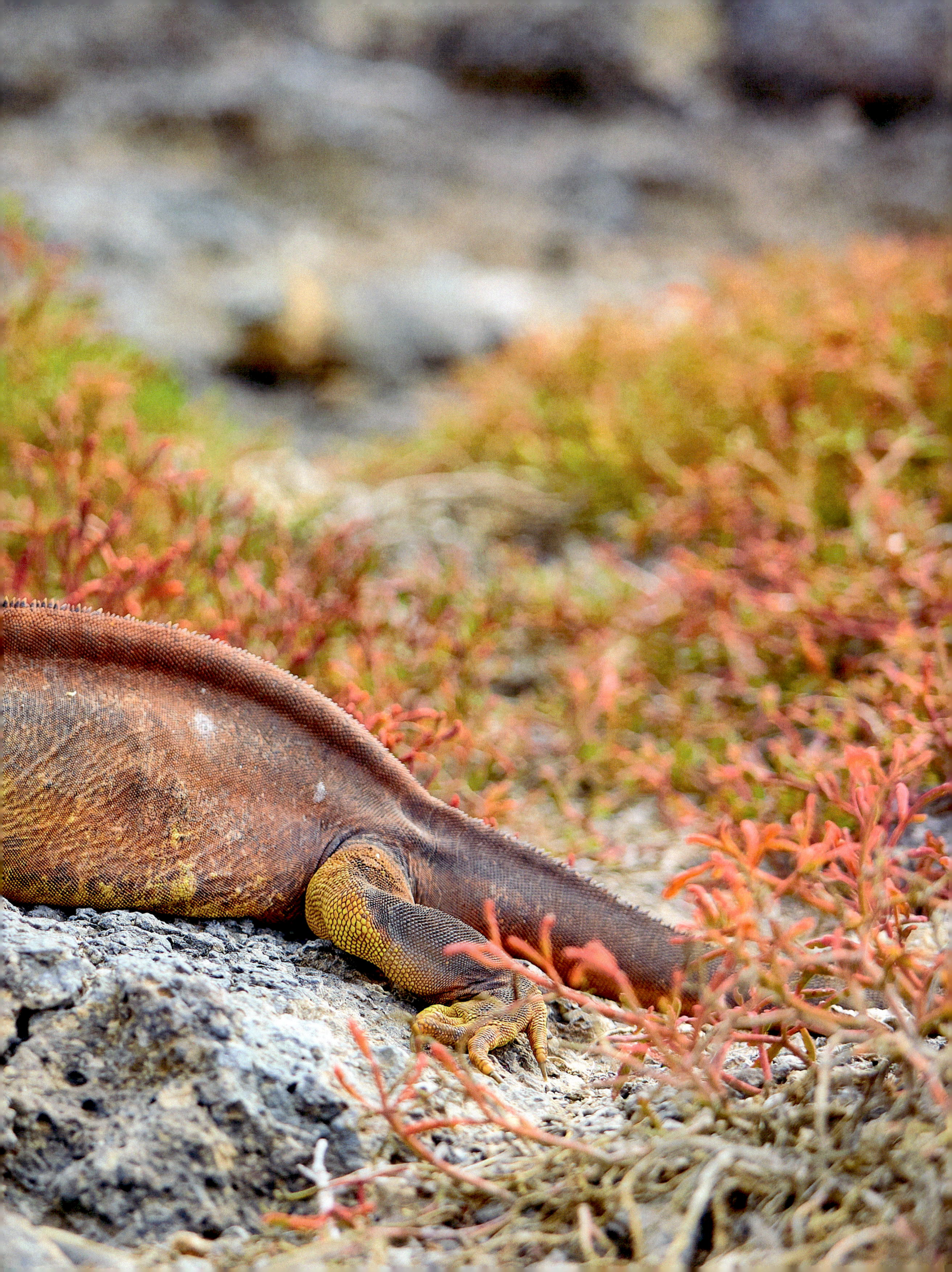

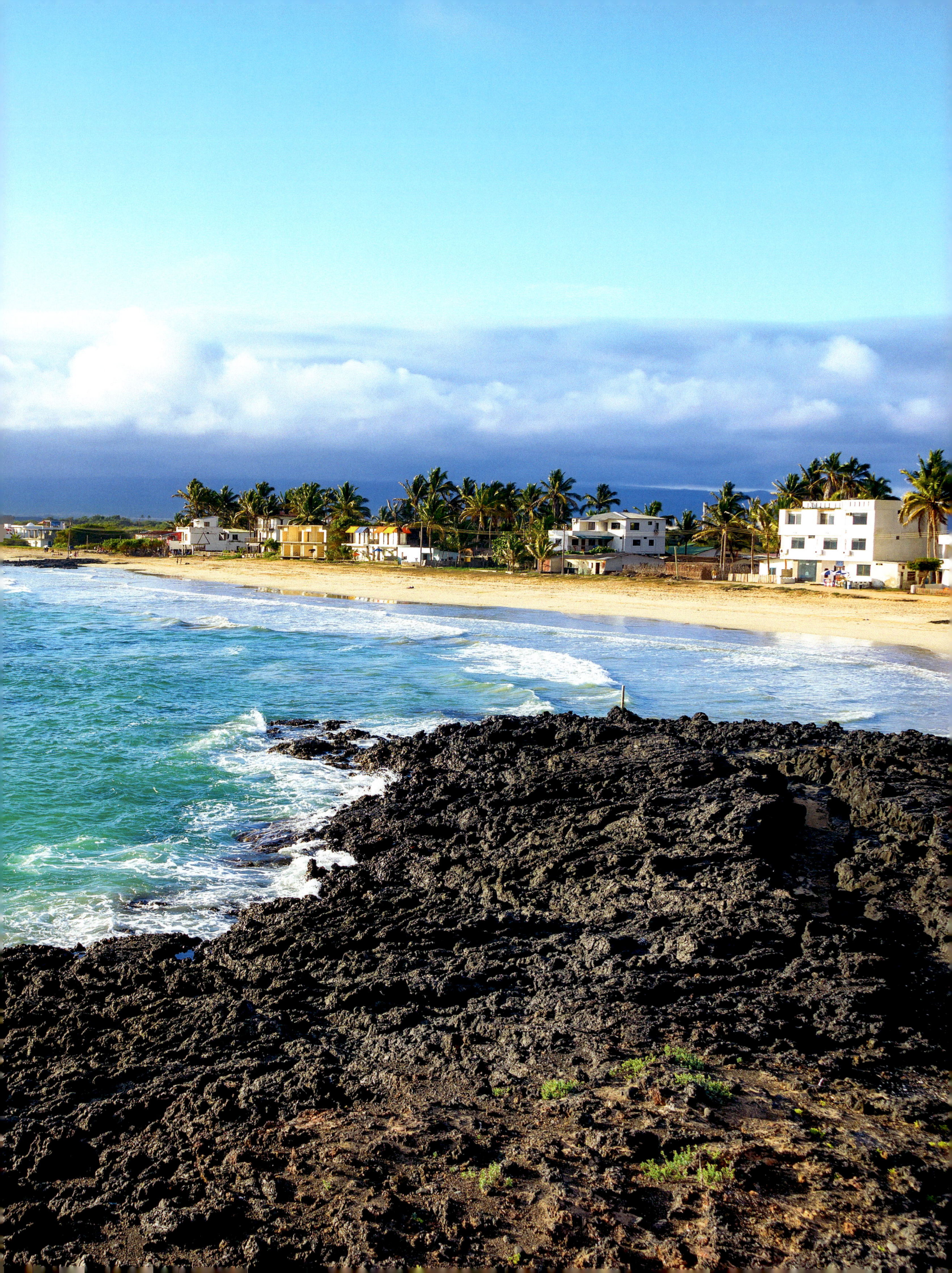

Human Settlements

The Galápagos Islands were officially discovered in 1535 by the Bishop of Panama. His ship had been blown off course by a storm as he sailed to Peru. He was not impressed by the place, saying it looked like 'God had rained stones' there. A legend remains that a fleet of Inca explorers had reached the islands a century before, but there is scant evidence for this theory. At first the archipelago was dubbed the 'Enchanted Isles' because they were so hard to find. Rumours developed that they were actually unmoored from the seafloor and floated around shrouded in cloud, only to reappear in unexpected places.

By 1570, the islands' location had been established and they were included on maps. They became a haunt of pirates who used them to restock their ships with water and food – giant tortoises were stowed aboard alive, as a source of fresh meat. By the 19th century the Galápagos had semi-permanent settlements used by passing whalers and the first permanent community were prisoners sent from the Ecuadorian mainland in 1832. The prisoners and assorted frontiersmen were there to greet Charles Darwin and the crew of HMS *Beagle* in 1835 and helped guide their explorations. Inevitably settlers brought domestic animals with them, which wreaked havoc on the natural wildlife. That legacy remains as the Galápagos Islands have become a world leading centre of ecological research, supported by an alliance – sometimes uneasy – with a lucrative tourist industry. Today the Galápagos Islands is a World Heritage Site and its land and oceans are highly protected.

Puerto Villamil
This picturesque coastal village is the largest settlement in Isabela. Even though it is the largest island, only 2200 people live here, and most of them are in this small settlement in the far south away from the volcanoes.

Pirate cave
This cave on Floreana was the earliest human settlement on the Galápagos Islands. It was used by assorted pirates, and there is evidence of fires having been lit inside. The first permanent resident of the islands is said to be Patrick Watkins, an Irish sailor who was marooned there in 1807.

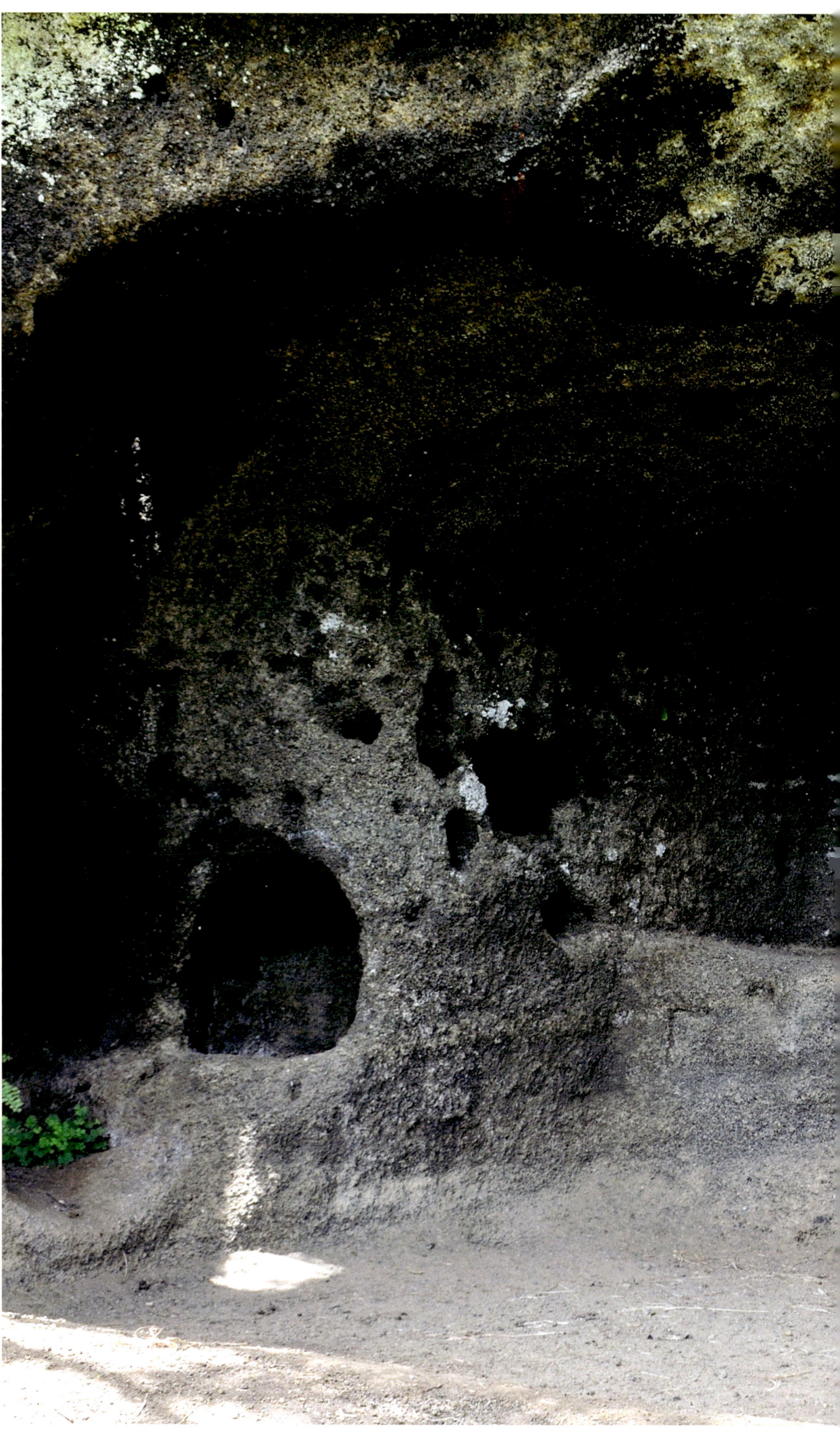

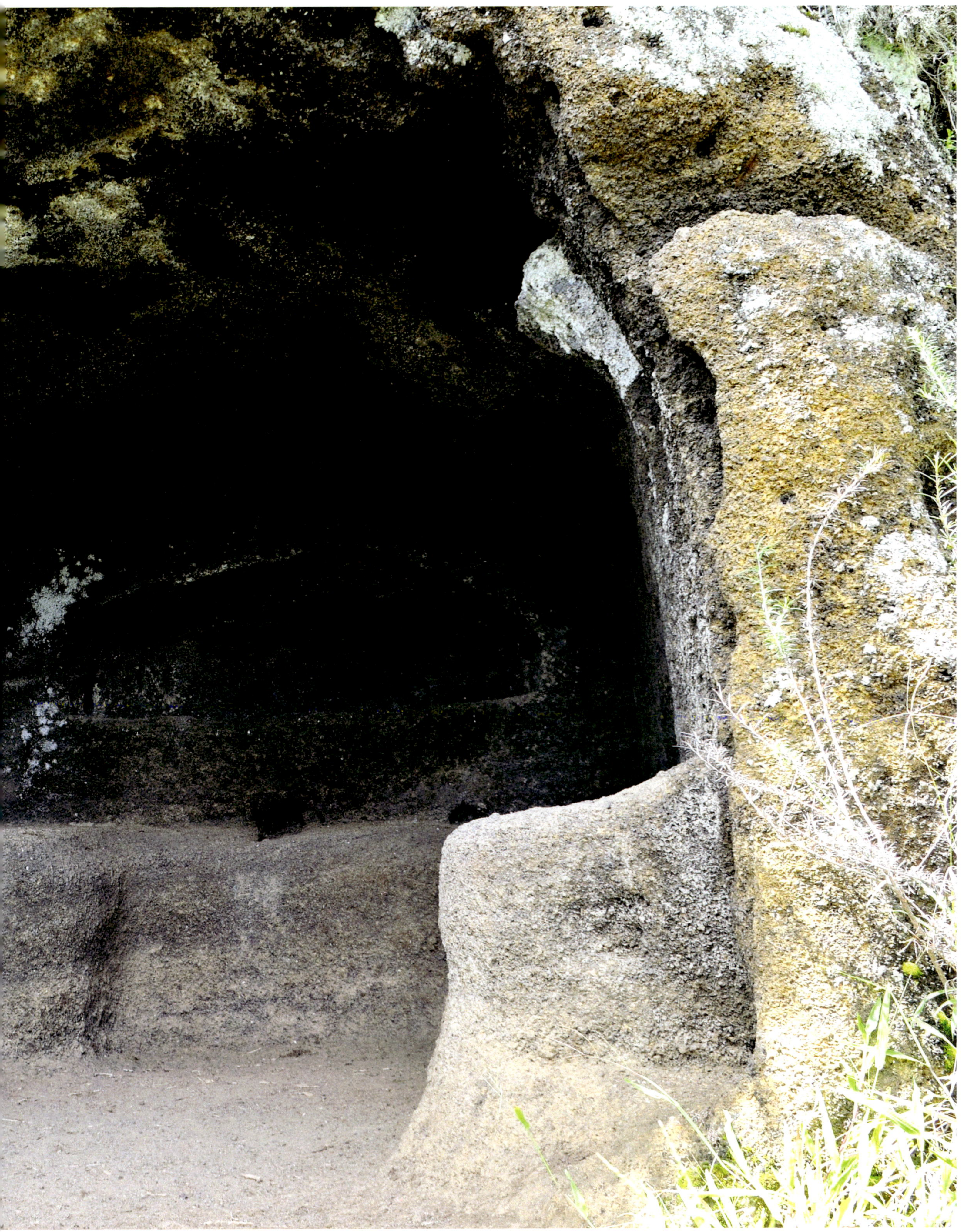

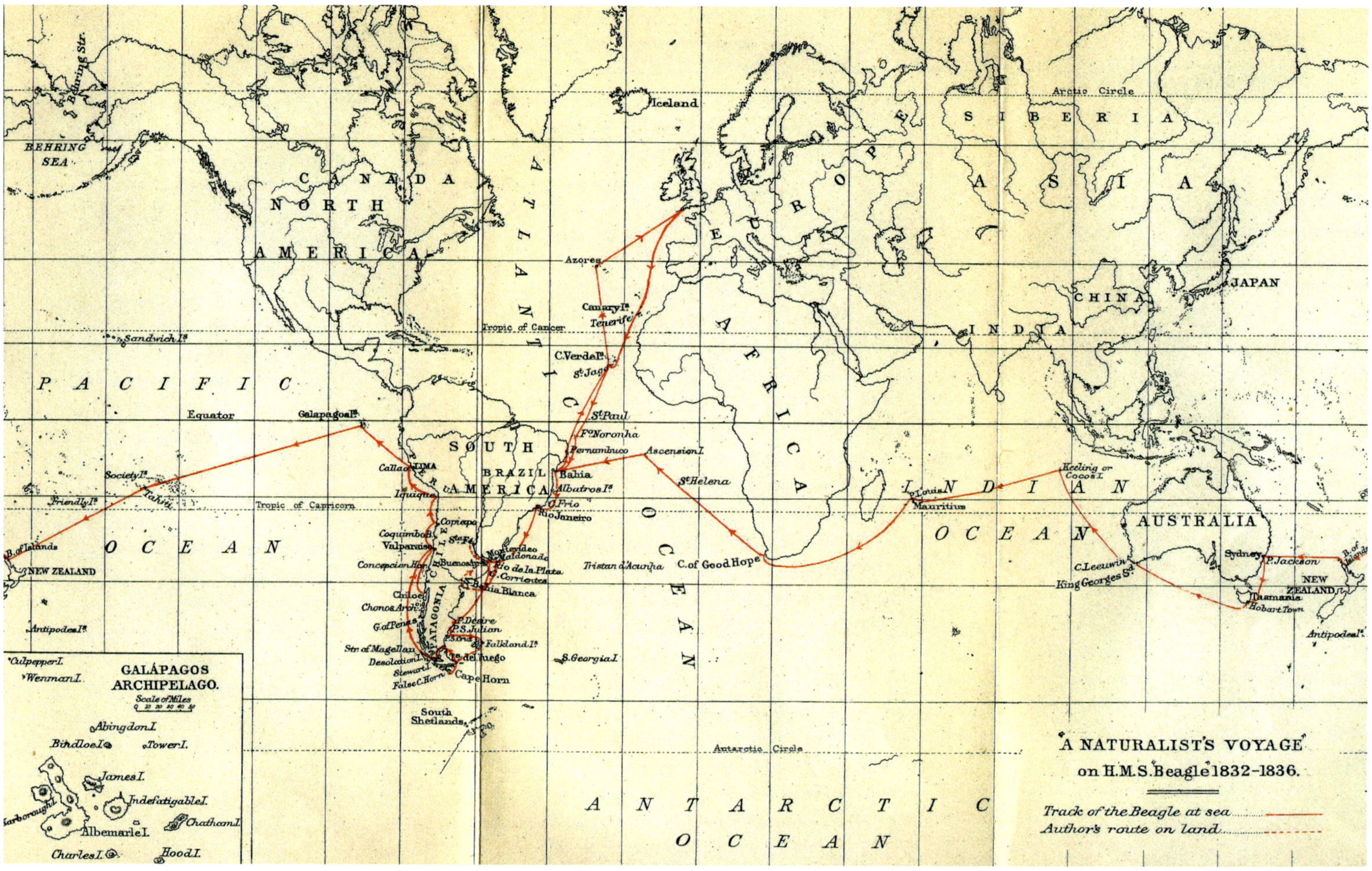

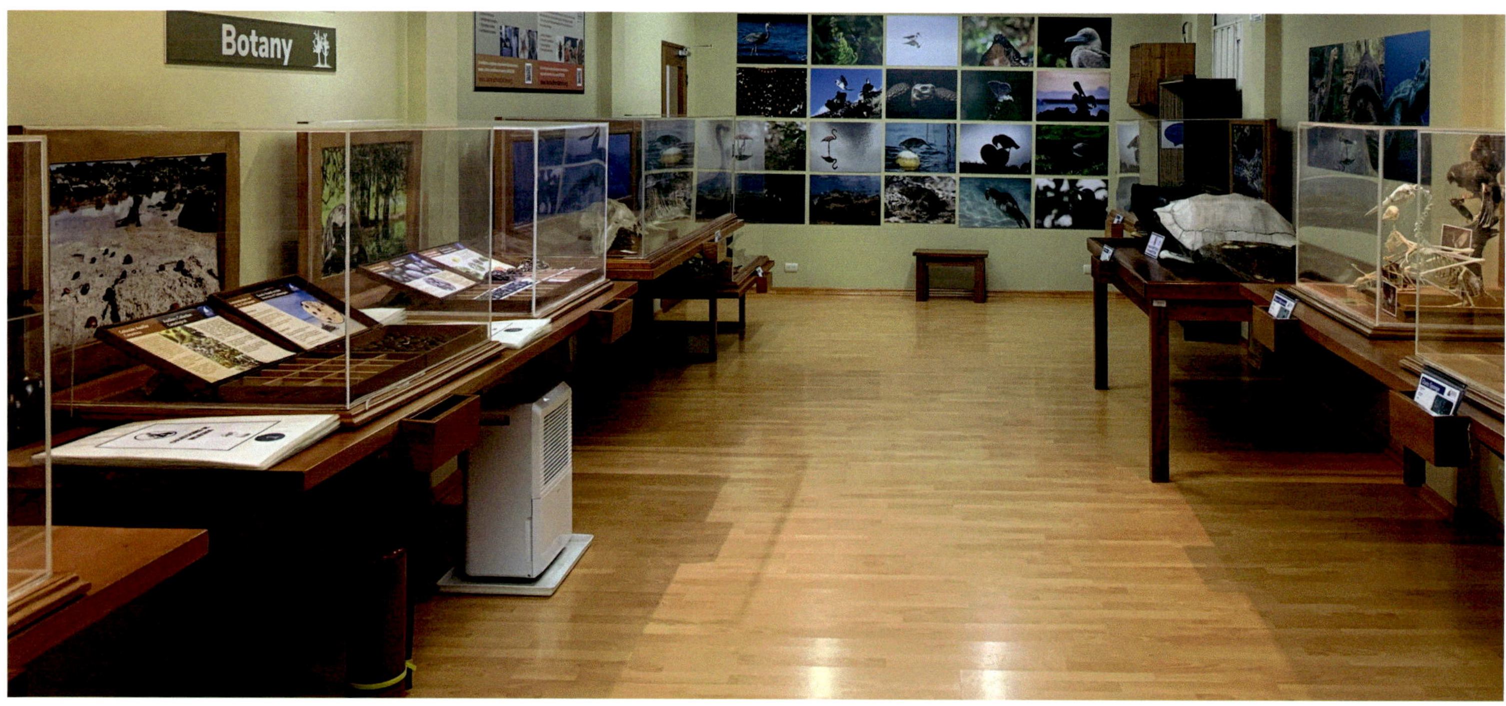

ABOVE TOP:

Voyage of HMS _Beagle_
This is the route of the second voyage of the naval research ship that took Charles Darwin to the Galápagos Islands. The five-year circumnavigation of the planet explored the islands of the South Pacific and Indian Ocean.

ABOVE BOTTOM:

Darwin's legacy
Today the Galápagos is a protected nature reserve and the waters around it are also managed to ensure the wildlife thrives. Conservation efforts are supported by the Charles Darwin Research Station on Santa Cruz.

OPPOSITE:

Charles Darwin
This photographic portrait of the English naturalist was taken by Julia Margaret Cameron in about 1868, long after Darwin had published his theory of evolution and become one of the most famous scientists in history.

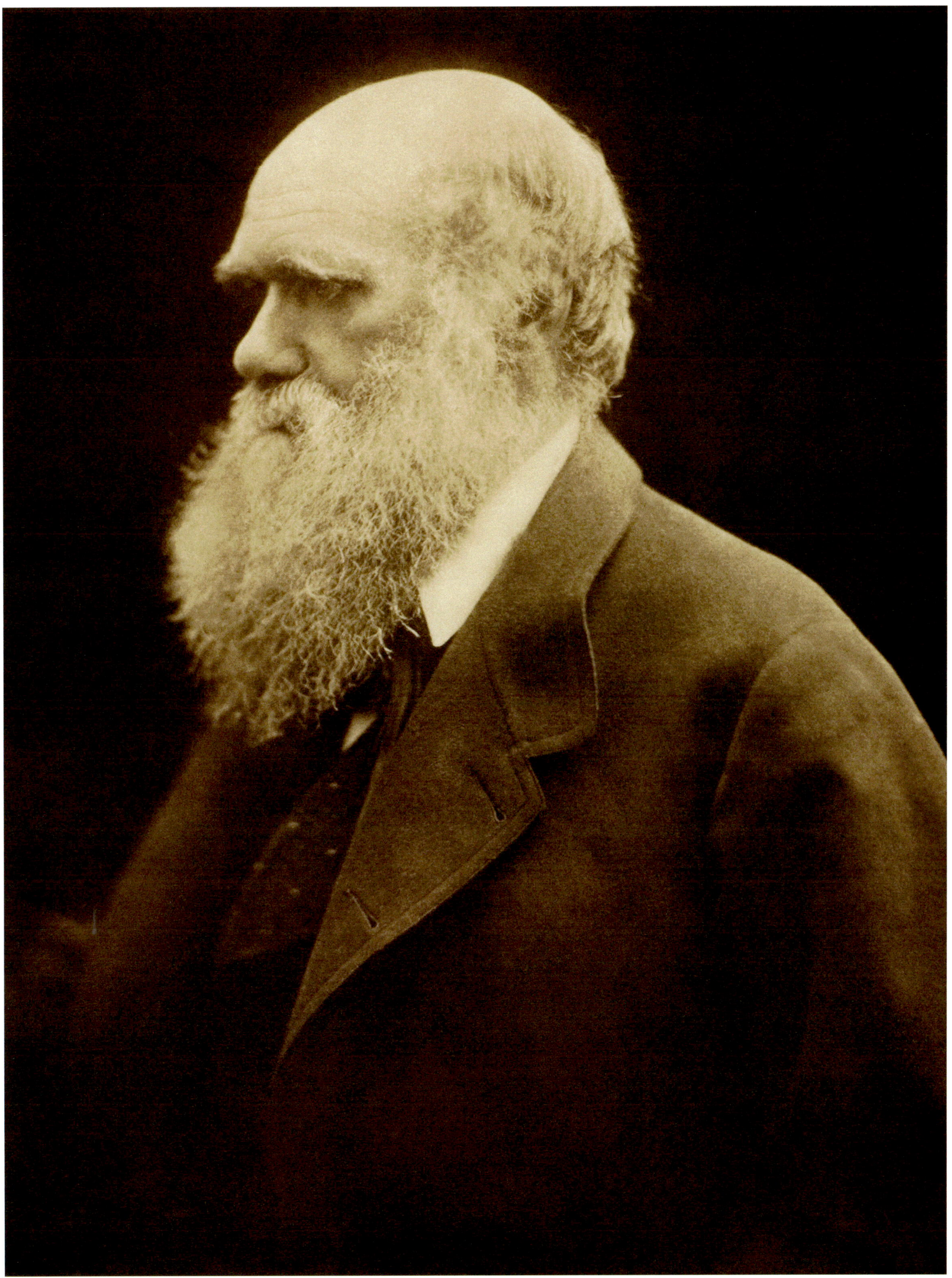

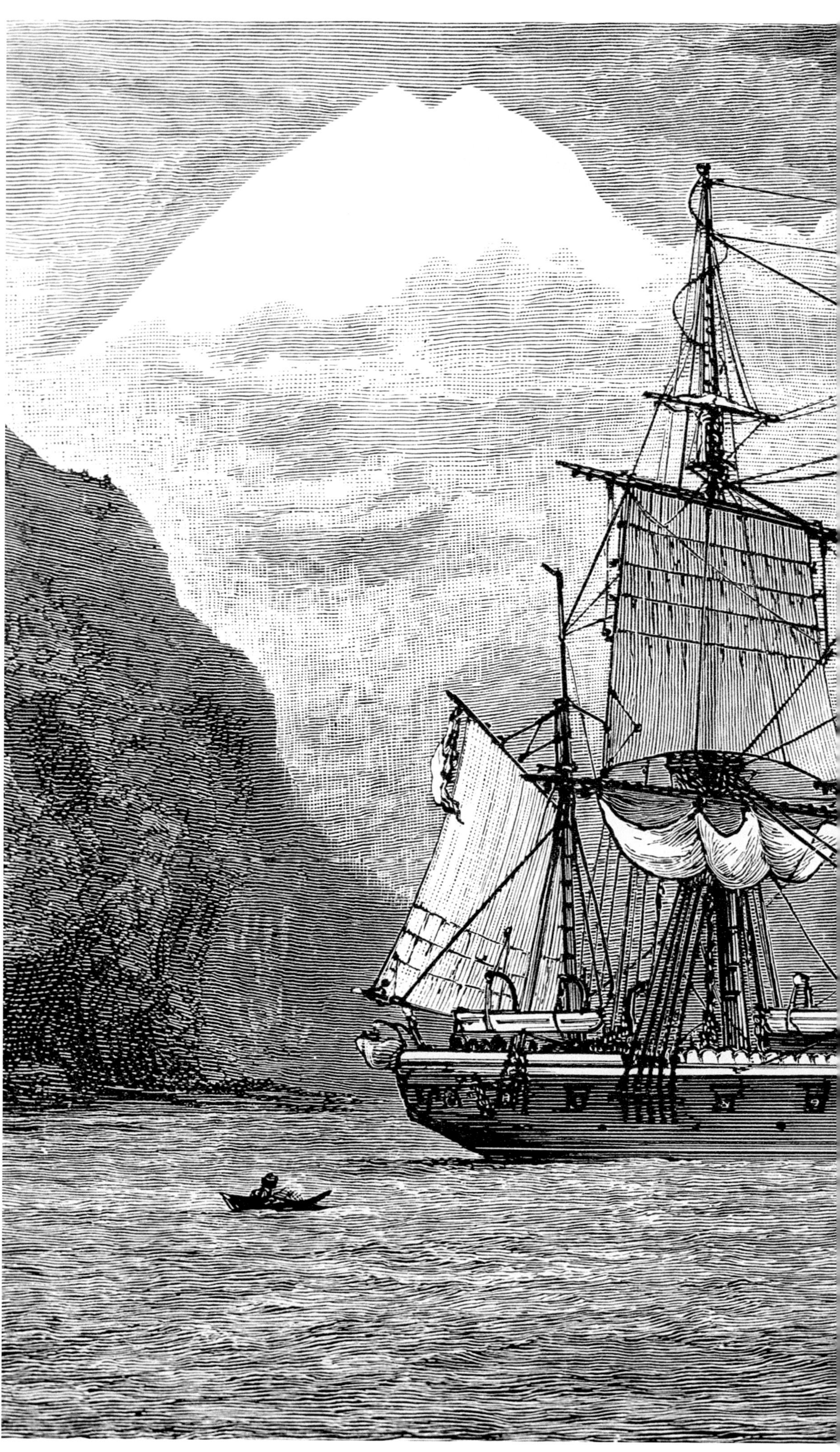

HMS *Beagle*
This reproduction of R. T. Pritchett's frontispiece from the 1890 edition of *The Voyage of the Beagle* shows HMS *Beagle* in the Straits of Magellan in front of the towering Monte Sarmiento peak.

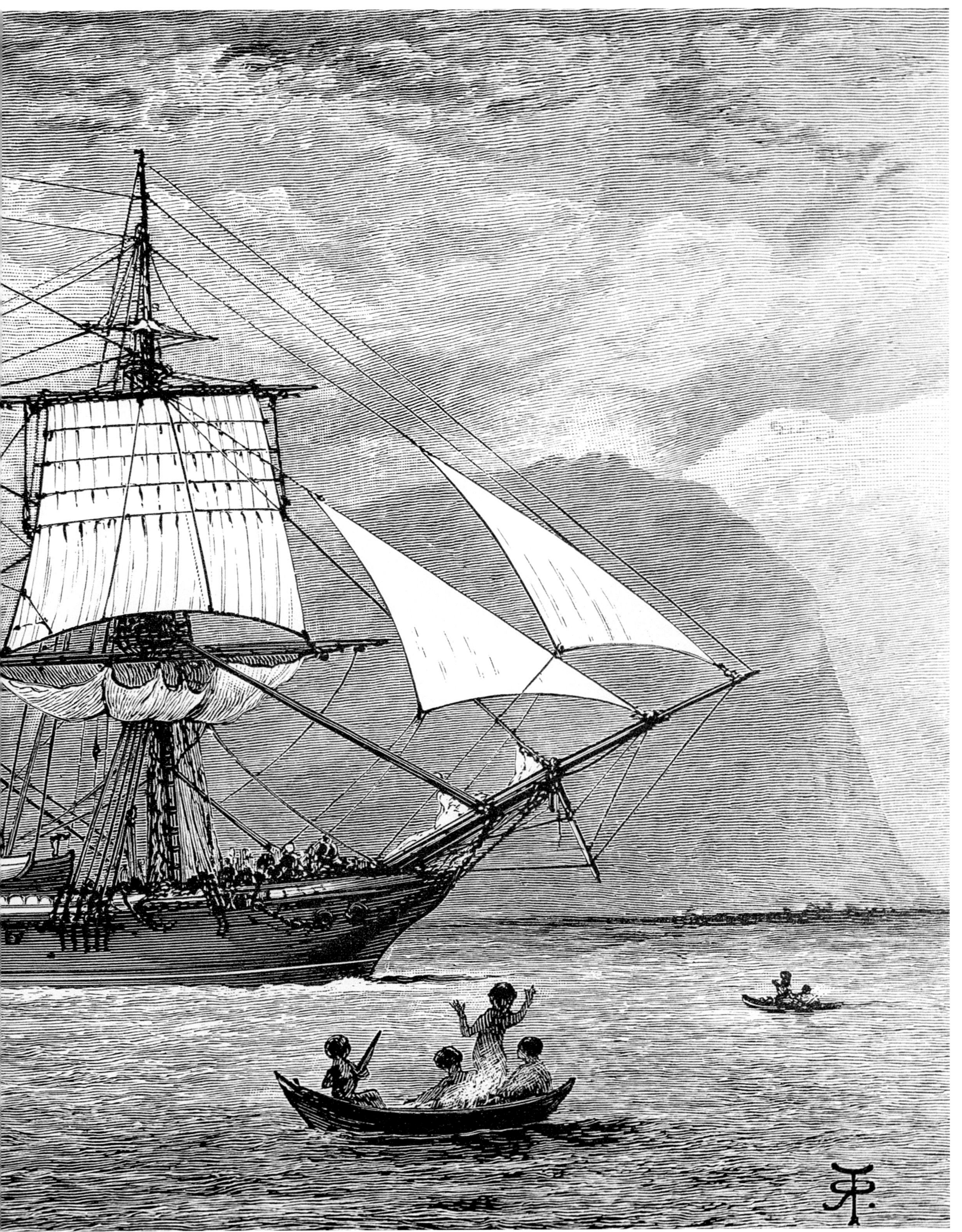

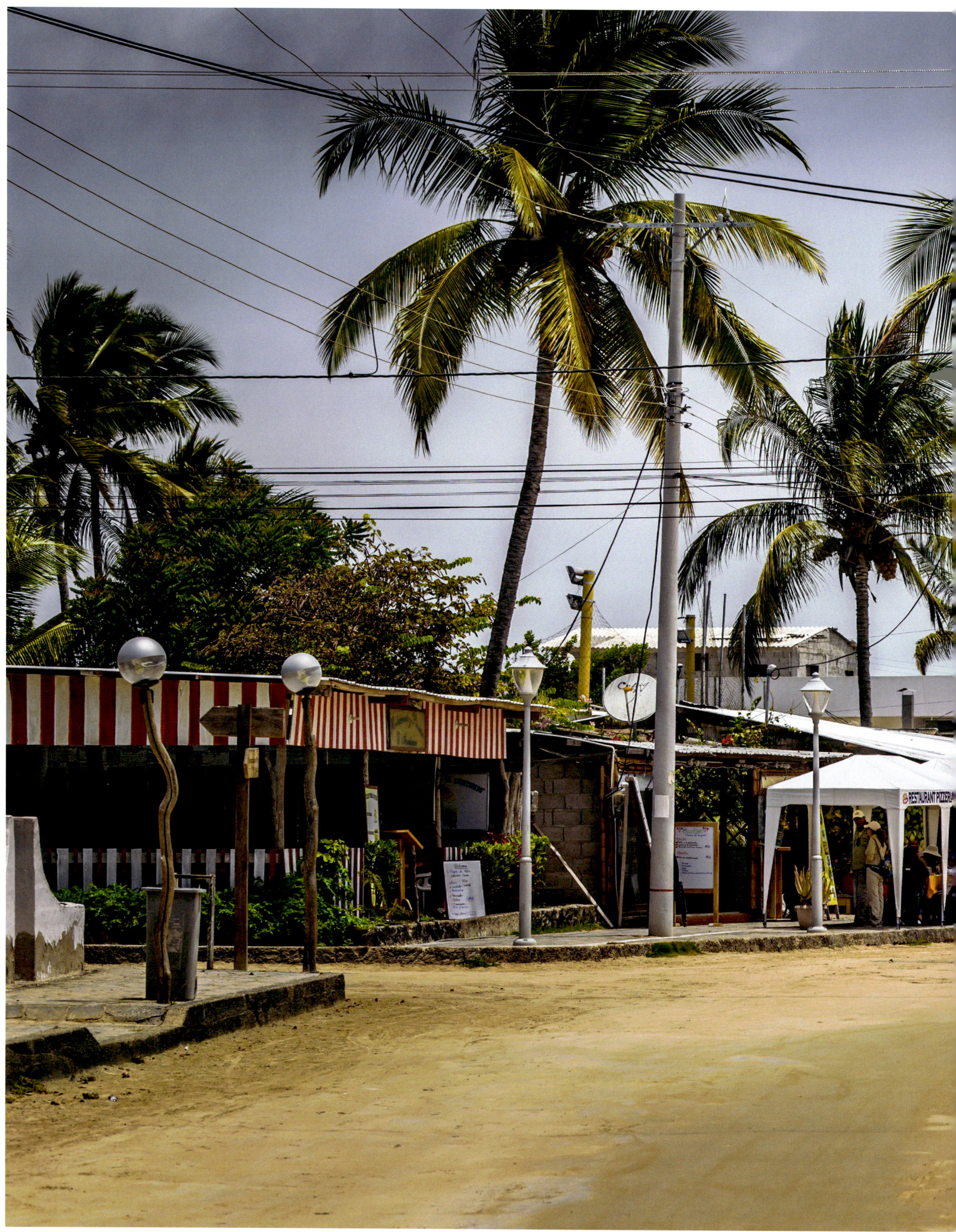

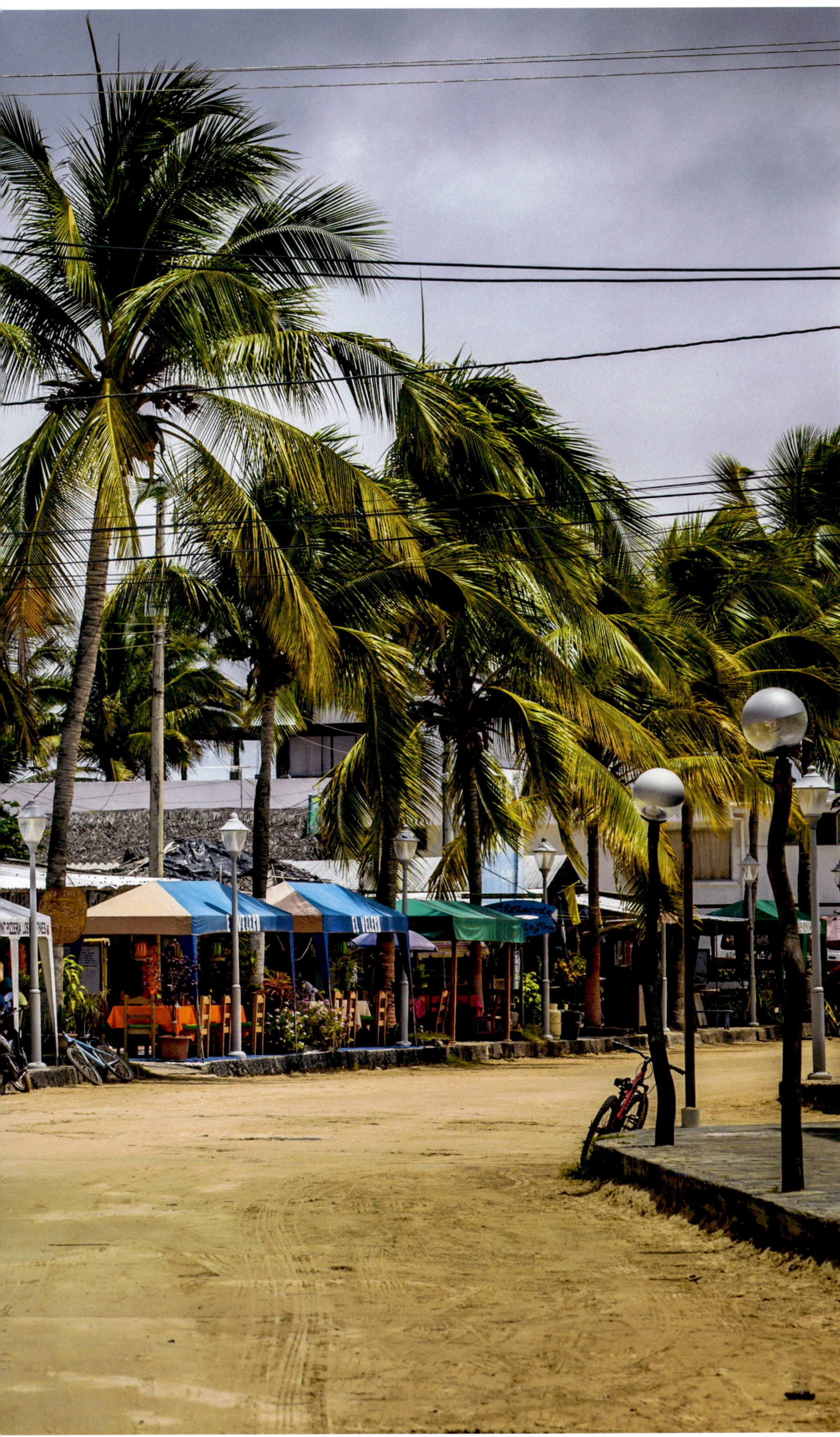

Tourist town
The main street in Puerto Villamil on Isabela Island has cafes and restaurants for visiting tourists. Visitors generally arrive by boat.

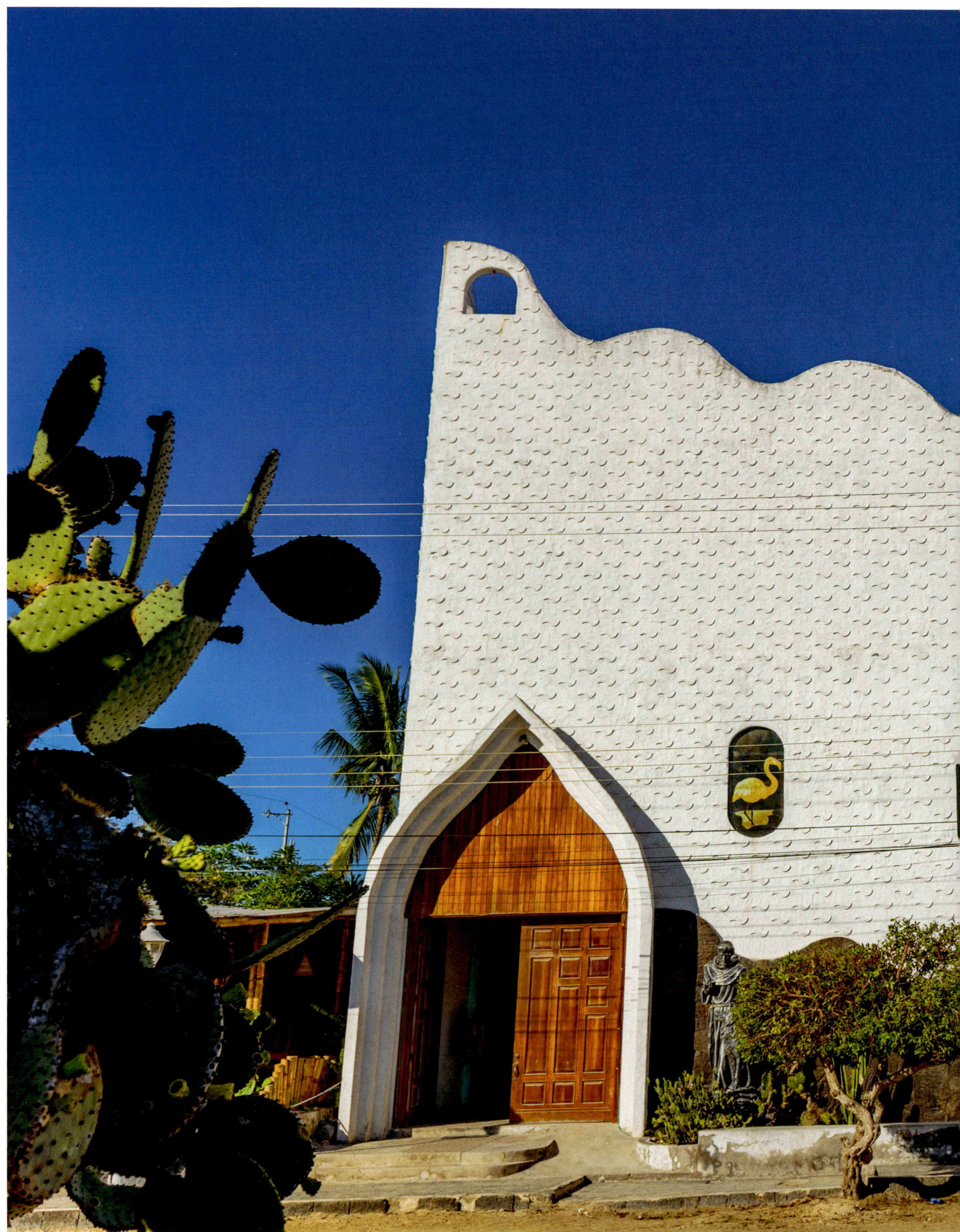

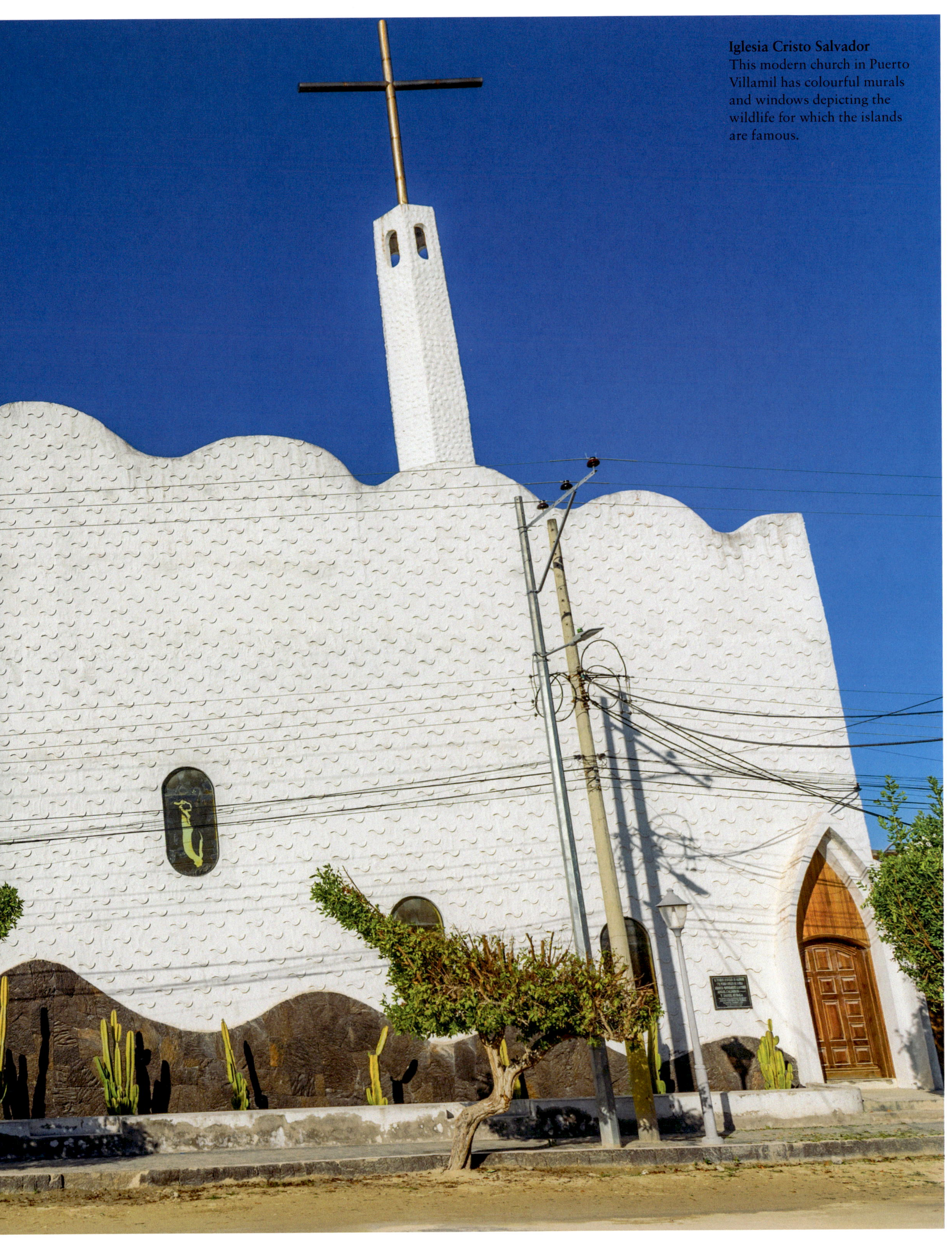

Iglesia Cristo Salvador
This modern church in Puerto Villamil has colourful murals and windows depicting the wildlife for which the islands are famous.

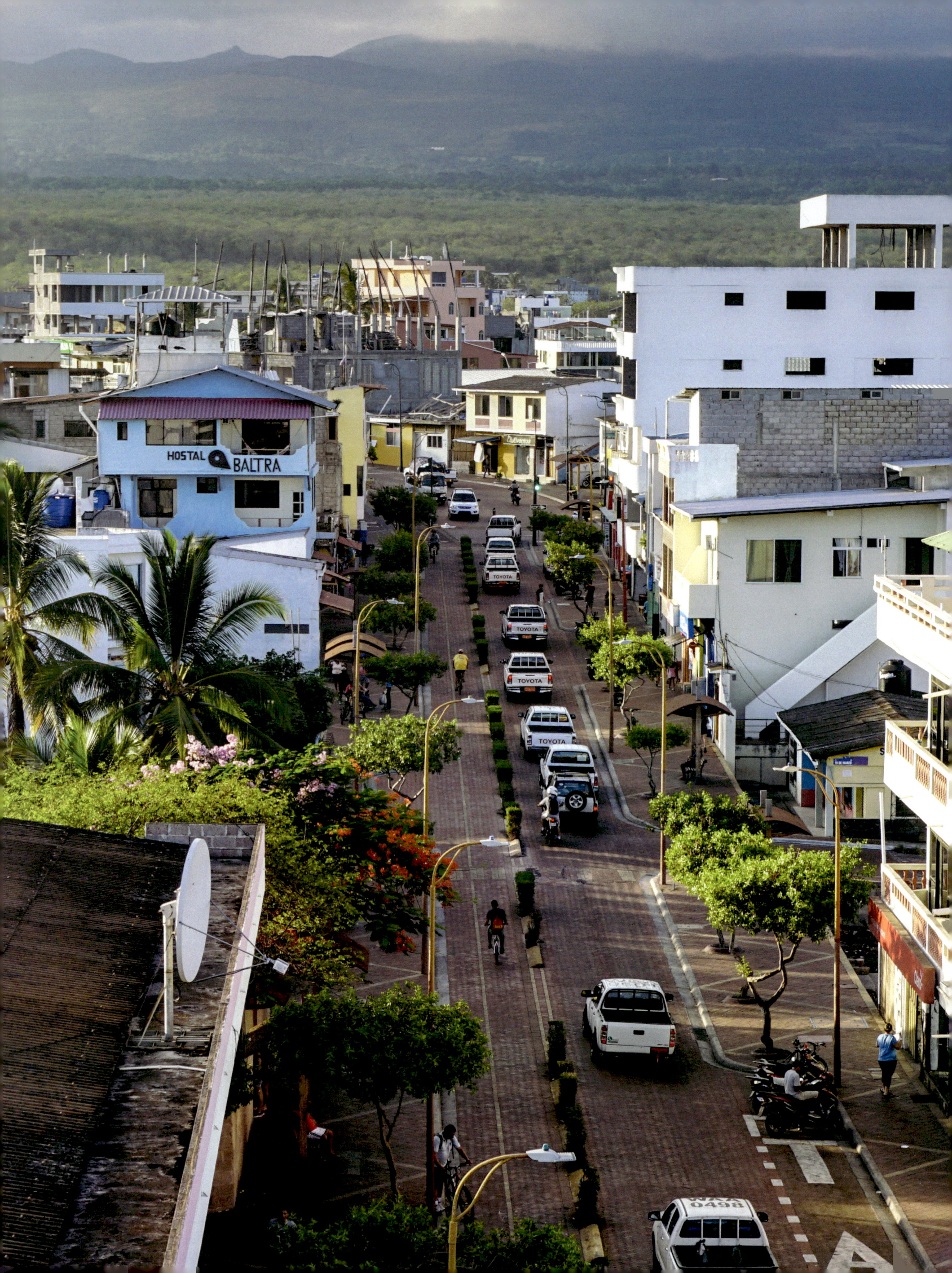
HOSTAL BALTRA
TOYOTA
TOYOTA
TOYOTA
TOYOTA
0498

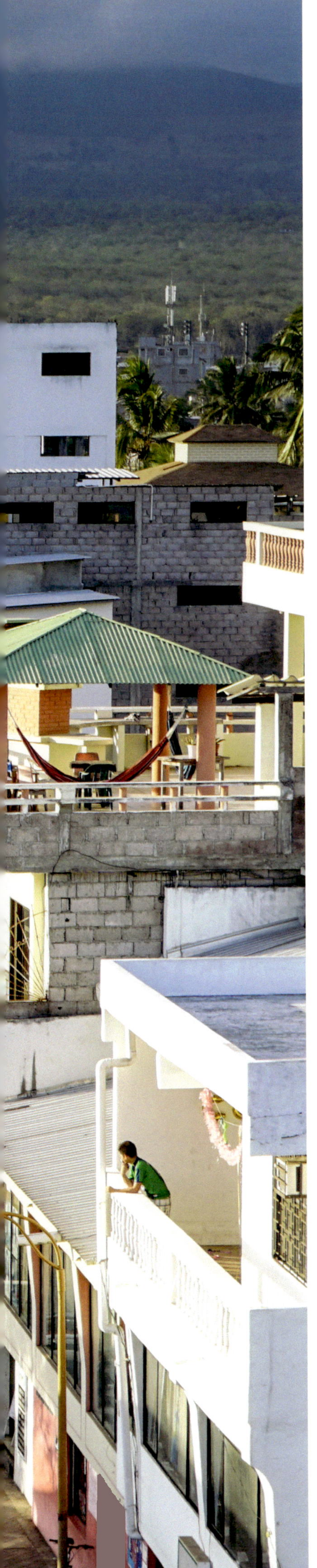

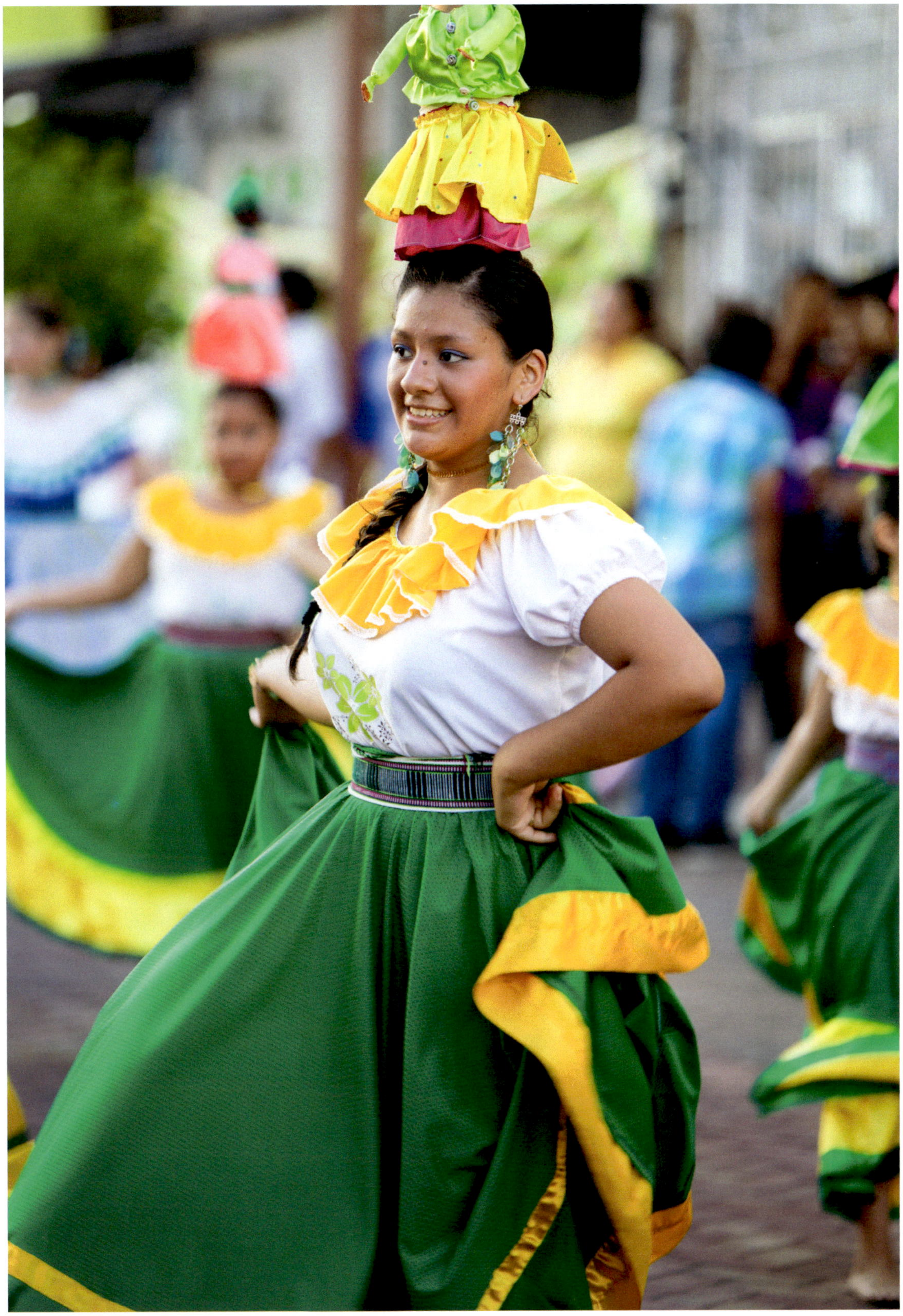

Puerto Ayora
Located in the south of Santa Cruz Island, this is the biggest town on the Galápagos, and is home to about half of the 33,000 Galapagueños.

Carnival costume
A Galapagueña performs in traditional costume during the annual carnival that takes place every February in Puerto Ayora.

Surrounded by wildlife
A gaggle of hungry pelicans
wait for scraps as fish are
gutted at the market in
Puerto Ayora.

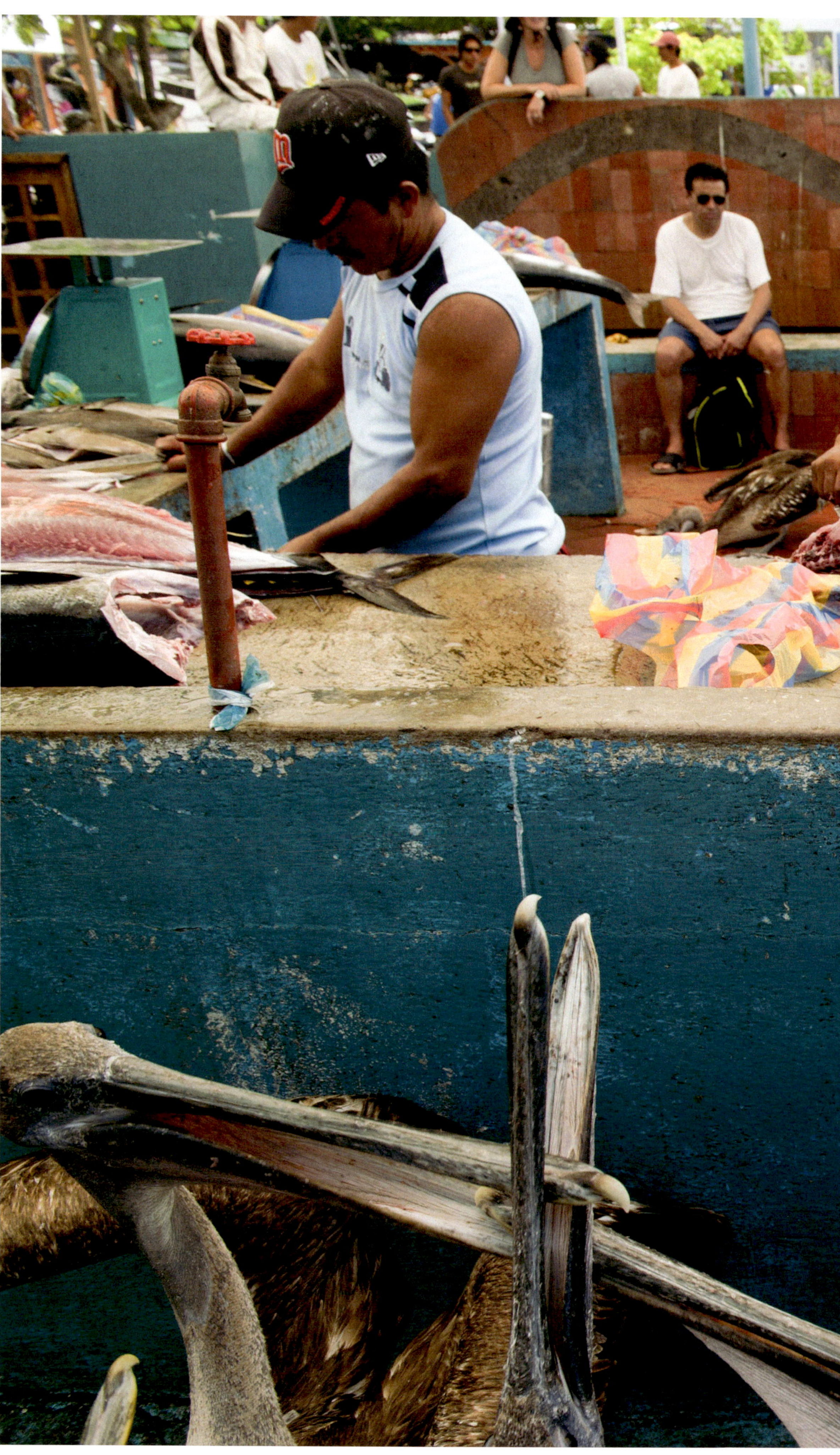

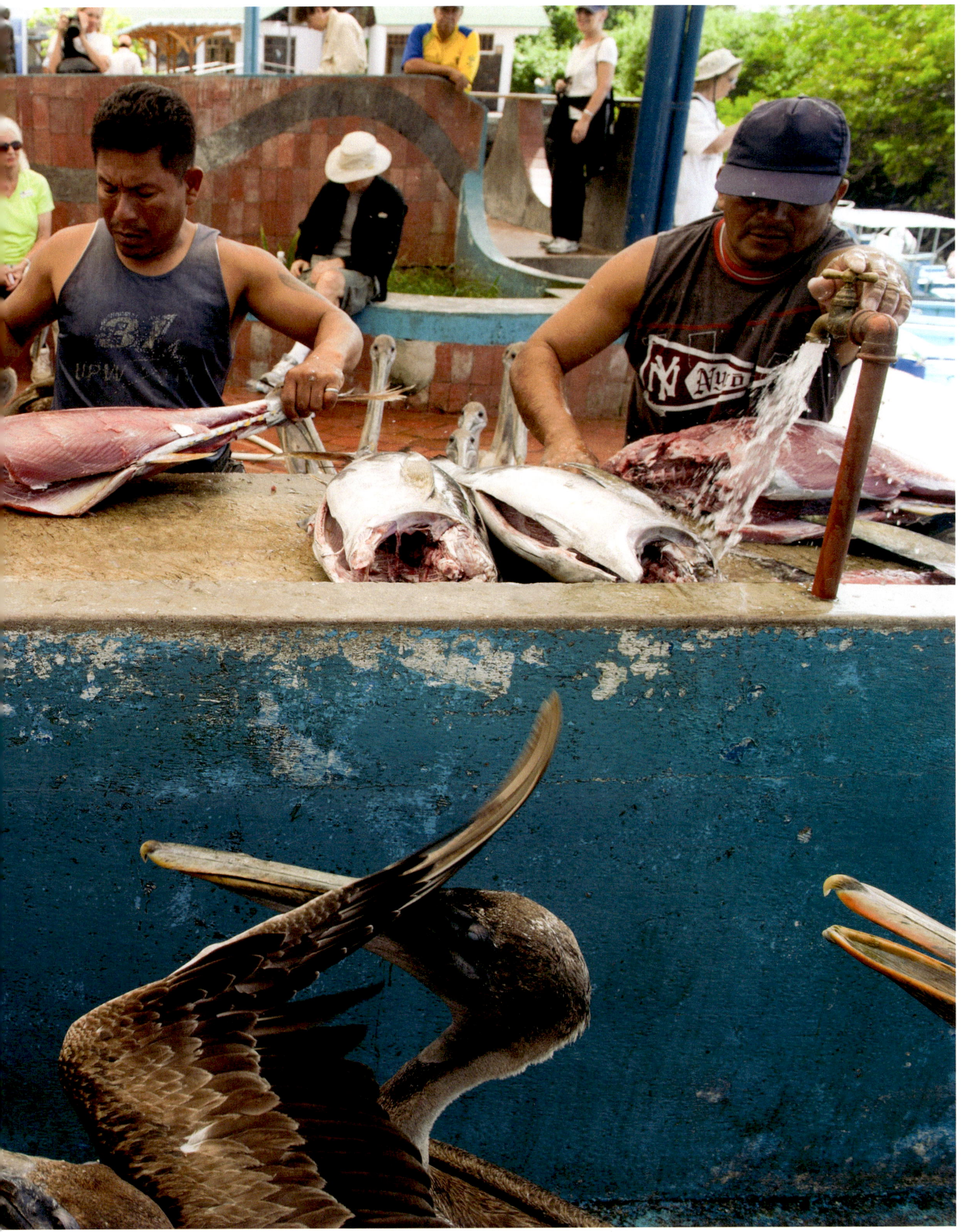

Important fishery
A tuna caught locally is butchered at the Puerto Ayora fish market. Outside of tourism, fishing is one of the main sources of income for the islands.

Sustainable methods
There are strict controls on how many fish can be caught in the protected seas around the islands. Large fish are caught using rods to reduce the chances that turtles and other marine life get caught up in nets.

Fishing
A local fisherman shows off an octopus for sale. There are around 1000 people living on the islands who have permits to fish.

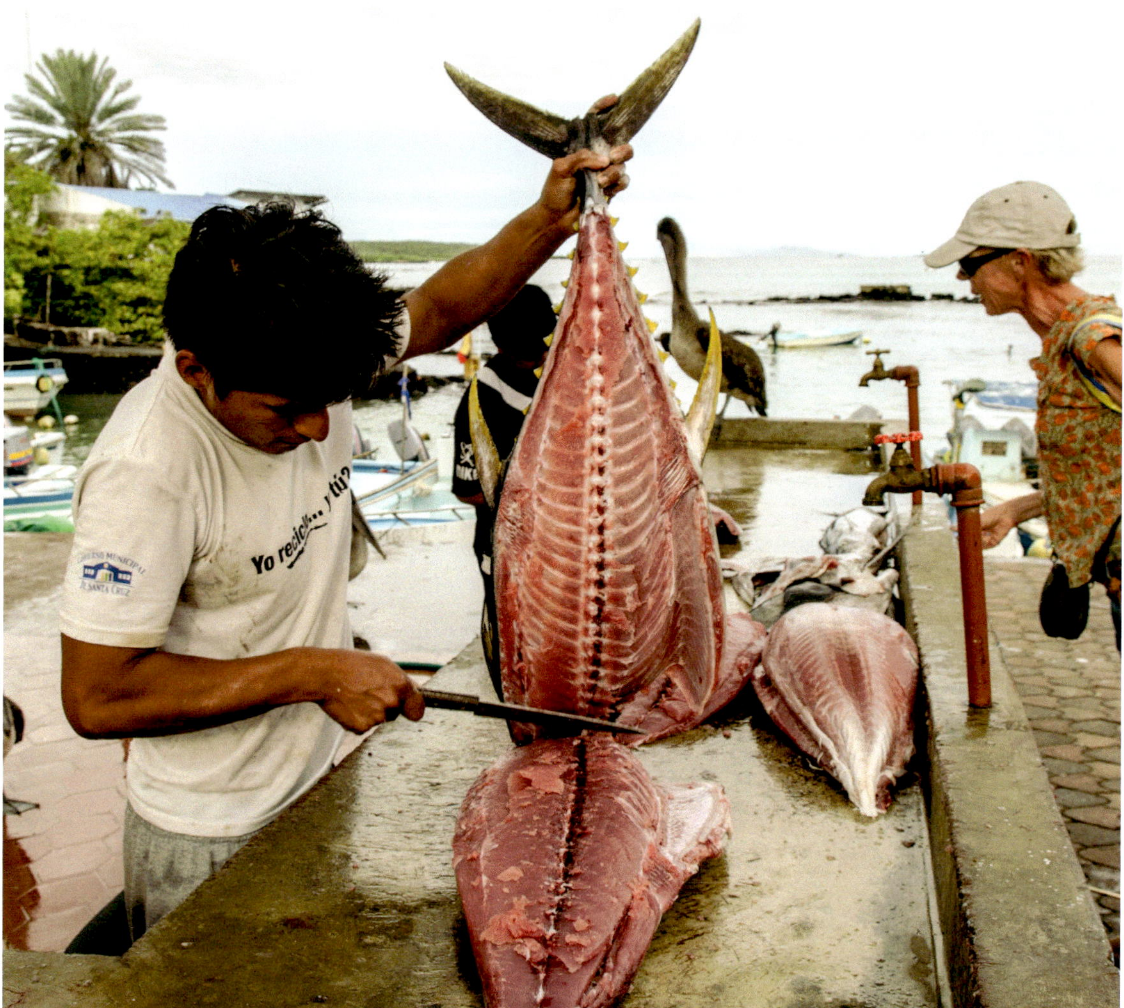

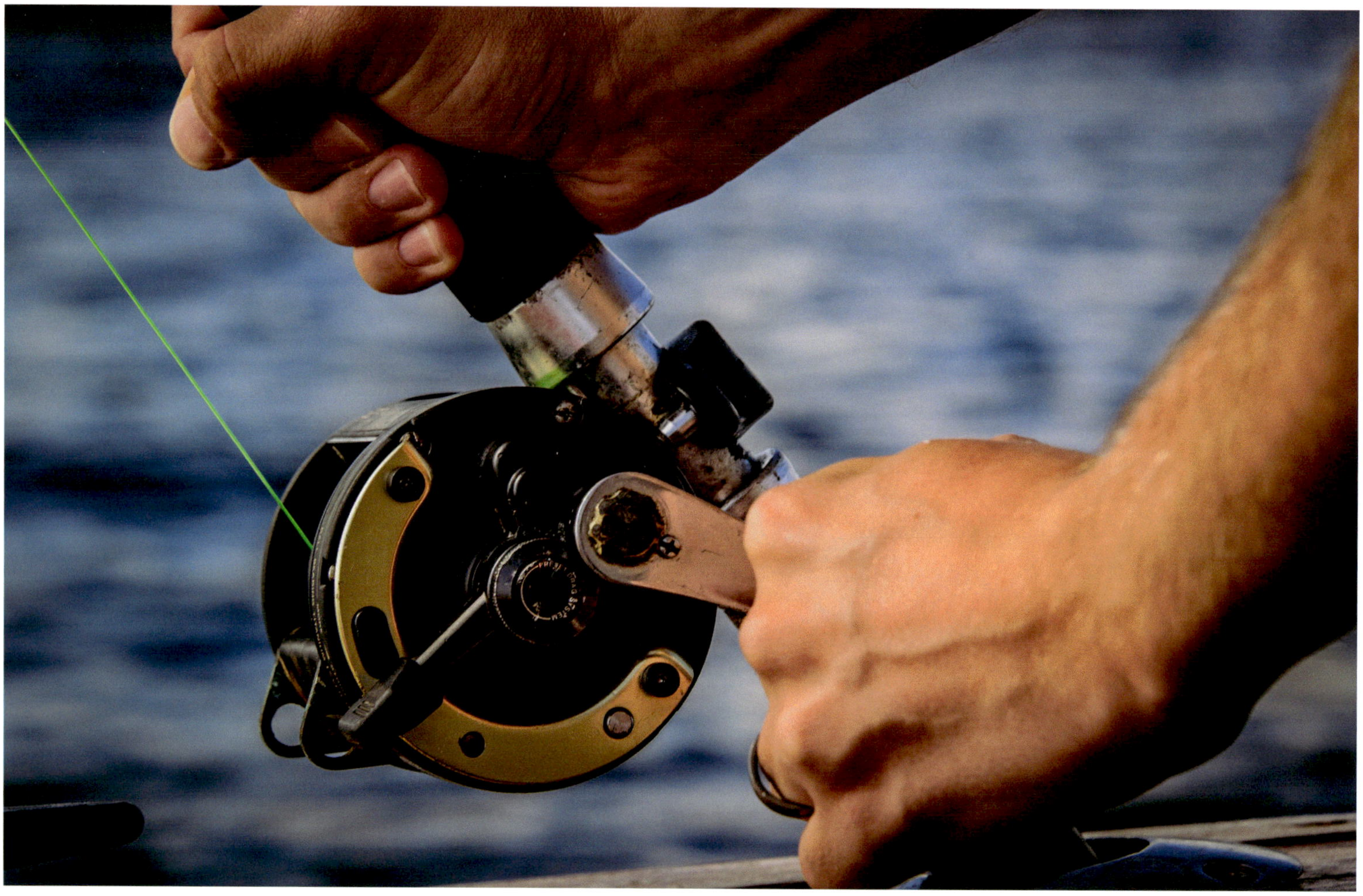

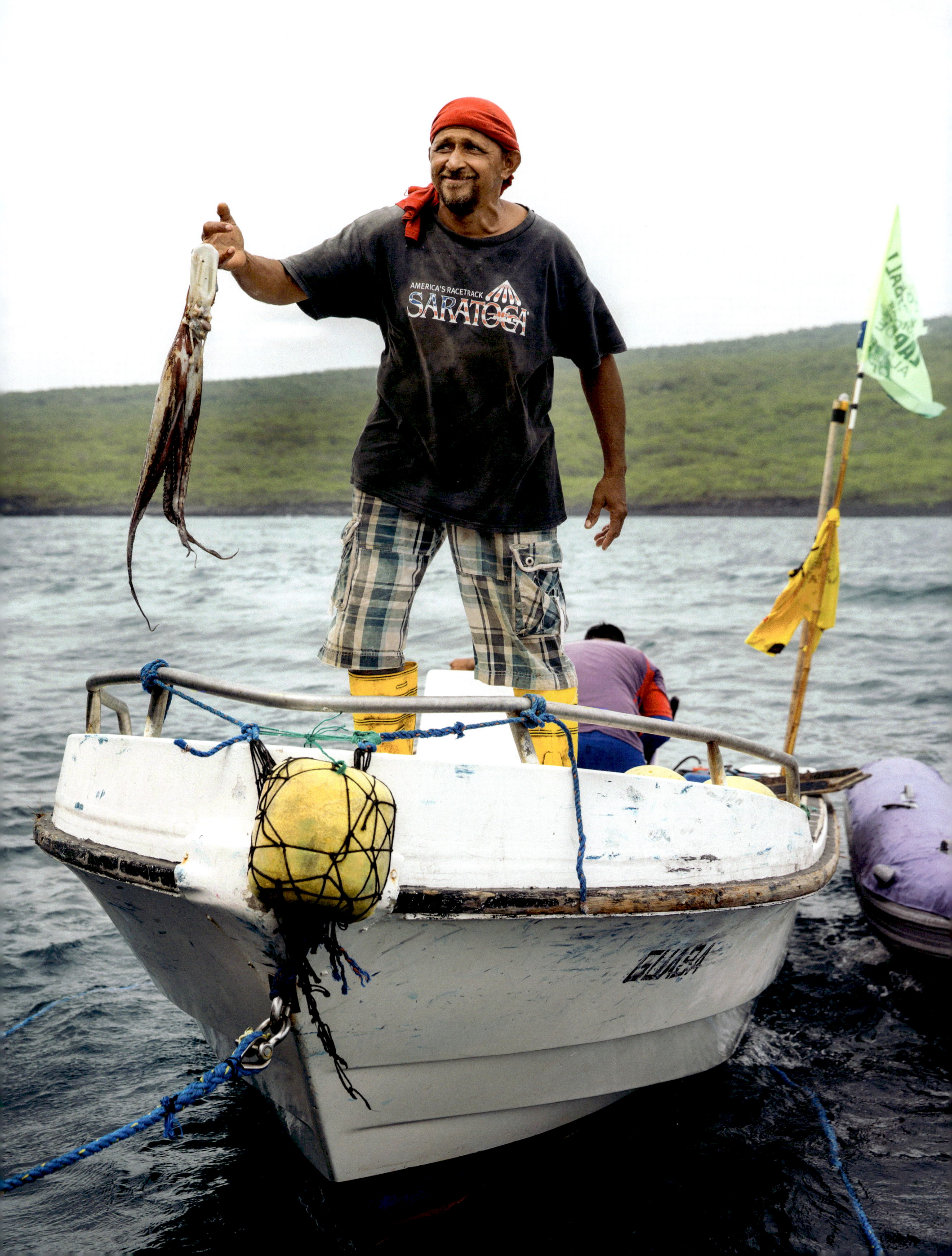

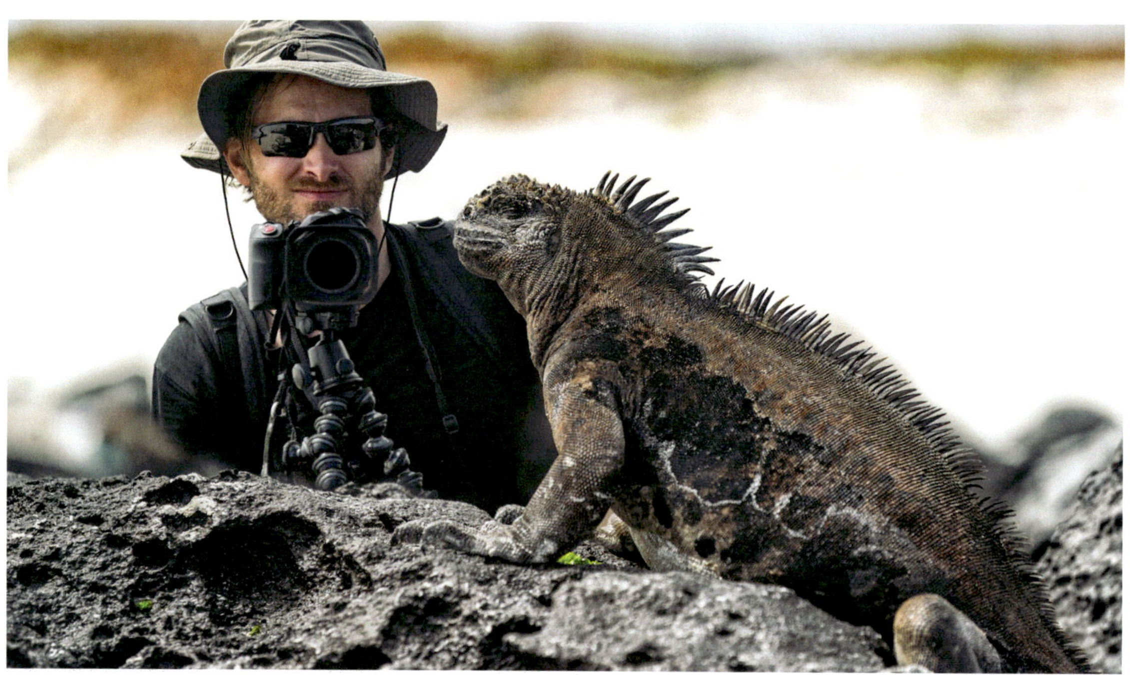

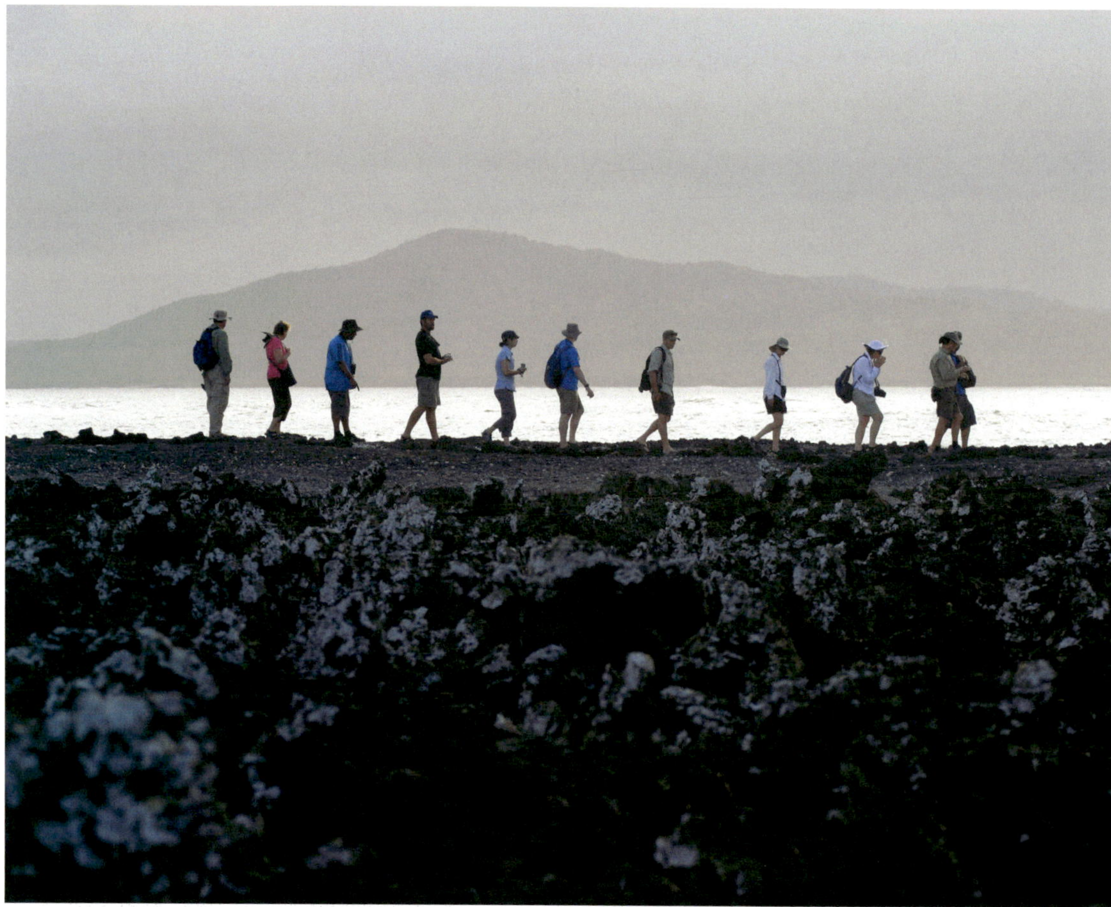

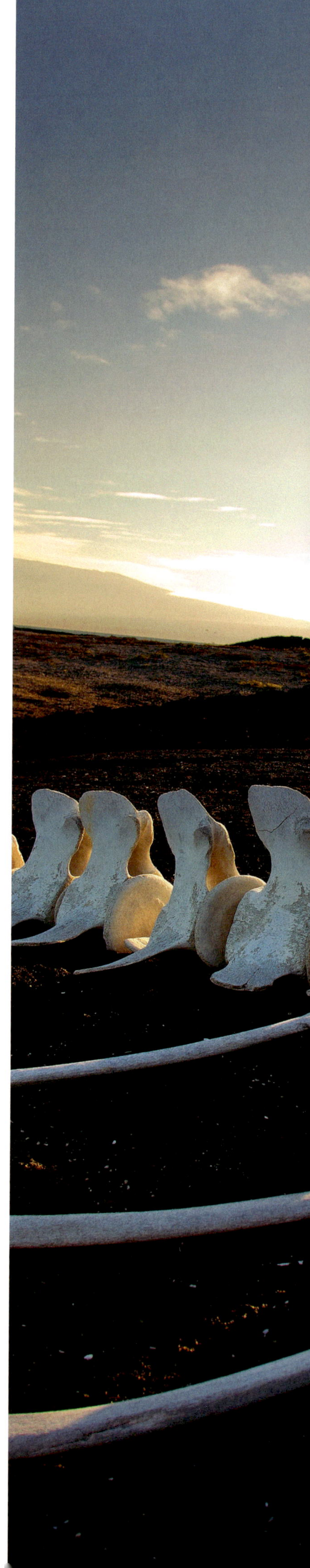

ABOVE TOP:

Ecotourism

By far the largest income source for the islands is tourism, with a quarter of a million people coming to see the marine iguanas and other amazing wildlife. The money raised ensures that the islands remain protected.

ABOVE BOTTOM:

Galápagos National Park

Only three per cent of land in the Galápagos, mostly around Puerto Ayora, sits outside the Galápagos National Park. The rest is left for the wildlife, and tourists are generally taken into the park by expert guides.

RIGHT:

Just visiting

Tourists stand by the bones of a whale on Fernandina Island. Tourists are not allowed to roam freely and visit any island.

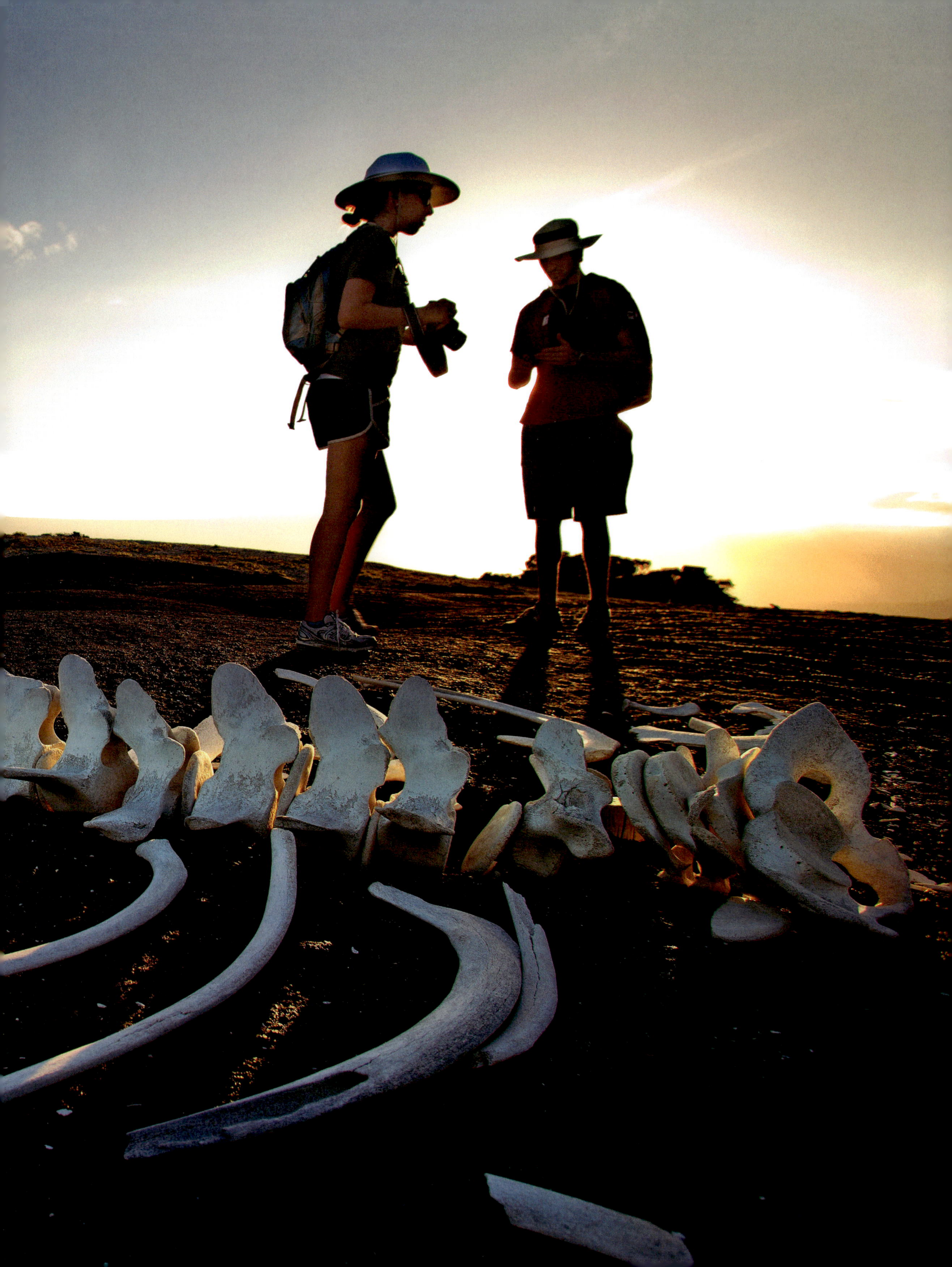

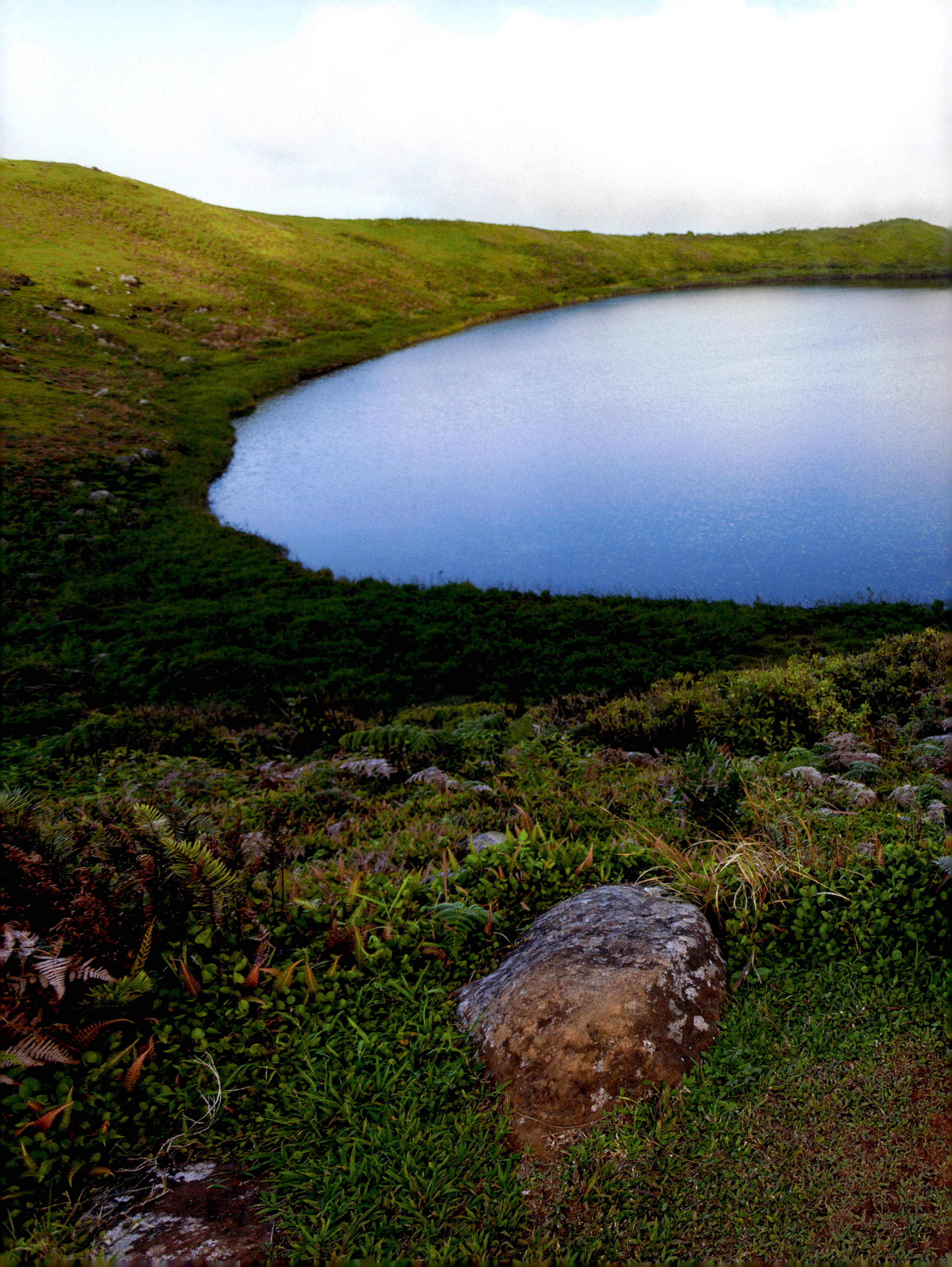

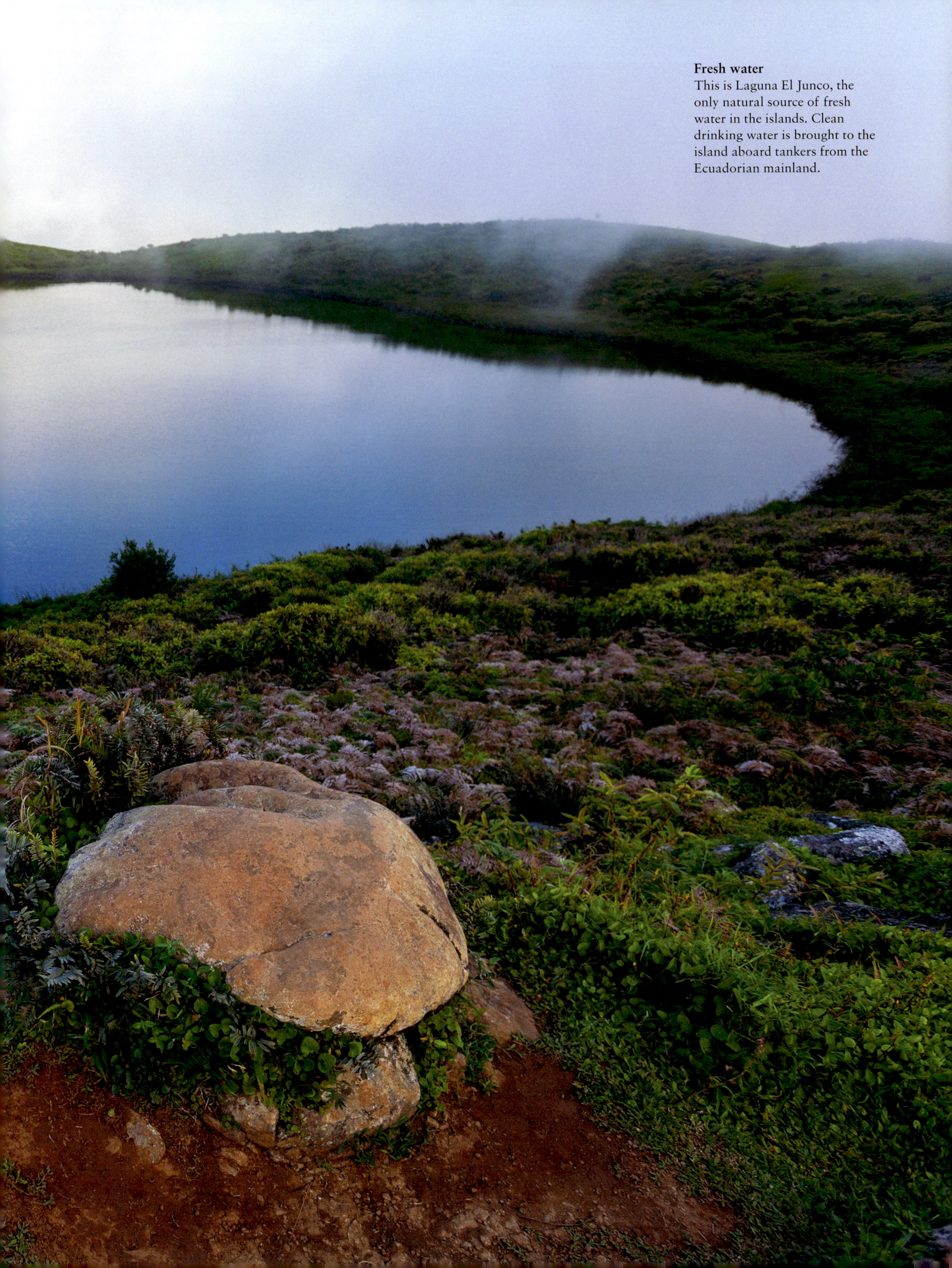

Fresh water
This is Laguna El Junco, the only natural source of fresh water in the islands. Clean drinking water is brought to the island aboard tankers from the Ecuadorian mainland.

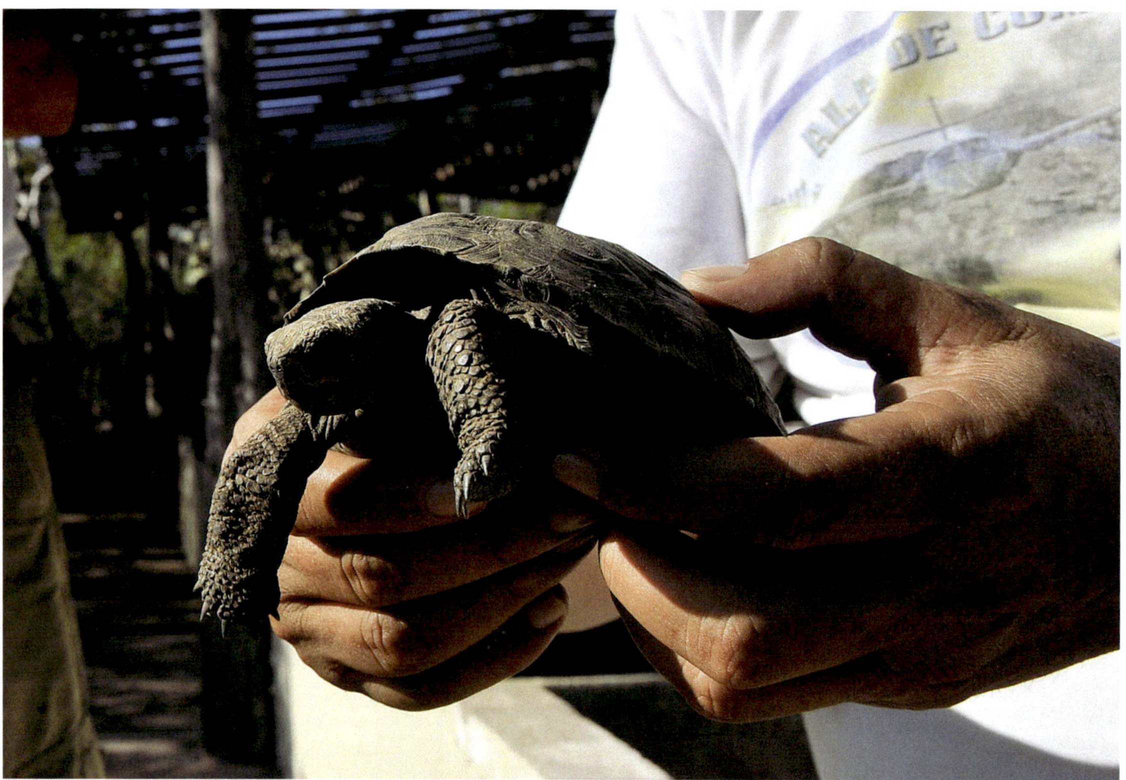

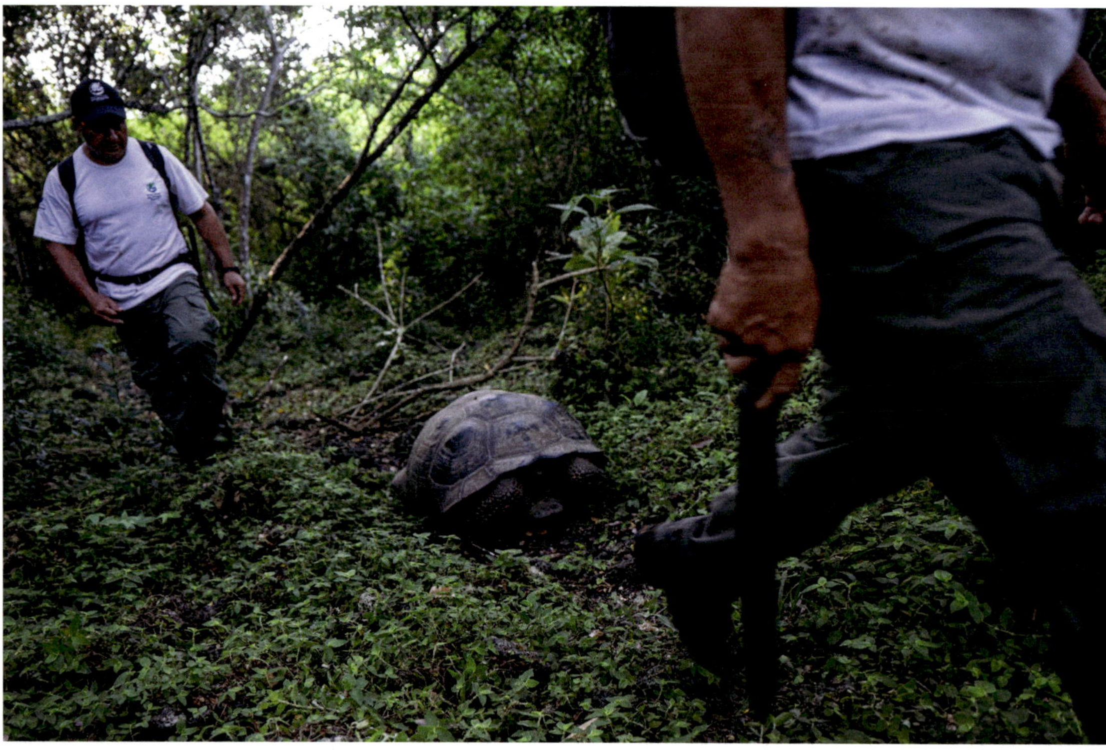

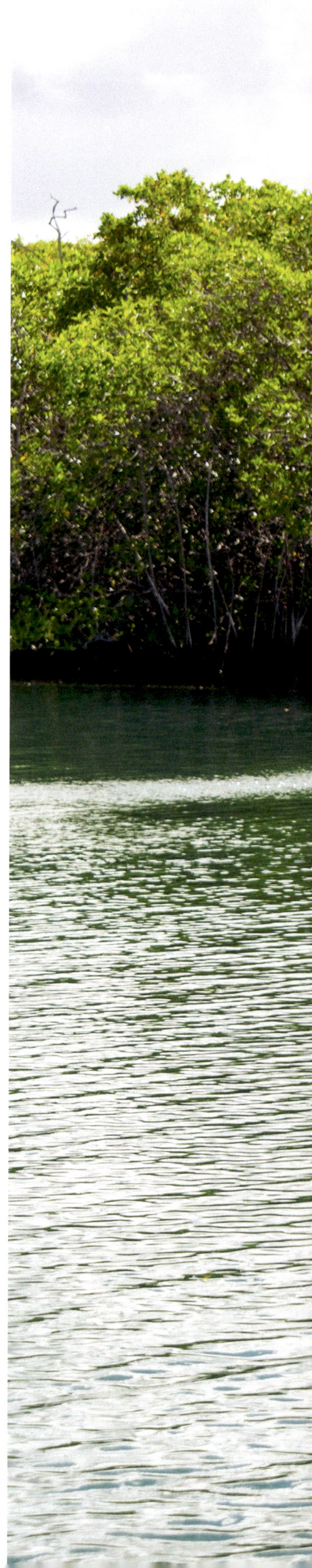

Conservation
A Galápagos National Park ranger holds a baby giant tortoise at a breeding centre in Puerto Ayora, which aims to boost the numbers of rare species.

To the rescue
Park rangers check in on a giant tortoise in the Galápagos National Park region of Santa Cruz island.

On the water
A flock of penguins accompany a boat full of tourists visiting a mangrove.

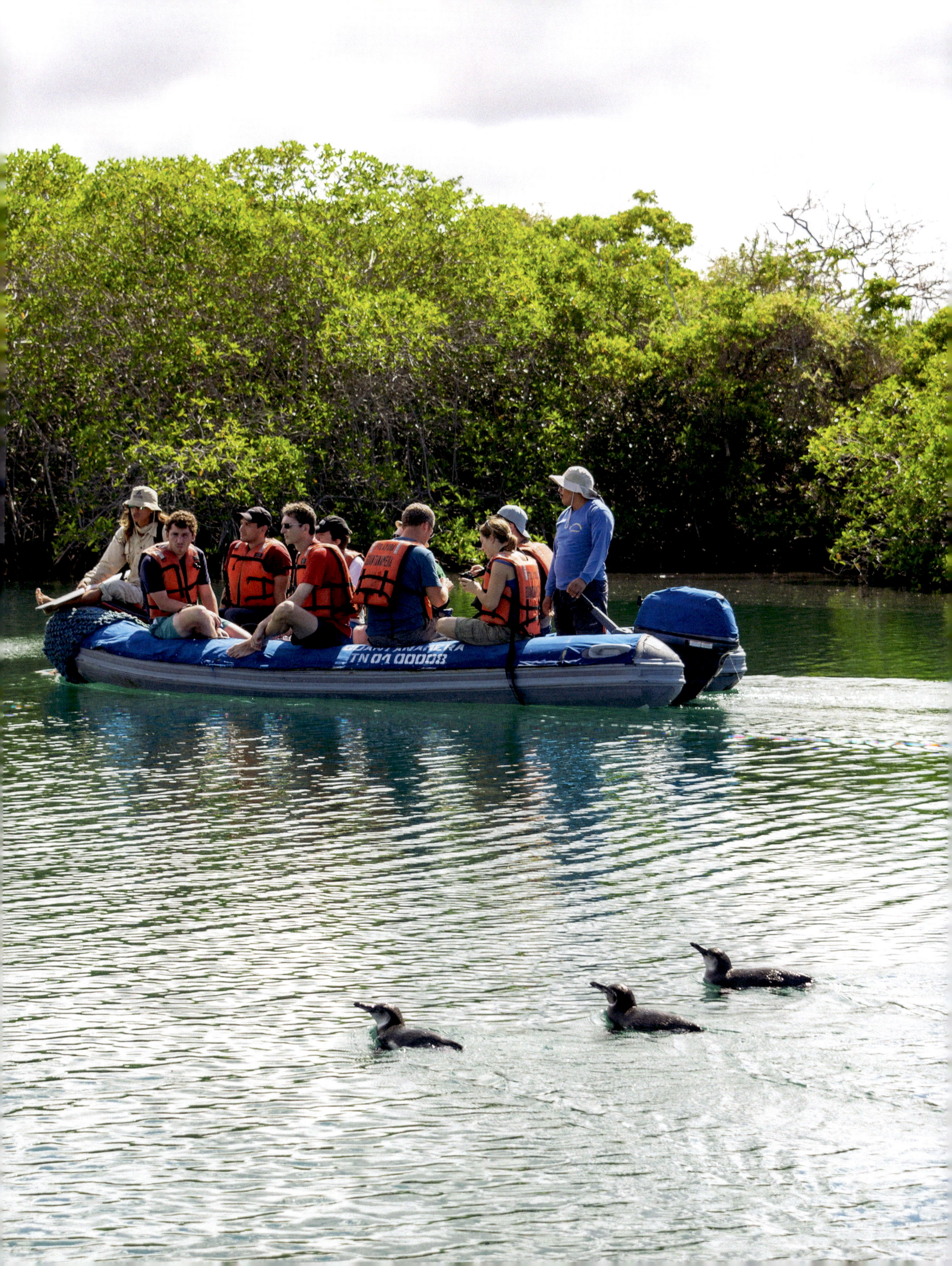

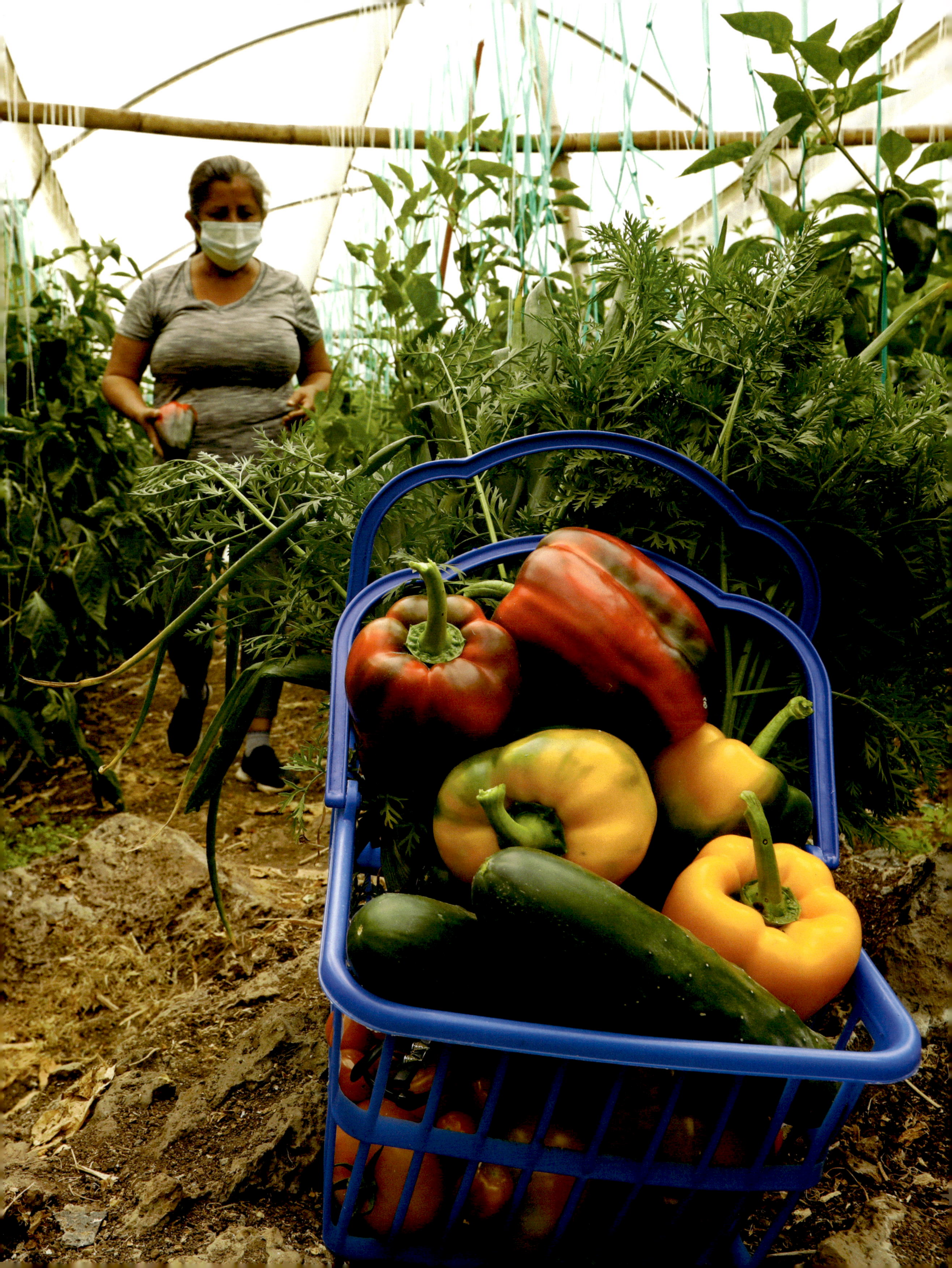

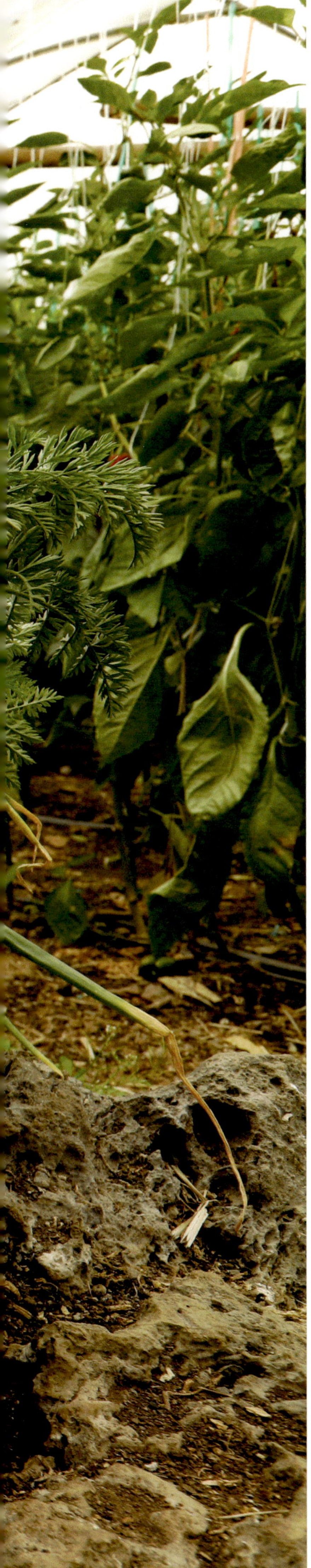

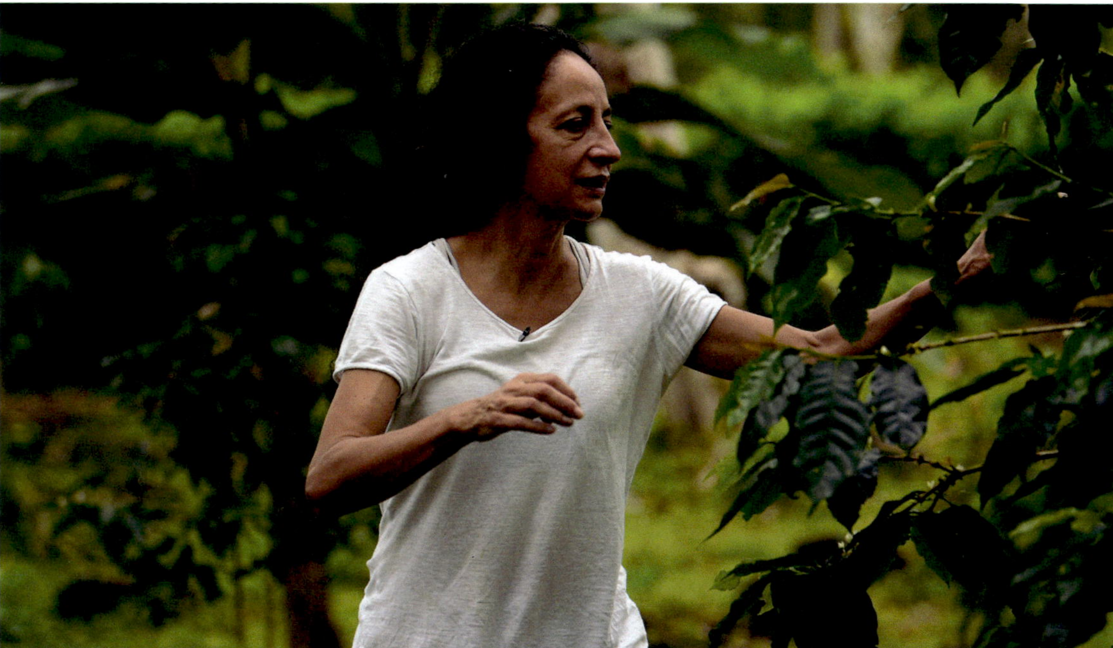

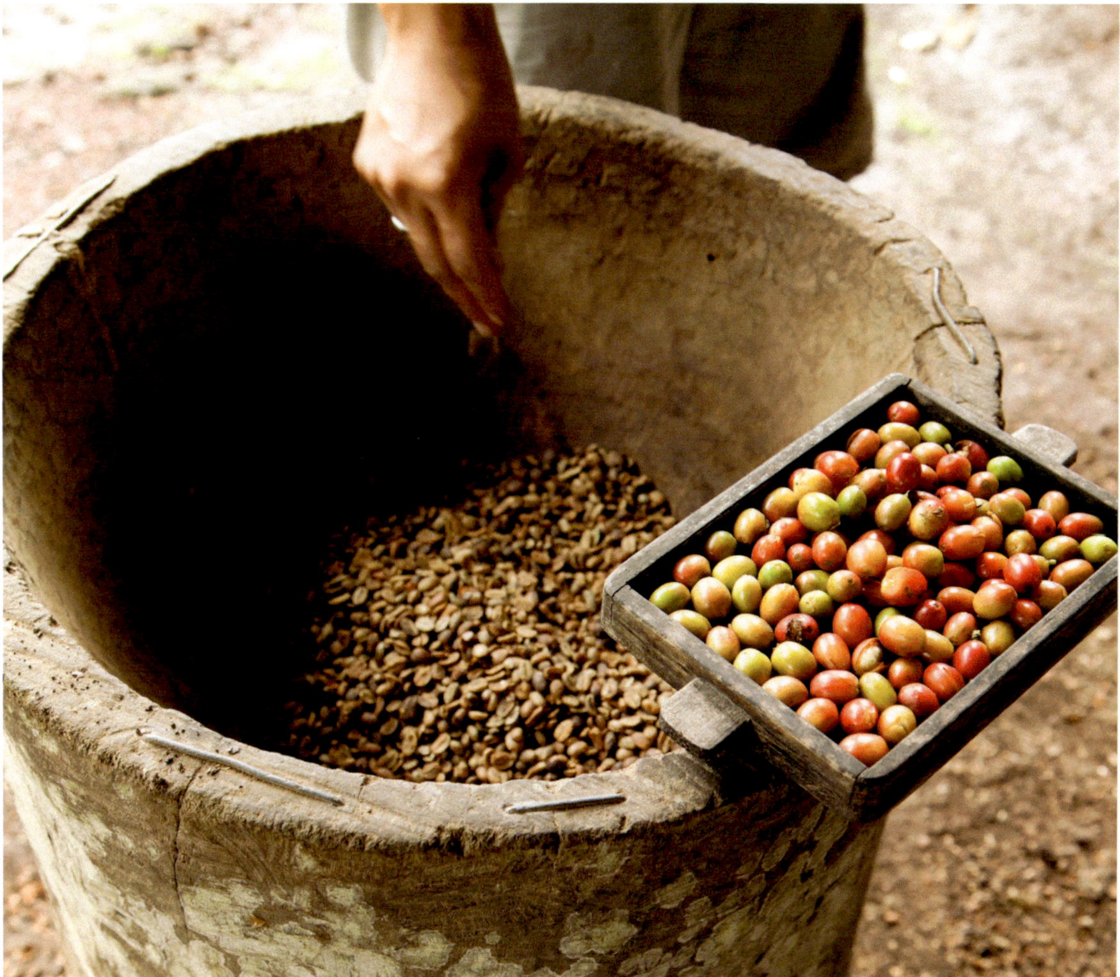

Farming

The hills around Puerto Aroyo are used for farming. Much of the islands' fruit and vegetables, such as these peppers and cucumbers, are grown locally.

Coffee plantation

Maria Elena Guerra tends to her organic coffee plantation on Lava Java farm in Santa Cruz. The coffee beans are only sold locally.

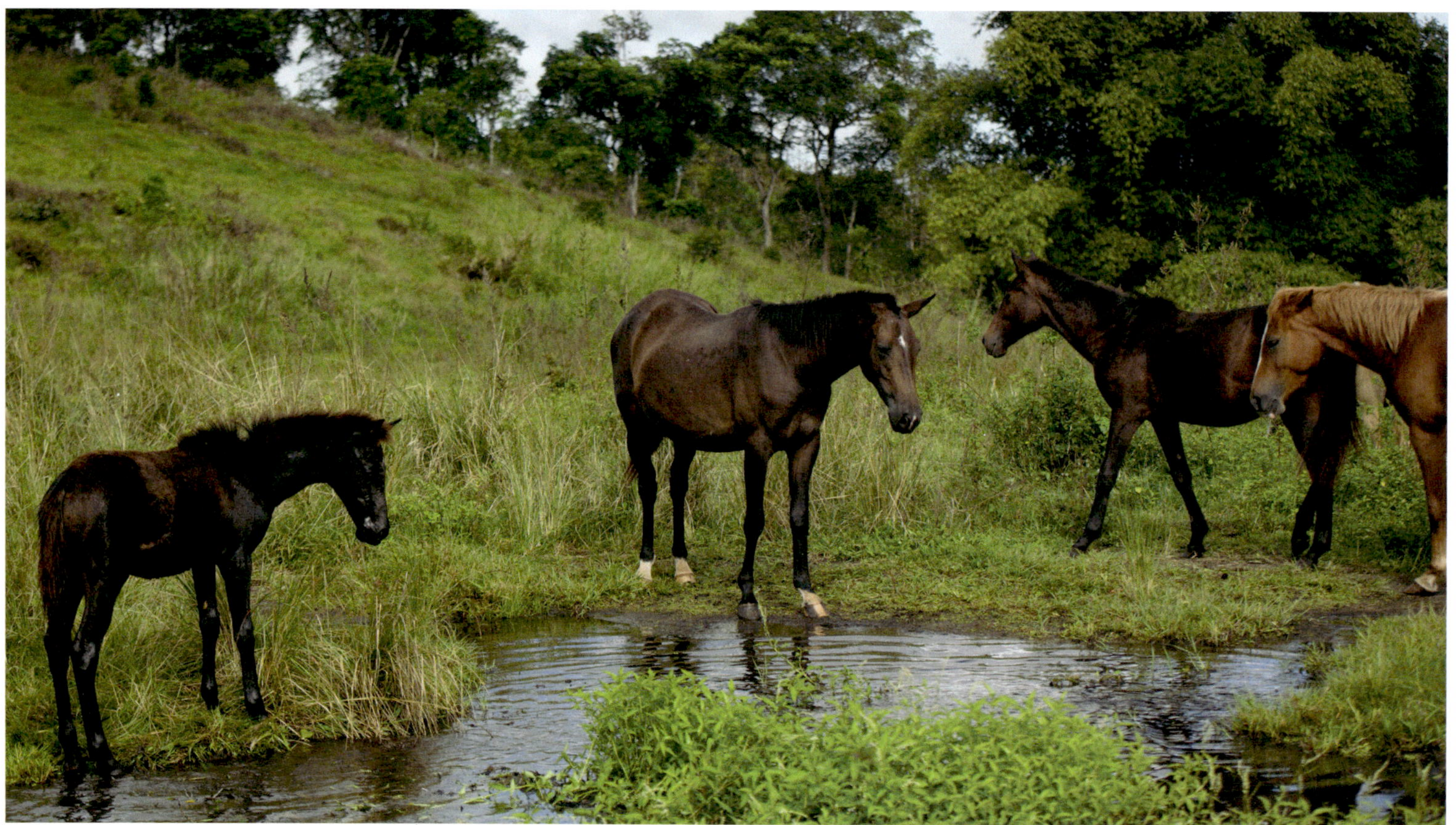

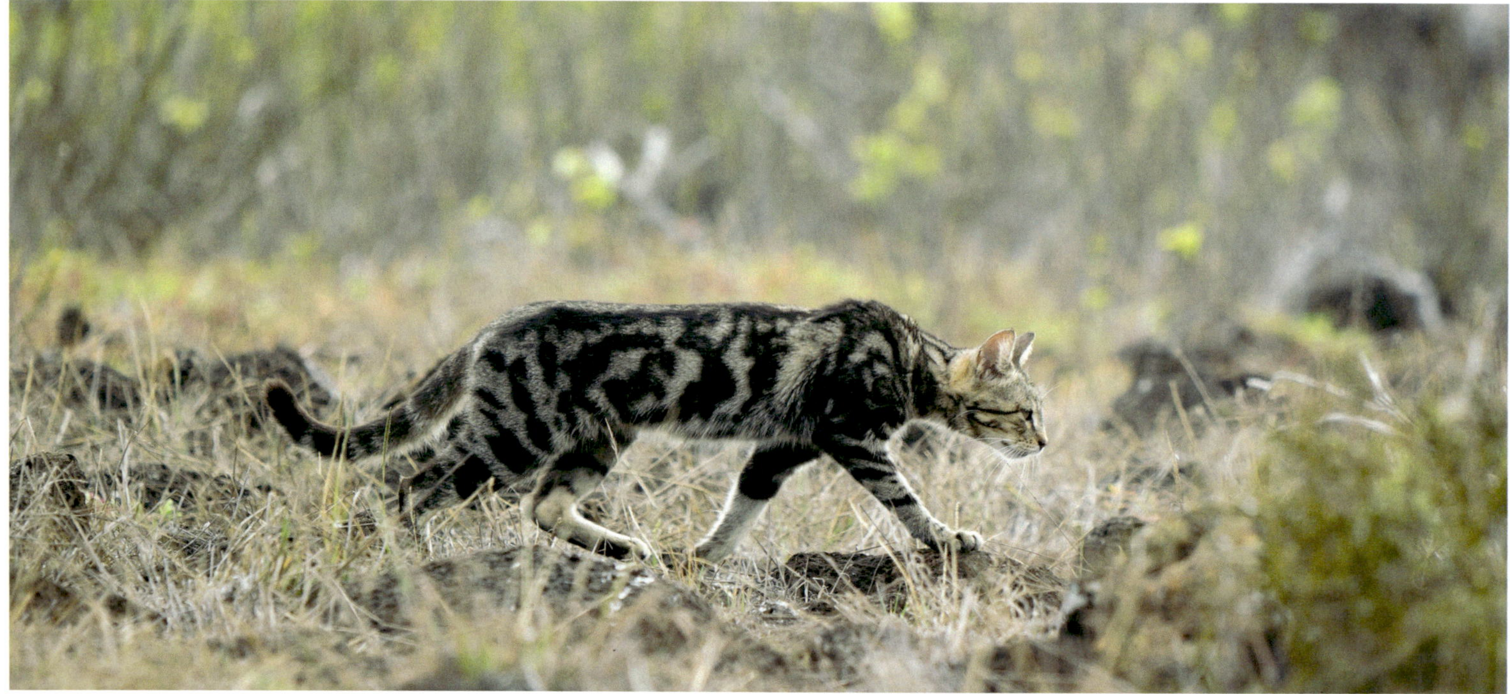

ABOVE TOP:

Wild horses

Horses and donkeys were brought to work on the islands in the 19th century. They are still used as beasts of burden, but many have also escaped to live in the wild.

ABOVE BOTTOM:

Feral cats

The pet cats of early settlers escaped and are now a dangerous threat to many bird and lizards species that have no natural defence against them. Conservationists are working to remove all feral cats from the islands.

OPPOSITE:

Invasive goats

Wild goats pose a threat to natural flora on the Galápagos. They eat native plants and create space for fast-growing weeds to take root. Trained Judas goats are used to track flocks. They are fitted with radio collars, so they can be tracked when they meet with fellow goats. The flock is then shot by marksmen in helicopters, all but the Judas goat, which is set free to find new groups.

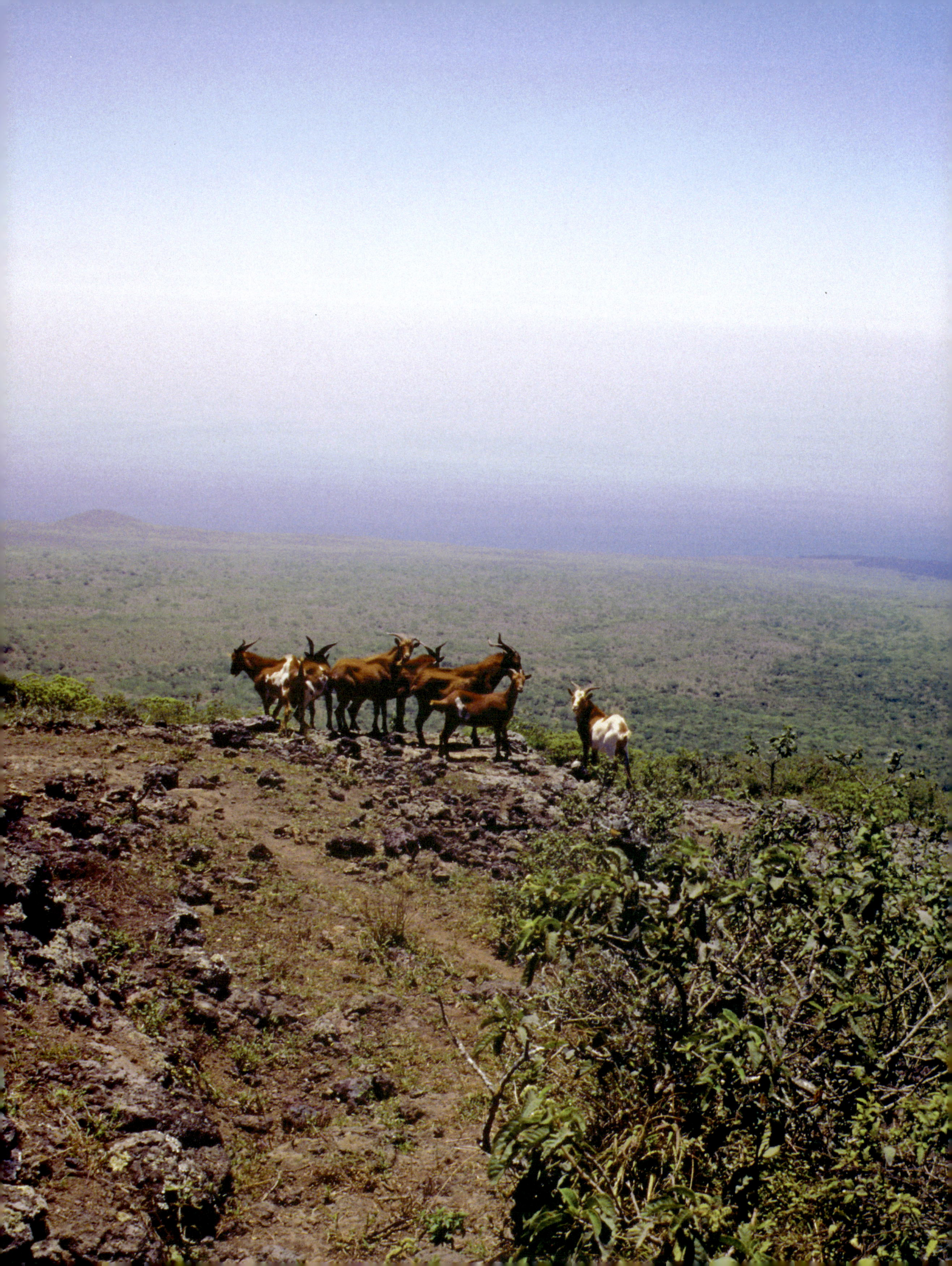

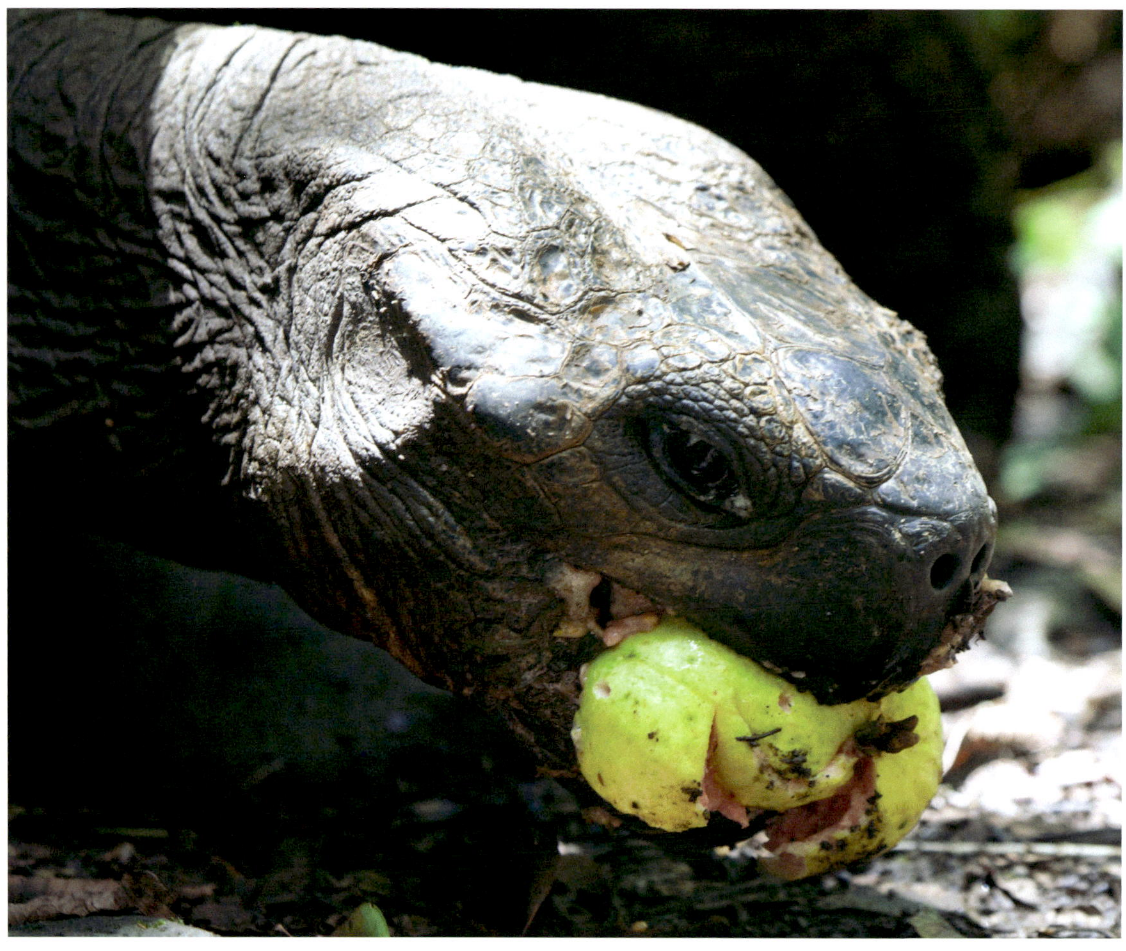

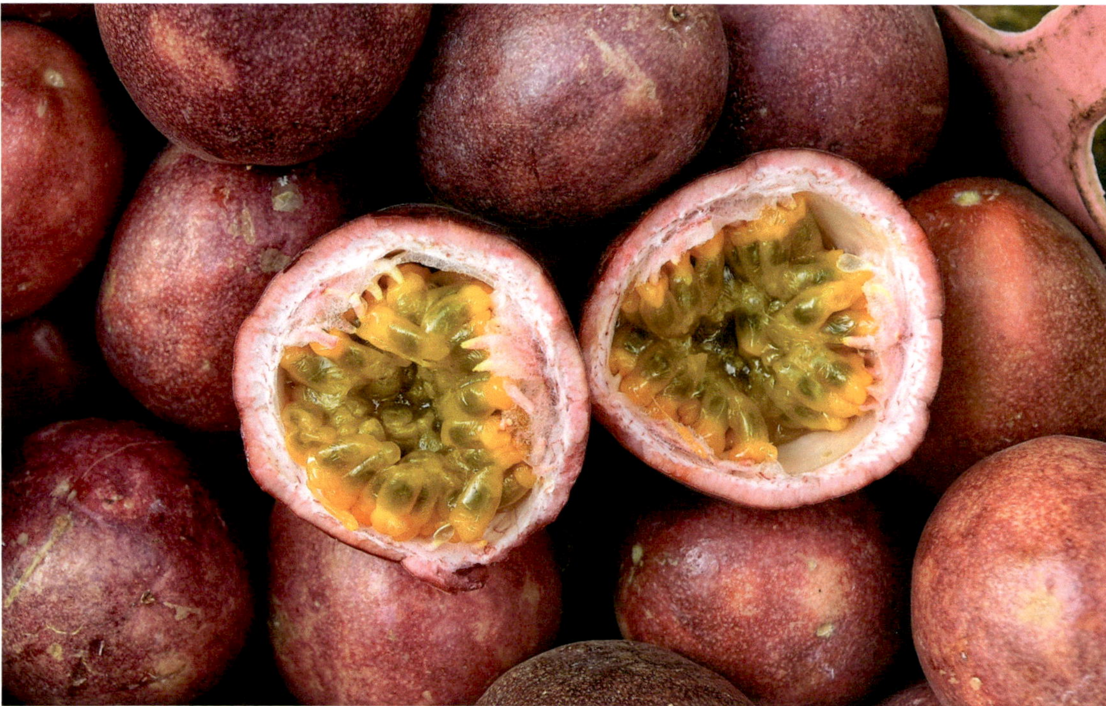

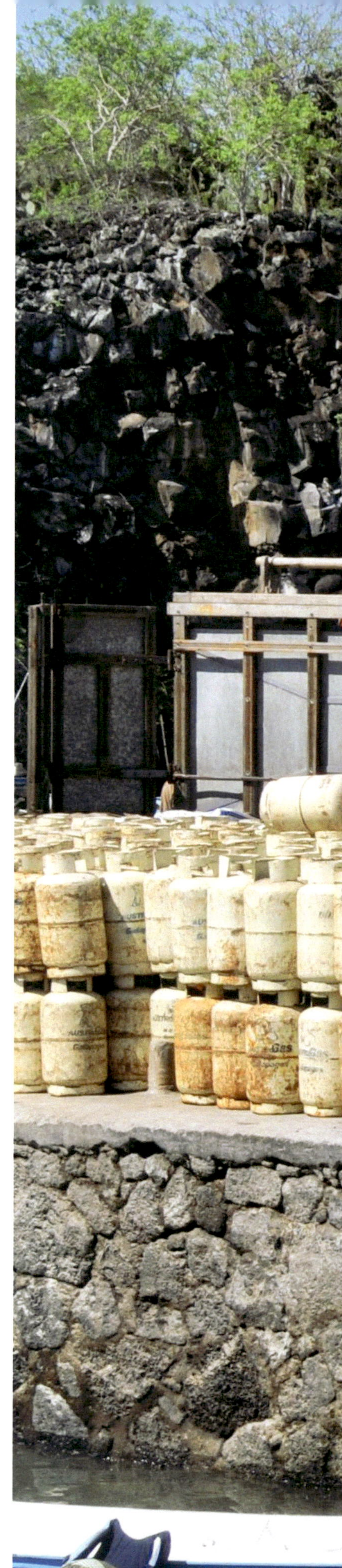

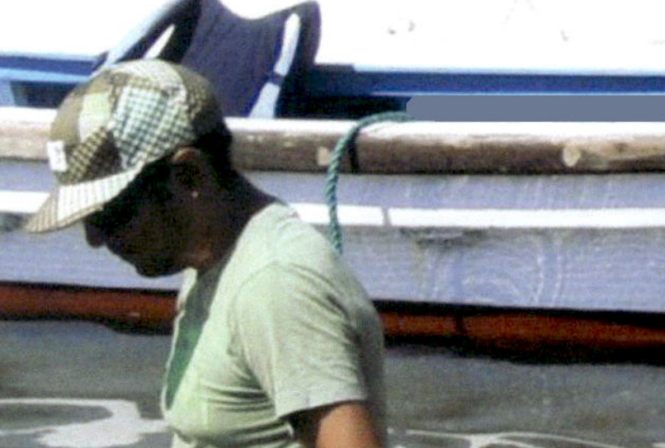

Pest plants

A giant tortoise eats a guava fruit. Guava is an example of a dangerous introduced pest plant that is spreading fast through Santa Cruz and other islands.

Forbidden fruit

Passion fruits are a popular tropical food enjoyed by tourists. However, if they eat this fruit on the Galápagos then they are banned from visiting many of the uninhabited islands until the seeds have passed through their system.

Import and export

Most of the food and all of the water and fuel used by the island arrives by ship. There is no room on the islands for a rubbish tip, so the rubbish has to be exported to the mainland.

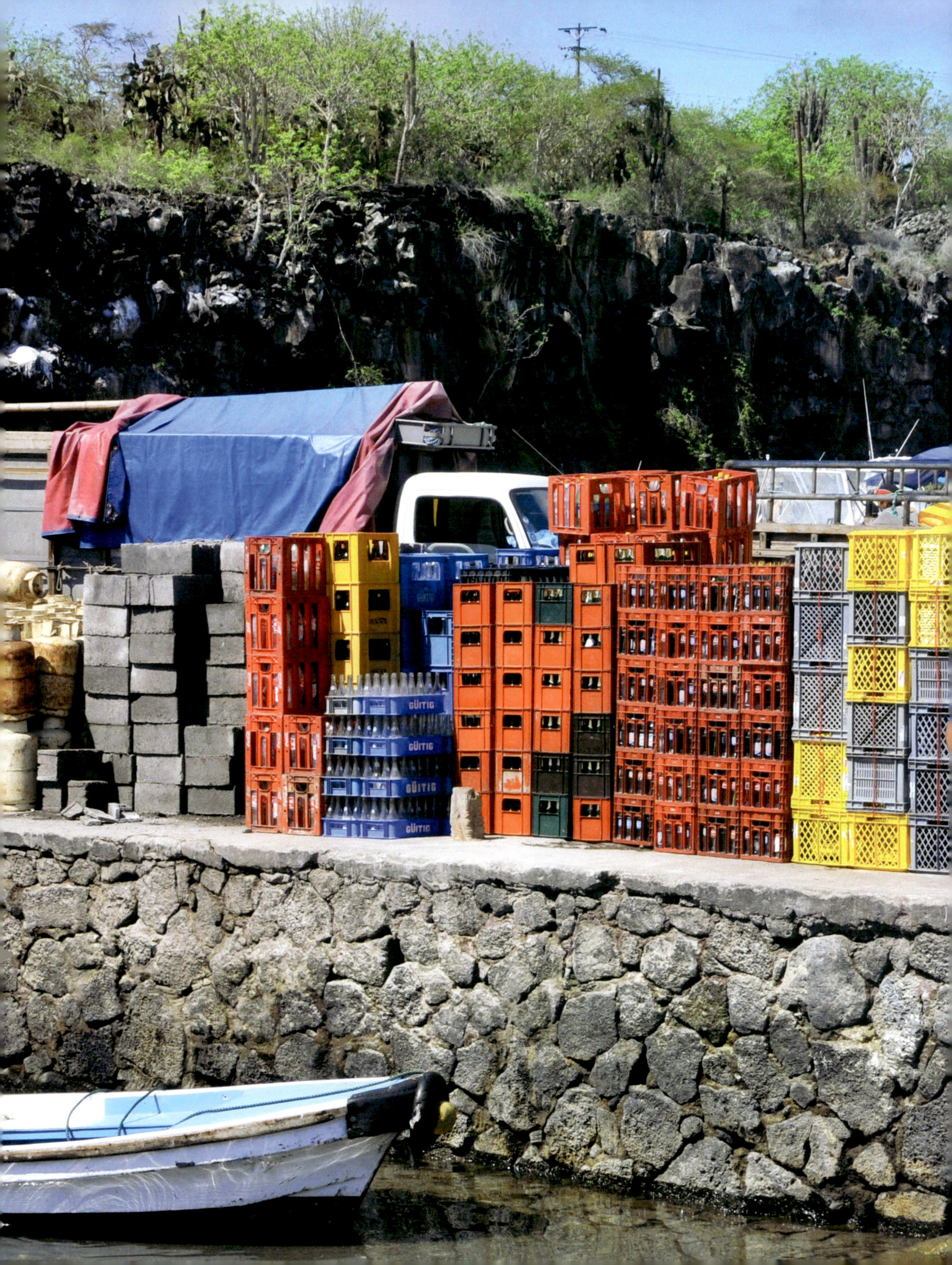

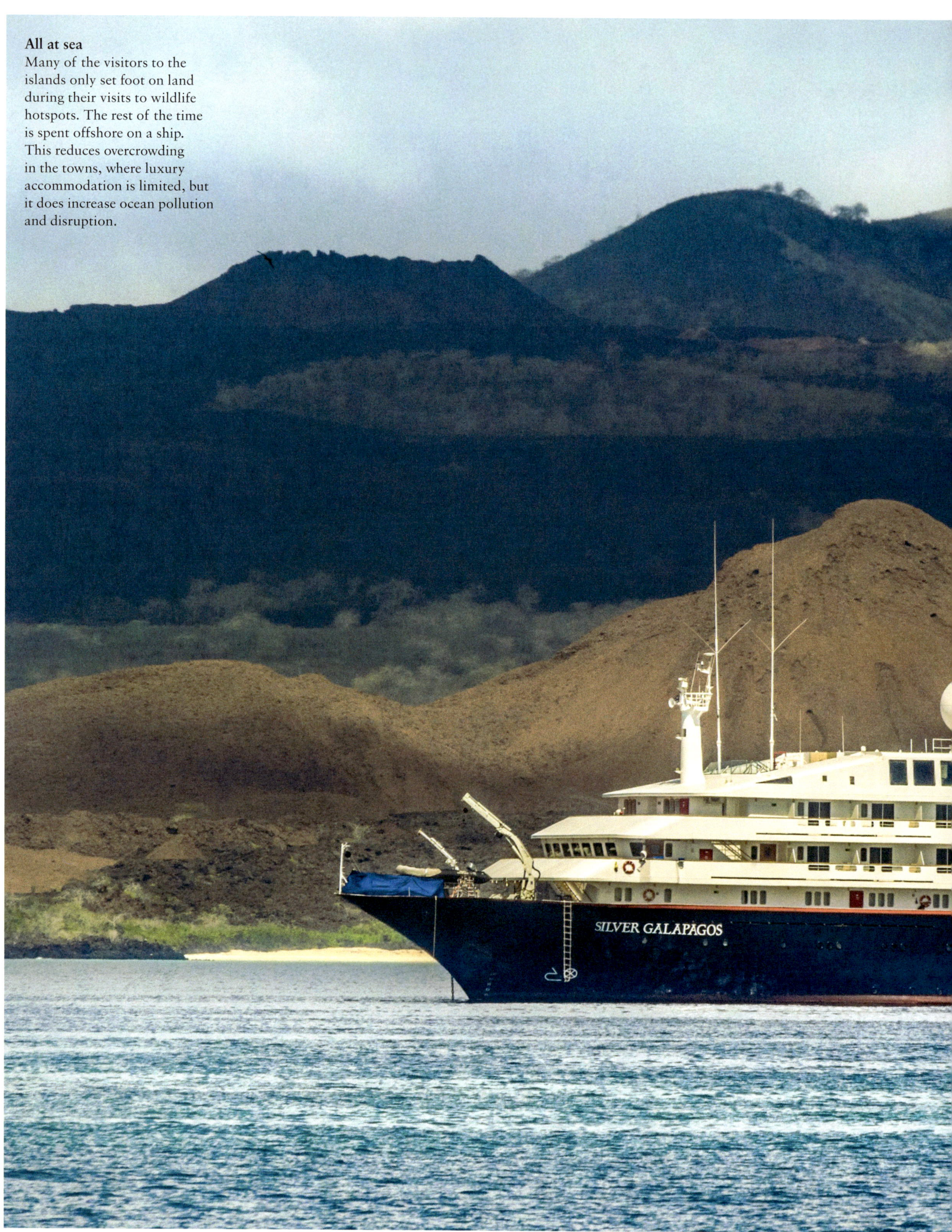

All at sea
Many of the visitors to the
islands only set foot on land
during their visits to wildlife
hotspots. The rest of the time
is spent offshore on a ship.
This reduces overcrowding
in the towns, where luxury
accommodation is limited, but
it does increase ocean pollution
and disruption.

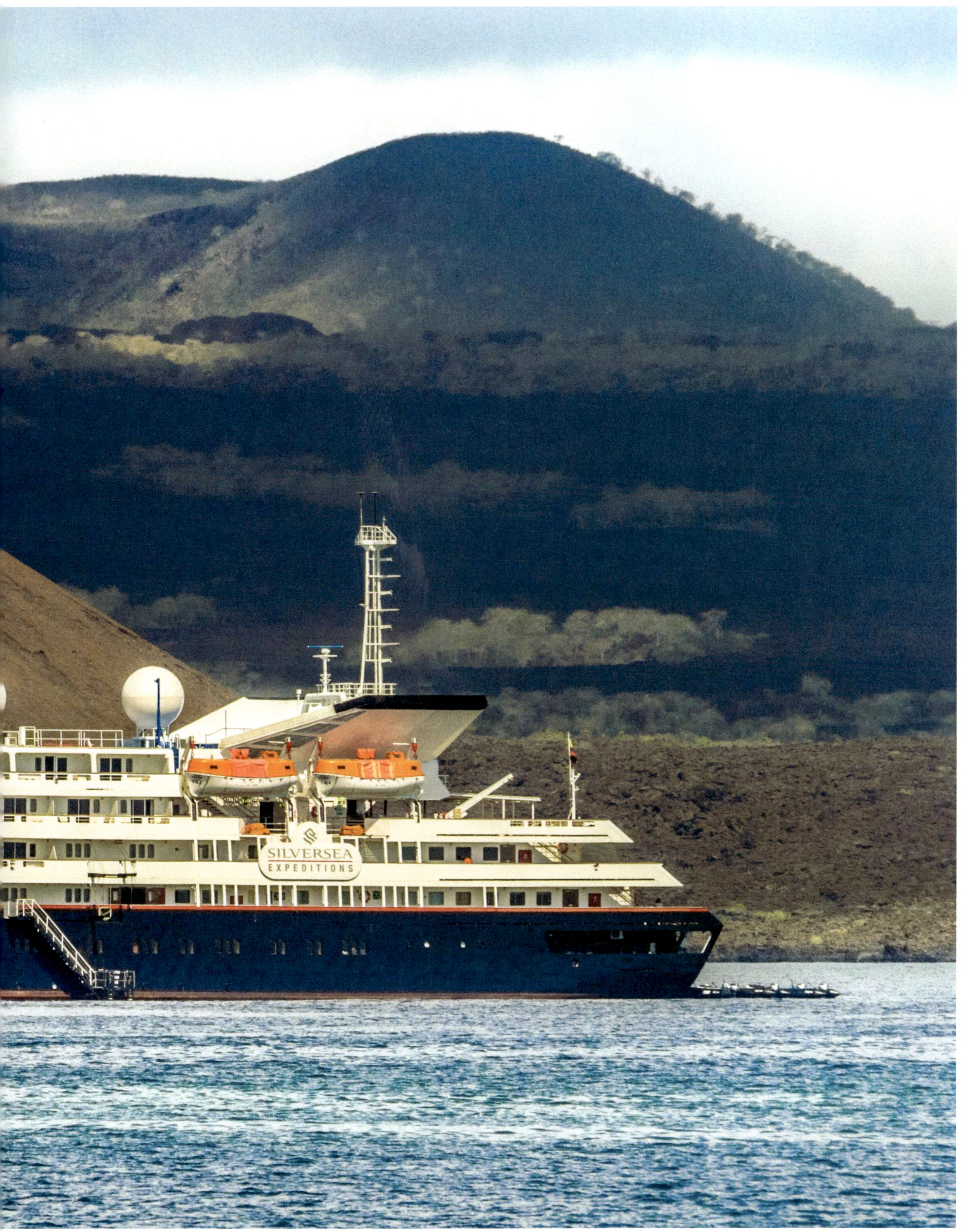

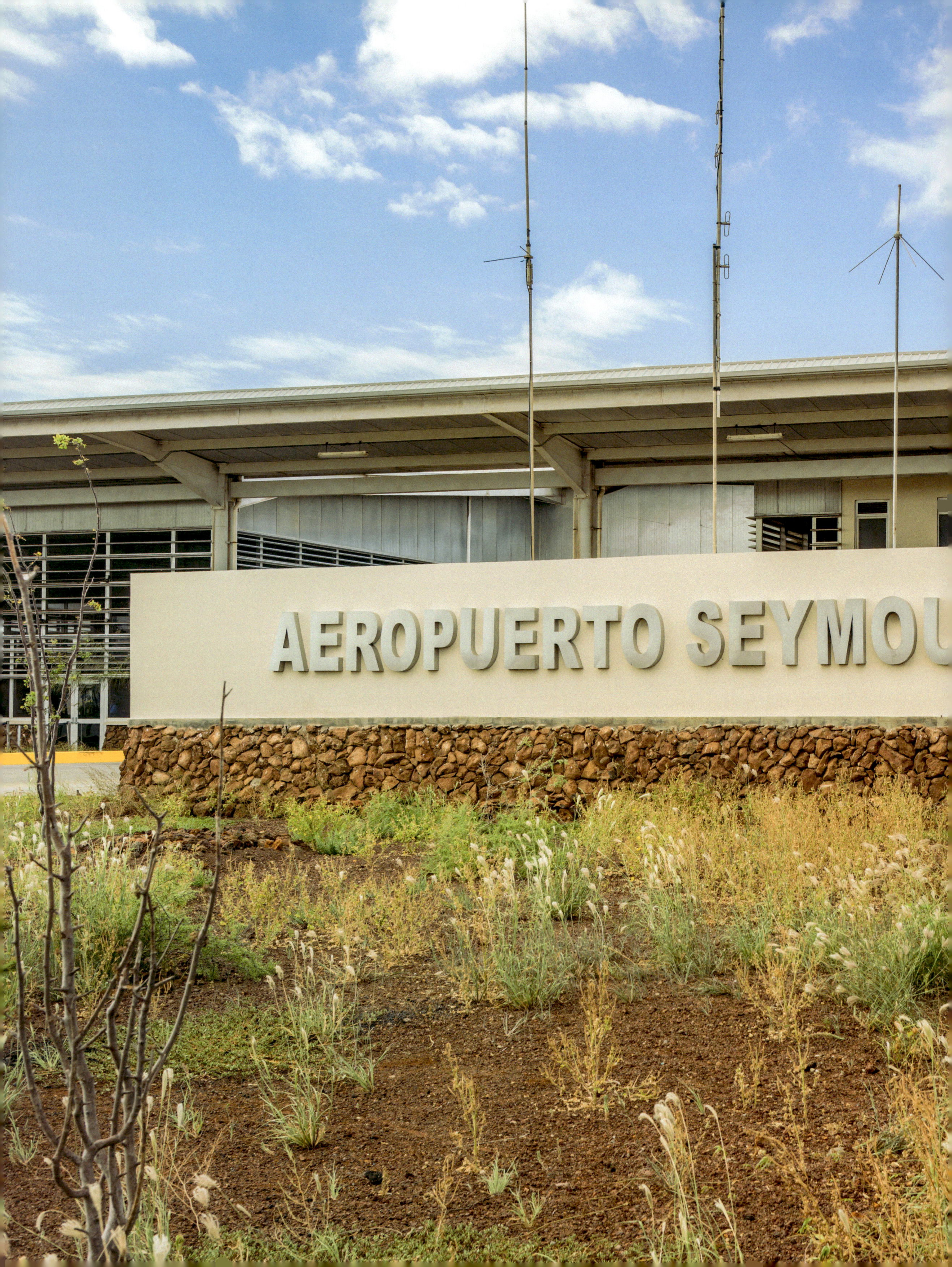
AEROPUERTO SEYMOU

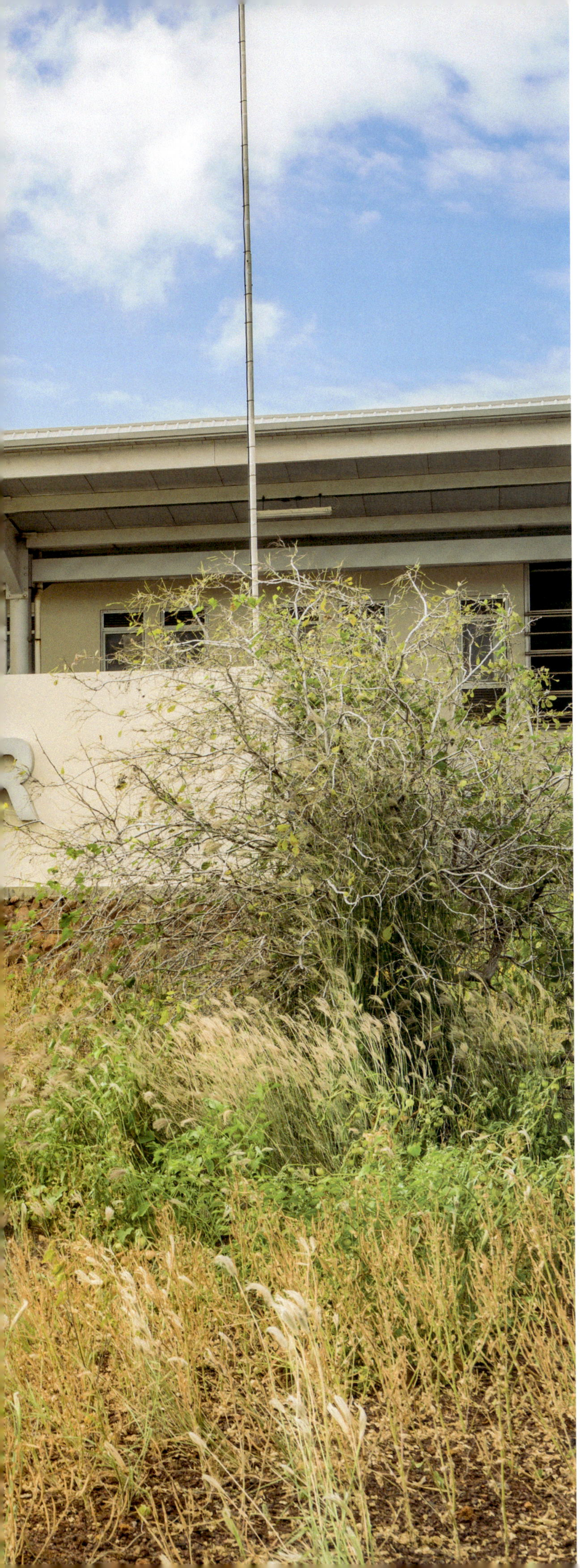

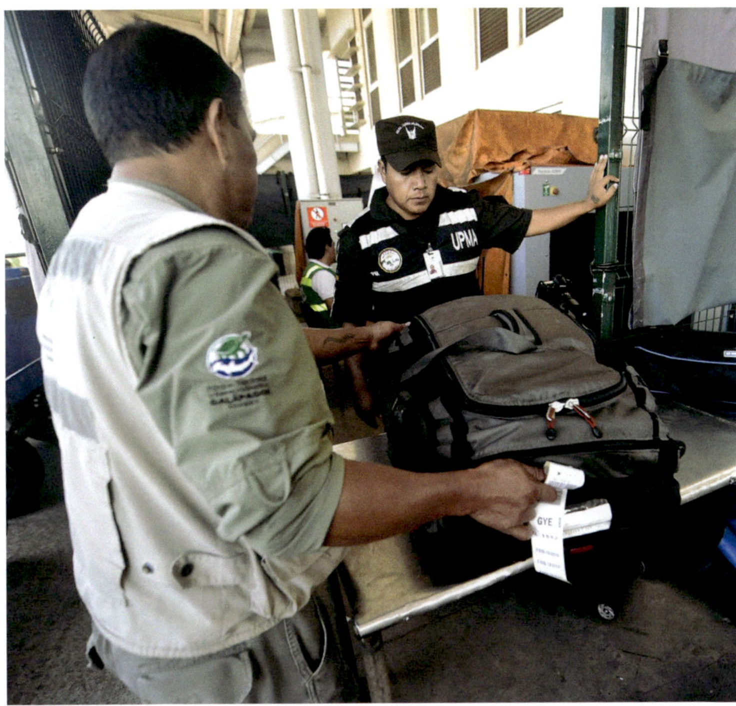

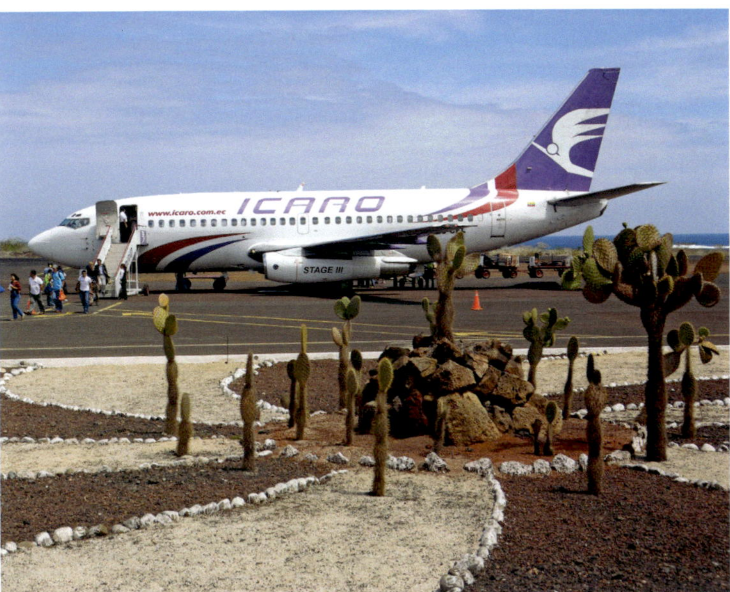

Airports

There are three airports on the islands. The main one is on Baltra, a small island near to Santa Cruz (originally a 1930s US airbase). This airport and another on San Cristóbal are big enough to serve passenger jets. The third airport on Isabela is used for smaller aircraft flying between islands. All arrivals come from the mainland of Ecuador, and the customs checks are mostly looking for animal and plant products that might contaminate the islands.

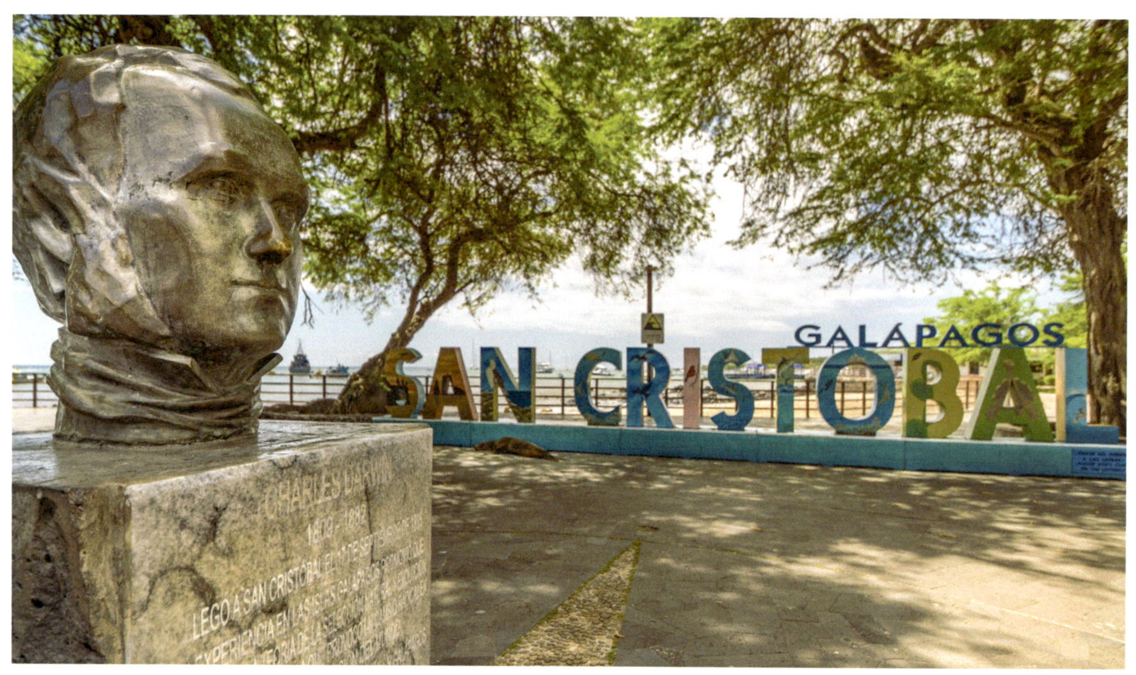

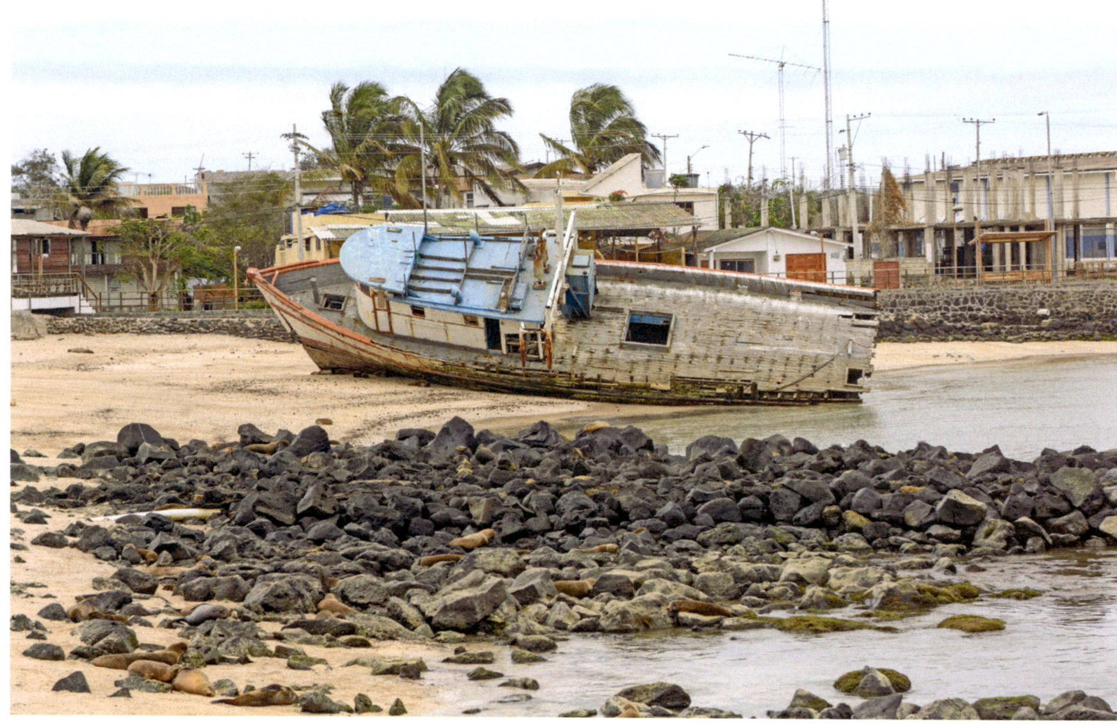

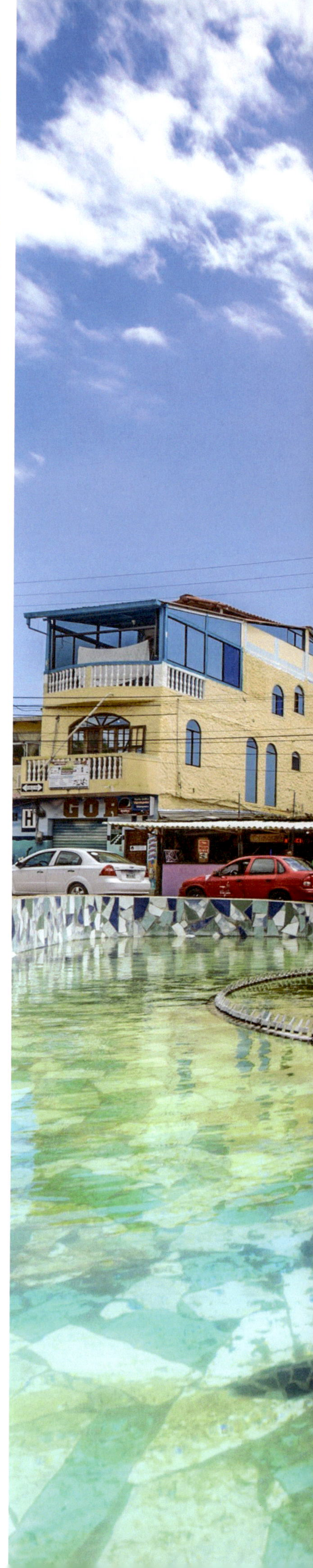

ALL PHOTOGRAPHS:
Puerto Baquerizo Moreno
This is the second-largest town in the archipelago located on San Cristóbal. This island was the first one visited by Charles Darwin, and his bust stands on the shore in Puerto Baquerizo Moreno. Fishing is a big part of the economy here, as evidenced by the town's swordfish sculptures.

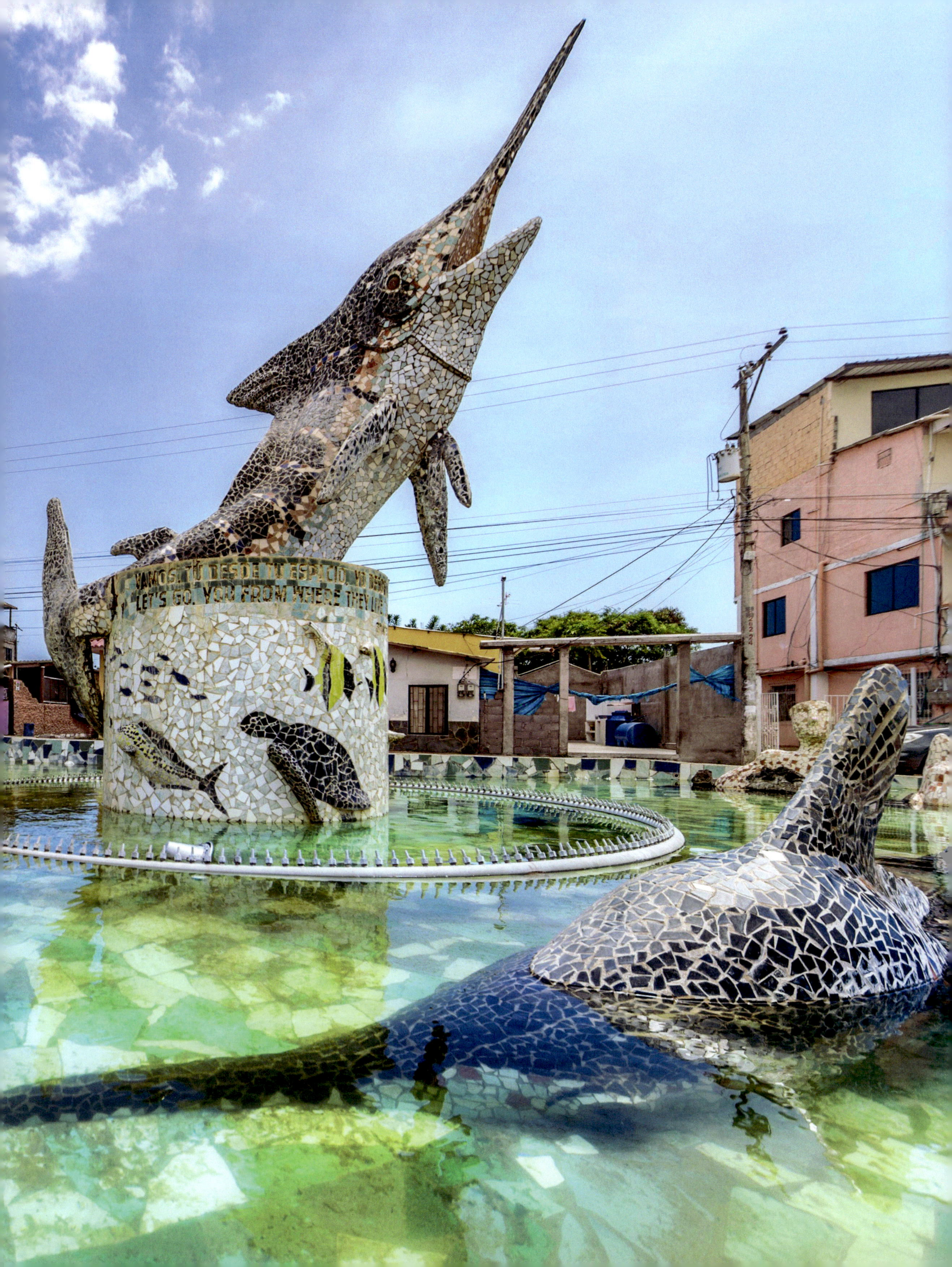

VAMOS. TÚ DESDE TU ESPACIO. YO DES
LET'S GO. YOU FROM WHERE THEY LIVE

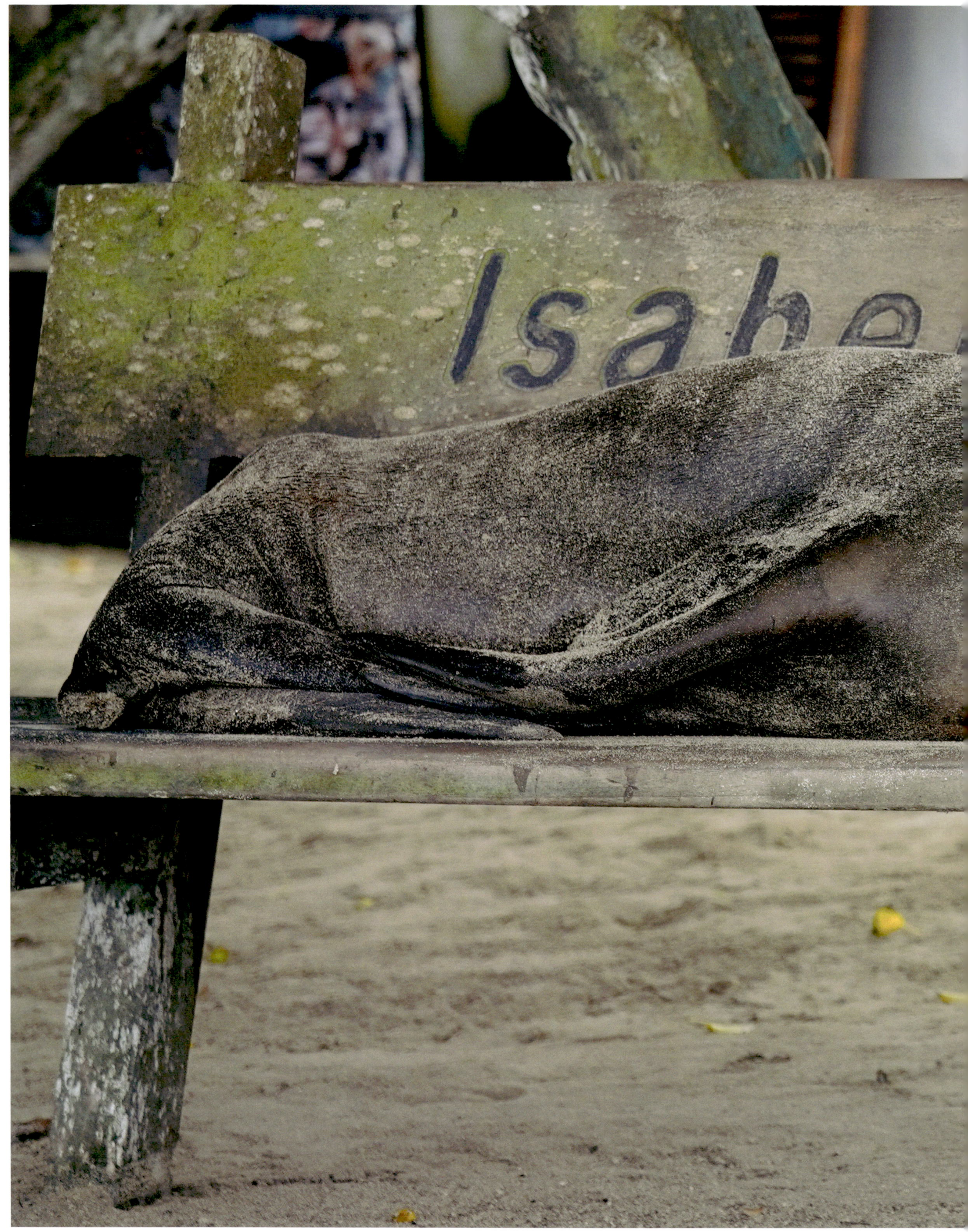

Isabe

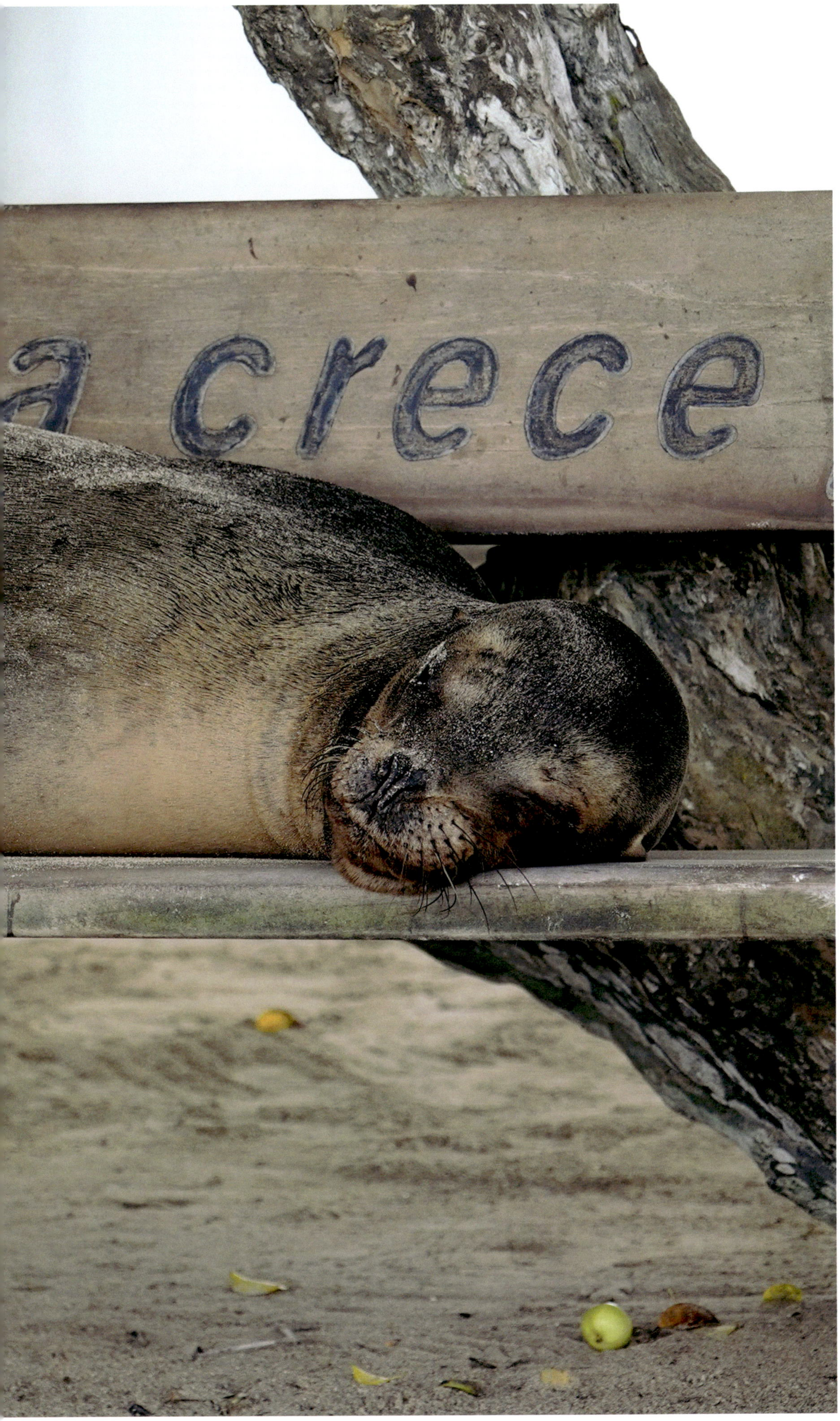

Taking it easy
A sea lion sleeps peacefully on a bench in Puerto Villamil on Isabela Island.

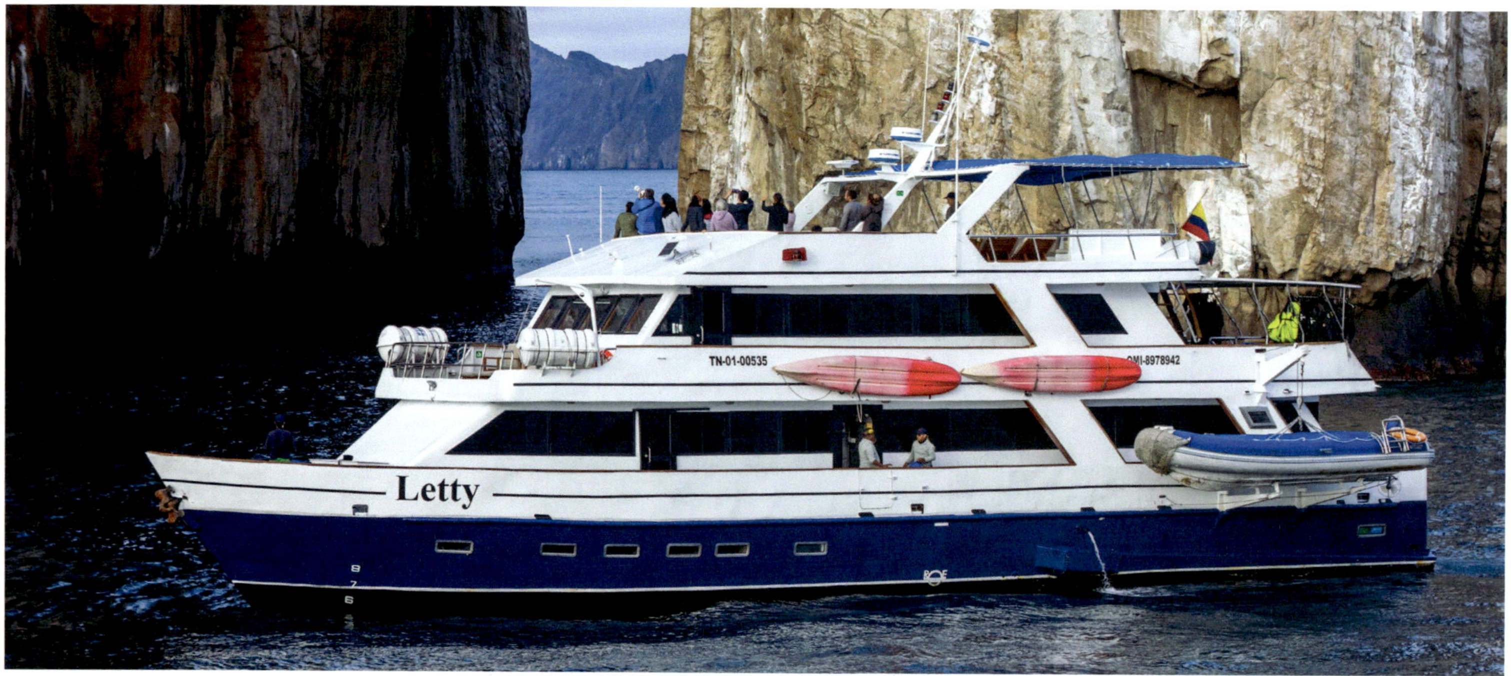

Photo opportunity

Tourists take photos of Kicker Rock which looms above them near the main island of San Cristobal. The rock is a haven for seabirds, and the waters around the volcanic edifice are a haven for sea turtles and other marine wildlife.

Wall of Tears

The dry forests of Isabela are interrupted by a tall dry stone wall. This is the Wall of Tears, the product of a penal labour camp set up on the island in the 1940s. The 8-m-high edifice is said to have caused the deaths of many of the workers that built it, and local people contend that ghostly cries can be heard coming from the stones.

Welcome

A sea lion greets a group of tourists arriving on Española, the southernmost and oldest of the main islands. This land has never been inhabited by people and visitors only stay for the day.

Hungry customer

A brown pelican visits the Puerto Ayora fish market in Santa Cruz looking for something to eat.

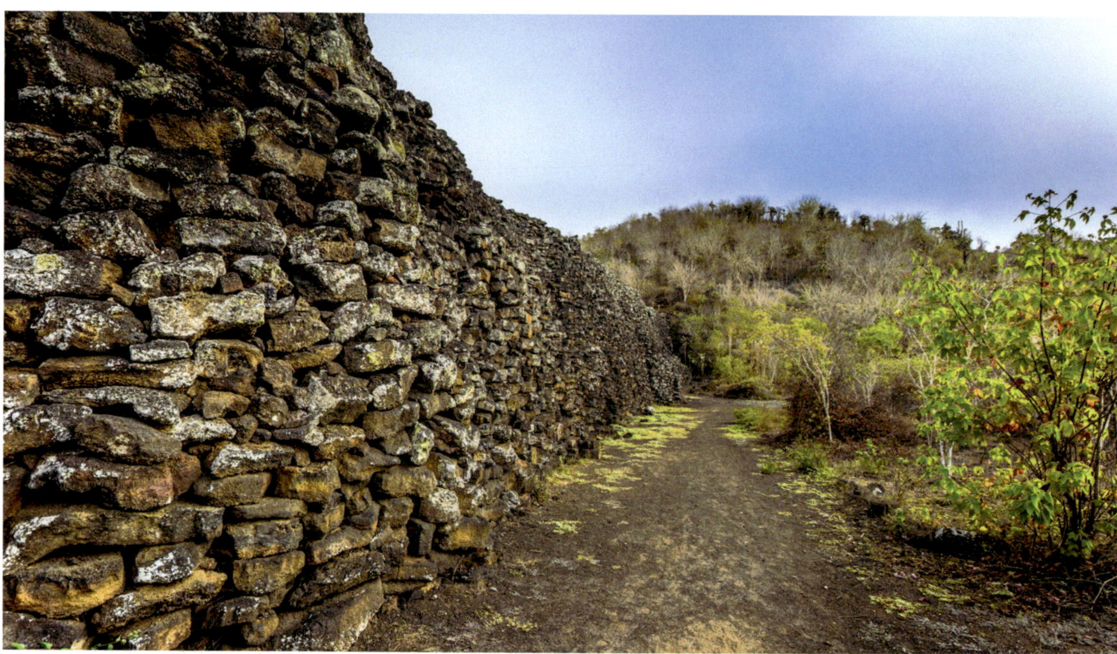

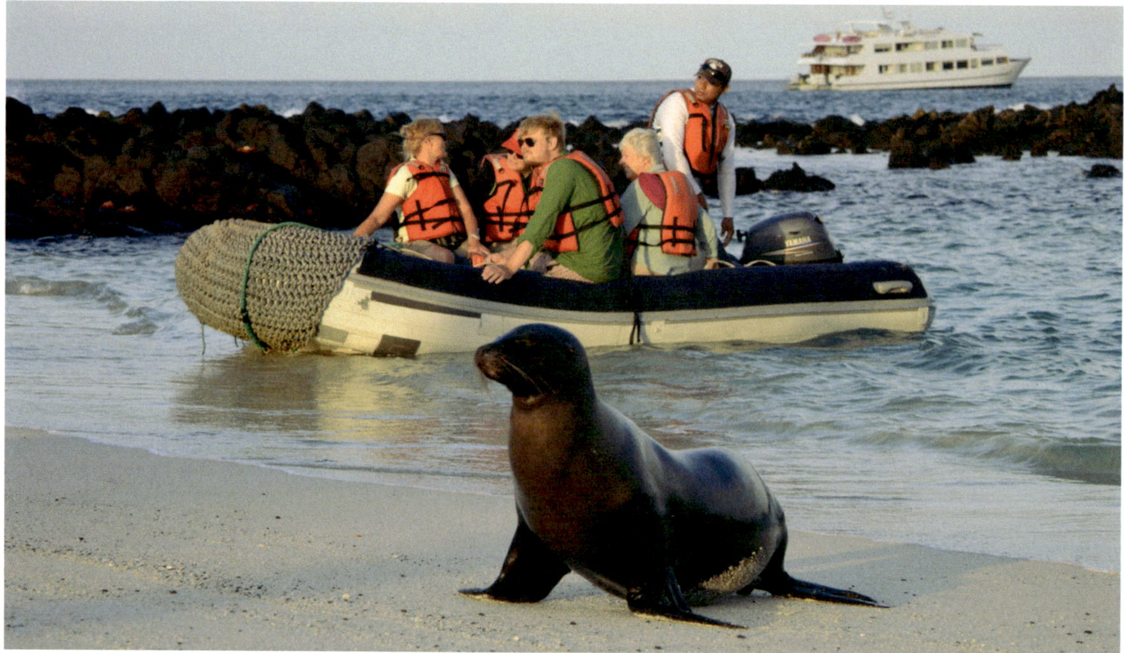

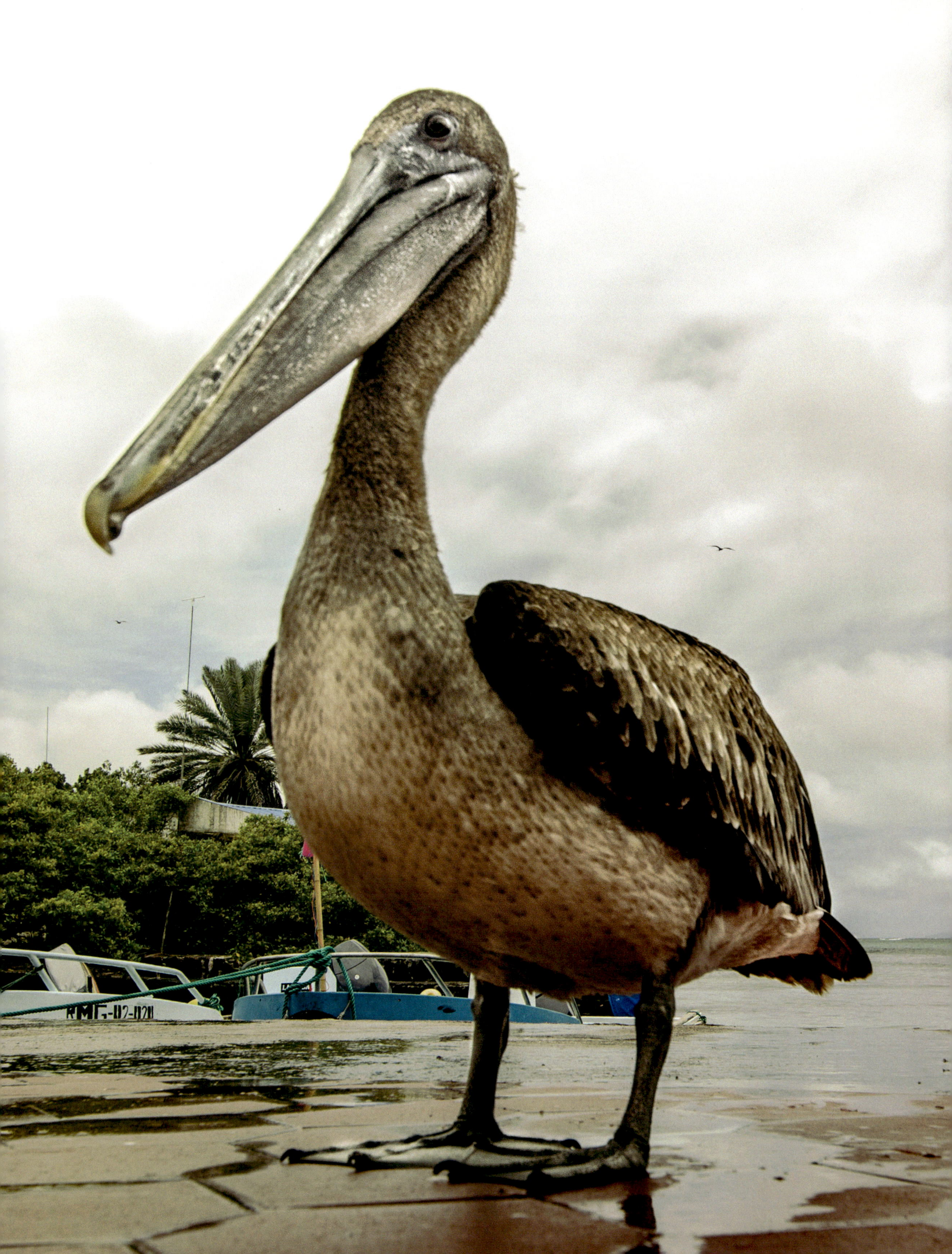

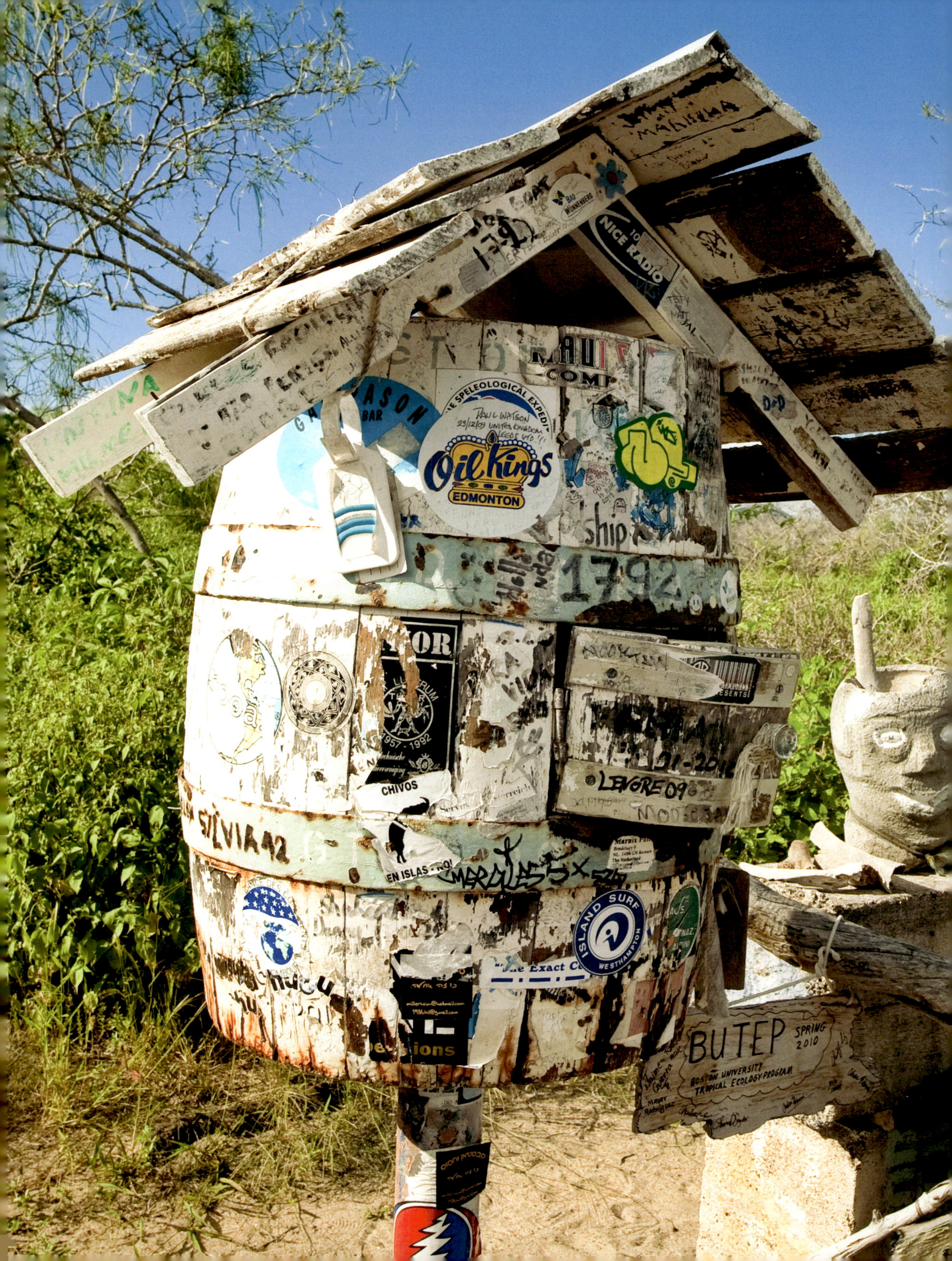

MADONNA
NICE RADIO
Oil kings
EDMONTON
GASON BAR
THE SPELEOLOGICAL EXPEDI
PAUL L WATSON
25/12/09 UNITED KINGDOM
ship
1792
CHIVOS
1957 - 1992
LEVORE 09
SILVIA 42
EN ISLAS - TO!
ISLAND SURF
WESTHAMPTON
The Exact C
BUTEP SPRING 2010
BOSTON UNIVERSITY
TROPICAL ECOLOGY PROGRAM

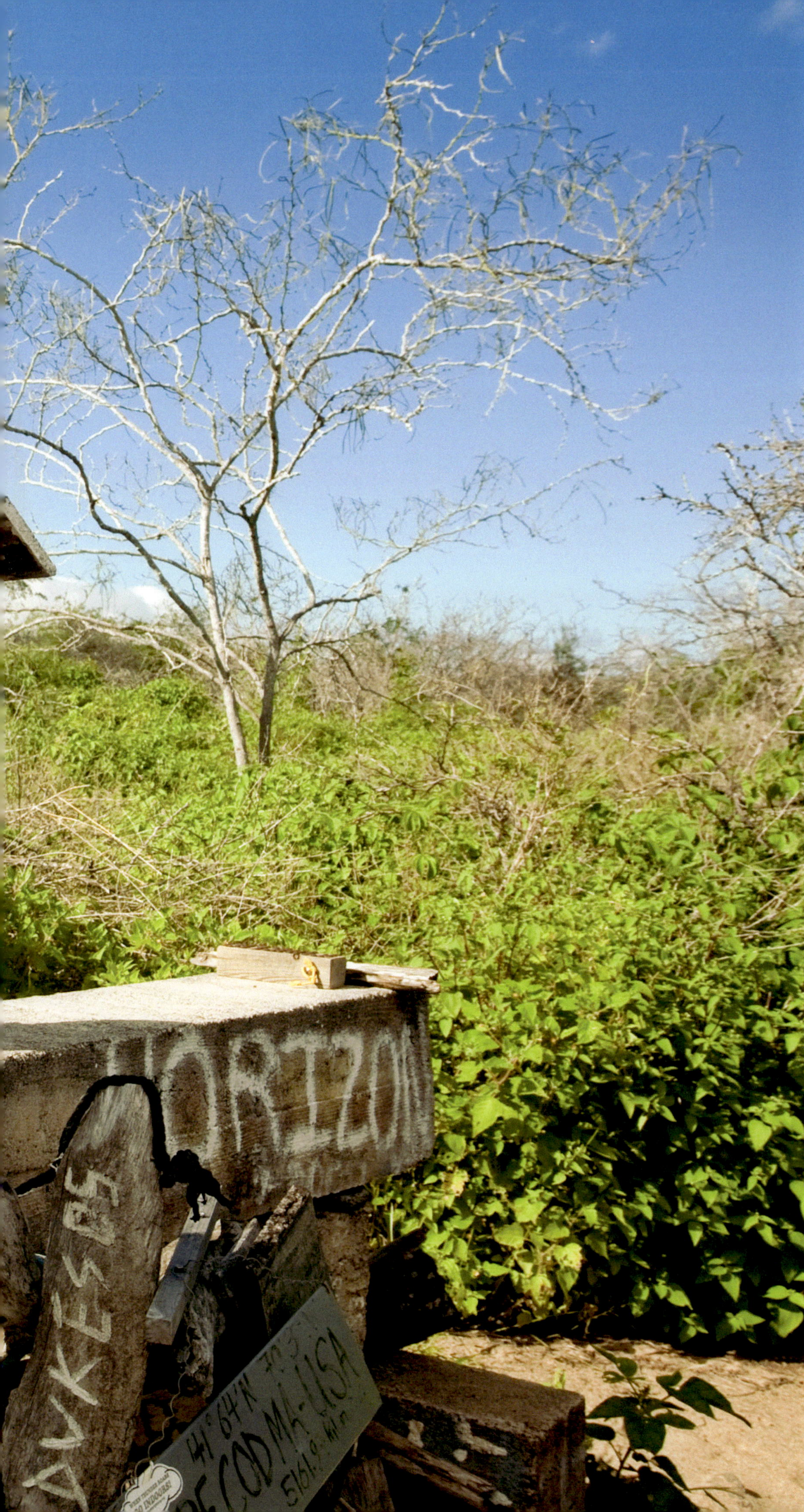

Post Office Bay

In 1792, a Royal Navy captain set up the first post barrel on Floreana. The idea was that crews could leave messages here when passing the islands, which could then be carried home by other ships heading in the other direction. This part of the coast became known as Post Office Bay, and a post barrel has been in service there ever since. Traditionally, any tourist that finds a card addressed to someone who lives near to their home can take it back with them on the condition that they hand deliver it to the intended recipients.

Picture Credits

Alamy: 14 top (robertharding), 25 (NASA), 28/29 (peace portal photo), 30 (Danita Delimont), 34 top (Sébastien Lecocq), 37 top & 38 (Rosanne Tackaberry), 46 bottom (Steve Allen Travel Photography), 50 (Andrew Pearson), 56/57 (Jeff Rotman), 59 (Danita Delimont), 60/61 (Tsuneo Nakamura), 62/63 (SeaTops), 64/65 (louise murray), 66 (Maridav), 70/71 (David Fleetham), 72/73 (Amar and Isabelle Guillen), 74 (Brandon Cole Marine Photography), 75 bottom (Amar and Isabelle Guillen), 80 bottom (imageBroker.com), 81 (David Fleetham), 84 (Minden Pictures), 85 top (imageBroker.com), 86 (SPP Images), 88 (Leon Werdinger), 92/93 (Cannon Photography LLC), 94 (F1online digitale Bildagentur GmbH), 100 (Danita Delimont), 103 top (Zoltan Bagosi), 106/107 (Minden Pictures), 108 bottom (Hudson Fleece), 110 top (Kseniya Ragozina), 111 (Stefan Rosengren), 113 top (John Holmes), 113 bottom (David Hosking), 120 (Minden Pictures), 125 both (Galapagos), 126 (MichaelGrantPlants), 128 top (MichaelGrantPlants), 128 bottom (David Hosking), 129 (GFC Collection), 132 top (Danita Delimont), 132 bottom (William Mullins), 133 (Cavan Images), 134/135 (WorldFoto), 136 top (Karol Kozlowski Premium RM Collection), 136 middle (GFC Collection), 136 bottom (Minden Pictures), 137 (Roland Knauer), 138 bottom (Chris Mattison), 139 (Bjoern Backe), 140 (KrystynaSzulecka), 141 bottom (Zoltan Bagosi), 142 & 144 (KrystynaSzulecka), 148 (Minden Pictures), 149 (David Hosking), 152 (Gordon Chambers), 156 top (imageBroker.com), 156 bottom (Malcolm Schuyl), 157 (Arterra Picture Library), 159 top (Christopher Vernon Parry), 159 bottom (Bill Coster), 165 (robertharding), 168 bottom (Krystyna Szulecka), 169 (David Hosking), 170/171 (Minden Pictures), 171 (Celia Mannings), 172 (Malcolm Schuyl), 173 top (Jason Bazzano), 173 bottom (Avalon), 174 (Carolyn Jenkins), 176 top (blickwinkel), 176 bottom (Auscape International Pty Ltd), 178 (imageBroker.com), 184/185 (Zoonar GmbH), 186 top (Chronicle), 196/197 (Design Pics Inc), 198 top (Renato Granieri), 199 (Cavan Images), 200 bottom (Olga Kolos), 201 (Barry Lewis), 207 bottom (Gail Tanski), 208 top (Keith Levit), 210 top (B.O Kane), 211 (Roussel Photography), 212/213 (Hemis), 215 bottom (incamerastock), 216 top (Hemis), 216 bottom (wildnerdpix), 217 (Hemis), 218/219 (Kriste Sorokaite), 220 bottom (Mark Green), 221 (Renato Granieri), 222/223 (Michael DeFreitas South America)

Alamy/Nature Picture Library: 7, 16, 18/29, 20/21, 22/23, 32/33, 40/41, 42/43, 44/45, 46 top, 58, 76/77, 85 bottom, 91, 99 both, 127, 164 both, 166/167, 168 top & middle, 177, 179 middle, 208 bottom

Art Institute of Chicago: 187

Creative Commons Attribution 2.0 Generic: 52 bottom (NOAA Photo Library)

Charles Darwin Foundation/Deep Ocean Research Program Generated using QPS Fledermaus mapping software using the Global Multi-Resolution Topography synthesis dataset (Ryan et al. 2009; GMRT v4.3.0 Oct 2024): 54/55

Dreamstime: 5 (Zachzimet), 39 top (Adwo), 39 bottom (Tonimunozcasas), 76 (Michael Zech), 95 bottom (Jonathan Green), 97 top (Wirestock), 97 middle (Martinmark), 97 bottom (Michael Zysman), 98 (Martin Schneiter), 101 top (Martinmark), 101 bottom (Donyanedomam), 104 top (Christianherzog), 104 bottom (Jiri Hrebicek), 114 (Brian Lasenby), 117 (Donyanedomam), 118/119 (Maciejbledowski), 121 top (Mrallen), 121 bottom right (Tangsphoto), 130/131 (Gonepaddling), 138 top (Fponceg), 141 top (Jirousek), 143 (Fotodorota), 146/147 (Danflcreativo), 153 (Donyanedomam), 155 top (Joncsontheroad), 155 bottom (Donyanedomam), 158/159 (Zachzimet), 160/161 (ndp), 162/163 (Alexshalamov), 205 (Jesse Kraft)

Getty Images: 8/9 (Benjamin van der Spek), 24, 36 (Keith Levit), 87 top (Wolfgang Kaehler), 89 top (Barry Lewis), 109 (Gerald Corsi), 188/189 (Bettmann), 204 top (AFP), 204 bottom (Ernesto Benavides), 206 (Carolyn Cole), 207 top (Rodrigo Buendia), 209 (Wolfgang Kaehler), 215 top (Rodrigo Buendia)

Patrick Mulrey: 52 top

Shutterstock: 6 (Rostasedlacek), 10/11 (zelvan), 12/13 (SL Photography), 13 top (Steve Barze), 13 bottom (RPBaiao), 14 bottom (Maridav), 15 (Gail Johnson), 26 top (sunsinger), 26 bottom (Jess Kraft), 26/27 (Florencia Colombatti), 31 both (Todamo), 34 bottom (Cris D), 35 (Paul Vowles), 37 bottom (cabiros), 39 middle (Marquicio Pagola), 47 (Arne Thielenhaus), 48/49 (Karol Kozlowski), 53 (Yarr65), 67 (Philip Garner), 68/69 (Molly Altschwager), 75 top (Ricardo Dias), 78/79 (Alex Vog), 80 top (Longjourneys), 82 (Brandelet), 82/83 (Joe Dordo Brnobic), 87 bottom (xagc), 89 bottom (Fotos593), 90 (Alex Vog), 95 top (NickThornton), 96 (doleesi), 99 middle (Marisa Estivill), 102 (CSNafzger), 103 bottom (SidWorld), 105 (Marisa Estivill), 108 top (Don Mammoser), 110 bottom (Jose Rui Santos), 112 (Michal Sarauer), 113 middle (Agami Photo Agency), 116 (npavlov), 121 bottom left (Pavaphon Supanantananont), 122/123 (Beto Santillan), 124 (Boris B), 145 top (Ekaterina McClaud), 145 bottom (Don Mammoser), 150 (Labetaa Andre), 154 (LouieLea), 175 top (Kanokratnok), 175 bottom (Boyd Hendrikse), 179 top (Kjersti Joergensen), 179 bottom (Sputnik Aloysius), 180/181 (Michal Sarauer), 182 (Jess Kraft), 186 bottom (K. Nakao), 190/191 (RPBaiao), 192/193 (gg-foto), 194 (Ekaterina McClaud), 195 (Watch The World), 198 bottom (IntoTheWorld), 200 top (Maridav), 202/203 (sunsinger), 210 bottom (thananya), 214/215 (Mark Anthony Ray), 220 top (BradleySmith), 220 middle (RPBaiao)